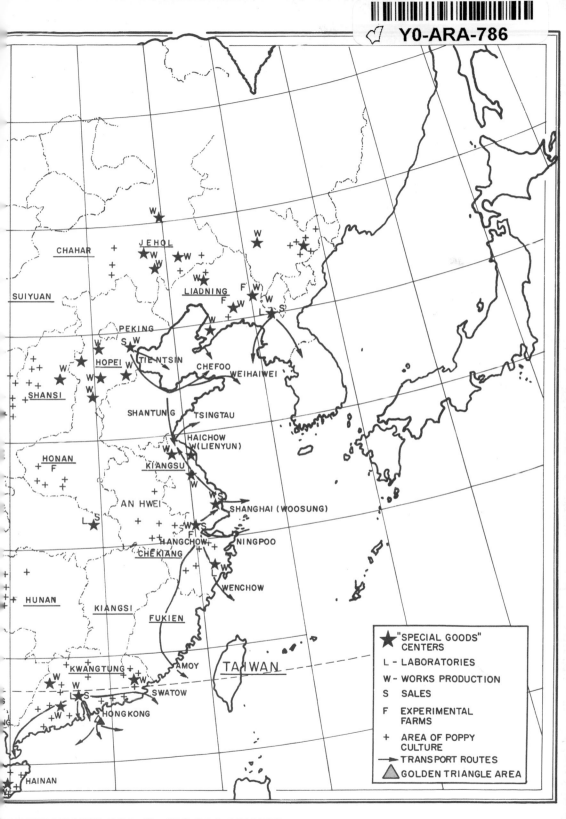

CHAHAR

JEHOL

SUIYUAN

LIADNING

PEKING

TIENTSIN

HOPEI

CHEFOO

WEIHAIWEI

SHANSI

SHANTUNG

TSINGTAU

HAICHOW
W(LIENYUN)

HONAN

KIANGSU

AN HWEI

SHANGHAI (WOOSUNG)

HANGCHOW

NINGPOO

CHEKIANG

WENCHOW

HUNAN

KIANGSI

FUKIEN

TAIWAN

KWANGTUNG

AMOY

SWATOW

HONG KONG

HAINAN

★	"SPECIAL GOODS" CENTERS
L	LABORATORIES
W	WORKS PRODUCTION
S	SALES
F	EXPERIMENTAL FARMS
+	AREA OF POPPY CULTURE
→	TRANSPORT ROUTES
▲	GOLDEN TRIANGLE AREA

DISTRIBUTION & FACILITIES

PSYCHO-CHEMICAL WARFARE

PSYCHO-CHEMICAL WARFARE

THE CHINESE COMMUNIST DRUG OFFENSIVE AGAINST THE WEST

A. H. STANTON CANDLIN

ARLINGTON HOUSE   NEW ROCHELLE, N. Y.

Library of Congress Catalog Card Number___73-10649_____

Manufactured in the United States of America

Library of Congress Cataloging in Publication Data

    Candlin, A   H   Stanton.
      Psycho-chemical warfare.

      Bibliography: p.
      1. Narcotics, Control of--China (People's
    Republic of China, 1949-   ) 2. Communist strategy.
    3. Narotics, Control of--International cooperation.
    I. Title. [DNLM: 1. Drug and narcotic control.
    HV5801 C218p 1974]
    HV5840.C6C35   338.4'7'61532312   73-10649
    ISBN 0-87000-214-7

To fight and conquer in all your battles is not supreme excellence. Supreme excellence consists in breaking the enemy's resistance without fighting.

—Sun Tzu

Contents

Foreword

The issue discussed in this work is one of the utmost gravity. It demands urgent attention on the part of the United States public, a public that has been undergoing some bad experiences lately from a monstrous evil, the international traffic in narcotics. This could be said of many other nations, similarly afflicted but to a lesser degree. One must realize that the threat in question has arisen not only because of weakness of moral fiber on the part of the victims and the cupidity that exploits that weakness, but also, to a very large extent, by a conscious design with political and military purposes in view.

It has been shrewdly remarked that the purveyors of opiates, of cocaine, the hallucinogens, or the synthetic drugs, whether they have been acting on behalf of the syndicates of organized crime or as independent operators, are the ultimate and most favored beneficiaries of the free-enterprise system since they are concerned with the single most profitable enterprise that it affords. Yet the activity in which they have been engaged is, by its nature, probably the one, next to total war, that can be relied on to wreak destruction on that system. Indeed, it could destroy the system utterly and create conditions that would result in its falling into the hands of its enemies, a situation the enemies have been trying to accomplish for years. Unless the polit-

9

ical and military aspects of the drug problem are properly assessed, as distinct from the purely social aspects, there is little likelihood of a particularly dangerous trend being reversed.

I have spent a good many years in the Far East (China and Hong Kong), in India, and in the Middle East, where my work has occasionally brought me to vantage points from which I have been able to gain a degree of insight into the narcotics traffic and its international ramifications. My duties have been in the fields of science and technology for the most part, and have also involved me sometimes in intelligence work. I have, particularly of late, been obliged to conclude that an especially formidable weapons system in extremely dangerous hands is being largely ignored and that, in this regard, "there are none so blind as those who do not wish to see."

As the Vietnam War has intensified and has approached an inevitable end, revealing the total inadequacy of U.S. preparations for it, the present situation has developed. It manifests a precipitous decline in U.S. service morale (army morale in particular), one that has been predictable for many years, and I have felt impelled to engage in the present analysis. In my capacity as a partner of Otran Research, Inc. I therefore undertook, as an unsolicited and voluntary research project in the public interest, an analysis that has eventually taken the form of this book.

In this work I have drawn freely on published source material in the press and on the numerous publications of the legislative and executive branches of the U.S. Government, as well as the books listed in the bibliography. I am also indebted to a number of private sources of data that I do not feel free to acknowledge, but to whom I am most grateful. I do wish to acknowledge with thanks, however, the contribution of Mr. Edward Jackson, who is responsible for the execution of the maps and diagrams. He, in turn, is indebted (as I am) to Mr. Chang Shao-jiun, a graduate of Utah State University, who has carried out important studies on the "people's communes" and who provided useful topographical advice. And I thank Mr. Henry W. Engel and Mr. David Franke for their invaluable editorial assistance.

As this book was going to press, interesting corroboration was provided by an escapee from the mainland, Mr. Wu Shu-jen. This man, an engineer, has identified and described a large opium processing plant in the Canton suburbs which he calls the "09 plant." This is located in a six story building, and is linked with a 3,000-acre poppy farm and employs some 700 persons. Wu, an excellent swimmer, was one of the lifeguards detailed to attend Chairman Mao when he went for a rather well publicized swim in the Yangtse some years ago.

In drawing the conclusions reached after the sifting of a great deal of information and evidence, I wish to make it known that my position is an individual one, arises from no sponsorship, and does not necessarily represent the view of any organization or group with which I may have been associated at any time.

A. H. Stanton Candlin

Norwood, Mass.

June 1973

Preface

For millennia the greatest nations and empires rested on the backs of slaves, and their fall was often connected with grave ethical questions and abuses associated with the treatment of slave populations or of individual slaves. Eventually a great movement succeeded and slavery appeared to be abolished in the civilized world, although it lingered in some countries in Asia and Africa. The main protagonists who succeeded in lifting this yoke were Great Britain and the United States. Unhappily, there are, in the Middle East and in Africa, some indications of relapse and an increase in slave trading, but at least the more advanced nations are free of that monstrous evil. It needs to be noted, however, in this regard, that another form of slavery, as distinct from traditional chattel slavery, exists on an extensive scale in the Communist countries.

Today an even worse form of bondage is threatening the world, and free societies, including that of the United States that played such a conspicuous part in freeing mankind from the ancient scourge of slavery, stand in deadly danger of being themselves enslaved. This danger takes several forms, but of these probably the most insidious menace is that of drugs. Drugs may, if unchecked in their onset, result in the destruction of all civilized values and the ultimate downfall of the countries that have contributed most to the emancipation of mankind. The monstrous evil that was slavery depended on the capture or the acquisition of *unwilling* victims, but the portentous fact about the new slavery of narcotic addiction that differentiates it from the previous form is that the victims, almost invariably, *do have freedom of choice.* Yet they deliver themselves into the chains of servitude that receive them and that lead to destruction.

As yet the fact is not recognized that, to a large extent, the psychotropic and narcotic substances involved in this assault on the fabric of society are being used deliberately, and with a merciless calculation, as weapons of warfare by unprincipled opponents of civilization. It is a warfare in which the casualties mount rapidly. It is the first full-scale war of its kind and the casualties almost all arise from self-inflicted forms of injury.

On a worldwide basis, drug addicts amount to many millions; scores of millions in fact. In the past, most of these have been located in Asia, but it may now be observed that the traffic in refined forms of opium that used to be sent from the Middle East and the Mediterranean area to the large and assured markets east of Suez has now been diverted westward and is flowing strongly into the Western Hemisphere.

In part this has been due to the entry into this lethal trade of Red China, a supplier operating on the largest scale. China's addition of the so-called "white drugs" to its vast export program (previously mainly opium) has now begun to saturate the markets formerly supplied with morphine and heroin arriving from Beirut, Marseilles, or other delivery points. Until 1952 it would have been correct to say that the primary motive of the Chinese Reds was economic. Since then there have been important planned political and strategic aims built into their policies, which were then conceived in terms of a twenty-year program (now almost achieved).

The scale of their operations has been enormous and they now produce and export far more than the rest of the world put together. The magnitude of Chinese operations has only been matched by the consummate skill with which they have succeeded, through bribery and intimidation at the highest levels, and by clever misinformation, in masking their intentions and their practices.

When a military commander contemplates an assault on a selected objective, it is a matter of principle and also, often, of historical record that his adoption of a convincing policy of deception is likely to achieve the most success so long as his opponent remains unaware of his intentions. It is for this reason that the Chinese Reds have adopted the ingenious political strategy of ensuring, through skillfully managed channels of information control and propaganda, that other countries, such as Turkey, should bear the burden of opprobrium.

As it happens, there is enough truth in the assertion that large amounts of heroin manufactured from Turkish opium find their way into the United States, now the primary target of the drug traffickers. But that is not the whole truth. The percentage of the total, usually given as 80 percent, is exaggerated. If the Chinese Reds were not supplementing the flow with their own contributions (which arrive mainly on the U.S. and Canadian Pacific coasts) and were they not, at the same time, dominating the important Asian market, the impact on the United States would be much less dangerous. The drug market owes its strength to the release of a large volume of narcotics originating in the Mediterranean that arrives in the Western Hemisphere instead of being routed eastwards.

"Papaverum Somniferum," the sleep-bearing poppy, or rather its extract, was known to the ancient Greeks as "Opion" and its effects as "Nepenthe." Their contemporaries in China knew of it, but only as a medicine, as a part of their pharmacopeia. It is said that the Dutch in Formosa played a major part in introducing its use as a social habit to the Chinese, when they mixed and smoked it with tobacco.

Realizing the ill effects of widespread use of this drug, both on the individual and on society, the Manchu government issued edicts against its use in 1729 and in 1790. These were not rigorously enforced. In 1800 they issued another, inveighing against importation of opium. There had been an import monopoly introduced by Portuguese traders during the eighteenth century and some of the Indian opium crop, planted under the "Mogul Raj," found its way into China. After both the Moguls and the Portuguese had passed from the scene, the East India Company continued the traffic; its pressure on the Manchu regime, with opium cargoes that were used principally as a "penetration aid" aimed at the virtual Chinese embargo on foreign trade, resulted in the Opium Wars (1839–42).

In 1858 the exports to China reached 10 million pounds of opium, but by 1906 domestic Chinese production had reached 44 million pounds while imports from India were at 7 million pounds. It was estimated, at that date, that some 27 percent of the Chinese population was addicted to the drug.

Morphine was discovered by a French chemist in 1803, and cocaine fifty years later by an Austrian chemist. They were intended to be used only as medicinal substances but soon became popular for other purposes, often through lack of understanding of the process of addiction on the part of the medical profession. Morphine, which constitutes the principal poisoning element in opium (8–15 percent) is manufactured without much difficulty from raw opium, but heroin, the most powerful opiate, is much more difficult to make and requires skillful chemical control. Synthetic heroin and cocaine have been produced from coal-tar derivatives.

Chemically speaking, these deadly substances are built up around

15

the pyridine base that contains five atoms of hydrogen, five atoms of carbon, and one atom of nitrogen, joined together in a heterocyclic ring. The complex structure of the opium group includes a three-ring compound, the so-called phenanthrene structure, united with the heterocyclic nitrogen ring with oxygen also included. The empirical formula for morphine is $C_{17}H_{19}NO_3$. The formula for cocaine is $C_{17}H_{21}NO_4$. In the case of heroin, whose preparation involves the use of acetic and hydrochloric acid, there is additional complexity, the substance being morphine-diacetylate (an ester) having the formula $C_{21}H_{23}NO_5$. Of the three, it is by far the most dangerous. It should be carefully noted that cocaine is derived from coca leaves and is not an opiate, although it is not dissimilar in some of its properties.

According to the physiologists who have studied the problem, the protoplasm contained in living cells is composed of proteins, water, and a small quantity of salt. The life process requires a regular supply of nutrients and oxygen, as well as the elimination of waste products. Some poisons attack the protoplasm itself. Others interfere with the life process. Some do both. These highly organized alkaloidal poisons combine readily with protein matter and easily penetrate the walls or sheathing that protect the cells. In consequence, there can be violent derangement of the activity of the cell and of the life process, as well as permanent injury to the structure.

The nervous system is the most highly organized part of the physical frame of the human organism and it has been noted that these complex alkaloidal poisons show their chief effect on the nervous system. Injury has been seen to take place both in the upper and lower portions of the brain.

These narcotics are soluble in fat; they can penetrate the fatty sheathing that usually protects the brain from the harmful substances that sometimes find their way into the blood stream. Thus the poison can quickly come into contact with the grey matter of the brain. The most noteworthy attribute of the narcotics has always been their well-publicized effect of deadening the sense of pain.

These poisons are said to attack the delicate, carefully protected organs of reproduction and can impair the sexual powers of the male; they can induce sterility in both sexes. The germ plasm that is essential to the continuation of life can become fatally undermined. It is a classical example of eco-suicide.

The symptoms of morphine addiction have been summed up as depravity of the mind; general debility; loss of weight and appetite; loss of sexual powers; sleeplessness; eczema; contracted pupils, diarrhea, alternating with constipation; and, finally, death through malnutrition. Heroin and cocaine are much more active. If unattended by skilled care the life of the addict may be short. The degeneration of the upper brain can be so rapid that the addict's character may disintegrate in a matter of months. Demoralization and a life of crime may result because of the desperate need for money to buy an expensive drug that only brings temporary relief from the acute physical torture that deprivation causes.

Transformation of character is particularly rapid in the young, and more so with cocaine and heroin than other narcotics. Very quickly, a young person "hooked" by either of these loses the results of family and home training. Self-respect, honor, decency, sense of discipline, ambition, truthfulness all melt away. Virtue and morality disintegrate and moral idiocy ensues. The necessity to secure the drug assumes absolute dominance over all other motives. To obtain it, the addict will not only advocate policies against the public welfare but will lie, steal, and murder without any feeling of compunction.

In addition to such antisocial traits, common to all addicts, the heroin addict has two special characteristics. First, for a short period after taking the drug he has *a sense of euphoria or of "exaltation of the ego."* This leads him to a frame of mind in which he looks upon himself as a hero. Under its influence, and in order to acquire money, he may commit daring robberies of the boldest kind. Cocaine has a similar effect. There are important military implications here for special service personnel on dangerous or one-way missions. In spite of their inherent heroism, Japanese kamikaze pilots were often drugged with a synthetic called "hiropon."

Secondly, the heroin addict has *a pathological urge, verging on a mania, to bring everyone else under similar addiction.* This is a general condition for most addicts, with all drugs, who are particularly gregarious. It is, however, a much stronger impulse with heroin than with any other, and the confirmed addict spends as much time as he can in trying to persuade others to share his condition. It is like a contagion and, if organized by unscrupulous promoters *for that purpose,* can spread through society like a chain reaction.

Also, there is *secretiveness.* When the drug supply (heroin) is easily accessible, so that withdrawal symptoms can be concealed, the addict is often successful in hiding his or her condition from family and most intimate friends. In most discussions of the problems connected with addiction to opiates, not nearly enough emphasis is placed on the long-term biological damage that can be transmitted through families or through the ranks of a community that has been decimated by the kind of social death arising from the abandonment of the concept of marriage and family life. Just as the unchecked advance of addiction can destroy an individual, so can a nation be destroyed by degradation and irrecoverable decline.

Even as early as 1925, in hearings before the House of Representatives, the Hon. Walter E. Linebarger made a statement that included the following:

Narcotic drug addiction is a serious universal problem which has become acute in America through the spread of heroin addiction. There are probably five times as many narcotic drug addicts in the world than there ever were slaves at any one time and the bondage is far more abject and far more dangerous.

America is being assailed by opium with Asia as a base, by cocaine with South America as a base, by heroin and synthetic drugs with Europe as a base. An unscrupulous traffic within joins the traffic from without. This deadly drug warfare, that from three sides and from the inside is striking at our citizens, our homes, our institutions, the very germ plasm of our people, is more destructive and biologically more dangerous to our future than would be united military warfare from these three continents.

Without knowledge of this peril, people, especially the youth, fall easy victims to organized exploitation. Delay will be costly to the Nation in life and character and the stability of our institutions. To the task of carrying out promptly an adequate educational program all good men and good women who love their country and love humanity, and all constructive organizations—private, semipublic, and governmental—should rally. Upon the result hangs the destiny of America and, in a large measure, the destiny of the world.[1]

These were prophetic and apposite words that are even truer today than they were in 1925, especially as the present situation is quite literally one of war.

Recently, on July 1, 1971, hearings were held at the Senate Foreign Relations Committee that were intended to contribute to the proposed legislation on narcotics contained in the Bills S. 509, S. 694, S. 1188, S. J. Res. 78, and S. Con. Res. 8. Opening the discussions, Senator Frank Church said

President Nixon announced only yesterday that the Turkish Government will ban the growing of poppies after the Fall of 1972. This is a welcome step, one that reflects the sense of urgency and concern evinced in Congress this year by the several legislative measures introduced to accomplish this objective. Senators and Representatives have been far more aware of the spreading plague of drugs abuse than the bureaucracy in Washington. This awareness has taken the form of a search for means to cut off the flow of illegal narcotics from abroad. I, for one, welcome the announcement that opium will no longer be grown in Turkey after 1972. I want to urge, however, that the administration explore every possible means to keep this year's crop and next year's crop from reaching the heroin factories and then the dope pushers in our own city streets.

It is also not enough to mark the progress made in Turkey. We must turn also to those nations in S. E. Asia that have become a major source of heroin both for our soldiers in Vietnam and for the United States. The evidence of the growth of opium in Burma, Thailand and Laos and its subsequent movement through these countries to South Vietnam, Hong Kong and to the United States cannot be controverted. This traffic cannot be allowed to continue.

... I believe that the Senate must amend the Foreign Assistance Act to provide sanctions for stopping the flow of illegal narcotics into the United States. Recipients of our aid must be pressed to cooperate in pursuit of this objective. From the various legislative proposals before the committee today, I am confident that we can report an amendment that will give the United States legislative help in stopping the flow of heroin. We can report an amendment that reflects the congressional sense of urgency about the drug threat.[2]

While the above statement is true, as far as it goes, it makes the very large assumption that the damage is being caused primarily by recipients of U.S. aid; also that they would be amenable to coercion by the threat of interference with that aid. Unfortunately, it, and the entire Senate document "International Traffic in Narcotics," ignores entirely the major question of massive and well-documented Red Chinese involvement, as do all other official pronouncements at the present time. Indeed, there is a virtual official blackout on the subject.

The first speaker at those hearings, Senator William R. Spong (Va.), added to the above:

... Not many years ago, drug use was a phenomenon of our inner cities. Unfortunately, we did not act with the programs necessary to deal with the problem in its nascent stages. As a result, we are faced with an epidemic which has reached into every American community and affected millions of American families of all economic levels. It is no overstatement to say that drug abuse today is a threat to the very survival of our nation.

... There is no easy solution to this problem. Our educational and law enforcement efforts are gaining ground in controlling abuse, but these programs alone are not enough. We desperately need expanded treatment and rehabilitation programs and most of all, we need to act vigorously to shut off illegal smuggling of drugs into this country.

It would be naive to believe that we can control the international drug flow through checks and border patrols alone. A State Department spokesman has estimated that only about 10 percent of the illegal traffic can be intercepted through law enforcement measures. We must begin to strike at the invader's base, the drug production and distribution centers outside the United States.[3]

In addition to the above, some graphic details were added by one of the other speakers, Congressman Charles B. Rangel (N.Y.):

The problem, in a nutshell, is that the heroin traffic coming from outside our borders is threatening to kill our cities one by one, not just in terms of the crime it fosters from addicts stealing to support their habit but, more importantly, in terms of the lives it destroys. *New York City is already dying of the malignancy. Other cities are on the death list, but Harlem, which I think reflects on a smaller scale what is in store for the rest of the nation, is in the terminal stage.*

... In Harlem...heroin has devastated the community fabric with pandemic virulence. This imported poison has pillaged and looted our businesses and people in Harlem at the rate of $1.8 billion a year. It has overtaxed and broken down our correction system so that overcrowded jails become little more than detoxification chambers for prisoners, 50 percent of whom are addicts, and classrooms of crime for the remainder.[4]

While much useful material was presented at the hearings in question and there was much alarmist information dispensed, no really clear picture of the international traffic in narcotics can be said to have emerged. The whole problem is stated in incomplete and unrealistic terms if the participation of Red China and its politico-military planners is omitted.

Since the actual sources and the degree of availability of drugs both need to be understood in making an assessment of the problem, the political drives of some of the suppliers need to be stressed, as well as some of the special circumstances that have favored the success of their distribution methods in the United States.

Some of these may be listed as:

(1) High purchasing power.
(2) The rise of collective patterns of behavior.
(3) Social vulnerability. Addiction to heroin, especially, can be associated with societies that are undergoing rapid social change and that contain conflicts between traditional and modern values.
(4) Progressive urbanization.
(5) Conflicts between racial minorities and between persons in different age groups. (To an extent, these have been deliberately accentuated.)
(6) Escapism. It needs to be remembered that the United States has been largely populated by emigrés, many of whom have been refugees from dangers or unfavorable conditions. To these the country has been, in the past, a sure haven and a source of comparatively easy and rewarding livelihood. This is no longer particularly applicable in either case. In the subconscious there is both apprehension and the seeds of disappointment. Drugs

20

provide a readily available means of escape and of support to an ego that is desperately unsure of itself in search of "identity."

(7) Preconditioning.

The social scientist is quick to fasten blame on the addict and he has the law on his side. There have been some extremely plausible theories, some of which include the insidious argument of collective guilt as a particularly potent solvent of public morale. However it seems clear that most of the blame needs to be apportioned to the real sources of the trouble: those veiled enemies whose inflexible purpose it is to bring down our society in ruins. In many cases, the psychological campaign against the mind of the public, a full-scale attack, can be linked with those who have conceived and are waging their devastating psycho-chemical offensive.

Of late, the troops in Vietnam have been the primary target, and some details of the operations and of our countermeasures will be found in these pages. The method of drafting men and rotating them in large numbers (when the buildup was at its height there were a half-million men in position) made the war of such kind that the great majority were often kept in a state of enforced idleness. Since the repatriation program has developed, the percentage of idle troops has been higher than ever. All who understand the inculcation and preservation of military morale are well aware that the U.S. military environment has been, as it were, made to order for propaganda and psycho-chemical attack. There has also been the added circumstance, highly favorable to our enemy, of a large and growing stream of returning troops, a proportion of whom have been "hooked" during the tour of duty.

The all-pervasive availability of heroin of the highest grade, at suspiciously low prices, has infused the largely inactive troops with a formidable degree of heroin addiction that was not dealt with in time and that would undoubtedly startle the country if it were made public. It is almost as if a "no-win" war had been planned somewhere to subject our troops, and ultimately our nation, to maximum exposure to this weapon. It is being wielded by a power complex that includes as elements the chiefs of the Red Chinese Intelligence and Political Warfare Services, members of clandestine organizations such as Chinese Triad and other secret societies, and organized crime syndicates in the Middle East, the Mediterranean area, the Far East, and the Americas.

Without doubt it was this situation that Chou En-lai had in mind when he incautiously confided to Nasser in 1965 the Red Chinese intention to strike at a U.S. "hostage army" in Vietnam, which from the Communist point of view should be as large as possible. The conversation has been reported verbatim in the new biography of Nasser by Mohammed Hassanein Heikal, the editor of *El Ahram*, who, in this instance, can probably be regarded as a completely reliable source:

21

We are planting the best kind of opium especially for the American soldiers in Vietnam... We want them to have a big army in Vietnam which will be hostage to us and we want to demoralise them. The effect which this demoralisation is going to have...will be far greater than anyone realises.[5]

The full implications of the last sentence have not been made clear as yet, but there seems to be more than a possibility that Chou had in mind the birth of a U.S. Revolutionary Army that, on its return, would challenge the established order.

The United States failure in Vietnam is one that may fully be compared with the "loss" of China during World War II when the United States was completely outmaneuvered by the Chinese Communist political planners. One of the major troubles in Vietnam has been the rigid and dogmatic orthodoxy of approach by the Army, which has placed its forces at a grave disadvantage when confronting an enemy dedicated to "Peoples' Revolutionary Warfare." While there had been much discussion about "counterinsurgency" and "special warfare" in the United States, and there had been good understanding of the subject in some professional circles, it was not possible to codify doctrine and to structure, train, and equip the armed forces in time to enable them to contain the threat in a reasonably economical manner, in spite of much talk of "cost effectiveness" in the Pentagon.

The armed forces have, in fact, performed well in Vietnam regardless of the insufferable restraints imposed on them by the inexperienced and often profoundly mistaken planners in whose hands lay the higher direction of the war. In the main these were not professional and trained military men but politicians and members of the new generation of pseudostrategists.

It has not proved possible for these, or even for the forces in the field, to analyze the problems of the war in depth and to apply them in time. Much time and energy has been spent on historical and politico-military research of a highly speculative nature that has had remarkably little to do with the specific problems of the real world. Thus what has notably been lacking is a capability to discern the real nature of the war and to react in time to developing trends in a highly original and constantly innovative form of warfare.

As the important lessons of the Vietnam War are learned and absorbed into the system of doctrine that will be officially adopted, there are grounds for grave concern that some of the more recent advanced and rapidly developing forms, such as urban guerrilla warfare and psycho-chemical warfare, may not command as much attention as they should. There is, in short, more than a possibility that, once again, obsolescent methods will be adopted and applied that would have been very effective in the '60s, if they had been in use in time, but will have, once more, little relevance to the urgent problems that we are likely to face in the '70s. It is most essential that a proper understanding be achieved now of the doctrine, strategy, and tactics of Communist China's narcotics offensive.

Preface
References and Footnotes

1. Hearings, U. S. House of Representatives, Dec. 16, 1925. Hon. Walter E. Linebarger (Committee on Education).
2. Hearings, Committee on Foreign Relations, United States Senate (92nd Congress), July 1, 1971. Senator Frank Church (Idaho), p. 25.
3. *Ibid.* Senator William B. Spong, Jr. (Virginia), p. 26.
4. *Ibid.* Representative Charles B. Rangel (New York), p. 58.
5. *Daily Telegraph,* London; quoted in "China's Secret Vietnam Plan," *Boston Herald Traveler,* Jan. 16, 1972. See also Mohammed Hassanein Heikal, *Nasser: the Cairo Documents* (New York: Doubleday, to be published). The full quotation is as follows:

When Nasser and Chou dined together in Alexandria on June 23 Chou said that he did not want Johnson to withdraw any American soldiers. On the contrary, he wanted the United States to send more and more of its young men to Vietnam.

"We are afraid that some Americans may press for a nuclear attack on China and we think that the American involvement in Indo-China is an insurance policy against such an attack because we will have a lot of their flesh close to our nails.

"So the more troops they send to Vietnam, the happier we shall be, for we feel that we shall have them in our power, we can have their blood. So if you want to help the Vietnamese you should encourage the Americans to throw more and more soldiers into Vietnam. We want them. They will be close to us. They will be our hostages."

One remarkable thing Chou said that night when talking about the demoralisation of the American soldiers was that "some of them are trying opium and we are helping them. We are planting the best kind of opium especially for the American soldiers in Vietnam."

Nasser looked at him in some disquiet, but Chou went on: "Do you remember when the West imposed opium on us? They fought us with opium. And we are going to fight them with their weapons. We are going to use their own methods against them. We want them to have a big army in Vietnam which will be hostage to us and we want to demoralise them.

"The effect which this demoralisation is going to have on the United States will be far greater than anyone realizes." (Author's underlining.)

Nasser felt that possibly Chou was exaggerating a little. But Chou had his plan absolutely clear in his mind. There was no doubt that he intended to do exactly as he said.

Chou's remarks had been provoked by a suggestion that he, Nasser, had made to the effect that he might protest against the massive U.S. intervention.

Later, Nasser told Mr. Harriman about this conversation and communicated to him the part about the Chinese desire for large numbers of U.S. troops in Vietnam; he did not, however, tell him about the revelation concerning psycho-chemical warfare.

Somewhat disturbed at what he had done, he confessed that he had spoken to Harriman:

"Do you really think you are going to defeat them? If you increase your troops in Vietnam, you are only going to play into your enemies' hands. Strangely enough, I've heard something from Chou En-lai, and *you are carrying out the Chinese plan precisely.*"

To Nasser's confession Chou made the rejoinder that he did not mind Nasser's telling the Americans because: "They are not going to learn anything. They are set on a certain course and nothing is going to change their minds."

24

1

Historical Examples of Narcotics Being Used as a Weapon of Political Warfare

History is replete with examples of the use of drugs to attain political ends. While the record is plainer and better documented in the Middle East than in other areas, much is also known about narcotics as a weapon of political warfare in the Far East. In this study, note will be taken of a few examples of such practices that can serve as an aid to fuller understanding of the purposes and the design that underlie the calculated assault on freedom now under way and gaining momentum every hour. This is the Chinese Communist psycho-chemical offensive against the Western order, in which the United States has been targeted as the main objective.

Americans, who have been thus singled out, are prone to ignore the lessons of history, tend to accept the concepts arising from "Social Studies," and are exceptionally vulnerable to this form of attack. They can, for instance, be easily persuaded of guilt of a personal or collective kind when the premises of guilt may not really exist. Their opponents understand particularly well the techniques involved in creating feelings of guilt, which they have used unremittingly as a means of subjugating their own populations. In different forms, the arguments and pressures are being generated within our own society with similar objects in view.

While it is, of course, important to attempt to analyze the domestic conditions that seem to favor the development of addiction to the variety of narcotics now in use, it is most important to recognize that their use does not depend essentially on need, arising from the impact of society on an individual, but much more on processes of promotion than most people realize. The epidemic that is now causing such acute problems can be attributed primarily to the characteristics of the drugs themselves, the motivation and activities of the purveyors, and, *lastly*, to the tastes and desires and weaknesses of the victims.

It will be instructive to consider, in this regard, examples of the use of drugs for political purposes, such as those provided by the sect of the Assassins in Syria, Persia, and elsewhere; the Roshaniyeh in Afghanistan (in areas now in West Pakistan); and, in more recent times, the Japanese narcotics or psycho-chemical warfare offensive. This last was launched in North China as a measure of preparation for the planned military assault that began, seriously, with the Marco Polo Bridge (Loukouchiao) incident in 1937. Consideration of these cases, and others nearer at hand, leads naturally towards informed understanding of the campaigns being waged against us today with marked success by elements of the Communist system of states. And, a most unfortunate situation persists so far not only with impunity but largely without attribution or any official recognition. The matter was handled differently until about 1962, before which year the United States showed signs of official comprehension of the problem. Since then, the threat has apparently been concealed from the public by persons who have evidently had the desire to cultivate better relations with the Red Chinese. The Chinese are the principal miscreants in this criminal conspiracy and they have been able, of late, to obtain protection and support in unexpected quarters.

This historical account begins with a brief examination of the case of the. Assassins.

Case "A": The Sect of the Assassins[1]

One of the earliest literary authorities to describe the strange and interesting sect that flourished in the Middle East between 1090 and 1256 A.D. and that called itself the Hashishyin was that remarkable chronicler Marco Polo, who wrote in his *Travels* of the sect of the Assassins:

> In the centre of the territory of the Assassins there are delicious walled gardens in which one can find everything that can satisfy the needs of the body and the caprices of the most exacting sensuality. Great banks of gorgeous flowers and bushes covered with fruit stand amongst crystal rivers of living water. About them lie ver-

dant fields and from the shaded turf burst bubbling springs. Trellises of roses and fragrant vines cover with their foliage pavilions of jade or porcelain furnished with Persian carpets or Grecian embroideries.

Delicious drinks in vessels of gold or crystal are served by young boys or girls whose dark unfathomable eyes cause them to resemble the houries, divinities of that paradise which the propnet promised to believers. The sound of harps mingles with the cooing of doves. All is joy, pleasure, voluptuousness and enchantment.

The Grand Master of the Assassins, whenever he discovers a young man resolute enough to belong to his murderous legions, invites the youth to his table and intoxicates him with the plant *Hashish*. Having been secretly transported to the pleasure gardens, the young man imagines that he has entered the paradise of Mahomet. The girls, lovely as houries, contribute to this illusion. After he has enjoyed to satiety all the joys promised by the Prophet to his elect, he falls again into a state of lethargy and is transported back to the presence of the Grand Master. Here he is informed that he can enjoy, perpetually, the delights he has just tasted if he will take part in the war against the Infidel as commanded by the Prophet.[2]

The Order of the Assassins was founded in 1090 A.D. by Hassan es Sabah, a Persian, who had been initiated into the doctrines of the Ismailis in Cairo, at the "Dar ul Hikmat" or "House of Knowledge." He had been of the household of the Fatimite Caliph al-Mostansir but was sent into exile in Egypt, having aroused jealousies by his large following. Before this, he had been a close associate of Abu Sadakah ibn Yussuf, the Vizier (prime minister) of the Caliph, who was a Jew and who arranged for the protection of Hassan while he traveled and sought converts in Persia.

At that time he seized the fortress of Alamut, on the borders of Iraq (as it is now) and Dilem, which he called the "House of Fortune." Calling himself Lord, or "Sidna," he founded a catechism and seven degrees of initiation for a body of followers who were divided into two hosts, the "self-sacrificers" and the "aspirants." Although, outwardly, a pious and dedicated Muslim sect, the secret aim of the Assassins was to destroy the faith from within. Its true initiates followed a monstrous and materialist philosophy that has been summarized as "to believe nothing and to dare all." Its aims were the acquisition of supreme power in the world by political murder and intrigue. To an extent, in its outlook, it was a throwback to the times of Karmath, a pagan and debauched period in the history of Arabia that preceded the triumph of orthodox Islam.

Originally stationed in Alamut, under the influence and the command of Hassan, who was frequently known as the "Shaikh ul Djebel" or the "Lord of the Mountain," there were three main categories of members of the Order. These were the "Dais," or missionaries; the "Rafiq," or disciples; and the "Fidayeen," the devotees. The last were the trained killers and wore ritual garments of red and white.

Hassan died at the age of ninety in 1124. Being without issue, he entrusted the future of the Order to Kia Buzurg-Umid, who was to inherit its spiritual and mystical aspect, and to Abu Ali al Quasvini, who assumed charge of the military and organizational aspects of the Order. The former became the second Grand Master.

Their methods brought them incredible success in a short space of time. By the time of the Second Crusade, the Christian military establishment had reached the conclusion that the Sect of the Assassins, being a mortal foe of Islam although outwardly professing that faith, could be used as an instrument to break the Muslim ascendancy in the Middle East, and that it held the key to the balance of power in that area. Most of the exploratory political work towards that end had been the responsibility of the Crusading Order of Templars, who had dealings with them in their fortress of Massyat in Syria. Eventually, an actual alliance was formed between their Grand Master and Baldwin II, the King of Jerusalem, aimed at the reduction of Baghdad.

This pact failed, and the original design formulated by the Templars came to naught. The eventual fate of the Assassins was to be destroyed as an important force by the Mongols under Hulagu Khan, who sacked Alamut in 1256. After that the Assassins remained largely underground, although they did, in fact, continue their mission of murder under the influence of the drug in the service of the Egyptian Caliphate. Some students of their history and of their decline claim to have detected an affiliation between them and the Thugs or "Phansigars" who were suppressed by the power of the British East India Company. The Thugs were certainly well acquainted with "bhang," a form of hemp related to hashish, and had a secret salutation "Ali bhai salaam." This seemed to be an anomaly in a sect whose primary impulse was to gratify the Hindu goddess Kali by human sacrifice. The use of the name of Ali seemed to suggest relationships with the Ismailis who, like all Shiahs, celebrate the festival of Muharram that commemorates the death of Ali.

Case "B": The Roshaniyeh (The Illuminated Ones)[3]

Another unorthodox Muslim sect was that of the Roshaniyeh (the Illuminated Ones), another outgrowth of the Ismailis. While the Hashishyin were, in general, the opponents of the Caliphate in Egypt, the Roshaniyeh were in opposition to the Mogul Dynasty in India (Hindostan) and were based in Afghanistan. Their origins can, also, be traced back to the Dar ul Hikmat in Cairo, but their beliefs were very different from those of the Assassins although their ultimate aims were somewhat similar. The founder of the sect was one Bayezid Ansari. In the sixteenth century, after his initiation as an Ismaili, Bayezid set up a school in the neighborhood of Peshawar. The emphasis was on the supernatural and on the attainment of mystical wisdom through "Khilwat" or meditation. It was a small movement and confined itself, as far as its full initiation was concerned, to about fifty disciples.

The ambitions of the Roshaniyeh were worldwide and their chief called himself the "Pir-i-Roshan," the Master of Enlightenment. His object was to take over the world by successive "illuminations" of different countries, beginning with Hindostan. These countries were to be infiltrated by groups owing allegiance to him, which would acquire the control of power wherever they might operate, whether this would be military, political, economic, or spiritual.

There was a considerable emphasis on drugs and their uses but the approach was a far more sophisticated one than the primitive addictions to hashish, sex, and violence encouraged among the "Fidayeen" used by the Assassins. It is believed that the Roshaniyeh used hallucinogens to promote mystical experiences among their converts. Also, while the Assassins certainly used women in their pleasure gardens, there is no record of women ever attaining positions of importance in that order. But among the Roshaniyeh there were evidently women admitted as initiates. They are supposed to have had an informed interest in poisons, with which their political assassinations were sometimes carried out, and also in aphrodisiacs. One of the features of the order, and a form of behavior that rendered it peculiarly offensive to the orthodox world of Islam, was licentious and orgiastic ritual in which unrestrained group sexual activity assisted the growth of the order among the unprincipled. Some of its most fanatical devotees were women, wellborn ones in particular.

There are, certainly, good grounds for comparing some of the social aspects of this strange community, which was ultimately broken up by the Moguls, and some of the modern "communes" in the United States and elsewhere. Some believe that after the last Grand Master, or Pir-i-Roshan, Omar Ansari, was killed by the pathan tribe of the Yusufzai, his son Abdul Qadir was able to carry on the succession in obscurity and that the beliefs and practices of the sect were transferred to Europe via the "Allumbrados" of Spain. These were suppressed by the Inquisition in 1623, but other underground elements are understood to have survived. Some believe that there may well be connections between the Roshaniyeh and such manifestations as the Bavarian "Illuminati" who sought world power through corruption and infiltration and are known to have been involved in the preparations for the French Revolution.

It is a far cry from the obsessions of the Assassins and the Roshaniyeh with narcotics and poisons applied to the task of world conquest and the Japanese drug campaigns that developed in China during the 1930s, but, in one sense at least, a historical linkage can be seen. Opium and narcotics were used by the Japanese, through their specialized agencies, to subvert the Chinese, preparing them for conquest and then maintaining them in a state of subjugation afterwards. Power was the common aim.

Case "C": The Japanese Narcotics Offensive

The Chinese national addiction for opium, which has been one of the most tragic features of life in that great country, can be traced back quite clearly to the advent of Muslim traders in the sixteenth century. Although known in the Chinese medical pharmacopeia for many centuries before that, the use of opium as a medium of pleasure rather than as a medicine is of comparatively recent origin.

It is said that the Arabs, who were familiar with ancient Greek medicine and who began trading with China about 900 A.D., brought opium to the notice of the Chinese during the reign of the Emperor T'ai Tsung (Sung Dynasty). At that period, the use in China was medical only and addiction was not recorded.

According to the historical record, opium smoking as a habit did not begin until the fifteenth and sixteenth centuries when Spanish and Portuguese traders brought tobacco to China and Southeast Asia via the Philippines. The Dutch habit of mixing tobacco and opium for smoking soon was widely adopted in Formosa and in other places in the Far East. Smokers used the pipe, and many proceeded to eliminate tobacco altogether to obtain the maximum effects from opium.

The authorities in China soon recognized that the use of opium was a social evil and the Emperor Yung Cheng issued an edict against its use in 1729. This was aimed only against smoking and did not imply legislation against the drug for legitimate medicinal purposes. In 1767 the annual import of opium into China was 1,000 chests (one chest = 160 pounds), and by 1790 about 4,000 chests were being imported. It may be assumed that the medical needs of China during that period were about 1,000 chests a year. The trade began mainly under the auspices of the Dutch, but the British supplanted them and, by the end of the eighteenth century, the British East India Company had a virtual monopoly. It should be noted that this monopoly was a going thing that they took over from the Mogul rulers of India.

By the end of the eighteenth century the Chinese had been cultivating a large domestic crop of opium for generations. The poppy and its culture had been introduced by itinerant Muslims coming into the

Empire through Tibet and Burma. Cultivation in Szechuan and Yunnan resulted. By about 1800 as much opium was being produced in China as was being imported.

However, this was illegal because the Emperor had issued edicts, prohibiting either growth or import, that were not repealed until 1860. His wishes were not respected, however, and, although difficulties usually existed in Canton, Chinese traders continually connived with British traders to land opium at other points. In the period 1820–30 there was an annual traffic of about 10,000 chests per year and in the period 1830–40 there was an approximate doubling of the amount imported.

The illegal opium traffic with China, promoted by England, has been portrayed by some as a deliberate attempt to debauch the Chinese population. In point of fact, it was really an attempt to ply a lucrative trade for which there was a strong demand in China, and it was resorted to as a means of keeping open trading channels that would, otherwise, have been closed. The Chinese state had a completely autarchic attitude towards the economy and saw no reason for and had no wish to import foreign goods.

One of the main effects of the opium trade was to precipitate an economic crisis through the constant drain of silver that was used to pay for opium imports. This was one of the Chinese grievances that led to the Opium War of 1839, fought because of affronts to the British that included the confiscation of a large quantity of opium in Canton. Britain won that war in 1842, and, by 1860, 85,000 chests were reaching China annually.

There was a rather general impression that Britain was forcing opium smoking on the Chinese by military means, but that is a gross oversimplification of the issues of a war that was waged over much wider questions. It must, however, be conceded that British merchants and, to an extent, their government regarded opium as a "penetration aid" that would lead to much more diversified, and even more profitable, trading.

John Quincy Adams, when he addressed the Massachusetts Historical Society in 1841, stated that

> Opium was a mere incident to the dispute but no more the cause
> of the war than the throwing overboard of the tea in Boston Harbor was the cause of the American Revolution.[4]

Indian opium was in great demand in China and much preferred, by those who could afford it, to the native product. Nevertheless, domestic production, as well as imports, grew by leaps and bounds and it can justifiably be said that, as the Manchu Dynasty declined, so the consumption and availability of opium increased. Its position as an important part of the economy was further recognized by the imposition of "likin," or internal tax, that, together with import duties collected by the China Maritime Customs, resulted in very large taxes becoming available. At the end of the nineteenth century it was estimated that $10 million a year were being paid by Indian opium imports alone.

As an indication of the growth of the domestic industry, in 1885, 83,000 piculs (one picul = 133 pounds) were imported from India (5,000 tons), at least as much as grown domestically; and, in the years between 1885 and 1900, domestic production soared. Indeed, by 1900, poppies were planted in most of the provinces of China and the production reached unprecedented heights—the annual harvest reached 300,000 piculs, a figure approximating six times that imported from India.

The remarkable rate of growth of opium production in China, together with the large-scale migration of Chinese overseas, led inevitably to considerable export of Chinese opium to numerous markets in the Far East that also absorbed Indian, Turkish, and Iranian opium. Towards the end of the nineteenth century a considerable trade in hard drugs such as morphine and heroin began, with its origins in the eastern Mediterranean area and in Europe. Narcotics of Western origin began moving in quantity from West to East. However, at the same time, an important market began in the United States.

Opium itself has always been especially associated with China as a major producing and marketing area, and where the Chinese have traveled, whether it be to Singapore or San Francisco, there have always been customers for the "Black Smoke."

Writing in *Japan and the Opium Menace*, Frederick T. Merrill has the following to say about their tastes in the matter:

> The oppressive conditions of life under which the majority of Chinese labor for a meager existence has further stimulated the consumption of opium. Education is deficient, ambitious instincts dormant; and the social distraction which the Occident takes for granted is available to less than one percent of the people. Opium smoking thus became the main form of relaxation. In addition to the euphoric effects obtained, the leisurely method of consumption and the social amenities which usually accompany its preparation were the most satisfactory way of relaxing after a hard day's toil. During the nineteenth century, the use of the opium pipe was an accepted custom particularly among the elders of the community.
>
> A more general reason for the extensive use of opium by the Chinese lies in the Chinese philosophy of life. Opium smoking is primarily stimulating but when many pipes are smoked the resulting intoxication sometimes produces dreams. The refinements of opium dreams have appealed greatly to the sensitive and sensuous Chinese people. The sale and purchase of opium is accompanied by the eternal bargaining which is a delight to the average Chinese.

Their fatalistic attitude towards life, their indulgence in earthly joys, all contribute to a tendency to use any pleasant stimulant at hand.[5]

So great was the interest in this commodity that the Chinese Government, under the Manchus, correctly estimated that it was not only a threat to the stature of the nation but even to its survival in a world of rather predatory nations. In consequence, once again, they returned to the task of restricting both the production and the consumption of opium within their own territories.

In 1906 Sir Alexander Hosie, acting on behalf of the Imperial Government, in his capacity as a member of the China Maritime Customs, carried out an inspection of China's opium-growing provinces after the Imperial Edict prohibiting the growing of opium went into effect. He was surprised and impressed to note that it had virtually stopped.

Interestingly enough, the measures of suppression were carried out following discussions that took place in Peking between Government of India officials and those of the Chinese Government connected with Tibetan affairs, after the Younghusband expedition to Lhasa in 1905. Agreement was obtained to cease export of Indian opium to China, the cutoff to be complete in ten years. That aim was achieved by 1913.

During the early days of the Chinese Republic, when the Central Government was very weak and the provinces were in contention between warlords, there was a rapid revival of opium cultivation. Opium served as a means of filling the war chests of the "Tuchuns" and "Tupans" who provided different forms of military government throughout the country. In spite of a heroic effort on the part of the Central Government, which by 1917 had almost succeeded in reversing the trend towards virtually unrestricted opium cultivation and trading, by 1924 the opium problem was as bad as ever.

In that year the office of the International Anti-Opium Association of Peking was obliged to report renewed and increasing cultivation in practically every province. Greed for opium profits was manifest everywhere and an air of breakdown of administration prevailed. To make matters worse, addiction to hard drugs had increased greatly.

It was at that stage that Japan entered the field as a major narcotics trader. In view of the extremely severe official attitude on the part of the Japanese Government, which resulted in very stringent controls for its own nationals, it is a matter of importance to note the laxity with which it viewed opium and narcotics trading in its own dependencies, such as, for example, Korea, or in areas of "special interest" such as North China or Manchuria. (See Appendix II.)

The political and military aggression that Japan launched against China was preceded by a calculated and highly effective preparatory campaign in that country. The campaign was intended to debauch the population, to weaken the national will to resist, and to corrupt the Chinese officials and the military whose duty it was to defend the country against the kind of incursions that ensued and that became inevitable after the annexation of Manchuria.

Unless some of the special features of Japan's drive on China are properly understood, it is quite difficult to visualize Japanese narcotic warfare against China in its proper perspective. It is, for example, quite useless, in the course of historical studies, to try to implicate the Imperial Government in the Japanese homeland in these reprehensible affairs. While there can be no doubt that a massive campaign of psycho-chemical warfare was waged against China as a preparatory "softening-up" process, this seems to have been conceived, planned, and executed by some of the more secret and chauvinistic elements conducting the Japanese effort in China, who had ample opportunity and means for independent action.

It is well known that much of the activity that led to the embroilment of Japan in China, and later in the full-scale war in the Pacific, started with the "Kais," or patriotic societies, of which there were many in Japan. Among these was the "Kokuryukai," or Black Dragon Society, that had defined Manchuria and North China as the earliest objectives to be assailed by Japan. Such societies, although they acquired many recruits from among the military, did, in effect, often act as a link between the military and the industrial and financial concerns whose united effort was important in Japan's drive towards the conquests of World War II.[6]

There is little point in exploring in depth the complexities and ramifications of that association except to note that the traffic in narcotics in the areas across which her armies and her navy intended to advance were exposed to the drug offensive well beforehand, and that it was carried out by what may be described as semiofficial, clandestine, and nonattributable means. It operated through a dangerous and predatory underworld peopled by a tough conglomerate of intelligence agents, criminals, and gangsters of all nations, as well as an increasing tribe of collaborationists and traitors among the Chinese themselves. Within this underworld, coordination and strategic and policy planning was the concern of specially designated personnel furnished by the "Kais." The whole movement was prophetic in its implications.

It is also necessary to recognize that, at times, the offensive encountered resistance in which the party being attacked tried to retaliate by attempting to corrupt or to implicate some of the actual aggressors through exposure or by blackmail. Such procedures were carried on against a background of extremely stringent legislation enacted by the Japanese, designed to protect their own population and nationals, and ensure their solidarity against the dangers arising from addiction. It can be said, in this regard, that moves and countermoves in this domain took on the nature of warfare that was being waged in a new dimension.

As early as February 14, 1919, an article appeared in *The New York Times* that said

> A charge that the Japanese Government secretly fosters the morphia traffic in China and other countries in the Far East is made by a correspondent in the "North China Herald" in its issue of Dec. 21st last. The correspondent asserts that the traffic has the financial support of the Bank of Japan and that the Japanese postal service in China aids, although Japan is a signatory to the agreement which prohibits the import into China of morphia or of any appliances used in its manufacture or applications.
>
> Morphia no longer can be purchased in Europe, the correspondent writes. The seat of the industry has been transferred to Japan and morphia is now manufactured by the Japanese themselves. Literally, tens of millions of yen are transferred annually from China for the payment for Japanese morphia.
>
> In South China, morphia is sold by Chinese peddlers, each of whom carries a passport certifying that he is a native of Formosa and, therefore, entitled to Japanese protection. Japanese drugstores, throughout China, carry large stocks of morphia. Japanese vendors look to morphia for their largest profits. Wherever the Japanese are predominant, there the trade flourishes. Through Dairen, morphia circulates throughout Manchuria and the province adjoining; through Tsingtao, morphia is distributed throughout Shantung Province, Anhui, and Kiangsu while, from Formosa, morphia is carried with opium and other contraband by motor-driven fishing boats to some point on the mainland, from which it is distributed throughout the Province of Fukien and the North of Kwangtung. Everywhere it is sold under Japanese extra-territorial protection.[7]

In the same article there were other references to opium as well as to morphia, and the author was under no illusions about the extensive and highly systematized illicit trading organizations behind the traffic and manipulated by Japanese:

> While the morphia traffic is large, there is every reason to believe that the opium traffic upon which Japan is embarking with enthusiasm, is likely to prove more lucrative. In the Calcutta opium sales, Japan has become one of the considerable purchasers of Indian opium. Sold by the Government of India, opium is exported under permits applied for by the Japanese Government; it is shipped to Kobe and from Kobe is transshipped to Tsingtao. Large profits are made in this trade in which are interested some of the leading firms of Japan.[8]

35

Among the many knowledgeable "foreigners" who lived in China, the late Putnam Weale (Lennox Simpson) knew more than most about opium and its political implications in China and the Far East. Writing in *Asia* in March 1919, he said

> At all ports where Japanese commissioners of Maritime Customs (in China) held office, it is undeniable that centres of contraband trade have been established, opium and its derivatives being so openly smuggled that the annual net import of Japanese morphia (although this trade is forbidden by international convention) is now said to be something like 20 tons a year, sufficient to poison a whole nation.

It was observed at about the same time by A. J. Macdonald, writing in *Trade Politics and Christianity in Africa and the East*, that

> In the North of China another evil is springing up. The eradication of the opium habit is being followed by the development of the morphia traffic. The morphia habit, in Northern China, especially Manchuria, is already widespread. The Chinese Government is alert to the evil, but their efforts to suppress it are hampered by the action of traders, mainly Japanese, who elude the restrictions imposed by the Chinese and Japanese Governments. China is being drenched with morphia. It is incredible that anything approaching the amount could possibly be devoted to legitimate purposes. It is said that in certain areas men are to be seen covered all over with needle punctures. An injection of the drug can be obtained for three or four cents. In Newchwang, 2,000 victims of the morphia habit died in the Winter of 1914–15. Morphia carries off its victims far more rapidly than opium. Morphia is not yet manufactured in any appreciable quantities in the Far East.[9]

Several sources of morphia existed at that time, including Great Britain and the United States, and as many as 600,229 ounces of the drug were shipped from the former to Japan in 1917. The United States supplied as much as 113,000 ounces to the same customer in the first five months of 1919. Japan was rather active at this period in acquiring surplus stocks that had been manufactured for legitimate purposes during World War I.

Thus, it can be seen that during the first two decades of this century there was a marked increase in the addiction of the Chinese and some others to morphine. The use of this dangerous drug was aggravated by shortages of opium, and opium smokers began to develop a taste for it. Within the same period, heroin began to make its appearance, as well as cocaine. Japanese pharmaceutical firms played a large part in developing a market in the Far East; there were large quantities of these drugs also carried from Europe, the Mediterranean area, and the Middle East having as their destination the Far East. The main consuming market was China, which was undergoing considerable sociological damage. Practically the whole of this traffic was illegal and is seen to be the more reprehensible when one considers that the Chinese Government (i.e., the Republic), founded in 1911, had taken very severe and firmly executed measures to try to suppress production of opium in China. This program was so successful that, by 1917, the British Minister in Peking was able to observe that most of the opium that had been under cultivation had been eliminated and that growth was, then, restricted to remote provinces.

However, it continued to be imported in large quantities and the condition was aggravated by the fact that China did not control her own customs service. In 1924 the International Anti-Opium Association of Peking reported a revival of opium cultivation throughout the country. It was believed that in 1919 about 900,000 ounces of morphine, largely of European manufacture, had been smuggled in, mostly from Japan. At this point the serious nature of addiction to "white drugs" rather than opium began to manifest itself, and the Japanese psycho-chemical offensive really began.

This deadly action was favored by the chaotic condition of China; the laws set by the Central Government were continually and openly flouted by the provincial warlords, many of whom were particularly interested themselves in narcotics production and trading as a means of supporting their private armies. Although the arrival of the Nationalist Government and its Northern Expedition were events that were destined to bring about a countercampaign against drugs, it took time for this to develop.

During the period 1932–37, one in which the influence of the Japanese Army (the Kwantung Army, in particular) began to extend itself southward from the newly acquired base in Manchuria that it had annexed in 1931, a great influx of Korean drug peddlers was observed in North China. At first they operated mainly in Hopei Province, which had been demilitarized as a result of the "Tangku Truce" (an accommodation on the part of a Chinese provincial government with the Japanese Army.) This resulted in the formation of a semiautonomous regime that became quite powerless in the face of the intensive smuggling operations that then began. Tientsin, especially, became a principal offensive base for the traffic in opium and heroin as well as morphine. The Japanese Concession at that Treaty Port became infested with innumerable dens, storage points, and laboratories for conversion of opium.

It was estimated, in 1937, that about 10 percent of the population of Tientsin was addicted to drugs and that the number was rapidly increasing. Most of the consumers were poor laborers, or coolies, who could ill afford the habit, although it was noticed that prices seemed to be surprisingly low. Heroin was sold quite cheaply (as it is today in Vietnam) and the addicts considered that they received more satisfaction from a dollar spent on heroin than from three dollars spent on prepared opium. Before long, the habit began to make inroads upon the more educated and wealthier Chinese, as was desired by the promoters of the traffic.

Within the Japanese Concession in Tientsin there were also, besides the hundreds of dens and small establishments connected in one way or another with the traffic, some really large and powerful drug rings, or syndicates, generally Chinese with some Japanese participation and enjoying Japanese protection.

An example of concerns of that kind was the "Sung Syndicate." This enterprise used to import opium from Jehol and convert it into morphine and heroin in the Japanese Concession (Tientsin). It specialized in supplying a number of retailing organizations manned by Koreans. Another concern was the "Chen Syndicate," whose principal activity was exporting drugs to Shanghai. Many of the businesses of this type were registered as Japanese firms, although owned and operated by Chinese. It may be noted, however, that the control of the retail traffic was wholly Japanese and that the people involved were either Japanese nationals, Koreans, or Chinese in Japanese employ.

The pattern that is today familiar to us in such countries as Burma, Laos, and Thailand was set in North China under Japanese auspices many years ago. In Indo-China whole regions have come under the sway of irregular forces sponsored by subversive political organizations (e.g., the Pathet Lao and the Neo Lao Haksat) and are traversed by opium convoys moving under guerrilla escort.

In the 1930s, consignments of drugs might be sent out, in Hopei, under escort of "puppet troops" in order to guard the freight from hijacking by bandits or by gangs of thugs employed by rival drug rings. One of the most famous routes was the road between Tangshan and Tientsin. The convoying forces had to be particularly wary of local garrisons or constabulary.

The so-called "demilitarized zone" between Hopei and "Manchukuo" was a vast reservoir of narcotics, and trafficking led from it all over China. There were hundreds of shops that were kept supplied by a horde of "salesmen" engaged in smuggling their wares in from Manchukuo. These were brought down by junk from the north and handled by such ports as Chinwangtao or Shanhaikwan. The shops were usually operated by Koreans or by Japanese. Peddlers were very active in the Shantung, Shansi, Chahar, or Suiyuan regions.

Some Japanese were obviously upset at the way this vast network had been set up. One of their representatives on the Opium Advisory Committee in North China contended, and it is believed sincerely, that Japan had no control, in the governmental sense, over Koreans in North China. The prevailing friction between the Chinese and the Japanese authorities in these controversial areas led to the traffickers being able to play these opponents against one another to their own advantage. Yet this situation was constantly aggravated by the fact that the Kwantung Army would usually support Japanese or Korean traffickers if they were challenged by the Chinese police.

The situation became much worse after the Japanese invaded and occupied North China after the Marco Polo Bridge incident in 1937. The Japanese population in Peking, for example, increased from 2,000-odd to about 30,000. They immediately suspended the strict regulations of the National Government for the control of opium and narcotics (Appendix I). A number of condemned and imprisoned addicts were released from confinement, together with some peddlers who had been apprehended. Opium traffickers, gangsters, prostitutes, and geishas commissioned to dispense opium and narcotics arrived in large numbers. At the same time, organized vice increased, with large numbers of brothels and cabarets that acted as centers from which drugs were dispensed and addiction promoted as a matter of policy. Very large numbers of retail opium shops, "t'u-tien" or "t'u-kao," were established everywhere, and heroin became freely available at ten cents a packet.

A further corroborating report of the situation at that time has appeared in a very recent book:

> Opium played an increasingly important role in the financial structure of the Japanese-occupied lands after the outbreak of the war. The clandestine character of the trade makes it difficult to come up with precise figures, but the testimony of numerous observers points to a sharp increase in opium trafficking after early 1937. Among those who noted the increase was the U.S. Department of Treasury attaché in Shanghai, one of whose assignments was to report to the Commissioner of Customs on narcotics traffic in China. In April 1937 he reported that "Japanese authorities" in North Chahar were issuing notices to farmers "in the name of local *hsien* magistrates," urging them to grow "the poisonous plant" and setting forth rewards (such as exemption from land tax for minimum cultivation and exemption from military service for cultivation of five *mou*). These crops, as well as those produced in other parts of Inner Mongolia and Manchukuo, were smuggled into North China by Japanese and Korean *ronin* who received "protection from the officials of the Japanese garrison troops in North China" in return for a percentage of the profits.
>
> The introduction of opium into North China was facilitated after

the war began by the establishment of the inappropriately named Opium Prohibition Bureau *(Ya-p'ien Chin-chih Chu)* whose main purpose was not in fact to suppress the narcotics trade, but rather to bring it under the control of the authorities through a licensing system. The reports of the Treasury attaché to this effect were later confirmed at the postwar Tokyo trials by both Japanese officers and Chinese puppet government officials. Of particular interest in this regard is the lengthy affidavit of Mei Ssu-ping, Minister of the Interior and one of the most important officials of the Wang Ching-wei administration. Mei denied what he termed "the current opinion" in China, that the aim of the Japanese narcotization policy *(ma-tsui cheng-tse; masui sei-saku)* was to create addicts in order to weaken and impoverish the Chinese. The plain fact was, he said, that the Tokumu-bu found the narcotics trade a useful way to supplement the "very limited funds" they were allotted to carry on their "extensive work."* Narcotics were also given or sold to "unscrupulous elements and even corrupt officials" for espionage purposes, Mei testified.

Mei distinguished between the trade in opium *(ya-p'ien)* and the trade in other drugs *(tu p'in)*, e.g., morphine and cocaine. The one he saw as largely the function of local low-ranking officials acting on their own, the other as a highly organized affair that represented a major source of funds for the Inner Mongolian puppet government. Moreover, he asserted, it was an open secret that proceeds from the opium trade were remitted to Tokyo for use as a "secret subsidiary fund" by the Japanese Government. It was not until 1943, according to Mei, that the Japanese Government took the first steps in a genuine opium-suppression policy, a move that was occasioned by a sudden outburst of public resentment and student demonstrations in China. (The economic adviser the Tojo Government sent to China in response to the crisis expressed his willingness to help the Wang regime suppress the opium trade provided it kept in mind that "opium profits were the chief source of revenue for the Mengchiang Autonomous Government (of Inner Mongolia.)"[10]

Shanghai Opium Capital

When Shanghai was attacked full scale by the Japanese forces in 1937, in addition to military operations many less conspicuous forms of aggression took place. Until then, in view of the extremely powerful, entrenched position of the major Chinese opium gangs based there that had resisted all attempts by the National Government to undermine

---

Tokumu-bu were the Special Service Units of the North China Area Army. Operated by Japanese Military Intelligence, they were largely independent from the area commanders. Their function was to supervise "civil affairs and political activities," i.e., bribery, corruption, political warfare, subversion, and so forth.

their position or to keep them under effective control, the Japanese had not reproduced the pattern that they had imposed on almost all of North China.

However, the nature of the military operations, and of the naval blockade that the Japanese were able to impose, completely disrupted the logistic networks of the large-scale opium traders and presented the Japanese with an opportunity to enter the opium and narcotics field in a much more direct manner. For example, there had been a good deal of opium coming down the main routes through Nanking and Hankow, which soon became completely blocked, and the immediate result was a great boom in opium prices. The Chinese traders attempted to exploit this even in the moment of great national reverses, by bringing in large quantities from Szechuan and from Yunnan. These shipments were made by important Chinese syndicates based on Swatow and working in collaboration with the hard-pressed opium tycoons in Shanghai.

The Japanese allowed this new trend to develop, and then cracked down on it after they had denounced it, deliberately and for tactical reasons of their own, to the China Maritime Customs. An immediate result was the exodus of a number of major opium magnates whose reign in Shanghai was at an end. One of these was a famous figure in the Shanghai underworld called Tu Yueh-sheng, who was immensely wealthy and connected with an important secret society called the "Ch'ing Pang" (Green Society). His flight to Hong Kong opened the door to Japanese operations in Shanghai, just as it marked the beginning of a new era when Hong Kong has assumed a much more important place, which it still occupies, in the half-world of narcotics trading.

Shanghai's special feature, which had often been noted during the warlord period, was that it was a most tempting prize for aspiring "condottieri." Even to hold it for a limited period with its opium "squeeze," one of the most rewarding of the spoils of Chinese civil war, was to obtain astronomically great profits. These the Japanese now intended to have.

There already existed, when they arrived, an organization called "The Opium Hongs' Union," an association of Chinese dealers who now found themselves in a difficult position because the Japanese had been able to isolate them. This, in effect, had been a "front" for a secret society called the "Hung Chi Shang Tang" that was on good terms with the Japanese authorities. They represented residual Chinese interests after the major operators had sought more peaceful surroundings.

Japanese narcotics policy in Shanghai was set by "Special Sections" attached to the Asia Development Bureau (Shanghai Coordination Office). It was operated by a Col. Kusumoto and a Mr. Suzuki who worked in close conjunction with the Japanese puppet government in

41

Shanghai known as the "Ta Tao" regime.

As the Japanese occupation was consolidated after the first invasions, many of the powerful syndicates in the Peking and Tientsin areas, as, for example, the "Chen Syndicate," moved to Shanghai. Narcotics became an important source of revenue that was paid to the "Consolidated Tax Bureau" and, insofar as the puppet regime was concerned, the industry assumed an official status.

Indeed, it even became a government monopoly. This can be recognized when it is remembered that the puppet organization, the North China Political Affairs Commission run by Wang I-tang, organized an Opium Suppression Bureau whose function was not, as might be surmised from its title, to eliminate the traffic but to control it as a monopoly. Another organ that functioned quite closely was a trade association called the North China Dealers Association.

Under the auspices of the North China Opium Suppression Bureau, a complex of branches was set up in Peking, Tientsin, Tsinan, Tsingtao, Kaifeng, Chefoo, Shihmen, Tangshan, and Tsiyuan. This was really a cover for Japanese military operations in narcotics trading, since almost all the personnel concerned with its operations through these branches were Japanese. Profits were shared between the puppet officials and their Japanese military masters.

It was evident throughout that these flagrant proceedings were, in a sense, carried out against the regulations and against the authority, whether residual or on its way out, of the National Government wherever the Japanese were moving forward. Once established, their narcotics empire became a feature of their rule that fastened itself on the subjugated, captive population.

Observers of the scene as it then was in China have often commented that areas that had been systematically cleansed of production or processing of opium (in North China) were rapidly relapsing into a far worse condition than before. It appeared that the Japanese, as a matter of policy, wished to cut down the production of opium in Manchuria, which had become a fully consolidated part of the Empire, and to supplement the sources from Jehol with new quantities to be grown in Mongolia (Suiyuan), where their influence began to be felt from 1938 onwards.

The control of Inner Mongolia (Mengchiang) by the Kwantung Army, as far as it went, resulted in a considerable increase of production, bringing that region into the forefront by the formation of the Mongolian Opium Company Ltd. This was entirely the creation of units of the KA, the Special Service Sections concerned with intelligence and political warfare, nominally on behalf of the then "Mongolian United Autonomous Government." That important monopoly had its main base in Kalgan, and brown heroin was at that time beginning to be produced in Kweisui and Paotow.

As might have been expected, the Japanese paid a good deal of attention to Nanking, the former capital. Before their arrival, the surroundings of that city and the Shanghai-Nanking-Hangchow triangle had been virtually free of opium, but, very rapidly, wholesale addiction was induced. This took place mainly as the result of the activities of the Opium Suppression Bureau, which fixed prices in such a manner as to enable opium imported from Dairen at $10 an ounce to be sold at $19 an ounce, thus netting enormous profits. Most of the heroin entering the region was sent in over the Tientsin-Pukow Railway from Dairen or Tientsin by Japanese couriers with the full connivance and the encouragement of the Army.

Under these auspices, opium from Iran and from Jehol and Mongolia began to make its appearance, and it was estimated in 1938 that profits of the order of $1,170,000 per month accrued from sales in the West Shanghai market alone. It was understood at the time that there was a good deal of contention between the Japanese Army and Navy over the volume of spoils that were being obtained by these means, which was not very surprising considering that the Army controlled the market and the traders, while, owing to its blockade, the Navy controlled a good many of the supply routes.

It was also obvious that, apart from the importance of the traffic in enabling the conquering power to get a strong grip on the collaborationist authorities that it set up, without the direct use of force, it enabled the armed forces to bribe the opposing armies and to collect intelligence. The Japanese attitude towards drugs was summed up in one of their guidance manuals that was issued to troops of the Kwantung Army in China:

> The use of narcotics is unworthy of a superior race like the Japanese. Only inferior races that are decadent like the Chinese, Europeans and the East Indians are addicted to the use of narcotics. This is why they are destined to become our servants and, eventually, to disappear.[11]

During the China War, the Japanese Armed Forces, especially the Special Sections of the Japanese Army, brought into being the new method of waging war that may be termed psycho-chemical warfare. Under those arrangements its principal characteristics were:

(1) It provided a means of exploiting Chinese susceptibility towards drugs, especially opium and its derivatives, whereby they could undermine the fabric of Chinese society and liquidate the authority and influence of the National Government whose jurisdiction was being displaced.

(2) By it they could weaken the Chinese will to resist at all levels.

43

Not only was the growing addiction at the "grass-roots" level a factor that favored their own advance but they were, also, able to shape the form of the puppet regimes that they sponsored, as well as breaking the resolution of opposing leaders.

(3) Also, using narcotics as a means of persuasion, they could recruit agents and collect military intelligence or conduct special operations.

(4) A means of raising revenue both for the puppet regimes and for themselves.

(5) A means of inducing collective defeatism among their enemies, procuring their defeat and keeping them in subjection once the decision had been gained. They viewed the dissemination of drugs in regions selected for conquest as a measure analogous to artillery preparation prior to an infantry attack. Thus their narcotics planning and operational planning were coordinated. However, this was clandestine.

(6) Recognizing the importance of the underworld of Chinese secret societies as a threat to the established order (i.e., theirs), they considered that partnership in narcotics trading with those interests provided them with a safeguard.

The Japanese psycho-chemical offensive took advantage of the resources that their conquering armies made available to them and thus projected their military operations into a new dimension.

The course of development of this weapons system has been surveyed in some detail, as has been the historical background of opium trading in China, in order to present a suitable foundation for the examination of current Chinese Communist activity. This will be seen to embody some of the characteristics of the Japanese effort, as well as some of the identical resources used by those pioneers in this new branch of warfare. However, Peking has greatly enlarged and refined the scope of such operations and can be shown to have embodied in its modern doctrine a good many of its own characteristic military conceptions. Yet, in a sense, both the Chinese Communists and the Japanese, who shared a common hostility to the Chungking Government during the war years, were contemporaries in their mobilization of the opium poppy.

At the very time that the Kwantung Army was saturating North China with drugs in the 1930s, the Chinese Red Army, where it was digging itself in in Yenan after the disastrous "Long March," was also engaged in planting the opium poppy and harnessing the new weapon to its primitive arsenal. The Reds have today brought it to a state of remarkable development, with a range rivaling that of the ICBM. It is striking hard and deep into the ranks of their opponents, who have not the slightest awareness of the strategy involved and whose highest

44

command is adding to the effectiveness of this murderous assault by denying that the Chinese are involved with narcotics in any way.

There are additional aspects that require examination and attention in the Chinese relationship to the United States domestic scene and to other areas in the Western Hemisphere. Our college campuses and ghettos have become suffused with a spirit of violence and this seems to be associated, at least in part, with a marked increase in consumption of and addiction to drugs on a scale never seen before. Marijuana (a close relative to hashish) and LSD have become general in their use, although few have sought to correlate in specific terms the political significance of what has amounted to a large-scale sociopolitical movement, or to interpret this as a major factor in what may be termed revolutionary potential. Consider, in this regard, another development that was recorded in the '30s.

Case "D": Marijuana and Mass-Revolutionary Violence

In 1934 an experiment was carried out in the United States to investigate the use of drugs in riot situations. It was under the auspices of the Comintern, the General Staff of the World Revolution that was ostensibly discontinued during World War II. The experiment involved the use of twelve college students as guinea pigs, who were given marijuana to smoke that had been delivered from Mexico. The object of the exercise was to combine the psycho-chemical effects of this now-fashionable drug with propaganda to incite student radicals against the New York police.[12]

The line that the incitement took was "Violence is the midwife of the Revolution...but violent action must be planned, controlled and disciplined." They were urged to take direct action and were led in a column to a place where there was a picket line and a demonstration connected with a strike in a button factory.

A "confrontation" resulted between the student demonstrators and some mounted police. The police were assaulted by these drugged students, who were equipped with small clubs through which nails had been driven, intended, mainly, as a means of injuring or goading the police horses.

At the same time, twelve *undrugged* youths approached from a different direction and joined in. During the melee that resulted it was obvious to the observers that the drugged group were far more effective than the undrugged one. The former were insensible to pain and also continued to struggle and resist vigorously after they had been arrested. As soon as they were in the police station, the ACLU appeared on the scene and bailed them out. All rioters were then taken to the Rand School of Social Science (listed as a Communist-run organization by the Federal Government) where they underwent medical and psychiatric examination. (Later the Rand School was absorbed by NYU.)

Two days later a conference was held having as its subject the use of marijuana as a conditioning medium for riots and revolutionary violence. It met in the headquarters of the League for Industrial Democracy (LID) at 112 East 19th Street. Leading personalities of the Communist Party, the Socialist Party, and Trotskyites, and Lovestoneites participated, as well as representatives of the LID.

It was made clear that all factional differences were to be set aside during the course of this briefing. The Fabian elements were acting, as it were, as a political umbrella, and the principal speaker was "Rosito Carrillo" (an alias) who stated that, after the election of Cardenas in Mexico, the left wing had taken over. He added that, in the future, they intended to outflank the United States by gaining control of Cuba in the southeast and then Canada in the north.

Carrillo explained that Mexico had been the proving ground for a new mental-conditioning technique that reinforced the strength of revolutionary masses in carrying out violent assaults against established authority. The idea was to use the controlled administration of marijuana to drug the instruments of their revolutionary purpose. Other narcotics had been tried but had proved inadequate. He stated that the Mexican and other Central American areas were an ideal proving ground, as they were the source of these psychotropic substances and the general population (especially the Indians) had long been accustomed to the use of marijuana and the chewing of coca leaves.

He explained that Pancho Villa, the Mexican revolutionary, used marijuana as a main instrument for conditioning his guerrillas while pursuing terror raids. He regularly allowed American leftist observers into his entourage. In the early 1930s Sandino, also a Red, promoted the major use of both marijuana and coca among his guerrillas in Nicaragua. There were both British and American leftists with him during his raids.

The experiences of both Pancho Villa and Sandino were analyzed by those American and British Reds and then applied further to the Mexican theater. In the 1930s the Mexican "Red Brigands" and "Workers Militia," after being systematically infused with marijuana, created such an impression of audacity that all opposition to them collapsed. The rank and file of the Mexican Army were also drug-induced to defy their officers. The successful performance of such "political zombies" was so complete that it surprised even the leftist manipulators. Carrillo emphasized that this planned mass narcotism offered a shortcut to the Red takeover of the United States.

It was further explained that until then marijuana was by far the best drug for promoting mass-revolutionary automatism. The elements of fear, apprehension, and indecision could be inhibited and the senses

46

tended to be anesthetized against pain or even the irritation of tear gas. It was found that instructions given by someone in authority were almost hypnotically fixed in the consciousness of the smokers. Indeed, the most detailed instructions could be "locked into" the reflex mechanism of the brain as long as the subjects believed in the idea of the revolution as an article of faith.

"Carrillo" mentioned that marijuana was of the same species as hashish and that the latter could be refined to any desired strength. It could be made concentrated enough to bring unconsciousness and even permanent brain damage. He explained that hashish had a long history as an impeller of violent action and had also been used extensively as a religious hallucinogen. It could be taken as a smoke, as a drink, or as a confection. It had been used in the Orient for more than 2,400 years and was an addiction with many millions of people. He named India, Turkey, the Arab World, East Africa, North China, South and Central America as areas inhabited by consumers of hashish.

He startled his hearers by telling them that distribution of hashish was a capital crime in Turkestan and the Caucasian areas of the U.S.S.R. Red leaders knew that mass use of hashish had a disturbing and debilitating effect on civilizations. He explained that it was a valued weapon in the Red arsenal to help undermine and topple the capitalist system but that, after the revolution, it would be necessary to extirpate its use (and, possibly, its users). He warned against excessive use of hashish by valuable revolutionary cadres.

Speakers arose and propounded a long-range campaign to arrange legal acceptance of marijuana and other similar drugs, using as an argument the right to freedom of individual choice. Some elements present—left-wing doctors, lawyers, news-media representatives, and even clergy—were urged to get a coordinated campaign running in which the public would be urged to accept and legalize the drug. A doctor commented on the effects of the substance and said that if a demonstrator were injured and captured, or killed, there would be no perceptible trace of the drug left as a basis for legal action. All other organic drugs leave traces that can be found during an autopsy. This conference ended with clenched-fist salutes and the singing of the "Internationale."

Next, immediate measures were taken to introduce the marijuana mass-violence technique into a number of revolutionary training schools. The New Workers School in New York City, for example, took the matter up under the prompting of Bertram Wolfe and Jay Lovestone. These were now professed Fabian Socialists but formerly had been members of the Comintern. Another center that became interested was Sidney Hook's International Workers' School. Others were the Brookwood Labor College of Katonah, New York; Commonwealth College in Mena, Ark.; the Highlander Folk School in Monteagle, Tenn.; and Camp Tamiment in Pennsylvania (operated by the Rand School).

Thus a program was begun that has had its effects on individuals now marching in the ranks of CORE, SDS, and SNCC. It has undoubtedly played a major part in the manifestations of campus violence and civic disorder that have been mounting in intensity for the last few years.

The meaning of those manifestations cannot be readily understood unless the doctrine, the strategy, and the tactics of narcotic warfare in its present form as an aid and an incitement to revolutionary action are related to certain political events with which they have been closely connected. Among these have been

(1) *The Tri-Continental Conference* held in Cuba in 1966.
(2) *The Continental Solidarity Conference* held in Cuba in 1967.
(3) *The Hemispheric Conference* held in Montreal in 1968.

All these had a direct bearing on Communist designs for the takeover of the Western Hemisphere by various subversive methods; but, in the light of the facts already given about the promotion of the technique of mass violence through the use of marijuana, the following program, in outline form, that was discussed during closed sessions of the Tri-Continental Conference is of special interest:

(Translation of the Secret Resolutions Passed at a Meeting of the Tri-Continental Conference in Havana, January 1966, about the United States.)

AS TO THE UNITED STATES OF (NORTH AMERICA).

...To coordinate the work of the Communist Party (CP), with all the kindred organizations.

1) At universities, labor unions, and negro groups.
2) To intensify agitation and propaganda, demanding from each Communist or sympathizer, especially those in the press media, radio, TV and public relations, in general the maximum results and efficiency as to make known the instructions and directives issued by the Bureau of Coordination.
3) To push forward with the utmost eagerness the pacifist campaign, more and more linking the youths in military age zealously caring to present the intervention of the Pentagon in Vietnam as a dangerous step towards an atomic war. To attack President Johnson, depicting him as a puppet of the monopolies controlling the military at the Pentagon and defending the right of the American nation to live in peace,

48

so that the money of the nation will not be squandered in imperialistic campaigns as in Santo Domingo and Vietnam. To praise the columnists, the congressmen and the newspaper people who are in favor of a Yankee withdrawal in Vietnam. To recruit a group of young pacifistic leaders taking good care that it will be made up by negro elements. To attack everyday the AFL/CIO as "yellow" labour organizations. To set up, at once, Communist and kindred "fractions" in the labour unions to work with all tactical sense, in accord with the teachings of Lenin, in favour of a Popular Labour Party headed by negro leaders.

4) To work for the dismantling of Yankee military bases in Europe, Asia, and Latin America, basing this campaign on the huge expenditures that NATO and other interventionist forces cost to the nation.

5) To cover up the conspiratorial tasks of the Communist Party especially in the United States behind the mask of peaceful coexistence.

6) *To back up resolutely the campaign of the drug addicts, defending it in the name of the respect for individual rights. To maintain completely apart the cadres of the Communist Party from the channels for narcotics and their traffic so that this source of income could not be linked with the revolutionary action of the Communist Party although we must combine fostering the fear of atomic war with pacifism and with the demoralization of youth by means of hallucinating agents.*

7) To brand as useless and false the Civil Rights Law, asserting that liberation and equality will only be possible for the negro through a Socialist Revolution that will bury the Imperialism of the white Yankees. To set up alliances as fast as possible with Puerto Rican and Latin American minorities in centres of studies, factories and sports. To emphasize the exploitation in which these minorities live, to become cannon-fodder sent to death in Vietnam. To avoid any fraternization with the Jews, accusing them of supporting imperialism in Israel, and elsewhere. To praise President Kennedy, opposing his humanist philosophy to that of the cow-boy Johnson who is pushing the world towards a nuclear conflagration. To praise the pacifist line of the Vatican as contradicting the attitude of the United States. To intensify raising funds all over the United States, because the guerrilla warfare in Latin America will have to be paid for fundamentally by the contributions of the Communists and their sympathizers in the United States. To spread the news that the KKK is represented in Congress, in the Pentagon, in the Judiciary and in the State Department.[13]

As a commentary on the case studies selected to provide historical background on psycho-chemical warfare, an example will be given of more recent historical significance, namely the bloody affair in Portuguese Angola in 1961. On the morning of March 15 of that year, bands of Angolese and Congolese irregulars suddenly made several well-synchronized and unprovoked attacks on a number of settlements in the Uige district. These resulted in the premeditated and wholesale slaughter, in the cruellest way imaginable, of 800 Portuguese citizens, black and white, including a number of women and children.

Unspeakable barbarities and mutilations were committed that were very fully and accurately documented by unimpeachable witnesses, and were duly reported to the United Nations. For example, as a part of his testimony, Vasco Garin, the Portuguese Ambassador to the UN, recounted

> A witness...heard the prolonged cries of agony of those being quartered, because the terrorists, their victims still alive, plucked their eyes out, cut off their heads, tore pieces of flesh from their bodies, disembowelled them and committed other bestial acts. Some whites, Mulattoes and Negros were skinned alive.
>
> The women, regardless of age, were dragged from their homes by the terrorists. Their children were snatched from them. The bodies of the innocent victims were then used to play ball with. All children's hands and feet were cut off....Girls were raped. All women, regardless of their age, had their clothes ripped off prior to being raped several times by bands of savages....These scenes occurred during the assault on the M'Bridge plantation. The name of the survivor who told the tale, who is still convalescing, is Manuel Lonco Neves Alves. The terrorists who assaulted that plantation were not known locally. The attack took place on March 15th.[14]

The worldwide propaganda that was disseminated about these events by the Communists and their supporters in the Western press was, of course, tailored to describe them as part of a spontaneous and popular outburst against the Portuguese African regime. Nothing could have been further from the truth.

This invasion was led by Robert Holden, a Baptist school-educated Bakongo Negro who, in 1954, had founded a body called the Union of the Peoples of Angola (UPA). He built this up under Communist auspices, receiving backing from their creatures Kwame Nkruma, Patrice Lumumba, and others, and directly from Soviet Ambassador Solod in Conakry. He also had Red Chinese contacts.

This murderous revolutionary was received in the United States in 1959, where he was treated with the utmost consideration by the State

Department and the CIA and was given both political and financial support. Later, his final recruitment and training operations in the Congo were undertaken with the direct backing of Lumumba, who provided his irregulars with arms taken from the stores left behind by the Belgian constabulary. The Bakongo, who were his main source of manpower, were incited by means of atavistic appeals to witch doctors, fetishism, and cannibalism. When they were actually committed to the outrages that were required of them, they were under the influence of drugs administered with professional skill by their commissars. The principal preparations used were variants of the cannabis or hemp plant (the marijuana family), described in Central Africa as "dagga." Lumumba is known to have favored the use of hemp preparations as a means of promoting terrorism and atrocities.

It is astonishing, and indeed most disturbing, to realize that these occurrences in Portuguese East Africa, and others like them, took place with the full, if somewhat naive, support of the United States. On March 16, the day after the Angolan massacres, Adlai Stephenson, the newly appointed Ambassador to the United Nations representing the Kennedy Administration, supported the Russian resolution for "immediate steps" to transfer all power to the peoples of Africa "without conditions or reservations..."

Consistent support of violent and subversive movements in Portuguese possessions followed, in spite of the fact that it was soon discovered that the lives of some 1,500 whites and 20,000 blacks had been claimed by the revolutionaries.

Chapter 1.
References and Footnotes

1. Arkon Daraul, *A History of Secret Societies* (New York: Pocket Books, 1969), pp. 11–12; Charles Heckethorne, *The Secret Societies of All Ages* (New York: University Books, 1965), Vol. I, pp. 116–122.
2. Yule and Cordier, *Travels of Marco Polo* (London: John Murray, 1903), p. 139.
3. Heckethorne, *op. cit.* pp. 123–125; Daraul, *op. cit.* pp. 262–277.
4. Frederick T. Merrill, *Japan and the Opium Menace* (New York: IPR/FPA, 1942), p. 6 (footnote).
5. *Ibid.*, p. 12.
6. Hugh Byass, *Government by Assassination* (London: George Allen & Unwin, 1943), Part III, pp. xii, xiii, xiv.
7. *The New York Times*, Feb. 14, 1919.
8. *Ibid.*
9. A. J. Macdonald, *Trade Politics and Christianity in Africa and the East* (1916), p. 229. Quoted by Ellen N. LaMotte in *The Opium Monopoly* (New York: Macmillan, 1920), p. 14.
10. *John Hunter Boyle, China and Japan at War, 1937–1945: The Politics of Collaboration* (Stanford, Calif.: Stanford University Press, 1972), pp. 99–100.
11. Merrill, *op. cit.*, p. 63.
12. Substance of "Marijuana and Mass-Revolutionary Violence" supplied to the author in private communication.
13. Translation of secret resolutions supplied by Professor Herminio Portell-Vila, former history instructor of Fidel Castro at the University of Havana.
14. Nathaniel Weyl, *Traitor's End* (New Rochelle, N.Y.: Arlington House, 1970), p. 151.

2

The Current Scene as it Affects
the United States
Domestically and Overseas

The exact number of illegal drug users and addicts in the United States is not known. At the end of 1969 a figure of 68,088 was noted in a publication issued by the Bureau of Narcotics and Dangerous Drugs, implying that there may be approximately one addict per 3,000 persons. The figure has been increasing since then and, in any event, reflects an extremely conservative estimate. New York is said to account for about 50 percent of the addict population, and if California, Illinois, and New Jersey are added, about 75 percent of those involved are accounted for.

Probably the most disturbing aspect of the problem, as it now confronts us, is that an attitude of growing permissiveness towards some of the reputedly less dangerous drugs such as marijuana (actually a most dangerous substance) or the barbiturates has been causing an increase in the use of hard drugs. Whole sections of the population that have been totally unaware of the drug problem have become enmeshed in it. Furthermore, most regrettable of all, it has been taking a heavy toll of the health, welfare, and even the lives of the young. At one time drug abuse could be confined strictly within the areas of law enforcement and medical activity. These are proving inadequate, and new

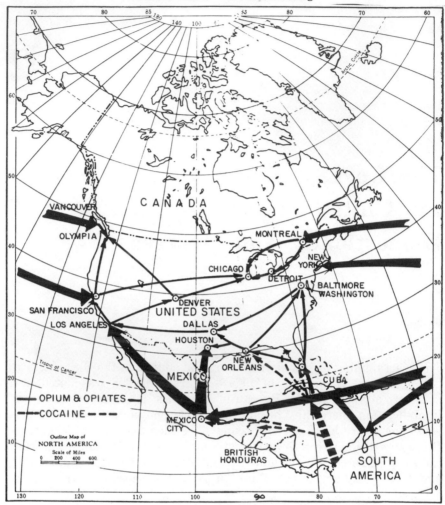

approaches are badly needed. One of the worst features of the matter is the way in which something that used to be regarded as degrading and beyond the social pale is becoming a criterion of respectability to a deluded but ever-growing segment of society.

In the government publication referred to above, stress very rightly was laid on the importance of economic loss and social disruption. According to the Bureau of Narcotics and Dangerous Drugs, and other observers, addiction drains millions of dollars from our economy. The average addict spends $30 a day for his drug, and this implies that for seven days a week, 52 weeks in the year, he or she would require about $10,950. When the addict is really "hooked" on hard drugs, a more realistic figure in this country would be $100 a day. This immediately results in crime, especially when heroin is involved, in view of the fearful imperatives that it exerts over its victims.

If theft is used to raise the money to satisfy a drug craving, the assumption is made that disposal of stolen goods is at an average rate of $1 in cash for $3-$5 worth of goods. Thus, a confirmed addict who needs to support a $30-a-day habit must steal $100 worth of goods a day or $36,500 a year. Obviously billions of dollars are involved in this drain on the productive resources of the country.

The economic arguments against drug abuse are, however, of minor significance when compared with the losses that can be listed under such headings as moral corruption, degradation, the total destruction of life and character that ensue from the use of drugs in forms of servitude utterly demeaning and destructive to a society such as ours. Involved in the whole question, but not particularly visible as yet, is the potential that is being stored up for the overthrow of the established order by various forms of revolutionary action. These, at present, may be considered to be in the formative, experimental, and training stages, although there are also indications that this program is well advanced. We live in the "Age of the Guerrilla" and, as will be seen, there are close affiliations between the doctrines of revolutionary warfare and the use of drugs.

Some of the findings in Vietnam are beginning to arouse quite valid apprehensions within this area of military study. The facts are extremely grave.

Early in June 1971, Rep. Seymour Halpern (R; N.Y.) told a Senate Labor Subcommittee on Narcotics: "Presently, I would say there are upwards of 60,000 GIs in Vietnam who are using hard drugs. Even this figure, I believe, is conservative. It represents 20 percent of the GIs in Vietnam, whereas firsthand estimates provided to me by those closest to the picture say it's close to 30 percent."[1]

These findings were the result of a trip to Vietnam undertaken by Halpern, Reps. Robert H. Steele (R; Conn.), and Morgan Murphy (D; Ill.). At the same hearings, Roger T. Kelley, Assistant Secretary of Defense, said, "We don't know how many military members in Vietnam use heroin and other drugs." He admitted, however, that addiction seemed to be spiraling upward, noting that, while in the whole of 1970 the U.S. military authorities investigated 700 cases of involvement with hard narcotics, the corresponding figure for the first *three months* of 1971 was 800. He added that, within the same period, "over 3,600 personnel asked for help under amnesty programs to overcome dependency on heroin."

He explained that one supposed reason for the increase in hard-drug addiction had been a crackdown on marijuana. The three congressmen emphasized that there were large quantities of heroin readily available to the GIs that they were led to believe derived from "corruption among high government officials."

By May 1971 an intensive antidrug campaign was under way in South Vietnam (New York Times, May 18, 1971). Two major difficulties that it encountered from the first were complete indifference and permissiveness among the Vietnamese who, for the most part, regarded drugs as perfectly normal and a personal rather than a public matter; secondly, there seemed to be some evidence of official connivance at high levels in the traffic.

The transport system delivering drugs to centers such as Bangkok or Saigon is an old one that has been functioning for a hundred years or more, but its efficiency has been greatly increased of late by the use of modern methods of transport such as aircraft and speedboats. There has been evidence that quantities of raw opium are being processed in clandestine factories in Vientiane, but suspicion has been growing that the exceptionally high grade of heroin that is generally available at very low prices may be coming from Red China itself, probably from Yunnan Province.

> The uniformity of packaging indicates a uniform source. These same plastic vials are virtually identical in any area of Vietnam. So either a criminal or an enemy element is involved. The purity of the heroin is astronomical but the price is low.
> There have, also, been strong indications uncovered by American officials, that there is a link between the heroin traffic and the United States-sponsored Royal Laotian Army, and which would be able to protect operations there and to provide some help in transporting the drug out. Opium is not prohibited in Laos.[2]

U. S. Army commentators have expressed the view that the prepared heroin is carried into South Vietnam by military and civilian air travelers. They are sure that one reason they have been unable to uncover many leads on smuggling and distribution in South Vietnam is because high-ranking Saigon officials are either engaged in the traffic or are protecting those who conduct it.

> Some of the criticism of official indifference toward drug smuggling is directed towards Tran Thien Khoi, chief of the national Customs Investigation Division and a brother of Premier Tran Thien Khiem...
> Another brother of the Premier, Tran Thien Phuong, is Director

of the Saigon Port, which is regarded by U.S. officials as a main point of entry.[3]

It is most important to note that the price of this heroin in Saigon is $20 an ounce while the same product in the U.S. costs $4,000.

A report was published in the *Sing Tao Jih Pao* of Hong Kong on August 6, 1971, to the effect that the Chinese Communists were launching a strong campaign to poison U.S. soldiers in Indo-China with narcotics. They had set up, for this purpose, an agency in the border region, near to Laos, North Vietnam, and Cambodia, to undertake the transportation and distribution of narcotics. Its policy was to offer a series of cut-rate prices for its products, chiefly heroin. The object was to push up addiction rapidly among the American troops and thus weaken their physical strength, erode their morale, and tempt some addicts to engage in espionage on behalf of the Communists. It was also hoped to earn dollars. The report added

> Dope has long been one of the major sources of foreign exchange for the Peking regime. The Chinese Communists have devoted vast tracts of farmland in the southwestern province of Yunnan and the northwestern provinces to poppy growing. They have built large-scale plants to process heroin and morphine. Narcotics from the Mainland are sent to Laos where they are sold or distributed without government interference. Then they are shipped to various Southeast Asian countries and Japan.
>
> Communist China has only a marginal surplus in its visible trade, amounting to some $166 M (U.S.) last year. Yet it has been lavishing large amounts of foreign exchange on economic and military aid to many countries. Without the foreign exchange from narcotics, it would not have been possible for the communists to afford such enormous expenditures.[4]

Gloria Emerson, writing in *The New York Times* of February 25, 1971, commented on the great availability of heroin, being peddled in Vietnam wherever there are convoys or concentrations of U.S. troops. The price of a small vial about the size of an airlines saltshaker is about U.S. $3.00. These vials can often be purchased by exchanging a carton of American cigarettes obtained for U.S. $1.75 in the PX.

It was reported at the brigade headquarters at Longbinh that the use of heroin in the unit had risen rapidly from 5 percent to 20 percent.

> Some GIs prefer to smoke the heroin which they mix with cigarette tobacco because, unlike marijuana, it has no distinctive aroma. It is said that few inject it into the veins. If they do not

smoke it they "snort" it; used like snuff, it is pushed into the nostrils and inhaled....

On the narrow road leading to the 90th Replacement Battalion where soldiers arrive in Vietnam and where they are processed to leave after one year, a small boy looking not much older than 7 sits under a poncho with a monkey on a leash and a bird in a bamboo cage. Not to be seen are the vials of heroin which he cheerfully sells....

At the tiny railroad station at Longbinh where there is a commuter train to Saigon for Vietnamese employees, a middle-aged Vietnamese woman in a green blouse and black pants sells watermelons. She also sells heroin which the Vietnamese call "White Opium."[5]

The U.S. authorities responsible for this problem have only comparatively recently become properly convinced of it. Earlier allegations made about drug abuse had, in fact, been rejected. There was a good deal of preoccupation with marijuana, resulting in worldwide investigation of 16,342 cases during the first half of 1970. During the same period the services examined 1,522 cases of involvement with hard drugs, of which 239 were in Vietnam.

During some hearings held by the House Armed Services Committee during August 1970, Frank A. Bartimo, an Assistant General Counsel of the Defense Department, indicated that

The recent "responsible" polls indicated, roughly, that 30 percent of the servicemen in S.E. Asia had tried marijuana some time before or during their service career, but that 70 percent of these were only casual experimenters. "I cannot emphasize too strongly," he said, "that by far the overwhelming majority of servicemen like other American youth are not drug users or addicts. They are clean-cut, upstanding individuals with a purpose in life." He criticized "bombastic statements" that have exaggerated the extent of drug addiction in the armed forces. Indeed, it had been asserted that there was a Communist propaganda policy to disparage our armed forces and to try and break their morale by tarnishing their reputation by unfounded allegations.[6]

During the same hearings, Rep. Durward G. Hall (R; Mo.), had said

Let none of us forget for one moment that some of these outrageous and unconscionable allegations and reports are much more than selling news media. They are, in fact, implanted there as a part of the planned deterioration of the esprit de corps, the morale, the command function and everything else of our armed forces by the Communist aggressor and there isn't the slightest doubt about that.[7]

However, the late Senator Thomas J. Dodd is on the record before his Committee on Juvenile Delinquency as raising questions connected with inattention to drug problems in the armed services and to subsequent difficulties after discharge.

One of the witnesses who testified before Senator Dodd was Jon Steinberg, who had been an Army reporter before joining the staff of Arlen Specter, the District Attorney of the Philadelphia District, as an administrative aide. He reported that drugs are used by the *majority* of young soldiers in South Vietnam and were lowering the Army's efficiency—also that drugs are easier to get than liquor. Steinberg, in the course of his report, said

> The military has taken an unrealistic look at the problem, doesn't recognize it as a problem and doesn't give it the proper treatment.[8]

This gist of his message was that, although the Army would not own up to the gravity of the situation, it was beginning to have an effect on operations. He had been told, during his visit to Vietnam, of several cases where guards on duty, having been "high" on marijuana, resulted in camps being overrun.

Steinberg emphasized that, after conducting a thirty-day survey in Philadelphia among persons arrested for drug offenses and violations (and who could not post bail), many had served in Vietnam, had taken to drugs there, and had been honorably discharged. He told the Dodd Subcommittee that GIs returning from Vietnam have great difficulty in breaking the habit because the variety available in Vietnam is much stronger than the local variety.

He considered that 80 to 90 percent of the younger GIs in Vietnam who experimented with marijuana either smoked it straight or laced it with opium. This often occurred on duty, and he had been told by Army psychiatrists about homicides and other aggressive behavior occurring while under the influence of marijuana.

There was, for example, the case of Robert J. Parkinson, an ex-marine sergeant. He had served a twenty-month tour of Vietnam and was quite unaware of drugs being used. When he asked for a second tour and found himself again in Vietnam (returning in August 1968), "pot was everywhere you looked" and he found his men smoking it on duty and becoming incapable of doing their jobs. Parkinson objected to the use of marijuana to such an extent that his men tried to kill him:

> I was blown up by my own men who rolled a grenade under my
> bed as I slept.

A bone in his foot was shattered, part of his intestines and liver were removed, and his diaphragm was injured.

Another witness before the Dodd Subcommittee, Dr. Robert Baird of the "Haven" in New York, has estimated that there are about 250,000 pot smokers, 25,000 heroin users, and 20,000 amphetamine users in the service. He has also expressed his opinion that the Red Chinese are heavily involved in this traffic and that their operations extend to this country as well as to Vietnam.

The Army launched a number of measures intended to control narcotics in Vietnam and their use by servicemen, which took effect in 1971 and continued after that. For example, Ambassador Ellsworth Bunker exerted heavy pressure on President Thieu, urging him to intensify control of movement and distribution of drugs. Thieu agreed to comply and replaced a number of senior officials who had been under suspicion of using their posts to abet smugglers and to profit by their transactions.

However, from the first there had been serious doubt about the efficacy of such measures, and the opinion was prevalent in U.S. circles in Vietnam that his responses were calculated more to placate the Americans than seriously to cut down the traffic. There was an interesting and rather significant example of the way in which the measures worked in the case of Pham Chi Tien.

This involved a senior member of the South Vietnamese Customs Service Fraud Suppression Branch who was known to be a user of opium and whom the U.S. authorities would have preferred to have removed from his post. In order to influence the Americans in his favor his chief ordered him to arrest Pham Chi Tien, a Member of the National Assembly, as he arrived at Saigon Airport with baggage containing 10 pounds of heroin and some opium. The official in question carried out his orders, which rested on information acquired through American channels in Laos whence the deputy had come. In consequence, he was decorated for efficiency and rewarded by an official dinner attended by the Americans who had asked for his relief from duty. However, they persisted, and he was, in fact, later posted to a far less critical appointment (New York Times, August 30, 1971).

His successor, Col. Cao Van Khanh, was very frank about the difficulties facing enforcement in a corrupt bureaucracy and indicated that he had "all kinds of people" on his force and was suspicious of the rich members. Both he and another keen and energetic police officer, Ly Ky Hoang, in charge of the National Police Narcotics Bureau, were aware of limits to their powers, especially as these involved the military. They had no powers to act in such cases except with military consent.

Naturally, in a country at war where most of the administration is in military hands, especially one in which the military have a long-established tradition of all kinds of smuggling and defalcations, this represents a very substantial curb on the powers of enforcement. A good deal of attention has been paid by such responsible individuals as Khanh and Hoang to the matter of heroin smuggling by air, and it is within that area that the most significant seizures have been made. Nevertheless, no impression whatever has been made by such measures on the general availability of the drug; it has, in fact, been becoming more prevalent all the time.

Col. Khanh is on record as having told U.S. newspapermen of his view that a good deal of smuggling was being carried out on South Vietnamese Air Force planes. As a result of tightening precautions at civil airfields, the traffic seemed to have shifted to military air bases, particularly Tansonhut and Danang. The Colonel displayed to visitors a permit, signed by Col. Nguyen Duc Khanh, authorizing a Mr. Hung (a Chinese) to enter and leave Danang Air Base by any means of transport. Tun Siu Hung is an overseas Chinese with a foreign passport, a person with a number of arrests connected with narcotics trading.

In all this, the Thais have presented a particular problem since, besides being the main channel through which most of the traffic flows in Southeast Asia, their armed forces have been active in fostering it. The official attitude seems to be a particularly permissive one. It has been reported that their troops have been observed openly selling heroin to Vietnamese in the neighborhood of their base in Longthanh. Their commander had refused to participate in mixed antinarcotics patrols conducted by Vietnamese and U.S. Military Police.

The view is expressed by many right-thinking Vietnamese that this aspect of the traffic can only cease when the Thais return to their own country. One of the complications connected with any attempts at control is the clandestine nature of many of the Vietnamese air operations. They are carried out under the terms of a Viet-Thai air agreement in which missions are flown to Thailand that are connected with secret Vietnamese Special Force activities on the Ho Chi Minh trail in Laos.

As yet, from a theoretical point of view, little has been said about the strategy and the tactics that underly the narcotics offensive. The enemies of the United States within the worldwide Communist movement, particularly those among the political planners of the CP(SU), have long recognized the difficulty of their task. But it should be remembered that with them time is no object and that the basic aims that were set in motion in 1917 and later reinforced by the Chinese component of the Trust were not new. They recognized the magnitude of the task before them, confronted as they were with a large potential adversary, the wealthiest country in the world, strategically protected by the oceans and a powerful navy and assisted by many allies.

They recognized that the country had great confidence and trust in its political system and its destiny. It had acted as a magnet towards which the oppressed of the earth had long made their way, where they had been made welcome and had been able to savor the successes of a prosperous and humane society. Such a great polity as that of the United States, equipped with the power of nuclear weapons (until recently on an overwhelmingly superior scale) and with what appeared, a few short years ago, to be a condition of unbounded confidence and invincible morale, certainly presented the Communists with the most difficult of all tasks that they had ever set themselves.

In other countries they had been able to avail themselves of the strategy of "class struggle," ideologically a part of the worldwide campaign that they had waged unremittingly in Europe with impressive results, and in the colonial and imperial territories of the European powers. In the United States, however, a country largely dedicated to the eradication of the idea of classes, and itself so opposed to the social structure of colonial and imperial systems that its support could be enlisted against them, the long-range planners were obliged to undertake a complete revision of their methods. Since they recognized that most of the forms of disruption and subversion they had promoted heretofore would not serve in the U.S. setting, they were obliged to seek new alternatives. They have settled, in the main, for two "contradictions": namely, the racial problem—the "color gap"—and the conflict between the young and the old—the "generation gap."

In addition to these, there are numerous other points of "contradiction," some more or less associated with the above, but others that are not so related. Examples are the points of cleavage in the armed services due to color, rank, etc., as well as alienation of the services from the body politic; racial minorities other than the blacks; the pitting of the sexes against one another by such means as "Women's Lib"; and the discovery and development of "countercultures" and disaffected members of the community. Of these, hippies and homosexuals are typical.

The fragmentation, division, and concurrent weakening of the fabric of American society by the discovery, initiation, and exacerbation of such divergencies has been carried out with skill and ingenuity, using all the resources of agitation and propaganda. Drugs have played an important part. On the whole, the task has been facilitated by a factor that has been eloquently and penetratingly explained by Marshall McLuhan: as a result of the all-pervasive presence of the media, a population that was originally founded on the basis of individuality and a sense of solidarity and neighborliness has become an electronically articulated and controlled crowd.

This crowd, under the constant pressure of advertising and other forms of suggestion or persuasion, has undergone a process of atrophy of its judgment and of its powers of resistance to undesirable ideas. Its further seduction in the direction of dissent or violent destruction of the established order is brought nearer.

In this situation, the plight of the young has become a particularly serious one. So much information and writing on the more obvious aspects of this problem are now available, as it relates to the assault on children in the schools and students on the college campus, that only the briefest account is given here.

There is something of a consensus that the present serious drug crisis in the high schools—primarily marijuana, LSD, mescaline, and a few others such as amphetamines and barbiturates—began about 1967. It is probably a fair observation that the rise of drug-taking within the high school community has coincided with the increasing process of integration and it has been aggravated by the great psychological stresses placed on all members of the younger generation by that process. In addition, there are those introduced by the awareness of the war in Vietnam, particularly as they have been presented to the country by highly organized campaigns of misinformation.

All who have studied the history of narcotics addiction in the United States realize that the original seat of marijuana smoking and even of heroin addiction has been the slums; it has been there that most of the pushers and distribution rings have been at work. Traditionally, it has been among the underprivileged and desperate black population that frustration and feelings of inferiority have led them, as elsewhere, for example in Asia, to seek escape by these fearful routes.

The habit has also been shared by the much more successful members of the entertainment world, who have nearly always been plagued by anxieties and stresses unknown to the more sedate members of the community with more assured forms of employment. Black youths of high school and college age, aware of the properties of heroin and accessible to "pushers" for generations, have, regrettably, been the primary means by which this menace has found its way into wider reaches of the body of society.

Indeed, before 1966 the extensive use of drugs was still largely confined to the criminal or normally addicted groups, aided by the small group of doctors who made a stealthy but successful living from the procurement of drugs for well-endowed wastrels or for decadents among the theatrical or film world. The whole question was considered not only illegal, as indeed it was, but essentially unclean and something to be concealed with a sense of shame. Paradoxically, it was the mission of the hippies and other freakish members of the population both to popularize and to confer a degree of social acceptability on the variety of drugs that were available in ever-growing quantities through new and rather wealthy marketing channels opening up at an unprecedented rate.

The psychedelic drugs, such as LSD, had never been associated with the black community, which, indeed, has had actual racial prejudices against them. But, as an alternative to marijuana, LSD's novelty and remarkable properties assured it an instant vogue, especially when a mystical and academic crank like Professor Timothy Leary of Harvard did great damage both to his country and to his profession by promoting the drug with the fervor of a convert to a new religion.

The actual reasons for the U.S. drug explosion are not easy to establish if only examined from the individual or domestic point of view. In the main, curiosity has been a primary cause. The word "drug," itself, has sunk deep into national acceptance by the presence of the ubiquitous drugstore associated with such desirable things as Christmas presents, ice-cream sodas, and the indispensible products necessary to an attractive way of life, as well as the large-scale "pill-popping" it makes possible. All, doubtless, have played a part. The narcotics themselves have been ruthlessly pushed, indeed foisted on society, often by addicts who have an almost missionary fervor in their search for customers and converts. Then again, U.S. society is no longer built around the needs and the performance of the individual but has become ever-increasingly collectivized. In consequence, some of the recent converts to drug-taking admit freely that they are now on the "scene" because of "peer-group pressure" and, incredibly, the sense of being out of things, social outcasts, if they do *not* participate.

As matters are, at present, every high school seems to have among its student body a small number of regular "buyers" who trade in drugs, most of whom are dealing in marijuana. They buy this from an established market in quantities of about a kilo downwards, and usually from contacts who may be relatives, friends, or persons engaged in similar transactions on college campuses. Some such individuals are even engaged, themselves, in illicit cultivation of the plant.

Marijuana and LSD are both relatively cheap and, therefore, generally accessible drugs. The expenditure is of such kind that most students can handle the cost either by diverting their allowances; asking their parents for handouts, ostensibly for school equipment, books, etc.; and, occasionally, by petty theft. The drug produces a euphoric, careless, and morally deadened mentality over a period of time, which can usually be relied upon to bring the user closer to the more dangerous drugs and, eventually, to their use.

Heroin in high schools is becoming a serious problem but as yet it occupies a position that still isolates its users. Marijuana is regarded with tolerance and on a communal basis, while heroin is not. Heroin is still quite difficult to obtain in schools, and it is feared. An addict or user is almost always much more on his (or her) own and unable to gain support or help from friends in the habit. It becomes impossible to finance the habit by any normal means. Costs are so high that systematic crime always results at once. Cases of theft occur, involving losses of school equipment all disposed of to promote the habit. Juvenile delinquency, sometimes quite violent in form, or shoplifting take place, undermining trust and affection that are so necessary in the upbringing of young people.

Countermeasures have been inadequate and often quite badly conceived. Official and educational films leveled at addicts and drug users in schools have been prepared with extraordinarily little understanding of the nature of the problem or of the mentality of the young victims, and have often been received with such derision that they have tended to promote the habit rather than to suppress it.

It is not realized widely enough that within our society a vortex has been set up that exerts an almost irresistible attraction towards many members of the community, young and old, and that a clinical or psychological approach will not really work. Careful study of the vortex itself is needed, as well as the hidden forces that keep it in motion.

Graduates of the high schools have been proceeding either to the college campuses or, sometimes, to the war in Vietnam. Both those destinations have been battlegrounds in which there has been free play of the forces behind the vortex. The consequences in both cases will be examined more closely in a subsequent chapter.

Chapter 2
References and Footnotes

1. Testimony by Rep. Halpern at Hearings before the Senate Subcommittee on Alcoholism and Narcotics, June 9, 1971. The testimony contained an extract from House proceedings, namely, the text of H.R. 8861, a proposed Armed Forces Drug Abuse Control Act.
2. *The New York Times*, May 18, 1971.
3. *Ibid.*
4. *Sing Tao Jih Pao*, Hong Kong, August 6, 1971.
5. *The New York Times*, February 25, 1971.
6. Hearings, House Armed Services Committee, August 20, 1970: "Drug Abuse by Military Personnel." Bartimo was also a member of a special Task Force on Drug Abuse in the Services.
7. *Ibid.*
8. Hearings, Senate Committee on the Judiciary, Subcommittee to Investigate Juvenile Delinquency, May 26, 1971.

3

Evidence of Red Chinese Complicity and Predominance in the World Pattern of Opium and Narcotics Trading

The World Picture

It has often been noted that increased consumption and abuse of drugs are problems that have arisen in the aftermath of wars. Traditionally they have been rightly regarded as aberrations or deviations from accepted patterns of conduct, or as infractions of law.

Therefore, it is the more disturbing today to realize that, to a large and growing community that is described as having set up a "subculture," drugs are becoming normal and accepted and a way of life regardless of any moral or legal considerations. The situation may, in a sense, be said to resemble the one in which society in the United States challenged the right of the state to enforce Prohibition, when large numbers of loyal citizens flouted the law. It was at that time that organized crime became a reality on the grand scale and acquired the organizational and financial capabilities that have led the "Organization," sometimes called the "National Crime Syndicate," to engage in international operations in narcotics trading. It is much to be hoped, however, that the dangerous parallel indicated above is not accepted as a true analogy, because repeal of most of our antidrug legislation would undoubtedly produce the gravest consequences.

The period after World War II has been no exception to the rule. In spite of the most strenuous efforts to restrain drug abuse, by national agencies and law-enforcement bodies and international agencies that have had a long history of effort, the problem has grown ever more menacing.

The most important factor in the maintenance of international controls is the 1961 Single Convention on Narcotic Drugs that was promulgated under the auspices of the United Nations. This stemmed from a number of previous international controls that had proved themselves to be quite effective in practice:

(1) *International Opium Commission, The Shanghai Conference 1909*

The first step in international control when thirteen governments met and drafted nine resolutions that led to

(2) *The Hague Convention of 1912*

This resulted in the definition of international usages and in preparatory steps towards legislation, and evolved the principles fundamental to international control of the drug traffic.

(3) *The Geneva Convention of 1925*

This met at Geneva in 1924 and 1925 in accordance with League of Nations requirements. Primarily concerned with the question of limitation of production under legal safeguards. Thirty-six delegations were involved. It set up the Permanent Central Board designed to exert statistical control. The United States had played the leading part in all such conferences but required special enabling legislation to attend this convention, not being a member of the league.

(4) *The Convention for Limiting the Manufacture and Regulating the Distribution of Narcotic Drugs, 1931*

An exceptionally important conference. Recognizing that previous measures had proven quite ineffective in some cases, such as a serious heroin leakage in Italy, it was able to evolve a system of estimates for production of narcotics.

In effect, it placed international controls on nationally owned industries. This was ratified by 73 countries by 1932.

(5) *The Convention of 1936 for the Suppression of the Illicit Traffic in Dangerous Drugs*

The 1961 Single Convention on Narcotics Drugs has sought to reduce leakages from farms *in countries that are governed by it* by establishing state opium monopolies that designate areas for legal poppy cultivation and by licensing individual farmers to grow the crop. This convention has only permitted export by those countries that were involved in legal export prior to 1961, these being Turkey, Bulgaria, India, Iran, the U.S.S.R., Greece, and Yugoslavia. The instrument that was created to maintain an overview of the situation and to monitor the degree of compliance of countries with the requirements of the convention was the International Narcotics Control Board. It should be noted that this board has no really effective powers of enforcement.

In effect, the degree of international control has been totally inadequate, for reasons that will emerge in the course of this account. Above all, in view of the extensive, irrefutable, and extremely disturbing reports that were furnished by the U.S. delegations and representatives to the United Nations Commission on Narcotics Drugs (in which the involvement of Red China was exhaustively documented), it is the more surprising that the deliberations and the activity of the INCB and the UN Commission have been so circumscribed whenever the Chinese factor has been called into account. On the whole, it has been virtually ignored; even, more recently, provided powerful political support by officials who deny any possibility of Red Chinese complicity in illegal narcotics trading. (Since the Peking regime bases much of its economy on this traffic, which is a particularly important source of revenue to it, in the strict sense this can hardly be called illegal.)

There are rather specific conditions of climate and terrain that favor the cultivation of the opium poppy. It is usual to find it in the irrigated flat terrain of mountain valleys. Often these are about 3,000 feet above sea level. There are very large regions in the Middle and Far East that have a suitable environment and, at present, there is a zone of cultivation of major importance extending from the Anatolian Plateau in Turkey to Yunnan Province in China. This zone includes the producing areas in India and adjacent areas in Southeast Asia such as Burma, Laos, and Thailand that merge with the major Chinese production base in Yunnan. Formerly Szechuan was considered to be the prinicpal growing area because Szechuan was favored by the existence of a large domestic market that no longer exists, but, in recent years, Szechuan

69

EUROPEAN ROUTES OF HEROIN AND MORPHINE TRAFFIC

70

has been totally surpassed by Yunnan Province. Yunnan is strategically located as the Chinese base from which most of their operations in the fields of political and military action in Southeast Asia have been mounted. It has provided the reservoir and the buffer stocks of opiates that have been indispensable to the permeation of Communist power into the tribal and guerrilla areas in Southeast Asia and for China's narcotics offensive against the U.S. troops in Indo-China and Thailand.

India, which has a good record of effective government policy and control of narcotics, has about 35,000 hectares under cultivation. Turkish poppy cultivation is understood to utilize some 12,000 hectares. It is interesting to note that Iran, which banned poppy production during the years 1956-68, decided to resume production and declared its intention of planting some 12,000 hectares that would be harvested in 1970.

In addition, there is a large subsidiary region taking in northwestern West Pakistan (now Pakistan) and northeastern Afghanistan that may be considered to be within the same geographical region as the adjoining Soviet Central Asian Republics; all of these contribute to the world total but on a lesser scale than other producing areas. Afghanistan and Pakistan are also involved in other aspects of drug traffic, such as hashish and its variants. Afghanistan in particular has been one of the meccas of the hippy movement, which to a large extent has been living off and dying from the ready availability of drugs there and in similar centers. Afghanistan has notably contributed to the export and worldwide distribution of drugs.

While Asia is dominated by the vast Red Chinese export drive, the degree of concealment is remarkable. For example, in a document—"The World Opium Situation," prepared by the Bureau of Narcotics and Dangerous Drugs and dated October 1970—presented before the "Conference on the Challenges of Modern Society" of the Atlantic Council, and from which the figures quoted above for India, Turkey, and Iran have been taken, little or no account is taken of Red China. On page 5 of this report there is the comment:

> The poppy acreage in Communist China is unknown but may well be less than it is in Turkey.[1]

In view of previous positions taken by that agency, and the wealth of information at its disposal obtained in previous years by its agents and contacts at great personal risk, this statement is the more amazing. However, it is consistent with the present tendency to placate the Peking regime. Actually, some current estimates of Chinese mainland poppy cultivation run as high as 600,000 hectares; even 400,000 hectares is a conservative lower limit.

Again, in the same report (which is unsigned) there is the statement:

> On the basis of the likely medical requirements for its vast population, production in Communist China can be estimated at 75 to 100 tons. Production in N. Vietnam is very much less. Pakistan, Japan, Bulgaria and Yugoslavia all produce very small amounts of licit opium. In 1969 Iran produced 9 tons.[2]

In the past there has never been a time at which the production and consumption of opium and its derivatives in China has been governed by medical requirements alone, even though, of course, opium in particular has been held in high regard for its alleged medicinal properties. In view of the historical record and the well-known, authenticated Chinese Communist attitude towards opium as an economic resource and as a weapon, the above remarks are particularly difficult to understand as emanating from a well-informed official quarter. It needs to be borne in mind that all production in Red China is considered "licit."

In the discussed report there is also the statement:

> The U.S.S.R. and China export none of their opium production, and the U.S.S.R. supplements its domestic supply with substantial imports from India. Exports of poppy straw also serve as medicinal raw materials. World exports amounted to 6,560 tons in 1968. with 98 percent from Turkey.[3]

This BNDD report estimates that the world's illicit production of opium is 1,250 to 1,400 tons annually. It states that

> The principal concentration of illicit production is in the Far East, with the other areas tending to rank in descending order of importance moving Westward. Together Burma, Laos, and Thailand account for an estimated 700 to 750 tons, or more than half of the world's illicit output, and Burma alone for 30 percent. Afghanistan-Pakistan is in second place as a producing region with an output of the order of 300 tons. Pakistan's production of 175 to 200 tons is about the same as India's. Turkey's illicit output, estimated at 100 tons in 1968 and 1969, may not be significantly less. Some opium is produced illicitly on a very small scale in Mexico and in some South American, North African, and Near Eastern countries. *Communist China's once vast illicit output dwindled to insignificance in the latter 1950s...There has been no evidence of any illicit exports of opium originating from the U.S.S.R. and the*

72

East Communist countries, or, in recent years, from Communist China.[4]

According to this interesting, but misleading, report the world market for opium and opiates has been subject to important and far-reaching changes within the postwar period, attributable to the following events:

> (1) The "shutdown of China's vast illicit market with the change of government there in 1949."
> (2) The "abolition of cultivation in Iran after 1955, coupled with the rapid suppression of China's illicit production at about the same time."[5]

It goes on to state that

> In response to abolition of poppy cultivation in Iran and the sharp reduction or possibly cessation of illicit cultivation in South China, new supplies were developed in Afghanistan-Pakistan-India, Turkey, and the hill areas of Burma, Laos, and Thailand.[6]

It may here be observed that while the primary producers are being acquitted of all blame and, indeed, whitewashed, countries that either are friends of the United States or uncommitted nations are subjected to unfavorable publicity and comment at the international level in a manner that might well give them offense and lead them towards less cordial relations with the United States. Thus countries are alienated that might be persuaded by diplomatic means or economic aid to become more friendly. Turkey is a particular case in point.

Chinese Complicity

The above survey has been provided to give insight into some of the broad aspects of the international scene and to note some of the modern developments in the U.S. official viewpoint. We will now examine more closely Chinese production and distribution, the largest contributor by far to the international traffic in opiates, operating worldwide on a much more substantial basis than ever before.

It has been reported that Chinese Communist opium cultivation began as early as 1928 when Mao Tse-tung set up his first major guerrilla base at Ching Kang Shan in Kiangsi. His orders to his cadres at the time were to "trade for supplies and poison the white areas." In this connection the term "white" was used in the classical Bolshevik sense, as it is applied to the term "White Guards."

73

Increasing pressure by the Kuomintang and economic difficulties forced the Chinese Communists out of Kiangsi and led to the abandonment of the Kiangsi Soviet when they embarked on the Long March in 1935. Arriving in Yenan in Shensi after a series of running engagements, the few survivors of the journey were practically at the end of their tether and badly needed some rapid economic means of rehabilitating themselves.

Yeh Ch'ien-ying, the chief planner of the Long March, who is now in power in Peking after the demise of Lin Piao, together with Mao and Chou En-lai was involved in the formulation of a plan for opium-growing operations in an area well known to be suitable. There was a ready-made market in areas under Japanese occupation that were thus accessible to the Chinese Reds. They also had in mind the possibility of challenging the authority of the National Government and its stringent narcotics regulations by trading within the areas remaining under its jurisdiction. Also they hoped to subvert its officials and to extend their influence.

Among the first of their activities in this program was the setting up of a special farm at Nanniwan, southeast of Yenan. It came under the jurisdiction of Brigadier General Wang Chen, then the commander of the 359th Brigade, a unit of the 120th Division that was commanded by Ho Lung. Wang Chen, before the Cultural Revolution, was known to be Minister of Agricultural Reclamation (a euphemism for narcotics production.)

The Nanniwan farm was only intended to be the pattern and the nucleus of a much more broadly based effort. Those who were responsible for the execution of the opium project soon designated special areas where they forced the peasants to plant opium. Within two years Mao was able to accumulate a large stock of opium and, in order to dispose of this, sent special agents into a number of potential consuming areas. The principal ones were Shanghai, Hankow, Wuchang, Peking, Tientsin, Canton, and Hainan Island. The agents were careful to conceal the traffic as much as possible in order to avoid unfavorable comment, particularly abroad.

A principal area of activity was the "Shen-Kan-Ning" border region where extensive planting had been completed by 1941 in areas well away from major highways. Other major regions of poppy production were the Luhsien-Tingpien-Yenchuan-Yenchang-Chinpien area in north Shensi, the province administered by Yen Shi-san. In west Shensi, the province within which Yenan was situated, they developed the Pienkuan-Hochu-Paoteh-Kofeng-Hsinghsien area, and in eastern Shensi the Hoshui-Chingyang areas. Another major region of development was the Panchih area along the Shensi-Ninghsia border.

In 1942 it was reported that within the thirteen border hsien of the Shen-Kan-Ning (Shensi-Kansu-Ninghsia)—Chunhua, Hsunyi, Yichun, Luhsien, Kanchuan, Yenchang, Yenchuang, Ansai, Chingpien, Suiteh, Tzuchang, Michin, and Hengshan—about 13,200 *mou* (1 acre equals 6.6 *mou)* were under opium. There were also known to be at least 7,000 *mou* in the provinces of Ninghsien, Chengning, and Chingyang. In addition there were 4,000 *mou* in Hochu and 47,000 *mou* in Linhsing and Paoteh.

According to the publication *The Chinese Communist Plot to Drug the World,*

> The Chinese Communists had long ago forced the peasants of Northern Shensi to plant opium, stipulating that after the opium was harvested two-thirds went to the Communists and the peasants kept the remaining one-third. However, the Chinese Communists still bought this remaining one-third (in other words they got the whole crop but paid for only one-third), and the peasants were not allowed to dispose of it as they pleased. In 1942 the Chinese Communists made the following rules on the purchase of opium:
>
> (1) Of those peasants who harvested over 60 ounces of opium, two-thirds were handed over to the "border area governments" and one-third was retained by the peasants but the total amount could not exceed 1,000 ounces. Consumption or sale of opium was prohibited in the "border areas."
> (2) Of those peasants who harvested 700 ounces of opium, the peasants were first given a bonus of 70 ounces and the remainder was divided in the same two-thirds to one-third proportion. Peasants who harvested 800 ounces were given 80 ounces, etc.
> (3) Of those peasants who harvested 1,000 to 5,000 ounces of opium, the peasants were given a bonus of 15 ounces per 100 ounces harvested and the remainder was divided as above.[7]

Some interesting particulars of Red China's involvement in the narcotics trade were provided by the veteran Far Eastern correspondent, the late Rodney Gilbert, in the September 15, 1956 issue of *National Review.* In this, Gilbert, who has been rated as one of the best-informed and reliable reporters, wrote

> There is no longer any doubt that Red China is by all odds the biggest contributor to the international illicit traffic in opium, morphine and heroin. And there is no doubt either that this is an offi-

cially promoted enterprise. Refugees who had been employed in the nefarious business have brought out full information about poppy cultivation, the smuggling of opium into Siam and Burma from government warehouses in Yunnan; the location of many factories that are under rigid Red policy control where opium is converted into morphine base, morphine and heroin; and the government patronage of the export traffic.

According to Gilbert, writing in the same article, two correspondents of a Chinese news agency were able to report conditions as they were in Communist-controlled territory in 1942, which indicated that the CCP had a long-term interest in the matter of poppy cultivation. These men traveled in the Red "border area" in June and late October 1942 and were able to gain insight into the Red Chinese opium traffic. At that time Mao and his minions were bottled up in Yenan and the parts of Shensi, Kansu, and Ninghsia on the north and a portion of Shansi on the west. They were held between the forces of General Hu Tsungnan (in Sian) and those of Fu Tso-yi in the north. They reported that the Communists had planted their first crop in 1941 and that it was gathered in 1942.

This was done under the closest military supervision. Mao's representatives took two-thirds of the crop and bought the remaining third at their own price. None was to be smoked within their territory but was for export only into territory under Chungking's control.

The size of the crop was a revelation to them, as was the tremendous profits that were being made. Greatly expanded production and improved marketing methods were then sought. The Communists issued instructions to all farmers throughout Shensi, Kansu, Ninghsia, and northern Shansi, in the territory under their control, that every farmer was expected to plant two-thirds of his arable land in opium poppies and one-third only in grain crops.

Local magistrates were notified that, before the next opium harvest, they would be required to supply sorting, packaging, and storage premises, as well as sales offices and transit accommodation for buyers from the government-controlled areas. It may be remembered that, at about that time, there was a vigorous campaign sponsored by such Red sympathizers as the late Edgar Snow and various State Department officials that Mao's contingents were not really Communists but were merely "agrarian reformers." In a certain sense it can be seen that, in fact, that is what they were.

When the traffic was fully under way, arrangements were set up providing military escorts for customers to the boundaries of the Red domain. The trade was exceptionally lucrative and included considerable revenue from a tax the Reds imposed on these shipments.

Their ventures did not proceed with the universal approval of the farmers in those areas, which were difficult to cultivate in any event. In the circumstances, there was a very marked reluctance on the part of farmers to cooperate in placing two-thirds of their land under poppy cultivation. Since those border areas have always lived under the shadow of famine, this was understandable. As a result, the "agricultural-reforming" Mao regime issued orders that any farmer that would not cooperate would be expropriated and the land leased to more compliant farmers. Needless to say, there was a good deal of opposition but this was dealt with ruthlessly in characteristic Communist fashion.

Sian, the provincial capital, was the nearest large city and soon became the primary opium market for the Reds in Yenan. The Nationalists previously had done a good job of cleaning up the area as a part of their nationwide drive to suppress the traffic. Indeed, it was not only the Japanese drive, with its narcotics offensive in North China, that prompted the Kuomintang to draft the stringent regulations quoted in Appendix I, but the alarming relapse produced by offensive trading operations instigated by Yenan as well.

Marshal Yeh Ch'ien-ying, who has been prominent of late in discussions with Henry Kissinger, was, from the first, one of the primary figures in strategic opium cultivation, suppression of peasant opposition to it, and the detailing of "opium guerrillas" whose function was to escort convoys to the borders of Communist-held territory. He was much concerned with "agrarian reform," namely the conversion of normal cropping into opium cultivation. Yeh and Chou En-lai, working together, bore the responsibility for the political and military planning for the "Sian Coup" of 1936 that played a major part in the preparations for the war with Japan that began the following year. Some believe that the corruption of the Nationalist forces based in the Sian area was accomplished by bribery based on Nanniwan opium as well as the most unusual arts of persuasion possessed by Chou En-lai.

There was much dissatisfaction with Yenan expressed by a number of bodies that had been profoundly disturbed by the relapse induced by Chinese Communist narcotics trading. For example, a strong protest was addressed to Mao himself by the Sian Press Association, which appeared in the local press in July 1942:

It is universally known that you have openly forced the people in the nine districts of North-Western Shansi and the ten districts of Northern Shensi Province to raise opium.... You are insane and you are blinded by the selfish lust to exploit opium to the full for nothing but profit regardless of its evil effects on the country and the people. This alone, apart from the other infamous things you

77

have already done, has made you the enemy of the whole nation. Are you not ashamed of what you have done.[8]

It may be noted that this accusation was made before Mao's opium-cultivation program had reached its maximum wartime peak, and that it was followed, shortly afterwards, by similar denunciations from the Bookseller's Union in Sian.

No notice was taken of this sinister development by almost all U.S. and other foreign representatives in China. On the contrary, an all-out campaign of whitewashing and supporting the Chinese Communists went on that coincided with systematic campaigns of vilification of the Nationalist Government. Today this same influence has again reached the highest circles of the U.S. government and is producing similar, but now infinitely more dangerous, distortions in public information and in policy.

As the expansion of their program of opium cultivation progressed, the Chinese Reds added to their primary base in the Shen-Kan-Ning Border Area another large-scale enterprise called "Huai-Tai-Hsi."

This was in Honan and took in the three hsien of Huaiyang, Taikang and Hsihua in the Shangchiu area. It was administered by the Hopei-Shantung-Honan Border Region and marched with the Japanese occupied areas. There exists an illuminating document that was issued on July 9, 1945. It enbodies the regulations for the cultivation of opium in Huai-Tai-Hsi and can be regarded as typical of similar regulations governing the operation of opium cultivation and traffic in all other so-called "liberated areas."

The full text follows:

Provisional Regulations on Opium Management and Taxation In Huai-Tai-Hsi Hsien Promulgated on July 9th, 1945.

(1) These regulations, formulated in accordance with the taxation regulations of the Shansi-Hopei-Shantung-Honan Border Area Government and the basic needs of this hsien, are aimed at intensifying the economic struggle against the enemy, lightening the burden of the people, controlling the export of opium, and earning currency to import necessities.

(2) A Central Opium Bureau is established in the major city of this hsien to provide unified administration over the operation and taxation of opium enterprises.

    a. Enterprises engaged in the production and sale of opium must periodically register with the Central Opium Bureau, file business tax, obtain business li-

78

censes and continue their operations under the supervision and administration of the Central Opium Bureau.

b. The Central Opium Bureau will establish, if the need arises, branch bureaus in other cities responsible for taxation and administration of opium concerns.

c. The Central Opium Bureau will designate a certain number of opium enterprises according to the volume of trade. When the number of enterprises exceeds the stipulated number, the hsien government will designate authorized enterprises from those which submit petitions and the remainder will serve as alternate enterprises.

d. Authorized opium enterprises may receive the following compensation:

(i) Brokers may collect 3 percent of the amount of the transaction as intermediary fees.

(ii) Brokers may collect 10 percent of the tax assessed as a bonus.

e. The Central Opium Bureau will appraise the performance of each opium enterprise in carrying out its operations in accordance with the regulations, and mete out the appropriate rewards and punishments. If necessary, the license of any enterprise may be revoked and turned over to an alternate enterprise.

(3) Merchants engaged in the opium trade must receive permission from the Central Opium Bureau or an authorized enterprise to export opium to other areas.

a. Persons desiring to purchase opium are required to register with the Central Opium Bureau or its authorized agents and to obtain a purchase permit.

b. Opium tax must be paid at the time of purchase and a tax receipt will be issued by the enterprise making the transaction.

c. In the case of opium being exported directly without going through a second party, opium tax must first be paid the taxation bureau and a tax receipt granted before permission is granted for export.

(4) Rate of taxation:

a. Opium will be taxed temporarily at 15 percent of the selling price.

b. Persons who exchange weapons and ammunition in lieu of the price of opium must pay a tax of 5 percent, but such exchanges are allowed only at the Central Opium Bureau or its designated agents.

(5) Fines:

a. Persons who falsely report the price of opium to illegally pay a lesser amount of tax must pay an amount equal to the lost tax plus a fine triple that amount.
b. Persons who purchase opium and attempt to smuggle it to outer areas without paying a tax must pay the appropriate amount of tax plus a fine triple that amount. Persons who attempt to smuggle opium directly from production without paying tax will be punished in the same manner.
c. In the case of purchasing opium from illegal opium enterprises (those which do not have business licenses), the seller will be fined an amount equivalent to 10 percent of the purchasing price, and the buyer will be fined the regular tax plus an amount equivalent to 40 percent.
d. In cases of persons dealing in opium outside the designated enterprises, the seller will be fined an amount equivalent to 20 percent of the purchasing price and the buyer will be fined the regular tax plus an amount equivalent to 50 percent of the purchasing price.

(6) Rewards:

a. Those who apprehend smugglers and other personnel who have left production will be rewarded by an amount equivalent to 10 percent of the fines incurred in cases of tax fraud and illegal sale of opium. These awards may not exceed $1,000 per person.
b. Merchants, enterprises, and the general public have the right to report cases of tax fraud and illegal sale of opium to the Central Opium Bureau. Rewards will be given at the rate of 20 percent of the fines incurred.
c. The right to assess fines is restricted to the hsien government or the Central Opium Bureau. Other agencies, groups or individuals are not allowed to impose fines.

(7) These Regulations are promulgated by the Shuiting Office.[9]

The above regulations were drafted specifically to govern the opium traffic in areas being evacuated by the Japanese and which the Communists were entering faster than the forces of the Nationalist Government could. This was because they were nearer. It may be noted that the Huai-Tai-Hsi area was primarily concerned with the opium traffic, while the other areas such as Shen-Kan-Ning had a good many other economic resources that the Communists were using.

Those who have studied the strategic and tactical aspects of Chinese Communist guerrilla bases and areas have, until now, been largely examining them from the point of view of the military potential and political significance that they represent. Lack of full understanding

80

of the technique of supplanting the authority of neutral states and of installing bases and sanctuaries that straddle borders has led to some highly unfavorable results in the Vietnam War, and the ultimate attacks on such base areas in Cambodia and Laos were undertaken far too late.

Had the initiative been taken against them at the outset, in concert with other measures, the outcome of that disastrous experience would have been very different. Currently, it must be recognized, with a full realization of the nature of the irregular-warfare mentality, that the economics of the development of almost all such guerrilla bases in the Far East, and in particular the tribal areas in North Thailand, Laos, Burma, etc., has been associated in large measure with the question of narcotics.

It must be appreciated, at the present time, that the vast complex of producing areas and logistic networks in Southeast Asia, in Burma, Thailand, North Vietnam, and Southwest Yunnan together comprise an enormous guerrilla-operated and -defended psycho-chemical warfare base, with its taproot well established on the Chinese mainland whence the bulk of the opium and its derivatives originate. The outlying countries are used as cover and as a means of ingress for the drug weapon to seek its marks. It cannot miss its marks—once the act of individual surrender is made, being self-inflicted, the wounds on the bodies and minds of the victims cannot be avoided. The weapon is intercontinental and among the deadliest fashioned by man.

Unfortunately an awakening to the realities of this situation has been long delayed. The attitude of U.S. officials, and those in other countries who have been playing a similar part, has had much to do with the delayed awakening. It is impossible to dissociate this fact from the current revision in U.S. Far Eastern policy, especially as it affects our relations with Red China.

As far back as 1962 a specific "early warning" of this threat appeared in the *Congressional Record* of March 20. At that time, in connection with countermeasures required to combat organized crime in the United States, Rep. William C. Cramer quoted from the *Tampa Times* of Friday, March 16, 1962, which carried an editorial called "Narcotics is Communist Weapon." Rep. Cramer said, in part:

> This editorial comments on recently passed Federal laws, which I cosponsored, not only last year, but for many years preceding, concerning the interstate transportation of syndicated criminals, gambling paraphernalia, broadening of the Fugitive Felon Act, and preventing the transportation of gambling information.
>
> The article further justifies the passage of further anti-crime measures, which are contained in my anti-crime bill, H.R. 6909,

and subsequent bills, to establish an Office of Syndicated Crime within the Department of Justice to outlaw the deduction as business expenses of the cost of operating criminal transactions interstate, to provide for court supervision and authorized wire-tapping and the obstruction of agency and departmental investigation, all related to syndicated crime activities.

As these weapons relate to narcotic traffic this editorial points out how the Red Chinese, through Cuban connections, are using narcotic traffic as a political weapon in an effort to spread the addiction and lower the morale and moral fiber of this country....

"One of the most difficult problems in dealing with Cuban refugees is to decide which are fleeing from Communist Cuba and which are using simulated flight as an excuse to enter this country to serve an ulterior purpose.

"This conundrum has been underscored in Miami where narcotic agents discovered persons posing as refugees operating a narcotic ring. Five arrests have been made and the Narcotics Bureau has pointed a finger of accusation at Red China as the source of dope being smuggled into the United States.

"Chinese Communists have played an important part in the Castro revolution since its success. Their presence in Havana is largely represented as providing technical assistance to the Castro government. But latest evidence uncovered by narcotics agents indicates that they have another purpose also. They are peddling dope, pushing drugs into the United States with the intent of spreading addiction and lowering the morale and moral fiber of this country.

"Unfortunately, the Red Chinese have allies here—the organized mob. Call it what you will—the Mafia, organized crime or the rackets—no one doubts the existence of a powerful crime combine in the United States. Its principal hoodlum leaders are known: some of their more "respectable partners" are not. The crime monopoly is engaged in gambling, prostitution, narcotics, labor racketeering and certain legitimate businesses where strong-arm tactics can be applied to curb competition.

"Congress just recently recognized the inability of local law enforcement to cope with this network of criminal activity by tightening Federal laws governing the interstate movement of criminals, gambling devices and crime profits. Attorney General Kennedy has asked for even broader powers to strengthen his hand against the mob.

"Meanwhile, the rackets are still doing business—and they are not above trading with the Communists....

"Narcotics officials report that opium from Red China is being channeled into the United States at several major points. Miami is one. The product is moved into the south Florida city from Cuba and is distributed to mobsters in major Eastern cities—New York hoods are prominent in this trade, many of them Cubans posing as anti-Castroites.

"We are confident that narcotics police units will be able to keep the opium business under control. But, inevitably some of the drug will find its way into... the hands of users both old and new.

"The refinement of the narcotics racket as a political weapon suggests a need for effective countermeasures. One step may be in furnishing the Department of Justice with the tools to strike even more swiftly and deeply at the very core of organized crime in the United States. If the machinery of vice and corruption is dismantled, the efficient movement of narcotics will be ended and the profit element in this criminal activity eliminated."[10]

An examination of this question in depth discloses that the deadly nexus connecting Chinese communism with organized crime in Europe and the Americas (including Canada) is the Chinese underworld, both on the mainland and among the overseas Chinese. The forces that need to be confronted are an operational alliance "of convenience" between covert Red Chinese intelligence instrumentalities, participating members of Chinese Secret Societies, and the hidden members of the alliance in the United States, sometimes called the National Crime Syndicate. The latter may not all know about the relationship, but in this enterprise the course has been charted by their higher command—*the Commission.*

Before examining the most important aspect of the international drug traffic, namely the nature of the higher command and the manner in which it conducts its worldwide operations on what might be termed the policy plane, it will be necessary to cite a few examples of the criminal aspect of this enormous complex of vested interests as these present themselves at the civic law-enforcement level. In doing this, it is not difficult to discern the continuing participation of the Red Chinese trading machinery that has, of course, adopted a practiced and well-executed attitude of concealment. It is highly questionable, for example, if many of their instruments have any idea as to the ultimate source of their involvement or even of the material that they handle.

It was reported by Commissioner Myles J. Ambrose of U.S. Customs on July 26, 1971, that narcotics worth nearly half a billion dollars were seized during the year that ended on July 30. This included 937 pounds of heroin, worth $409 million on the street.

This enormous quantity was taken in during the course of 503 separate seizures and amounted to more than the total quantity taken in the previous eight years. While there is cause for satisfaction in the improved efficiency of the Customs Service, there is also reason to suspect that imports have been considerably stepped up.[11]

During the same year, customs agents were able to seize 360 pounds of cocaine with a street value of $49.2 million. In the previous year only 108 pounds were taken in the course of eighty-eight seizures. There were also seizures of marijuana and hashish, which brought the street value of the taking to $492,512,598, while the addition of some opium and LSD brought the value to the half-billion mark.

The largest haul of heroin during 1971 was made at San Juan, Puerto Rico, when 247.5 pounds were found in an automobile, in hidden compartments. This was also the largest single haul in the 182 years of operation of the Customs Service. There has been marked improvement in the intelligence branch of the Customs Service of late, and an increased awareness there, as elsewhere in government, of the imperative need to cut off supplies as near the source as possible.[12]

The U.S. Bureau of Narcotics, particularly when it was under the direction of Henry J. Anslinger, has had an enviable record of success in combating the traffic in narcotics and in analyzing the higher policies of the major traffickers. These findings, particularly as they impinged on the Mafia, or "Cosa Nostra," and its associated organizations, proved to be of great value in drawing in the attention of other agencies and thus strengthening the processes of law enforcement against the infractions of organized crime in other areas than narcotics.

The U.S. Bureau of Narcotics has been charged with the responsibility for detection and investigation necessary to prevent violations of the Federal Narcotic and Marijuana Law and the Opium Poppy Control Act. Its actions aimed at suppressing the drug traffic in all aspects has led it to activity at both the interstate and international levels. The bureau has, for many years, been particularly aware of the major source of the international traffic in opiates located in Red China, and has considered this to be a particularly dangerous and insidious form of the international scene as it affects both Canada and the United States.

As an example of the domestic operations that have led them to that conclusion, the following may be cited. This was a well-known case involving George W. Yee of San Francisco and a society called the "Hip Sing Tong." The Bureau of Narcotics concluded, in January 1959, an investigation of the smuggling into the United States of 270 pounds of heroin over a period of time by a gang of twenty-one conspirators. Twelve of these were living in Hong Kong, Macao, and Shanghai and were able to evade U.S. action and the criminal indictment returned against the gang by the Grand Jury of the U.S. District Court at San Francisco.

In the course of the investigation documents were seized that proved that all the heroin originated in the Szechuan Province of mainland China, which has long been noted for its opium production. The drug was smuggled into the United States through a number of different ports, via Hong Kong, and the average price paid by the receivers in the United States was $360 an ounce. The operation had been masterminded by George W. Yee of San Francisco, proprietor of a clothing store and President of the Hip Sing Tong of that city. He had, as an associate, a previously convicted trafficker, Jung Jim of Portland, Oregon.

Another figure in the case was Chung Wing Fong, who had also been President of the Hip Sing Tong. There was another organization that figured in the case called the "Bing Kong Tong" of Portland, Oregon, which was concerned in the adjudication of disputes arising from the distribution of commissions arising from this illegal traffic. As in other parts of the world, members of Chinese secret societies in the United States, which are called tongs or lodges, are often deeply involved in illegal activities such as the drug traffic. It must be borne in mind, however that tongs have an extensive "legal" side as well. However, prostitution and trading in drugs are among their more lucrative pursuits.

In the case described, there had been an extremely careful investigation of the affair before indictment. In part this had involved undercover operations in which an agent of the Federal Bureau of Narcotics had been able to penetrate a San Francisco element of the Hip Sing Tong, as well as another similar organization in Oregon, and to obtain conclusive evidence of the whole operation. From confessions obtained from defendants in this case, absolutely reliable confirmation was obtained of the logistic path taken by the heroin in transit from Szechuan to Shanghai, thence to Hong Kong and the United States.[18]

This was not an isolated case, and it may be noted that earlier, in June 1957, the Bureau had been able to seize some brick-type heroin in New York that proved to be a part of larger consignments that had come in through the West Coast. The imported drugs were being widely diffused throughout the country by a skillfully planned criminal network located at strategic points.

Another celebrated case was that which became known as the George Douglas Poole Case. This involved the smuggling of large quantities of Red Chinese heroin into the United States and resulted in the conviction of thirty conspirators. It is interesting to note that, although there has been no doubt as to the Chinese Communist source of the shipments in the case, the distribution network of the Poole Group was originally set up by a certain Anthony J. Longobardi and two other U.S. merchant seamen in 1948, even before the Chinese Communists were in power. Poole was not one of the original founders of the operation, but joined forces with Longobardi shortly after it began. They took advantage of sources in a number of Oriental ports, mainly Hong Kong.

The arrangements made by this consortium consisted of a fund, subscribed to by all members, for the purchase of narcotics whenever a member of the ring (they were almost all merchant seamen), knew that he was about to sail. This member acted as courier for the organization; he would contact a dealer in Hong Kong or some other port when the ship docked, and he would take on a shipment. This he would hide aboard his ship until after it had passed its last port of call, usually Honolulu, after which he would remove the drugs and sew it into an article of clothing. On arrival in the United States, the garment would be exchanged with an identical garment worn by the receiving courier who would board the ship at the port of destination.

In those days the known quantity of drugs smuggled by this ring was considered significant, being estimated at 70 kg, although that was believed to be only a fraction of the amount shipped. Today it would be considered small in comparison with current scales of operation. Current operations are a tribute to the relentless promotion of the traffic by policy planners at the source and to the disturbing growth of addiction in the country.[14]

During 1958 the Bureau of Narcotics made two seizures of drugs also known to have originated on the Chinese mainland. In New York, narcotics agents, local police, and Customs officers arrested a curio dealer called Yu Hong Ting and his wife, Leung Tam Yong Sing. Small quantities of heroin were discovered in the shop in various hiding places, amounting in all to about 50 ounces. This was a processing and packaging center that obtained its narcotics in Shanghai from a seaman called Lim Yew Ming.

The raid was connected with other investigations that had previously been carried out by the Japanese police. On February 18, 1958, the latter seized 28 ounces of pure heroin from a Chinese called Lin Po Huai, an individual said to be from Communist China although resident in Japan. The heroin had similar characteristics to that seized from Yu Hong Ting in New York, namely 86 percent purity, similar appearance and consistency, matching infrared spectrum and melting point.

Shortly afterwards, on August 27, 1958, there was a seizure of 25 pounds of crude opium from three Chinese seamen. The origin was unknown but was considered to be Red China, with Hong Kong as a transshipment point. The traffic in raw opium to the United States is not very large but may always have an important aspect as it affects the lives and sometimes the loyalties of Chinese residents in the United States. All the above cases serve to underline the fact, understood at the time and, indeed, much earlier, that the major source of all illicit international narcotics trading was, and still is, Communist China.[15]

In 1952 the Bureau of Narcotics made its position quite clear when it addressed reports to the United Nations calling to the attention of the UN Commission on Narcotics Drugs the nature and the extent of the traffic. Anslinger, then U.S. Narcotics Commissioner, is more recently on record, in the February-March 1961 issue of the *Military Police Journal*, as follows:

> The major source of the international illicit narcotics traffic has been and still is, Communist China. Literally tons of narcotics are being smuggled into Burma, Thailand, Hong Kong and Macao for evil use in those areas and for transshipment to Japan, the Philippines, Canada and the U.S.
>
> Ever since 1952, we have called to the attention of the United Nations Commission on Narcotics Drugs the enormous illicit traffic in narcotic drugs pouring out from the Chinese Mainland to many countries of the world. We have repeatedly brought the traffic originating in Communist China into sharp focus. We have supplied the UN with information regarding seizures within the United States of illicit narcotics originating directly from Red China or which were transmitted through other Far Eastern countries before arriving in the United States.
>
> Some Far Eastern countries have specifically labeled Red China as the source of narcotics they have seized. Other countries in that region, however, have been somewhat reluctant to speak or report in this same candid fashion before the United Nations Commission on Narcotics Drugs.
>
> (Parenthetic Note: Hong Kong has always been exceptionally cautious in its attribution of any consignments of drugs, proceeding through the colony, to Red Chinese sources. Also, since the assassination of President Kennedy, there has been in the U.S. a somewhat unaccountable extreme reluctance to confirm the large-scale participation of the Chinese Communists in narcotics trading. There had been uncompromising denunciation until then.)[16]

Commissioner Anslinger also mentions in his article that the 1959 George Yee conspiracy was reported to the 15th Session of the UN Commission on Narcotic Drugs and that in 1959 approximately 15½ tons of raw opium was seized in the Far East. Of this quantity, 8 tons had been captured by Thailand, which was also able to intercept about 687 kilos of opium in seven consignments between November 7 and December 19, 1958. In the period between March and November 1959 they seized 1,142 kilos. They described the source of these quantities as being "beyond the northern frontier."

At the same time, the Government of the Union of Burma reported cases of seizure that totaled about 2½ tons of opium that they considered to be of Yunnanese origin or possibly, in part, from the Shan States of northern Burma. Malaya claimed at that time to have been able to impound 2 tons of opium from the same source and, concurrently, there were large seizures in Hong Kong from the same source.

In the same article in the *Military Police Journal*, Anslinger states further

> The United States Delegation to the 1960 Geneva Meeting publicly took the position that the bulk of these opium seizures originated in Red China specifically and not within this vaguely defined (Yunnan-Shan States) region.
>
> Our delegation to the United Nations cited its concern at this traffic because, although much of this opium is consumed by addicts in the Far East, a large portion of it is used as raw materials for the illicitly manufactured heroin which is smuggled to the United States. We also observed that, on occasion, raw opium is smuggled to the United States directly from the Far East. In March 1960, for example, two kilograms of raw opium and prepared opium were seized from Chinese traffickers in New York City.... The opium was smuggled directly from Hong Kong but since there is no opium production there, the true origin was probably Red China.[17]

Besides the trade in opium and heroin, another highly important aspect of the matter is the movement of morphine-base, or crude morphine. This material is, of course, the intermediate stage between crude opium and the final derivative, heroin.

On August 26, 1959, Nationalist China reported the seizure of 1⅛ kilos of morphine blocks bearing the impressed symbol "999." Shortly before, the Hong Kong police, on July 14 of the same year, had seized 8 kilos and 346 grams of similar blocks with the same trademark. Earlier still, they had taken in two suitcases on a BOAC liner arriving from Bangkok with 35 kilos of morphine-base bricks and some powdered morphine. The bricks were stamped "999" and the powdered-morphine packages had a stamp bearing the letter "A" and metal seals stamped with Chinese inscriptions indicating Shanghai as the source.

Mr. Anslinger comments in this connection:

> This evil traffic in narcotics has a tremendous adverse effect on the welfare of the United States. It is regrettable that other countries who also suffer from this Red Chinese dope traffic refuse to place the blame where it correctly lies. We can only hope that eventually circumstances will permit all countries to join with our country in using the medium of the United Nations Commission on Narcotics Drugs and other international forums to marshal world opinion to force Communist China to stop this traffic in poison and death.[18]

In view of this and other similar fully documented statements made by Commissioner Anslinger to the United Nations, it is the more remarkable that in recent years there has been an almost complete continuation of that world position. If anyone makes accusations of this kind against the Peking government and its activities in the field of narcotics trading, there is a smokescreen of official denials that the Chinese are engaged in any such activities. It is stated that the Chinese are "austere" and incapable of any such thing. The facts of the case, for which many dedicated officials have risked their lives, and the official views of the most responsible and highly informed officials are set aside. In so doing, grave doubts are thereby cast on the evidence and the processes of law that have taken place in the courts over many years.

It is well, however, to note certain foreign commentators who have added further verification to the earlier official point of view expressed with such conviction and such forthrightness by Mr. Anslinger.

In September 1960 the following editorial appeared in the *Saturday Evening Post:*

> It is well known that many of the supposedly fanatical students whose rioting prevented President Eisenhower from visiting Japan last Spring were putting on a great show for something like eighty cents a day, but there is less knowledge of the source of the money. It would appear that much of it came from the profits on Red China's sale of dope—heroin mostly—smuggled into Japan.
>
> The news that such funds were to be made available to Japanese agitators against Kishi and the American Treaty was printed in the Orient last March, notably in *Free China and Asia,* a journal published in Taiwan (Free China).
>
> That Red China has been exporting huge quantities of opium and all its derivatives in all directions is common knowledge. The Jap-

anese police have, for many years, complained that the profits from Red China's dope sales to Japan—estimated about five years ago to be $30,000,000 a year—were going in part to the support of Japan's Communist Party. The payoff came when President Eisenhower's proposed visit to Japan triggered off Communist-inspired riots.

More than forty years ago Lenin declared that any kind of dirty work that forwarded the Communist cause was justified by what he called Bolshevik ethics. But the sale of dope in a neighboring country and the use of the proceeds to foment riots against that nation's foreign relations is a new approach to diplomacy. Just why this dirty Communist business should be said to have destroyed American prestige in the world is outside our understanding.[19]

The above assertions are supported fully by information coming from a multitude of sources, but for the purposes of the argument—that Red China, far from being a country that is guiltless and is being maligned by such accusations, actually is heavily involved—two further sets of observations only will be examined here. The first is the deliberations of the Senate Internal Security Subcommittee on "Communist China and Illict Narcotics Traffic," in 1955. The other is evidence provided by an expert witness, Richard L. G. Deverall, formerly representative in Asia of the Free Trade Union Committee, AFL, in his book *Mao Tze-tung Stop This Dirty Opium Business*. Deverall, who has held positions such as Chief of Labor Education for SCAP (Supreme Commander Allied Powers), had unusual opportunities of gaining insight into the problem. He also testified in the SISS hearings.

The hearings were held on Tuesday, March 8, 1955, with Senator James Eastland in the Chair. In the course of the testimony the following discussion took place:

> Mr. ARENS (Assistant Chief Counsel). Now on the basis of your numerous sources of information can you tell this subcommittee what was the annual opium production of China prior to the takeover by the Communists in 1949.
> Mr. ANSLINGER. It was about 2,000 tons and was rapidly declining.
> The CHAIRMAN. You have good reason to believe, Doctor, that your estimates are accurate?
> Mr. ANSLINGER. We have observed conditions in China for the past 20 years. At the time that the Nationalists were in power we had fairly accurate sources of information. Generally our information checked with the governmental authorities.
> The CHAIRMAN. Now, since the Communists took over China has that production increased?
> Mr. ANSLINGER. We have every reason to believe that it has in-

creased because of opium derivatives which are being smuggled out of China into the United States and other countries, and also because of large seizures of opium that are occurring, particularly in Southeast Asia, which unquestionably have their origin in the southern provinces of China.

The CHAIRMAN. What is your estimate of present opium production in Communist China?

Mr. ANSLINGER. Well, we would estimate that, according to long experience, at about 6,000 tons.

The CHAIRMAN. Now, is it your testimony that part of the opium is smuggled into the United States?

Mr. ANSLINGER. Most of it would be smuggled in the form of heroin, which is a derivative of opium and is the most powerful opium derivative known, it being about five times more powerful than morphine. Heroin is not used in this country medicinally and is not manufactured....

The CHAIRMAN. Now when you mentioned smuggling into this country do you include the Hawaiian Islands?

Mr. ANSLINGER. I include the Hawaiian Islands, yes, sir.

The CHAIRMAN. Does much of it go to Hawaii?

Mr. ANSLINGER. A great deal of it is going to Hawaii. We have noticed a rather heavy concentration of heroin there in the past three years with a long list of traffickers.

The CHAIRMAN. How can you tell that that opium comes from Communist China?

Mr. ANSLINGER. Now I am speaking of heroin. Because we have pretty clear lines of identification insofar as heroin coming from the clandestine factories in France, Turkey, Lebanon, or Italy are concerned and we know where the routes are.

Now the only possible source from which you can get heroin in Hawaii is Communist China. There is no other source of heroin....

The CHAIRMAN. Now does much of that heroin get to the Pacific Coast of the United States?

Mr. ANSLINGER. There is a great concentration of Communist heroin in California. Some of it has come East of the Rockies. We have identified it in a certain way which I can't disclose to you, but we certainly know that it is Communist heroin for the reason that it is almost pure.

Now we know that it isn't Mexican heroin. We can't always identify Mexican heroin, but Communist heroin is identifiable.

Now the heroin that we get in New York after it gets around street level is probably 4 or 5 percent pure, 95 percent adulterated. Out on the Pacific Coast we found heroin in the illicit traffic which is 85 percent pure.

Unfortunately, some of the addicts who have been accustomed to using heroin coming to the East don't realize that the peddler

91

probably sold them this very pure Chinese heroin and there have been deaths...

The CHAIRMAN. Now, you speak of Communist China production at 6,000 tons a year. How does that compare with world consumption for medical purposes?

Mr. ANSLINGER. World consumption for medical purposes, according to the United Nations and according to the experts, is roughly between 600 and 700 tons. That is for the medicinal needs of the whole world.

The CHAIRMAN. Then the production of Communist China is today 10 times what we would consume throughout the world for legitimate purposes?

Mr. ANSLINGER. I would say that that was a very conservative estimate.

The CHAIRMAN. What is the special trade bureau of the Ministry of Finance in Communist China?

Mr. ANSLINGER. According to our information, that was a bureau set up under the Ministry of Finance, directed by a man named Po I-po who was the Minister of Finance, in order to promote the sale of opium and heroin and the distribution. And, in that connection, under that bureau there is the so-called opium prohibition bureau of China.

The CHAIRMAN. Now what you are saying is that the Communist Government of China is directing the sale of opium and heroin throughout the whole world?

Mr. ANSLINGER. We have made that statement three or four times at the United Nations, and there has been no refutation except denials, but certainly all the enormous trade that is taking place out of Communist China would have to have official direction. Otherwise it could be slowed down. The Nationalist Government was able to slow it down.

The CHAIRMAN. Now, this bureau directs the sale and distribution of narcotics in international trade, does it not?

Mr. ANSLINGER. Yes sir.

Mr. ARENS. Doctor, what principal ports do these narcotics move out of China?

Mr. ANSLINGER. They move out through the ports of Canton, Dairen—Dairen in the North, Canton in the South—and most of the seizures that we have have come out of Hong Kong.

The British authorities have exerted special efforts in order to stop the traffic through Hong Kong as an in-transit port. I would also say that the British information generally confirms what we have in relation to the traffic inside China....

Senator JENNER. Doctor, what was the narcotic situation in Japan prior to the Communist takeover of China?

Mr. ANSLINGER. Japan never had addiction problems up until

1950. I think that they started out at zero then and they probably have a very tragic heroin situation which is worse than ours. Their arrests went from zero to 2,500, and a number of the arrests of important traffickers were Communist leaders in Japan who were apprehended selling narcotics, selling heroin.

The Japanese Government has found it necessary to increase their force of agents throughout Japan, and the number of arrests and seizures of heroin in Japan today is, to an old-timer like myself, just a little frightening.

Senator JENNER. Where does this heroin come from?

Mr. ANSLINGER. The heroin is all coming from China. It is not produced in Japan.

Japan, of course, probably did more or less the same thing, sending heroin into China, but there is a lot of this coming in from North Korea; there is a lot of heroin coming in from North Korea to Japan and, of course, some of it finds its way as a backwash into the United States.

Senator JENNER. Would you recount to this committee an incident concerning Lee Chin Swee, I believe is the way you pronounce it, known as Kee Chin, who was a specially trained bureau agent for the Communists.

Mr. ANSLINGER. Well, he was a key man in charge of the branch office of the Special Trade Bureau and he was doing quite a bit of trafficking in Japan. I think that at the time of his arrest he was operating two laboratories.

He was seized with something like 42 pounds of heroin. He was one of the traffickers who moved out of Communist China into Japan and organized it there.

Mr. ARENS. How many addicts are there now in Japan? I understood you to say there were virtually none before the Communists took over China.

Mr. ANSLINGER. Well I would judge from the reports that are sent to us by the Japanese experts, I think from their own reports that they would estimate about 25,000.

Mr. ARENS. In just a period of time since 1949 when the Communists took over in China, is that correct?

Mr. ANSLINGER. Just in a period of 5 years.

Mr. ARENS. Now, Doctor, what part does North Korea play in the illicit narcotics traffic?

Mr. ANSLINGER. There again, North Korea is one of the largest opium-producing centers in the world. North Korea has produced most of the opium for Japan before the war.

There were large factories in Seoul which the army seized at the time of the occupation. North Korea has been the source of a great deal of heroin and opium which has been smuggled into South Korea and Japan.

Now, for instance, there were three South Korean police officers, police chiefs, in our bureau recently and they reported that they had arrested some 2,400 young Communists who had been trained in a school in Rashin, who had come down to South Korea as refugees, smuggled through the lines with heroin in one hand and gold in the other, gold for the purpose of corrupting officials, heroin for the purpose of spreading addiction. And to show you cause and effect, we have sent to our hospitals here young men who were addicted under the program.

Mr. ARENS. Is there a concentration of effort by the Communists and their narcotics agents around the United States military installations in the Far East?

Mr. ANSLINGER. There is considerable trafficking around those security areas.

Mr. ARENS. What are the principal target areas of the Chinese Communists in their narcotics drive?

Mr. ANSLINGER. Well, certainly Japan and South Korea. Japan would be number one. In Southeast Asia, the country that is getting the worst of it is Thailand, with Burma and Vietnam getting it, and around Singapore; around the Straits Settlements there is a very, very substantial traffic that is coming down through Burma from Yunnan.

Mr. ARENS. Now, is your information based, in part, upon seizures made in these areas by the authorities?

Mr. ANSLINGER. It is based in large measure on reports made by those various governments to the United Nations. Some of the seizures we know about are corroborated by this, some are not reported. We get a good deal of information from that part of the world.

Senator JENNER. Doctor, may I ask this question: I believe you stated earlier in your testimony that the Chinese Communists have sponsored and are promoting this illicit trade?

Mr. ANSLINGER. Yes, sir.

Senator JENNER. And I believe that you stated that the primary purpose for the government sponsoring and promoting this illicit trade in narcotics is money, strategic materials, and the demoralization of the West. Is that a fair statement?

Mr. ANSLINGER. Demoralization also of the Southeast Asian countries.

Senator JENNER. Now, is it fair to ask you what the United Nations think about that kind of situation and what they are doing about it?

Mr. ANSLINGER. Well, sir, I think that as far as the United Nations go on narcotics they have done a magnificent job in the control of, for instance, the synthetic narcotic drugs. If it were not for the United Nations, the world would be flooded with synthetic narcotic drugs and there is a system of limitation of manufacture, control of distribution, all over the world which is supervised by the United Nations and there is not very much you can do about Communist China except to put the pitiless spotlight of publicity right on the problem.

Now that is the only thing we have been able to do at the Narcotics Commission.[20]

The remarks by Mr. Anslinger, in response to his interlocutors in the hearings in question, are quoted "in extenso" because of the extremely authoritative standing he has had in this field, comparable to that held by the late J. Edgar Hoover in national security. There can be no doubt of the full authenticity and complete accuracy of the information contained in this testimony insofar as the complicity of Red China in worldwide narcotics trading was concerned. Also, the great importance and the responsibility of the United Nations cannot be stressed too strongly, the more so perhaps today when the Red Chinese have a delegation in the UN and are members of the Security Council. Reference should be made, in this connection, to the fully documented reports submitted to the UN by the U.S. Government that appear in Appendix IV, Sections "A" and "B," and to the extremely halting protestations and denials of the Chinese Reds, conveyed to the UN via their then representatives the Soviet delegation, which are also furnished as Appendix IV "C." While the Chinese mainland press has, from time to time, made references to addiction there and measures of suppression, the substance of Chinese denials is based on statements that they now have no *domestic* problem such as China once had. At no point have they ever denied the allegations that they are engaged in massive overseas trading operations.

Somewhat later, after the Soviet Union had been involved in a dispute with the Chinese Communists, they ceased to defend the Chinese Communists from charges of participation in the narcotics traffic. This was shown by an article that appeared in *Pravda* on September 15, 1964, that charged the Red Chinese authorities with support of an extended program of opium growth in Yunnan Province. The author of the article claimed to have seen vast fields of poppies under cultivation and charged that some half-billion dollars a year came into the hands of the leaders of China from the illicit sale of narcotics. The statement was also made that the traffic was encouraged so the resulting opium would find lucrative markets outside Red China.

As is well known, the day-to-day activities of the Bureau of Narcotics (or BNDD) involve great personal danger to its agents, who, of necessity, operate at close quarters with the criminal elements who carry on the drug traffic. This fact was underlined at the Senate Internal

Security Subcommittee hearings from which the above quotations were abstracted, because one of the persons who testified was described as a "nameless" undercover agent of the Bureau whose identity had to be protected.

The testimony of "Nameless" is quoted, in part, below:

Mr. ARENS. And did you perform a special assignment on behalf of Commissioner Anslinger in connection with the smuggling of narcotics from the Far East into the West Coast?

The WITNESS. Yes, sir.

Mr. ARENS. Now, would you first of all please, sir, kindly recount experiences and incidents of seizures in Japan, of narcotics traceable to Red China...

The WITNESS. Yes, sir. The flow of heroin into Japan from Communist China began in 1947 at the same time that it did into South Korea. By 1948 there was considerable traffic and by 1949 great numbers of the smugglers from Communist China were being arrested.

In December of 1949, 729 grams of heroin, which is about two pounds, were seized on the seaside of Japan from smugglers who had purchased it from a Communist trading store in Gen San, North Korea. That was the first big seizure that we had that was directly traceable to Communist China.

Then we had another seizure on the Japanese seaside in 1950 of about 1,900 grams, which is about four pounds, that was smuggled into Japan by marine sea products personnel and in that investigation we found that they had a regular smuggling route established from a North Korean port into Japan and then they took the railroad down into Kobe and Osaka, where at that time the traffic had reached considerable proportion.

Then, in October, we made a seizure in Tokyo of 450 grams, which is about a pound, from two Japanese. These two people happened to be more or less of the crying type, which was unusual—that is, they furnished additional information immediately, and we were able to arrest the chief of the Communist Party for the Southern Island of Japan, Kyushu.

And this man, whose name is Yamamoto, had obtained the heroin from a courier who operated out of Rashin, North Korea. And this courier was, according to our information, one of the most powerful men in Rashin in the Communist echelon. The chief of the Communist Party in Kyushu had brought the heroin to Tokyo and furnished it to two other officials in the Communist Party to dispose of it to obtain funds for their operations.

Then in 1951, in February of 1951, we had information that there was a big shipment of heroin coming in and we were able to seize 10 pounds of it in Kobe. It was only a third of the total amount that had come in: 30 pounds had reached Japan at Kure, which is near Hiroshima, and this heroin was labeled with the lines Global Brand being manufactured in Tientsin, China.*

The package itself bore the seals of the laboratory, as did the wrapping paper on the outside, so that if the package had been opened you could tell readily that it had been opened. That was one of the biggest seizures that had been made up to that time.

Following that, shortly after that, we seized 676 grams, which is about a pound and a half, that had been smuggled in by Chinese through the Tokyo International Airport, and this heroin was the first that bore the Red Line brand and after that we became very familiar with this particular kind of heroin from Communist China.**

The tag, the Red Line tag, was always found within the package of heroin.

In April, we received another two pounds of this Red Line brand from Chinese in Tokyo, and it also bore the Red Line label. In all these seizures that I am mentioning, the principals were Chinese; in fact, the arrest statistics showed that 40 percent of the traffickers arrested were Chinese and Koreans.

In considering that, you have to remember that there were only about 35,000 Chinese in Japan and about 400,000 Koreans, numbering about four-to-one in favor of the North Koreans. So that with a small segment of the population of about 85 million they were accounting for 40 percent of the arrests.

Then in 1952 the Red Line brand heroin showed up again in Kobe. We got about a pound and a half that time, and we had another seizure in Kobe of about four pounds of this Red Line brand, and with respect to this seizure the Japanese authorities said the smugglers were suspected to be Communists and the smuggling was the strategy of the Chinese Communists.

And they added that the smuggling of narcotics has increased, aiming at the dejection of the Japanese people. That was from the Japanese authorities themselves. In connection with this seizure of four pounds in Kobe, the same ship was reported to have discharged 170 pounds of heroin at Yokohama. And following that incident one of the Chinese that was instrumental in the smuggling of this committed suicide.

Mr. ARENS. What is the narcotics situation, Mr. Witness, in Southeast Asia?

The WITNESS. Well they certainly have their problems because literally floods of narcotics out of China are going down through Southeast Asia into and through Southeast Asia.

---

*Misprint for Lion's Global Brand.
**Misprint for Red Lion Brand.

Mr. ARENS. You are, of course, familiar with the global strategy of the Communists to penetrate into Southeast Asia, are you not?

The WITNESS. Yes, sir.

Mr. ARENS. Is it safe to speculate that the narcotics drive is the artillery which precedes the Communist agents going in, the political agents, to undertake to foment discord in Southeast Asia?

The WITNESS. I would say that was a political question; but certainly narcotics demoralize, there is no question about that.

Mr. ARENS. What about Thailand?

The WITNESS. There is traffic in Thailand and out of Thailand, considerable traffic.

Mr. ARENS. Can you give us a little bit more information with respect to the traffic penetration of Thailand by the illicit narcotics traffic?

The WITNESS. Well of all of the opium, I wouldn't say all but almost all of the opium seized there comes from Communist China, and recently we have had big seizures of crude morphine which is the worst stage or intermediate stage of processing morphine for heroin. From the crude morphine you are able to make heroin very easily....

Mr. ARENS. Now would you kindly recount the circumstances on narcotics seizures on the West coast, of narcotics coming in from Red China.

The WITNESS. ...In 1949 the trafficker in Hong Kong that the Commissioner mentioned established a so-called cut-off into the United States for heroin, and through a system of letters and telegrams, more or less coded, they were able to effect receipt and delivery of this heroin.

In other words, the cut-off would receive the heroin and deliver it to someone he did not know so that it would be impossible, so they thought, to establish a line back to the source. This man was in Hong Kong, this source of heroin was in Canton and Shanghai, and all together that we know of, they were able to bring in some 400 ounces of heroin in this one transaction....

Mr. ARENS. Is the penetration of narcotics from Red China on the West Coast of the United States substantial?

The WITNESS. Yes, it is substantial.[21]

As can be seen from the carefully worded nature of the replies by Commissioner Anslinger and one of his agents, underlying them was a wealth of official information of a kind that could not be revealed more specifically because of their sources. Most of the sources are international and a slip could compromise individuals and possibly lead to their deaths.

In view of the vital need for an overall perspective on the whole drug question, there is an obvious demand for a wide-reaching review of international police records and for the setting up of a public information policy designed to divulge in much greater depth than has been done heretofore the supply and political aspect of the international traffic in narcotics. This should be on a scale comparable to that which, most fortunately, has now developed in connection with the social and domestic aspects of the drug problem. Without its counterpart describing the political and criminal aspects, and assessing the nature and magnitude of this world threat, the whole question cannot be seen from a fully balanced point of view.

Another extremely important witness with full insight into the problem, based on direct experience in Asia, has been Richard Deverall. This gifted and highly informed man was, in the mid-'50s, the representative in Asia of the Free Trade Union Committee of the AFL and was, at one time, the Education Director of the United Auto Workers-CIO and Chief of Labor Education in SCAP (Supreme Commander Allied Powers).

In the course of the testimony to the committee quoted above, Deverall provided a wealth of information on the labor situation in Japan, of which he possessed almost unparallelled knowledge, and on the political aspects of the Japanese trade union movement.

In his remarks Deverall brought out important but relatively little-known aspects of the relationship between Communist penetration of Japan and the activity of organized Japanese labor and the Japanese academic world. He also examined in some detail the use of drugs by the Chinese and North Korean Communists in their subversion of Japanese society. Some of this latter testimony is of unusual interest because it explores a little-understood subject, the question of preconditioning of potential addicts of the harder drugs by the use of synthetics:

> Mr. ARENS. Then if you would kindly get into the next phase, your narcotics smuggling.
> Mr. DEVERALL. In answer to Mr. Arens' question on narcotics, in 1951 is the first mention by Japanese of heroin entering Japan from North Korea, the first mention that we find on the part of Japan, and that is the beginning of the second phase of drug smuggling into Japan to gain funds for the party, and that was the beginning of the illegal, illicit heroin traffic into Japan's four islands.
> Mr. ARENS. So our record is clear, when does this period begin of their narcotics smuggling?
> Mr. DEVERALL. I would say 1950–51, when the Japanese first began reporting heroin entering into Japan illicitly, probably from Korea or northern China.

Mr. ARENS. What is one of the objectives or what are the objectives of the Communists in penetrating Japan with narcotics?

Mr. DEVERALL. Well, I think they have several objectives. One very obviously is to, I think, inflict as much damage as possible—what you might call psychological demoralization—on Japanese, especially Japanese youth. The major portion of the heroin addicts or heroin users are young people. It is one of the tragedies of the postwar period.

One purpose, I think, has been this penetration and corruption of young people. A second purpose, and I think it diabolical, is the need of Red China for American dollars to pay off its credits to the Soviet Union.

Mr. ARENS. Do you have a document there, an exhibit, which is pertinent to the second point?

Mr. DEVERALL. I do, sir. This is a document from my file but this is printed in Peking. The title is "The Sino-Soviet treaty and agreements signed in Moscow on the 14th of February 1950," published in Peking by the Foreign Languages Press, dated 1952.

Now in this document, in article 3—I may say this was signed on the February 14, 1950, by the late Mr. Vishinsky and the present premier of China, Mr. Chou En-lai.

In article 3, this was regarding a loan to China, a credit of 300 million American dollars. Article 2 says:

"The Central Peoples' Government of the Peoples' Republic of China shall repay the credit mentioned in article 1 together with the interest thereon in deliveries of raw materials, tea, gold, and American dollars."

Mr. ARENS. Now, Mr. Deverall, do you have documents there which demonstrate the growth and extent of the illicit traffic in Japan from Red China of opium and other dangerous drugs?

Mr. DEVERALL. I do, sir. I left Tokyo this past Monday, and last Monday morning I had an interview with friends in the Narcotics Commission of the Japanese Ministry of Welfare, the chief and his very brilliant assistant, Mr. Nakahama, and they furnished me with a copy of the 1954 report of the Government of Japan on illicit traffic in narcotics....

This is the Japanese Government's annual report for 1954. One striking thing is that the number of arrests and prosecutions for violations of the narcotics laws of Japan has increased 45 percent in the last year.

Mr. ARENS. Over the preceding year?

Mr. DEVERALL. Yes, sir. And I talked with the chief of the narcotics bureau in Tokyo about this and said "Would you say the drug traffic is increasing, decreasing, or being controlled?"

And he said, "I cannot say that it is decreasing, I cannot say it is being controlled, it is increasing."

And I might say he added, he or Mr. Nakahama, I forget which one of them, told me that the influx of heroin from North Korea is sharply increasing, that they are detecting more and more of it in Japan.

Mr. ARENS. In passing, may I ask you this. Has there been in the recent past a new drug introduced in Japan?

Mr. DEVERALL. Yes, sir, if you would like to talk about it later, the name of the drug is hiropon. It is not a narcotic, it is a stimulant drug like benzedrine, but later, if you will, I would like to tell you that it is one of the most horrible weapons used by the Communists in the Far East.

Mr. ARENS. What are the number of users of hiropon in Japan?

Mr. DEVERALL. At the end of 1954 it was estimated that one to two million out of a population of 88 million were using hiropon, and I think that many thousands of the one to two million are addicts.

Mr. ARENS. That is one of the weapons of the Red Chinese in penetrating Japan, right?

Mr. DEVERALL. I think I can introduce evidence that would give very strong indication of that.

Mr. ARENS. Would you just tell us in a word, we will get on to this a little later on—just in a word, what is the effect of hiropon on the human system and upon the mind?

Mr. DEVERALL. Hiropon—the first effect is a stimulation of ability to work for hours and hours without any fatigue.

It then begins to affect the heart and the liver, facial twitches, overanimation, then delusions—this is a very dangerous period in which the victims rape, murder, kill, steal. We have had the most horrible crimes in Japan in the last year, all connected with hiropon. A hiropon victim will have the delusion that someone is trying to kill him, and he will meet you and if you happen to fit the delusion you are struck down and murdered on the spot, and when the man comes off the drug he says, "I do not know why I did it, I have no idea."

Mr. ARENS. And how is it administered?

Mr. DEVERALL. By injection into the blood stream. The final end result is insanity, incurable.... Hiropon, a stimulant drug, is made from a drug well known to us called ephedrine hydrochloride.

Mr. ARENS. I mean, where does it come from?

Mr. DEVERALL. Well, the ephedrine, we make a little ephedrine in our country, mainly for nasal passages and the treatment of rheumatism, but the ephedrine in the Far East is primarily coming out of Red China.

I may say that I have some photographs here which we have secured from friends in Hong Kong, in which I have ephedrine being sold in Hong Kong and Macao. The bottled container has a leaflet extolling the qualities of the drug and the leaflet itself says the main source of ephedrine is North China....*

Mr. ARENS. What are the Japanese told by the left wing in Japan as to the source of hiropon?

Mr. DEVERALL. The general propaganda, as I have read it in translation from the Japanese Communist press, is that they have repeatedly alleged that hiropon is the result of the occupation's policies and is purely an American device....

Mr. ARENS. Now, will you kindly tell the subcommittee some of the techniques of this smuggling of narcotics and drugs and other commodities?

Mr. DEVERALL. Well, I think that you should divide that into the routes and the methods.

Mr. ARENS. All right, sir.

Mr. DEVERALL. If I may. The general route is the beginning of the Communist China phase. The bulk of narcotics coming into Japan, I think it is only safe to say, were coming in through Hong Kong. Hong Kong and Macao. Hong Kong is a British colony beneath Canton, and Macao is a Portuguese colony adjacent to Hong Kong, the same area as Canton.

Well, the early route was apparently through there, but then there has been a shift a few years ago of bringing drugs through Southwestern China from Yunnan into Burma and from Yunnan through Siam, through Bangkok, across Hong Kong into Tokyo. In the early phase, 1950-51, the main vehicle used was boats. Smuggling by boat. Lately the traffic has changed much more to smuggling by aircraft.

Now, in this regard, the Japanese told me when I was leaving last Monday that in their estimation the Bangkok-Tokyo route is a rather important one, and I was rather distressed a few weeks ago to get a report that a young American Air Force sergeant had been arrested at the Hong Kong airport with a satchel full of heroin and, I think, cake morphine and watches that he was smuggling. He was a member of the military group in Bangkok and had evidently been seduced or enticed into carrying the stuff and thinking that as an American he could get away with it. He had been from Bangkok to Hong Kong with the stuff and was apprehended and arrested with the narcotics and watches in his possession.

I think there is one case—and there are many others. There are other rumors that there are other sources and officials of other countries are also part of the Bangkok-Hong Kong-Tokyo run of narcotics. They tell me, the Japanese, that this Yunnan through

---

*There is a Chinese plant called "Ma Huang" that contains ephedrine and that has long been used by the Chinese for medicinal purposes.

Hong Kong to Japan run is now a very important source of drugs entering Japan. The other main source is directed out of North Korea through Niigata and west coast cities into the Tokyo-Yokohama area which is the market, the hub of the narcotics market in Japan....

Mr. ARENS. How about the seamen's clubs? To what extent do they play a part in this scheme of the techniques?

Mr. DEVERALL. This is a new device that is growing out of Red China in the major ports of China.

The Chinese seamen's union which is, of course, a Communist-controlled organization, has constructed so-called seamen's clubs in Tientsin. We have photographic evidence from Red Chinese sources of the seamen's club there, and foreign seamen entering these ports are wined and dined, free room, free board, free dance, free girls, free everything, and the implication I would draw from this is (1) It is useful in promoting Communist propaganda and (2) I think it indicates a deliberate attempt, a very clever attempt by the Chinese to soften up foreign seamen and find out those who might be susceptible to running a few packages of drugs to some other country. I might tell you—I cannot name the source in Japan that told me this—that we discussed this problem with one man who knows very much about Japanese seamen's problems and he said that the young seamen have been so well treated by the Chinese seamen's union there that they have been rather taken in by the propaganda, and the conclusion I think one can draw from this is that the increase in foreign trade with Red China will directly increase the danger of narcotics smuggling. Any foreign trade, in any way, with Red China I think would be automatically suspect as a carrier for narcotics.[22]

These remarks are all the more pertinent today when not only a staggering increase in the volume of international narcotics traffic in the Far East has taken place but increased trading with Red China seems to be in prospect. The recognition of that country by Canada, its entry into the United Nations, its purchases of modern transport aircraft, and massive illegal entry of thousands of Red Chinese nationals into North America all add up to a considerable augmentation of the threat that the witnesses perceived so clearly in the mid-'50s.

Details of narcotics addiction in Japan that they furnished are of great topical interest, since they expose and underline the manner in which a positive policy of promotion of narcotics by the Communists has been able to make rapid headway in a country that, literally, had no addiction problem but that did possess social conditions that favored it in the postwar period. These were brilliantly exploited by the skillful Red Chinese and North Korean preparation and extension of the traffic, soon producing an intolerable aggravation of the situation and considerable demoralization and political disruption in Japan.

Richard Deverall has been a particularly reliable and well-informed witness of this process who has paid the closest attention to the origins of the traffic in Red China and the complex patterns of worldwide trading. His official post in the occupation of Japan and his close contacts with many labor leaders all over Asia provided him with an almost unparalleled opportunity to obtain an informed view.

Much of this he has exposed in his short study, *Mao Tze-tung Stop This Dirty Opium Business*. In that work, based on his five years of close study, Deverall came to the firm conclusion that Red China was engaged in massive production of opiates, was promoting the worldwide distribution of these substances, was partly motivated by economic motives, but was also engaged in a politico-military offensive of a particularly reprehensible kind.

His small book contains a mass of well-sifted evidence, and two quotations will be given by way of illustration:

> The Opium Prohibition Bureau office in Tientsin is the center of a huge network of agents and smugglers all over the world who are trading Red Chinese opium and heroin for souls and dollars. It is also a matter of record that offices in Harbin, Rashin (North Korea), Shanghai, and Canton handle both production and export, while an office in Peking ties together the financial aspects of this giant Red Chinese-North Korean opium smuggling operation. Most of the raw opium needed for this vast operation is grown inside Red China and North Korea. But it also seems to be a fact that the Sino-Soviet agreement of 1950, which provided Red China with a credit of U.S. $300,000,000 to help prepare Red China for its launching of the Korean War, included as part of the credit U.S. $240,000,000 worth of opium (about 4,000 tons) originally seized by the Russian Army in Manchuria in 1945 from Kwantung Army stocks.[23]

and again:

> The evidence which we have reviewed is conclusive: (a) chemical analysis and the physical appearance of many seizures establish the fact that they came from stock cultivated only in Red China and/or North Korea; (b) enormous seizures of drugs in Malaya, Hong Kong, South Korea, Japan and the United States have generally been traced back to Red China and North Korean ports; (c) arrested smugglers like Akira Ito and many Chinese in Japan have

104

given narcotics agents full details on their operations—details which have later been checked by the police and the narcotics agents and found substantially correct; and (d) both Red Chinese and North Korean sources directly or indirectly have admitted the existence of the opium and heroin export racket.[24]

From time to time there have been important items of corroborative evidence from Free China, whose writers have shown deep insight when they have reviewed the problem and whose information, although often regarded much too lightly, has largely been confirmed by other sources.

Writing in *Free China Review* on March 7, 1965, a staff writer, Teng Yen-pin, under the caption "Hong Kong is Principal Distribution Center of Peiping's Opium Offensive," describes the manner in which "Hong Kong today is apparently the principal distribution center of the world-wide opium trade conducted by the Peiping regime.

"The usefulness of the British Crown Colony as a distribution center for their narcotics—opium, heroin and morphine—is exploited to the full extent. The Chinese Reds poison the world and at the same time earn large amounts of foreign exchange.

"Adjoining the Chinese mainland, Hong Kong is an ideal place for Chinese narcotics exports. Within the colony, reports on the arrests of dope-smuggling rings and the arrests of addicts are almost daily events and seldom arouse public attention. Hong Kong does not produce opium. Where do the narcotics come from?"

In his article, Teng briefly reviews the international scene, listing the eleven nations and territories known to be producing opium: Soviet Russia, India, Turkey, Czechoslovakia, Pakistan, Japan, Bulgaria, Burma, North Korea, North Vietnam, and the Chinese mainland, and mentions the fact that the first six had supplied statistics on production to the United Nations Narcotics Commission. However, he points out, the last five had consistently refused information.

Teng adds:

> The so-called "Department of Social Affairs" of the Chinese Communist Party has been in full charge of the production and sale of opium. The "Commission for Foreign Trade" is in charge of the management. The Chinese Communist "Political Bureau" is in supreme command. Poppy plantation areas include Yunnan Province in Southwestern China and Shensi and Kansu Province in Northwestern China as well as Inner Mongolia. At the same time the Chinese Reds have reportedly established a unified organization with Burma, North Korea and North Vietnam to coordinate production and sale. Peiping is the boss.

The main route of the large-scale smuggling to Europe and Africa is via Albania, the only East European ally of the Peiping regime.... Some nine Red Chinese freighters call at Albanian ports every month.

Interpol international police in Paris, the responsible authorities in many countries and Nasser of the UAR know it... When Nasser, who maintains diplomatic relations with Peiping, says no to such smugglers, the road to Africa leads through Paris and Marseille.[25]

Another article that appeared in *Free China Review*, on October 25, 1964, mentioned that "The Mao Tse-tung regime in Peiping is offering the free world—called 'consumer lands'—the best morphine, heroin and opium at the lowest prices as 'consumer goods' as West Berlin's International Press Service has reported."

A careful review of all the published evidence of many expert and reliable witnesses, and of the numerous documented criminal cases that are a matter of public record, produces such an overwhelming case against Red China that any attempt to defend that country against the allegations of complicity is futile. The Chinese do not attempt even to do this themselves.

A more recent form of denial, other than flat repudiation such as appears at the beginning of this chapter in the BNDD document called "The World Opium Situation"—namely, to state the rapid decline in mainland production in the late '50s and early '60s—cannot be seen to have even the flimsiest basis of support. This is obviously impossible when the ever-growing volume of seizures is taken into account, as well as the growing realization of the nature of the unprincipled attack on the U.S. troops in Vietnam.

When these facts are examined and correlated with the disturbing facts of domestic addiction in the United States, it is not possible to support the carefully fostered explanation that this scourge is almost entirely the result of the impact of Turkish heroin processed by Sicilians and the Union Corse in the neighborhood of Marseilles. While there has been an impressive and skillfully conducted campaign of public misinformation and of information control of a most subtle kind—in order to conceal the realities of the Red Chinese "connection" and to pin the responsibility on friends and allies of the United States by means of slander—the underlying facts of the case completely belie such measures. Today there is, without doubt, an awareness forming in the minds of the public about the significance of the drug menace, the massive involvement of the Red Chinese regime, and of its motives in this sinister traffic.

An important case that was investigated at about the time the Red Chinese export drive was really gathering momentum was one in which two kilograms and 136 grams of morphine were found in the possession of a USAF enlisted man named Marshall R. Wilmot, who was seized on June 14, 1959. The investigation that followed was a joint one in which personnel of the U.S. Air Force Office of Special Investigation (OSI) and personnel from Japan, Hong Kong, and Free China all collaborated. According to the Japanese press, which was well informed about this and other similar cases, Wilmot was a member of a criminal narcotics ring that had been responsible for smuggling drugs from Communist China to Japan, amounting to $278 million in value over a ten-year period.

Yet another case involved Lee Edgar Sartain of Honolulu. Sartain was arrested for a misdemeanor and was found to own a suitcase containing one kilogram and 54 grams of heroin. He was a bar owner and theatrical proprietor who was constantly seeking outlets within the United States for heroin that he was procuring in very large quantities from Red China.

Another aspect of the narcotics menace that came under discussion in Geneva was drugs as a factor in political warfare. It had been found in the course of the arrest of about 700 Communist infiltrators and agents entering South Korea from North Korea that all of them had narcotics in their possession intended for use in raising funds for fifth-column operations. In all, about 70 kilos were involved that were worth about $700,000. One of these seizures was linked with the Wilmot affair.

Most of the information presented so far in this chapter deals with policies, events, and findings in the 1950s and early '60s, during Phase I of Red China's 20-Year Plan. Further particulars appear in Appendixes IV "A" and IV "B." There, some statements made by Commissioner Henry Anslinger are quoted *in extenso*, as they serve to outline the objectivity, the dedication, and the sense of international duty, as well as the efficiency, of the Bureau of Narcotics of that period. Considering the scale of resources it had at that time, its achievements were the more remarkable.

It is necessary, however, to examine some more recent statements and items of evidence that point even more conclusively to the shameless and utterly ruthless aggression promoted by the Chinese Communists, assisted by their principal accomplices in Asia, North Korea, and North Vietnam. All three have been heavily involved in psychochemical operations at one time or another, but Red China most of all.

As was noted previously, one of the most important and revealing statements in this connection was the strangely unguarded statement made by Chou En-lai to Nasser in 1965 (see pp. 21 and 23). The implications of this confidence have now been borne out in the devastating heroin epidemic in Vietnam that began in 1970, and whose political and military motivations have been becoming all too obvious of late. (See below pp. 261-266, General Walt's findings, Chapter 6.)

Speaking on this subject on April 12, 1972, Representative Philip R. Crane (R; Ill.) said

> At a time when there is a euphoric feeling that peace may be at hand with the Communist Chinese, a feeling not borne out by the fact that the Peking government continues to sponsor subversion and terror throughout Asia, one important question remains unanswered and, to a large extent, unasked. That question is this: how involved is Communist China in the flow of narcotics in Southeast Asia and elsewhere in the world?

Continuing, after reviewing the evidence, Mr. Crane added in conclusion

> At a time when thousands of young Americans are becoming addicted to heroin and other dangerous drugs, it is incumbent upon our government, if it is sincere in its desire to stem the tide of such drugs, to investigate the possible involvement of Communist China in their production and distribution.[26]

These observations have been echoed by a good many journalists and publicists, as well as by professional men in various disciplines. Numerous comments have also been forthcoming from political and military figures both in the United States and abroad.

The present-day form of the problem was, indeed, foreshadowed by a strikingly similar statement made in 1961 by Representative Frank E. Worth (D; Penn.) when he referred to Communist "Dope Warfare" waged by the Red Chinese against American and other UN troops during the Korean War. He said that narcotics were "peddled at bargain prices by young women pushers near all military installations in Korea." The narcotics were of high quality and of considerable strength and purity. In connection with this, the Japanese police arrested some 2,000 pushers near U.S. installations in Japan. As a direct result of that offensive and of growing Japanese concern about a completely new problem of heroin addiction—which had never existed before on any perceptible scale in Japan, and which was directly traceable to the offensive use of drugs—the Japanese hurriedly set up a National Committee to defend the country against the traffic. Its Chairman was Tsusai Sugawara. Of all people, the Japanese were the least likely to be skeptical about this mode of warfare.

According to some of the statements issued by this committee, which, in view of the breach that was developing between the U.S.S.R. and Red China, were featured by the *Pravda* correspondent in Tokyo (Ochinnikov), the Chinese Reds were supposed to be making some $170-million profit from drugs. Of this sum, 25 percent was supposed to go towards the support of the Japanese Communist Party and to other illegal activities in that country. The Japanese at that point estimated that the gains from the whole Chinese narcotics traffic were $500 million; as much as two-thirds of the drugs were being shipped into the United States via West Coast ports, with San Francisco as the main point of ingress. Chinese heroin in Japan was fetching $4,000 a pound in 1960. There was also a considerable amount of opium being imported into Japan, perhaps 2,000 to 3,000 tons a year.

In 1964, Sugawara, in his capacity as Chairman of the Japanese National Committee for Struggle Against Drug Addiction, said that Peking had become the world's principal producer of opium poppies. This committee, and other bodies that the Japanese created to control drug addiction, deserve much credit for having beaten the heroin problem in Japan. Now that the two countries are moving closer together, it remains to be seen whether that situation can be sustained.

Another witness in Asia to the important political and social significance of the Red Chinese "connection" has been the chairman of the Labor and Immigration Committee of the Senate of the Philippines. That official stated, on April 30, 1966, that the value of narcotics arriving illegally in his country from Hong Kong and Singapore was $1,161,290. He left no doubt in his hearers' minds about the intent behind the traffic, and he accused the Chinese Communists of attempting to narcotize the bodies and minds of the Filipinos, cause social disruption, impede the development of the economy, and to promote disaffection and the spirit of rebellion in the Philippines. At the time of writing, the Philippines are under martial law and a revolt is ongoing, a situation bearing out many warnings given earlier by vigilant Filipino officials who have had much experience in matters of this kind.

Among the well-known writers on the subject of Red Chinese narcotics trading has been De Witt Copp, who, among his many articles, contributed one that appeared in *Human Events* on October 16, 1971. In this, the author referred to a British Government document that gave, as a 1969 estimate, the total amount of illicit opium being cultivated in the world as 5,000 tons per year. Of that figure, some 3,500 tons per year was supposed to be coming from Red China. In his article, Copp said, "No doubt, the authenticity of the British document will be challenged...." However, supporting evidence is offered by a ranking official of the Dutch Narcotics Bureau and Jacques Kiere of the French Bureau of Narcotics and Dangerous Drugs.

The Dutch official declared that "Smuggling of Red Chinese narcotics is on the increase in Holland. The main points of entry are Rotterdam and Amsterdam in that order. The drug usually seized is heroin. Ninety percent of the crew members apprehended have been Chinese. Several of the ships involved have been Red Chinese. Our laboratories have verified that the drugs originate in Communist China."

According to Jacques Kiere, "The Bureau has always stated that Communist China is involved in poppy cultivation and illicit drug trade. We have much evidence for that."[27]

Closer at hand, the well-known radio commentator Jeffrey St. John announced on the CBS radio network on February 23, 1972,

> Ever since the establishment of the Chinese Reds on the Chinese mainland, they have been actively involved in drugs. However, it has only been in recent years that narcotics have served a specific ideological end, coinciding with the mushrooming of the drug problem in Western nations like the United States.[28]

Another knowledgeable source, now prominent in the press, is Lt. Gen. V. H. Krulak (USMC, Ret.), who, speaking at the 43rd Annual Conference of the Copley Newspapers at Borrego Springs, Calif., on February 14, 1972, said

> The Chinese Reds do want hard money and opium is probably China's greatest export staple. They are doing everything they can to improve and expand opium culture, and it is estimated that they earn about a billion clandestine dollars a year from their dope sales.[29]

General Krulak is comparatively recently retired and obviously had the fullest access to intelligence sources bearing on the subject during his period of service in Vietnam.

According to the well-informed and accurate *Washington Report* issued by the American Security Council (issue of January 13, 1972), the Hong Kong police have stated that there was a 1,000-percent increase in illegal drugs smuggled out of Red China into the Free World. Most of this was reputed to be opium, and the Hong Kong police seized 12,500 pounds in 1971 as compared with the 877 pounds they captured in 1970.

Very recently, an interesting and important first-hand account of opium cultivation in Red China has been provided by a reliable witness, a refugee from the mainland called Miss Yuan Mou-ru. Miss

Yuan testified on May 17, 1972, before the House Foreign Affairs Committee (Subcommittee on Asian and Pacific Affairs) in Washington, D.C. According to the report that was subsequently issued:

> Miss Yuan was born in Szechuan Province of China. Both her parents were medical doctors... Miss Yuan herself is an engineer with a degree in mechanical engineering from Chungking University. Because of differences with university authorities, Miss Yuan was classified as a "rightist" and was assigned by the Communist Party to work as a laborer and in factories for some ten years. In May 1969, Miss Yuan escaped from the People's Republic of China by way of Burma.[30]

In the course of her account of her experiences, Miss Yuan said

> My route of escape from China to Burma is via Yunnan Province. I rode through Lu river valley [Nu Chiang, the headwaters of the Salween (author's note)]... I saw with my own eyes the Chinese Communist Liberation Army growing opium in that area. So were the Burmese Communists and their mountain army under Chinese Communist influence. It did not surprise me because the Chinese Communists, in order to defeat "American Imperialism," have never hesitated to employ whatever means available to them. They would be glad to see their enemy degenerate and collapse without firing even a single shot.[31]

Miss Yuan has also mentioned that very little is known about opium cultivation among ordinary people on the mainland because of the high degree of secrecy attached to it.

Also recently, a useful and informative short publication called *Chinese Opium Narcotics—A Threat to the Survival of the West* was published. Its author, Prof. J. H. Turnbull, is the head of the Department of Applied Chemistry at the Royal Military College of Science, Shrivenham. Dr. Turnbull is particularly well informed on the international drug trade and its strategic and psychological-warfare implications. He has no doubt about the participation of Red China as a major factor, although his estimate of Chinese capacity is a conservative one. It may be noted that in producing this exposition of the situation, Dr. Turnbull has been acting in his private rather than in his official capacity. He has had, of course, access to much more information than most and has the following to say about Asia:

> The focal area of the Far Eastern narcotic traffic lies in the border states of Burma, Thailand, Laos and North Vietnam. In 1967,

a United Nations survey team estimated the area's opium capacity at 1,000 metric tons annually. These states, with the exception of Thailand, share a common frontier with South East China. Addiction to opium is indigenous and unofficial poppy cultivation is widespread. Any major drives to check the growing traffic in this area has the twofold problem of controlling opium production and stemming the stream of narcotics in transit from South East China en route to Bangkok and Hong Kong.[32]

Here, Dr. Turnbull gets to a major aspect of our current problem but, unfortunately, as he is well aware, there are a good many other routes out of China used by the traffic:

Burma achieved independence in 1948 as a union of five minority states. The country is high on the Communists' list for subversion. The military government in Rangoon under General Ne Win adopted a policy of neutrality between East and West. The Burmese Communist Party was outlawed in 1962 and has gone underground. The presence of a strong central government in Burma has unfortunately not achieved political stability in the country as a whole. The tribes in the hill provinces continue to strive for more independence from Rangoon. Communist subversive activities in the Chinese frontier areas of Burma and Laos foster unrest and undermine the authority of the Burmese Government. These political factors aggravate the problem of narcotics control in Burma.

Official figures based on 1969 estimates show that Burma produces about 180 tons of opium annually.... The total annual production capacity has been estimated at some 400 tons, of which some 300 tons leave the country illicitly. The major poppy-growing areas lie in the Kachin and Shan States which share about 1,200 miles of frontier with the South Eastern Provinces of China. The Burmese Government has had difficulty in curtailing the production of opium in these states because of weak administrative control from Rangoon. Some success has been achieved, however, by the introduction of wheat cultivation to replace the large acreage of poppy fields. At the same time, communications across the Salween River are being improved, and joint measures to control the border traffic in opium have been agreed with the governments of Laos and Thailand. *Unfortunately the Burmese Government is powerless to control poppy cultivation across the ill-defined frontier with the Yunnan Province of China. The major problem remains in stopping the illicit through-traffic in opium smuggled across the Yunnan-Burma border en route to the port of Rangoon.* (Italics added)[33]

In his treatment of the "Role of Red China," Dr. Turnbull makes the following observations:

112

Communist China's narcotic drive is directed broadly at the major industrial societies of the Free World. In purely commercial terms these offer obvious targets, since they provide both large, affluent markets, and potential sources of hard currency. The looser structure of the free societies renders them more vulnerable to exploitation than the tightly controlled Communist economies. Commercial enterprise, absence of travel restrictions, and uninhibited self-expression are factors which weaken the resistance of the West in this respect. Those industrial societies which have in addition endemic addiction on a large scale are particularly susceptible. From a purely commercial point of view the most attractive markets for Chinese narcotics are Japan and the United States.[34]

However, there are also the other aspects of the matter, which are those with which this work is particularly concerned:

The production of drugs for export on a global scale provides the Chinese with a valuable source of income, and a powerful weapon of subversion. The subversive aspects of the Chinese drug drive have three basic aims: to finance subversive activities abroad; to corrupt and weaken the people of the Free World; and to destroy the morale of U.S. servicemen fighting in Southeast Asia. Chinese Communist subversive activities are mainly financed with profits of the narcotics trade. In Hong Kong alone, a 1970 estimate by the Narcotics Investigation Division of the Police quoted some 1½ million HK $ monthly. This money is deposited in the Bank of China in Hong Kong. It is used to purchase machinery from Europe and to finance secret agents serving in the Far East....

The border area between Yunnan, Burma and Thailand has become a major international distributing centre where illicit distributing companies enjoy the covert protection of the Chinese Ministry of Foreign Trade. The importance of this source of supply in the global drug-control problem has enormously increased now that Turkey has been virtually eliminated as a major producer.[35]

Although Dr. Turnbull takes account of such estimates of Red Chinese production of opium as the figure of 8,000 tons that has been quoted by a Russian source, he tends himself to doubt this figure and gives as his own estimate 2.5 million kilos of opium a year, 2,750 tons.

This figure, which he derives by a simple computation based on a chosen figure of a yield of 5 kilograms (kg) per hectare on a known figure of area under cultivation, he describes as a conservative estimate. In the view of this author, it is an underestimate since it is known that about 2,000 tons a year are consumed in Japan while the figures for Malaya, Hong Kong, and the Phillippines, when added, raise the figure well toward 2,750 tons.

Another recent author who has written reliably on the subject has been Ch'in Yung-fa, a contributor to the serious and important periodical *Issues and Studies* published by the Institute of International Relations in Taipei. His latest article, called "The Economic and Political Significance of Chinese Communist Production and Exportation of Dangerous Drugs," appeared in the March 1972 issue.

This is an extremely factual and informative article that, as well as providing useful historical background, contains some significant tables showing the main features of Red Chinese production and the nomenclature of their products. As far as the volume of production is concerned, Mr. Ch'in writes

> It is estimated that the Chinese Communists process about 10,000 tons of narcotics a year. From 1952 to 1957 the annual production and sale totalled about 2,000 tons but it increased to 8,000 tons a year between 1958 and 1964. From 1965 to the present, the annual export has been 10,000 tons, earning a net profit of over U.S. $800 million per year.[36]

This would appear to be about right, and tribute must be paid at this point to the scholarly objectivity of the research workers and analysts in Taipei, who can throw more light on the situation on the mainland than anyone with the possible exception of the Russians. The latter have an uncanny knowledge of the state of affairs there that is not surprising in view of the extent of their involvement. There is, unfortunately, a tendency to ignore or even to disparage writing and information coming from the Republic of China. It is an attitude that has always been present but that has become more pronounced of late, possibly because of the changes of U.S. policy in the Far East and the misfortunes that these have brought Taiwan. Nevertheless, I have, over the years, sustained a high faith in the basic integrity of the Republic of China in all aspects of its conduct of affairs. And the scrupulousness of the scholarship on Taiwan is not surprising when the strength of the Confucian tradition there is so evident. I have often been in a good position to check and corroborate the information that Taipei has made so freely available, and have no hesitation in attesting to its accuracy in most cases. I am, in fact, indebted to several Chinese sources for essential parts of this work.

Another scholarly commentator on this important and controversial question has been Dr. Stefan Possony of the Stanford Research Institute, who also made a contribution to *Issues and Studies* not long ago.

This was called "Maoist China and Heroin" and the article appeared in the November 1971 issue.

Dr. Possony sets the keynote of his brief study with this opening:

> Nikita Khrushchev reportedly once called Mao Tse-tung an "opium dealer." By contrast, the press in the Free World has time and again absolved Peiping from any complicity in the illicit drug trade. For more than ten years Free World governments, including the government of the United States, have remained strangely silent on this touchy subject. The more one studies the matter, the more the conviction grows that the governments of the main democratic states were very slow in recognizing that a drug epidemic has been in progress, and that till now they have avoided investigating the causes and conditions of this tragedy. Interest centered on the question of why an individual takes to drugs? This question has been given as many answers as there are "schools" of psychiatry, psychology and sociology. But all these hypothetical replies cover only portions of the truth.[37]

In this article, fully accepting the idea of Red Chinese involvement in the worldwide aspects of the drug traffic, Dr. Possony attempts to work out the scale of that involvement by means of some rather speculative calculations—that they are rather tentative he himself admits. At the outset he makes some especially pertinent observations about the continual recurrence of the "magic" figure of 80 percent that has, until recently, been repeated over and over again as an article of dogma whenever the matter of heroin imports into the United States has been discussed. He writes

> Whatever the quantities of opium that came out of Turkey during the period when the Middle Eastern and Turkish supplies were being reduced, heroin consumption went up in the United States and all over the world. This consumption grew at a very steep rate and in some places was doubling in less than one year. It is this extraordinary increase in heroin consumption which gave rise to the talk of a heroin epidemic.
>
> With a dynamic growth of consumption in the U.S. and elsewhere and a constant reduction in the output of Turkish opium the contributions of Turkey cannot possibly have remained static at the 80 percent level.
>
> Experience suggests that whenever a "magic figure" is cited for many years in a row, the analytical process must have gone off the track. Be it noted that Turkey is an ally of the United States, that given their own serious problems, the Turkish authorities have

been cooperative, and that the criticism on the basis of a fictional figure has not improved our relations with that ally.[38]

Dr. Possony continues:

There can be no serious doubt that the Maoists conducted a drug offensive during the early '50s which, among other things, was directed against American soldiers. This finding may or may not be of purely historical interest. If there were any evidence that the Chinese Communists abandoned the illicit drug business, the information would have historical significance only. Unfortunately, no such evidence has been obtained and none has been even suggested. Beginning in the early 1960s, the subject, which originally had attracted great attention, became an "unsubject," to paraphrase Orwell. It is thus painfully obvious that we did not remember—and did not want to remember—the lesson we learned during World War II, the Korean conflict and the occupation of Japan. Consequently, our unpreparedness, when a narcotics offensive hit us again in 1970, should not elicit any surprise.[39]

After briefly reviewing some of the principal characteristics of the Red Chinese narcotics program, Dr. Possony attempts a numerical analysis, from his view, of the scale of operations. Taking a productivity factor of five kg per hectare, he examines the figures given by the *United Daily News* of Taipei of March 1965, namely a rise of opium production on the mainland from 3,500 tons per year in 1950 to 10,000 tons by 1965. He then states his opinion that these figures are unrealistic and that somehow an extra "nought" has slipped in. He therefore brings his own estimates down, saying that the actual rise during the time span is from 350 tons per year to 1,000 per year.*

Then Dr. Possony attempts an estimate of world heroin production, which he computes in order to determine an approximate rate of production in Red China, by a brief calculation that includes a factor for what he considers to be "known" heroin production. Examining the addiction rates in a number of places—1:300 in Stockholm and 1:70 in Hong Kong, 1:27 in Puerto Rico and 8 to 1,000 in Great Britain—he assumes that the addiction rate worldwide (i.e., in the Western World) is 1.5 per 1,000 and that, therefore, the number of heroin addicts in a population of, say, 1 billion is 1.5 million addicts, "in all likelihood a low estimate." Then, using a figure of 80 grams per year as the requirement of each of the addicts, he calculates that these will require

---

*Note, however, that in 1949 the production was known to be about 2,000 tons per year.

120 million grams of heroin a year—120 metric tons. Then, noting that only 20,000 kg of heroin are accounted for by knowledge of existing plants, he maintains that 100,000 kg of heroin are unaccounted for. He also believes that 1,350 tons of illicit opium are similarly unaccounted for, both of which he believes can only be coming out of Red China.

His conclusions, which are of unusual interest, are as follows:

1. The world heroin market probably is, in round figures, about 100,000 kg of high-grade heroin.*
2. Between two-thirds and four-fifths of the high-grade heroin sold on the international market is and can only be supplied by mainland China.
3. Some of the opium and morphine base supplied by countries other than mainland China are utilized under Maoist direction as part of the overall Chinese Communist operation. This is particularly true of the opium grown in the no-man's land in the mountains of Southeast Asia and of morphine production and drug logistics handled by "overseas" Chinese.
4. As indicated by the probable size of the market, the average heroin (or heroin-opium) addiction rate of East Asia, Western Europe, and North America, considered as a single population, lies between 1 and 1.5:1,000.
5. In terms of production, the Chinese Communists have the capacity of replacing suppliers who, like Turkey, may go out of business. They also are able to satisfy a larger market and/ or growing market demands.
6. The Maoist drug penetration is undertaken for economic and strategic purposes. The heroin offensive appears to have been accelerated in 1965.** [40]

I am, on the whole, in general agreement with most of Dr. Possony's findings, but I maintain that Possony has considerably underestimated the total production of opium under Chinese Communist control and on the export market, and that he has tended to overestimate the gross export volume of high-grade heroin produced in Red China.

Of course all estimates of this kind, necessarily based on incomplete knowledge, are of empirical value only and subject, eventually, to cor-

---

*The figure of 100,000 kg is an adjusted figure, derived after the original estimate of 100,000 had been scaled down to 80,000 which added to 20,000 gives this.
**1965 was the year of the Chou/Nasser conversation.

roboration or disproof by findings achieved by entirely different and more positive methods.

Yet, whatever the level of production of these baneful substances by the Chinese Communists, the fact is incontestable that the Chinese are heavily engaged in the business and that they are dominating the world's markets, although their operations are cleverly hidden from view. They do seem to be producing some 10,000 tons or more each year and to be earning profits of the order of $600 to $800 million a year and adding substantially to their gold reserves on an ever-increasing scale.

The most surprising feature of the Red Chinese narcotics problem is the manner in which its very existence is denied by those who hold the primary responsibility for suppressing the traffic. Yet these latter also profess the strongest disapproval for the nefarious international traffic and blame it on almost anyone except the real operators—allies for preference. This question will be discussed more fully below in Chapter 7.

The detailed processing data on the chemistry and technology of opium and its derivatives, most importantly that pertaining to heroin, are primarily confined to the research and development reports of company and, in some cases, government laboratories. While such data are not in wide circulation, there are a few sources that are more available.

An interesting popular treatment of small-scale methods of producing heroin has been provided by Alvin Moscow in a book called *Merchants of Heroin* (New York: Dial Press, 1968). This is an account of the Mediterranean heroin industry and it traces carefully the operations of the opium/morphine/heroin growth-production-transit-marketing process. Moscow goes quite carefully into the process by which heroin is manufactured under conditions of secrecy in the south of France.

That author has been far more painstaking in his reporting than have been some other nonqualified (i.e., non-chemist) authors who have been known to confuse acetic acid with acetic anhydride, two very different compounds, and who not only make gross errors revealing ignorance about chemical technology, but also underrate the difficulty of the process and of maintaining the quality of a high-grade chemical product. For example, a recent official report has attempted to persuade the public that the processes are about as simple and as easy to run as the manufacture of bootleg whiskey. This is far from being the case. Although small-scale heroin-manufacturing processes can be run on a routine basis by laboratory technicians with the requisite degree of skill, if any sustained operations are required, more highly qualified chemical supervision is also required, which becomes mandatory if larger-scale operations are in view.

However, the Moscow picture is not the only one that exists and one should understand, when considering the problem, that there are, broadly, three kinds of production:

(1) *Full-scale.* Professionally controlled and supervised production on the industrial scale under factory-type conditions and with full access to research and manufacturing information. Generally speaking this would be either the operation of a pharmaceutical-type plant in which a permissive government allowed the overproduction of a dangerous drug or the operation of an officially sponsored or owned plant under security conditions or controls. (Capacity 200 kg/week and up.)

(2) *Semi-scale.* Manufacture of heroin under clandestine conditions using maximized procedures imposed by limits of secrecy, availability, and type of premises. Not particularly mobile, but subject to periodic transplantation. Not necessarily directly controlled by fully qualified scientific staff—skilled lab technicians enough to run routine manufacture, but ultimate professional participation essential. This would be of particular importance in a rural or "undeveloped" area, especially when establishing manufacturing standards and procedures, modifying process conditions, replacing or ordering equipment, etc. Could be either urban or suburban, but improbably rural. (Capacity 100 kg/week maximum.)

(3) *Small-scale.* Installation for manufacture of heroin under clandestine conditions and limited availability of premises. Possibly operated as a satellite or dispersal of plants of type 2. Capable of producing a high-grade product when operated by lab technicians or chemistry students. Capable of operating under urban, suburban, rural, or even under primitive conditions. Rather mobile. (Capacity about 25 kg/week.)

It needs to be emphasized that types 2 and 3 do not lend themselves to protracted and sustained production campaigns because of health and other reasons. Thus, the prediction of the annual capacity of these, and even plants of type 1, is not easy, and manufacture can be subject to fluctuations in rate for various reasons requiring insight to understand their impact on output.

The French authorities have been able to crack down on half a dozen plants within the last three years, but it seems that none of those yet raided fall into category 1, the only kind capable of sustained and really

119

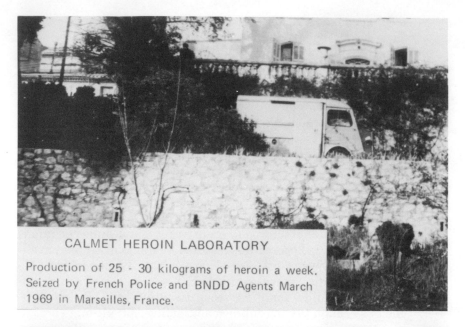

CALMET HEROIN LABORATORY

Production of 25 - 30 kilograms of heroin a week.
Seized by French Police and BNDD Agents March
1969 in Marseilles, France.

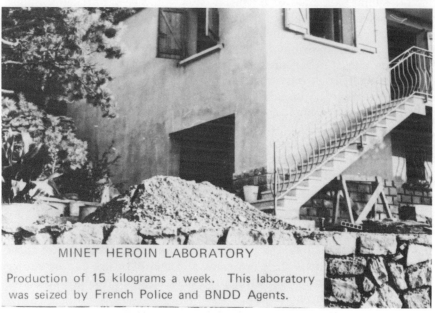

MINET HEROIN LABORATORY

Production of 15 kilograms a week. This laboratory
was seized by French Police and BNDD Agents.

Two clandestine laboratories of the mobile type.

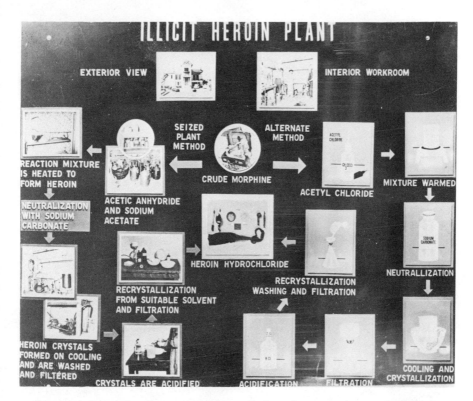

ILLICIT HEROIN PLANT

EXTERIOR VIEW — INTERIOR WORKROOM

SEIZED PLANT METHOD — CRUDE MORPHINE — ALTERNATE METHOD

ACETYL CHLORIDE — ACETYL CHLORIDE — MIXTURE WARMED

REACTION MIXTURE IS HEATED TO FORM HEROIN

ACETIC ANHYDRIDE AND SODIUM ACETATE

NEUTRALIZATION WITH SODIUM CARBONATE

HEROIN HYDROCHLORIDE

SODIUM CARBONATE — NEUTRALLIZATION

RECRYSTALLIZATION FROM SUITABLE SOLVENT AND FILTRATION

RECRYSTALLIZATION WASHING AND FILTRATION

HEROIN CRYSTALS FORMED ON COOLING AND ARE WASHED AND FILTERED

CRYSTALS ARE ACIDIFIED — ACIDIFICATION — FILTRATION — COOLING AND CRYSTALLIZATION

substantial production campaigns. It has been estimated that these plants, run by French criminal elements, amount to perhaps twelve in all and that the total production of which they are capable would be some 15,000 kg per year if undisturbed.

Although attempts are being made at present to portray the French "connection" as the product of illegal and criminal conspiracies started just after World War II by members of the U.S. forces in Europe and the Corsican gangsters whom they met, this is only a half-truth. While it is quite true that such contacts were made, these did not result in much collaboration at the time. Indeed, most of the early revival of the heroin-export industry took place in Italy and flourished with Mafia and Cosa Nostra stimulus until the Italian government cracked down on the Mafia. It was this that led to the expansion of the industry in Marseilles, largely a recent affair since 1965, although of course smaller quantities had been processed there before that.

In Italy, Turkish and Iranian opium was processed and, while there was some clandestine small-scale production, there was also manufacture under industrial conditions in plants of type 1 that involved illicit

121

CALMET HEROIN LABORATORY

Storage areas and equipment in the mobile heroin laboratories.

diversion of the product into the international channels. That country is, today, far less cooperative than France in combating the traffic, and perhaps this can be traced to Communist influence in high Italian government circles.

Taking into account both Corsican expertise in heroin manufacture and the strength of the Union Corse in Indo-China, where there have been decades of lawless activities of all kinds, there seems to be a marked possibility that this powerful group has been operating some processing plants in Southeast Asia, perhaps in Laos, Thailand, or even South Vietnam itself. Their professional skills could even have resulted in manufacture being conducted by Chinese (say Chiu Chau) collaborators in those countries. Possibilities exist that these operations may

MINET HEROIN LABORATORY

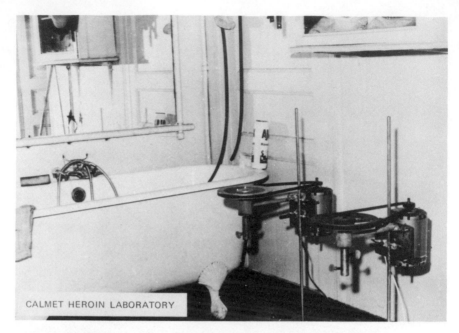

CALMET HEROIN LABORATORY

Reaction area. Stirring and decantation phase of heroin
manufacture.

extend beyond Thailand into Burma, especially the Shan and Kachin
areas, where the authority of the Rangoon government only weakly
extends and where whole tribal areas come under the dominance of
Peking because of the strong influence that the Chinese Reds exert
on tribal rulers.

However, the plants involved in these areas would only in a few
cases come into category 2 and would for the most part be in category
3. In such cases clandestinity could also be accounted for by the protection of corrupt officials, a situation endemic in Asia. Also, the public
attitude, unlike that of the former Chinese government's, has been one
of almost complete permissiveness toward drugs.

Therefore, assuming there are some six to nine plants in the "Golden
Triangle" or neighboring areas, it is extremely unlikely that the production of high-grade (No. 4) heroin could possibly be undertaken at
a rate exceeding 10,000 kg per year. In Hong Kong there have been
reports of No. 3 being made, and occasionally No. 4, but internal
security in Hong Kong is tightly supervised and the attitude of the
authorities of a kind that leads to such enterprises being short-lived.

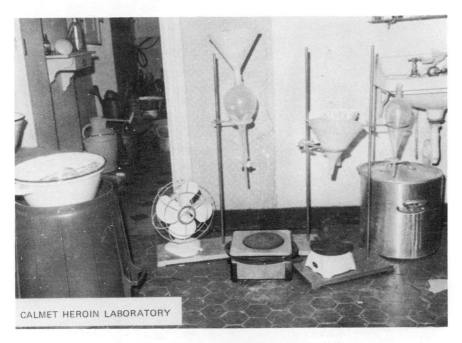

CALMET HEROIN LABORATORY

The extraction phase.

At the very outside, a maximum of some 5,000 kg per year can be assumed, and even this is probably an overstatement.

Adding the 15,000 kg produced in Europe, the 10,000 kg produced in Southeast Asia and the 5,000 kg originating in Hong Kong, this gives a figure estimated for *officially recognized* producing areas. It would be instructive to see how this figure fits in with the demand that exists. In the United States, until quite recently, the figure of 60,000 heroin addicts has often·been given by official reports. Today it needs to be revised, and even the more recent official figure of 600,000 is likely to be quite out of date, particularly when the impact of returning war veterans on the U.S. scene is taken into account; 700,000 addicts is a more likely estimate today. Does the figure of 35,000 kg of heroin per year (30,000 *officially recognized,* plus another 5,000 from other sources) match the demand of the U.S. addicts alone if it were *all* imported to the U.S. and denied to the addicts in other countries? Or what is the number of addicts that such an amount would sustain?

A simple calculation provides an instructive result:

35,000 kg equals 35,000,000 grams (gm).

Vacuum filtration.

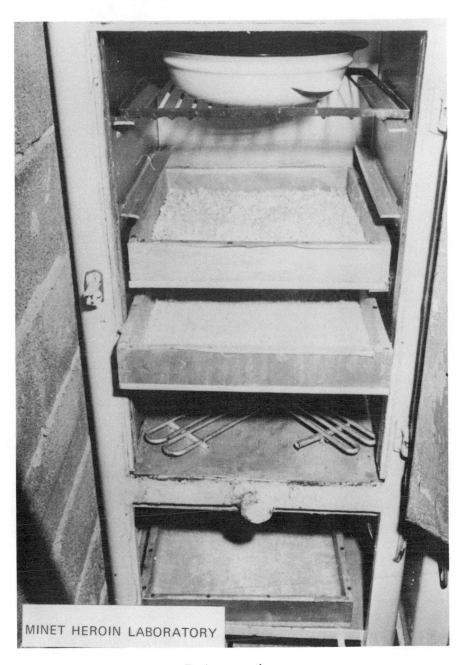

MINET HEROIN LABORATORY

Drying operations.

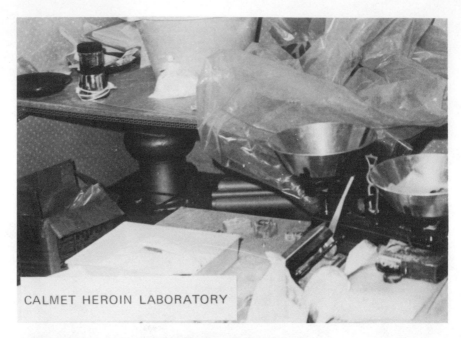

Packing the heroin.

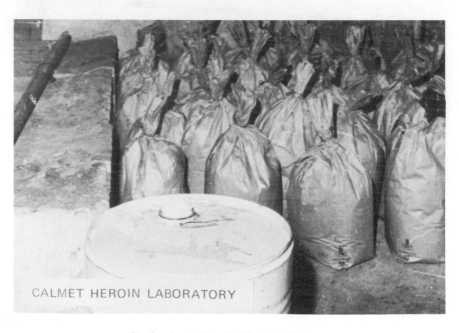

Packaging of the finished product.

In order to estimate the number of addicts that the above amount would sustain, it is necessary to divide the figure by 80 since 80 gm per year is an accepted number for the consumption per year per head. Dividing, we obtain a figure of 437,500 addicts, which is actually less than the total number of addicts now known to be in the United States and far less than the total addiction in the Free World. Obviously there is heroin arriving in large quantities from another source that is not identified by official analysts—at least not since 1962.

With the figure for addiction in the United States running as high as it does, it would probably not be too much to assign a figure of two addicts per thousand for the Free World and, since the area in question has a population of about one billion people, the figure of some two million addicts is reached. To satisfy these addicts (again using the figure of 80 gm per year) would require an amount of 160,000 kg per year of heroin on the world market. If one subtracts from this the figure of 35,000 kg from known sources, derived above, there remains 125,000 kg per year available on the world market and deriving from (officially) unknown sources. This would require 1,250 tons of opium a year. The total amount of opium known to be grown in the general area of the Golden Triangle is less than this and, in any event, large amounts of opium and morphine from there have already been taken into consideration. Since Turkey, as a grower, is already phased out, *the material in question can only come from Red China.* Also, the rate of production argues that it could only be produced in plants operating on the basis of category 1.

A good many different estimates have been made about the amounts of opium produced "legally" by Chinese standards but illegally in terms of world usage. The quantity of 10,000 tons per year is usually given by analysts of the Republic of China, who also assert that Peking is thus able to earn about $800 million in foreign exchange. This figure has been supported by Soviet sources, some of whom come down to 8,000 tons per year. In his short study called "Maoist China and Heroin" (discussed above), Dr. Possony reaches the conclusion that the above figures are much too high and that an export volume of some 1,200 tons per year is more likely.

Another well-informed author who has provided a different estimate is Prof. James Turnbull, the British author of *Chinese Opium Narcotics,* also discussed above. Dr. Turnbull, a scientist in official employ, sets his own estimate of total production for export at 2,750 tons, describing it as a "conservative estimate." Still another British writer, Ian Greig, in his particularly important book *The Assault on the West,* supports the Taiwan figure of 10,000 tons per year. It is this author's

129

impression that Greig's highly factual book, undoubtedly compiled in great measure from official sources, is exceptionally accurate.[41]

Another approach to the matter of estimates is based on the area reported under cultivation, assuming that this is reasonably accurate, while also bearing in mind that the quantity of 10,000 tons a year is quite small by traditional Chinese standards. In making this approach, the figure chosen for productivity of land under poppy cultivation is important. Dr. Possony selects a figure of 5 kg per hectare. This would seem to be a very pessimistic figure, since even such comparatively unscientific cultivators as the Afghans can get well over 20 kg, sometimes 27 kg, and in the Soviet Union even higher yields have been reported.

The Chinese program is an extremely large one; it has the full resources of very highly skilled and well-qualified agricultural scientists at its disposal, as well as standardized cropping methods and unlimited manpower. For the purposes of this analysis a higher figure, 10 kg per hectare, will be used.

Figures for acreage under cultivation vary and are generally given as about 5 million to 9 million mou by Chinese sources who have had occasion to study the question intensively, and sometimes at close quarters.* The figure of 6.6 million mou may be chosen as a reasonable median estimate, which gives exactly one million acres. This is approximately 400,000 hectares, which gives a figure of 4,000 tons of opium being produced if the reasonable figure of 10 kg per hectare is adopted; i.e.,

400,000 hectares x 10 kg equals 4,000,000 kg—say 4,000 tons

Some (including Dr. Possony) consider that a yield of 5 kg per hectare is a reasonable approximate figure because of fertilizer shortages. However, since yields of over 20 kg per hectare are obtainable in a number of other countries and the Chinese Reds have been placing a high priority on their opium crop, and the total area is extremely small compared with other areas under cultivation, there is most unlikely to be a shortage. Therefore 10 kg per hectare would seem to be a reasonable figure. It needs to be noted that, although 4,000 tons is much less than the 10,000-ton figure often given, it is derived from *known* acreage. The total area under cultivation is often quoted as being higher than one million acres. Besides, the production from Burma and the "Triangle" should be added.

---

*A mou equals 0.15+ acre.

Heroin—An Approximate Estimate by Addiction Data

It has been suggested that the total addict population in the Free World that should be taken into account for targeting purposes is perhaps one million persons. For purposes of rough calculation an addiction rate overall of say two per thousand may be assumed. This gives the possibility of about two million heroin addicts. Taking a somewhat lower estimate of annual requirement per addict than the figure of 80 gm per year given above—namely 60 gm per year—the quantity of heroin can be set at two million x 60 or 120 million gm. This is about 120 tons per year.

It has been noted above that the total estimated production for heroin-producing areas in southern France and the Far East comes to 15,000 kg (Europe), plus 10,000 kg (Southeast Asia), plus 5,000 kg (Hong Kong), or 30 tons.

This seems to indicate a quantity of 120 minus 30 tons, namely 90 tons, for heroin on the world market that should, supposedly, be charged to Red Chinese production. There may, of course, be other sources but these are as yet unknown.

It is emphasized that these figures are highly tentative and demand corroboration by other, more positive, means of verification.

Chapter 3
References and Footnotes

1. Report issued by the Bureau of Narcotics and Dangerous Drugs: text of lecture delivered to Conference on the Challenges of Modern Society (the Atlantic Council), October 19 and 20, 1970, p. 5.
2. *Ibid.*, p. 9.
3. *Ibid.*, p. 11.
4. *Ibid.*, p. 16.
5. *Ibid.*, p. 22.
6. *Ibid.*, p. 22.
7. *The Chinese Communist Plot to Drug the World* (Taipei: Asian Peoples' Anti-Communist League [APACL], 1972), pp. 16–17.
8. Quoted in article by Rodney Gilbert in *National Review*, September 15, 1956.
9. Ch'in Yung-fa. "The Economic and Political Significance of Chinese Communist Production and Exportation of Dangerous Drugs," in *Issues and Studies* (Taipei: Institute of International Relations, March 1972).
10. *Tampa Times*, Friday, March 16, 1962. (In *Congressional Record*, March 20, 1962.) Inserted by Rep. William C. Cramer (R; Fla.).
11. *The New York Times*, July 26, 1971.
12. *Ibid.*
13. Henry J. Anslinger, "The Red Chinese Dope Traffic," in *Military Police Journal*, February-March 1961, p. 3.
14. *Ibid.*, p. 4.
15. *Ibid.*, p. 4.
16. *Ibid.*, p. 5.
17. *Ibid.*
18. *Ibid.*, p. 6.
19. Editorial, the *Saturday Evening Post*, September 1960.
20. Hearings, Senate Internal Security Subcommittee, "Communist China and Illicit Narcotics Traffic," 1955. Statement by Mr. Anslinger, pp. 1–7.
21. *Ibid.*, Testimony of an anonymous witness, "Nameless," employed by Bureau of Narcotics, pp. 14–17.

22. *Ibid.*, Testimony of Mr. Richard Deverall, pp 32–47.
23. Richard Deverall, *Mao Tze-tung Stop This Dirty Opium Business* (Tokyo: Toyoh Printing and Bookbinding Co., 1954), p. 67.
24. *Ibid.*, p. 75.
25. Teng Yen-pin, "Hong Kong is Principal Distribution Centre of Peiping's Opium Offensive," *Free China Review*, March 7, 1965.
26. Text of broadcast by Rep. Philip R. Crane, quoted in Allan C. Brownfeld, *The Peking Connection: Communist China and the Narcotics Trade* (Washington, D.C.: The Committee for a Free China, 1972), p. 3.
27. *Ibid.*, p. 16.
28. *Ibid.*, p. 2.
29. *Ibid.*, p. 4.
30. *Ibid.*, pp. 21–22.
31. *Ibid.*, pp. 22–23.
32. James Turnbull, *Chinese Opium Narcotics-A Threat to the Survival of the West* (Richmond, Surrey, England: Foreign Affairs Publishing Co., 1972), p. 9.
33. *Ibid.*, p. 9.
34. *Ibid.*, p. 12.
35. *Ibid.*, p. 15.
36. Ch'in Yung-fa, *op. cit.*
37. Stefan Possony, "Maoist China and Heroin," in *Issues and Studies* (Taipei: Institute of International Relations, November 1971).
38. *Ibid.*
39. *Ibid.*
40. *Ibid.*
41. Ian Greig, *The Assault on the West* (Richmond, Surrey, England: Foreign Affairs Publishing Co., 1968).

4

The Red Chinese Connection—
The Higher Command of the
Chinese Narcotics Traffic

The Current Situation in Red China

Until mid-September 1971 Red China was being ruled by a powerful military caucus consisting of a dominant faction of the Peoples' Liberation Army (PLA) run by Lin Piao on behalf of Mao Tse-tung rather as if it were an outsize bodyguard. Often called the "Fourth Army Clique," this organization had been comparatively successful, after the intervention of the PLA towards the end of the "Cultural Revolution," in projecting its influence into almost all other organs of government (such as the Revolutionary Committees in the provinces that had supplanted their predecessors, the Party Committees) and also into various ministries with economic and industrial functions (such as those run by the State Council, in turn run by Chou En-lai). It had also moved into a position of dominance in the educational system, such as it was.

The Fourth Army Clique, ostensibly fully loyal to Chairman Mao but secretly working against him, had succeeded in capturing the main levers of power that formerly had been in the hands of the official Party apparatus (the CCP). Until he was ousted, the CCP was run by Mao's rival and successor to his State Chairmanship, Liu Shao-chi. The Fourth Army Clique was only one, but it was the most powerful of

134

the seven military factions into which the PLA was divided. For the time being, because of various compacts between leaders, notably an understanding of convenience between Lin Piao and Chou En-lai, there was an armed truce between rival factions. But the superficial appearance of stability hid deep fissures within the body politic. This armed truce was broken by the onset of a series of dramatic events that began, insofar as the public was aware of them, on September 13, 1971.

On that day, all civil and military aircraft on the mainland were suddenly grounded and the usual national celebrations for October 1 were abruptly canceled. Lin Piao, Defense Minister and "heir apparent," vanished completely, as did almost all other high-ranking personalities of the regime. The only conspicuous exception was Chou En-lai, who continued to be in evidence although appearing somewhat harassed. Then there was the mysterious and still largely unsolved affair of the fugitive aircraft.

This was the transport plane, a VC-10, that crashed in Mongolia with all its passengers, said to be nine in number, reported dead. Their identity has been a matter for speculation and some have suggested that Lin Piao was among them, attempting to escape to the U.S.S.R. after disagreements with Chairman Mao.* Some have suggested that he was totally at odds with Mao about the forthcoming U.S. Presidential visit, having no wish to be on hand when such a visit took place. Others have gone so far as to say that he was involved in a plot to oust Mao and to seize power himself, being tired of waiting; others maintained that he had made several attempts on Mao's life.

It now looks as though the aircraft contained the ambitious Huang Yung-sheng of the General Staff; Wu Fa-lin, Deputy Chief of the General Staff and Air Force Commander; Li Tso-peng, Deputy Chief of the General Staff and 1st Navy Commissar, together with officers of their staffs. The bodies and documents aboard fell into the hands of the Russians who have been quite uncommunicative about the affair. They have undoubtedly had a considerable fifth column in Red China.

For some time before these dramatic events, it had been reported that General Yeh Ch'ien-ying, a Deputy Chief of the General Staff, and Chen Yi, former Foreign Minister who died recently, had frequently clashed with Lin Piao, whose power and even whose legitimacy as heir to Chairman Mao they had called into question. Yeh Chien-ying, after the sudden political demise of Lin Piao, then began to appear as the senior ranking "visible" military figure who was much in evidence during the Presidential visit. He is one of Chou En-lai's oldest friends and is now working in the closest partnership with him.

---

*Now officially confirmed—but doubtful; there are reports that he may still be alive.

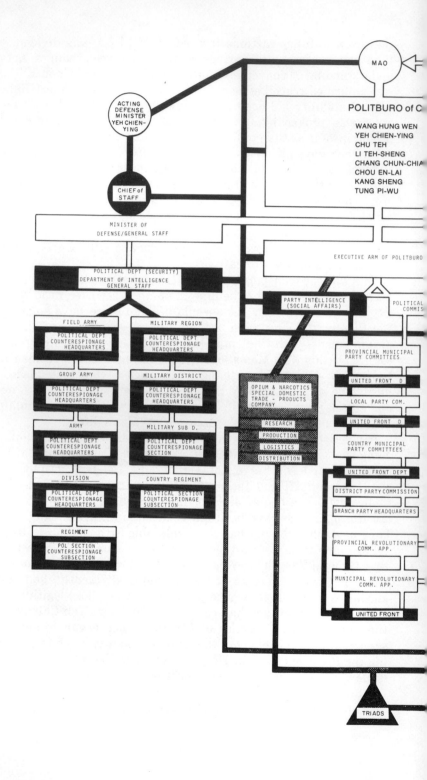

MAO

POLITBURO of C

WANG HUNG WEN
YEH CHIEN-YING
CHU TEH
LI TEH-SHENG
CHANG CHUN-CHIA
CHOU EN-LAI
KANG SHENG
TUNG PI-WU

ACTING
DEFENSE
MINISTER
YEH CHIEN-
YING

CHIEF of
STAFF

MINISTER OF
DEFENSE/GENERAL STAFF

EXECUTIVE ARM OF POLITBURO

POLITICAL DEPT (SECURITY)
DEPARTMENT OF INTELLIGENCE
GENERAL STAFF

PARTY INTELLIGENCE
(SOCIAL AFFAIRS)

POLITICAL
COMMIS

FIELD ARMY

POLITICAL DEPT
COUNTERESPIONAGE
HEADQUARTERS

MILITARY REGION

POLITICAL DEPT
COUNTERESPIONAGE
HEADQUARTERS

PROVINCIAL MUNICIPAL
PARTY COMMITTEES

GROUP ARMY

POLITICAL DEPT
COUNTERESPIONAGE
HEADQUARTERS

MILITARY DISTRICT

POLITICAL DEPT
COUNTERESPIONAGE
HEADQUARTERS

UNITED FRONT   D

LOCAL PARTY COM.

OPIUM & NARCOTICS
SPECIAL DOMESTIC
TRADE - PRODUCTS
COMPANY

UNITED FRONT   D

ARMY

POLITICAL DEPT
COUNTERESPIONAGE
HEADQUARTERS

MILITARY SUB D.

POLITICAL DEPT
COUNTERESPIONAGE
SECTION

RESEARCH

PRODUCTION

LOGISTICS

DISTRIBUTION

COUNTRY MUNICIPAL
PARTY COMMITTEES

UNITED FRONT DEPT

DIVISION

POLITICAL DEPT
COUNTERESPIONAGE
HEADQUARTERS

COUNTRY REGIMENT

POLITICAL SECTION
COUNTERESPIONAGE
SUBSECTION

DISTRICT PARTY COMMISSION

BRANCH PARTY HEADQUARTERS

REGIMENT

POL SECTION
COUNTERESPIONAGE
SUBSECTION

PROVINCIAL REVOLUTIONARY
COMM. APP.

MUNICIPAL REVOLUTIONARY
COMM. APP.

UNITED FRONT

TRIADS

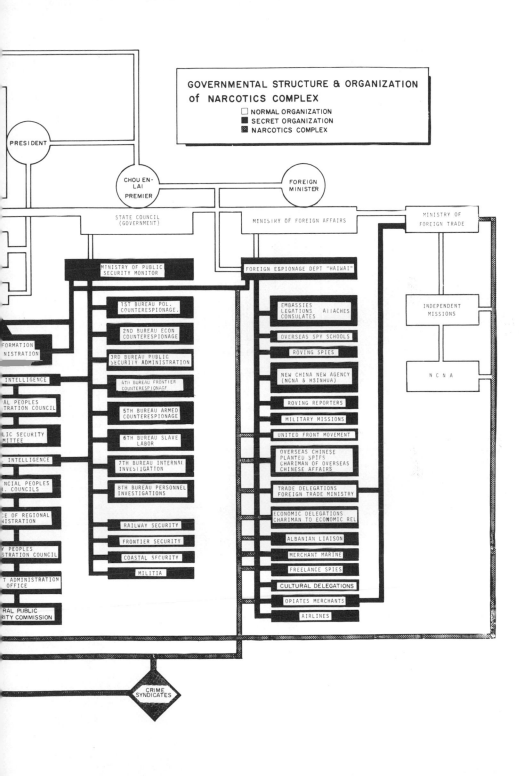

GOVERNMENTAL STRUCTURE & ORGANIZATION
of NARCOTICS COMPLEX

☐ NORMAL ORGANIZATION
■ SECRET ORGANIZATION
▨ NARCOTICS COMPLEX

PRESIDENT

CHOU EN-LAI
PREMIER

FOREIGN MINISTER

STATE COUNCIL
(GOVERNMENT)

MINISTRY OF FOREIGN AFFAIRS

MINISTRY OF
FOREIGN TRADE

MINISTRY OF PUBLIC
SECURITY MONITOR

FOREIGN ESPIONAGE DEPT "HAIWAI"

INDEPENDENT
MISSIONS

FORMATION
NISTRATION

1ST BUREAU POL.
COUNTERESPIONAGE.

EMBASSIES
LEGATIONS ATTACHES
CONSULATES

INTELLIGENCE

2ND BUREAU ECON
COUNTERESPIONAGE

OVERSEAS SPY SCHOOLS

AL PEOPLES
TRATION COUNCIL

3RD BUREAU PUBLIC
SECURITY ADMINISTRATION

ROVING SPIES

NEW CHINA NEW AGENCY
(NCNA & HSINHUA)

N C N A

LIC SECURITY
MITTEE

4TH BUREAU FRONTIER
COUNTERESPIONAGE

INTELLIGENCE

5TH BUREAU ARMED
COUNTERESPIONAGE

ROVING REPORTERS

MILITARY MISSIONS

NCIAL PEOPLES
. COUNCILS

6TH BUREAU SLAVE
LABOR

UNITED FRONT MOVEMENT

CE OF REGIONAL
NISTRATION

7TH BUREAU INTERNAL
INVESTIGATION

OVERSEAS CHINESE
PLANTED SPIES
CHARIMAN OF OVERSEAS
CHINESE AFFAIRS

Y PEOPLES
STRATION COUNCIL

8TH BUREAU PERSONNEL
INVESTIGATIONS

TRADE DELEGATIONS
FOREIGN TRADE MINISTRY

T ADMINISTRATION
OFFICE

RAILWAY SECURITY

ECONOMIC DELEGATIONS
CHARIMAN TO ECONOMIC REL

FRONTIER SECURITY

ALBANIAN LIAISON

RAL PUBLIC
RITY COMMISSION

COASTAL SECURITY

MERCHANT MARINE

MILITIA

FREELANCE SPIES

CULTURAL DELEGATIONS

OPIATES MERCHANTS

AIRLINES

CRIME
SYNDICATES

POLITICAL INFILTRATION AGAINST FOREIGN COUNTRIES

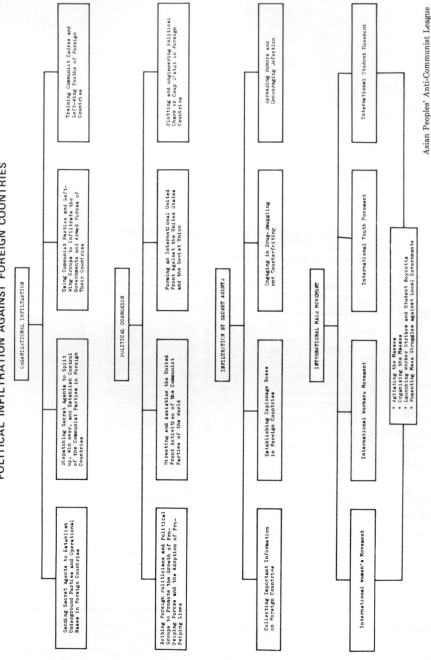

ORGANIZATIONAL INFILTRATION

Sending Secret Agents to Establish Underground Parties and Operational Bases in Foreign Countries

Dispatching Secret Agents to Split up, Win over, and Establish Control of the Communist Parties in Foreign Countries

Using Communist Parties and Left-Wing Groups to Infiltrate the Governments and Armed Forces of Their Countries

Training Communist Cadres and Left-Wing Youths of Foreign Countries

POLITICAL CORROSION

Bribing Foreign Politicians and Political Groups to Promote the Growth of Pro-Peiping Forces and the Adoption of Pro-Peiping Lines

Directing and Assisting the United Front Activities of the Communist Parties of the World

Forming an International United Front Against the United States and the Soviet Union

Plotting and engineering Political Chaos or Coup d'état in Foreign Countries

INFILTRATION BY SECRET AGENTS

Collecting Important Information on Foreign Countries

Establishing Espionage Bases in Foreign Countries

Engaging in Drug-Smuggling and Counterfeiting

Spreading Rumors and Encouraging Defection

INTERNATIONAL MASS MOVEMENT

International Women's Movement

International Workers Movement

International Youth Movement

International Student Movement

* Agitating the Masses
* Organizing the Masses
* Launching Worker Strikes and Student Boycotts
* Fomenting Mass Struggles against Local Governments

Asian Peoples' Anti-Communist League

ACTIVITIES AGAINST FOREIGN COUNTRIES

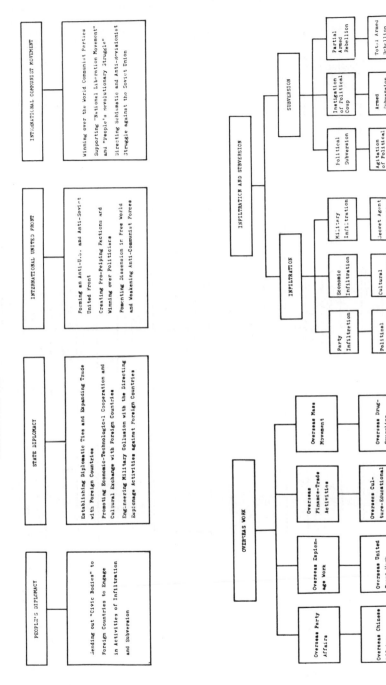

PEOPLE'S DIPLOMACY

Sending out "Civic Bodies" to Foreign Countries to Engage in Activities of Infiltration and Subversion

STATE DIPLOMACY

Establishing Diplomatic Ties and Expanding Trade with Foreign Countries

Promoting Economic-Technological Cooperation and Cultural Exchange with Foreign Countries

Engineering Military Collusion with the Directing Espionage Activities against Foreign Countries

INTERNATIONAL UNITED FRONT

Forming an Anti-U.S. and Anti-Soviet United Front

Creating Pro-Peiping Factions and Winning over Politicians

Fomenting Dissension in Free World and Weakening Anti-Communist Forces

INTERNATIONAL COMMUNIST MOVEMENT

Winning over the World Communist Parties

Supporting "National Liberation Movement" and "People's Revolutionary Struggle"

Directing Schismatic and Anti-Revisionist Struggle against the Soviet Union

OVERSEAS WORK
- Overseas Party Affairs
- Overseas Espionage Work
- Overseas Finance-Trade Activities
- Overseas Mass Movement
- Overseas Chinese Affairs
- Overseas United Front Work
- Overseas Culture-Educational Activities
- Overseas Drug-Smuggling

INFILTRATION AND SUBVERSION

INFILTRATION
- Party Infiltration
- Economic Infiltration
- Military Infiltration
- Political Infiltration
- Cultural Infiltration
- Secret Agent Infiltration

SUBVERSION
- Political Subversion
- Instigation of Political Coup
- Partial Armed Rebellion
- Agitation of Political Chaos
- Armed Subversion
- Total Armed Rebellion

Asian Peoples' Anti-Communist League

ECONOMIC INFILTRATION AGAINST FOREIGN COUNTRIES

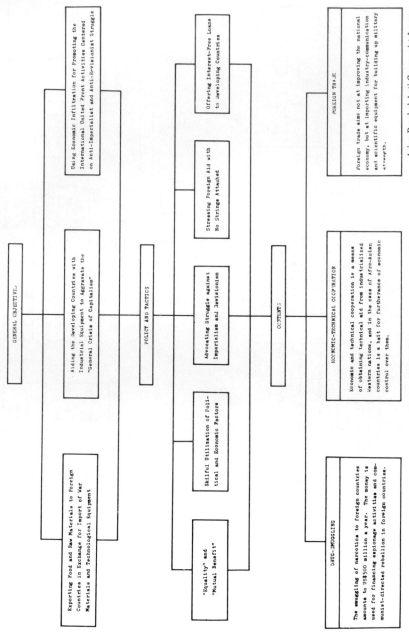

GENERAL OBJECTIVE

Exporting Food and Raw Materials to Foreign Countries in Exchange for Import of War Materials and Technological Equipment

Aiding the Developing Countries with Industrial Equipment to Aggravate the "General Crisis of Capitalism"

Using Economic Infiltration for Promoting the International United Front Activities Centered on Anti-Imperialist and Anti-Revisionist Struggle

POLICY AND TACTICS

"Equality" and "Mutual Benefit"

Skilful Utilisation of Political and Economic Factors

Advocating Struggle against Imperialism and Revisionism

Stressing Foreign Aid with No Strings Attached

Offering Interest-Free Loans to Developing Countries

CONTENTS

DRUG-SMUGGLING

The smuggling of narcotics to foreign countries amounts to US$500 million a year. The money is used for financing espionage activities and communist-directed rebellion in foreign countries.

ECONOMIC-TECHNICAL COOPERATION

Economic and technical cooperation is a means of obtaining technical aid from industrialized western nations, and in the case of Afro-Asian countries is a bait for furtherance of economic control over them.

FOREIGN TRADE

Foreign trade aims not at improving the national economy, but at importing industry-communication and scientific equipment for building up military strength.

Asian Peoples' Anti-Communist League

CULTURAL INFILTRATION AGAINST FOREIGN COUNTRIES

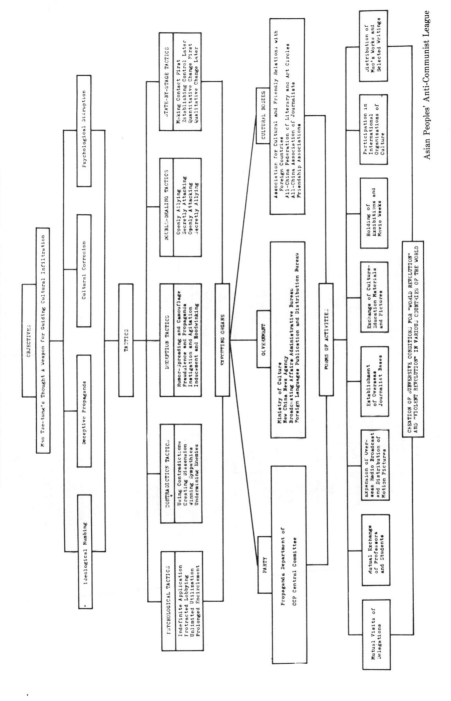

OBJECTIVE: Mao Tse-tung's Thought A Weapon for Guiding Cultural Infiltration

Ideological Numbing	
Deceptive Propaganda	
Cultural Corrosion	
Psychological Disruption	

TACTICS

PSYCHOLOGICAL TACTICS:
Indefinite Application
Protracted Lobbying
Unlimited Utilization
Prolonged Encirclement

CONTRADICTION TACTICS:
Using Contradictions
Creating Dissension
Winning Sympathies
Undermining Enemies

DECEPTION TACTICS:
Rumor-spreading and Camouflage
Fraudulence and Propaganda
Instigation and Agitation
Inducement and Hoodwinking

DOUBLE-DEALING TACTICS:
Openly Allying
Secretly Attacking
Openly Attacking
Secretly Allying

STAGE-BY-STAGE TACTICS:
Making Contact First
Establishing Control Later
Quantitative Change First
Qualitative Change Later

CARRYING ORGANS

PARTY
Propaganda Department of
CCP Central Committee

GOVERNMENT
Ministry of Culture
New China News Agency
Broadcasting Affairs Administrative Bureau
Foreign Language Publication and Distribution Bureau

CULTURAL BODIES
Association for Cultural and Friendly Relations with
Foreign Countries
All-China Federation of Literary and Art Circles
All-China Association of Journalists
Friendship Associations

FORMS OF ACTIVITIES

Mutual Visits of Delegations	Mutual Exchange of Professors and Students	Expansion of Overseas Radio Broadcast and Distribution of Motion Pictures	Establishment of Overseas Journalist Bases	Exchange of Culture-Education Materials and Pictures	Holding of Exhibitions and Movie Weeks

Participation in International Organizations of Culture	Distribution of Mao's Works and Selected Writings	

CREATION OF SUBVERSIVE CONDITIONS FOR "WORLD REVOLUTION"
AND "VIOLENT REVOLUTION" IN VARIOUS COUNTRIES OF THE WORLD

Asian Peoples' Anti-Communist League

MILITARY INFILTRATION AGAINST FOREIGN COUNTRIES

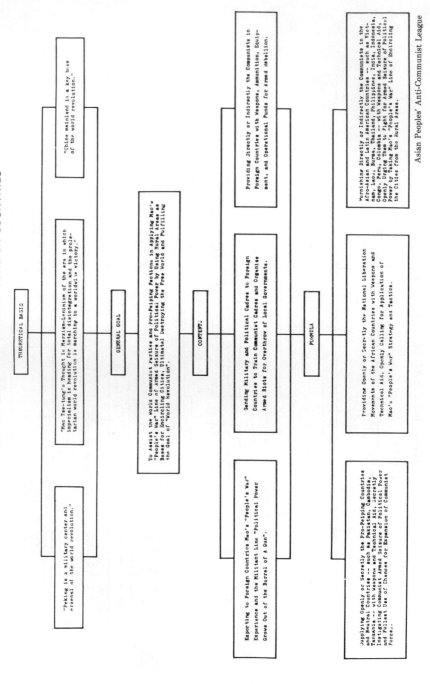

THEORETICAL BASIS

"Peking is a military center and arsenal of the world revolution."

"Mao Tse-tung's Thought is Marxism-Leninism of the era in which imperialism is heading for total disintegration and the proletarian world revolution is marching to a worldwide victory."

"China mainland is a key base of the world revolution."

GENERAL GOAL

To Assist the World Communist Parties and Pro-Peiping Factions in Applying Mao's "People's War" Line of Armed Seizure of Political Power by Using Rural Areas as Bases for Encircling Cities, Ultimately Destroying the Free World and Fulfilling the Goal of "World Revolution".

CONTENTS

Exporting to Foreign Countries Mao's "People's War" Experience and the Militant Line "Political Power Grows Out of the Barrel of A Gun".

Sending Military and Political Cadres to Foreign Countries to Train Communist Cadres and Organize Armed Riots for Overthrow of Local Governments.

Providing Directly or Indirectly the Communists in Foreign Countries with Weapons, Ammunition, Equipment, and Operational Funds for Armed Rebellion.

FORMULA

Supplying Openly or Secretly the Pro-Peiping Countries and Neutral Countries -- such as Pakistan, Cambodia, Tanzania -- with Weapons and Technical Aid, Secretly Instigating Communist Armed Seizure of Political Power and Fullest Use of Chances for Expansion of Communist Forces.

Providing Openly or Secretly the National Liberation Movements of the African Countries with Weapons and Technical Aid, Openly Calling for Application of Mao's "People's War" Strategy and Tactics.

Furnishing Directly or Indirectly the Communists in the Afro-Asian and Latin American Countries -- such as Vietnam, Laos, Burma, Thailand, Philippines, India, Indonesia, Congo, Peru, Colombia -- with Weapons and Technical Aid, Openly Urging Them to Fight for Armed Seizure of Political Power by Taking Mao's "People's War" Line of Encircling the Cities from the Rural Areas.

Asian Peoples' Anti-Communist League

INTERNATIONAL UNITED FRONT

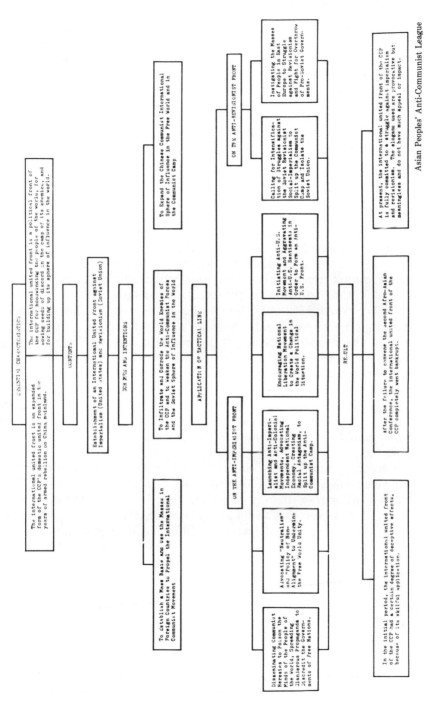

ESSENTIAL CHARACTERISTICS

The international united front is an expanded form of the CCP's domestic united front in the years of armed rebellion on China mainland.

The international united front is a political front of the CCP for hoodwinking the people of the world, for sowing seeds of discord in the camp of its enemies, and for building up its sphere of influence in the world.

CONTENTS

Establishment of an International United Front against Imperialism (United States) and Revisionism (Soviet Union)

SCHEMES AND INTENTIONS

To Infiltrate and Corrode the World Enemies of the CCP and to weaken the Anti-Communist Forces and the Soviet Sphere of Influence in the World

To Expand the Chinese Communist International Sphere of Influence in the Free World and in the Communist Camp

APPLICATION OF TACTICAL LINE

To Establish a Mass Basis and use the Masses in Foreign Countries to Propel the International Communist Movement

ON THE ANTI-IMPERIALIST FRONT

Disseminating Communist Heresies to Poison the Minds of the People of the World, Spreading Slanderous Propaganda to Discredit the Governments of Free Nations.

Advocating "Neutralism" and "Policy of Non-Alignment" to Undermine the Free World Unity.

Launching Anti-imperialist and Anti-Colonial Movements, Advocating Independent National Economy, Creating Racial Antagonism, to Split up the Anti-Communist Camp.

Encouraging National Liberation Movement to Create a Change in the World Political Situation

Initiating Anti-U.S. Movement and Aggravating Anti-U.S. Sentiments in Order to Form an Anti-U.S. Front.

ON THE ANTI-REVISIONIST FRONT

Calling for Intensification of Struggles against the Soviet Revisionist Social-imperialism to Split up the Communist Camp and Isolate the Soviet Union.

Instigating the Masses of People in East Europe to Struggle against Revisionism and Fight for Overthrow of Pro-Soviet Governments.

RESULT

In the initial period, the international united front of the CCP had a certain degree of deceptive effects, because of its skilful application.

After the failure to convene the Second Afro-Asian Conference, the international united front of the CCP completely went bankrupt.

At present, the international united front of the CCP is fully committed to a struggle against imperialism and revisionism. The slogans used are provocative but meaningless and do not have much appeal or impact.

Asian Peoples' Anti-Communist League

Since these two men, apart from the remote and rather unearthly Mao Tse-tung, were the principal figures who participated in that strange interlude, the Presidential visit, it would be well to examine them and their significance more closely. Recently I was privileged to have a first-hand account from a retired U.S. Army officer, Col. Roy McNair, who acted as interpreter between General Marshall and Chou En-lai when they met in 1945. The course of the Chou approach was, and is, highly indicative of the nature of the man, who is disingenuous and insidious to the highest degree.

"Oh General!" he exclaimed, on being introduced to Marshall, "I wish I could convey to you something of the sense of expectancy with which we have been awaiting your arrival. This is because, as you know, your President, Mr. Truman, has described you as your country's leading citizen." (Marshall swelled visibly at this point.) Chou then added, quickly, "You should also know General, that we have in our historical writings a saying that when a great power intervenes between lesser ones, it cannot avoid taking a position within the pattern of power at issue, and thus influencing the course of destiny."

In other words, Marshall was to be captivated by flattery and enlisted by the Chinese Communists as an ally in order to further their designs. The process was not really completed until Chou had had a further series of discussions with his victim. These usually took place after dark at Marshall's quarters, always after he was tired from a hard day and after he had retired for the night. Chou and his interpreter, Huang Hua, now serving in a special capacity in the United Nations, had no compunction at intruding late at night, and were soon able to indoctrinate their man, exploiting his egotism and his extreme ignorance of China.

So much is known and has been written about the remarkable Mr. Chou (who has evidently achieved a position of dominance in Peking, although, of course, it may not last) that it is not proposed here to describe his background at length. However, for those who have been exposed to a good deal of flattering information about him, it is well to know that in the 1920s he was head of the Chinese Communist Party's "Crimson Squad" in Shanghai, a terrorist and extermination unit modeled on the Russian Tcheka that had, earlier, contributed to his Party training. He was known to have killed some of his victims with his own hands.

A friend of mine, a former British official who used to meet Chou frequently in Chungking during the war when the latter was a liaison officer with the National Government, once observed that Chou was the most inspired and gifted liar that he had ever met and a *most successful diplomat*. The informant was at that time a diplomat himself, one who had spent some thirty years in China, a circumstance that helped him to assess the remarkable qualities of the Chinese minister who, in my opinion, is equipped to describe wide circles around any opponent that the United States is likely to pit against him at present.

In all probability, Chou's most remarkable exploit, working in close conjunction with his friend and associate of many years standing, Yeh Chien-ying, was the Sian Coup that took place in 1936. At that time Chang Hsueh-liang, known as the "Young Marshal," son of the late Marshal Chang Tso-lin, Warlord of Manchuria until he was murdered by the Japanese, was head of the Tungpei Army.

That was a force that had originated in Manchuria and that had been detailed by Generalissimo Chiang Kai-shek to fight the Communists who were then based on Yenan (Shensi). The Communists were then practically at the end of their tether after the "Long March," which had been planned in its military aspects by Yeh Chien-ying. During an action between the Tungpei troops and the Communist forces near Yenan, a Tungpei brigadier was captured and then returned after he had been thoroughly indoctrinated with the reasons for a truce and a "modus vivendi" between the opposing forces. He was also provided with a letter from Chou En-lai to the Young Marshal.

The purport of the letter was that the Chinese were committing national suicide by engaging in fratricidal warfare while the country was being assimilated by Japan. As the Young Marshal was only too well aware, a total Japanese success in China seemed to be an imminent possibility—the more so because he and his men had already lost their birthright and their homes to the invaders. The letter also urged that all Chinese, of whatever political beliefs, should now close their ranks against a common enemy. Chang Hsueh-liang fell for the argument, which was well presented, and his ensuing inaction soon brought Chiang Kai-shek to Sian to discover the reason for this.

There the Generalissimo found himself a prisoner of his own subordinate and thus, in effect, of his mortal enemies in Yenan. Naturally, he was relieved, as were many others, to discover that their aim was not to eliminate him, as he believed at first, but to persuade him to resist the Japanese at once, before he had destroyed the Communist forces and, instead, accept the Communists as wartime allies. Chiang knew full well the long-term aim that this implied was designed to oust him by using their device of the "United Front," which he had defeated once before. Consequently, he resisted the proposals for a while. However, other members of his government and his family soon joined him in Sian and, with grave premonitions of the troubles lying in the future, he accepted the terms. It can be seen, in the light of subsequent events, that this agreement was to cost him the country.

While the comparison may not be a very exact one, there are certain similarities between the situations of 1936 and 1972 that would bear watching. On both occasions the Chinese Reds were at the end of their rope. On the first, after the "Long March," usually portrayed as an epic but actually an ignominious flight, only about 25,000 survivors of forces totaling some 130,000 had reached Yenan, where they were menaced by two enemies, the Nationalist Government and Japan, each incomparably stronger than the Reds. Today, once again they are in a state of near bankruptcy, having experienced daunting losses of many different kinds, both of political and economic nature. The effect of the "Great Leap Forward" on the economy has been catastrophic and the economy has not yet recovered, if indeed it can under such a system, without massive outside assistance. After the convulsions and destructive turmoil of the "Cultural Revolution," until the American President's announcement of his forthcoming visit, there had been the semblance of a trend toward improved stability, enforced by the preponderant military power of the Lin Piao faction.

Since the September Crisis, the linchpin of Mao's precarious tenure has been pulled out and a rich prize awaits the onset of the various cliques and factions. They have not made, as yet, any major or obvious moves, although the country is seething with unrest and conspiracies of all kinds. Ironically, the Presidential visit has contributed to the maintenance of the tenuous positions of Mao and Chou who may, of course, themselves become estranged before long, particularly in view of the extremely uneasy relationship that exists between Chou and Chiang Ch'ing (Mme. Mao). As the visit was portrayed as a humiliation of a great power that was supposed to be sending its President to pay his respects to Mao Tse-tung as if he (Nixon) were a vassal, this enabled Mao and Chou to gain a great deal of "face," a priceless commodity in China even today.

These observations have been made in order to provide a short sketch of the situation in Red China (today) and to underline the fact that the existing higher command is of a provisional nature only. It may be subject to sweeping changes before long. Leadership in China tends to attach itself to major vested interests within the country such as the peasantry, the PLA (Peoples' Liberation Army), the atomic energy industry (State Council), or the narcotics complex. This last, being a major and extremely lucrative source of power and influence and also tied in with the Chinese intelligence community, is a particularly important factor in Chinese domestic politics. It is also a cardinal influence in the conduct of Chinese foreign relations in such aspects as the financing of unrest on the American campus or the actions of Arab guerrilla terrorists in the Middle East or beyond.

Yeh Chien-ying and Chou En-lai, both of whom have been deeply involved in the Chinese intelligence community and its activities for many years, have been, in consequence, very much concerned with the planning, the production, and the marketing and distribution of narcotics. Even though Lin Piao has gone, it is doubtful if the ideas that he expounded in his well-known speech "Long Live the Victory of the Peoples' War" have been abandoned. It would be strange if this were the case, since they were quintessentially Maoist in all respects. That speech envisaged an assault by stages on the "cities," namely the advanced areas of Europe and North America, from the countryside, the underdeveloped nations that the Chinese intend to consolidate by means of guerrilla armies operating under the Maoist canon of "People's Revolutionary War."*

The means by which their ascendancy can be built up, or so they reason, would be through subversive organizations and United Fronts of the kind that have sponsored recruitment, training, supply, and command through special missions. Such are the White Flags in Burma, the Neo Lao Haksat or Pathet Lao in Laos, the Free Thai Movement in Thailand, the Terrorists in Malaya, the CCO (Clandestine Communist Movement) in North Borneo, and many others.

Planning and executive action of the kind needed to bring these into being has been largely a task entrusted to special agencies within the complex of the CCIS (Chinese Communist Intelligence Services). This form of activity, the waging of war within the "fifth dimension," exclusive of the four of space and time, has always been closely coordinated with a skilled, large-scale operation in international narcotics trading and the gold and dollars accruing from it.** The drugs themselves have also been applied directly to the conflict since they are seen as an important means of softening up the communities and social systems under attack.

In carrying out its subversive programs of this kind, conceived as a part of the Chinese-directed world revolution, such policies and actions have often brought the Red Chinese into a state of confrontation with the Soviet Union in many areas abroad. Local representatives of

---

*If the essential meanings of the concept "War of the countryside against the cities" be closely examined, one of the most intriguing elements of the strategy is the devastating blow that can fall on urban communities, launched from the poppy fields under Red Chinese control in their own country, and in the areas of guerrilla activity and militant intrusion in Southeast Asia.

**See article by author, "Warfare in the Fifth Dimension," in *Brassey's Annual* (London: Wm. Clowes, 1971).

147

the KGB, stowed away in embassies or consulates, have often found themselves so busily engaged in complex counterintelligence activities against their erstwhile Red Chinese partners that their own planned activities have had to go under a lower priority or even to cease.

The Chinese have been handicapped by a number of significant disabilities in installing the kind of intelligence apparatus needed by a great modern power. Among these disabilities are

(1) There is very great difficulty involved in the delivery of true and objective information to consumers in high positions in an exceptionally dogmatic and tyrannical central government.

(2) There is the ever-present racial problem—Chinese can be rather conspicuous, especially in Europe. Also, the present-day operatives both in China and abroad have a great deal to learn about the ways of foreigners. However, thanks to certain major shortcomings of U.S. education in the China field, now that the barriers are coming down they are able to cultivate large numbers of potential fifth columnists.

(3) There tends to be an innate aloofness among the Chinese that, in a national sense, expresses itself in isolation and that militates against the maintenance of really adequate penetration abroad. At least in the pre-ping-pong era, such was the case.

(4) More than most intelligence establishments, the Red Chinese apparatus tends to look down on its agents (a common failing). It has difficulty in inspiring loyalty among those who really know it and act for it except by highly coercive or compulsory methods.

(5) Their whole governmental machine is ridden with pathological suspicions and rivalries and as such is severely handicapped in its efficiency. This is also a common trait of other countries as well. Here it is a lethal quality that often acts against their national interest, since it is extremely difficult for a talented and successful individual to operate for any length of time without incurring jealousy or enmity.

Since the mid-'50s, the Chinese Reds have been trying to make serious inroads into Europe; they are in strong rivalry with the Soviet Union not only in Eastern Europe and the Balkans but in Western Europe, particularly in France and Italy. One early step that they took was to found an espionage instructional center in Berne, Switzerland, operated discreetly in conjunction with the embassy there. Initially, they concentrated on providing cultural and social "background" to raw graduates of the language schools and cadres from instructional units on the Chinese mainland. Recently, they have been going in for more advanced aspects of intelligence work such as special weaponry, sabotage, infiltration, policy subversion, operational "trade-craft" in an unfamiliar Western setting, and the control of networks. The handling and use of narcotics from an economic, paramilitary, or psycho-chemical-warfare standpoint is implicit in almost all such operations.

Although the emphasis in this study is on the methods of the Red Chinese Intelligence Services and, in particular, their participation in the operations connected with the international drug traffic, it needs to be remembered that, not only have the Soviet special services carried out a great deal of research into the use of drugs as aids to espionage and to the promotion of civil disorder and revolution, but many Chinese have attended Soviet training establishments. Chinese methods and training have thus been influenced a good deal by background provided by the Communist Party of the Soviet Union (CPSU), although of course the Chinese Reds have been able to furnish a good many original ideas and practices of their own. Sometimes the operatives of the U.S.S.R. have been able to profit by those methods, but, on the whole, it seems to be the case that the Chinese have decisively rejected some of the longer-established Russian methods.[1]

To gain perspective in this rather prescribed area, the following details on Soviet intelligence training would appear to be relevant. Within the U.S.S.R., selection of intelligence personnel may be from within the party ranks whence they are channeled into special duty; their personal particulars are forwarded through the "Partorgs" (Party Organizers) to the "Orgleaders" of the District Secretariats.

After a good deal of observation and personnel work (i.e., screening) the particulars go on to the Cadre Commission of the CPSU. Approval of the selectee is accorded by the head of the Cadre Commission of the Recruiting Division. The candidates, who know nothing about this, then come under the attention of the KGB who, by all the tricks of their trade in provocation, get to know the candidates and attempt to test their party loyalties. This is known to be an exhaustive and time-consuming operation.

Even after selection, the candidates do not know what has happened to them and only that they have been singled out for special training. This takes place at the Marx-Engels School in Gorki, near Moscow. That establishment has to be differentiated from the Marx-Engels Institute in Moscow, which is an ideological research and training institute run by the Central Committee of the CPSU. The Marx-Engels School is a covert training organization whose functions are totally unobvious even to the students who undergo training there.

Its purpose is to isolate trainees from the outside world for several months and, in effect, to terminate any private life that they have had until then. They are then exposed to a particularly arduous series of courses of physical, mental, and ideological conditioning designed to bring out the characteristics needed for their future duties as secret-service operatives abroad or as KGB personnel at home. In general, the training there lasts four months, sometimes six, and students are obliged to sign the most stringent security undertakings about their work there.

Actually, training at the Marx-Engels School, the first stage in a Soviet intelligence operative's career, is merely preliminary, covering ideological and character-forming aspects only as an extension of the prior elaborate selection process. However, without it being at all obvious, the training staff are known to attach great importance to this initial phase of instruction. It is during this course that decisions are made about the real potentialities of the prospective agent and the most likely and rewarding field of specialization that the student can undertake. Decisions depend on a highly experienced and sophisticated system of rating and grading the trainee.

However, even after successful completion of the initial phase of training, the second stage, although more "professional" than the first, is still rated as preliminary instruction. Indeed, final disposition of the student and the nature of the more advanced training he can be permitted to undertake is deferred until after the second stage of preliminary training. This takes place under more clearly defined and explicit conditions when the nature of his prospective duties is no longer concealed from him. The location is in the Lenin Technical School at Verkhovnoye, which is in a wilderness about 90 miles from Kazan, near the border of the Tatar Autonomous Republic.

At Verkhovnoye the emphasis on physical and psychological conditioning continues and it includes instruction in unarmed combat, jiu-jitsu, karate, boxing, wrestling, etc. This is combined with commando-type assault training (two weeks—six hours daily).

The unarmed combat and physical training courses are followed by small-arms training of an intensive kind. The short musketry course, which includes the use of rifles, pistols, and submachine guns, lasts about a week and is then followed by an intensive course in the use and handling of explosives, which takes five weeks. Instruction is given in demolition—practiced on buildings, bridges, and other structures. A wide variety of explosives is used and there is instruction in the manufacture and use of homemade bombs and explosive devices. There is also some instruction in bomb detection and disposal. Some of this course covers sophisticated areas of instruction such as muffling explosions, selective demolition, blowing of safes and strong rooms, design calculations and estimation of charge weight, and positioning of charge clusters. There is also consideration of sabotage devices, small concealed charges, and so forth.

Specialized intelligence training then begins after these intensive preliminaries. This starts with "pharmaceutical" courses on the art of preparing doped or poisoned drinks, food, sweetmeats, cigarettes, etc. Candidates are given full instruction on the choice of drugs for specific purposes and on their physiological effects. This is followed by electronics and signals courses that include the tapping of telephones and the doctoring of recordings. The students are made into adepts in the uses of limpet microphones and wire recorders.

Next, there is intensive instruction in the use of portable R/T and W/T transmitter-receivers of all kinds, particularly some portable models designed for espionage work. This includes the use of special high-speed transmission techniques. Courses extend to training in codes and ciphers and in message discrimination. They have exhaustive practice in the use of call signs and message layout. Much attention is paid to servicing and repairing sets and other specialized equipment.

Finally, there are intensive and highly professional courses in photography. Students become skilled in photomontage and retouching, in copying drawings, blueprints, maps, etc. They are also taught how to convert microfilms into microdots and the employment of these.

In all, courses take about twelve months, ending in extremely stringent qualifying examinations. Even if all these are passed—and almost all students pass—there is no guarantee that the candidates will be accepted for secret-service work abroad or for domestic duties with the KGB. The disposition of the graduates is determined by the deliberations of a selection board that usually meets after the students have departed to a rest center called the Octyabr Recreation Center at Kyslovodsk in the Caucasus. In general, the annual class graduating from Verkhovnoye numbers about 3,000 and provides the U.S.S.R. with about 2,000 men and women considered suitable for "assessment duties" (i.e., pre-mission-briefing periods in Moscow), while the remainder go to the KGB.

"Assessment" implies more than briefing, as a matter of fact, but the term describes in noncommittal fashion a long process, usually lasting about a year, during which the operational and administrative staff are able to make decisions affecting the best use of the individual. But if the selectees ever believe, at that point, that they are fully trained, they are mistaken.

Before the Soviet spymasters at the Center permit agents to operate abroad, they must undergo specialized regional training in a unique category of intelligence schools of a kind that do not exist on anything like a comparable scale outside the Communist countries.

Probably the most interesting of these is Gaczyna. This establishment is situated along the southern part of the Tatar Autonomous Republic, lying about 100 miles southeast of Kuibyshev. It covers an area of about forty-two square miles. It is a top-secret place—one that is protected by unbelievable security precautions. In effect, those entering are already on foreign assignment because they soon find themselves in territory that bears little resemblance to the areas they have left. Elaborate efforts have been made to make Gaczyna and other places like it into precise replicas of the kinds of territory within which the students will eventually operate.

Gaczyna is charged with the special responsibility of providing highly trained Soviet agents who may function abroad as spymasters within the English-speaking world.

Consequently, it is divided into sections as follows:

N. W. Area	—	North American Section
N. Area	—	Canadian Section
N. E. Area	—	United Kingdom Section
S. Area	—	Australian, New Zealand, Indian, and South African Sections

Those who enter these different sections are completely segregated from one another because it is here that postgraduate training is attempted in the way of life within the country of assignment. Instruction and conversation is invariably carried out in the language of that country and even the diet is matched. It is here that the student acquires his or her new identity. Incredibly, the process usually takes *ten years*. The reason for this is that the policy planners of this remarkable method believe it takes that long for a new and implanted identity to become really imbedded so as to be proof against hostile interrogation or other hazards. Although it might be thought that such training ought to be rather ineffective, since the environment seems to be too constricted, results have proved otherwise. Indeed some outstanding Soviet successes have been scored by this and other similar places.

The first five years are spent on "familiarization" and specialized education, including even business courses and instruction in Western common law, but the last five years are spent in intensive training in codes and ciphers. They become thoroughly familiar not only with crytographic principles but also with the operational codes in current use and an elaborate call-sign system. This is at the same time a "refresher" course for methods and practices already learned at Verkhovnoye but also a much more advanced attainment.

Tied in with this more elaborate instruction in cryptography, there is also advanced instruction in communications, transmitting and receiving on a wide range of sets, repairs, etc. There is a good deal of emphasis on the use and conversion of commonly used articles of everyday life into containers for transmitting or storing microfilms; e.g., talcum powder boxes, hair cream bottles, toothpaste tubes, cigarette lighters, bottle corks, shoes, and so forth. It is worthy of special note that there seems to be a marked similarity between the process of concealment and transfer of information through a chain of cut-outs or dead drops, strongly reminiscent of almost identical methods and procedures involving transfer of heroin rather than of information.

Other similar establishments than Gaczyna cater to different requirements. For example, there is in Byelorussia a school called Prakhova. This is situated about seventy miles northeast of Minsk and is even larger than Gaczyna. Prakhova's mission is to train master spies who have been detailed to work in Norway, Sweden, Denmark, Finland, the Netherlands, Austria, Switzerland, and Germany.

The Latin countries are taken care of by Stiepnaya. This is located some 110 miles south of Chkalov and lies along the north border of the Kazakh Soviet Republic. The "local color" pertains to France, Spain, Italy, Portugal, Brazil, Argentina, and Mexico.

Counterparts also exist to deal with Asian and Middle Eastern races. These, respectively, are Vostocznaya, which lies about 105 miles southeast of Khabarovsk, and Novaya, lying about ninety miles southwest of Tashkent.

Since the Soviets do not trust any of their satellites, they maintain highly organized systems designed to spy on them much as if they were enemy countries. There is evidence that the forms of infiltration and subversion that are used are a source of continuous irritation within the Communist group of countries. It will be remembered, in particular, that many years ago there were acute difficulties of that sort in Yugoslavia.

The principal establishment engaged in training personnel for this kind of assignment is Soyuznaya, a place about the same size as Prakhova that lies about eighty-five miles southeast of Tula. It deals with Czechoslovakia, Poland, Bulgaria, Hungary, Rumania, Albania, and Yugoslavia. Far Eastern countries such as China, Japan, Indonesia,

Mongolia, Korea, Malaysia, Burma, Vietnam, etc., are catered for by the important establishment called Kytaiskaya that is situated about seventy-five miles south of Irkutsk, near Lake Baikal and the Mongolian border.

It needs to be emphasized at this point that all of these schools are concerned with espionage or other related aspects of the intelligence function. There are, of course, many other establishments that instruct in associated fields such as political-warfare training of guerrillas and propagandists. Sometimes there are transfers in special cases from one type to another. In earlier days this type of posting was more frequent and many Chinese Communists of the older generation have undergone diversified training in a number of such schools.

Formerly this was an advantage in China, but in recent years there has been a good deal of suspicion of and downright persecution of graduates of Soviet training establishments. They have often fallen out of favor, particularly since the Kao Kang episode in Manchuria. Kao Kang was the Communist Party functionary occupying the senior Party post in Manchuria who, together with Jao Shu-shih and others, was purged in 1953 for anti-Party activities and because he had been accused of heading a "Right Opportunist Clique." He was supposed to have been on particularly good terms with the Russians.

All the above observations refer to the highly professional aspects of training applying to the recruitment and development of the more important categories of "spymasters" who are intended to operate under "deep cover." There are, of course, a good many less-comprehensive arrangements connected with the selection, development, and training of the locally recruited agents and dupes who make a large contribution to the achievement of Soviet designs. In many cases the support of such people is dependent on their virtual total ignorance about the realities of the Soviet Union, and the leadership there is sophisticated enough to realize that such people are better kept at a distance, where they are.

The Chinese, although they have a number of schools modeled to an extent on those run by the Russians, where they reproduce in general the main features of the curricula, do not really subscribe to the idea of building an illusory world around their trainees on their home territory. Being Chinese, they feel completely detached and take their zone of separation with them when they go abroad. Any local color that they require, they prefer to acquire on the ground, if possible, and they are, in consequence, rather careful about the persons they select for service abroad and these persons' loyalties. Also, they are, or so far have been, obliged to pick up many of their agents in foreign countries, although it now seems likely that they will be installing arrangements to cater to the increasing numbers of Canadians and Americans who will find their way to Red China.

Their principal training centers are believed to be at Mutankiang (Manchuria), Tungchow (near Peking), Kweisui (Suiyuan), Foochow (Fukien), Hangchow and Mokanshan (near Shanghai), Tsingtao (Shantung), Kashgar (Sinkiang), Tali (Yunnan), as well as innumerable smaller training centers.

It must be recognized, in this regard, that the Chinese have had many centuries, indeed millennia, of experience in conspiratorial activity and in espionage. It is only necessary to read the observations of that military sophisticate Sun Tzu who, about 500 B.C., described principles of intelligence work that have not changed very much to this day. The formative influences in the various organizations of their modern intelligence community have been the outlook and methods of a number of important secret societies that have played an important part in their history. These have been brought up to date by a process of adaption of extremely effective and proven methods. Both the services and their traditions can be traced back to the extraordinarily successful arrangements that were instituted by the Tartars during their mission of world conquest, and under whose yoke the Chinese and the Duchy of Suzdal–Muscovy both fell.

The watchword of both these successors to the aspirations of the Great Khans is still conquest. One of the countries that has felt their impact rather heavily has been India, which has become increasingly aware of a mounting threat from across the Himalayas. Normal military operations apart, over the past few years the Chinese have been setting up in Tibet the machinery for the type of political or special warfare that has always characterized Chinese Communist operations and which, until understood, has proved so difficult for regular military forces to contend with. Using Tibet as the base, their long-range programs have been directed at Afghanistan, Nepal, Sikkim, and Bhutan, as well as at India itself. So far, the programs primarily have been concerned with various forms of preparatory infiltration. The means that have been devised for the purpose, when examined, provide useful examples that can be regarded as typical of the many other operations directed into target countries on an increasing worldwide scale.

In the case of Tibet, the Red Chinese intelligence and political-warfare services took advantage of the "17 Point Agreement" of May 23, 1951, that had been drafted with some of these functions in mind. That pact provided for a significant merger between the old Foreign Affairs Bureau of the Tibetan Government and the Office of the Assistant in Charge of the Central Peoples' Government in Tibet. Thus, it was hoped, the vestiges of the sovereign state machinery of the country could be shaped so as to provide a cover for their own operations. The combined bureau that resulted also had linkages with a number of Communist intelligence enterprises of an international nature and, overall, the arrangements that were set up to push their policies had the following organizational structure:

1. Foreign Affairs Office
2. Border Affairs Office
   a. Yatung Office
   b. Lammo La Office
   c. Tsona Office
   d. Gartok Office (controlled by Tihwa, Sinkiang)
3. Training Establishments
   a. Staff Training School
   b. Tibetan Language School
   c. Trade School
   d. Infiltration Training School
      i. India Infiltration Class
      ii. Nepal Infiltration Class
      iii. Bhutan and Sikkim Infiltration Class
4. Espionage Bureau
   a. Transport Section (Movement Control)
   b. Conference Section (Meetings)
5. Mining Research Office (Resources)
6. Land Survey Office (Military Topography and Mapping)
7. Meteorological Bureaus (Air Condition and Weather)
8. Communications and Technical Service Section[2]

The operations of the Foreign Affairs Office were conducted under the management of an "Advisory Bureau" run by Chang Ching-wu, who received his orders from Peking. The name "Border Affairs Office" was a cover for intelligence operations aimed at the border areas of Nepal, Bhutan, Sikkim, and, most of all, India. This was responsible mainly for infiltration and agent-running.

It has been noted that the personnel chosen by the Chinese to work in these areas mostly have been teams recruited in provinces on the borders of China and Tibet that have bilingual or multilingual populations: Yunnan, Kansu, Sinkiang, Kham, and Amdo. Instruction has been given to personnel in the language schools, or other counterpart establishments, in English, Nepali, Tibetan, Hindi, and Bengali.

In 1962, when the Indian Army encountered the Peoples' Liberation

Army (PLA) and lost a good many prisoners to the Chinese, the captives were greatly surprised to find themselves being interrogated by fluent linguists speaking all the dialects of the Indian Army. They were housed in prison encampments that had obviously been built for the purpose and completed in good time before the Chinese assault on India. However, in their haste to address themselves to wider objectives that they had set, the Chinese had seriously underestimated the effort they would need to consolidate their Tibetan base first. Also, they had reason to be disappointed in the Russians, from whom they had expected military supplies that would enable them to make a much more effective showing in the western, or Ladakh, sector of the campaign. In view of the palpable Soviet designs on India, it is far from surprising that they were disobliging at that juncture.[3]

It is through people such as those just described that the traffic in narcotics is handled, as it is in the case of the tribal regions in Assam and neighboring areas that are being exploited by the Chinese. There are other, more direct, supply routes from Yunnan into Burma that perform a similar function, also used for subversion and social disruption combined with the corruption of officials. China cannot afford operations as extensive as those that have been undertaken without the economic and "mind-bending" resources that it can commit through recourse to the opiates.

Chinese Intelligence Organizations

Basically, the Red Chinese intelligence community is divided into four distinct parts, which are, however, closely coordinated in their operations. This operates through a system of personnel management such as has been known to exist in other countries, which places key men in dual or multiple roles, transcending the obvious administrative boundaries.

The four major parts are:

I. "Hai Wai Tiao Cha P'u," or "Hai Wai"

This is the Overseas Intelligence, or Foreign Espionage, Department. It is a partly overt, partly covert organization within the structure of the Foreign Ministry, and is divided into two main branches: (a) "Ching Pao" (intelligence collection), and (b) "Teh wu" (operations). This department is the highest guiding organ for the collection of international intelligence, but it is actually under the control of the Department of Social Affairs, for whose personnel it often provides cover.

II. The Department of Social Affairs—"Kung Hsiung Hutung" (Bowstring Alley)

This particularly elusive but most interesting agency is the CCP's own master intelligence service that has always been responsible to the Politburo or the State Council. It is by far the most powerful of all the bodies since it controls the Ministry of Public Security under the Government Administration Council. Also under its jurisdiction are "Hai Wai," all the organs of security under the Department of Political Affairs at all levels of the PLA, and the intelligence organizations belonging to the Office of the General Staff. (This arrangement is similar to that existing within the Soviet system between the KGB and GRU).

III. "Kung An Chu" or "Pao an Chu"

This is the Ministry of Public Security that functions under the control of the State Council and under the Department of Social Affairs. It is responsible for counterespionage, police, and the secret police administration within the country. It performs the functions discharged within the U.S.S.R. by the KGB with respect to border control, "exits and entries," and the management of slave and "correctional" labor. There are numerous members of this organization functioning in embassies abroad, charged with security responsibilities. It is a very large organization, emanating from the very highest Central Party HQ and spreading downward to the lowest party organs. "Kung An Chu" has had its difficulties during the Cultural Revolution and its aftermath and some believe that considerable restructuring is in progress.

IV. Department of Intelligence of the Office of the General Staff

This is the highest directing organ for the collection and evaluation of intelligence in the Chinese Communist forces. It works in very close concert with the Ministry of Public Security and the Information Administration.* It controls two main systems, one of which is found in the field armies and the other within local military districts; both have similar organizations. Military security is supervised by a body called the Department of Protection of the Peoples' Liberation Army. This

---

*Certain functions are embodied in all four organizations that do not fall clearly under the jurisdiction of any particular department. An example is provided by the Information Administration.

performs security functions at all levels and includes the Department of Political Affairs that provides the commissars. The role of commissar is exercised rather discreetly and inconspicuously, as a rule, because the Chinese Communist forces are particularly well aware of the importance of apparent autonomy and integrity of the chain of command.

The Information Administration is in part a research department active in the information and propaganda fields and it is also charged with certain security functions. It operates at exceptionally high levels and has its own representatives abroad who often operate under cover of economic and purchasing missions. There is another organization working in the information and propaganda fields, the Department of Information of the Ministry of Foreign Affairs, with which the Information Administration has close connections, but a distinction needs to be drawn here between State and Party instrumentalities.

In August 1952 it was said that the Information Administration was abolished and its responsibilities divided between the Foreign Ministry and the Department of Social Affairs. However, although its main tasks may have been thus apportioned, it is not likely to have been abolished altogether in view of certain of its interests and contacts. It is considered by some to be much involved in such arcane matters as cryptography, theoretical aspects of psychology, applied psychology, and various forms of covert and deceptive practices. It may be noted that since about 1953 the Department of Information of the Ministry of Foreign Affairs has become subordinate to the Department of Social Affairs and often provides cover for its agents at posts of foreign deployment.

There are two principal security agencies:

1. The Office of the Peoples' Procurator General (Judiciary)
2. The Department of Protection of the Peoples' Liberation Army (mentioned above)

The former is vested with the supreme advisory power to ensure strict observance of the law by all institutions, as well as by the nationals of the country. This is the highest agency that supervises and regulates all aspects of thought, speech, and behavior of the Communist cadres and people. It plans, prosecutes, and conducts purges when necessary. The offices of the organization, down to "hsien" level, work closely with those of the public-security directorate. Naturally it is deeply involved in the task of suppressing the domestic use of narcotics or any other irregularity connected either with production, processing, or distribution of drugs in terms of the public ordinances.

The Department of Protection of the PLA is a security organ placed under the Department of Political Affairs. It functions both overtly and covertly, providing both commissars and information networks at all levels. It has two different systems that operate in headquarters and military districts, and another in the field army by party members even down to squad level. This contains a multiplicity of informer networks that check up on one another at all times, often producing a particularly corrosive effect on morale. Also, it comes directly under the supervision of the Department of Social Affairs.

Persons that have been most associated with the development of the Chinese Communist secret services as a whole and that have had a major part in the conception and execution of the opium and narcotics offensive as a weapon of psycho-chemical warfare are Kang Sheng, Lo Jui-ching, and Chou En-lai.

Originally, when the Chinese Reds began their party organization program in Yenan, they set up a Bureau of Central Protection (i.e., a security directorate). This was abolished in 1938 and a new approach was made to the problem of security, more oriented toward a war on two fronts—against Japan as well as the National Government. It was then that the Department of Social Affairs was set up and placed under the Politburo.

As originally constituted, its affairs were conducted by two main committees, the Working Committee of Enemy Area (against Japan) and the Working Committee on Friendly Area (against the government); both were coordinated by Kang Sheng (alias Chao Yung). After the war with Japan, both of them were replaced by the Central Committee for the Extermination of Traitors—sort of a Chinese counterpart of the Russian SMERSH *(Shmert Shpionam)*.

Kang Sheng may be regarded as the leading specialist in security intelligence since the death of Lo Jui-ching. A Shantung man, Kang was originally called Chao Yung and has had a long and close association with Chou En-lai. His parents were well-to-do and belonged to the landlord class. After graduating from Shanghai First Provincial Middle School, he became an early recruit to the Chinese Communist Party, which he joined in 1926. He was active in the organization of strikes and, after an arrest in 1930 and a short period of detention, he was posted by the CCP to Soviet Russia for training with the NKVD in various fields of intelligence, espionage, and security. He worked there during the period 1930-33. His training was completed in 1933 but he stayed on for another two years working on secret projects under the auspices of the Comintern.

During the latter period he returned to China on several occasions, going to Yenan and to Shanghai in connection with planning of the projected Central Intelligence Department of the CCP. Later, on his return, he was put in charge of this department as well as being made Secretary of the Central Committee of the Party. He also became the Principal of the Party School for the Rectification Campaign ("Cheng Feng"). It is believed that his work during the period 1933–34 was also connected with important Soviet agent-running and network installation operations in the Far East. War with Japan was imminent and the Soviets were engaged in setting up their intelligence machinery in China and Japan. This, to an extent, involved collaboration between Soviet agencies such as NKVD and GRU and some surviving agents of the former German Imperial Military Intelligence Directorates. In the period of gestation of the "Black Reichswehr" and of Soviet/German cooperative ventures such as "GEFU," there had also been important intelligence liaison; a good many *Nachrichtendienst* files had been handed over to the Bolsheviks by Col. Walter Nicolai.

Kang was deeply involved in the first rectification campaign, which involved a good deal of literary activity that resembled later upheavals such as the "Hundred Flowers" and the "Cultural Revolution." Since he had a hand in all of them the resemblance is not surprising. Quite recently he has been rather invisible and rumors have been getting around that he has been purged—an improbability. What is much more likely is that, being now rather old, he is husbanding his strength. It is extremely likely that he played a major part in the exposure of the Lin Piao heresy because it was known that he and two others had warned Mao about Lin some six months before the September crisis.

Chou En-lai himself had brought Soviet intelligence techniques into China after a spell of training, research, and planning in Moscow, whence he returned after the CCP Party Congress in 1928. Chou set up an organization called "Chih Wei Tui" (Crimson Guards),* a name that is not to be confused with "Hung Wei Ping" (Red Guards). He assumed the post of Director of Operations and Planning, using as his deputy Ku Shun-chang, a Shanghai craftsman who was a trainee of the Russian Tchekists in a center that they operated in Vladivostok (a so-called Spetsotdyel). The latter had a well-earned reputation as an experienced and competent thug. At that time the mission was basically a defensive one because the Kuomintang had the initiative and it was necessary for the CCP to set up a protective network to safeguard its members and the operations in which they were engaged.

---

*Essentially a terrorist organization.

Before long, Ku was caught by the Kuomintang and lost to the party.

It was after this loss that Kang Sheng received the opportunity from Chou that started his career, beginning with his joining the "Chih Wei Tui." He joined Chou in Shanghai, but soon moved with him to Kiangsi where a new base was set up after Shanghai had become too dangerous for them. During World War II, Kang was engaged in covert operations against both the Japanese and the Nationalists, although primarily concerned with long-range aims of seizing power after the Japanese defeat.

After the war, during the period 1945–47, Kang was involved in a series of extremely important and delicate intelligence maneuvers in Soviet Russia, East Germany, Czechoslovakia, and Poland. In Asia he was much concerned with the development of party programs and in liaison with the pro-Chinese faction surrounding Sukarno in Indonesia. It is known that he had a good deal to do with the preparations for the Korean War.

In 1965 Kang became a Vice Chairman of the Standing Committee of the National Peoples' Congress and assisted Teng Hsiao-ping and Liu Ning-yi in conferences with Moroccan Communist leaders visiting Peking. Also, he was Director of the Cultural Affairs Committee of the PLA during 1966/67, which aligned him with the Chiang Ch'ing and Chen Po-ta group that ran the Cultural Revolution. After that he was described as a member of the standing Committee of the Polit-buro and "Chief Intelligence Officer." Since mid-1970, Kang's position and functions have become quite obscure and it has been rumored that, like Chen Po-ta, he has fallen out of favor.

It is not easy to establish the truth of this, but speculation exists that he had become involved in a power struggle with Lin Piao or per-haps that he had even fallen foul of his old chief, Chou En-lai. The latter theory was based on the evident fact that Kang had obtained a strong grip on foreign affairs through his deployed Social Affairs network during the period of diplomatic withdrawal arising from the Cultural Revolution. Now that Chou has been pursuing a much more positive foreign policy, that position, it has been argued, is no longer tenable. It is quite premature to accept either of these two explanations or the idea that this powerful and extremely capable specialist in se-curity and intelligence matters is out of the running. It seems much more likely that he has been engaged in resisting attempts by the Fourth Army faction to seize power, and in protecting both Mao and Chou from forces acting against them.

Another important figure, one of considerable consequence at the present time, is Yeh Chien-ying, who has emerged as the most prominent soldier since the disappearance of Lin Piao. He is a lifelong friend of Chou En-lai, experienced and highly trained in the intelligence field. He is also reputed to have had much to do with the production of opium within military areas for which he has been responsible, and for the use of opium in subversive operations. After the sudden demise of Lin Piao, Yeh remained as the only visible member of the PLA of any evident standing and Chou En-lai's military partner in maintaining stability at a time of crisis when Huang Yung-sheng and numerous other military leaders disappeared.

Interestingly, both Yeh and Chou En-lai share a penchant for acting and drama. The latter has had quite a degree of success as a female impersonator. Theirs is not a detached interest in the stage but it can be directly linked with the use of drama as a medium of propaganda and as an important adjunct in intelligence training.

Lo Jui-ching is another significant name in recent Chinese Communist history, especially its intelligence aspects, although shortly after the Cultural Revolution, probably as a result of differences with Lin Piao, Lo was dismissed from his post of Chief of Staff and was reported to have committed suicide soon afterward (1967).

By 1949, as Chief of Staff and Deputy Minister of National Defense, it had become known that Lo was regarded as Mao's security chief. Nobody in the history of the Chinese Communist party can claim to have achieved as much power through knowledge of intelligence matters plus the powers of repression as Lo had by 1964 when he was at the peak of his career. It could be seen that Lo was a threat to the future position and designs of Lin Piao when the latter succeeded Lo's discredited chief, Peng Teh-huai, who was dismissed from his post as Defense Minister in 1965.

In November of that year Lo disappeared and was not heard of again until he was replaced by Yang Chen-wu as Chief of Staff. His arrest took place in November 1966 in Szechuan, whence he was transferred to Peking to undergo public humiliation at the hands of the Red Guards. It is believed that he may have "committed suicide" in 1967 by "falling from a window." It was remarked that long before his own final misfortunes, Lo had been much perturbed by the fate, in Russia, of Beria, whom he had admired and whose end he dreaded for himself.

Lo Jui-ching was strongest in the area of operations rather than policy and probably had as much to do as anyone among the senior Communist leadership in China with setting up the links with the international criminal underworld on which so many of China's foreign operations have depended. Especially after the quarrel with Russia, these activities were based on the urgent Chinese Communist need to develop a large and skilled body of professional criminal contacts who were, themselves, fundamentally at war with the Western societies in which they lived. Although such elements, especially in the United States, were essentially beneficiaries of the free enterprise system and stood in the long run to lose by such an association, it was possible for the Chinese to form an alliance with organized crime. The latter could not resist the terms they could secure and the availability of Red China's opiates any more than did the territorial magnates of China's traditional secret societies, who as early as 1933 had made an alliance with Mao during his Chingkangshan period.

It will be remembered that in 1936 Mao appealed to the patriotism of the "Ko Lao-hui" (Elder Brother Society), and asked for its support against the Japanese and the Kuomintang. The appeal read as follows:

Brothers of the Ko Lao-hui.

Recently, the mortal enemies of our Chinese nation, the Japanese imperialists, have been constantly increasing the ferocity of their savage robber actions to swallow up China. Not only have they occupied our four northeastern provinces but they have gone further and established *de facto* control over the whole of Northern China. They have not merely engaged in smuggling, thus ruining the whole of our economic life and increasing various forms of suffering such as bankruptcy and unemployment, but they have sent more than 50,000 additional soldiers into Northern China. All these political and economic methods are calculated to turn China into a second "Manchukuo," to make of Northern China a base for assault on all of China. Moreover, they are, just now, engaged in carrying out a ruthless invasion of North-western, Central and Southern China, and endeavouring to swallow up all of China and turn it into their colony; they want to turn our 400,000,000 brothers into their slaves and beasts of burden. The grievous misfortune of the loss of our state and the extinction of our race is already singeing our eyebrows; we find ourselves before an imminent crisis in which life and death, survival or ruin are at stake. Apart from a few traitors who are selling out their country ("Han-chien mai-kuo-tsei"), there is no one among those Chinese who are unwilling to be slaves without a country whose bosom is not filled with rage, and who does not want to wage a war of resistance to the death against Japan! Today, the military leaders of the south-west, Li Tsung-jen, Ch'en Ch'i-tang, etc., have raised the banner of resistance to Japan, and moved their armies northward. Moreover, they have demanded of the Nanking Government and Mr. Chiang Kai-shek to go forth and do battle against Japan. The anti-Japanese national revolutionary war has entered a new stage.

Formerly, following the principles "Restore the Han and exterminate the Ch'ing,"—"Strike at the rich and aid the poor"—the Ko Lao-hui participated actively in the anti-Manchu revolutionary movement of 1911. The revolution in northern Shensi has also benefited from the considerable aid, support and active participation of comrades from the Ko Lao-hui. Comrades such as Hsieh Tzu-chiang or Liu Chih-tan are not only leaders of the Red Army; they are also exemplary members of the Ko Lao-hui. This revolutionary spirit, these heroic feats, must be manifested even more widely in today's heroic struggles to save the country and save ourselves....

The Soviet Government is the government of the oppressed people of China. We have the responsibility to receive and to protect all those who are persecuted and threatened with arrest by the Kuomintang Government. Consequently, the Ko Lao-hui can exist legally under the Chinese Soviet Government. Moreover, we have established a reception bureau for the Ko Lao-hui for receiving all the heroes, brave fellows and courageous fighters for upright causes who are unable to maintain themselves in the white areas. We hope and request that the lodge masters and grand masters of the various lodges in all parts of the country and our brothers among the brave fellows on every hand, will send representatives or come themselves to discuss with us plans for saving the country. We await them with enthusiasm, and will give them a hearty welcome! We proclaim loudly:

Show us the revolutionary spirit that characterized the Ko Lao-hui in the past.

Let the Ko Lao-hui and the whole of the Chinese people unite to strike at Japan and to restore China!

Long live the liberation of the Chinese people.

The Chairman of the Central Government of the Chinese Peoples' Soviet Republic:

Mao Tse-Tung
July 15, 1936[4]

Governments have almost always taken a dim view of societies, associations, or sodalities whose objectives are unclear and that can foment internal disorder or sponsor activities running counter to the established forms of law and order. In China the authorities have always been plagued by secret societies that keep an eye on the prevailing dynasty and move in to drag it down if for some reason it has become unsatisfactory.

These societies have often been important and it is not, perhaps, as widely understood as it might be that Dr. Sun Yat Sen himself was successful in bringing down the Manchus mainly because he was a high-ranking and senior member of two such societies, normally on unfriendly terms but whose joint energies he was able to mobilize. This function of providing a rather dangerous type of political opposition to the many forms that despotism has taken in China is part of an extremely old tradition. However, it has largely been obscured by the more mundane and day-by-day activities of these bodies, which today generally can be categorized as racketeering of a reprehensible and particularly lawless kind.

In 1845 a document called "An Ordinance for the Suppression of Triad and other Secret Societies" was issued in Hong Kong on January 8, about three years after the Treaty of Nanking by which Hong Kong was ceded to Great Britain. There had been an influx of Chinese labor into the new colony; characteristically a number of guilds and trade associations were formed, as well as an increase in the membership of the Triad Societies that had existed there even before the British arrived.

When they have arisen in China in the past, the secret societies have usually formed a part of a counterculture in opposition to the established order. That order, in imperial times, traditionally depended on the "Heavenly Mandate" (T'ien Ming) of the emperor, on the official interpretations of the Confucian ethic, and on the powers of control of the population possessed by the state. However, be it noted, Confucianism contains approval of revolutionary situations in which a weakened or corrupt dynasty is overthrown; indeed, it imposes a duty on the people to do that. Often the criteria by which the dynasty was judged were set by the societies. Somewhat naturally the authorities took a jaundiced view of them and often tried to suppress them, but never with complete success.

The Mandarinate that ruled China in the name of the Emperor was a powerful machine, the preserve of the "scholar-gentry." It called the secret societies, the "mi-mi hui," by various terms of opprobrium such as "Hsieh Chiao" (vicious sects), "Yao Chiao" (perverse sects), "Chiao Fei" (criminals or brigands), "Yin Chiao" (obscene sects), and "Wei Chiao" (pseudo-religions). Often the Mandarinate displayed considerable skill in handling them. For example, the "Boxer Rebellion," so-called because its members called the organization "I Ho Ch'uan"* (which means "Illustrious Fists of Harmony"), began by being anti-dynastic. The court officials of the Dowager Empress Tzu Hsi, a Manchu and therefore a foreigner in the eyes of all patriotic societies, were able to divert its efforts exclusively against the European and American "interlopers" into the Middle Kingdom. This actually caused it to lose a good deal of goodwill from other organizations such as the Triad.

The Triad, that powerful and classic body, went by a number of different names, such as the "San Ho Hui" (The Society of the Union of the Three Elements[Heaven, Earth, and Man]), the "San Tien Hui" (The Society of the Three Dots), the "T'ien Ti Hui" (The Heaven and Earth

---

*There is an organization by this name in the New York underworld today.

Society), the "Hung Men" (Gate of Hung), the "Hung Chia" (Family of Hung), the "Hung Pang" (Hung Party). The word "Hung" can be interpreted to mean "red" (the color of the Ming Dynasty) or may be given another meaning; there is a homonym that means "flood." This may be a hidden name, of which all such societies are rather fond.

The "T'ien Ti Hui" and the "Pai Lien" (White Lotus Society) were, perhaps, the ones that the Manchu Dynasty feared most and that experienced the most repressive measures in consequence. Others were the "Ta Tao Hui," a branch of the White Lotus; the "Tsai Li Hui" (The "Within" or "Observance" Society); the "Hung Hu-tze" (The Red Beards); the "Hung Chien Hui" (The Red Spears); the "Ko Lao-hui" (Elder Brother Society); and the Ch'ing Pang (Green Circle).[5]

The Ko Lao-hui played a particularly important part in the overthrow of the Manchu Dynasty, and Sun Yat Sen was a prominent member. So also was Chu Teh, who became Red China's Commander-in-Chief. Another prominent Chinese Communist soldier, Ho Lung, now supposed to be in exile in the Soviet Union, was a member, as was his father before him. In the 1930s there was a tendency to think of both the Green Pang and the Red Pang as one and call them "Ch'ing Hung Pang," which was a mistake but one that was made through something of an identity of interest that they possessed in Central China, the Yangtse Valley, and Shanghai.

At that time the societies had achieved their mission to destroy the Manchus and now had no role that could be fitted into their traditions. These had permitted rather unbridled methods of fund-raising, on the principle that the end justified the means, and this somewhat naturally led them into organized crime, as previously mentioned.

Today there seems to be something of a rededication on the mainland itself and bodies like "I Kuan-tao" are in action against the Chinese Communists. As yet, however, that trend has not been able to impress itself fully upon similar groups abroad, which still are largely working in their own interest or in those of their individual members.

Before leaving the subject of these noteworthy bodies, it may be relevant to provide particulars of the oath of loyalty taken as a rite by a prospective member of the Triad:

Chief:	What have you come here for?
Answer:	To join the Heaven and Earth Society.
Chief:	You are deceiving; your thoughts are not as your speech.
Answer:	I swear that I am good in faith.
Chief:	Then swear (the candidate then taking paper burned it while he repeated his assertion).

Chief:	Are you acquainted with the rules of our society?
Answer:	Yes. I understand that I am required to take an oath by drinking blood.

Then, after a question by the chief—

Candidate:	I promise not to divulge the secrets of this society to anyone, under penalty of death.
Chief:	Truly?
Candidate:	Truly.[6]

After that the candidate would drink a cup of wine containing a drop of blood taken from all members present, with which was mingled one of his own. This rite conferred membership.

In view of the links between the Chinese underworld and criminal organizations abroad, it is intriguing to examine the details of the initiation of Joe Valachi into the Cosa Nostra, as provided by him to the FBI and recounted in the *Valachi Papers:*

> Mr. Maranzano (the Chief) said to everybody round the table "This is Joe Cago," which I must explain is what most of the guys know me by. Then he tells me to sit down in an empty chair on his right. When I sit down so does the whole table. Someone put a gun and a knife on the table in front of me, I remember the gun was a .38 and the knife was what you would call a dagger. After that, Maranzano motions us up again and we hold hands and he says some words in Italian. Then we sit down and he turns to me, still in Italian and talks about the gun and the knife. "This represents that you live by the gun and the knife," he says "and you die by the gun and the knife." Next he asked me, "Which finger do you shoot with."
>
> I said "This one" and I hold up my right forefinger. I was still wondering what he meant by this when he told me to make a cup out of my hands. Then he put a piece of paper and lit it with a match and told me to say after him, as I was moving the paper back and forth. "This is the way I will burn if I betray the secret of the Cosa Nostra." All of this was in Italian. In English Cosa Nostra would mean "this thing of ours." It comes before everything—our blood family, our religion, our country....
>
> So Joe Bananas comes to me and says, "Give me that finger you shoot with." I hand him the finger and he pricks the end of it with a pin and squeezes until the blood comes out.
>
> When that happens, Mr. Maranzano says, "This blood means we are now one family." In other words we are all tied up.[7]

Such rites of blood brotherhood are common enough and occur all over the earth. The Chinese conception of "face," combined with the

ILLICIT NARCOTICS TRADING PYRAMID

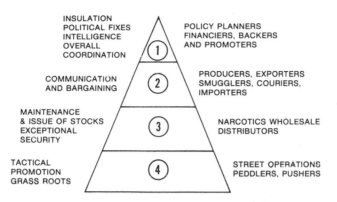

INSULATION
POLITICAL FIXES
INTELLIGENCE
OVERALL
COORDINATION

① POLICY PLANNERS
FINANCIERS, BACKERS
AND PROMOTERS

COMMUNICATION
AND BARGAINING

② PRODUCERS, EXPORTERS
SMUGGLERS, COURIERS,
IMPORTERS

MAINTENANCE
& ISSUE OF STOCKS
EXCEPTIONAL
SECURITY

③ NARCOTICS WHOLESALE
DISTRIBUTORS

TACTICAL
PROMOTION
GRASS ROOTS

④ STREET OPERATIONS
PEDDLERS, PUSHERS

IN STAGE I OF PYRAMID THE INNER CIRCLE OF THE INTERNATIONAL
NARCOTICS CARTEL CONFER, REGULATING PRODUCTION CEILINGS AGAINST
MARKETS CONTROLLING BROADLY DIRECTION AND VOLUME OF FLOW, ALSO
DIVISION OF SPOILS. THE MATCHING OF POLITICAL AND CRIMINAL AIMS—
HIGH LEVEL CORRUPTION.

IN STAGE II OCCURS THE DETAILED MANAGEMENT OF THE PATTERN OF
FLOW CONSISTING OF MAIN OR SUBSTANTIVE TRANSACTIONS OFTEN MASKED
BY COVERING OR DIVERSIONARY MOVEMENTS AND SMALL-SCALE MULTIPLEX
DIFFUSIONARY MOVEMENTS.

STAGE III INVOLVES BUFFER STOCKS IN ORDER TO STABILIZE MARKET
COUNTERPART TO PRODUCERS' BUFFER STOCKS. PERMITS SWITCHING OPERATIONS
AND CLOSURE OF SUSPECTED CHANNELS.

STAGE IV FINAL DELIVERIES TO PROSPECTS OR ADDICTS. IN THIS LIES
THE DEVELOPMENT OF THE HEROIN CHAIN REACTION.

NOTE: AT ALL LEVELS SECURE METHODS OF COMMUNICATION
USED. SOME CRYPTOGRAPHY, BUT GREAT RELIANCE ON
MEETINGS AND IRREVOCABLE AND ENFORCED AGREEMENTS.
FULL USE OF DEAD DROPS, DOUBLE CUT OUTS — "LETTER
BOXES," CONCEALED MESSAGES IN ADS, ETC. MODERN
LARGE-SCALE NARCOTICS TRADING BY ORGANIZED CRIME
IS SAFEGUARDED BY (A) SPECIAL ATTENTION TO
CORRUPTION OF NATIONAL OFFICIALS, OFTEN AT HIGHEST
LEVELS; (B) DIVERSIFICATION OF EFFORT I.E.,
COMBINATION OF THE TRAFFIC WITH GAMBLING; (C) USE OF
SWISS OR OTHER NUMBERED ACCOUNTS, ACQUISITION OF BANKS—
COLLATERAL TRADING IN GOLD.

idea that membership in the Triad or another such society implies a sort of rebirth into a new kind of family, coincides closely with the conception of "omerta" (manhood) that governs the behavior of Mafiosi or members of its newer form, the Cosa Nostra. The latter disposes its membership in families that are the operational and territorial units on which its power is based. The Ch'ing Pang and other socieities use the term "Mountain" as a synonym for "Family." One of the current concerns of Mao Tse-tung, that often comes into his speeches, is a fear of "Mountaintop-ism."

Since it has long been known that the Mafia actively participates in the international drug traffic, it is necessary to understand the shades of difference between the Mafia proper, the "Cosa Nostra," and the "Organization." In discussing them it is essential to recognize that there is a distinction that must be drawn between the "Old Mafia" that has been a traditional and established complex of organizations in Sicily and the "New Mafia" that has owed its existence to the greater scope for illegal operations and modernized crime in the United States. Although ethnically similar, members of these two organizations owe their allegiance to entirely different hierarchies and belong to entirely separate families. There is also a considerable difference in their codes of behavior. "Cosa Nostra" really does signify a structure separate from the Mafia in Sicily itself. The term "Organization" is used as a loose description and describes roughly what has been called the "National Crime Syndicate" (NCS). This includes the Cosa Nostra, or at least parts of it. The NCS is essentially a crime cartel linked by a network of operational agreements resembling treaties.

The latter conditions have resulted in the revival or reconstitution of Mafia operations in Sicily, arising from collaboration between the Mafioso who were members of the "Onorata Societa" in Sicily and gangsters in the United States who can trace many of their traditions, and certainly their descent, from the parent body in the Mediterranean.

It is not as well known, perhaps, as it should be that the Mafia in Sicily, after it had practically been immobilized by the Italian Fascist regime, owed its new lease on life to wartime collaboration between the U.S. intelligence services and members of the Cosa Nostra, some of whom were serving sentences in prison when their services were sought out under the exigencies of war. Therefore, in effect, the liberation of Sicily meant its virtual subsequent government by Mafiosi, since all mayors appointed by the Military Government were members of the Societa Onorata. This came about through the acceptance of a list submitted by Don Calo Vizzini, Chief of the Mafia, in recognition of services rendered to the invading Allied Forces. The introduction had been effected by "Lucky" Luciano, who had been released from prison for the purpose and flown into Sicily at an early stage of the invasion.

The situation thus created enormously favored the revival of the Mafia on a large scale and its participation in Sicily and in the Mediterranean generally in a greatly intensified narcotics traffic. Fabulous profits would be guaranteed by anticipated addiction on a wider scale than had ever before existed in the United States and in Canada, where there was much more purchasing power than in Europe or the Mediterranean area.

It should not be supposed, however, that either Sicily or Europe was an exclusive preserve of the Mafia. There is an infinite complexity of organizations involved, including the important Union Corse, the Corsican gangsters traditionally concerned with heroin-refining operations in the south of France, as well as numerous Arab, Greek, and Turkish participants. On the other hand, because many of the operators have Italian names and are of Mediterranean origin, suspicion has often been leveled at the Cosa Nostra when this has been unjustified. However, that in itself has been a safeguard of another kind.

It should be remembered that while U.S. Naval Intelligence, under the imperatives of operational necessity during World War II, promoted "Operation Underworld" that, in an unforeseen manner, led to the widening of the channels that brought heroin in ever-increasing amounts into the United States, in another theater the same institution was dealing on the terms of the closest intimacy with Tai Li in China. The latter, for similar operational reasons, had special relationships with the Ch'ing Pang and opium gangsters in Japanese-occupied China. This was "another kind of war" that, be it said in all fairness, was practically a closed book to the inexperienced and well-intentioned American members of SACO, the Sino-American Cooperation Organization, who had no real insight into the actual aims of their Chinese colleagues. These aims had more to do with the postwar period than with the war with Japan, whose end result was a foregone conclusion long before the surrender took place.

Since the war and the accession to power of the Chinese Communist regime, the entry of Red China as a political force in the Mediterranean area has been rapid. The Chinese have established an important base in Albania and have made intensive efforts to gain influence in the Middle East within the Arab countries. Like the U.S.S.R., they have been conscious of the importance of military aid in the form of armaments and of training and advisory missions in the Arab nations. In the course of their operations they have also sought to use narcotics as a means of gaining influence, but have been becoming more and more aware of the kind of opposition they will be obliged to overcome in the furtherance of their aims.

Their activities have brought the Red Chinese agents into the closest touch with operatives of the Mafia and other criminal syndicates in Europe, the Mediterranean region, South and Central America (countries like Mexico, Cuba, and Guatemala), as well as Canada and the United States.

One of the countries that has played a major part as a meeting ground for Chinese agents and representatives of the National Crime Syndicate (including Mafia and Cosa Nostra members) has been Mexico. This has been the case especially since the advent of the Castro regime, which involved changes in the patterns of flow. Formerly Cuba had been a main base from which Meyer Lansky, the chief financial boss and so-called "Chairman of the Board" of the National Crime Syndicate, had operated.

Although the Cosa Nostra has been prominent in the international traffic and has had its own discreet links with the Chinese machine (for example, Santo Trafficante of the Florida "Family" toured Vietnam, Hong Kong, and Singapore in 1970), there are a good many interests and groups involved, as there must be. The intellectuals, the planners of these worldwide operations, both on the Chinese side and among their numerous and increasing supporters, realize that there is safety in complexity. This enables large numbers of independent operators to make immense profits. The considerable sums involved in the successes of a highly organized system of liaison and collaboration between the Chinese producers and the diversified interests that undertake distribution often find their way into banks in Switzerland, some of which seem to have a degree of Communist, or even criminal, control.

Recently it appears that even Israel has been used as a base for the traffic and it has been alleged that Israeli cooperation permitted transit of drugs through that country consigned to Egypt. On March 2, 1971, the Egyptian police seized two tons of hashish and morphine, worth $9 million, on the Island of Hamata that were on their way from Israel to Egypt.[8]

Meyer Lansky has himself left the United States and attempted to obtain Israeli citizenship under the provisions of the "Law of Return," but he was unsuccessful in his aim. With him in Israel were reputed to be two of his lieutenants from the National Crime Syndicate, Max Courtney and Frank Ritter, who left the Bahamas because of impending indictments. Some of Lansky's known associates in the eastern

Mediterranean area are supposed to operate under Albanian passports.

Ian Fleming, the well-informed author of the popular series of James Bond novels, created a world of fantasy that was the playground of that sophisticate in eroticism and violence. That fantasy world has caused mild amusement to the professionals in the intelligence area, who usually conduct their affairs somewhat differently but who sometimes comment that the full truth, if it could be told, would be even stranger.

However, it is well to note that the late Ian Fleming was an individual who, in his time, had more insight into the underworlds and half-worlds of which he wrote than most professional criminologists and who had, it would seem, underneath all the persiflage, a serious and important message for his worldwide readership—a message that recurs like a *leitmotif* time and again in his scintillating productions.

This message was essentially a simple one, but the kind that should not be ignored by those who have any responsibility toward the fate of civilization, because it is a true observation. It is that, at the highest levels of international politics, there is a field of action where international crime and politics converge. Fleming pointed continually to the Caribbean as the principal seat of that convergence.

Enough has been said earlier of Cuba, Mexico, Puerto Rico, and other Caribbean islands and territories to indicate that this is a region of the most intense importance to those who traffic in narcotics of all kinds and who have the aim of introducing them to the greatest of all markets—the United States. The traffic is indissolubly linked with gambling and prostitution, and is of gigantic proportions, backed by the most powerful financial interests.

To obtain some notion of the resources of organized crime in the United States, an alliance or system of alliances between the well-known Mafia/Cosa Nostra machinery and lesser-known but extremely active "mobs," almost all of whom have recognized Lansky as their financial overlord, it is necessary to make a few comparisons with large-scale operations of a more legitimate nature. It has been estimated that if all the profits of the ten largest corporations in the United States were pooled together and the gains of such giants as General Motors, General Electric, Dupont, Standard Oil of New Jersey were combined, the total profits would reach some $7.5 billion a year. On the other hand, the takings of the National Crime Syndicate, it is said, would reach about $22 billion; some say more.

Just as the big corporations spend a considerable amount of their resources on advertising, lobbying, etc., the organized criminal element, embarrassed by the extent of its financial success and chronically faced with the problem of how to dispose of or to conceal

173

its gains, is intensely preoccupied in using its funds for various forms of suppressive publicity, misinformation, propaganda directed at attracting customers towards its wares, outright bribery at the highest levels, and the acquisition of influence of a kind most calculated to safeguard its operations. In Asia there has long been a serious problem connected with the wholesale corruption of governments, beginning at the top; the practice now seems to be becoming more normal in countries where it would have been unthinkable only a few years ago. The methods are subtle, indirect, and practically invisible, but they exist nonetheless.

The whole matter has been made much easier by a veritable invasion of the financial world. A company that has caused a degree of curiosity in this area is called International Overseas Service. It is based on Switzerland and therefore is able to evade the operations of SEC. As a parent company, it owns a host of subsidiaries that are said to have, together, holdings amounting to some $2 billion in mutual funds. The purpose of this organization is to buy stock for anonymous customers all over the world. It is particularly active in casino investment; for example, in the Caribbean, in Resorts International, the corporation operating on Paradise Island that used to be known as the "Mary Carter Paint Company." Through the intervention and assistance of International Overseas Service, it is possible for extensive conveyancing operations to take place in the United States and for the real ownership of property to be concealed. Other financial houses that appear to be involved in transactions that would be of interest to gangsters are the Bank of Commerce in Nassau, the International Credit Bank of Switzerland, the Bank of World Commerce, and the Exchange and Investment Bank, Switzerland.

Concealed accounts and the transactions that arise from them have been the cause of much concern in the United States. In 1969 Representative Wright Patman of the House Banking and Currency Committee, with the cooperation of U.S. Attorney Robert Morgenthau, drafted a bill that would force U.S. citizens to report investments made through International Overseas Service and similar organizations. Hearings were projected on this subject by the House Banking and Currency Committee but were never held. It seems that the Nixon administration was opposed to the bill. Treasury Department officials, who had originally been in favor of the bill, suddenly changed their minds. They expressed the view that the bill would create too much paperwork for the banks.

There was a good deal of criticism at the time and the result of the failure to back the legislation was that Robert Morgenthau was dismissed. He has been rated as the most effective prosecutor of both the Mafia and the National Crime Syndicate. Because of the intense dissatisfaction caused by this situation, the Nixon administration gave ground somewhat and the Treasury Department announced that it would again support the bill if some concessions were made. Chairman Wright Patman at first charged that the concession would leave loopholes through which organized crime could continue to operate, but in the end he accepted the changes.

In the course of these proceedings, Morgenthau not only was concerned with the investigation of Swiss banks and the operations of gangsters belonging to the NCS, but he wanted to tighten up the laws regulating the flow of money to Switzerland from the United States. A clash soon developed between Morgenthau and Attorney General John Mitchell and, in spite of being the most effective prosecutor of the Mafia and the other elements of organized crime, he was abruptly dismissed.[9]

However, in spite of Morgenthau's insistence on the crucial importance of Switzerland to international criminal transactions, there are some who believe that perhaps undue stress is placed there and that attention also could profitably be directed elsewhere. For example, Interpol, the international police information clearing house situated in St. Cloud, Paris, gives Swiss banking houses a rather clean bill of health. It is, of course, well known that these banks are extremely cautious and are also exceptionally well informed. Although the freedom and secrecy they allow are of unusual value to international criminals, and the services they afford, such as free convertibility of gold, are of great value to dealers in narcotics, they are bothered by the vigilance of the Swiss bank officials. It is conceded that crime could easily operate just as well without them.

No one can deny that the multifarious operations of narcotics suppliers, shippers, laboratories, and smugglers in Red China or Lebanon, France, Italy, Mexico, New Orleans, Vancouver, Montreal, or New York are often paid out of Swiss banks. Nevertheless they are also served by similar facilities in Hong Kong, Beirut, Paris, Rome, or the United States. Methods of concealment vary, but the process goes on just the same. Besides, there is the especially useful resource known as the "Latin American Loophole" in which much of the big money earned by the American gangsters is hidden away.

Earned by racing or numbers rackets, by big-time gambling, prostitution, or drugs, these enormous profits find their way from New York or Las Vegas to the Bahamas, or more likely to Panama, Montivideo, or other known centers whence the money can easily be "borrowed" back in order to finance legitimate enterprises in the United States. Latin American banking houses of that kind are quite as difficult to investigate as those in Switzerland and have the reputation of being far more sympathetic towards the aims and activities of the criminals whom they serve.

Gold is an exceptionally important commodity that, in some of its aspects, is inseparable from the international traffic in narcotics. The Chinese Reds are extremely active in acquiring gold to build up their reserves, and obtain much of it by exchanging it for narcotics. Macao has been greatly involved in this and the Chinese now have virtually complete control of the Colonial Government, officially Portuguese but subservient to their wishes. This is a circumstance that favors many of their less reputable dealings.

Transactions in gold are both legal and illegal. Legally, they are carried out in such centers of international gold trading as London or Zurich, but they also proceed illegally from such places as India, Vietnam, Thailand, the Philippines, and other Southeast Asian countries. Red Chinese reserves are reputed to be well over $2.5 billion and their annual import of gold is supposed to be $100 million or more. The metal is extremely important to them as a means of payment for subversive activities abroad and for obtaining strategic commodities.[10]

Methods of smuggling have been perfected through generations of practice in which the greatest ingenuity has been shown by the criminal traffickers, with an immense advantage over their opponents in the field of law enforcement. Shipping is, par excellence, the preferred method of transporting drugs.

The actions and procedures that characterize the liaison and the maintenance of operational control between the field activities of the Red Chinese members of the international drug cartel and their counterparts within the Western world are among the most closely guarded secrets in the world. They are virtually impenetrable since they are protected by more than mere legalistic means such as Official Secrets Acts, security undertakings, and the governmental sanctions and punishment associated with these.

Instant death, or sometimes a more protracted route to the grave, is the usual means whereby this latter-day Moloch claims as victims those who betray the Trust or turn against it and are found out. Faced by the certainty of such a fate, and knowledge of the ever-readiness of ruthless powers to inflict it, whether by the Department of Social Affairs, or the Organization, or the Union Corse, or perhaps concerted action by them all, those in the know are silent. It is particularly disturbing that this kind of silence is now beginning to be detectable in quarters where it would be least expected.

Joint transactions of the varied elements of the cartel, whether at the operational, the policy, or the financial level, thus protected, usually involve a great deal of personal contact and many conferences where important and delicate negotiations are involved. Nothing can be committed to writing; codes or ciphers are regarded with suspicion or contempt by professional conspirators, who have a lower regard for them than that held by governments. Such agreements need to be personally negotiated, sealed by verbal agreements, and witnessed by the parties involved.

Sometimes, when major decisions are to be made, new trends begun, or shifts in policy or in the world logistics pattern are afoot, these are signaled by conferences of representatives of the Cosa Nostra families or, on the Oriental side, by the "sworn brothers" of clandestine organizations that are similarly engaged. Examples of the former are provided by such gatherings as the famous Appalachin affair (the Appalachin Convention, 1957) and the Acapulco Convention of 1967. The former was an all-U.S. affair, while the latter was attended by members of the Organization, the Cosa Nostra, and Canadian gangsters, as well as others.

Another liaison feature, as maintained by the higher management of the international traffic, has been the use of special representatives, resident or traveling personal "aides" or plenipotentiaries, acting in a special capacity. One personality whose functions in such a capacity should be noted was the late Virginia Hill, a native of Alabama, who seems, for a number of years, to have been a deployed or traveling representative of Lansky, responsible to the well-known yet shadowy figure of "Joe" Epstein, a big gun of the U.S. underworld. This woman, understood to have died in exile in Austria, discredited and abandoned by her principals in the United States, is supposed to have been most actively involved with the operations of numerous international traders in narcotics. Many believe that she was a courier and intermediary, operating at the very center of the financial web owned by the Organization, first in the United States, later in Mexico, and then, finally, in the neighborhood of Switzerland, at a time when many new routes were opening up in Eastern Europe. The range of her travels included Japan and Hong Kong.[11]

For a good many years Virginia Hill was a close associate of Mrs. M. J. ("Mom") Chung, a notorious member of San Francisco's Chinatown who was known to run an abortion clinic and who was suspected of trafficking in drugs, a simple activity for her to undertake since she was a doctor. Dr. Chung seems also to have acted as a courier for the Organization in the late '40s and early '50s.

The last message this tarnished queen of the underworld sent to the country of her birth was on October 15, 1965, with the return address: Virginia Hill Hauser (Hauser was the name of her Austrian [fourth]

husband), Hotel Havana Libre, Havana, Cuba. It was addressed to the
U.S. Treasury Department, Internal Revenue Service, Tacoma, Washington, U.S.A., and read

To the INTERNAL TAX SERVICE;

These are my last words to you because I am God dam good and
tired of your persecution. I wish with all my heart never to set
foot in your so called Free World. You know as well as I do that
I owe you nothing. If anything you owe me something. And if you
are still looking for gangsters why don't you start in at the top
in the White House and work down. Put them all in jail and the
world will be a lot better off. So — — you and the whole United
States Government.

(signed)Virginia Hill Hauser

She had gone to Havana via Prague.

The Asian scene is, of course, well stocked with shady characters,
a good many of whom have already been mentioned. At present the
far-flung members of the Chiu Chau "family" seem to be in the ascendant, extending from coastal areas in South China through Hong Kong
and Macao as far as Bangkok, Saigon, Rangoon, and even further. With
these, such "neocolonialists" as Frank Furci, a Mafia expatriate who
has operated from Hong Kong using a restaurant as a front, and William Crum, a long-time Far Eastern adventurer, formerly of Hong
Kong but now a resident of South Vietnam, have been having their
dealings, although these may be indirect.

What has been very clear since about 1960 is that the Mediterranean
traffic has greatly intensified its assault on the Western hemisphere,
in accordance with the Maoist slogan of the "East Wind prevailing over
the West Wind." This is largely because of the greatly increased export
availability of Chinese drugs to the Eastern markets that used to be
supplied from the West.

The complexity and ingenuity of the methods of transportation have
burgeoned, and the task for those concerned with the suppression of
the traffic, always difficult, has been rendered even more onerous. It
is also far more risky because of the participation of particularly high-
powered intelligence and terrorist organizations that live both with and
by this monstrous empire of politically oriented crime.

Those who plan the methods of course have the fullest availability
of modern instruments of systems analysis and operational research,
as well as using the most modern means of transportation and concealment. Particular attention has been paid to systematic use of the

178

mails. Mail transmission of packages unconsciously is abetting the cause and the aims of the international conspirators, both by forwarding high explosives intended to destroy the victim by inflicting instantly fatal wounds and by the delivery of packets of heroin to disrupt the society of its enemies.

This presents unusually difficult preventive problems, for the volume of mail traffic is so enormous that effective supervision becomes well-nigh impossible. For example, many firms operating internationally are involved in components manufactured abroad. They receive delicate components carefully packed, often protected by elaborate styrofoam formers. Such formers lend themselves especially well to the concealment of small consignments of narcotics, which cumulatively can amount to very large amounts. It may be noted that one of the first measures instituted by the Kennedy Administration, which had the result of exposing the country to an invasion of this kind, was a series of relaxations on foreign mail, notably printed matter, that favored the opening up of direct postal traffic from the Chinese mainland.

At present there is a great deal of dissatisfaction among those who have troubled to keep themselves informed about the activities of the Hong Kong Seamen's Union. This is an organization, thoroughly riddled with Red Chinese agents, that is being used as a means not only of smuggling narcotics but as a vehicle for large-scale illegal immigration into the United States and Canada. More will be said about this menacing development that has grown rapidly in the last few years. It is one that is obviously being operated as a part of the worldwide Chinese narcotics offensive against the stability of our society. There are evidences of a disturbingly paramilitary nature about these operations.

There exists a small book in Chinese called *Supply of Narcotics and Spying Work,* written by a refugee from the Chinese mainland and published in 1955. The author was formerly with the "Department of Overseas Work" and a CCP cadre; he provided the following observations on the Chinese Communist policy towards foreign intelligence work and agent-running:

> a. All experienced spies must be good at smuggling drugs and all able drug smugglers ought to shoulder important responsibilities in intelligence work.
> b. It would be easy and safe to turn smuggling organizations into front organs for the intelligence network.
> c. It is necessary to strengthen the political knowledge of drug smugglers so that they can advance from the stage of "working for money" to that of "struggling for the revolutionary cause."

d. With the flow of narcotics into a place, many underground organizations are bound to spring up and they are the best components of the intelligence network.

e. Bribed officials in various countries should be encouraged to encourage their friends to receive bribes.[12]

Discouraging signs abound that the activity described above is being proliferated with great success by the Chinese Reds on a worldwide scale. Their outlook is also quite similar to that possessed by their partners in the international underworld who are acting, out of financial greed, in the wider interests of the projection of Chinese power into the Western Hemisphere.

Mao and his followers have been fond of repeating the slogan that "power grows out of the barrel of a gun," but the evidence is continually mounting that they also believe it grows out of the point of the hypodermic needle.

Chinese Communist visible and significant entry into Europe as a factor in political affairs began about 1955–56. The Chinese set up a trade mission in East Germany (Potsdam) that seemed somewhat inactive; but this can be explained by the extremely secret nature of their operations that were, at that stage, primarily concerned with exploratory work in the field of scientific and technical "liaison." Somewhat naturally, sensing certain inhibitions on the part of their Soviet ally, they were rather interested in exploring the possibility of exploiting East European scientific manpower as well as purchasing refined equipment.

However, it seems that they soon came to the conclusion that their stations in East Germany had numerous drawbacks due to Soviet interest in their activities, and, before long, they carried through another aspect of their planning by concentrating a strong group in Switzerland. Some of the earliest and most indicative discoveries concerning their operating procedures came to light when it was apparent that they were using their new facilities to reach a rapport with some of the tribe of international criminals and operators who have always been active in such enclaves as Switzerland and Liechtenstein.

This situation has been well described by Edward Hunter in his exceptionally accurate *The Black Book on Red China.* Mr. Hunter writes

A dispatch that cast a lightning flash of light over this undercover situation was written by Frank H. Bartholomew, president of United Press International, and published in the *New York Times* of July 19, 1958. Western diplomats and counterintelligence agents in Switzerland, he reported, noted a startling increase in

180

financial transactions at Berne related to Red China's illicit drug traffic with the West. He quoted one such source as saying:

"This traffic, much of it routed through Italy, is promoted by the Reds for the dual purpose of helping finance the heavy costs of the spy organization and inflicting on the Western countries an intensifying problem in narcotics. The money runs into incredible figures."

Only a few weeks before, a trial had taken place in Zurich in connection with probably the biggest narcotics haul in world history. Heroin from Red China valued at between $30,000,000 and $50,000,000 on the black market was seized in Switzerland. A Swiss, Turk and Italian were imprisoned and heavily fined and another committed suicide. All were agents of the Communist crime syndicate.

International police forces point out that drugs are a more effective medium of exchange than gold in the world crime network. Money requires the use of bank checks and other incriminating records. Drugs do not, and have the added advantage of passing "for what the traffic will bear." Red China, confronted with the lack of hard currency dollars—and the need for a safely clandestine medium of exchange—has resorted to narcotics instead of money to finance its subversive activities abroad. The Moscow-Peking Axis operates in complete harmony with that other criminal network, the Mafia. Bartholomew's dispatch pointed to the enormous flow of dope from Communist China, saying:

"Although the total is hard to ascertain, there is reason to believe that the communists send out an average of $1,000,000 a week from Switzerland to spies, provocateurs, and contraband traders for their work in the Western democracies."[13]

At that time there was still a degree of collaboration between the two Communist giants and there was good reason to believe that the U.S.S.R. was also involved in the traffic. Both operators are exceptionally careful; they protect their stocks, their networks, and their personnel by highly skilled security methods as long as their people remain "in line." They ruthlessly eliminate them as soon as they do not. Of the two, the Russians are the more circumspect. Their volume of trading is considerably smaller.

These pages are primarily concerned with Red Chinese participation in the international drug traffic. However, it must be observed that the Soviet Union is far from free of opprobrium in this regard. In spite of vigorous and frequent denunciations of its former partner, the Chinese, in opium-, morphine-, and heroin-smuggling operations in Korea and Japan, it is still involved in the trade.

The Soviet operators do not produce and distribute on the same heroic scale as the Chinese, but there are continual indications that they have substantial commitments that are carried out with the greatest circumspection and secrecy. Some insight into the kind of activity in which they are engaged is provided by the interesting and rather bizarre case of Edouard Batkoun, whose vicissitudes in Canada and in France have recently become a matter of public knowledge and speculation, although there has been a virtual blackout of press coverage in the former country.

However, *Human Events* (Washington, D.C.) made a reference to Batkoun in its issue of July 3, 1971:

> Are the Russians entering the international drug trade? That question was being asked last week at the Bureau of Narcotics and Dangerous Drugs after Canadian officials seized 115 pounds of heroin on a Soviet liner arriving in Montreal. An Algerian national was charged with smuggling heroin valued at $30 million on the illicit market—but investigation is continuing to determine the extent of Soviet involvement in the scheme.

Four months after his arrest, the defendant was acquitted by a Montreal court after he claimed that he had no knowledge of the heroin which had been, he asserted, planted in his Fiat car. The car was picked up as it was being unloaded from the M.V. *Pushkin.* He contended that the "plant" must have been made before he embarked the vehicle at Le Havre.

Having successfully eluded Canadian justice, Batkoun was deported to France where he was immediately arrested by the French police. He was accused of exporting heroin from France and finally convicted after a protracted trial and sentenced to fifteen years imprisonment.

During his trial, it transpired that Batkoun was a well-known member of the French Communist Party and that he was an agent of the subsection "Groupement Cinq" of the Soviet KGB. It may be noted that, at the time of the Canadian trial (when he was acquitted), rather extensive coverage was provided by the French publication *Valeurs Actuelles.* This quite comprehensively revealed Batkoun's background as a courier for "Group 5" of the KGB, which has the known mission of breaking down the moral resistance of prominent people in the Free World by the offensive use of drugs and by means of sexual entrapment. Batkoun frequently traveled on the *Pushkin* and had had frequent contact with a Cuban Communist, Ramon Gutierrez, who had at one time been enrolled in the *Freie Universität* in West Berlin.

In one of the articles in *Valeurs Actuelles*, dated November 10, 1971 (published during the period of the trial in Montreal), mention was made of introductions that Batkoun had been given to Canadian Communist Party cadres and to the Cuban Consul General in Montreal. It was also revealed at the time that he had in his possession, when arrested, a list of 2,000 heroin addicts in Canada, many of whom were prominent civil servants, artists, radio and television entertainers, and university professors.

The French press, which followed the case in the Canadian and French courts, expressed surprise that Batkoun could have been dealt with so lightly in Canada. It is most disturbing to think that the kind of permissiveness shown may have something to do with the growing anxiety on the part of the Canadian government to appease the Soviet government and to avoid any situations that might give it offense. In short, Canada may be said to have developed an attitude toward the drug traffic, as carried out by Communists whatever their particular shade of red, somewhat similar to that existing in the United States when the matter of Red Chinese participation is under discussion or investigation.

It is important to recognize that these closely linked, mutually articulated forms of aggression—psycho-chemical warfare and subversion/terror "liberation"—are complementary to one another, and that the worldwide narcotics cartel, secretly dominated by the Chinese Communists, works closely with the Communist-operated liberation and terrorist groups worldwide. There are, of course, the most elaborate methods in use to prevent them from being identified with one another. One of the more obvious of these is the systematic attempt to hide behind false trails and libelous accusations.

Of late it has been particularly obvious that a new "Terrorist International" or an "International Murder Incorporated" has been operating with increasing activity and determination. The limited aims of "particularist" groups such as the IRA or the "Black September" often are made to merge with and to further the much wider aims of the Soviet and Red Chinese world strategies.

It would, in fact, be a great mistake to underestimate at any time the extent and the intensity of Red China's ambitions in the Middle East and in the Arab World, which it recognizes clearly as a region whose control is necessary for the achievement of its designs on the world stage.

To this end, several years ago the Chinese established as their intelligence HQ in the Arab World a particularly highly charged embassy in Damascus. This post, a beachhead on the threshold of the Balkans and of East Europe, has had the task of promoting the formation of

Arab splinter groups, organizations, and "fronts," as well as guerrilla movements. One of these curiously has been named CIA (Chinese Islamic Association).

The Chinese have been most assiduous in combating Soviet influence and ascendancy with the Arabs, which now is beginning to wane. They have been especially active in Egypt and there was a great deal of trouble in that country in 1965 with the pro-Peking Arab Communist Party. The ACP was caught up in a plot to assassinate President Nasser in December 1965, only a short while after Chou En-lai had made the visit during which he committed his indiscretion of confiding to the Arab leader the Chinese intention of subjecting the U.S. forces in Vietnam to psycho-chemical attack. In the uproar that followed the discovery of the plot, the Egyptian Government came across and investigated links between the Chinese embassy and the Arab accomplices who were under suspicion. The Red Chinese ambassador left in a hurry, as did the local representative of NCNA (New China News Agency) who was accused of financing the operation.

Activities of this kind fall within the sphere of operations of a group of departments on the Chinese mainland appropriately described as bodies concerned with the development and maintenance of "cultural relations." A lesser-known but extremely important personality at the essential working level in the Chinese Communist Intelligence Service (CCIS), often connected with the more detailed aspect of operations and planning, is a most interesting man, Tsou Ta-p'eng, who has spent a lifetime as a professional intelligence operative working for the Peking Reds.

A native of Manchuria, where he was born in 1900, Tsou has been one of the most successful members of the Social Affairs Department. There he served under Kang Sheng and Li K'o, who were his superiors at the time of the Sino-Japanese War and World War II. In the postwar period he worked in Manchuria as mayor of Chang Ch'un and concurrently was head of the Information Administration Bureau and the Liaison Department of the Peoples' Revolutionary Council.

Tsou is known to have been one of the leading specialists in "United Front" operations. His skills have been widely used in the organization of a sort of expanded "cover" for a number of interlocking intelligence departments and projects that were planted within a catchall called the "Commission for Cultural Relations with Foreign Countries"; of this he was a founding member. Later, he was to become vice-president of this body, while simultaneously he was vice-president of a nonofficial body called the "Chinese Peoples' Association for Cultural Relations with Foreign Countries."

For the last few years he has been in a central position from which he could wield considerable influence, since he has been operating on official (i.e., governmental), party, and nonofficial levels.

Aside from the operations and the interests of the CCIS indicated above, that service has performed functions particularly vital and valuable to a backward country avid for rapid progress towards superpower and world status. Associated with that status it holds the acquisition of strategic nuclear-weapons capabilities and delivery systems.

Although specialists have been impressed by the circumstance, not many members of the greater public are aware of the triumphant success of the Red Chinese Defense Ministry and the State Council within the nuclear field. The planners and managers of the program have been able to deliver serviceable weapons of both high and low yields at a rate that has been matched nowhere else. In part this has been due to their adopting from the start the novel approach of aiming to acquire fusion weapons first, before the development of fission weapons. In other countries fusion weapons have been developed after the completion of the fission program.

In view of China's scientific backwardness in 1949 (at least so far as formulating and executing scientific policy aimed at the increase of state power), the performance of the Chinese weaponeers in mounting such an expensive program can be accounted for only by their obtaining manufacturing know-how of a kind available abroad rather than at home. Much of this must have been purchased "off the hook." Furthermore, there must have been an unexpected availability of massive financial resources that could be assigned to these ends.

In part the bill has been met by the blood and sweat of countless toiling peasants engaged in large construction projects, but there has also been a liquidity conferred by the tainted currency earned by the Red Chinese narcotics complex. Those earnings, in gold and foreign exchange, have made available to the research staffs and the development and production teams large quantities of sophisticated instruments and equipment quite unobtainable either in the U.S.S.R. or on the mainland. In addition, there has been the participation of certain foreigners who must be given full credit for an extremely impressive and dangerous program being conducted on a large scale. That program explains the Chinese preoccupation with penetration into Central Africa, with the Congo and Katanga as major objectives.[14]

Also, what could be more satisfactory to the Red Chinese planners than their large-scale program of narcotics exports. On the one hand, it underwrites their ascent to world eminence as a major military power, providing them with the foreign exchange to buy strategic assets (and services) from their opponents. On the other hand, it rots away the fibre and deadens the will of their opponents, breaking up the very foundations of their enemies' society.

Chapter 4
References and Footnotes

1. J. Bernard Hutton, *The Subverters* (New Rochelle, N. Y.: Arlington House, 1972), Ch. 3.
2. A. H. Stanton Candlin, *Tibet at Bay* (New York: The Asian-American Educational Exchange, 1971), Ch. 5, "The Chinese Military Base in Tibet."
3. In this connection, see B. N. Mullick, *The Chinese Betrayal* (Bombay and Calcutta: Allied Publishers, 1971).
4. Translation. See Jean Chesneaux, *Les Sociétés Secretès en Chine* (Paris: Archives Juilliard, 1965).
5. W. P. Morgan, *Triad Societies in Hong Kong* (Hong Kong: Government Press, 1960).
6. *Ibid.* A number of initiation ceremonies are given by Morgan.
7. Peter Maas, *The Valachi Papers.* (New York: Bantam Books, 1969); p. 94.
8. Frank Messick, *Lansky* (New York: Berkley Publishing Corp., 1971). This short study goes a long way towards explaining the policy-making and financial control exerted by Lansky in a position whence he coordinated the action of the Cosa Nostra and other elements of the National Crime Syndicate.
9. T. R. Fehrenback, *The Swiss Banks* (New York: McGraw Hill, 1966), chapter, "Les Rackets Internationales."
10. See Timothy Green, *The World of Gold* (New York: Walker and Company, 1968).
11. E. Reid, *The Mistress of the Mafia (The Virginia Hill Story)* (New York: Bantam Books, 1971).
12. *The Chinese Communist Plot to Drug the World* (Taipei: Asian Peoples' Anti-Communist League [APACL], 1972).
13. Edward Hunter, *The Black Book on Red China* (Washington: Friends of Free China Association, 1958), Chapter 9, "The Red Crime Combine," pp. 115–116.
14. Leo Yueh-yun Liu, *China as a Nuclear Power in World Politics* (London: Macmillan, 1972).

5

The Scope and Policies
of the Red Chinese Opium
and Narcotics Industry

Economic Aspects of Red Chinese Narcotics Trading

When the Chinese Reds came into power in 1949, they took over a country that had been at war since 1937 and that had been ravaged by civil wars for many years before that. A decade of war with Japan, plus Japan's occupation of large parts of North China and the coastal areas, had deprived the country of its main industries. The United States, after Pearl Harbor, had not been able to provide supplies to the National Government in any really meaningful way because of logistic difficulties, political sabotage, and other priorities. However, in spite of the predilection of influential U.S. policy-making circles for the Chinese Communists, the arrangements made with the U.S.S.R. at Yalta resulted in the removal by the Russians of almost all of the industrial plant in Manchuria. Most of this had been set up by the Kwantung Army as its industrial base. The Russians were not prepared to leave such a strong arsenal, to be developed further by their new allies, in the vicinity of the Maritime Provinces.

Thus, the Chinese Communists inherited a bankrupt country almost destroyed by war and urgently requiring reconstruction and rehabilitation; nearly all Chinese outside party circles wanted nothing more than peace and an opportunity to work towards recovery. Since the national currency was in a deplorable condition and there was very little purchasing power, acquisition of foreign currency, by any means possible, was an urgent necessity.

After initial discussions between Stalin and Mao in 1950, it was obvious that the route for the Chinese Communists would be a series of plans beginning with the First Five-Year Plan (inaugurated in 1952). Because the Soviet Union was not disposed towards giving credit on favorable terms and could not, in any event, afford much aid to China, in view of its own war damage, Mao was obliged to cast about urgently to find other means of raising revenue.

One obvious and immediately available source appeared to be the large number of Chinese living overseas in areas other than Taiwan. At first many of these did not really know where they stood vis-a-vis the Chinese Communist regime and, in many cases, without proper knowledge about it, tended to welcome the change. In the first five years or so of its existence, a certain national pride asserted itself even among the Chinese who had no use for communism (this included persons both inside and outside). The attitude stemmed mainly from the evident desire of Mao to claim great-power status for China. It should also be remembered in this regard that the Chinese Communists sought (and rather successfully for a short while, until their hold on the country was firmer) to speak of their "line" as being one of "democratic centralism" that even included some opposition elements. Even the impact of the Korean War, that was in no way likely to improve the prospects of overseas Chinese, called forth further aspects of this form of admiration, grudging but none the less real.

In all, about fourteen million Chinese were living abroad in the first half of the decade 1950–60 and it was to these that Mao turned for support in assisting him to obtain foreign exchange. Of that number, about one-half, say six million, were living in Thailand, which has the largest single minority, while about another two million were in Hong Kong. The latter have always been a special case and, as the tyranny on the mainland has mounted, more and more Chinese have fled to Hong Kong until there are, at the time of writing, about three million refugees. Yet even there, at the outset, there had been a sizable section of the community in support of the Reds.

There were, in addition, many overseas Chinese in Malaya (particularly in Singapore), in Brunei, Sarawak, Burma, India and Pakistan, in Ceylon, the Philippines, Korea, and Japan. In spite of immigration policies, there were even a few in Australia and New Zealand. Besides these, there were significant and wealthy overseas-Chinese communities in the United States, particularly in San Francisco and New York City. Similar communities also existed in Europe and even in Africa.[1]

Traditionally, the Chinese, wherever they have been, have been noted for their devotion toward their own place of origin within China and have generally (rich and poor alike) been able to trace their ancestry back for many generations. Because of the influence of Confucius, and other social traditions, their family ties have always been particularly strong. In consequence, there has been a considerable influx of wealth from Chinese sources abroad that has favored the development of the Chinese economy.

This has taken the form of gifts, direct remittances, investment in industrial and commercial undertakings in China, and extensive participation in issues of private or Government bonds or securities. Remittances considered as falling within these categories have often amounted to as much as U.S. $1 billion a year, and a reliable average, compiled over a number of years prior to 1949, would be about U.S. $750 million per annum. According to the *Hong Kong Standard,* in its issue of January 16, 1954, the figure for remittances through Hong Kong as gifts in 1949 was about U.S. $1 million per month. However, by 1953 these large remittances had fallen off to a mere trickle and the reasons are not far to seek.

While appraising their economic situation in 1949, a report by Po I-po, Vice-Chairman of the Committee for Financial and Economic Affairs of the Government Administrative Council, stated on December 2

> In some areas, over 50 percent of our economy was destroyed as compared with pre-war years... For this reason, we must no matter how difficult our situation may be, accumulate sufficient funds, systematically, and in a planned way, so as to be able to restore production.[2]

During the deliberation that gave rise to this report, Chen Yung, a member of the same committee, said

> The people are looking forward to one thing that the government, though in difficulty, will find means to stabilize currency and prices to some degree.[3]

What was wholly remarkable about the approach to the situation, and highly indicative of the nature and aspirations of the Chinese Communist regime, was that, in spite of the state of bankruptcy in which they found themselves, and their need to recover, the Draft Budget for 1950 that was set out in that report was in all respects a war budget. It included, for example, a proposal that 38.8 percent of all revenue be earmarked for military expenditure, with an added 23.9 percent for investment in state-owned enterprises, mainly heavy industrial projects constituting the foundations of a powerful base for their new war industries. Despite more than 60 percent of their revenue being thus allotted for war purposes, only 4.1 percent was to be set aside for "culture, education and public health."

This, of course represented a very different attitude from that which the ordinary people of China had been led to expect from their new mentors. Those who set the above objectives knew perfectly well that they could only be achieved by the blood, sweat, and tears of countless victims, many of whom would lose their lives in the effort.

However, the nature of that budget is not altogether surprising when one realizes that the Red Chinese, impatient to embark on their self-appointed task—the mastery of Asia and the expulsion of the United States and the colonial powers from that region—were preparing for war in Korea in 1950. The job of shouldering the military budget necessary for the anticipated war in Korea, and other enterprises such as the Tibetan invasion, was tackled in the following manner:

1. The primary sources of revenue available domestically to the Chinese Communists were, as noted by Chen Yung in the proceedings that gave rise to the report, "public grain" and taxes. It may be noted that "public grain," until the first collectivization programs had been implemented, consisted of as much grain as they were able to requisition or to seize from the peasants.
2. The collection of as much "extra wealth" as they could extort from all industrial and other workers in the country. This could be described as wholesale despoliation of the property of the population, including even the possessions of the poorest.
3. Emulating the action of the Kuomintang during the Sino-Japanese War by issuing National Bonds. Just after they came into power, even before the provisions of the 1950 war budget came into effect, the Communists drew up a plan for the issue of "Victory Bonds." These were in "parity units" corresponding to six catties of rice, one-and-a-half catties of wheat flour, sixteen catties of coal, or four feet of cloth. Tremendous pressure was exerted on the whole population to buy these bonds and a drive

was launched overseas to force them on Chinese all over the world.

Not only were the unwilling and frightened investors on the mainland coerced into this form of investment, but their relatives abroad were, in effect, blackmailed into buying the bonds by being told that if they did not comply with the request to purchase them, those at home would probably experience difficulties with their new government. Needless to say, there was a significant response and, during 1950, large sums were remitted to the mainland in exchange for worthless bonds.

The next economic blows to fall on the hapless population of the mainland were those connected with confiscatory tax collecting and "land reform" at the point of the gun. Knowing something of the terrific pressures being exerted on their unfortunate kinsmen, overseas Chinese desperately tried to help them and, in some cases, even went bankrupt. Their attempts failed for the most part, and it soon became clear that there had been wholesale massacres, particularly during the early stages of the Korean War. It has been estimated that fifteen million perished.

As might have been expected, the Chinese Reds rapidly forfeited any sympathy or support they may have had from overseas Chinese, who had been deceived by them and who had learned of their infamous behavior towards the peasants and others who had been foolish enough to entrust them with power. It had become necessary, therefore, in order to tap fresh sources of foreign exchange, for the Reds to build up their opium producing, processing, and exporting industry on a priority basis. This was undertaken by the Department of Overseas Trade, but the export program was planned in conjunction with the various intelligence services whose interests were involved. Active exploratory work began in 1951 as far afield as Europe, where it was intended that distribution would be coordinated by trade missions as soon as these were ready.

An indication as to the way the wind was blowing was provided by a short but extremely significant passage that appeared in the *Chi Yin Daily News* of Hong Kong on October 18, 1952:

> The Chinese Communists have concentrated all the opium from different parts of the mainland in South China for sale abroad so as to obtain foreign exchange. The sale at two certain places has been greatly increased and, at the same time, organisations have been established in Kwangtung and Kwangsi Province to undertake the transport of narcotics and work in collusion with traitorous merchants overseas.

Henry J. Anslinger, then U.S. Commissioner of Narcotics, made like references in one of his numerous reports on these activities by Li Choy Fat,* one of the principal miscreants:

> Late in 1952, it became firmly established that the movement of gold and narcotic smuggling were closely connected and Communist-inspired. It was also discovered that the same traffickers were shipping strategic war materials to Communist China.
>
> The *Pakhoi* which arrived in Yokohama in July 1953 was found to have 6,495 grammes of heroin on board. The Japanese and Chinese involved in this confessed that they were in collusion with a dealer in Hong Kong.
>
> Eighty-four grammes of raw opium were seized on the *President Wilson* in February 1953, also of Hong Kong origin. Also the *Sancola* was boarded in Kobe and 3,682 grammes of opium found aboard.
>
> Within the same period there were dramatic discoveries in Hong Kong itself where the police produced in court 256 pounds of raw opium and 86.5 pounds of heroin.[4]

The First Opium Policy Planning Conference in Red China

Red China's new Finance Minister, Po I-po, who was also a member of the North China Military District Council, announced the details of the First Five-Year Plan late in 1952. This program to expand heavy industry and the armaments base of Red China was highly dependent, at that time, on Soviet assistance that was secured on rather unfavorable terms. In order to obtain the foreign exchange needed to service their loans, the Chinese Communists felt obliged to raise money, as quickly as possible, by narcotics trading. This was also envisaged as a means of improving their purchasing power for trading in instruments and strategic materials to be obtained outside the Soviet bloc.

Already, the trade in opium and narcotics had been placed under a subsidiary trade division of the Ministry of Trade, run by Yeh Chih-chuang, who had been concerned with Chinese Communist narcotics operations even during the Yenan days. Details of export were entrusted to Wang Feng-chih, head of the Hopei Opium Prohibition Bureau. The general policy from the outset was to

1. Suppress opium traffic in private hands and to prohibit its use by Chinese on the mainland.

---

*Li Choy Fat was deported from Hong Kong on June 26, 1952.

2. Convert all poppy cultivation, processing of opium, and manufacture of hard drugs into a government monopoly controlling all such products for export.

A prominent figure at the beginning of the campaign was Wu Chi-ho, who dominated an organization called the Jehol Agency, located administratively under the Central Tobacco Monopoly Bureau.

The counterpart in South China was called the South China Trade Bureau, based on Canton; it was run by Wang Jui-feng. From the outset Macao and Hong Kong were singled out as entrepôts for the traffic.

On December 5, 1952, Po I-po (Finance Minister) presided over a highly secret meeting that was held in Peking and was attended by Yeh Li-chuang (Chief of the Foreign Trade Division), Yao I-lin (Vice-Chief of the Commercial Department), Chen Hsi-shih (Vice-Chairman of the Southwest Military Political Committee), Liu Hsiu-feng (Chairman of the North China Financial and Economic Committee), Hsiu Hsian (Vice-Chairman of the South China Financial and Economic Committee), and a few others.

This important conference, which started new policies in the opium and narcotics fields, showed that for the fiscal year 1952 revenue obtained from the sale of narcotics was about U.S. $70 million. Of this sum, about $30 million were retained by the mainland while the balance was spent on party activities abroad, including subversive activity and collection of intelligence. The largest outlets for such activities were Southeast Asia, Japan, and the United States.

It was reported that the drugs of that period were being shipped (when dispatched directly) via Tientsin and Tangku in North China and by Kwangchowwan and Nampo Island, southeast of Yanchiang, Kwangtung Province. Over 1,000 tons of crude opium were thus dispatched from Kwangchowwan during the period June 1951–June 1952.

Until that conference, foreign sales of opium and narcotics had been handled directly by the Finance Division of the Chinese Communist regime, but it was then decided to transfer operations to the Overseas Trade Division. At the Narcotics Conference the following decisions were made:

(1) Qualities and grades of narcotics gathered from various districts will be standardised... Under the new system various sorts of opium will be standardised.

(2) Export promotion regulations are established and private concerns are permitted to participate in the transport and sale. Moreover, discriminatory prices are established so that merchants may be encouraged to sell narcotics abroad more aggressively.

(3) Powerful leaders are being sent, secretly, to various places to encourage sales activities, especially in Tokyo, Singapore, Bombay, and other places. For this purpose the Social Division (i.e., Party Intelligence, Secret Police) and the South China Bureau of the Communist regime have decided to select those most experienced in selling narcotics and to place them in charge of promoting sales.[5]

In connection with (3) above, it is a matter for special note that General Yeh Chien-ying, the only visible ranking member of the PLA after the fall of Lin Piao and others of his military faction in September 1971, was made Commander of the South China Military Region in 1952; was Vice-Chairman of the Central South China Military and Administrative Committee (CSMAC), appointed December 1949; and the Secretary of the First Political Study Center, South China Bureau. In these posts, as well as others, he would have been particularly concerned with the recruitment of agents and their briefing for such assignments. He is a very close associate of Chou En-lai.

It is a matter of history that after the Chinese Communists arrived in Yenan on the completion of their Long March, it did not take them long to launch an opium-cultivation program. While it was explained that the primary objective was a medical one, the levels of cultivation and the pattern of distribution belied it. The fact that this cultivation was being used as an instrument of political warfare was apparent to all. Most of the development initially took place in what became known as the "Shen-Kan-Ning Special Area."

The planning of opium culture followed the same trends in politico-military doctrine (formulated by Chu Teh and Mao Tse-tung) that led the Chinese Communists to set up guerrilla bases that spanned provincial or even national boundaries. They were the prototypes for the complexes in Laos and Cambodia and the narcotics-producing and -exporting "special areas," such as the "Triangle" or Burma-Thai-Laotian complex adjoining Yunnan.

When the Communists came into power in 1949, the extent of the crop on the mainland was about 1,000 to 1,500 tons per year, with very little being exported except accumulated stocks. Opium and even other narcotics were still being imported on a wide scale from the West, although unsettled conditions had produced a serious decline in purchasing power. The Chinese Reds were, however, intensely conscious from the earliest days of the tremendous potentialities of a large narcotics industry designed for the export trade. It was a means of obtaining foreign exchange to finance their industrial expansion and weapons programs and also of debauching their political opponents and buying influence within countries that they wished to subvert.

Under their policies, planning, and management, the opium poppy has been cultivated on an ever-increasing scale and with continually improved techniques, linking the produce with a steadily expanded processing base aimed at the production of immense amounts of "hard" derivatives. Domestic consumption, concurrently, has been ruthlessly suppressed. Up-to-date estimates of the annual national production place the overall figure at about 10,000 tons per year. While this is, of course, a very large amount and considerably larger than the rest of the world's production put together, it must be realized that the quantity does not represent an advance in terms of output over that which existed in earlier times.

For example, in 1900 the corresponding figure would have been much higher, perhaps as high as 25,000 tons per year. The essential difference, however, is in the fact that exports then were comparatively small and there was no coordinated national production program. Today, all the resources of the state lie behind the production and refining logistics and final distribution of the largest single narcotics industry in the world, entirely directed towards foreign markets.

The Chinese Communists used to be called "agrarian reformers" by their idealistic supporters and fellow-travellers in the United States and elsewhere. Certainly there was some meaning in this epithet when it is considered that enormous tracts of territory that otherwise would have been productively cultivated with staple crops were producing poppies instead. That crop has brought in wheat from Canada and Australia but, so far, few have begun to count the cost in terms of impaired health, death, riots, and civil unrest.

Those who estimate the total revenue paid into the Red Chinese exchequer by this kind of foreign tribute, which has been growing at a great pace, place it as high as $800 million per year. This may be slightly high and a safer figure would be $600 million. Substantial amounts of this foreign exchange have been allotted to the purchase of critical scientific equipment, instruments, and strategic raw materials essential to their advanced-weapons programs.

The 1952 Opium Policy-Planning Conference also drew up a 20-year plan (See Appendix VI). This recognized three phases:

Phase I (1950-56): Development of the Base
Phase II (1956-63): Establishment of the Movement Pattern
Phase III (1963-71): Realization of the Objectives

In conformity with the requirements of Phase I, the opium plantations on the mainland are divided into two different categories:

195

(A) *Ordinary Opium Farms* (Appendix V, Table I)
(B) *Special Opium Farms* (Appendix V, Table III)

Ordinary Farms are operated by the civil population under government supervision, while the Special Farms are public or state-operated enterprises. The latter are sometimes managed by troops or by special governmental organizations such as health departments, agricultural departments, or scientific institutes.

Opium cultivators in category A may obtain loans from local "peoples' banks" for seeds, fertilizers, and implements, but the produce is sold to one customer only, the government. Extremely close watch is maintained to ensure that there are no leakages to the general population. Such farms are supervised by inspectors and a system of norms or quotas exists, with incentives for those who can overfulfill the norm. In general, this consists of various forms of prestige or "face" that can be given to successful performers.

There has been much research and a number of scientific institutes have been ordered to carry out a comprehensive program of experiments in opium cultivation and in the science and technology of producing derivatives. Among these have been the Academy of Sciences and its own facilities; the Institute of the Agricultural Sciences, Anhwei; the Agricultural College, Kweichow; North-West Agricultural College; Yunnan University; several agricultural colleges in Yunnan; and Szechuan University. (Many of these should be listed under Category B.)

There is an active personnel-exchange program between different areas so that an interchange of experience and diffusion of skills may result. Exhortation and propaganda are continuous. Special attention has been paid to refining processes since 1950 and extensive use has been made of the "gangsters" who had worked for the Japanese during the occupation. In the earlier stages of the program there used to be collaboration between technicians falling within the above category, newly trained personnel, and Russian specialists.

In consequence, about thirty "Special Products Refineries" have been established in Peking, Tientsin, Dairen, Mukden, Chinchow, Kopeikou, Yenchi, Shanghai, Chekiang, Hankow, Chungking, Sinkiang, Tibet, Sikang, Kunming, and Kwangtung. The brands and products of these refineries are listed in Appendix V, Table V. Their function is to manufacture products such as morphine, heroin, and some synthetics.

Initially, in 1950, the Chinese Communists set up a "Trade Center of Narcotics Exports" in Wantse village, Chungshan County, Kwangtung, close to Macao. Retailers and distributors of mainland-produced opium and other narcotics in Hong Kong and Macao signed contracts in secret with the local "mobsters," criminally disposed members of Triad and other organizations who would be receiving their drugs inside a "security zone" prior to distribution. As is generally the case during periods of negotiation and dispute resulting from such transactions, there were disturbances and crimes of violence, and investigations were provoked. Towards the end of the year, the UN intervened by disclosing this illegal but brazenly conducted traffic and issued an open warning to those engaged in the trade.

This resulted in the closing of the Trade Center of Narcotics Exports and a new policy for clandestine operations was developed. In consequence, the Chinese Reds began calling their produce "Special Goods." They set up a "Special Domestic Products Trade Company" in Peking, with a large number of branches. This organization handles what is essentially a criminal trading enterprise. It is also a political warfare operation with worldwide ramifications involving conspiratorial relationships with many international crime syndicates.

It is operated, at its highest echelons, by the Central Committee of the Chinese Communist Party, which uses as instrumentalities the Foreign Trade Commission and the Ministry of Foreign Affairs. There is, as might be expected, strong participation by the Chinese intelligence community—which has considerable operational resources to contribute to the traffic, as well as having a very large vested interest in the results of its transactions.

The affairs of the Special Domestic Products Trade Company are conducted by the commercial attaches in the Red Chinese embassies abroad; the attaches are, in effect, in charge of the distribution and sale of "Special Goods." As a result of the recommendations of the numerous universities and research institutes whose intellectual resources have been mobilized in the interests of the combine, together with the experience that has been accruing in clandestine operations, in the last seven years or so there has been a great improvement in logistics and the overall techniques of handling the product. In addition, there has been a skillfully promoted program of publicity in consuming areas such as the United States to conceal the nature and sources of the traffic and to throw potential critics off the scent by diverting the blame to other sources—for example, Turkey and France, and, more recently, the Golden Triangle.

Study of Red Chinese guerrilla operations, extended by recent disclosures of their theory and methods of designing, constructing, and manning "transnational" base areas such as those in Cambodia, shows that most of the concepts of movement and penetration as worked out in their doctrine for irregular operations have also been applied to the paramilitary assembly and distribution of narcotics from such base

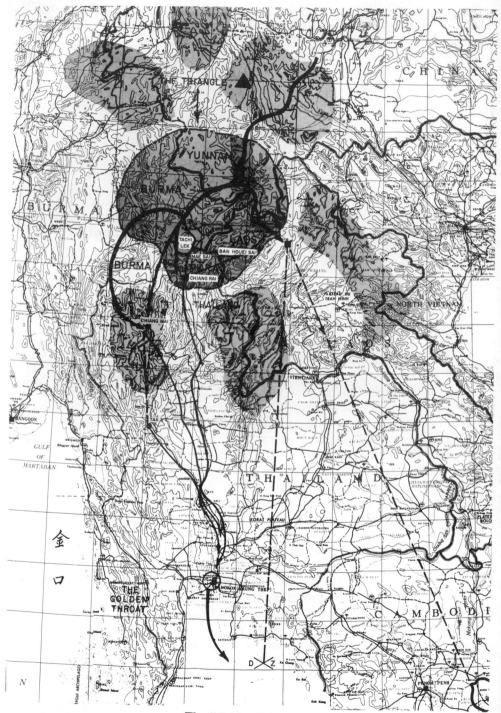

The "Golden Triangle"

areas. A good example of the type of complex is the one the Chinese Reds have set up as an enclave at the junction of the Thai, Burma, Laos, and Yunnan frontiers.

To conceal the actual source of the opium (or at least to play it down), a number of processing and production plants have been set up outside China's national boundaries. Also, the term "tri-junction" has been encouraged, implying involvement of Burma/Thai/Laos without, be it noted, Yunnan, which is in point of fact the principal source.

As is well known, the government of the Union of Burma has been having great difficulties with a number of tribes in Northern Burma; tribes such as the Shans, Kachins, and Karens have been opposing the central government with their elusive private armies. In Thailand there is a corresponding "Free Thai Movement." Merged with the Burmese area of disaffection and the section of the Yunnan border and its hinterland concerned with export operations, an enclave exists within a special area described as a "no man's land" or an "extra-juridical zone." This is a major center of world narcotics operations and the private armies of the tribal chieftains provide it and its logistics with the security that is required.

The pattern of distribution and delivery of the opium and other narcotics, and the constantly changing networks, has a relevance to the subversion and underground warfare that has been directed toward such countries in Southeast Asia as Laos, Cambodia, Thailand, Malaysia, North Borneo, and even Indonesia. Just as the viability of numerous private armies was maintained by opium revenue in the China of the warlord period, so today there is a complex pattern of "Popular Fronts," "National Liberation Armies," and the numerous tribal chieftains who are making considerable fortunes from their profitable dealings with the Chinese Communist intelligence and political-warfare machinery.

Mention was already made of the extreme brazenness shown by the Chinese Communists when they were beginning the export of their drugs to Hong Kong, and the openness with which they set up their export headquarters near Macao. This was certainly matched by a particularly intriguing proposed transaction that drew an official comment by the British Government (not the colonial government of Hong Kong, be it noted). In late 1950 Great Britain released the following statement addressed to the United Nations:

His Majesty's Government has received information that representatives of the Chinese Government have approached the Imperial Chemical Industries (China) Ltd. of Prince's Building, Hong Kong, with a view to disposing of 500 tons of opium via Hong Kong.

The representatives have indicated that the Chinese Government is anxious to dispose of the opium by intimating that a suitable buyer shall receive all facilities necessary to expedite the transaction. The Imperial Chemical Industries has refused the offer.[6]

In this connection it is interesting to note that the quantity of 500 tons was enough to supply the entire legitimate needs of the world for a period of about fifteen months.

At about the same time, an official Opium Monopoly Bureau was set up across the border from Hong Kong and, as in the counterpart near Macao, the marketing staffs at these two stations on the Chinese mainland were soon in touch with potential buyers in Hong Kong, offering them drugs at extremely low rates. These suppliers referred openly to their parent government department as the "Poison American Imperialism Drug Monopoly Agency."

That the agency had a long reach was apparent as early as 1950, when the Japanese government became extremely disturbed about the entry into that country of large shipments of drugs that indubitably had their origin in Red China. In November 1950 the Japanese police arrested five prominent members of the Japanese Communist Party while they were arranging for the disposal of a quantity of heroin in a teashop.

The funds to arise from this sale were intended to finance party operations. This, and an ensuing series of similar raids, proved conclusively that this was not ordinary criminal activity but calculated subversion that could be linked directly with the Peking government. In August 1958 the Japanese press, which had been following these proceedings with interest and concern, reported that the police had about 600 "big names" on their lists, connected with Red Chinese attempts to penetrate their country, using the drug traffic as a medium.

Since the circulation of dollars in Japan was high at the time, owing to the presence of the U.S. forces there, it was also quite apparent to U.S. officials that the traffic was diverting very large sums in U.S. currency into the hands of the Communist Party in Japan. They concluded that this income was needed to maintain a large underground in being that was engaged in propaganda against the defense treaty with the United States (agitation designed to shift the orientation of the country away from the U.S. and towards Red China, to promote trade even in prohibited strategic goods, and to harden Japanese hostility towards the United States). In this connection, General Matthew Ridgeway, Commander-in-Chief of U.S. forces in Japan, felt obliged to state the following in an official report on March 10, 1952:

Investigations of arrests and seizures in Japan, in 1951, proved conclusively that the Communists are smuggling heroin from China to Japan and using the proceeds to finance party activities and obtain strategic materials for China.[7]

It was also noted at the time that the agents of the Chinese Reds were "particularly anxious" to dispose of the heroin to American troops, coordinating this with a propaganda campaign that attempted to smear young American soldiers as being dope addicts.

More recently, in October 1970, the Chief of the Narcotics Investigation Division of the Hong Kong Police stated that in 1969, 10,500 pounds of opium, 310 pounds of heroin, and 250 pounds of morphine had been seized, all of which had come from the Chinese mainland. In making such statements, however, the officials of the Hong Kong Government are careful—for obvious reasons—not to make direct accusations against the original suppliers. Yet the particulars, marking, and superscriptions on materials being consumed in Hong Kong, or reexported from that free port, speak for themselves.

There are three main brands of heroin obtainable in the underground market of Hong Kong: "Number 3," "Number 4" (this is now the commonest, also obtainable in South Vietnam), and "Golden Eagle." In small local refineries four brands of heroin have been produced in Hong Kong—"White Rose," "White Dragon Pearl," "Pigeon Mark," and "Powder King." In the first half of 1969 opium was sold in Hong Kong at H.K. $ 90 per ounce, while in the latter half of the same year the price fell to H.K. $ 60 per ounce owing to high availability of supplies. Heroin brought H.K.$ 190 per ounce. Early in 1970 the Narcotics Investigation Division of the Hong Kong Police and the Smuggling Investigation Unit of the Hong Kong Industrial and Commercial Bureau tightened their measures of control and there was an appreciable fall in the quantity of imports from the mainland, so much so, in fact, that local dealers were obliged to call in supplies directly from Singapore, Thailand, and Malaysia.

In order to understand the extreme difficulties under which the authorities operate in Hong Kong, one must know the nature of the free port of Hong Kong, as well as the fact that there exists, based on Hong Kong harbor, a large fleet of several thousand junks that greatly assists clandestine or unobtrusive traffic with the China coast. However, the Hong Kong Government manifests a superlative skill in dealing with Chinese matters; it is informed to a high degree about most subterranean activities in and near the colony and even farther afield.

Some of the dealers and refiners in Hong Kong are Hsueh Pu-yuan, Li Chien, Tung Ya-fa, Tung Yi-kang, and Huo Ying-to (a wealthy merchant); in Macao, Han Shen and his brother Han Shih-hao, Yeh Kan-fu and his nephew Yeh Chih-chun, Yang Shih-kang, Kuo Fu-sheng, Tao Chuan-tien, and Liang Chang. In Thailand, the "999" brand of morphine base is produced under franchise arrangements by Wang Chin-piao (alias Yang Liang-fu), Li Si-kuei, Chang Kuang-ai, and Chang Chan-ao (alias Chang Ming-san); the "Camel" brand by Wang Hai-san and Chao Lao-si; and the "555" brand by Cheng Yao-sheng and Ting Sung-tsai. These three brands are exported to many countries exclusively through the agent and distributor Cheng Yao-sheng.

Involved in actual transport operations from Thailand are Ma Ah-shing, Ke Yu-tsai, Kung Chih-chung, Tai Jui-Ken (these are seamen); Lu Chi-tung (alias Chiao Chi-lu), Liu Ah-si (alias Liu Pao-chang), and Liu Chieh (these are ships' personnel). They, and many others, are narcotics smugglers on the runs between Hong Kong, the United States, and Japan.

As might be expected, Yunnan, by virtue of its position and its traditions (much influenced by drugs and the drug traffic), forms a main component of the trading base. Within the province there is a principal military base at Chen K'ang that is concerned with the military and intelligence aspects of opium trading. One of its leading personalities, said to have been in charge of logistic arrangements to Burma, is Wang Ch'eng. Early in 1970 Wang was known to be negotiating with a Burmese Communist leader with the Chinese name of Peng Chia-sheng in reference to the construction of a morphine plant in the Gyogon area.

Agreement was not reached because of an implied conflict of interest. At present Wang Ch'eng buys opium produced in Burma that is imported into China to be processed in morphine refineries in Kunming. Another Burmese Communist leader, Lo Hsiang, is engaged in similar activities.

The Chinese Communist regime has very stringent legislation against domestic consumption of narcotics and also against internal trading such as used to be carried on in free markets. Although the Kunming market has been closed for several years, there is still a black market in opium in Kunming that attracts customers even from Shanghai, Nanking, and Chungking.

When the Red Chinese narcotics question is under discussion, one must understand that the terms "legal" and "illegal," "licit" and "illicit" have unusual meanings. For example, it is often stated that the Chinese have ruthlessly stamped out opium in their country (which is true enough when consumption or trade are meant). Similarly, statements are often made by fellow travelers of the Chinese and by State Department spokesmen that there is no illicit export of opium from

Red China. Since the Peking Government regards massive export as perfectly legitimate, this is quite correct.[8]

Routing

At present, Red Chinese narcotics exports follow four main routes:

(1) East China Route
(2) South China Route
(3) West China Route
(4) North China Route

(1) East China Route

Shanghai is the main center, Amoy is next in importance, and Hong Kong is the main entrepôt. From Hong Kong deliveries are channeled to the Middle East, to Australia, Europe, the Americas, Southeast Asia, and even Taiwan.

(2) South China Route

Canton is the main center and the other export stations are Shenchuan, Shihchi, Humen, Nantou, Chungshan, Shehkou, Lachiwei, and Hainan. There is a service by motor boats from Humen and Nantou to Hong Kong and Macao. The cargo is first delivered to Inner Lintin Island and thence to Macao or to Tayushan, an island near Hong Kong. From Tayushan cargo is delivered to Hong Kong or Kowloon by a service of fast speedboats. In Macao the company called Nankuang Hong is the headquarters of narcotics transactions dealing in wholesale shipments with a minimum quantity of 10,000 ounces. Deliveries for Macao are frequently made on the high seas in the neighborhood of Tankanshan, close to Macao. There are a number of extremely wealthy and influential wholesale dealers in Hong Kong.

Work was begun in November 1969 on Lachiwei Island, near Hong Kong and Macao, on a port that was finished in April 1970. Narcotics are delivered there from Canton in small warships (described as gunboats), packed in wooden cases bearing seals marked "Defense Ministry." There are about four to six deliveries a month and the whole area is a security zone that requires prior clearance for foreign ships that arrive to take on the cargo. This may also take the form of arms shipments.

(3) West China Route (also called Southeast Asian Route)

Chehli, Lungchuan, Tengchung, and Wanting are the main centers. Consignments are transported via the border areas of Vietnam, Thailand, Laos, and Burma to Burma, Cambodia, Laos, South Vietnam, Thailand, Malaysia, and Singapore. There may be further movement to Indonesia, Hong Kong, Macao, and other destinations. Quantities may also be sent via North Vietnam to Cuba, Albania, and some African countries such as Tanzania (Zanzibar). The dealers who use this route consider it to be the most profitable and call it the "Golden Throat" (Chin Kou). It has been, so far, the main line of logistics for Chinese Communist narcotics operations aimed at the Free World.

It should be noted, however, that the Chinese Reds are currently extremely interested in stepping up their shipments and that their recognition by Canada, Italy, and Ethiopia is producing some alternatives. For example they have considerable interest in operations through Pakistan towards the West. They will need more civil aircraft in order to do this.

(4) North China Route

Tientsin is the main center while Tsingtao, Weihaiwei, and Dairen are the export ports. The main destinations are Japan and Korea. Within Japan, transshipment stations have been operated in Kyushu, Hokkaido, Kobe, and Osaka where there are active Communist "apparats." Cargo may be transported via North Korea to East Germany and thence to European countries. Alternatively, it may be sent via North Korea to Cuba, Albania, and African countries.

Logistics

(A) Smuggling Methods

1. Seamen and pilots may be used as carriers. Often ships have specially designed hiding places.
2. Fishing boats are extensively used. Cargo is discharged, usually at night, in quiet coastal target areas. It may be left in the water, marked by floats prior to recovery by divers or frogmen.
3. Cargo may be parachuted from light aircraft at designated points at night.
4. Submarines are sometimes used to deliver goods at distant destinations. Cargo may be discharged in containers through torpedo tubes or escape hatches.

5. Under some conditions, it has been found necessary to mix the narcotics with flour, spices, sugar, or soap. After delivery, laboratory technicians dissolve the mixture and extract the drug.
6. Cotton cloth may be soaked in morphine and then dried. The absorbed morphine can be leached out.
7. Cargo can be specially packed with misleading labels for concealment in tins, toothpaste tubes, plaster figures, plastic goods, etc.
8. Official visits, good-will delegations, and cultural exchange groups are frequently used.
9. Careful concealment of storage is arranged at destination and great care in final consignment and delivery is taken.
10. Much use is made of vehicles. There are elaborate techniques for concealment in body work, gas tanks, etc.

(B) Logistics Security

One must remember that the distribution networks are a complex that combines elements of the Chinese intelligence services, members of Triad and similar societies, and international crime syndicates. The distribution networks are especially skilled in evasion, deception, and covert operations. Care is observed that personal contact is avoided between the directing Communist cadres and agents, between agents and distributors, and between distributors and retailers, and that a secure system of "cut-outs," letter boxes, and code messages is used throughout. Channels are multiform and continual alternations are in effect to maintain secrecy.

Objectives of the Red Chinese Narcotics Traffic

(1) Revenue

A primary aim is the acquisition of foreign exchange. In 1952 leading party members in the National Planning Commission and the Ministry of Foreign Trade and leading cadres from South and Southwest China attended a highly secret conference in Peking. The main item on the agenda was "How to Increase National Income by Exporting Narcotics." Since that meeting a greatly augmented program has been developed that has increased growth and production, refining and export. In fact, the fiscal intake from the narcotics trade has become one of the three principal sources of revenue. These developments have been noted by the head of the U.S. Bureau of Narcotics, Henry J. Anslinger, who has placed his findings on record on a number of occasions, expressing the view that intensive cultivation of the opium poppy has been undertaken in order to obtain foreign exchange.

This attitude has been supported by the findings of the Japanese Government, where the head of the National Narcotics Control Committee of Japan, Tsusai Sugawara, has stated that the annual Red Chinese export of opium to Japan amounts to Y60 billion, rather less than one-third of the Chinese export of the drug. Formerly there was considerable heroin addiction among Japanese but countermeasures have been proving rather successful.

The Russians have also commented with increasing displeasure on the Red Chinese intensification of their large-scale opium-growing and narcotics-export program. According to an article published in *Literaturnaya Gazeta* in 1969 (No. 12), written by a B. Bulatov, the annual production of opium on the mainland is about 8,000 tons per year.

(2) The Financing of Subversive Activities

Those who are best informed about Chinese Communist activities abroad know well that they are largely financed by profits accruing from the narcotics trade. A statement was made by the Chief of the Narcotics Investigation Division of the Hong Kong Police in August 1970 that the Chinese Communist take from narcotics trade in Hong Kong is over U.S. $1.5 million per month and that the entire amount is deposited in the Bank of China in Hong Kong. This is a Communist-owned bank; it has a closed and secret annex within which has functioned the headquarters of the CCP on Hong Kong.

It should, perhaps, be noted that the account in question seems only to be concerned with *local* transactions. In addition, vast profits are deposited that arise from worldwide distribution operations that rely on Hong Kong's characteristics as an entrepôt and free port. There is a constant and heavy flow of goods in transit.

To use Southeast Asia as a major theatre of political penetration—the establishment of Communist "infrastructures" and "parallel hierarchies," as well as "wars of liberation"—Red China has depended to a major, even decisive, extent on narcotics revenue. In Burma, Laos, and Thailand, Chinese Communist couriers and agents have been selling narcotics to tribal and other leaders and pro-Communist organizations such as the Pathet Lao and the Free Khmers at attractive and, indeed, exceptionally low prices. Generally speaking, for transactions of this kind, the fixed price is seven ounces of gold or U.S. $30 for one kilogram of raw opium.

According to a Reuters dispatch of November 30, 1970, Chinese Communist guerrilla troops acting in liaison missions were using "miracle medicine" to cure pain among simple villagers. This was reported to be morphine, and by its use they have succeeded in gaining confidence, food, and shelter from the local inhabitants. Using this support to build up the kind of conditioned civic environment recognized by all serious authorities as the essential popular base from which successful guerrilla operations can be mounted, they have been carrying out vital preparations for such operations by caching food, munitions, and stores in the villages. These constitute the resources they will need when the time comes to launch full offensive operations.

To further such moves they have been relying to a large extent on the "Triangle" mentioned above (p. 197), which has become the major base in Asia of the Chinese Communist Party's international narcotics trade. In Southeast Asia, in such countries as Burma, Malaysia, Singapore, and Indonesia, there are about a dozen large companies that deal in the distribution of opium and narcotics. They are enormously wealthy and have excellent credit and banking facilities, in some cases involving participation or ownership. They enjoy a very high degree of local protection and privilege not entirely due to their own resources. It is understood in some cases that, acting discreetly, the Ministry of Foreign Trade in Peking has advanced very large sums that have been used to bribe the high officials whose complaisance or connivance is required.

In addition to the types of guerrilla operations already mentioned, gains have been made in other areas of political action conceived in terms of civic disruption. The basic aim is to alienate and to place under attack particular segments of the population, notably the young. The physical conditioning that results from addiction, when combined with the psychological conditioning imposed by various communications media (underground papers, etc.), induces varying degrees of moral idiocy and social irresponsibility that culminate in dangerous forms of political activism such as arson, bomb-throwing, and the like. Perhaps the victims of this program would be less cooperative if they realized that they are regarded as totally expendable by those who intend to use them.

(3) Corruption and Undermining of the Will and Morale of the People of the Free World

Within the last five years there has been a particularly disturbing rise in the number of drug addicts in the Free World who have shown a precipitate decline in physical and mental condition. Only the briefest outline is to be given at this point, fuller discussion being deferred. As examples that may be cited of the incidence in some Far Eastern areas, it is noted that in Singapore and Malaya alone the consumption of narcotics (mainly opium) amounts to about 1,000 tons per year. In Japan the corresponding figure is about 3,000 tons per year, in spite of stringent regulations, and in Hong Kong about 800-1,000 tons per year. It has been estimated by Dr. Donalief Loubie, Associate Professor of the Medical College of Cornell University and Director of the New York State Addict Reformatory, that 10,487 of the 12,049 male inmates of the Hong Kong prisons are drug addicts. In December 1968 the Hong Kong Narcotics Abstinence Committee, as a result of an investigation, expressed an opinion that the figure for male and female addicts might be as high as 65,000. This is a very high figure for a community that has a population of about 3 million, and may even be an underestimate.

(4) The Corruption and Demoralization of U. S. Servicemen

While the level of addiction of U.S. troops and other servicemen in South Vietnam and other Asia theatres had been known for some time, it did not begin to be a matter of public or international concern until 1970. It then became apparent, as a result of hearings within specialized Committees of the U.S. Senate and of investigations by the executive branch, that the U.S. contingents in Vietnam were coming under a particularly deadly and insidious form of attack. It was shown in particular that

(a) The Chinese Communists were selling, through intermediaries, large quantities of heroin, of the highest quality, at very low prices in Vietnam. The price quoted is usually about $20 per ounce, while the price within the U.S. could be as high as $4,000 per ounce. The material is 90 percent to 100 percent pure. The rate of casualties, which has been rising at a very high figure, reflects the comparative inactivity of U.S. troops during the repatriation and "Vietnamization" phase of the war.

(b) In 1969, the casualties caused by overdoses of heroin averaged two per per month. In 1970, in the period January to October, they increased to an average of two per day. For 1971 the figure is somewhat higher, being sometimes as high as ten per day. Investigators began by the end of 1970 to speak of addiction as assuming epidemic proportions.

As a comment on the above, while there are grounds for some satisfaction that the salient features of the situation have now been recognized and extremely vigorous measures are being taken by the three services in Vietnam, nevertheless there are dangerous possibilities of "follow-through" action by our opponents that will be related to returning veterans.

Some of the most striking successes that have been achieved during the war have been those attained by the enemy on the U.S. "home front." These have included the formation of what are, in effect, potentially rebellious paramilitary organizations composed of veterans who have been caught up in antiwar movements. Many of their members are perfectly sincere and loyal citizens who are profoundly mistaken in their opinions and who have been influenced by insidious and specious arguments and by plausible misinformation. When the matter of addiction is built into this situation, a serious danger to internal security emerges. An individual who has become enslaved to heroin, originally obtained at easy prices, will do anything whatsoever to secure the commodity that, on his return, he finds completely out of his reach except through channels that would want above all else to launch him against his own country. The variants are infinitely menacing; they could reach far beyond mere civil disturbance into situations that threaten security through espionage or sabotage.

The Planned Expansion of the Chinese Mainland Opium Industry and its Present Organization

Before the formulation of the 1952 Opium Policy Planning Conference there had been little coordination of overall production of opium. However, immediately after the accession of the Communist regime to power, a secret instruction was addressed to all provinces through the local Party Committees to "guide and effectively control the existing areas of opium cultivation." In order to foster the industry, arrangements were made to enable the general public, i.e., the farmers, to obtain seeds, fertilizers, and even agricultural loans.

The planting was strictly controlled and the pattern of planting regulated. The Reds bought up the entire crop after it was harvested. The participants in the program at first were rather reluctant farmers who did not care to see their arable land put under crops of this nature; but, if they showed the slightest sign of impatience or protest, which they often did, they were immediately dispossessed. In this manner, large numbers of "reliable" cultivators, usually ex-soldiers or party activists, were put in their places and the cultivation of the poppy began to acquire status.

After the 1952 plan, which began to take effect in the following year, it was clear to all who had any comprehension of these developments that the Party attached the highest importance to the project. Measures were instituted to improve the nature and the prospects of the product. These were both qualitative and quantitative: careful selection of poppy seed became a matter of priority research and great new areas of cultivation were allocated.

In order to obtain the best poppies, research programs in plant breeding were instituted at the Anhwei Agricultural College, Yunnan Higher Agricultural School, and Kweichow Agricultural College. Somewhat later Szechuan University and the Agricultural Research Centre of the Academy of Sciences also became involved. In 1954 arrangements were made for a national opium production plan that included the planting of 200,000 tan of poppy seeds (1 tan equals 133 1/3 pounds), from which the extent of the enterprise can be gauged.

From the outset, it was decided that the sowing and cropping practices of Yunnan, the methods of fertilization and collection of sap used in Manchuria, and plant selection as practiced in Szechuan would provide the best standards and traveling teams went over all growing areas to instruct the cultivators. There was a concerted drive instituted for much more acreage.

However, the traditional pattern of Chinese agriculture, based on a family system and landlord-tenant relationship, together with free marketing of agricultural produce, was quite unsuited to the centrally coordinated and executed plan for the narcotics industry, and the first type of collective farms were not much better. It was not until the large-scale setting up of "People's Communes" and large mechanized "State-Operated Farms" that conditions began to fall into line. Before 1952 the total area under opium was about 2 million mou, but by 1956, it was up to 4 million mou. After the "Great Leap Forward" there were further increases, and by 1972 some 5 million mou were under the poppy. The Communists inherited a national production of about 1,000 tons per year in 1949. By 1953 this had climbed to 2,000 tons per year. In 1956, 5,600 tons per year was achieved; by 1972 the figure had risen to about 10,000 tons per year. This was not a particularly large figure by Chinese standards, but the remarkable and unique aspect of the industry was now the extent of modernization of the research and of the refining and processing of the raw opium, and the fact that it was destined for export. Winter cropping is used, since the plant is resistant to cold weather.

There is an emphasis on secrecy. Attempts are made to conceal the presence of opium crops by planting poppies with other plants, either by interspersing or surrounding them by higher plants. Movements of persons are strictly controlled in the neighborhood of opium-growing areas.

In the past, when the domestic market was important, Szechuan was particularly significant as a growing area, but this has now subsided and it has been replaced by the newer primary producing areas such as Yunnan and Kwangtung. The latters' situations are far more favorable to export requirements. In 1966 a particularly successful plant became available in Yunnan as a result of selection and plant breeding, and instructions were passed in the following year for more than 200 communes to cultivate this strain. Production is being considerably expanded in Yunnan, which, as the base area and a component of the "Golden Triangle," is exceptionally important from the international point of view.

The Chinese Communists have 2,300 "hsien" or districts on the mainland and they have described 179 of them as "important opium-growing areas." Of these 9 are in Northeast China. There are 11 in North China, 35 in West China, 38 in Central China, 4 in Szechuan, 35 in the Yunnan-Kiangsi-Kweichow area, 4 in Sikang-Tibet, and 34 in Kwangtung. Of the 1,000 State-Operated Farms, 60 are growing opium; of the 75,000 communes, 318 are growing opium.

The above results derive from the management of an "Opium Prohibition Bureau" that was set up in 1949 as soon as the Chinese Communists came into power on the mainland. It had the following executives: Po I-po (Chief of the Finance Division), Yueh Chih-chuang (Chief of the Trade Division), and Wang Fen-chi (Chief of the Hwapei Opium Prohibition Bureau). Although the first two names are those of important political "bosses" with long experience in the narcotics trade, the actual details of licensing and trading—namely the operational aspects of the project—were, from the start, the responsibility of the last named.

In view of the essentially covert nature of the enterprise, the Opium Prohibition Bureau (in effect, a state monopoly in its branches) exists under a variety of different names that are often changed for purposes of security. In the Tientsin area, a particularly important one, being the principal opium-, morphine-, and heroin-exporting region in North China, the Bureau is called the "Yuta Concern" and is located at 5 Aomen Lu, 10th Ward, Tientsin.

The head of "Yuta" has been from the start Wang Tsu-chen, who has with him as Managing Director Li Tsu-feng. They have as an active partner Sung Han-chen. The two first were formerly bandits, Wang having had his origins in the Nanking Area. Li has been a prominent leader of gangsters in the "Tseng Jen Wang" clique. Sung is, however, a Tientsin man and a notorious dealer in opium.

While Tientsin is the leading center in North China, its counterpart in South China has always been Canton. There, from the outset of the

211

Communist regime, the trade has been in the hands of the "South China Trade Bureau," called "Lin Chi Hang" and run by Wang Jui-fang.

In the Wuhan area near Hankow, the "Hangkow Agency of the Central and Southern District Tobacco Bureau" handles narcotics questions and both storage and transport are managed there by Lo Wen, Chief of the Accounting Department of the Central and Southern Army District. He is well known to Yeh Chien-ying, who for a considerable period was in command of that area.

At Shihkiachwang there is an important storage depot that existed before the Communist takeover and that had been used by the Japanese. It has been in the charge of Kua Hua-jen. In Northern Shensi, Kung Liang has been in charge of planting, harvesting, and processing, and is also responsible for the management of the Northern Shensi Warehouse. In the Jehol district, Wu Chih-ho has been in charge of the "Jehol Agency," which used to be called the "Jehol Tobacco Bureau." It supervises cultivation and processing of opium.

Shanghai was formerly China's opium capital, where there had been a number of important and powerful organizations engaged in opium and narcotics trading. Since the Communists took over, for the most part, these have fled and private opium trading is prohibited except where there is a special dispensation connected with export activity. Chu Yu-lung, who has been Chief of Public Security in Shanghai, has also been head of a special liaison office whose function has been to maintain contact with potential buyers of opium. This great seaport is still important to the traffic in view of the number of foreign ships that call there. Among the measures taken to enlist foreign seamen as smugglers have been the formation of special seamen's clubs and other facilities.

In spite of rigid controls against domestic consumption or internal dealings in opium and narcotics, Shanghai is, in fact, a most important export base, although only in a functional sense since the controls and the formulation of policy now lie elsewhere. The city is in the middle of the great complex of Kiangsu, Chekiang, and Anhwei, all of which are producing areas. There are considerable differences of quality in the opium converging on Shanghai from various sources, and the quality of opium for export is inspected by a laboratory attached to the Shanghai Hygienic Department that has been under the management of Lin Siu-hao. Actually, the produce of the three provinces mentioned above is largely in the hands of Cheng Lao-san, whose title is Director of the Opium Prohibition Bureau for Kiangsu, Chekiang, and Anhwei and who is reputed to be the most important opium dealer in the Chinese Communist regime. Cheng, who has been called the

"King of Opium," has a particular responsibility for coordinating the trade to Japan and directing the distribution networks.

Great attention has also been paid to maximizing the value of their opium crops through advanced research in the chemistry of refining and diversification of opium byproducts. This phase of development began seriously in 1960 although, in part, the groundwork had been laid long before by scientific liaison cautiously established through contacts abroad with Europe, Canada, the United States, and South and Central America.

To some extent this involved the recruitment of former collaborationists with the Japanese, who had worked for the invaders and had useful experience in the areas of refining, processing, and inspection. Even some Russian narcotics specialists were recruited, as well as some Germans.

There has been a sizable expansion of "special-products processing factories," already-existing ones being enlarged while new ones were added. Some thirty or more factories were soon in operation in Peking, Dairen, Mukden (Shenyang), Chinchow, Kupeikou, Yen-chi, Shanghai, Hangchow, Hankow, Chungking, Kunming, and in Kwangtung, Sinkiang, and Tibet. Some estimates now place the number of such installations as high as seventy-two, some of which are, however, dispersals of main establishments.

Appendix V consists of five tables, carefully and accurately compiled. These tables show the location and prevalence of Red Chinese opium farms, both regular and special, the communes engaged in growing opium, the refineries, and the brand names of the narcotics produced. In addition to the refineries and laboratories listed, there are said to be twenty-one more located throughout all areas of the mainland.

The trend seems to be toward certain improvements in refined opium and morphine production. Some informed sources consider that the emphasis on morphine suggests export of this commodity in bulk for refining nearer the market. Use of Albania as an entrepôt for morphine base headed for further treatment by the Union Corse and other Marseilles illicit refiners may have the motive of keeping up the myth of Turkish preponderance in heroin. If that can be sustained even after the imminent decline in actual Turkish exports, and further exacerbate relations with that sensitive and deeply offended ally, the Communist purpose will have been served.

However, the above remarks apply only to main products. It is considered by some that the Chinese Reds have an important ongoing program in synthetics. Research is also said to be proceeding into some of the opium derivatives other than heroin.

From the time that the Chinese Communists came to power they regarded the narcotics trade as being of such outstanding importance that they built into their plan of operations arrangements to operate on a basis broad enough to involve the following Ministries, Boards, and Departments. Many of them come under the jurisdiction of the State Council headed by Chou En-lai:

(1) The Ministry of Agriculture
This ministry, which is responsible for the operation of State Farms, has a particularly important role in the cultivation of opium.

(2) The Committee for the Review of Austerity
A widespread organization with branches all over the Chinese mainland, this specialized agency has played an important part in the supervision and development of opium and the opiates.

(3) The Ministry of Commerce
All "Special Products" and "Native Products" companies that come under the purview of this body are concerned with the assembly, storage, purchase, exchange, and booking for export of opium and opiates.

(4) The Ministry of External Trade
This maintains "External Trade Companies" abroad that have the responsibility of handling the export of narcotics among their other products.

(5) The Central Government Production Board
A programing, statistical, and management body that takes its production targets from other agencies connected with economic planning.

(6) The Ministry of Finance
A key role is fulfilled by this ministry that handles appropriations connected with the financing of the narcotics industry and is responsible for the collection of taxes on drugs.

(7) The Ministry of Foreign Affairs
This plays an important role in the marketing of narcotics abroad through special representatives, through information policy, and through political intrigue aimed at foreign governments.

(8) The Ministry of Public Security
This ministry has a large responsibility in the supervision of the processes of the manufacture of narcotics.

(9) The Ministry of Forestry and Reclamation
This body has an important role to play, particularly in the promotion of frontier colonization and opium cultivation in remote areas.

There are, besides, such organizations as the "Overseas Chinese Affairs Commission," involved in relations with Chinese living abroad, the "Committee for the Promotion of International Trade," often used as a cloak for clandestine activities, and the news agencies NCNA (New China News Agency) and Hsinhua. The Academy of Sciences also plays its part. The primary and crucial role of the intelligence agencies is reviewed elsewhere (Chapter 4).

Export and trading in opium and narcotics by the Chinese Communists can be divided into domestic and foreign operations. In domestic operations, on the mainland, the handling of the goods in all aspects is a matter for secrecy. Although, as indicated above, there is a wide base of cooperation between public bodies, in this field there exists a conspiracy of silence that is not difficult to impose in a state such as the Chinese Reds have installed.

All the above organizations have special transport and personnel that are detailed for such duties. The PLA and Public Security Forces are often involved in convoy and movement, while "Road Clearance Orders" are issued to enable opium and narcotics to pass freely without examination through security checkpoints. They are often given innocuous labels, and control documents that describe them as "pharmaceuticals," "industrial chemicals," "chemical intermediates," and the like.

Foreign operations need to be completely clandestine because of the stringent international restrictions that exist, and the need for security is even greater. It is an easy matter for the Chinese Communists to deceive or to bypass their own officials, but the task becomes far more difficult abroad. Here the whole affair is an underground matter, although it is often made much easier by corruption of foreign governments at the highest levels. The methods include:

(1) *Smuggling*—by sea or by air.
(2) *Transport by charter party.* This involves the cooperation of shipping companies either knowingly or unconsciously through specially designated personnel abroad. Transport of opium and narcotics from China to Europe is often managed through official channels. An example may be cited—movement of narcotics from Tientsin to Poland by means of the "China-Poland Steamship Company" that was formed in Red China in 1951.
(3) *Use of support by Communists abroad* qualified to play a part in the trade.
(4) *Collaboration with international organized-crime syndicates* that have formed associations with the CCP.
(5) *Use of foreign posts deployed by parent organizations on the mainland,* such as "Purchasing Commissions," NCNA, etc.
(6) *Abuse of the diplomatic privilege* through the illegal use of dip-

lomatic bags or by the use of diplomats as couriers carrying narcotics.

(7) *Use of normal branded merchandise* as a cover for the traffic, either by concealment or by impregnation.

(8) *Transmission by mail.* Normal postal services abroad are frequently used when camouflaged merchandise is sent to customers abroad.

(9) *Forgery or reproduction of trademarks.* Often goods are consigned with misleading well-known brands or trademarks and packaging characteristics.

Much attention has been paid to the commercial aspect and the practices needed to promote the trade, especially where risks are high. In general the Chinese Reds work by:

(1) *Subsidies*
When foreign-exchange rates are low, subsidies are granted to foreign buyers so that transactions will not be affected by exchange fluctuation.

(2) *Sales on Credit*
Minimal deposits, or even no deposits, are required of potential buyers when they place orders. However, the normal practice is to collect 30 percent of the total buying price at the time of sale, followed by 20 percent when the goods are delivered. The balance must be paid within a fixed period. All payments except those in cash or in gold must be made through designated banks.

(3) *Most-Favored-Customer Treatment*
Special arrangements are made that depend on the nature and circumstances of sale. When purchases are made of narcotics in quantities greater than 3,000 ounces, usually a discount of 8 percent is offered. If the quantity is over 10,000 ounces, the discount is 10 percent. As regards a relative difficulty imposed by local conditions at particular localities, 25–30 percent discounts are offered when risk is involved. It may be noted that Hong Kong, Macao, Japan, and Indo-China are excluded from such arrangements. Where trading is slow, 20–30 percent discounts are also offered.

It is a matter for special note that while the United States is regarded as a soft, or medium-hard rather than a hard target, in view of the political rather than the overriding economic aims in this case, special favor terms are given of a 25–35 percent discount. These are com-

216

parable to rates given for "absolute hard" areas regarded as next to impossible.

Estimates of the volume of export have been made, as follows:

Opium

Sold in Asia: about 46 percent of all opium exported.
Sold in Australia: 6 percent.
Sold in the Americas: 33 percent.
Sold elsewhere (i.e., Europe, etc.): 15 percent.

Morphine

Sold in Asia: 30 percent of all morphine exported.
Sold in Australia: 8 percent.
Sold in the Americas: 32 percent.
Sold elsewhere (i.e., Europe, etc.): 30 percent.

Marseilles is well known as the heroin capital of Europe and has until quite recently played an especially important role in the refining and distribution of that drug. Heroin has generally been supposed to be almost exclusively produced from Turkish opium, transported to Marseilles through Syrian, Lebanese, or other channels via Sicilian and Corsican criminal organizations. While of course there is truth in this assumption, it is a dangerous half-truth because that ancient seaport has always had worldwide connections. It has been a primary link, through shipping and through airline connections, with Southeast Asia and the Far East, as it has been with the Western Hemisphere. Thus the opium or morphine coming in from Turkey has for years been supplemented by the same commodities sent in from the Far East as well. In this traffic, the role of Chinese production from the mainland has been in the ascendant, helped especially by the rise of Albania in the role of a European satellite of the Peking regime.

The principal reasons for the importance of Marseilles in this activity have been

(a) Its situation on the Mediterranean, readily accessible to traffic from the Eastern portion of that sea.
(b) Its important Atlantic trade with the United States and Canada.
(c) Its highly skilled, versatile, and competent criminal underworld. This is related to a large Corsican element.
(d) Its situation as a primary center of the French perfume and cosmetics industry. This makes for the availability of trained chemists.

217

It can be said that the Corsicans bear to France something of the same relationship that the Sicilians bear to Italy, and that just as Sicily has the Mafia, so does Corsica have the Union Corse. To a remarkable degree, members of both those organizations understand the art of keeping their own mouths shut and closing the mouths of others. Their chosen method is quite often murder. In both cases it is necessary to take account of the politico-criminal nexus.

For example, it is rather important to realize that collaboration between General de Gaulle and his following and criminal elements in the south of France played an important part in the successful landings in the Toulon and St. Raphael areas and in the capture of Marseilles from the Germans in 1944. To a very large extent, the smoothness of operations was due to the highly effective opposition provided by determined groups of the French Resistance, many of whom were Corsican gangsters with whom de Gaulle's emissaries had been in touch. For decades, Marseilles' underworld had been dominated by these Corsicans, whose leadership had been provided by the Guerini brothers, the Venturi brothers, and the Francisi and Orsini families.

It is, unfortunately, a matter of record that when the Allied Armies began operating offensively in the Mediterranean theater, among the U.S. contingents were a large number of persons of Italian, Sicilian, or French extraction who were highly interested in founding "connections" of a profitable nature—if necessary none too legal. While, of course, the "French Connection" was no new thing and there had been a thriving drug traffic before the war between the south of France and the United States, this had been almost completely cut off by the war. It was now to revive in a much more dangerous form after a transitional phase in which Italian production played the primary role.

Being particularly aware, in recent years, of the joint importance of Turkey and Marseilles in the scheme of things, and of the catastrophic rise of addiction in the United States, the Bureau of Narcotics and Dangerous Drugs has not only been putting pressure on the Turks through diplomatic channels but on the French as well.

That pressure began in 1969 and was accompanied by a good many articles in the French press alerting the public to the gravity of a problem that had not, as yet, made its mark in that country. France had experienced no domestic addiction problem in any way comparable with that existing in the United States.

Positive French reaction really began with the accession to power of Georges Pompidou, after the passing of de Gaulle from the French (and international) political scene. Because of Pompidou's understanding of the importance of the problem and the need for international collaboration, the French Minister of the Interior, Raymond Marcellin, visited the United States in July 1970. In consequence, in January 1971 a most important joint protocol was signed by the U.S. and French governments designed to effect cooperation. Since the headquarters of Interpol, the international police organization, is at St. Cloud, these moves augured well for the prospect of more effective international collaboration as well as more bilateral cooperation.

The French government began at once to revamp its measures for suppression of the traffic and appointed Raymand le Mouel as Narcotics Squad Chief in Paris, while Marcel Morin was put in charge of antinarcotics operations in Marseilles itself. There was a marked expansion of personnel of the departments concerned with the problem. In Marseilles a tightening-up of customs precautions was instituted under Chief Inspector Jean le Carré.

However, it must be understood that until then, in France, a situation existed that had been singularly favorable to the existence of the traffic. To a large extent it may be attributed to the wartime fall of France and its aftermath.

The situation in question may be described as a highly undesirable interpenetration, and even fusion, of interests between the underworld and the security services. All who have any real knowledge of the most secret operations of governments realize that the necessary basic clandestinity bears a marked resemblance in method, but not aim, to operations conducted by the criminal underworld. Experienced and enlightened countries spend a good deal of time and effort in defending their security services, maintaining their essential integrity in the face of the ever-present threat of capture by competing organizations of a similar nature within the politico-military field of those within the underworld of crime. In the case of France, there have been within recent years certain failures of this kind that are fully understandable. However the French must be given the greatest credit for recognizing the state of affairs in their characteristically realistic manner and engaging in strenuous efforts to rectify matters.

Within the area of the problem there have been the following components:

(1) The professional criminal underworld.
(2) The S.D.E.C.E. (Service de Documentation et de Contrespionage). As its name suggest, this is a combined secret service with a responsibility for covert collection of foreign intelligence and also for protection of metropolitan France—an organ of internal security.
(3) A.S. (Action Service) or Service 5.
(4) S.A.C. (Service d'Action Civique).

(5) H.C. (a group known as Honorables Correspondants).

The last are a supernumerary reserve of qualified persons with intelligence experience who have been used as a cadre to provide special services as required.

S.D.E.C.E., A.S., and S.A.C.

It has been noted in Chapter 3 that the Chinese intelligence services have, in their short career, become thoroughly interwoven with criminal elements in the course of foreign operations. In part this has been due to the sudden and rapid expansion of their worldwide operational posture, as well as important but little-known or recognized fluctuations in their fortunes. Before World War II, although quite effective, their intelligence and security services were somewhat parochial and, even now, the aggregate has not completely outgrown the attitude.

Perhaps it may be mentioned here that both the CIA and the German services are "postwar" and that this period has been one of great difficulty for the construction and management of properly organized and aligned instrumentalities of this kind. It has been, after all, an "Age of Betrayal."

Thus the French have not been alone in their employment of unsuitable personnel. Their important new agency the S.D.E.C.E. has been expecially plagued by the actions of the agents referred to above as the H.C. or Honorables Correspondants, many of whom have proved to be adventurers. In addition, a particular problem was introduced by de Gaulle himself. S.D.E.C.E. was growing rapidly during that period-in-the-wilderness known as the "Hegira" when Charles de Gaulle was out of office after the war. It was the grave threat to the Republic presented by the result of the Indo-China War and the attrition of the Algerian War that brought him back.

Well aware of little-known aspects of U.S. involvement in both those wars, of a kind that he felt was strongly against French interests, de Gaulle's prejudices, mordant enough during World War II, became even more marked. They took a sufficiently rabid form to enable dubious advisers such as André Malraux to gain ascendancy over him and to propel him in the direction of China and the Soviet Union and away from NATO commitments.

As far as S.D.E.C.E. was concerned, this involved the recruitment and placement of an entirely new cadre of French intelligence officers. Their mark was personal fealty to de Gaulle, whose attitude has been well summarized by the remark that he made to Harold Nicholson during his wartime period in London—"La France entière c'est moi." The result was that at times his faithful followers in the S.D.E.C.E. seemed indistinguishable from their opposite numbers in the KGB or the GRU, a phenomenon that was a source of the greatest anxiety to other members of S.D.E.C.E. with more traditional or orthodox views.

On the accession of Georges Pompidou, measures were instituted to remove this uncertain element that had no further claim on employment. For this purpose a man of great integrity, Colonel de Marenches, was given a mandate from the President of France to undertake a much-needed purge. This, of course, brought a great deal of annoyance and discomfiture to those who were removed, and to elements of the H.C. who were affected by the process and who in some cases seem to have reacted strongly in consequence.

The man who was principally concerned with the removal of the unwanted elements from S.D.E.C.E. was an excellent and highly respected French intelligence officer, Colonel Paul Fournier. Col. Fournier became known to the general public for the first time as a result of the extraordinary de Louelle affair. The main features of this *cause célèbre* in the field of international heroin trading and of the "French Connection" were as follows.

Roger de Louelle, a French citizen, left Paris by air on April 14, 1971, and after registering in a hotel in New York City left for Port Elizabeth in New Jersey to collect a Volkswagen camping vehicle that was awaiting him there. Unknown to him, the vehicle had previously been searched by a U.S. customs officer, a young lady named Lynn Pellettier, who had discovered in it 96 pounds of heroin. On arriving to claim the vehicle, de Louelle was arrested immediately.

Under subsequent police investigation and questioning, he became aware that if he were to plead guilty and to furnish depositions, i.e., to cooperate fully with the police, he would only be liable to a sentence of five years rather than the likely sentence of twenty or thirty years. On reflection, de Louelle decided to plead guilty. He explained that he had been called on the phone on December 15, 1970, by Col. Paul Fournier of S.D.E.C.E., his former chief during his period of service with that body.

As a result of that conversation, he complied with a request to rendezvous with a man unknown to him, whom he met a few days later and who asked him if he would smuggle 44 kilos of heroin into the United States, for which he would receive $50,000. He said that he believed this was being done by S.D.E.C.E. for official purposes and he acceded to the request, particularly as he needed the money.

He was instructed to arrange for the purchase of the vehicle and provided with an advance for this. Also he was asked to make arrangements to ship it to the United States. The final arrangements for the purchase of the Volkswagen camper were not made until mid-February. Then, in March, he drove it to Pontchartrain, near Paris, where he met another man driving a green Simca, from which the 44 "keys" of heroin were transferred.

De Louelle then drove the vehicle to le Havre. There he arranged to ship it to Port Elizabeth and, on the following day, he phoned Fournier and told him about the arrangements and gave him the name of the hotel where he proposed to stay. Fournier called him on April 3 and instructed him to fly to New York on the following day and then to pick up the vehicle at Port Elizabeth on the 5th, after which he should drive it back to his hotel, where he would be contacted.

These facts were in a statement made by de Louelle to the New York police, an officer of the Bureau of Narcotics and Dangerous Drugs, and to M. Chaminades, a French consular official. There was, of course, an immediate crisis in Franco-U.S. relations, which tested rather strongly the accord that had been reached between the two governments in January—and it seems strange that the coup in question should have taken place just when it did.

The response of the French Government, in view of de Louelle's serious accusations against a serving member of the S.D.E.C.E., was to send him a big questionnaire. This, under advice from his U.S. lawyer, he declined to answer because of the Fifth Amendment, something that the French, of course, do not have. Indeed, some of the U.S. officials involved in the case succeeded in having an injunction drawn up for Fournier, who was charged by a U.S. Grand Jury. The French Government was asked to extradite Col. Fournier in order that he might be tried in the United States. Naturally both Col. Fournier and his government ignored the injunction and the extradition request.

The whole affair remains something of an unsolved mystery, although de Louelle's confession has been accepted by the U.S. authorities and has led to his receiving a light sentence. Some entertain the theory that a group of disaffected ex-S.D.E.C.E. officers, in a vengeful mood, were out to "get" Fournier and that, while de Louelle may have been perfectly assured that he had actually been working on behalf of Fournier, his instructions were really issued from some other quarter.

There is another theory. Earlier, in the period 1967–68, Col. Fournier had been head of Section R-6 of the First Bureau of S.D.E.C.E., that being the Far East/Asia desk. In that capacity he was responsible for issuing a report on CIA air logistics activities, which he said had been using its private airline, Air America, as a means of moving narcotics in Southeast Asia. He stated, in that report, that they were running raw opium from the Golden Triangle (Laos/Cambodia in particular) in order to support unbudgeted operations in the theater. It seems that S.D.E.C.E. had been infiltrated and the report leaked back to CIA. This caused considerable hostility that conceivably might have taken the form of reprisals against Fournier calculated to jeopardize his career.

On the other hand, there also seems to be a possibility that this may have been a "Desinformatsiya" or "DEZA" operation conducted by the Russians, who may not have liked the reforms introduced by Col. Fournier and may have wished to fix him, halt the organizational changes, and becloud U.S.-French relations in the process. Certainly it would seem to have been the height of stupidity on the part of the CIA to go about damaging an official whose principal responsibility was the task of "rectifying" S.D.E.C.E. and bringing it back within the U.S. and Western framework. But stranger things than that have happened in the interrelationships of intelligence services, whatever "side" they are supposed to be on.

The Fournier case is covered at comparative length because it illustrates particularly well some of the special problems encountered by the French and others that need to be resolved before much progress can be made in dealing with the narcotics menace.

Both Action Service and Service d'Action Civique have been Gaullist security organs that served as "muscle men" in defending the movement against the threats emanating from the left-wing demonstrations then common in France, or any other threat such as, for example, the assassination of de Gaulle by the OAS. A heavy price was paid by the recruitment into the security services of an undesirable type of person, a situation extraordinarily difficult to eradicate.

But, be it noted, the influence of the Marseillan-Corsican underworld extended much further than S.D.E.C.E. and Metropolitan France. Indo-China has always been a theater of operations for Corsicans, who have interested themselves in a good many lucrative pursuits ranging from gold and armaments brokerage and currency swindles of various kinds to prostitution and the narcotics traffic.

In particular, Laos has always played a central role in most of these activities, and not the least in the opium trade—both as a producing area and as a transport route for opium during the war in Indo-China.

It has been the development of the war situation in the Far East, with full U.S. participation, that has provided such golden opportunities to the members of the Mediterranean underworld and that has also underwritten the operational alliance between its members and the biggest gangsters of all, the Chinese Reds. The business in which both are interested, for somewhat divergent motives, is one where trails must be obscured and where concealments and cutouts are absolutely necessary. The Golden Triangle is the world's outstanding and most complicated device of this nature. It serves the important purposes of hiding the extent of Red Chinese participation in worldwide trading and of providing a buffer, or "cordon sanitaire," that intervenes between them and their allies in the Western underworld. The overseas-based Chinese gangs and entrepreneurs act as middlemen, ably assisted by a multitude of corrupt officials and complaisant part-time smugglers of all kinds.

The range of operations is astounding and has been greatly facilitated of late by trends in Canada and the United States that have resulted in political recognition of Red China by the first and an evident wish to follow suit on the part of the United States. These changes in political alignment have provided opportunities for the Red Chinese regime to acquire bases in the Western Hemisphere and to get to close quarters with the avowed adversaries whose destruction at Chinese hands they have often predicted.

Chinese narcotics operatives, in joint collaboration with such allies of convenience as the Mafia, the "Organization," and the Corsican Union, have availed themselves of existing channels of supply and distribution. They have augmented the supply of opiates for mutual benefit to themselves and their coadjutors, and there are some areas of exploitation where essentially pioneer work has been undertaken, particularly on the West Coast. It is, perhaps significant that when the Institute of Pacific Relations was exposed as a Communist-infiltrated "front" some years ago, it took refuge in Canada in the Vancouver area.

That great Pacific port has, within recent years, become an advanced base of Chinese Communist penetration into North America. It has been used extensively as a springboard for clandestine but extremely hostile actions against the United States itself.

Of these, one of the most insidious and dangerous has been the massive influx of illegal Chinese immigrants into the United States, which has now reached startling proportions. While it is difficult to be certain about the figures, some well-informed estimates have placed the total as high as 25,000. Most of them are individuals who have jumped ship at a Western seaport such as San Francisco, Los Angeles, or, especially, Vancouver, and who have used the Chinatowns of those ports as an entry point. Many have proved to be members of the Hong Kong Seamen's Union. There is some evidence that a large proportion of these men are trained guerrillas who have come in with quantities of narcotics and money to assist them in their missions, whatever those may be. A fair number of them who have made their way into the United States have entered by means of the long, undefended border between that country and Canada. Further details of this remarkable and most disturbing migration will be provided later in Chapter 7 and Appendix IV, Section C.

It must not be thought that operations of the kind briefly outlined above are confined to the West Coast. There is abundant evidence that the Chinese Reds are particularly active in Canadian provinces farther east, especially in Toronto and in Montreal, where they have been able to acquire a surprising measure of local support.

In the United States, their membership in the United Nations and thereby the ability to set up an important base in New York have drawn attention to quite remarkable activities engaged in by members of their security services, such as the "Social Scientists" from "Bowstring Alley."* One such case has been brought forcibly to the attention of the U.S. public. Unfortunately that public has been so exposed to the accounts of the numerous acts of criminal violence that occur all the time that the major significance of certain recent events in New York's Chinatown has not, as yet, been fully understood. It is a matter of high importance that the following facts are not only widely known but that a correct estimate is made of their wider significance to the security of the United States.

For the information and extracts that follow, on what may be called the "Kwa Lin Case," the author is indebted to the work and writing of two investigative reporters on the staff of the *New York Daily News*, Paul Meskil and Frank Faso. Quite recently these well-informed and reliable writers collaborated on an article that appeared in the July 1972 issue of *True*. This article, entitled "Peking's Spies in America," is certainly sensational in its nature but it is important to those who wish to acquire an up-to-date and realistic understanding of the actual state of U.S.-China relations. I have gone to some pains to assure myself of the accuracy and authenticity of the facts revealed in the article, which I now consider to be incontrovertible.[9]

The Kwa Lin Case involves the actions in the United States and Canada of a Red Chinese network engaged in collecting hostile intelligence and in subversive operations that are a serious threat to the security of these countries. Kwa Lin himself is a Chinese thug who has been employed by the Department of Social Affairs but possibly was operationally responsible to the "Hai Wai" organization in North America.

Kwa Lin is the name by which he was known when he was registered as a merchant seaman in Hong Kong some years ago, and that he also

---

*The members of the Chinese secret service are under the Bureau of Social Affairs, and their headquarters address in Peking translates as "Bowstring Alley."

used when he joined the Hong Kong Seamen's Union. He has been known, however, by other names, such as John Lee (which appears on the forged passport that he has recently been using), Daniel Ton, Tong Tom, Lin Tze, and others. This Red Chinese agent first arrived in New York City in the summer of 1970, after which an epidemic of murders among the Chinese population began. Clearly, Kwa was carrying on in the long-established traditions of the Shanghai "Crimson Squad" in which Chou En-lai had played so prominent a role in the 1920s.

In order to understand fully the motivation and background of the murders one must realize that the Hong Kong Seamen's Union has, through its membership, provided the bulk of the illegal Chinese immigration into the United States. In their article, Meskil and Faso have described the situation as follows:

> Under pressure from Washington, the Turkish Government is burning illegal poppy fields and the French Government is trying to close the heroin factories of Marseilles. Red China has high hopes of taking over the heroin trade. Proceeds from this billion-dollar business will be used to finance China's espionage and propaganda activities.
>
> Chinese junks and fishing boats transport heroin, cocaine and opium from the mainland to Hong Kong where much of it winds up in the seabags of HKSU members. In fact, all the Chinese dope smugglers seized by American and Canadian authorities in the past two years carried HKSU cards.
>
> The door through which Chinese aliens, agents and narcotics smugglers enter North America is Vancouver, British Columbia, Canada's third-largest city and main Pacific port. Cargo and passenger ships from all over the world dock at Vancouver, where Chinese sailors can easily disappear in the city's teeming Chinatown.
>
> At least two Vancouver travel agencies serve as fronts for smuggling and spy operations. They make travel and hotel arrangements for ship-jumping seamen smuggled across the U.S. border into Washington, Michigan, New York and New England. Further, a restaurant in Montreal and a barber shop in New York City have been identified in official reports as key links in the alien-smuggling chain.
>
> In putting together the pieces of the puzzle, investigators found Chinese seamen involved in a wide range of crimes including espionage, forgery, counterfeiting, narcotics violations and at least a dozen murders in the U.S. and Canada.
>
> The murder epidemic began soon after Kwa Lin arrived in New York in the Summer of 1970. Then, in less than two months, four Hong Kong seamen were killed in the city.

First victim was 17-year-old Willie Wong, a courier for the spy network. He entered the U.S. illegally in 1969 with a small quantity of narcotics which he delivered to a contact in New York's Chinatown. Ordered to return to Hong Kong for a new assignment, he refused. He was ice-picked to death in August 1970, on a crowded Chinatown street.

Two nights after Willie Wong was hit, Hong Kong seaman Sing Hop, 27, was strolling along Park Street when a small neatly dressed man shot him three times in the head. In Hop's room, a few yards from the corner where Willie Wong died, detectives found a forged U.S. passport and documents proving that he was a Red Chinese agent.

The third target, Kuee Tang, 31, was shot dead September 9, 1970, when he emerged from a Chinese social club on Canal Street in downtown New York City. The New York Police Intelligence Division described the club as "a known gambling establishment frequented by illegal aliens including seamen engaged in smuggling, narcotics and intelligence gathering operations." The same report identified Tang as "a Communist courier and illegal alien involved in narcotics operations and a card-carrying member of the Hong Kong Seamens Union."

Eleven days after Tang's murder Jerry Ginn and Larry Wong were gunned down outside the Sun Sing Theatre. Investigators reported that Ginn and Wong also were involved in narcotics smuggling and had kept some of the proceeds for themselves. Wong recovered and told Federal agents about the espionage network. His story convinced investigators that all four killings were carried out by an enforcer for Peking's Social Affairs Department.

It may be noted, parenthetically, that the shooting of the two men (just above) was witnessed by an FBI agent who was tailing them after they had emerged from the theatre at 6:30 P.M. on September 20, 1970. The agent in question had a good view of the assassin but did not break his cover by attempting to arrest the assailant in view of the paramount importance of the investigation he was conducting into the drug traffic. The article continues:

After the assassin fled to Montreal, he checked into the Mei Chow Hotel in the city's Chinese section. There he was contacted by a man called Jack Wong, one of the top Chinese agents in North America. Wong was in charge of the Canadian end of the spy-and-smuggling operation. His chief lieutenants were Chinese but he also employed Canadians to transport ship-jumping seamen.

Kwa Lin and Jack Wong made separate but related trips to the U.S. in October 1970. Kwa Lin and another agent drove to Seattle on Oct. 18 in a car supplied by one of the Vancouver travel agencies. They carried forged Canadian passports that enabled them to cross the border without question. They returned to Canada the next day after a Chinese seaman called Choy Lung had been shot dead in Seattle's Chinatown. Choy, a spy network courier, was killed because he had pocketed $18,000 he was supposed to deliver to a contact on the West Coast.

A week after Choy Lung's murder, Jack Wong and a chauffeur/ bodyguard drove from Vancouver to Seattle on the first leg of a 3,000-mile cross-continent journey that included stops in St. Louis and New York. They held clandestine meetings with Chinese business men, college professors, leaders of militant Maoist groups and others useful to the espionage network. Their every move was observed by U.S. counteragents.

The point may be made here for the benefit of those who are unfamiliar with intelligence practices, that networks in a target country are managed from an adjacent country for valid security reasons. Therefore, in accompanying his subordinate Kwa Lin into the United States, Wong committed a serious breach of procedure and a lapse from normal security practice. In fact, it would be surprising if, in an excess of zeal or even a sense of crisis, he did not disobey the instructions under which he was supposed to operate.

Despite the important nature of his appointment, Wong, although he had had a considerable amount of success in operating his traffic in illegal immigrants and narcotics, had already seriously compromised Red Chinese operations by other shortcomings in technique. Again quoting Meskil and Faso:

> Upon his return to Montreal in mid-November, Jack Wong learned that his alien-smuggling operation was in trouble: a courier had been caught as he crossed the border near Lynden, Washington. Federal agents reported that he had a HKSU card and "numerous intelligence papers on him when apprehended." Additionally, several other Chinese seamen had been picked up in the U.S. including nine who had come ashore from a fishing boat near Blaine, Washington, and five who had been caught in Vermont. Two more had been found frozen to death in woods along the Canada-New York border.

The trouble arose because Wong had entrusted a good many of his border-crossing and infiltration operations to a Canadian ex-convict called Donald Levac, with an extensive police record for offenses such as dope-smuggling, gunrunning, and hijacking. Levac double-crossed Wong and denounced him to the Canadian authorities. This did not help him at all because it resulted almost at once in the murder of two of his men and, in June 1971, of a Chinese associate and himself.

Wong was finally deported from Canada. Although suspected of a number of murders, there was not sufficient proof for a conviction. Kwa Lin continued with his tasks and on June 20 was responsible for the death of another Hong Kong seaman, called Lee Wing Sung, who apparently wanted to escape from the Red Chinese network. Kwa was arrested shortly afterwards by the Royal Canadian Mounted Police and turned over to the CIA.

It is pointed out in the article that the crimes described above are only a part of the role Red China's agents have been playing in the United States. In addition, they have been engaged in a campaign of harassment and intimidation of loyal Chinese-Americans. No mention is made of tactics of this nature that undoubtedly are also being used against citizens of the Republic of China, who have been displaying most commendable composure and single-mindedness in the face of an extremely menacing situation.

The threat that is of concern to the Nationalist Chinese is the expressed desire on the part of the present Japanese Government to normalize relations with the Peking regime. This would also have the effect of destroying Taiwan's security, because its defense, under the U.S./Republic of China Treaty, relies on the use of Japanese bases in the event of a military threat against Taiwan from the mainland. The terms of a new relationship between Red China and Japan could completely nullify the existing peace treaty with Japan that was signed by the Republic of China over and above the terms of surrender that were signed earlier. This would constitute a political disaster of the highest magnitude, pregnant with the most ominous possibilities for all overseas Chinese and even perhaps for peace in the Far East.

At present there are about 20 million overseas Chinese, very few of whom have any desire to be absorbed by Peking. They are singularly free of the illusions that, for no really explicable reason, are held about the Chinese Reds even among intelligent Westerners. If they ever become exposed to the unrestricted influence of Peking, forces would be let loose in the world that could probably only be checked by the most drastic and least desirable measures.

The United States is not only exposed to this imminent threat but to another that is beginning to be somewhat more discernible in the Caribbean. It was mentioned above (Chapter 3) that this is an area in which the closest partnership has been evident between international politics (Communist machinations) and international crime, that is, moves made by the "Organization" to facilitate the entry and distribution of narcotics from many sources. Recently this situation has been further aggravated by an increasing number of South American coun-

229

tries becoming channels of transit. The longest-established trading base has, of course, been Mexico.

Mexico has been notorious for many years as a primary source for the extremely large quantities of narcotics that have been imported into the Southwestern States, into Florida, and into Gulf ports such as New Orleans. Among the commodities handled, perhaps the most characteristic of the country itself has been marijuana, which has been of the greatest importance to the multitude of dealers involved and to the large number of customers in the United States. The volume of customers is very hard to estimate, but the figure of 20 million has been given as the number of persons who have at least tried the drug.

The marijuana Mecca in Mexico is Tijuana, 15 miles south of San Diego. Additionally, it is a major source for the entire drug traffic in California, which has a large and growing drug-addicted portion of its population. There are, for example, about 20,000 known heroin addicts and probably many more who are unknown. The main source of heroin—native heroin, that is to say—is the state of Sinaloa on the West Coast, half way between the border and Mexico City.

Tijuana and the Baja Peninsula were virtually isolated from Mexico twenty years ago. Traffic to the area came via Arizona and by sea and air across the California Gulf; these routes controlled the direction of the narcotics traffic between Arizona, Texas, Baja California, and Tijuana. Today the main line runs across from Culiacan, the capital of Sinaloa State, to Tijuana and then across the border to San Diego and Los Angeles and thence points East. This provides a much-favored route with considerable appeal to smugglers who don't care for the higher costs and much more risky methods of ingress and transmission in running direct to the East Coast.

Border Patrol agents in New Mexico and Texas for some time have been reporting huge shipments of narcotics carried over the Mexican border into the United States, consigned to college campuses. When intercepted, these have often been found to be part of a mix consisting also of Communist propaganda literature and sometimes even weapons. Skillful professional methods of concealment have been in evidence, such as the immersion of plastic bags of heroin inside gas tanks.

The direct traffic through Mexico is also, of course, supplemented by an even more direct traffic to the coast of California, involving operations by the type of Chinese seamen mentioned above, by others who do not jump ship, and by fishermen. These have been observed bringing in exceptionally pure-grade heroin that they have been distributing at an unusually low cost. There are even cases on record in which they have given away the drug to hippies.

Mexico can provide an almost classic case study for social or political scientists with an urge to know the aspects of the narcotics traffic: the techniques of smuggling, which are highly developed there; the system of "mordida" (a Mexican term describing bribery, corruption, and illegal practices, usually involving officials), in which protection and graft take advanced forms; the economics of drug dealing and peddling in which an exceptionally wide range of products is handled. In addition, there are the stimulating tales that can be heard about the characteristics of the smugglers and their opponents (sometimes disguised accomplices) on both sides of an unusually picturesque frontier, the U.S.-Mexican border.

Considerable fortunes have been made in recent years, particularly from marijuana, always a sizable export from Mexico. However, there is a long-established opium industry that was originally brought to the country by Chinese immigrants: its derivatives formed the basis of many patent medicines in the last century. It is a matter of record that drug addiction about 1900 was extremely heavy; some say that addiction to opiates at that time was possibly as high as 500,000 or more.

The base from which the trade was carried out was a complex in the provinces of Sinaloa, Sonora, and Chihuahua, the best area climatically. There was also the district of the Sierra Madre Occidental in Sinaloa. Nowadays it is also grown in Durango, Jalisco, and elsewhere. There has always been a profusion of a low-grade brown heroin that has a reputation with addicts for unusual strength (about 80 percent). The reason is that it is quite often available in an unadulterated form. It is not quite as pure as the European or Hong Kong heroin that has also been finding its way there, and it has been reported that attempts are made to disguise the pure No. 4 by adulterating it slightly and adding a colorant such as cocoa or instant coffee, when it can pass for Mexican. The Mafia, some Cubans, and, more recently, Chinese traffickers from the mainland have been appearing. This is not surprising, because for a number of years the Chinese Reds have maintained an important series of posts in Mexico that are, in part, related to espionage in the United States, also to guerrilla warfare and political activities, at least some of which have been connected with Cuba. As usual, the opiates traffic is closely interrelated. More recently, Chinese attention has been claimed by Canada, as already noted.

Canada, an unusually sparsely populated country, yet abounding with mineral and other riches, seems to have exerted a particular fascination on the Chinese Reds. There have been a number of circumstances that have favored them, such as the influence they have been able to wield invisibly both in that country and the United States. They have poured illegal immigrants into Canada, many of whom have been under orders to infiltrate into the United States over the long, undefended border, some taking heroin with them just as some of their precursors used to cross from North Korea to the South, often ending up in Japan. Estimates vary, but it is believed that some 30,000 have come in, most of whom have ended up in the United States. For the present the "control" is being wielded from Canada. The Chinese are active on the Eastern seaboard but the port of Vancouver is an especially active center.

The situation is likely to become even more troublesome when the impulse to increase trade with Red China has resulted in their acquisition of sizable numbers of Concordes or Boeing 707s or other long-range aircraft. When Shanghai and Vancouver or San Francisco are linked, the drug traffic may expand greatly.

Chapter 5
References and Footnotes

1. For overseas Chinese, see: Victor Purcell, *The Chinese in Southeast Asia* (London: Oxford University Press, 1951). Lea A. Williams, *The Fate of the Overseas Chinese in Southeast Asia* (New York: McGraw Hill, 1966). Gunther Barth, *Bitter Strength* (Cambridge, Mass.: Harvard University Press, 1964).
2. Richard Deverall, *Mao Tze-tung Stop This Dirty Opium Business* (Tokyo: Toyoh Printing and Bookbinding Co., 1954), p. 10.
3. *Ibid.*
4. Remarks of Henry J. Anslinger to UN Commission on Narcotics, April 1953, as quoted in the *Congressional Record*, August 4, 1971.
5. From Henry J. Anslinger and William Tompkins, *The Traffic in Narcotics* (New York: Funk & Wagnalls, 1953), pp. 93–94.
6. Statement quoted in Edward Hunter, *The Black Book on Red China* (Washington: Friends of Free China Association, 1958, p. 116.
7. *Ibid.*, p. 119.
8. The sources from which the data on the narcotics production and trading complex of Red China have been compiled are Hong Kong, Japan, Malaysia, and the Republic of China. The author has been able to avail himself of correspondence with a number of private contacts.
9. Frank Faso and Paul Meskil "Peking's Spies in America," *True* (magazine), July 1972.

6

Survey of the Current Pattern
of Action in Asia

One of the major dangers that lie hidden in war and conflict—one that is seldom recognized by statesmen and military planners—is that the protagonists, in the heat of the struggle, often begin to interchange their characteristics and end up by resembling each other. The Ukrainians, exposed to the full impact of conquering Mongol hordes, became Cossacks whose cavalry tactics began to resemble those of their adversaries. The subjugated princes of Suzdal-Moscow escaped from the Tartar yoke by using the Oriental duplicity they learned from their overlords, the Mongol Khans, whose very techniques and ambitions their descendants possess today. The English, impressed by the Welsh and their deadly practice with the long bow, became themselves a nation of bowmen as the French learned to their cost at Crécy and Agincourt. History is replete with innumerable examples of this strange phenomenon of conflict-induced interchange of characteristics. One of the more interesting and imaginative inquiries into the process was that highly suggestive and provocative book *The Roman and the Teuton* by Charles Kingsley. This work advances the idea that the Teutonic urge towards armed conquest that erupted in the two world wars that plagued the first half of the twentieth century can be traced back to the conquest of Rome by the early Teutons.

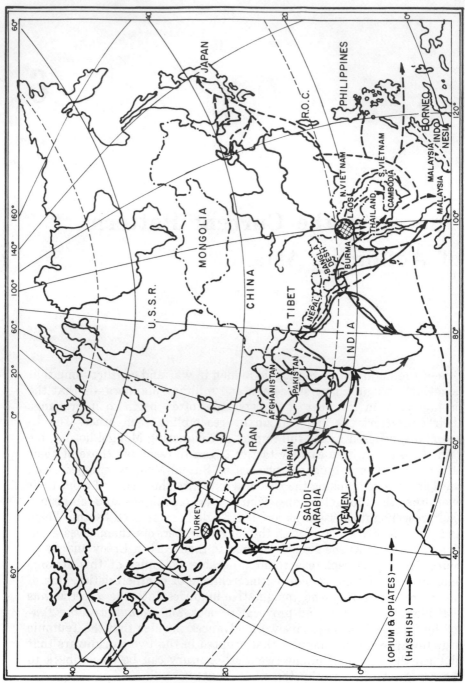

Asian Routes—Narcotics Traffic

(OPIUM & OPIATES) ‑‑‑
(HASHISH) ⟶

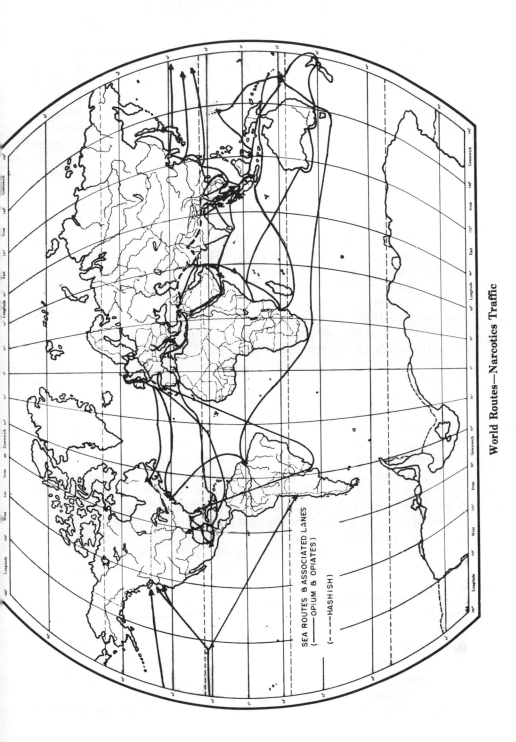

SEA ROUTES & ASSOCIATED LANES
(——— OPIUM & OPIATES)

(— — — HASHISH)

World Routes—Narcotics Traffic

235

Since the danger is a very real one, those who manage wars and have a high regard for their own national identity and values should be fully aware of this transposition. It is particularly important when one party to the conflict wishes to remain always on the defensive. This provides an aggressive opponent, who is thus able to retain the initiative, with the opportunity of impressing more of his own nature on his adversary than he would receive. It is especially the situation in the case of Communist-sponsored protracted conflict, doubly so because of the ideological impulse of Communists to proselytize. The effects of such missionary effort have been noted by observers of the French war in Indo-China and the subsequent one in Algeria.

In their professional zeal to match their adversaries on their own terms, the French military, without fully realizing the transformation that had come upon them, were so infected by the insidious and contagious thought of Mao Tse-tung that they ranked among his most assiduous disciples in the practice of "La Guerre Révolutionnaire," which they attempted to use as a defensive instrument in the "Peoples' War" that claimed their attention. Most regrettably they went so far with the ideology and the cult of ruthless and unbridled violence characterizing this mode of warfare that they adopted—officially be it noted—the practice of torturing prisoners, a circumstance that became more widely known during the Algerian War than the practitioners of this variety of special warfare would have wished.

That more of the revolutionary dynamic of the Maoist canon had transferred itself to "les Paras," for instance, than could readily have been foreseen by the French Establishment was evidenced by the very real fear of a military coup d'état in metropolitan France itself. When matters of this kind are under review it should not be forgotten that the Chinese Reds have specialized, probably more than any other military power, in the seductive art of turning their opponents round, and even acquiring effective command over them by the strategy and tactics of the United Front.

If this remarkable characteristic of our Asian opponents is borne in mind, it is perhaps less surprising that one finds whole sections of the community in Massachusetts who have evidenced a desire to go and live among the poor inoffensive North Vietnamese who have been treated with such violence by what they fondly believe to be unprovoked U.S. aggression in Asia, or that whole sections of the student population and younger generation in the United States are already militant and active fellow-travellers of the murderous Viet Cong. Perhaps phenomena of this kind, which are of course by no means confined to the United States, will eventually be recognized for what they really are—the propagation of world revolutionary action by extremely

236

CHINESE COMMUNIST GUERRILLA BASES FOR GUERRILLA AND POLITICAL WARFARE OPERATIONS - EXTENSION AND APPLICATION TO OPIUM AND NARCOTICS TRAFFIC.

I. GUERRILLA WARFARE AREA (SCHEMATIC)

SUPPLIES AND SUPPORT
HOME TERRITORY

⊠ SANCTUARY
Ⓢ STRONGHOLD
FB FORWARD BASE
GWI GUERRILLA WORKSHOPS & INDUSTRIES

OFFENSIVE OPS.
TARGET COUNTRY
OFFENSIVE OPS.
FLANKING NEUTRAL COUNTRY

ORIGIN AND SYMBOLIC ARCHTYPE CHINGKANGSHAN. THE FULLY DEVELOPED VERSION PLANNED TO STRADDLE BOUNDARIES PERMITTING ACCESS TO TARGET AREAS AND TO IMPLANTED 'INFRASTRUCTURES' AND PARALLEL 'HIERARCHIES' (DOCTRINE-DOMESTIC REVOLUTIONARY WARFARE)

THE GUERRILLA WARFARE AREA AS A BASE FOR CONQUEST

A. EARLY EXAMPLE (WW II)
'SHEN-KAN-NING'
SHENSI-KANSU-NINGHSIA
BORDER AREA. A BLUE
PRINT FOR REPRODUCTION
AND EXTENSION OF COMMUNIST
POWER IN CHINA AND ULTIMATE
CONQUEST.

. ORIGINAL PROTOTYPE MODIFIED IN
CASE OF HUAI-'AI-HSI AREA.
HUIPANG-TAIKANG-HSINHUA ('HONAN')
FOR OPIUM RAISING... NARCOTICS ANALOG
TO CHINGKANGSHAN.

OFFENSIVE OPS OPERATIONS
GUERRILLA TACTICS
TERROR - PROPAGANDA
ORGANIZATION OF
REVOLUTIONARY
MOVEMENT

SUPPLY BASE
N. VIETNAM
OPS. VIETNAM
LAOS
SUPPLY ROUTES
HO CHI MINH TRAIL

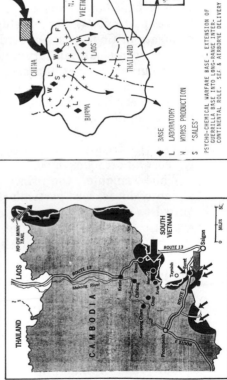

IV. THE GOLDEN TRIANGLE (SCHEMATIC) NARCOTICS BASE

◆ BASE
L LABORATORY
W WORKS PRODUCTION
S 'SALES'

PSYCHO-CHEMICAL WARFARE BASE - EXTENSION OF
GUERRILLA BASE INTO LONG-RANGE INTER-
CONTINENTAL ROLE. SEF & AIRBORNE DELIVERY

CHINA, BURMA, LAOS, N. VIETNAM, THAILAND, S. VIETNAM

HK, JAPAN, HAWAII, CANADA, U.S.
'MILITARY POSTINGS'

'COUNTRYSIDE' VS. 'CITIES'
'CONDITIONING' LEADING TO DEMORALIZATION &
FRAGMENTATION OF TARGET SOCIETY URBAN
GUERRILLA WARFARE & REVOLUTION.

SIMILAR ARRANGEMENTS FOR LAOS, CAMBODIA & THAILAND.
(DOCTRINE: PROJECTION OF REVOLUTIONARY WARFARE - NATIONAL
LIBERATION MOVEMENTS OPIUM USED AS A FORM OF CURRENCY AS A
MEANS OF DEADENING AND CORRUPTING OPPOSITION.)

III. 'MAP ILLUSTRATING APPLICATION OF DOCTRINE OF GUERRILLA BASES IN INDO-CHINA.

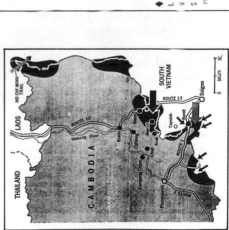

THAILAND, LAOS, HO CHI MINH TRAIL, CAMBODIA, SOUTH VIETNAM
ROUTE 13, Mekong River, Saigon, Phnompenh, Kompong Cham, Kratie

MILES 50

skilled and subtle exponents of the art of overcoming the established order. In this process, the political use of drugs has been playing a particularly prominent role of late.

Since there is rather widespread public agreement—not only among the free citizenry of the Western nations and their allies in Eastern countries, but even among the subjugated Communist masses—that the characteristics of the Communist power against which we have been contending are not really for us, it is most important to recognize the need for great circumspection against acquiring more of those characteristics than have already appeared in our midst. The fact should not be ignored that France, the U.S.S.R., the United States, and China all have experienced revolutionary action at critically formative historic periods and that, in consequence, there exists latent potential that may erupt when it is no longer desirable and least wanted. The French experiences in Indo-China and North Africa can, in short, be portents for the United States.

It is well known, for example, as often happens in war, that an alliance of expediency was made in the '50s between the French Army (more particularly its intelligence services) and certain criminal elements in Cholon, a vice-ridden suburb of Saigon. The effectiveness of such secret paramilitary underworld enterprises as the Binh Xuyen was so great in what appeared to be essential security operations and in breaking up the cellular Communist substructure of South Vietnamese society that a new military trend was started. General Salan and Col. Trinquier were the officers whose names were most associated with this change, which involved the mobilization and training of special service troops, "Forces Suppletifs," on an entirely new and certainly most unorthodox model.

While Trinquier, the principal architect of these developments and a man of ideas, was particularly well versed in the kind of tactics required to oppose Communist uprisings with minimal resources, and was also inspired by ideals of patriotism, some of the steps that he took in Indo-China opened a whole Pandora's box that has not yet been closed. Unfortunately, this often happens when the doctrines of "the end justifies the means" and "necessity knows no law" become fully embodied in military doctrine. When leadership is principled these moral traps can be evaded.

One of Trinquier's more interesting moves, when faced with difficult problems of economic and logistic support to be obtained through regular channels, was to divert some of the profits of the burgeoning opium trade of Indo-China into the military coffers of the MACG (acronym for French special forces in Vietnam: Mixed Airborne Commando Group). In particular, he was out to gain the loyalty of the strategically placed and doughty hill tribesmen on the borders of Laos (the Meo) by buying their opium.

The underlying tragedy in this aberration, which in itself seemed but a minor one at the beginning, is that with it a dike collapsed that before long permitted a flood of opium through Thailand into Indo-China. It was a flood of unprecedented proportions and momentum although, of course, the traffic itself on a large scale was nothing new. The rate of the effusion from its sources and the pattern of flow throughout the region and beyond was what had been radically changed.

The increase in momentum was spurred by the enormously improved communications pattern provided for the traffic by military participation and by the greatly increased accessibility of Indo-China. This last came about with the unprecedented volume of air traffic, both military and international, in and out of Bangkok and Saigon, now among the busiest airports in the world. Within the more recent period after the United States supplanted the French in Indo-China, there has grown up an even further increased air traffic and a corresponding multiplicity of airfields.[1]

Here it may be noted, parenthetically, that that extremely well-informed specialist in the art of irregular warfare, Major General Edward Geary Lansdale, writing in his recently published book *In the Midst of Wars*, puts a rather charitable interpretation on the French military opium policy. In that work, he states

> Some memories of my Indochina visit* have stuck with me. There was the hasty trip to a foreign legion outpost on the Plaine des Jarres to observe a sudden Vietminh invasion of the area— only to discover that the Communist invasion had been called off when the French preclusively bought up the opium crop in the region and thus denied it to the enemy. (Ever since, I have noted how Communist military forces of the North Vietnamese or Pathet Lao became active in that region every year at opium harvest time. The opium now pays for many of their battalions and divisions.[2])

Lansdale was certainly no friend of the French in Vietnam and was cordially disliked by them, so that this testimony is valuable.

In dealing with the important matter of French, and even U.S., involvement in the expansion of the logistics pattern of narcotics delivery through Southeast Asia, it is highly significant to realize that the visible forms of the traffic, its diffusion, and its ramifications, both inter-

---

*Lansdale was in Vietnam on a short visit in 1953. He was based on the Philippines at the time.

nally within the region and externally in the direction of its delivery, are effects rather than causes.

Some deeply concerned but incompletely informed students of the problem have accepted the myth of Red Chinese noninvolvement and believe the entire source of the floods of opium, morphine, and heroin flowing through Bangkok and Saigon on their way to their remoter customers is located within the Golden Triangle. This they believe to be both a growing and refining area that is now the world's greatest, since Turkish opium is on its way out and, supposedly, the heroin industry in Marseilles is also on the decline. These are very speculative and misleading assumptions.

On the contrary, almost all the evils that came out of the recesses of Pandora's box came from far beyond the northern borders of the Golden Triangle, which may be likened only to the lid of that fatal receptacle. None can deny that the lid provides its own contribution, since opium is grown in quantity in the Triangle. Its tonnage has been mounting and some now place it as high as 1,000 tons per year. Morphine has been produced there for some years and there are now supposed to be some plants producing heroin. Nevertheless, the scale and nature of those facilities, which have been installed there only recently, could not possibly account for the great heroin "epidemic" that struck the U.S. troops in South Vietnam with such fury in 1970.

In order to achieve the results that took place then, the most detailed planning and "consumer research" (i.e., intelligence) must have been employed. The standardization of the product, the uniformity of packaging in neat plastic vials (without brand labels), the faultless synchronization that characterized the operation, distinguished it clearly for what it was—a military offensive. It was also launched as a reprisal after the Cambodian expedition and during the ensuing Laotian adventures. It fell on the troops when they were most exposed to an assault of this nature, during the period of intense Vietnamization and large-scale withdrawal of U.S. effectives.

It would not have been possible to conduct this operation without large buffer stocks of heroin—stocks of such size they could not be accounted for by the four small-scale heroin plants that have been alleged to be located at Ban Houei Sai, Ban Houei Tap, Tachilek, and Vientiane.

The supply in question could only have come from a major source—one established for some time, willing to dispose of this valuable material at cost price or even at a loss, and that had been able, over a period of time, to build up an extensive buffer stock of the purest heroin. The only source that could conform to these criteria was the

Special Products Trading Company of Red China, a source that has been disregarded altogether for political reasons.

In order to understand and interpret the lessons to be drawn from the pattern of action discussed below it is necessary to know that:

(1) The main source of most of the opium and narcotics entering the Southeast Asia region is Red China.

(2) The Golden Triangle plays a vital part in the delivery of the above main flow of narcotics towards its remoter objectives and possesses the character of an advanced base in a guerrilla area. This provides a complex that screens the origins and the politico-military import of the traffic.

(3) Southeast Asia, having been targeted for acquisition and control by the Chinese Reds, is, therefore, being exposed to the full impact of the narcotics menace; and that this takes the form, as intended, of addiction on the part of its chosen victims, of wholesale corruption and connivance by criminals (often highly placed) and of greatly misguided individuals, some of whom, regrettably, are supposed to be on "our side."

This is an effect, not a cause. It can be closely compared to the effects obtained in North China when the Japanese special-service organizations began softening up their target areas or to similar actions by the Chinese Reds and the North Koreans when they used narcotics offensively in Korea.

(4) This region now indeed represents the major threat of the long-range Red objectives.

Heroin and other hard drugs are a comparatively new problem in South Vietnam so far as the U.S. forces are concerned. It began in serious fashion in 1970. In addition to air operations by smugglers, now beginning to be better understood, in spite of serious deficiencies in air-traffic control, a great deal of transport of drugs is also being carried out by sea. The whole long South Vietnamese coastline is suspect at every point, and a good deal of heroin has been coming in on fishing boats and on ordinary merchant vessels. There are also a number of suspicious craft that favor Quinonh, Nhatrang, and Danang as unloading points and that appear suddenly and then rapidly pull out to unknown destinations. They may operate illegally from Singapore, Hong Kong, or even Taiwan. Direct transshipment is unnecessary and the technology of mooring submerged "draccones" (buoyed containers), etc., is sufficiently advanced to provide sure methods of retrieval and further forward movement to onshore delivery points.

It is generally accepted that most of the control, policy planning, and financial aspects of the traffic are the concern of a shadowy community of Chinese race. They take control of the opium (or narcotics) as it leaves the hill tribesmen who grow it in the Shan States or similar tribal areas, or who receive it from Yunnan in Southwest China. They arrange for its transport, escort, and processing where necessary, and deliver it to marketing areas and "rings." By means of a widespread network of "clan" or "Tong" connections extended throughout Southeast Asia, they dispatch and market it, while bribing officials as necessary, and often at the highest levels, to protect their operations.

In this regard, accusations have been leveled at a good many senior South Vietnamese, specifically against General Ngo Dzu, commander of Military Region II, and even against former Vice-President Nguyen Cao Ky and President Thieu. None of these have been substantiated and have drawn strong denials.

According to *The New York Times* of July 17, 1971, President Nguyen Van Thieu described as "shocking and slanderous" an NBC report that alleged he was using funds derived from the illegal drug traffic to advance his election campaign. His press made the following statement:

> This concrete example of journalistic irresponsibility which enables sensationalism to prevail over truthfulness is a disgrace to the journalistic profession and, willingly, or not, has helped the Communistic saboteurs who have been trying to undermine the prestige of the Republic of Vietnam.

Phil Brady, broadcasting for NBC, charged both Thieu and Ky with profiting from the drug traffic and that the South Vietnamese police were pushing drugs. He stated that the biggest pusher was Lt. Gen. Dan Van Quang, Thieu's special assistant for military and intelligence affairs. Brady accused Ky of having made a fortune from smuggling gold and narcotics while in charge of the air force. However, during his vice-presidency, according to Brady, he was supposed to have delegated these activities to trusted air force associates.

United States reactions in Vietnam were negative, claiming that there seemed to be no evidence to support such allegations. It was noted that similar statements had been made about other Vietnamese figures in the past but had been discovered to be unfounded. They admitted that the traffic must have an immunity conferred upon it from high levels. Accusations against Maj. Gen. Ngo Dzu were under investigation. According to Brady, Dzu was a scapegoat. These serious charges against Dzu and others followed the visit of Representative Robert H. Steele to Vietnam.

It is, of course, important to recognize that a psycho-chemical operation such as we are witnessing in Vietnam needs to have, in order to be fully successful:

(1) Complete clandestinity; e.g., the actual sources of drugs should be concealed as far as possible or be attributable to other sources such as neutral or "allied" countries.
(2) A highly organized propaganda and rumor network, providing "disinformation" of a kind able to implicate or to compromise personnel on the opposing side, preferably at high levels.
(3) Vulnerability on the other side. This is a condition that can be fostered by policies of preparatory conditioning through study of drug habits or recruits. The use of lead-in drugs such as marijuana assists the development of addiction to harder drugs. This vulnerability can be and has been fostered by publicity and propaganda methods.
(4) A military situation in which large numbers of the opposing troops are often on inactive duty and there exists either a maximum flow of incoming draftees, being the replacements for large numbers of returnees from the theatre, or a large rundown.
(5) A condition on the home front of the opponent in which price differentials can impose an intolerable situation on addicts, who can be enrolled in clandestine activities favoring an enemy on their return.

Considerations of this kind obviously require that the utmost caution must be exercised in listening to rumors that are passed concerning allied personnel of whatever rank, and against the alleged sources of drugs. Particular vigilance is obviously necessary against involvement, conscious or otherwise, in assisting either transport or distribution of drugs that may affect the morale or efficiency of U.S. forces.

Often U.S. personnel become engaged in the traffic and are subject to prosecution. One such case was that of Major Delbert W. Fleener, USAF, a much-decorated pilot who had flown Ambassador Ellsworth Bunker and Gen. William Westmoreland. Fleener had been arrested because he was suspected of having transported 859 pounds of opium between February 21 and 24, 1971. Charged and convicted of having ferried the drug between Bangkok and Saigon, a court in Salt Lake City was obliged to consider a sentence of up to fifty-years imprisonment.*

*See Appendix VII.

In a recent report by the U.S. Provost Marshal of the Military Command in Vietnam that was submitted to Ambassador Bunker and General Creighton Abrams, there are observations on addiction, placing it at about 10 percent to 15 percent (on heroin). In the report are the following statements:

> Although there is not sufficient proof, at this time, to warrant a discussion of individual names, it is quite apparent to American law enforcement personnel that the degree of sophistication in which the traffic in drugs—especially heroin—has been achieved, could not exist without at least the tacit approval, if not the active support, of senior members of GVN [Government of Vietnam].
>
> Masterminding this trade are the financiers, a group which may comprise high level, influential political figures, government leaders or moneyed ethnic Chinese members of the criminal syndicates now flourishing.[3]

An interesting analysis of the problems connected with narcotics trading within the context of the war was furnished by *The New York Times* of June 6, 1971. In part it purports to be based on CIA reports. In these, the CIA claims to have identified about 21 opium refineries in the "border area of Burma, Laos and Thailand" that "provide a constant flow of heroin to American troops in South Vietnam." These plants are understood to be operated and defended in Burma and Thailand by insurgent armies and their leaders.

In Burma, the interest involved is the puppet Shan State system that has been built up under Red Chinese auspices while, in Thailand, it is the Thai Liberation Movement under the same direction. In Laos, it is believed that elements of the Royal Laotian Army are actually involved. In this region, the Triangle, which also includes a part of Yunnan, are grown most of the opium and narcotics finding their way to South Vietnam and other Southeast Asian countries. Exclusive of Chinese production, about 700 tons per year are grown in the region while 400 tons per year are grown in Burma alone. These tonnages are being expanded and the overall production for 1971 may have reached 1,000 tons.

Apparently, the processing plants and refineries that, up to 1970, had been producing refined opium, morphine base, and No. 3 smoking heroin have been converting their processes to deliver No. 4 High Grade Pure White Heroin. The change is said to have coincided with the phase of the Vietnam War involving Vietnamization and the disengagement of U.S. forces. The immobilization of large numbers of troops in base areas, awaiting repatriation; the combination of purchasing power plus increased leisure; the mounting frustration and discontent of the men under psychological stresses induced by propaganda, have all contributed to the formation and development of an exceptional market.

It is difficult to resist the conclusion that the augmentation of the traffic and the availability of the strongest heroin at unaccountably low prices are a part of the enemy doctrine of psycho-chemical warfare intended to produce addiction among as many GIs as possible and to have them carry this back with them to the United States.

It was stated in *The New York Times* of June 6, 1971:

> Most of the narcotics buyers in the "Tri-Border Area" are ethnic Chinese who pool their purchases, but no large syndicate appears to be involved. The opium, morphine base and heroin purchased in this area finds its way eventually to Bangkok, Vientiane and Luang Prabang, where additional processing may take place before delivery to Saigon, Hong Kong and other international markets.[4]

There is widespread awareness of an unceasing traffic in raw opium and morphine base from northeast Burma and Thailand, smuggled into Bangkok and sent from there to Hong Kong by fishing trawlers. Such vessels, carrying cargoes of one to three tons, move at the rate of about one a day to Lamma Island (near Hong Kong and under Chinese Communist jurisdiction) where there is transshipment into Hong Kong by junks based on that port.

> Opium and derivatives move through Laos and are transferred from the Mekong River refineries by river craft and vehicles to Ban Houei Sai, further downstream on the Mekong from Laos, and are transferred from there to Luang Prabang or Vientiane. A considerable amount of the Laotian-produced narcotics is smuggled into Saigon.
>
> An increased demand for No. 4 heroin also appears to be reflected in the steady rise in the price; for example, in mid-April 1971, the price in the Tachilek (Burma) area of a kilo of No. 4 heroin was reported to be $1,780 as compared with $1,240 in September 1970.[5]

The CIA report noted by *The New York Times* rather strangely does not refer to availability of Red Chinese opium and narcotics to the transport and distribution networks, although it is well known that Yunnan Province is a major exporter. Again, according to the CIA report in question:

Northeast Burma is identified as the largest producer and processer of raw opium in the border area. Burma's #4 refiner is located in the Tachilek area, and in 1970 converted 30 tons of raw opium into refined opium, morphine base and heroin.

The opium harvested in Shan, Wa and Kokang area is picked by caravans that are put together by the major insurgent leaders in these areas. The caravans, which can include up to 600 horses and donkeys and 300–400 men, take the opium on the southeasterly journey to the processing plants that lie along the Mekong River in the Tachilek-Mai Sai, Thailand, Ban Houei Sai, Laos areas. Caravans carrying up to 16 metric tons have been reported.[6]

Twenty-one refineries in this area have been identified, seven of which are reported to be capable of processing the opium to the heroin stage:

> The most important are located in the areas around Tachilek (Burma); Ban Houei Sai (Laos) and Nam Keung (Laos) and Mae Salong (Thailand).
> The best known, if not the largest of these factories is the one at Ban Houei Tap (Laos) near Ban Houei Sai which is believed to be capable of processing some 100 kilos of raw opium per day.[7]

It is known that the opium and its derivatives crossing Thailand from Burma, en route to Bangkok, proceeds out of such towns in northern Thailand as Chieng Rai, Chieng Mai, Lampang, and Tak by a variety of means of surface transport by road and river.

> The opium is packed by the growers and traded to itinerant Chinese merchants who transport it to major collecting centers particularly near Lashio and Ken Tung.[8]

There is, of course, widespread fear of Red China in all the neighboring countries of Southeast Asia. Thus, quite apart from the extremely subtle and skillful methods of the Chinese Reds to conceal their involvement, there is an effective information barrier created by that fear. This attitude is shared even by such well-informed and determined governments as that of Hong Kong, which, for obvious reasons connected with its relations with the mainland, consistently plays down the magnitude of the Chinese effort and the role of the Colony as a principal entrepôt.

An interesting comment appeared in the *Washington Star* of January 5, 1972, which quoted Mrs. Helen Bentley, Chairman of the U.S. Maritime Commission, when she referred to the statement of Chou En-lai to Nasser in 1965 that was mentioned by Hassanein Heikal, the editor of *El Ahram:*

Chou En-lai told Nasser the American soldiers are trying opium and we are helping them. We are planting the best kinds of opium especially for the American soldiers in Vietnam. We want them to have a big army in Vietnam which will be hostage to us and we want to demoralize them. The effect which this demoralization is going to have on the United States will be far greater than anyone realizes.[9]

Reference was also made in the same issue to a friend of Mrs. Bentley's in Saigon, who wrote to her:

If profit is the incentive (for narcotics coming from North Vietnam) and with the high unemployment rate here—about 20 percent or more—then why is an uncut drug sold at cost when cutting would increase the profit margin?[10]

In regard to the revelations made by *The New York Times* based on CIA reports, while it would be a logical development to expect the installation of heroin-processing laboratories in the tribal areas, there are grounds to doubt the probability of such a large number of installations designed to turn out No. 4-grade heroin in such regions. The production of morphine base from crude opium is a comparatively crude process that could, certainly, be carried out there on a wide scale. However, the degree of chemical sophistication required to supervise No. 4-grade heroin production is unusually high. Also, there is a continual demand for chemicals and equipment that are not readily available in such outlying areas and would be conspicuous if they were.

While it would certainly be of value to the Chinese Reds to create the impression that an important opium-processing and refining industry has grown up in the Triangle area, and they themselves have shown great skill in organizing "guerrilla industries" (some of which are quite sophisticated), there is still room for considerable doubt that the Chinese Reds have gone to the trouble to organize the complex described above. It would, however, be of the utmost value to their own official attitude that they are in no way involved to have the account widely believed.

This is, of course, only a part of an elaborate worldwide campaign of misinformation and information control relating to the problem of narcotics as intensified by massive Red Chinese participation in the international traffic. The campaign extends high into U.S. Government circles, where extremely thorough measures are being taken, for political reasons connected with the "New China Policy," to prevent the public from being informed about China's actions.

In view of the numerous deaths from drug abuse that had been taking place in Southeast Asia, the army instituted a system of amnesty for drug takers who would turn themselves in, and a Department of Defense general directive affecting all service personnel was issued in July 1971.

Very full details of the amnesty, recuperation, and detoxification programs have appeared in the press and much emphasis had been placed on medical testing, urinalysis, and so forth. The processes, aimed at prevention and cure, have been well thought out and quite effective but they have been adopted much too late. At times they have been run in such a manner as to have an impact on morale. Like all measures of this kind, these programs have tended to generate evasions and they certainly cannot, as yet, be regarded as being foolproof.

Burma, Thailand, and Laos

In Burma, the component of the Golden Triangle is the Shan and Wa States. They are a primary source of opium (estimated at about 800 tons per year), and a transit area for Chinese opium from Yunnan coming down the Burma Road or otherwise. During British imperial rule they had been managed on a tribal basis through the sawbwas or chiefs and run by skilled and practiced methods of indirect rule. That these practices were highly successful was proved during World War II when the tribesmen of the hills, who felt themselves to be utterly different from and indeed alien to the Burmese of the South, gave unstintedly of their loyalty and friendship to the Allies fighting the Japanese in their country.

Their heroism and military prowess as irregulars played a vital part in the recovery of Burma and its opportunity to gain independence. But they were ill-requited for their efforts and have, in general, been at cross-purposes with the Central Government of the Union of Burma ever since. This situation has provided the Chinese Communists with a great advantage in their attempts to penetrate Burma.

Northern Burma, where the Chinese have been operating for the most part, differs completely from Thailand in that the former is part of a succession state to the colonial system in Southeast Asia, while northern Thailand is part of a country that has been sovereign and independant for centuries, having been preserved from foreign subjugation by Anglo-French rivalries that the Thais were quick to exploit.

However, all the components of the Golden Triangle south of the Yunnan border have two common characteristics:

(1) A considerable reduction in the administrative authority of the central government in each area.

(2) A significant permeation of Communist influence by means of "United Fronts" or paramilitary organizations, all of which have the objective of destroying and supplanting the central government.

In all components, Red China has been able to intrude into areas of considerable strategic value that have enabled the Chinese to use communications routes to support their military operations in South Vietnam and elsewhere. The Chinese have been in effective control of the area, a circumstance that has permitted growth of the opium poppy on the widest scale, which, in turn, has provided them with the means of controlling most of the populations. They have also been able to augment their own volume of opium production, possessing thus a strategically positioned base for worldwide export and diffusion of the combined production of opiates, in themselves the key to widespread aggression through espionage, terrorism, and guerrilla warfare.

The Chinese Reds have not been the only Chinese on the scene. After the collapse of the Chinese Nationalist Government in 1949, a number of its troops, surviving units of the Eighth Army under General Li Mi and elements of the Ninety-third Division, Twenty-sixth Army, retreated into Burma and Indo-China.

Of these, the part that moved into Indo-China was interned by the French, but the troops who went to Burma decided to remain as settlers (or, more correctly, "squatters"), using Meng Hsat near Tachilek as their base. The Burmese government was not at all in favor of this and there was a period of hostilities during which the Chinese bickered with Burmese forces based on Kengtung.

But the latter were too preoccupied with their own operations against tribal rebellions in the Shan States to pay much attention to their Chinese visitors, who were, in any event, rather a formidable proposition to tackle. These former Chinese Nationalists, or "KMT" (Kuomintang) troops as they have generally been known, were, in the early '50s, deployed in the Wa States (Mong Mao) and the Kokang Area. After a few diversionary and harassing excursions into Yunnan, which proved somewhat disappointing to them, the KMT stragglers began to settle down to a garrison life in Kengtung. They are now more aptly known as CIF, Chinese Irregular Forces.

At first the Ne Win Government had been seriously alarmed. It was trying to obtain a modus vivendi with its dangerous northern neighbor and felt that any such plans would be impossible of achievement if they harbored an alien force that used Burmese territory as a base for sorties into Yunnan. On the other hand, when the CIF forces changed their posture and opted for a more static existence, the Burmese were even prepared to concede, privately, that their guests could fulfill a useful role in defending the frontier, which was becoming extraordinarily vulnerable because of tribal disaffection. Besides, if they resorted to the classical means of paying their way—the kind always practiced by Chinese warlords, cultivating and supporting the transit of opium through the area that they controlled—this might even bring other advantages.

It is well known that practically the whole economy in these remote upland areas has been based on poppy cultivation, since other agrarian productivity is remarkably low. Thus, what has happened in recent years is that there has been a very marked intensification of the effort put into poppy cultivation in Burma, for the following reasons:

(1) The independence of Burma and the removal of the restraints placed on poppy culture by British District Officers has opened the way to increased cultivation.
(2) As a result of the political changes mentioned above, there has been an extremely intensive clash between postcolonial Burmese nationalism (i.e., Rangoon) and tribal independence movements resisting central authority.
(3) That clash has been exploited by the Chinese Reds, who have had their own ideas how it could benefit them through the hold they could develop in the Shan and Wa States by opium production.
(4) More recently, a market of wholly astonishing dimensions has been opening up as a result of the arrival of hundreds of thousands of U.S. troops in South Vietnam and the opening of a vast U.S.-dollar pool in Southeast Asia, together with enormously improved channels reaching to the United States itself. The skills of Chinese promoters and marketers of opiates in meeting this opportunity has highly impressed the hill peoples.

In the Shan States there has always been a history of rugged individualism and disaffection shared by such peoples as the Nagas (who live in both Burma and Assam), the Kachins, Karens, and others. By the late 1950s and early '60s, an unpopular policy of Burmanization had produced a primitive insurgent movement that was led by the interesting General Sao Gnar Kham, a Shan chieftain who was killed in December 1964, after which a good deal of strength went out of the movement. Before that, the Shan National Army, SNA, had gone in for intensive opium cultivation and trading with the objective of buying arms and equipment for the movement. While this seemed to be a complete economic success, it proved, as always, double-edged.

Although they were able to procure the arms they needed, they found that the opium with which they were purchased was, as usual, a source of discord, alienating officers and tribal chiefs from their subordinates, promoting rivalries and quarrels over profits, creating chaos and decline.

One of their most successful leaders was Chan Shee-fu, who became far more interested in the opium traffic than in the nationalism the drug was originally supposed to serve. Chan set himself up in a particularly prolific growing area at Vhing Nhu in the Wa States where, as an independent operator, he is said to have established a morphine plant. In attempting to export on a large scale to Thailand, he soon found himself at odds with the CIF opium guerrillas.

Originally there were about 12,000 KMT troops under General Li Mi. Their posture in North Burma and their activities hostile to Red China were an embarrassment to the Burmese government, which made representations in the UN. That body passed a resolution in 1953 condemning the Chinese emigres in Burma and demanding that they leave. General Li Mi left for Taiwan in 1961 and about half his men were evacuated as well, leaving the other half, now completely disowned by the Republic of China, to their own devices (almost all connected with opium in one way or another).

Those who stayed remained in position after this split, subdivided into three independent factions. The sector that they occupied together from then on was a strip of the Burma/Thai border stretching from Amphur Fang to Amphur Mae Chang. They are constituted as follows:

(a) Chinese Third Army.
     About 5,500 strong—led by General Li Wen-huan (former commander of the Nationalist Third Army).
(b) Chinese Fifth Army.
     About 3,000 strong—led by General Tuan Shi-wen (former commander of Nationalist Fifth Army).
(c) First Independent Unit.
     About 500 strong—led by General Ma Ching-ko.

These three military forces and their generals have trading and political contacts with all governments in the area: Burma, Thailand, Laos, Cambodia, and Vietnam. All are well armed and have impressive inventories of light automatics, submachine guns, mortars, and rocket launchers, plus the usual small arms and grenades. They also possess large numbers of vehicles: trucks and jeeps, motor craft and aircraft, as well as mule transport. The CIF organization has a record of fairly continuous minor operations against Shan leaders, such as Chan Shee-fu, who has been regarded by them as a dangerous competitor and a man consumed with delusions of grandeur. They also fight against Chinese Communist forces who have made occasional forays within the area. In April 1971 there was a battle between the CIF troops and the People's Liberation Army. The latter intruded into Burma and attempted to pick up an opium convoy with 400 men that was moving from Kengtung to Chang Dao in Thailand, where there is reputed to be a factory. All the equipment of the CIF, except for some obtained in the early 1950s from U.S. channels, has been acquired through opium sales or transport.

The CIF troops often have serious differences and armed clashes with local tribesmen who grow and attempt to convoy their own opium. The Haws are a case in point; there is said to have been a fierce battle with them in 1967 in which 400 were killed. In 1970 there were reports of similar trouble with the Meos. Later, in September 1971, the CIF made a foray into Thailand, ostensibly to assist the Thai government against Meos whom they alleged to be heavily infiltrated with Communist agents. That may well have been true, but it also may have been slightly unnerving to Bangkok which is anxious not to rock the boat. Almost all Asian governments who know they are on the menu are deeply concerned by the U.S. withdrawal from Asia and do not wish to provoke the Chinese Reds unnecessarily.

Another hazard that the CIF troops sometimes have to face is the KKY, a sort of Home Guard that the Burmese Government has established in Kengtung. This situation is made even more complicated by the fact that these units, raised to oppose Shan tribal insurgency, have themselves become involved in the all-pervasive opium business. Indeed, it is said that the KKY own a refinery at Kwang Htat (Burma) that produces No. 3 heroin. The Tachilek area is reputed to harbor several heroin refineries, the largest being at Kwang Htat. Three others are supposed to exist, run by Chinese, one of which is two miles northwest of Hawng Luk while another is at the Nam Hok River four miles north of Mong Ko. A third lies at the junction of the Nam Hok with the Mekong. All are on Burmese territory and have been set up, it is said, quite recently because the Laotian Government, under U.S. pressure, has cracked down on operations in its own territory at Phong Saly.

Not all Laotian refining capacity has been eliminated as yet and there still may be two installations—at Luang Prabang, the old capital, and at Sayaboury. It is also reported that Generals Tuan and Li Wen have refineries of their own in North Thailand on Tam Ngo and Dae Salong mountains. "Pink" heroin or concentrated morphine base and "white" No. 4 heroin are made locally. This list sounds impressive and many are now being led to believe that the world's center of heroin manufacture has shifted into the Triangle because a campaign of publicity has been launched to that effect. In fact, none of this activity fits in with the timing of the surge of heroin deliveries to the U.S. troops in Southeast Asia. That could only have come from larger, longer-established sources that have profited by the existence of a screen of small, "low profile," but nevertheless discernible plants in this deceptive region.

The "Plain of Jars" in Laos has been in the news over the years. Western followers of Laotian events have been puzzled as they have tried to follow the bewildering steps of the princely saraband in that disputed domain where Prince Souvanna Phouma and his half-brother Prince Souvannouvong have often been locked in a strangely repetitious form of indecisive combat.

Actually this contest has by no means been as meaningless as it has appeared because, apart from Laos' strategic value as an annex to the neighboring Ho Chi Minh trail and the defended flank of that line of supply into South Vietnam, it is also an opium-growing area. The battles that have often been waged there, in which General Vang Pao, the leader of "L'Armée Sécrète," has been a participant, have quite clearly been connected with the poppy harvest, a major objective for all concerned. On our side it has been a matter of "denials."

An excellent description of the situation in Laos has recently been given by General Walt in his interesting testimony to the Senate Internal Security Subcommittee:

> General WALT: Right up at the northern extreme of the Laotian territory. The area includes Phong Saly Province in the far north, Samnueu Province in the northeast, and the Plaine des Jarres in Xiengkhoang Province. There was a time when these producing areas were divided more or less evenly between the Meos under Pathet Lao or Communist influence and the Meos loyal to the Government in Vientiane. But as the Pathet Lao, with heavy North Vietnamese support, have extended their areas of control, the anti-Communist Meos have been forced out of their opium lands and onto the plains so that today the opium-growing areas of Laos are overwhelmingly under Communist control. The opium agriculture

in these areas, like all other agriculture, is under the village management of Hanoi-trained cadres.[11]

(Note: with matters as they are at present 90 percent of the opium-growing areas in question are under Communist control.)

General WALT: In addition to the locally produced opium which was picked up from the hill people by ethnic Chinese entrepreneurs, horse and mule caravans brought large quantities of opium into Laos from Burma. The opium was moved to processing laboratories at Ban Houei Sai and other centers; then the opium, morphine and heroin was moved out, generally by plane, to Thailand, Vietnam, and Hong Kong.

Why did the Laotian Government not move sooner to deal with the opium traffic in its country? There are several reasons that help to explain the lag, sir.

The first reason is that, until recently, the Laotian attitude towards opium was as tolerant as were Western attitudes 100 years ago. Opium was not a serious problem among the Laotian peoples and the heroin problem was nonexistent. There was no law against growing opium or merchandising it and no law against processing opium into morphine or heroin. And so, a handful of senior officers, including Gen. Ouan Rathikone, former commander of the Laotian Army, could line their own pockets by engaging in the opium trade. General Rathikone was retired from the Army last July.

Second, there was the Government's almost total preoccupation with the war that has ravaged their country for more than a decade now. Beginning as a domestic insurgency, this war has in recent years evolved into an open invasion by North Vietnam involving as many as five divisions of the North Vietnamese Army at times. For a small country of three million people, the many scores of thousands of military and civilian casualties have had a devastating impact.

On top of this, the Government must cope with some 235,000 refugees who have fled from areas under Communist control. In the light of these facts, perhaps some allowance should be made for an attitude which accepted the war and the refugees as the Government's first priorities.

Third, there was the factor of corruption and vested interest. There can be no question that many well-placed people in Laos, both Laotian and ethnic Chinese, were making a good deal of money out of the opium business and doing it without violating any law.

With the major scandals that we have had in some of our metropolitan cities, reaching up all the way to police inspectors and judges, we are not exactly in the best position in the world to lecture other countries on corruption. But it is a fact that corruption tends to be far more widespread in low-income countries. When police inspectors and judges who make $20,000 and $25,000 a year succumb to temptation in our own country, we should not be surprised when their counterparts in other countries who work for bare subsistence salaries succumb in substantially greater numbers to the temptation of big money.

Fourth, there is the fact that opium in Laos did not become a problem that vitally affected American interests until the heroin epidemic hit the American forces during the summer of 1970.

It took several months before we realized what was happening and it was getting on to mid-1971 before our war against the heroin epidemic in Vietnam went into high gear. It was about this time that we began to use our influence to persuade the governments of Southeast Asia to join us in more vigorous measures against the opium traffickers.

All governments tend to move with a certain time lag. On the whole, I believe that the governments of Laos, Vietnam and Thailand must be given credit for moving quickly and dramatically since we first raised the issue with them on a top-priority basis.

Looking at the situation which existed a year ago in Laos, no one could be blamed for deciding that ingrained attitudes ran too deep to make any serious improvement possible. But then things began to happen.

The strength of the American reaction to the news of the heroin epidemic among our servicemen in Vietnam persuaded the Laotian leaders that they could no longer afford to remain indifferent or unmotivated if they wished to retain American support. And so, on November 15, 1971, the Laotian Legislature took the revolutionary step of passing a law banning the production, sale or use of opium. *All of the Meo deputies, following the leadership of Gen. Vang Pao, voted affirmatively on this measure.* [Underlining added]

Even before the law was passed, the Laotian Government had acted to curtail refinery operations, destroying two refineries and seizing large quantities of drugs in the process.[12]

It must be understood that there has been a considerable amount of distortion of information and doctoring and slanting of news in the U.S. press and also in other recent publications that bear on this problem. For example, the CIA has come under fire and has been accused of being deeply involved in the opium and narcotics trade, providing transport facilities and protection. Similar accusations have been leveled at Gen. Vang Pao. It is normal practice for Communists to accuse their opponents of precisely those activities in which they themselves

Narcotics Routing and Communist

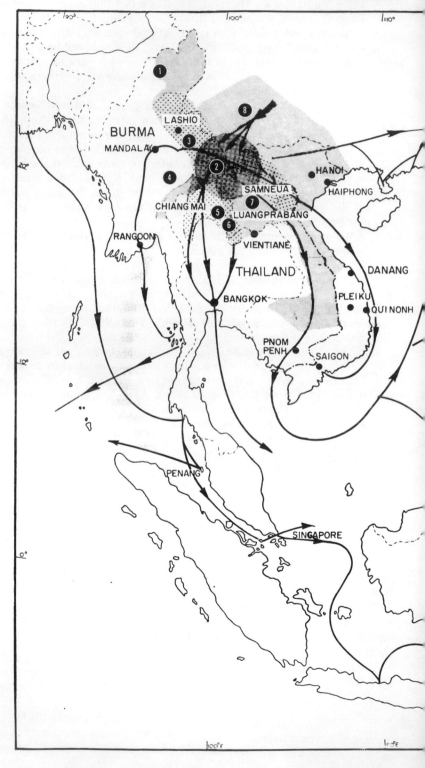

Penetration — South East Asia

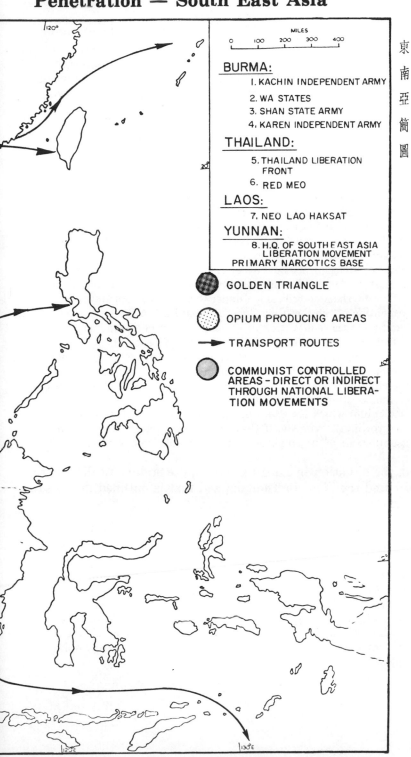

MILES

0   100   200   300   400

BURMA:
1. KACHIN INDEPENDENT ARMY
2. WA STATES
3. SHAN STATE ARMY
4. KAREN INDEPENDENT ARMY

THAILAND:
5. THAILAND LIBERATION FRONT
6. RED MEO

LAOS:
7. NEO LAO HAKSAT

YUNNAN:
8. H.Q. OF SOUTH EAST ASIA LIBERATION MOVEMENT PRIMARY NARCOTICS BASE

GOLDEN TRIANGLE

OPIUM PRODUCING AREAS

TRANSPORT ROUTES

COMMUNIST CONTROLLED AREAS - DIRECT OR INDIRECT THROUGH NATIONAL LIBERATION MOVEMENTS

東
南
亞
簡
圖

are most deeply engaged, and this is a good example of that technique in action.

There are absolutely no inhibitions on their part to engaging in opium trading, and indeed every inducement to do so, since it is both profitable and also damaging to their opponents. Whatever method may be employed to bring that about, even if, by our standards, it is a monstrous crime, is to them a meritorious act since it serves to bring their objectives closer.

General Walt continues in his testimony with the following:

> It is, of course, true that the Meo tribesmen whom we supported were opium cultivators, as were the Meo tribesmen on the Communist side. Virtually all Meos in both Thailand and Laos grow opium—because they have done so for generations, because they use it as a medicine and as an euphoric drug, because it is their one cash crop, and because it can be stored against hard times....
>
> While there was much criticism of the fact that the Meos on our side were engaged in opium agriculture, I have thus far come across no criticism of the Pathet Lao and the North Vietnamese Communists for condoning and even encouraging the cultivation of opium by the Meo tribesmen under their control; nor have I seen any mention of the fact that General Vang Pao's Meos have largely discontinued the cultivation of opium because of Vang Pao's crop substitution program going back a number of years; in the second place, because the Communist advance has forced them out of their traditional lands, which were suitable for poppy cultivation, onto the plains, which are not suitable for poppy farming. Nor have I seen the question raised as to the ultimate purpose and destination of the opium which the Meos under Pathet Lao control are known to be growing. Obviously, if they are growing opium, they are not consuming all of it; some of it must be sold somewhere.[13]

Indeed, the situation in Laos has been quite similar to the one that has confronted the Meos in Thailand and that is outlined in the same testimony:

> The government has pushed its efforts to the point where it has aroused open resentment among the Meos, making it markedly easier for the Communists to recruit Meo tribesmen for the guerrilla insurgency which has plagued northern Thailand for a number of years now. The Communists come to the Meos and say to them in approximately these terms: "The government is trying to prevent you from growing opium poppies, which you have always done and which is your right. They are trying to take your only cash crop away from you. Come with us and we will let you grow opium poppies."

On the basis of such agitation and with cadres trained in Hanoi and Peking, the Communists have been able to establish fairly effective control over a strip of land perhaps 150 miles long by 25 to 50 miles wide along the northernmost portion of the Laotian frontier [i.e., on the Thai side of the Lao frontier—Candlin].

The Communists have about 3,000 guerrillas in the area who are extremely well equipped. We were told that they have AK47 rifles which are comparable to our M-16s, 60 and 81 mm mortars, B40 rockets, 57 mm recoilless rifles, and rubber landmines and booby traps similar to those used by the Viet Cong. There is reason to believe that the movement is directed from China, among other things because the supporting propaganda operation, the Voice of Free Thailand, is located there. The Voice of Free Thailand has transmitters capable of reaching all the way to Bangkok and it carries sophisticated programs of music, news and propaganda in both the Thai and Meo languages.[14]

Besides the station mentioned by General Walt there has been another called the "Voice of Thai Revolution." This is a Thai Communist radio station set up by the Chinese Reds in southwest China that has continually broadcast particularly virulent anti-United States speeches and that has consistently been inciting the Thais to rise up and overthrow their government. In 1966 the late Marshal Chen Yi, Chinese Communist Foreign Minister, predicted that they intended to have a full-scale war of liberation running in Thailand within the year. The border area mentioned by General Walt is, in the main, the Khaopipunnam mountain massif that stretches from northern Thailand to Loey Province in northeast Thailand. The forces are mainly Meos in the north but Thai communists in the southern sector. They have, on the whole, been operating somewhat independently of each other. Both have been paying their Chinese backers in opium.

Another commodity that has been a very active part of the economic scene in Laos has been gold.

References have already been made to the special role gold plays in all irregular military operations. It is used as a means of storing wealth and as a means of exchange when transactions in narcotics or in arms are involved. It is a particularly important commodity when the countries in the theater of operations do not have strong currencies.

Since Laotian currency is notoriously weak and subject to fluctuations, there have been a number of attempts to support it. One method has been through the operation of an exchange-stabilization fund that involves the United States, Britain, Australia, and Japan. Because of the prevalence of U.S. dollars in the area, whether contributed by the U.S. Government, by normal processes of transfer from U.S.

servicemen in Southeast Asia, or by illegal transactions, there is a corresponding influx of gold (about two tons a week) mostly from Switzerland. This is because Vientiane is a free market and the government imposes a mere 3 percent duty. This favors the accumulation of large stocks of gold by rich individuals in Laos and also the backloading of a good deal of the precious metal to Red China in exchange for its opium and narcotics exports arriving via the Burma Road, the direct southern route out of Yunnan, or from Bangkok.

The Chinese Reds have been particularly aware of the great strategic importance of Laos as a central, pivotal area, not only of great defensive value because of its position vis-a-vis South China, but also of high value as a potential offensive base from which full-scale attacks can be launched against several neighboring countries. It has been a corridor for their war supplies into Vietnam and also a clearing house through which their own economic position can be consistently improved.

Their efforts at expansion in Burma have been prodigious though not much publicized. The isolationist Ne Win administration, disturbed by what it sees of Chinese expansionist tendencies, has been doing what it can with its limited resources to stem the tide. Despite a number of high-sounding undertakings, such as the Sino-Burmese Friendly and Nonaggression Treaty and the Sino-Burmese Boundary Agreement, there has been stealthy and continuous encroachment of the kind experienced by Laos, except that the progress so far has not been comparable.

However, the Chinese have helped the Burmese Communists raise an army. They have trained a leader called Lo Hsiang, who has been put in charge of a force called the Burmese Army Corps, planned in conjunction with a body called the Burmese National Liberation Front. Lo Hsiang and his cadres, and members of the other organization, have had extensive training by the Chinese Reds at centers at Pao-Shan, Teng-chung, and Wan-tien in Yunnan. There has been an intensification of this activity of late and during the period July–December 1968 a considerable movement began among the border tribesmen of the Shans, the Kachins, and Karens, from whom eleven battalions were formed under the direct control of the Vice-Commander of the Yunnan Military District, General Chu Chia-pi. The Chinese also maintain a school for subversives and agitators at Shun-nin in Yunnan that has an intake of about 3,000 per year.

This tribal rebellion was supported by an incursion of two PLA battalions in May 1969 in the Chin Province. There has been a long record of rivalry between Red Flags (pro-Russian) and White Flags (pro-Red China), but signs are appearing that they are beginning to collaborate.

It has been movements of this kind that have stirred the CIF units into action and distracted them from their more normal pursuits.

During the visit of the Subcommittee to Investigate the Administration of the Internal Security Act's Special Task Force on the World Drug Situation (headed by General Walt) to the critical areas in Southeast Asia, an unusually interesting event took place. This was the agreement signed between the Royal Thai Government and the CIF forces in Thailand to the effect that the former would grant all Chinese belonging to the CIF (Chinese Irregular Forces) "resident" status if they would desist from their opium-smuggling activities and accept conditions of resettlement based on a land grant, some financial support, and various forms of aid.

Remarkably, the Chinese, in earnest of a wish to accept the terms, turned over to the Thai Government 26,245 kilograms (more than 26 metric tons) of opium for public burning. At market prices the consignment would be worth $3 billion. In spite of allegations by journalists, to whom these unfortunate Chinese expatriates could never appear in anything except a sinister light, that the destruction of this large quantity of opium was a put-up job and that only five tons of opium mixed with other substances was destroyed, the incident seems to have been genuine enough. The episode was arranged by the Bureau of Narcotics and Dangerous Drugs, whose representative, William Wanzeck, stationed in Bangkok, seems to have assured himself by more than adequate sampling and inspection that it was all opium. This affair, on March 7, 1972, may indeed constitute a portent for the future role of the Triangle in Southeast Asia. It is, of course, rather soon to make any predictions and the author can remember similar events that took place in North China that were hailed as the beginnings of the end of opium. Yet it was a good many years before any results were visible, although it was certainly true that the Nationalists under Chiang Kaishek, who were behind those burnings, were very serious in their intentions and were able to make very appreciable reductions. (See in this connection [the CIF/Thai opium burning] Appendix IXC.)

General Walt, in the course of the Senate hearings, made a particularly important observation central to the theme of this book in expressing his views on the heroin epidemic in Vietnam in 1970:

> Mr. Chairman, now I would like to go to the country of Vietnam.
>
> When the heroin epidemic broke in June 1970, it caught both the American authorities completely unprepared. New programs and new command structures and new techniques had to be devised starting almost from scratch, to deal with the epidemic and to bring it under control.

The rapid rate of American withdrawal makes scientifically accurate judgments difficult. There is, nevertheless, no question but that we have made enormous progress in dealing with the problem. My associates and I were enormously impressed by what we saw of the urine-testing program, the detoxification program and the educational program that is going on in South Vietnam today. Because it would take too much time to describe these programs adequately to the subcommittee, I plan to submit a written report covering our findings later on, sir.

We were also favorably impressed by the concrete evidence of progress made by the government of Vietnam over the past year in developing its interdiction and law enforcement capabilities....

On May 18, 1971, by virtue of a presidential decree, an interministerial committee was created under the Ministry of Justice encharged with the responsibility of stopping the traffic in narcotics in South Vietnam...

I heard on the news this morning, sir, that President Thieu has signed an edict now making the death sentence mandatory for the trafficker in dangerous drugs and narcotics....

One final observation, sir. The Government of Vietnam has taken the stand that the heroin epidemic was a Communist operation. Under these circumstances, a Vietnamese officer or governmental official would stamp himself as the worst kind of traitor in the eyes of his countrymen if he were caught participating in the drug traffic and this is a very powerful form of disincentive.

Sir, I would like to bring up the topic of the heroin epidemic among the American Armed Forces in Vietnam.

In Vietnam the prime focus of the investigation was on the heroin epidemic. We wanted to find out as much as we could about the epidemic itself and about the effectiveness of the countermeasures which had been instituted in the fields of detection, rehabilitation and education.

The epidemic hit in the month of June, immediately after our Cambodian incursion had devastated the enemy sanctuaries and supply caches in the Parrots Beak Area. Almost overnight heroin of remarkable purity—94 to 97 percent—became available in unlimited quantities to the American Armed Forces in the Saigon area, initially at a price of $1 a vial, later at an average of $2 a vial. I am talking about a vial, sir, that small vial I had here this morning that contained anywhere from one fourth of a gram to 0.15 or one-seventh of a gram, was selling for $1 a vial.

Within two months the epidemic had spread to cover virtually the entire country.

Within a few months' time, death from heroin overdoses among our servicemen climbed from two a month to almost 79 a month. There are varying estimates as to what percentage of our armed forces became involved in the epidemic, but certainly it ran into many, many thousands. Naturally it varied from unit to unit. Maj. Jerome Char, psychiatrist for the 101st Airborne Division located in I Corps, estimated in a statement to the Senate Juvenile Delinquency Subcommittee that 40 to 50 percent of the men in his division had either experimented with or were hooked on hard drugs. Although the official estimate was substantially lower, it was clear that we were confronted with a situation of catastrophic dimensions.

The heroin was sold in the streets in plastic vials of similar manufacture, and all the heroin was of closely related appearance and purity. At wholesale level, all of it was uniformly packaged in sealed 135-gram plastic bags.

It is my information that the vials which first appeared on the streets of Saigon contained 0.15 gram, which is about eight times as much as a New York addict takes in one injection. At a very early date, however, it began to appear on the streets in quarter-gram and half-gram vials. In this country—here is half a gram here, sir—in this country a half-gram of heroin would be enough for 25 injections for an addict.

Everyone agreed that the operation appeared to be highly coordinated and centralized. Some people or some group must have established virtually simultaneous contact with scores of Chinese ethnic entrepreneurs and other criminal elements throughout South Vietnam and prepared them to receive large quantities of heroin, for distribution through the armies of street urchins, both boys and girls, who had until then been merchandising marijuana for these sellers of drugs.

Senator Gurney: How much would these half-gram vials cost in Saigon on the street?

General Walt: Starting—they were $2 and then they got up to $3 in a year's time.

Senator Gurney: And how much would they cost in New York on the retail market?

General Walt: About $200.

Senator Gurney: About $200?

General Walt: Yes, sir.

Senator Gurney: So I take it the low price, according to your testimony, is indicative that it was some sort of a large-scale, coordinated program to get the heroin out at far below the usual cost in order to hook large numbers of our soldiers; is that correct?

General Walt: Mr. Chairman, I don't think they were selling it for profit; I think they were just selling it for material reasons and I indicate that here later on, sir.

Senator Gurney: Go on, General.

General Walt: Apart from the fact that this kind of explosive nationwide launching of a heroin sales-promotion campaign is simply not in the pattern of criminal operations, the pattern I have described here raises two very basic questions:

If the operation was organized by some Asian Mafia, it would be natural for the profit motive to predominate.

Why, if the operation was criminal in origin, did they sell stuff that was 94 to 97 percent pure, when people manage to get high in New York on 10-percent heroin? Why didn't they dilute it?

Why did they sell it for $1 or $2 a vial when no GI who was hooked or who wanted to experiment with heroin would have batted an eyelash at paying $5. Cash was one thing the boys over there had—there was loose change. And it makes even less sense when one considers that in March–April, just before the epidemic broke, similar vials were sold for $10 to $15 each.

This appears to be a program.

The economics of the heroin epidemic call for very careful scrutiny. While estimates of the rate of profit at different stages of the market vary considerably, it would appear reasonable that the street urchins, in order to sell vials for $1, were to purchase them for 50 cents each. The markup in each stage of the sales process is substantially higher than this in the United States. Similarly, the wholesaler, in order to sell them for 50 cents, was probably able to purchase the heroin content for approximately 25 cents.

At the time the heroin epidemic broke, a kilogram of heroin was selling for roughly $1,300 a kilo—2 2/10 pounds-or $1.30 a gram; a half-gram, therefore, cost the master entrepreneur 65 cents while a quarter-gram cost 32 cents.

Whoever was selling heroin to the ethnic Chinese entrepreneurs in Vietnam at a price which permitted sales at $1 per vial was taking a heck of a beating financially; he wasn't making any money. They probably began to make some money, however, at the point where the street price of a vial went up to $2. They at least broke even.

All of this doesn't make sense from the standpoint of the criminal obsession with profit. It does make sense, however, if the operation was political in origin, because then it would only be natural for the organizers to want to hook as many GIs as possible, as hard as possible, and to hook them moreover, on a habit so expensive that they would have to engage in far more crime than the ordinary addict to feed the habit once they returned home.

The Communists had so much to gain from such an operation. First of all, it was clearly bound to have an immediate demoralizing effect on our forces in Vietnam. Second, it was bound to have a highly demoralizing long-term effect on American society. Third, and perhaps more important in terms of the Vietnam War, it was bound to provide grist for the mill of "let's get out of Southeast

Asia immediately" propaganda. At the height of the heroin epidemic the situation was so bad that many parents who had previously backed the President's policy joined the clamor to get out of Vietnam, fearful that if we stayed there much longer all our American boys would return as drug addicts.

All of this so far is deductive; hard evidence is difficult to come by. In Saigon the MACV [Military Assistance Command, Vietnam] officer who briefed us told us that they had thus far found no hard evidence tieing Hanoi or the VC to the epidemic. On this point, I would like to quote the commentary of a senior general concerned with the drug problem in Vietnam:

"How the hell do you get hard proof of the VC's movement of several hundred pounds of heroin into Vietnam when for years we were virtually certain but couldn't prove that they were moving thousands of tons of military supplies through the port of Sihanoukville?"

Had the VC decided to organize the heroin epidemic which hit our forces in the summer of 1970, it stands to reason that they would not have had VC vendors in the streets; this they left to the street urchins and mama sans. Nor would they have been involved with traffickers at the next level up; this they left to the ethnic Chinese entrepreneurs who are traditionally willing to lend themselves to shady undertakings which promise a profit. If they had played any role at all, it would have been far, far back on the other side of the Cambodian or Laotian frontier, operating through a handful of principals who could not clearly be tagged as Vietcong.

But the absence of evidence is not absolute; there are some items of definite evidentiary value.

We had occasion to examine the reports of interrogations with three different VC defectors who claimed to have knowledge relating to large-scale opium cultivation in North Vietnam and in one case, of Vietcong involvement in the heroin epidemic.

One defector, who came over on August 25, 1971, said that while he was attending the COSVN military-political school in May of 1970, that is at the time the heroin epidemic in South Vietnam was breaking out, he had participated in some frank discussion on the North Vietnamese use of drugs as a direct means of undermining the morale and efficiency of U.S. forces. COSVN, I should point out stands for the Central Office for South Vietnam. This is the secret Communist headquarters which has been masterminding the entire war in South Vietnam.

The defector said, among other things, that North Vietnamese combat reconnaissance activities were often undetected because security forces at defense installations were visually impaired by the use of drugs. While he had no direct knowledge of how the drugs were distributed in South Vietnam, the interrogator in a summary statement said that the defector was cooperative and appeared sincere throughout the interrogation and that control questions revealed no attempt to deceive the interrogator....

All the senior Vietnamese officers with whom I discussed the matter are convinced that the heroin epidemic was essentially political rather than criminal in origin. They are convinced, in short, that the Communists were behind it and that they were using it as a weapon against our armed forces.

This conviction is shared by a number of American officers of general rank who have been concerned with the drug problem, and also by other high-ranking officials.

In traveling around the world I also encountered a number of senior Western officials who follow the world drug situation closely and who told me confidentially that they were convinced from the circumstances of the Vietnamese epidemic that the Communists were behind it.

Certainly the evidence points to the need for an intensive study of the origin and nature of the heroin epidemic among the American Armed Forces in Vietnam.[15]

Hong Kong

It was mentioned earlier that Shanghai used to be considered the opium capital of China, particularly before the Japanese occupation. Today, the character of the Chinese opium industry has changed from that of an agricultural enterprise, linked with rather primitive transport and traditional marketing arrangements, to that of an immense state enterprise of an increasingly industrial character. Shanghai has long lost its supremacy and if any city is to be regarded as the opium capital it must be Peking itself. Hong Kong however, is, next to Bangkok, unquestionably the leading Far Eastern city involved in the drug traffic, although primarily as an entrepôt and a clearing house; no narcotics are grown there, and processing is at a minimum and generally of a transient nature. There is a good deal of addiction, but the primary fact of life there is large-scale distribution on a worldwide basis, as is to be expected from a place with a Chinese population of over three million, geographically but not politically a part of Kwangtung Province, adjoining one of the main opium-growing areas of China.

One of Britain's few remaining Crown Colonies, Hong Kong was itself one of the principal gains in the Opium Wars with China and has always been associated with the traffic although few of its European inhabitants have been particularly aware of the fact. Originally, before the large-scale traffic from India into China was halted (by 1919), the Colony played a large part in the importation of the drug into China, where Indian opium was highly prized. In the period after World War II the flow has been reversed and the accent is on export trade.

Many have noted that Hong Kong, since 1945 and the return of British administration after a brief period of Japanese rule (when an immense efflux of Chinese population occurred), has altered in character and has changed from a rather torpid and sluggish colonial outpost into a particularly fast-moving and busy seaport and airline junction. Indeed, it seems to have acquired many of the characteristics of the former Chinese coastal treaty ports, including the international settlement in Shanghai.

With that transformation, however normal and legitimate it may be, there has also come about a major participation in worldwide narcotics operations, from which it had been free for many years. Most of this is entrepôt trade, in which the nature of the free port that exists there has lent itself, conveniently, to the designs of the many criminal operators who have been able to use it just as they did the International Settlement in Shanghai years ago.

It must be realized that in more senses than one Hong Kong is a hostage to fortune, since most of the food and even a large proportion of the water needed by the Colony is brought in from the mainland. The recognition of Red China by Great Britain has brought prosperity to Hong Kong, since it has served many purposes regarded as essential by the Communist regime. It provides a means of ready access to the outside world; it provides purchasing facilities; and it brings in much of the foreign exchange vital to Chinese purposes. Less conspicuously, it is also a kind of golden funnel through which astronomical quantities of raw opium and narcotics flow to a wide range of consuming or target areas.

Although no opium is grown in Hong Kong, a good deal is smoked by its swollen Chinese population, most of whom are refugees from the mainland. The extent of the popularity of the Chinese Communist regime can be gauged by the inescapable fact that some 1,000 refugees a month are currently coming into Hong Kong from neighboring parts of the mainland. If internal travel there were not greatly restricted there would be many more. Most of them are prepared to face a long and dangerous swim through shark-infested waters rather than stay under intolerable conditions. A good many more do not arrive and their bodies are often washed up in Hong Kong waters.

The Hong Kong authorities are very well informed about the activities of their large population and the extent of its addiction to opium or other narcotics. Their attitude is a rather tolerant and benevolent one. So long as the volume of the traffic does not impinge on the population in such manner as to promote dangerous or violent gang warfare on an intolerable scale, or threaten the internal security of the Colony, they take the whole question calmly. It is unfortunate, however, that they cannot do more to avoid the consequences or discourage the traffic, especially since they know reasonably well the extent of the very considerable flow-through of drugs (without really admitting the access to such knowledge) and even the most probable destinations of much of the traffic. There is, in fact, a heavy ransom being paid for the continued existence of the Colony. It may be noted that this situation is likely to change considerably when worldwide trading with Red China is resumed through more normal channels.

Nevertheless, the Hong Kong Government does what it believes to be possible in the circumstances. For example, among the early émigrés from Shanghai to Hong Kong was an important trafficker called Li Choy Fat, a prominent member of the Ch'ing Pang society. This individual went into partnership with two other traders of long standing, Li Sui-po and Kwok Kam-chi, to set up the firm of Li Choy Fat, which soon became a very large-scale narcotics-smuggling operation.

The procedure was as follows: narcotics came into Hong Kong by sea aboard vessels of all sizes, ranging from small junks to large passenger liners, where members of the crew were in league with the firm. Use was also made of charter planes and even regular airline flights. It has been stated by Henry J. Anslinger, who was certainly in a position to know during his office as U.S. Narcotics Commissioner, that "it is reasonably safe to say that there is not an airline operating either to or from the Colony which has not been used by narcotics smugglers." Late in 1952 it became firmly established that movements of gold and narcotics smuggling were closely connected and Communist-inspired. It was also discovered that the same traffickers were shipping strategic war materials to Communist China. Li Choy Fat was deported to Taipei, where he was sentenced to fifteen-years imprisonment.

One of Li Choy Fat's partners, Li Sui-po, had previously been active in Shanghai, where he had worked with another opium gangster called Wu Sze-pao of 70 Jessfield Road (International Settlement). This address was in a district infested with crime and vice of every description, of the lurid kind for which Shanghai used to be famous. It was known as the "Badlands" and was an area of especial concern to the Shanghai Municipal Police, a remarkable body that was continually plagued by crimes of violence that went on there, including many murders connected with the extensive and continuous trading in narcotics. While operating in Hong Kong as an exile from Shanghai, Li acted as an agent and a trader in the well-known Chinese Communist brand of heroin known as "Red Lion."

Kwok Kam-chi, also mentioned above, is a Fukienese who has had many contacts in Communist China in both Fukien and Kwangtung, and who played a prominent part in building up the traffic into Hong Kong from the mainland. Besides smuggling in opium, morphine, and heroin in large quantities, he also set up a heroin factory in the Colony, which led to his arrest in December 1952 and to his deportation. At the time, the *Chi Yin Daily News*, a Chinese newspaper in Hong Kong, printed the following:

> The Chinese Communists have concentrated all the opium from different parts of the mainland in South China for sale abroad so as to obtain foreign exchange. The sale at two certain places has been greatly increased and, at the same time, organizations have been set up in Kwangtung and Kwangsi Provinces to undertake the transport of narcotics and to work in collusion with traitorous merchants overseas. The details of the intrigue were exposed in detail July 7th, 1952 and since that time the authorities have paid special attention and for the past three months have exerted great efforts in their investigations. It is understood that Kwok and a number of traffickers have left for Japan within the past two months.[16]

Other firms that have employed persons who have been deeply engaged in the trading in narcotics in Hong Kong have been the Tin Shing Company, the Chan Brothers Company, the China Syndicate and Company, and the Sung Hoi Company. An individual called Chan San-yuk, who was a manager in the last two companies, and several other Chinese were charged with piracy when they were discovered to be planning the seizure of the SS *Nidar* on her way to Japan and her delivery to the Chinese Communists. One of Chan's associates at the time was the well-known narcotics trader Judah I. Ezra, who had been deported from the United States after serving a sentence after conviction for smuggling.

Late in 1952 it was found that China Syndicate and Company made an offer to L.Y. Goh and Co., a broker, to deliver 200 tons of opium from Communist China, acting on behalf of a bogus Swiss firm. China Syndicate claimed to be able to deliver very large quantities of opium at Shum Chun near the Hong Kong border. It also offered quantities of heroin for sale on reasonable terms.

At that time the Chinese Communists were desperate for foreign exchange and were engaged in setting up their opium and narcotics industry. A part of that process, aimed at increasing their exports to the maximum possible extent, was the setting up of an airline with passenger and freight service that, from the first, carried opium and narcotics as well as other export articles. This service was called the Chinese Peoples' Aviation Company and operated from Peking to Kunming and Canton via Nanking. It was noted by the Hong Kong authorities that on December 20, 1952, a plane belonging to that airline brought in a load of 25 cases of opium of 62 catties each from Kunming to Canton. This was for export through Macao.

That this was a part of a much larger and regular traffic was evidenced by a news dispatch from Canton on October 16, 1952:

> Four hundred and fifty cases of raw opium arrived in Canton from Yunnan Province on Oct. 4th, 1952. The cases of opium, all of which were sealed by the "Provincial Peoples' Government of Yunnan," were consigned to a certain firm in Yat Tak Chung Lu, Canton. It was learned that this firm is owned by Ch'en Keng and a certain Yang who is Ch'en Keng's personal representative in Canton. It was also learned that this opium was intended for Hong Kong and Macao.[17]

Another article from Hong Kong reported on the growing activity on the mainland near South China's traditional export bases in that area:

> The 8th moon of the lunar calendar is the time for the planting of the poppy and the Chinese Communist authorities are taking into consideration conditions in various areas in fixing tariffs on poppies cultivated. The Kwangtung Communist leader Yeh Chien-ying on Sept. 3rd issued secret instructions to authorities in the various hsien and municipalities in the province to the effect that since the prohibition of poppy cultivation could not be fully enforced in the remote and hilly areas they might as well enforce the policy of seeking prohibition through taxation so that the people would be made to abandon poppy cultivation voluntarily (sic).*
>
> The taxation rate of 280 catties of grain for every 100 poppy plants was fixed, and tax evasions would be severely punished. The news amounted to the lifting of the ban on poppy cultivation and peasants in various parts of Kwangtung were elated.
>
> In the scores of "hsiang" in the suburbs of Canton, it was stated that all the dry fields would be devoted to poppy cultivation since it brought a greater yield than rice cultivation.[18]

---

*It may be noted that Yeh Chien-ying, whose career is examined elsewhere in this study, has become the major military figure in Peking since the demise of Lin Piao.

This last conception is one that has played a very large part in Red China's opium economics, because imports of wheat from such countries as Canada and Australia have been paid for by opium and narcotics-trading profits derived from areas that have been concentrating on the more lucrative planting of poppies.

To have a better understanding of the significance of Hong Kong and its role on the international scene, one must know the historical background of the Colony, taken against the wider aspect of Far Eastern affairs. It has been noted above, for example, that there was a close relationship between events in Shanghai during the China War, the form of the traffic there, and later developments in Hong Kong. This was because, when the Japanese descended on Shanghai, one of the major objectives of their assault was control of the flow of drugs into and out of that port.

One of the personalities whose positions was adversely affected by the Japanese successes in Shanghai and in Central China was the celebrated Tu Yueh-sheng, who had been, until then, the opium king of Shanghai and who was reputed to have enjoyed special privileges through connections in high government quarters. From his secluded but luxurious home in the French Concession he controlled an immense and fabulously profitable traffic entering the great port from Yunnan, Szechuan, and other domestic sources, as well as imported opium from such other supplying countries as Iran. Opium was the main commodity but he handled other drugs as well. The organization that he ran was enormous, extending up the Yangtze Valley, and was also deeply involved in other unpleasant activities such as slave-trading and prostitution.

There was a scandal in 1933 that caused a good deal of excitement in Shanghai because it involved French personnel in the municipal government who were shown to be in collusion with Tu. The cause of these revelations was the seizure of several hundred tons of Iranian opium, some of which had been converted into heroin. The raid was carried out by the troops of the 19th Route Army who, under General Tsai Ting-kai, had distinguished themselves by heroic resistance to the Japanese when they attacked Chapei; this was an early incident that anticipated the Marco Polo Bridge affair that launched the China War. Tu was forced out of the French Concession into Nantao, where his business flourished until it was struck down by Japanese rivalry in the same field.

A most significant factor concerning Tu was his high position (he was said to be Grand Master) in the important secret society the Ch'ing Pang, or Green Circle Gang, mentioned above in Chapter 4. This had, as one of its most important activities, the manufacture, transport,

271

and sale of opium and narcotics under carefully controlled clandestine conditions. Since many important figures in the business, social, and even official life of Shanghai were members of this gang, the opium trade was conducted under particularly safe and efficient arrangements (until the Japanese irruption).

Tu also occupied a particularly useful post, that of the most important member of the official Shanghai Opium Suppression Bureau. As a result, a particularly anomalous situation arose in which the Green Circle found itself acting as a sort of enforcement agency controlling the movements of rival opium shipments. This was done through a highly illegal holding company called the "Special Goods Association," whose actions resulted in the levy of an unofficial tax or "squeeze" on opium of ten cents a tael over the legal taxes.

One of the better-informed writers with intimate knowledge of the Far East has been Percy Finch, who had the following to say about Tu and his organization in Finch's highly informative book *Shanghai and Beyond:*

> During World War II Du [an alternative spelling] transferred his headquarters to Chungking, leaving his gangs to find refuge in the mazes of Shanghai's underworld. After the war he was back again, the same man of mystery, power, public benevolence and high finance, with a new plan. To his manifold accomplishments he added a neat labor management formula, never tried in the West but immensely successful and profitable in the East. With the city struggling to recover from war losses Du established boss rights over Shanghai's 600,000 industrial workers by grabbing control of a number of key unions with Nanking's blessing, before they had recovered from wartime stagnation. To his *Who's Who* success biography, he added the presidency of the Chinese Cotton Guild, the employer's association. Between the two, he reduced labor friction to a minimum, inaugurating a new era in industrial relations and vastly expanding his empire until the Communists wiped it out. His efforts were given government approval and what amounted to international recognition when one of Du's lieutenants was made head of Nanking's Chinese Labor Organization and represented China at International Labor Organization conferences. When he died in the British Colony of Hong Kong, Du acquired further merit, to employ a Chinese phrase, by forming the subject of an obituary notice in the ultra-respectable *London Times* with the subheading "Finance and Politics in Shanghai," which shrouded the corpse in utmost decorum and rectitude. A *New York Times* correspondent in the heyday of Du's postwar empire had the temerity to ask the old man if he were an opium trader. Du looked hurt. "The impression that I deal in opium is erroneous," he replied. "It

is true that some members of the Green and Red Societies deal
in opium but not on my orders.[19]

The answer was an interesting and typical one. Whenever they are
taxed with similar activity all such persons and organizations will only
admit that some members are involved as individuals or small independent groups, but the parent organization is not—however they continue to enjoy its usually effective protection.

Mr. Finch also makes another reference to Tu (Du) and to Chinese
Communist interest in drugs, and to the situation in which some but
not all drug traffickers found themselves after the accession to power
of the new government:

> Du Wei-sung's gang was scattered, Du himself fleeing to Hong
> Kong when the Reds took Shanghai. Many members fell into the
> hands of the conquerors and were executed in the purge for their
> political sins and their part in Chiang Kai-shek's suppression of
> the Communists. Not all, however, were liquidated. One of Du's
> associates, possessed of all the secrets and business knowledge of
> the opium trade was arrested and dragged before a peoples' court.
> He publicly repented his anti-Communist activities, according to
> a report put out by Peking, whereupon he was admitted into the
> Communist fold for purposes known only to the calculating realists
> in the palaces of the Forbidden City.[20]

It should be noted here that Tu and his organization, for all their
extremely questionable background, played a significant part in the
Chinese war effort, especially in the fields of intelligence and of special
operations. Comparison can, perhaps, be made with the wartime collaboration between U.S. Naval Intelligence and "Lucky" Luciano in Operation "Underworld."

Needless to say, a great deal of the local sale of opium and narcotics
in Hong Kong is in the hands of members of secret societies that themselves are also frequently involved in the wider international aspects
of the traffic. However, their operations are carried out with such skill
and their security is so good that significant evidence of the depth of
their participation is particularly difficult to find.

As has been mentioned above, in Chapter 4, although societies such
as the Ko Lao-hui (Elder Brother Society), the T'ien Ti Hui (Heaven
and Earth Society), and Hung Society (Flood Society) have been
documented and have become quite well known as entities, little is actually known about their actual nature. In general, they suffer from
rather split personalities. While their original aims were laudable in
general and of a patriotic nature, as is always the case with secret

organizations in which the leadership has powers of life and death over the membership, in the long run situations of degeneracy and corruption have become common that lead rapidly into the maelstrom of organized crime.

It is not at all easy for persons unaccustomed to the ways of Chinese populations to visualize the complexity of the situations arising from the actions of societies of this type that are generally bound up with the problems of Chinese labor and employment conditions. The British authorities in such areas as Hong Kong, Malaya (now Malaysia), and Singapore have had a long and close contact with them, extending over generations. Indeed, it was the understanding the British have been able to attain that enabled them to resist successfully the attempts at the overthrow of the civil power in Malaya (1946–57), in North Borneo in 1960, and in Hong Kong in 1966. Unmistakable signs of Chinese Communists intentions of breaking the power of the Hong Kong Government, as they had destroyed that of Portugal in Macao, had been detected in time and the proper precautions were taken. For one thing, the British realized that the preponderant Chinese intelligence effort in the Colony was being carried out by *domestic* mainland agencies as if Hong Kong had already been absorbed.

Although Mao is supposed to have destroyed the power of these societies on the mainland, it has been ascertained from refugees that they still exist in strength and almost all are opposed to the Peking regime. Many newcomers to the Colony soon find themselves affiliated with foreign branches of organizations that are in extreme official disfavor across the border. There are supposed to be about 200 societies known to the colonial administration in Hong Kong, but a closer inspection reveals that often there are alternative names for the same organization or names of different sections or subsections of the same organization.

It has been the general custom to refer somewhat loosely to almost all of these as the Triad Societies, a term that has arisen from the trinity of the elements—Heaven, Earth, and Man. In the period immediately preceding the Japanese assault on Hong Kong in 1941, the British attempted to enlist on their side some of the Hong Kong Triad interests (as they did, also, in Malaya) and were successful in splitting the local Triads, ironically, into three groups. One of these was willing to work against the Japanese when they had been influenced by Admiral Chan Chak, the liaison officer representing the Chungking Government. Another group was actively prepared to help the Japanese take the Colony, while a third was neutral and intended to see what would happen. The second group was a dangerous fifth column whose existence was known and which was kept under observation. It was known as the "Wo Group" and a number of its members were arrested and put in custody before the Japanese attacked.

When the Japanese had taken the Colony, they used this element and others like it to support their rule, which was never a popular one and which caused an immense exodus. Their embodiment in the Japanese scheme of things conformed to a policy pattern set for the Chinese secret societies within their own area of conquest. This was drawn up by their puppet Wang Ching-wei, who formed an organization called the "Five Continents Hung Family" (named after the Hung Society). Yet their operations in this field turned out to be a total failure and they were often betrayed by those whom they thought they had captured.

They were actively opposed in the Shanghai area by the Ch'ing Pang, elements of which stayed behind although the top management kept well away from the Japanese. Li Choy Fat, mentioned above, eventually became the head of the Ch'ing Pang after the death of Tu, and its membership grew rapidly in Hong Kong after the Communists took Shanghai and drove a good many of that city's gangster population to take cover in Hong Kong.

The very powerful Ch'ing Pang enclave that developed in Hong Kong had its main area of influence in the district between Causeway Bay and North Point. Causeway Bay, be it noted, was a point of concentration of Hong Kong's junk fleet, amounting to several thousand vessels. For a time, the behavior of the Ch'ing Pang was open and rather shameless. It ran a large number of brothels and nightclubs in which a full gamut of activities such as extortion, blackmail, prostitution, and narcotics ran wild. It sobered up a good deal after Li Choy Fat was dealt with and, today, is much more discreet in its operations. It is particularly strong in the Tsimshatsui area of Hong Kong and it seems very possible that it has changed its policies from an original concern with the exploitation of local and other Far Eastern markets for the much more important and basically more rewarding long-range export operations associated with the immense invisible flow of drugs through Hong Kong.

Their original practices in the building up of local protection rackets in Hong Kong were a continual source of irritation to the law enforcement authorities there. Hong Kong authorities found the transit and long-range trading operations much less interesting since they had less direct impact on the Colony, caused no addiction there, and, indeed, tended to postpone the day when China will reclaim the Colony. Local authorities certainly have not failed to note that the Peking govern-

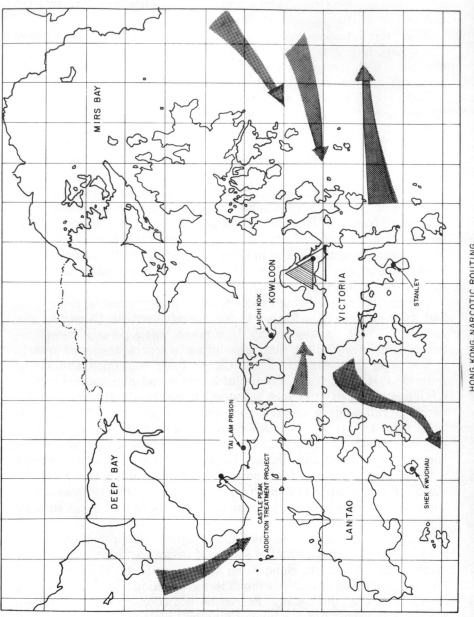

MIRS BAY

KOWLOON

VICTORIA

LAICHI KOK

STANLEY

TAI LAM PRISON

CASTLE PEAK
ADDICTION TREATMENT PROJECT

DEEP BAY

LANTAO

SHEK KWUCHAU

ment now frequently refers to Hong Kong as a part of Kwangtung, a definition that is faithfully echoed by their fellow travellers abroad. The Ch'ing Pang, the Wo Group and the 14K group are all heavily involved, through some of their members, in the long-distance game and, since they do not thus menace the public health or internal security of the Colony on the short term, they continue to get away with it.[21]

It has been seen in Chapter 1 that the opium gangsters of Shanghai and other parts of China in the prewar and early World War II period operated in such manner as to have both firms and semiofficial bodies "fronting" for them. In modern terms, the possibilities offered by internationally operating commercial organizations are of the greatest value.

In practice, this implies the establishment of perfectly normal-seeming import/export companies having legitimate trading activities, but which contain within themselves a highly secret department that handles narcotics transactions. These are usually the sphere of operations of a "private office," the exclusive domain of an inner circle, with specially selected persons within the organization, usually members of the same secret society, "in the know."

Such companies often operate in collusion with other in-groups, forming a tightly knit network or complex of the cartel type. In some cases they are privately owned, in the sense that they are technically independent, but in other cases the concerns are set up by the Communists either directly or operating through "illegals."

The Chinese Communist "takeover" in Macao has favored them in this kind of operation and one of the major components in the network of drug-trading companies trafficking in their interest has been the Nankuang Company. Similarly, in Hong Kong there exists the Huajun Company, among others. In Bangkok there is the Hsinfu Company; in Rangoon, the Tungfang Company; and in Saigon, the Huichung Company.

Several of these maintain branches and agencies in Singapore where, in addition, there is an especially important branch of the Bank of China. The Bank has within its organization key personalities of the Departments of Overseas Trade and of "Social Affairs" who maintain an overview of the situation as well as channeling the profits.

Chinese Communist designs exist to convert Singapore into a sort of Southeast Asian Cuba and, since the failure of their designs in Indonesia when their plot to murder all the most important military leaders miscarried, they have been giving Singapore much more attention. This phase of their designs has been made somewhat more promising by the separation of Singapore from Malaysia.

277

The activities of such companies and organizations are very wide-ranging and have their counterparts in other countries. One of these is an active Japanese concern called the Mitsuichi Company. So far, in spite of a rising ground swell of Japanese commercial opinion, there has not been much permeation of the Japanese economy by enterprises of this kind. However, in view of current developments and with the prospect of increased commercial traffic between Japan and the mainland, the organizing of a good many joint ventures can be foreseen that will, in effect, be "united fronts," operating under company law yet engaged in a good deal of illegal business. These will be a new and rather dangerous form of Trojan horse. All will have their invisible channels connecting them with various widely deployed "Overseas United Front" offices.

Hong Kong and Macao, as well as Singapore, are active centers of secret-society activity, some of which is connected with the drug trade. In this regard there exist the Shanghai Society, the Chaoshan Society, the Hainan Society, and the Kwangtung Society.

Addiction in Hong Kong is very heavy. The population is now well over three million, about two-thirds of whom have come in since the Communist regime took over. Of these it has been estimated that about 150,000 to 200,000 are users of drugs. Just as in the United States, there is almost no addiction in the rural areas, but this is no source of comfort in Hong Kong since about 80 percent of the population is urban. As happens elsewhere, there is a close correlation between the extent of addiction and the incidence of crime; also, the criminals are to be found among both the users and the suppliers of drugs.

One of the particular difficulties connected with the use of narcotics in Hong Kong is that very many Chinese have always tended to regard opium as a sort of patent medicine that can cure most ills. In these circumstances, the attitude of the police and law enforcement generally in the Colony is one of deterrence rather than rigorous and punitive prohibition, except in the case of flagrant irregularities. There is a highly organized public-information system attempting to warn possible victims of the habit of the dangers that they face.

There is also an effective correctional-treatment system that often includes confinement of addicted prisoners as an opportunity to cure them. As an example of this there is the well-run prison at Tai Lam in the New Territories that handles some 700 persons, about a quarter of the Colony's addicted prisoners. There are other institutions where addicts are treated, such as Stanley Prison and Chi Ma Wan Prison. In addition, there are a few voluntary treatment centers such as the Castle Peak Center, a psychiatric hospital, and the Shek Wu Chau Center that started in 1963.

In spite of all efforts made by the Hong Kong Police to protect the Chinese population from the influx of drugs, it must be noted that about 90 percent of the incoming prisoners are dependent on drugs and more than half are committed for drugs, while most of the remainder were convicted for crimes undertaken to pay for their addiction in one way or another.

Within the last ten years there has been a most disturbing trend away from opium towards harder drugs. The Colony now has what is probably the highest hard-drug addiction rate in the world. Some estimates place the figure as one in fifty or higher, of the four million inhabitants, being either an opium or a heroin addict. This would place the figure at about 80,000 addicts and of these some of the more alarmist commentators have estimated that three out of four are on heroin.

Originally, when opium was the staple, it was quite expensive and a commodity that few Chinese in Hong Kong could really afford; but the present situation is one that places a premium on crime because the drugs now craved are well out of economic reach. Most Hong Kong addicts need at least $10 a day and this means criminal association. Inevitably many of these people become directly involved in selling or pushing drugs, and can thus earn enough. Often husbands and wives participate, and even the children, some of whom become addicted to hard drugs at the age of eight or nine.

A consequence of this kind of situation quite often is the repudiation of the individual and his family by his own parents and family, a fearful calamity in Chinese circles adhering to the traditional Chinese ways still prevalent in Hong Kong. The outcasts then join the wide community of the depraved and debased underworld or counterculture that has made narcotics a way of life almost to the exclusion of all other interests.

This is a social tragedy of the highest magnitude—one that can only serve as a terrible warning to other countries where there are signs of similar trends that are now still in their early stages. There is no hope for a society in which large segments of the population forsake productive or creative employment or occupation in order to follow a path of utter dissipation and waste. Hong Kong has been the goal of many seekers of freedom from an intolerable and merciless tyranny on the other side of the border at Shum Chun. It is a tragedy—and a mockery of the good intentions and the essential public spirit of the British Colonial Government in Hong Kong—if refugees now find themselves menaced by another form of servitude that is becoming all too prevalent. Clearly the prosperity of the port, with the need for skilled labor in its thriving new industries, cannot really support idle and vicious residents whose attitudes can only retard the objectives of their neighbors.[22]

The government is more than aware of the magnitude of the problem and, although little is said, is extremely uneasy about its wider implications. Hong Kong is now a major port, with a world outlook that follows naturally from its extremely wide range of commercial contacts. Ultimately, still being administered from London and thus coming under the jurisdiction and legal provisions issuing from Parliament, the Colony has to subscribe to numerous international treaties, conventions, and agreements relating to the control of narcotics. However laudable some of the efforts towards local remedial action may have been, it cannot really be said that a particularly active effort has been made towards the implementation of these agreements.

It is an undeniable fact that the social services and the law-enforcement efforts that have been made are quite inadequate. In spite of limited manpower, however, the Hong Kong Police Narcotics Bureau has had a high degree of success in seizures, particularly since an evident intensification of traffic through the Colony began in 1966. In that year local sources in Hong Kong claimed that the surge was taking place because the Chinese Communists were increasing their export drive coincidental with a precipitous decrease in price. Tons of opium were arriving in Macao and Hong Kong wrapped in 52-ounce packages that were sold at HK$35 per ounce. This represented a cut from HK$100 per ounce, which would argue that only government-subsidized dealing on the largest scale could account for the drop.

On May 5, 1966, a British-registered ship, the SS *Tong Kock*, arrived in Hong Kong from Shanghai with 400 pounds of opium aboard concealed in a fuel tank in the engine room. This was seized and four members of the crew apprehended. The opium had been enclosed in sealed tins immersed in the fuel.

About three years later a Hong Kong-registered junk was boarded in harbor and 4,320 pounds of raw opium and 66 pounds of morphine were found on board. This was valued at HK$12 million (US$2 million) and was packed in 60 plastic bags and gunny sacks contained in cleverly concealed cardboard boxes. According to the police chief responsible for the raid, the opium would amount to about 5.2 million doses while the morphine, converted to heroin, would be equivalent to some 900,000 "shots." He added that this was the second-largest haul of narcotics in the history of their operations, the largest having been in February 1965, when they were able to get their hands on two and a half tons of raw opium and morphine. Four men were taken into custody. The official view, at the time, was that the consignment was intended for domestic consumption in Hong Kong rather than for re-export. The authorities would not reveal the source, but said cryptically, as usual, that the "fact that the goods were seized on a junk might indicate that they came from a limited distance."

The larger seizure in 1965 was made ashore in Kowloon at a chicken farm and amounted in all to 4,600 pounds of opium and about 400 pounds of morphine. The materials had been smuggled into Kowloon in bamboo segments. In all probability it was on its way into the notorious "walled city" of Kowloon.

There were some extremely impressive seizures during 1971. By December 10 the HKP Narcotics Bureau had seized some 13,500 pounds of drugs worth about HK$60 million, an almost tenfold increase over the amount captured in the previous year, which amounted to only 1,400 pounds valued at HK$8.5 million. According to the police, the breakdown was 12,500 pounds of opium (previous year 877 pounds); 660 pounds of morphine (previous year 170 pounds); 162 pounds of heroin (previous year 31 pounds); 191 pounds of barbital (previous year 303 pounds); and 75 pounds of marijuana (previous year 53 pounds).

As usual there was no attribution of the source of the drugs as being Red China, but a spokesman expressed the view that the greater part of these drugs had come in by sea from Southeast Asia, originating in the Golden Triangle area. In 1970 there had been 12,395 drug raids, 14,000 arrests, and 16,011 prosecutions. During the first nine months of 1971 there were 10,648 raids and 12,857 prosecutions. During the month of November, in a single seizure, 2,700 pounds of raw opium and about 420 pounds of morphine were taken from a truck in Kowloon.

Those who are responsible for promoting the traffic in opiates that passes through Hong Kong, and also the authorities there, do not care to have it known that the real source of the greater part of the traffic is the Chinese mainland. In part, for this reason, there has been the elaborate construction of the vast base now known as the Golden Triangle, although a far more accurate and descriptive title would be the "Yunnan Area," one that was used consistently during an Australian conference on the traffic in narcotics held in Melbourne in October 1971.

Another reason of policy for concentrating their main base in Southeast Asia, besides a natural desire to have it close to their enemy, is that the Chinese, looking ahead to the period when they will be recognized and have diplomatic relations with the United States, will then have much less need for Hong Kong since their own ports will be more open. If, for example, through their new membership on committees in the UN that exist for the purposes of extinguishing the last vestiges of colonialism, they were suddenly to lay claim to Hong Kong, it would be logical for them to have parallel trading channels that could continue the traffic uninterrupted.

An estimate of the productivity of the Golden Triangle area has been made by Dr. William Geddes, Professor of Anthropology at Sydney University. In his capacity as a member of a UN team advising the Thais on their narcotics problem, Professor Geddes has calculated, after a survey of opium-producing areas in Thailand, that these are capable of producing about 145 tons per year. This is based on aerial photographs. His overall estimate for the whole region is over 1,000 tons per year, amounting to over 100 tons of morphine or heroin per year at total conversion.

As for opium itself, it is doubtful that there is a constant demand now in Hong Kong in excess of eighty tons per year, but there is little doubt that the amounts entering and leaving by transshipment are very much larger than this; some say as high as 2,000 tons a year. Some of the opium is undoubtedly converted into morphine and heroin covertly in the Colony, as raids on small plants have proved.

The most active component among the Chinese population in Southeast Asia, South China, and Hong Kong is the community known as the Chiu Chau, who originated in the Swatow area. These are a ruthless, clannish, and cunning community with Mafia-like characteristics and deep involvement in secret and criminal organizations. It is believed that there are some six major importing groups in Hong Kong today whose activities range well into the Golden Triangle or Yunnan Area. In the Colony there are supposed to be four retailing syndicates that deal with distribution, two of which are on the island of Hong Kong, while two are based on Kowloon.

The walled city of Kowloon has a particularly active narcotics traffic. Problems induced by that traffic, as well as others, pre-existent, made the Hong King government propose some years ago to flatten the walled city and replace it with housing projects. Unfortunately this did not prove possible because the Peking Government was in a position to assert ownership and proprietary rights in the area, which is an enclave whose ultimate ownership is shrouded in legal confusion. The turnover of one syndicate operating there is said to be $100,000 per day.

No account of the Far Eastern scene is complete without some reference to its important gold market, in which Hong Kong and Macao play substantial roles. Gold is one of the principal reasons for narcotics traders to be in the business.

The gold traffic operates on a sort of Hong Kong-Macao axis. The Hong Kong government has imposed legislation that controls the import or export of gold but, characteristically, as with so many other transactions in the Colony, arrival and departure do not come under this ruling and the incomparable facilities for *transit* of all goods in that free port are of the utmost use to the gold-trading fraternity. In Hong Kong the prime movers are Commercial Investment Company, Mount Trading, and Premex, who are, in effect, brokers who order consignments from Australia, South Africa, London, or elsewhere.

They have extensive dealings with a concern called the Cambista Seng Heng, a bank in the Avenido Almeido Ribeiro in Macao, and transshipments are made from Hong Kong to Macao by the fleet of the Hong Kong Macao Hydrofoil Co. The most interesting part of the whole puzzle (and puzzle it certainly is) is a remarkable organization called the Sindicato de Ouro, which operates for trading purposes under another name, the Wong Hong Hon Company. For many years this company was operated by a most interesting character, Dr. Pedro Jose Lobo, a considerable figure in the world of gold trading. After the demise of Dr. Lobo in 1965, he was succeeded by Roque Choi and Y.C. Liang (Liang Cheong). Another important figure linked with these latter is a well-known banker Ho Yin, who is involved in practically everything that Macao can offer, certainly a very wide range of options. All transactions of this group are wrapped in the deepest mystery and, in view of the legislation imposed by the Colony of Hong Kong, there is a total absence of meaningful statistics about gold movements. Similarly nothing is known about the fate of the innumerable gold bars that find their way into the vaults of the Sindicato de Ouro. As far as anyone knows they just stay there. More than a suspicion exists that a good many of them find their way through Bank of China channels into Canton, but those who really know about this subject will say nothing. On the other hand, it is widely believed that a good deal of the gold that comes into Hong Kong in the first place, but which cannot be *imported* as ingots (all of which are numbered and listed), may well return there in other forms and in substantial quantities. The goldsmiths and jewellers of Hong Kong know about this, as do some of the bankers, but they are just as reticent as their neighbors in Macao.

It is a curious and noteworthy fact that the two areas most notorious in the world of narcotics trading, namely the Middle East and Southeast Asia (with the Far East in concert), are regions in which very important gold markets and trading posts exist. In the former, it is primarily Beirut and Dubai, at the entrance to the Persian Gulf. It may also be observed that both these areas are regions of unrest and of protracted conflict. One of the most inexplicable paradoxes of our time is that both the British and the U.S. governments have expressly forbidden their nationals to own gold sovereigns and dollar coinage, once legal tender. These now find their way abroad in enormous quantities to places like Vientiane or Kuwait, where they are buried in the ground by Chinese, Corsican expatriates, Thais, or Laotians, or Palestinian and other Arabs. They are regarded so highly that a large number of clandestine mints exist to counterfeit them. And their principal use seems to be as backing for intrigues to deprive the West of its position in the world of petroleum, or to finance terrorist or guerrilla movements. Such movements are bent on harassment of the powers who minted or designed the coins or on outright conquest or expropriation of their property and/or rights of possession from Puerto Rico and Panama to Hong Kong and Brunei.

At one time gold was the touchstone of financial stability and a recognized prop of the established order. Since the Chinese Communists have become one of the most active purchasers of gold, especially on the London market since 1965 (a significant year and a turning point in their narcotics program, be it noted), and Arab terrorists are being paid in it, gold seems to have been flooding into the hands of those who are the self-professed destroyers of the established order.

In passing, it should be mentioned that New York City, unquestionably the narcotics capital of the United States, is also its primary gold-storage and trading point where, in the vaults of the Federal Reserve Bank of New York, there is a vast store of the precious metal held on behalf of many governments, some private persons, and also the International Monetary Fund.

Japan

It has been noted that Shanghai is an important exporting base for narcotics, situated in the middle of the three producing areas of Kiangsu, Anhwei, and Chekiang, and that the principal figure to be connected with the traffic in recent times has been Cheng Lao-san. Cheng, whose title is Director of the Opium Prohibition Bureau for the above three provinces, is reputed to be the most important opium dealer in the Chinese Communist regime. He has sometimes been called the "King of Opium," and has held a particular responsibility for coordinating the trade to Japan and directing the distribution networks there. There are those who are convinced that his charter also extended to operations in Korea, undertaken with a view to subsequent movements into Japan.

The organization set up in Japan subordinate to Cheng has been, in the main, based on Tokyo and Kobe. Its chief has been Li Chin-sui. Operations can be said to have begun seriously in 1949 when a consortium formed by Li Tien-cheng, Kuo Chu-hsiu, Lan Kuo-cheng,

Pao Wen-han, Pao Jui-sheng, Liu Kan-lung, and Hsieh Chan-mu, all Chinese Communists who had been working in Japan, returned to the mainland in a ship they had purchased. Of these, Pao Jui-sheng soon returned to Japan in order to operate the distribution (and intelligence) networks the group had left behind in the country. It seems that Japan had become rather too "hot" for the others.

However, they, and especially Li Tien-cheng, have been in the habit of negotiating directly with Cheng Lao-san for supplies of narcotics consigned to Japan and to other markets such as the Philippines. Of these, Li Chin-sui was "wanted" by the Japanese police after a quantity of heroin was seized aboard the MS *Hermaline* in Kobe in 1951. It was not a large consignment, being barely four pounds in weight, but it was believed to be part of a single order of which 170 pounds had already been delivered. The deal had been the result of a purchase by two Chinese, Hsieh Chun-mu and Hung En-chu. The latter, with an associate called Hsu Yu-fu, was arrested at this time for trafficking in heroin. Simultaneously, Li Tien-cheng was arrested in Hong Kong. He had the same kind of relationship with Li Chin-sui as that held by both Hung and Hsu.

In April 1952 a Japanese called Shibata Tatsuo was arrested in Tokyo when attempting to sell 720 grams of heroin, charging a price of Y290,000 for 110 grams. This he had obtained from Lo Chung-chung, a subordinate member within the ring operated by Cheng Lao-san. Seized during these investigations were 676 grams of heroin of the Red Lion brand (known to be manufactured in Tientsin), then later 706 grams, and finally 1,313 grams. Packages with the Chinese factory numbers 00016 and 00019 were taken in July 1952, and in October of that year packages bearing the numbers 00017, 00018, and 00021 were seized.

An individual named Chen Kun-yuan was then identified, living in Hongo Meguro, Tokyo, who was found to have a close working relationship with Cheng Lao-san. The latter had been particularly active during the period 1949–52, when he shipped large quantities of heroin to Tokyo. Before moving from China to Tokyo he had been able to send into Japan 120 pounds of heroin, delivered by air and packed in half-pound rubberized bags. He is reputed to have paid the pilots of commercial aircraft Y700,000 for each flight during which the consignments were packed in the pilots' personal luggage and then delivered by hand to the Meguro ward where Chen was to base himself.

Chen was a well-known personality in the narcotics-trading half-world in the Far East and was the leader of a gang in Central China during World War II. His activities were ended by the Nationalist Government, which arrested him in Szechuan and confiscated his effects.

However, later, under the Chinese Communist regime, Chen was able to start again with his trading in heroin and is said to have amassed a fortune under their rule.

Two other Chinese, Chang Liang-tung and Tao Tsing-kang, have been working under Chen in the opium trading he has been conducting in Japan, Singapore, Malaysia, and even, it is said, in parts of China. About one-half of their heroin is delivered to Japan. He has a Korean subordinate who is concerned with transactions in Korea and Soviet Russia.

A head of the Red Chinese underground in Japan has been Li Chin-sui, who seems to have been an "illegal" rather than a Party member. As a result of large-scale trading he has been able to return large profits to the mainland. For some time, Li has been operating a commercial-front organization called the Yung Tung Trading Company. This is actually an element of the Ministry of Trade and Commerce (State Council) that was set up for strategic trading such as the purchase of medical stores, computers, and advanced scientific instruments for the military programs. In exchange for these it exports narcotics.

Also it is said that there has been an affiliation between Kiu Kan-lung and members of the family of Li Sui-sen, a well-known trader who was arrested in Yokohama in October 1951. These are Shanghai-based dealers. Hsieh Chun-mu was known to have been connected with Kaji Wataru and Mitsuhashi Masao, who were exposed as Japanese agents of Red Chinese intelligence. Although there have been numerous cases of Japanese who have become involved in the traffic, the prevailing pattern has been that the instigation of the traffic and the management of its operations has remained in the hands of Koreans and Chinese, primarily the latter.

In the early 1950s there was a particularly brisk trade being carried on by a group of some forty experienced smugglers from the Tientsin office of the Overseas Trade Division. The principal port of exit was Tangku, while Kyushu was the port of entrance. China was receiving, in exchange for its narcotics, return cargoes of gasoline, steel ingots, automobile parts, and electronics equipment.

It was also this same ring that was caught trading in Red Lion brand via Hong Kong (876 grams), as reported in a SCAP (Supreme Commander Allied Powers) report of March 10, 1952. There was also the case of a similar seizure in Japan of 30 pounds of heroin smuggled by sea from Hong Kong. Some of the packages seized bore wrappers marked "Duro-Well Pharmaceutical Laboratory, Lions' Globe (Brand), Luck St., Tientsin."

In order to understand properly the present status of the drug menace as it affects the United States directly, within the North American continent itself, as well as U.S. military interests both in Asia and in Europe, it is extremely important to review the Japanese case. Japan, next to the United States, has been a primary area of attack by the U.S.S.R., and all party activities, particularly subversive operations in Japan, must have been fully known to the Communist Party of the Soviet Union. The Soviets, until the breach with the Chinese Reds, supported them in all their denials about the drug traffic. The Chinese only entered the Korean War after the obvious failure of the North Korean offensive that resulted from U.S. intervention. However, there can be no doubts about the planned nature of any action and the close coordination that then existed between Chinese and Soviet military staffs.

Although the Korean War was waged on conventional lines, neither the Russians nor the Chinese neglected the highly important matter of subversive and paramilitary organizations aimed at providing a revolutionary infrastructure for Japan. It is incredible, in view of the U.S. military presence in the country at that time, that they were able to achieve such a striking degree of success. This can be attributed to the weakening of the Japanese security system as a result of the outcome of the war, a basic unfamiliarity by Americans with Asian security operations, and the difficulty of building a free system—which was the wholly estimable aim of the United States in Japan—without the opportunity being created for highly undesirable activities on the part of those whose intent was to bring about a takeover of Japan after U.S. power and influence had waned. This has, of course, been one of the underlying aims of the Vietnam War.

Indeed, it was necessary for the Chinese Reds and their North Korean allies to gain experience—both in the delivery of various narcotics to target areas in the much more accessible Japanese islands, and by studying closely the U.S. military-security machinery in order to circumvent it when future operations such as those in Vietnam would warrant this. It is obvious from a survey of the evidence that the Chinese Reds, who have no scruples and are governed in nefarious activities of this kind by the Leninist conception of Bolshevik ethics (if it is not possible or if it is too expensive to use clean methods of fighting, dirty ones will do just as well), were pleased to be able to pay the Japanese back in their own coin: in short, to wreak vengeance on them for their narcotics offensive delivered in the 1920s and 30's. The facts were certainly closely observed by U.S. officials connected with the defense of the Far East, but the Korean War was one in which the emphasis was on conventional methods of waging war. Thus, coordination between narcotics and related morale operations mounted by the Chinese seems to have been missed. The consequences for the U.S. military contribution to the Vietnamese War have been grave.

To gain perspective on the question and to assemble even further evidence of Chinese culpability as artists in the conduct of hypodermic warfare, some of the assessments and analytical observations of Richard Deverall are of special and, indeed, unique value, as has been noted earlier in Chapter 3. Deverall was certainly not among those who were deceived by appearances and his comments are penetrating. Deverall states

> The two major victim countries of the world today are Japan and the United States of America. The evidence regarding this dirty opium business proves beyond a peradventure that much of the opium and heroin arriving in both Japan and the United States comes from factories in Red China and/or North Korea. And the transmitting station is the British Colony of Hong Kong, with the Portuguese Colony of Macao running a poor second—although Macao is also host to part of the smuggling racket sending the dirty drugs from Canton across to Okinawa and Japan proper.[23]

In the same work the author points out the important but little-known fact that the U.S. higher command in the Pacific theater was acutely aware that wherever the Japanese forces were deployed, and particularly in the "East Asia Co-Prosperity Sphere," they took narcotics with them not for their own use (although of course there were cases of addiction among them) but mainly to bring down the new subjects of Japan.

> Drug addiction in Japan seems to have grown rapidly in post-war Japan despite the stern action of the Allied Occupation in trying to curb or eliminate any drug addiction. America's expert, Anslinger, has pointed out, the huge areas occupied by the Imperial Japanese Forces during the Pacific War were areas in which opium and other narcotics were not only used but even encouraged both to secure revenue and to spawn corruption and degeneracy among whom the militarists expected would become colonial subjects of the leader of the so-called "Asian Co-Prosperity Sphere." For that reason, the U.S. sponsored a series of conferences beginning in 1943 to plan for immediate action to suppress the drug traffic in the Far East the very minute the hold of the Imperial Japanese Forces was broken. Despite all precautions, and as an official Welfare Ministry note explains (cf. editorial in *Nippon Times*, September 10, 1953) post-war addiction has increased and there are now 40,000 narcotics users in Japan. Another source charges that the actual

number of drug addicts is 100,000 *(Nippon Times,* November 4, 1953), while a third source says the number is as high as 300,000 *(Tokyo View,* September 1953). Whatever the actual figure, all agree that it is high—and higher than pre-war days. Indeed, the Welfare Ministry has announced plans to build a narcotics-addict hospital in Tokyo to accommodate 200 persons at one time *(Nippon Times,* September 10, 1953).

Drug addiction in pre-war Japan was rather sternly dealt with in Japan proper. But, during the war, the deployment of Japanese forces all over China and the Far East seemingly played a part in bringing about increased Japanese addiction: so too the use of strong stimulants such as *philopon* (or *hiropon)* during the war on the part of airmen on service, as well as war industry workers who were forced to take drugs in order to keep awake on the job and avoid accidents—these and other reasons made straight the path at the end of the war for a rise in the craving of many persons for the unnatural state produced both by stimulants such as *hiropon* and such narcotics as heroin. Indeed, as many narcotics authorities have pointed out, the continued use of *hiropon* or benzedrine disorders the nerves and body functions to such an extent that the next step is to narcotics addiction, heroin being both the logical development and the most dangerous of all.[24]

Deverall quotes an observation made by Anslinger in Anslinger's own book, *The Traffic in Narcotics,* pp. 70–71:

"The traffic in smuggled heroin had attracted the authorities' attention for the first time at the end of 1947. During 1948 it had increased and in 1949 had attained considerable proportions. In 1950, 1978 grams of heroin had been seized at Konosaki, on the Japanese coast. It had been brought into Japan by a group of North Korean Communists with the help of Japanese accomplices. At the same time 729 grams of heroin bought from a Communist company at Genzan, in North Korea, had been seized at Niigata, also on the (west) coast of Japan. The total heroin seized in 1950 had been 10 kilograms, or three times the amount seized in 1949."

The UNO narcotics expert then declared: *"The chief of the Communist Party in Kyushu, implicated in one of the seizures, had said the heroin had been given him by a North Korean called Kyo Son, a member of the Central Committee of the Communist Party of Rashin (North Korea)"*[25]

At about this time SCAP in Japan issued a report dated March 10, 1952, in Tokyo, concerning this question, that was also quoted by Anslinger in a memorandum dated April 15, 1952, issued in New York City.

Anslinger's memorandum was addressed to the Chairman of the UN Commission on Narcotics Drugs:

> Investigations, arrests, and seizures in Japan during 1951 proved conclusively that the Communists are smuggling heroin from China to Japan, and are using the proceeds from the sale thereof to finance party activities and to obtain strategic materials for Red China.... Approximately fifty percent of the total seized in 1951 was either definitely labelled with a Chinese address...or else marked with a known pre-war brand of Chinese heroin. Other seizures were traced by the statements of arrested Communists who stated the heroin was being sold to raise funds for Party activities.[26]

Again Deverall:

> During 1953, the Japanese police revealed some details of the smuggling ship *Itsukushima Maru*, a 10-man-crew, 190-ton vessel operating between Japan and Red China. Bristling with guns and with a machine gun in the cabin of the master, the police reported that the ship had made a score of trips returning morphine, opium and guns from Shanghai. Thousands of watches had been smuggled to Japan although they do not bring in as many dollars as the heroin or the opium. The police reported that one year of operations had netted the smuggling group a neat Yen 10,000,000 profit.
>
> ...Again, the Japanese narcotics agents early in 1954 broke up a ring (Tokyo, *Mainichi Shimbun*, March 17, 1954) smuggling narcotics from Hong Kong to Iwakuni and Kobe—to the former by air, to the latter by sea. A Hong Kong report notes (Hong Kong, *Kung Shang Jih Pao*, January 8, 1954) that Japanese small craft have been increasingly noted landing at Lap Sap Mei, a Red Chinese-held island off the estuary of the Pearl River. It is said that the Japanese, Korean and Chinese smugglers bring textile machinery and other valuable items which are exchanged for Chinese goods and raw opium....
>
> Again, the raw material for *hiropon* is seemingly coming in through Hong Kong. One example is seen in the police raid late in 1953 which resulted in seizure of enough ephedrine to manufacture 150,000,000 ampoules of *hiropon* (Tokyo, *Mainichi Shimbun*, December 18, 1953). Chinese in Hong Kong were involved, as were Chinese in Japan. In a police raid at Yokohama, six Koreans were arrested in what appeared to be a *hiropon* factory. (Tokyo, *Nippon Times*, November 10, 1953).
>
> All available evidence in Japan indicates that Chinese and Koreans predominate in both the opium and heroin rackets and the introductory-stimulant-drug racket of *hiropon*. Thus Japanese

arrests of narcotics violators from January through to November of 1952 included 24.6 percent Chinese and 16.8 percent Koreans (p. 6, remarks of Mr. Anslinger, *op.cit.*). Figures for the entire year of 1953 indicate that Koreans constitute 22.2 percent of all persons involved, with Chinese at 19.4 percent (Tokyo, *Nippon Times*, February 15, 1954). The Tokyo Metropolitan Police report their narcotics arrests in 1953: out of a total of 149 some 68 were Koreans and 39 Chinese.[27]

In testimony that he presented before the U.S. Senate Subcommittee on Internal Security, Deverall said, with regard to trade union developments in Japan:

> During November–December of 1949, the new Chinese Communist Government sponsored in the city of Peking a WFTU conference which discussed the "liberation movement of the colonies and semi-colonies" of Asia. The military, aggressive character of this alleged labor conference can easily be seen by reading the manifesto of the conference which advised the workers of Asia: "When you can no longer carry on your action in the cities under the white terror, you join the areas under partisan control to rally their units."
>
> In Japan, the Communists subsequently joined with North Koreans in launching a series of violent disturbances preparatory to the Korean War. In the Philippines leading officials of the CLO left Manila to pack a rifle with the Huks in the hills. In Vietnam, South Korea, Malaya, Indonesia and Upper Burma Communist armed aggression against local government was intensified.
>
> WFTU backing of guerrilla warfare was only one tactic. The second tactic in Peking was the organization in Peking of the liaison bureau of the WFTU. Based on Red China and hiding behind the banner of the All China Federation of Trade Unions, this liaison bureau has woven a network of intrigue, corruption and subversive propaganda. The liaison bureau consists of 5 sections and 4 offices. The most important section, that responsible for the guidance of secret Communist operations throughout Asia and the Far East is directly under a Russian. His assistant is a Japanese. *Another vital section, the so-called fifth section, is the economic-financial controlling trading organisations outside China. The Chinese Chiang Ch'ing* heads it; and again the No. 2 man is a Japanese, the former actor Ganemon Nakamura.*

---

*The author doubts whether Mr. Deverall was aware of the fact, when he submitted the above testimony, that Chiang Ch'ing was Mme. Mao Tse-tung. At that time she was an extremely obscure figure little known in the West, not as she is now. It is perhaps not very surprising that she should have an ex-actor as a deputy since she, herself, has been a film actress.

The second vital section, it should also be noted, is engaged in the dirty narcotics business out of Red China which has as one of its principal targets the country of Japan. Opium and heroin smuggled to Japan and sold mainly to young Japanese is providing the WFTU secret organizations in Japan with hundreds of millions of yen to carry on their operations of spreading camouflaged WFTU propaganda and corrupting some labor leaders into accepting the Red Chinese line designed for Japanese labor.

As the Korean population of Japan is less than one percent, the Chinese only a tiny fraction of one percent, it is quite obvious that the dirty opium business in Japan is largely in the hands of Chinese and Korean dope-pushers. And, as the successful seizures indicate, the heart of the business is concentrated in two areas, the Tokyo-Yokohama Area in which 77.35 percent of all heroin seizures took place in 1953, and the Kobe-Osaka Area which accounted for 18.47 percent of the heroin seizures during the same period (p. 12, Annual Report for Welfare Ministry, 1953).[28]

The three criteria that underlay the choice of these two areas were

(1) Being very large urban areas with great concentration of population, there is at once a ready-made market and a region providing suitable cover for clandestine operations.
(2) Both are seaport areas, enabling deliveries to be made.
(3) Both areas are near large American bases that in each case are objectives of the traffic and markets.

As a part of the traffic, a particularly vicious crime- and vice-sodden environment grew up in these areas, organized to produce demoralization of U.S. servicemen and simultaneously to degrade the civilian population adjoining the bases. This rendered the U.S. armed services particularly vulnerable to skillfully mounted hostile propaganda campaigns designed to portray GIs as an influence promoting and supporting the drug traffic rather than being victimized by it. Precisely the same technique has been employed more recently in Indo-China.

When considering the facts connected with the situation in Japan in the '50s, it must be realized that the psycho-chemical offensive then launched in Japan and in South Korea was directly related to the Korean War, and also that, at that time, the North Koreans had been trained for and launched on South Korea.

It should, perhaps, also be noted that the WFTU is the entirely Communist-run international trade union movement that must be sharply distinguished from the ICFTU that is the international federation of trade unions with which are affiliated almost all free trade unions outside the Iron or Bamboo Curtains.

The Japanese have been particularly plagued by a group of synthetic drugs falling within the aminobutene group, of which the following have been recognized:

1. Alpha-6-dimethylamino-4, 4-diphenyl-3-acetoxyheptane and salts.
2. Alpha-6-dimethylamino-4, 4-diphenyl-3-heptanol and its salts.
3. Beta-6-dimethylamino-4, 4-diphenyl-3-acetoxyheptane and salts.
4. 3-dimethylamino-1, 1-di-(2-thienyl)-1-butene and its salts.
5. 3-ethylmethylamino-1, 1-di-(2-thienyl)-1-butene and its salts.
6. 6-Methyl-delta 6-desoxymorphine and its salts.

Of the above, 3-dimethylamino-1,1-di-(2-thienyl)-1-butene hydrochloride had been manufactured in Japan with the trade names of Orton, Kobaton, Shikiton, and Takaton; it was a source of great trouble to the Japanese authorities, who considered that it had a particularly baneful effect on society. *Hiropon* itself was also manufactured in Japan, in large quantities, with a high degree of addiction, although now largely abated. *Hiropon* was prepared from ephedrine hydrochloride, often supplied through Hong Kong from the mainland as Star Brand, produced by the New Asiatic Chemical Works Ltd. in Shanghai. The tablets in this preparation are a neutral sulphate with the following formula:

$$(C_6H_5 \ CH\text{-}OH\text{-}CH_3 \ NH\text{-}CH_3)_2: \ H_2SO_4$$

Its manufacturers claim remarkable properties for it as a medicament for all kinds of complaints, but it is as an intermediate for the preparation of a most dangerous stimulant that it is most widely known.

In Japan *hiropon* has played something of the same role as the central stimulants Preludin, Methedrine, and Ritalin elsewhere. These are aphrodisiac stimulants; the last in particular has proved to be an unmitigated disaster in Sweden, where it has been used a good deal intravenously. Full particulars of this form of self-inflicted madness are provided by Dr. Donald B. Louria in his highly informative and authoritative work *The Drug Scene*.[29]

For the purposes of this study it is not the erotic aspect of these substances that is of primary interest. The factor of significance to psycho-chemical warfare is that drugs of this kind have played an important role, when used on a sustained basis, as preconditioning agents leading to other narcotics, notably heroin. That at least, has been the case in Japan, and neither the source nor the intent behind the traffic has been in any doubt to the properly informed.

There is still another important aspect that has been insufficiently realized—the doping with these stimulants of partisans and terrorists who can be given particularly impressive degrees of endurance, artificially increased vitality, and murderous propensities untrammelled by the slightest humanitarian impulses. This matter will be discussed below in the section dealing with the Korean aspects of the narcotics problem.

Yet in spite of the tremendous assault on Japan launched with such intensity by the Chinese Reds and the North Koreans in the '50s, there are grounds for some satisfaction. Although the Japanese did, in fact, develop something of an epidemic of heroin addiction under the extraneous pressure put on their society, they have been able to get the situation under control. Since 1964, when they had at least 50,000 known addicted (and possibly many more), they have been able to reduce the figure to only a few thousand now.

The methods they have used are certainly worthy of close study. For one thing, the Japanese have a remarkable tradition of efficient internal security and law enforcement and their departments charged with these responsibilities have been both competent and ruthless. Their legislation has been exceptionally stringent: the penalty for smuggling or selling heroin can be as much as ten years and an individual found with heroin in his possession can be held for thirty days without bail.

In addition, the Japanese Government has been able to evoke a response from its citizens that is based on the national character—known to be extremely amenable to discipline and possessing a strong basis of national pride. In appealing to this pride, and also subtly causing the addict or the suspect to lose face and to have a sense of being an outcast from society, an almost infallible method has been formulated. Naturally this can only be made to work in such manner in a country that has a highly defined and accepted social structure.

Nevertheless a situation of vigilance must be maintained there because most of the Communist infrastructure, designed with long-range purposes in view, remains concealed below the surface pattern of life. The Nixon shocks were extremely severe, all the more so because the Japanese have far fewer illusions about China than does the United States. The current policy of normalization is highly perilous.

Korea

While the Japanese authorities were always very strict about the use of narcotics in their own country, there was an element of laxity in their colonies. It is known, for example, that the drug traffic was a highly profitable pursuit in Korea during their four decades of rule there prior to World War II.

In a noteworthy report delivered by Henry J. Anslinger at the 8th Session of the UN Commission on Narcotic Drugs, in New York on April 15, 1953, the attention of the Commission was drawn to the established fact that in 1951 Korean employees of the North Korean Trading Co. stationed in Pusan were employed in opium and heroin trading on behalf of Red China. On August 23, 1952, 333 grams of heroin were seized that were known to have come from North Korea. Similar seizures in Seoul had shown that the heroin readily obtainable there was of a kind commonly received from Communist China.

The Soviet Union that today is reacting strongly to Chinese narcotics trading—now often denouncing it—actually participated in the traffic just after World War II for political and strategic reasons. When Soviet occupation forces arrived in Pyongyang, they not only authorized but encouraged the production of opium poppies because they believed that they would gain both valuta and psychological advantages by directing narcotics sales in South Korean and Japanese target areas. As early as 1945 they entertained the aim of "liberating" South Korea by force as a means of threatening Japan itself. Consequently, they viewed drug transactions as a form of softening up, or as "artillery preparation," for their assault, which came to be mounted by North Korean troops in 1951.

During the Korean War itself, after the UN forces had succeeded in crossing the Yalu and occupying Pyongyang, they uncovered there 300 boxes of raw opium in storage buildings owned by the Ministry of Commerce. They also captured a large quantity of morphine, sufficient to fill two or three rooms of approximately 10'x12'x8' in size. This was enough to identify the official nature of the sources of opium, morphine, and heroin in North Korea that had been troubling South Korea and Japan. It also became quite evident at the time that Kim Il-sung was personally involved in the traffic, which was resumed shortly afterward when the UN forces withdrew to positions south of the 38th Parallel.

For further information on the pattern of Korean narcotics trading, reference may be made to Appendix IVB-II, which summarizes the salient features. The traffic has been made all the more dangerous by traditional acts and capabilities of the Korean "Ronin," as a particular kind of assassin or bravo has been known to the Japanese. The latter have always had reason to accord a high degree of respect to the militancy and personal bravery of those Koreans with whom they have had to deal.

Along these lines, there has recently been created a Special Task Force raised, trained, and operated in North Korea. So far it has not had any particular success, but one must concede that it has not as yet been used to the extent possible. This Special Force is known as the "124th Unit."

It is an interesting and somewhat unique body about 6,000 strong whose main headquarters is in Pyongyang but whose disposition is in six bases. Its operational H.Q. is at Tokkol Sungho District, Pyongyang, and there are also the following: 1st Base, Sanggok-ri, Yonsan-kun; 2nd Base, Siksong-ri, Sangwon-kun; 3rd Base, Taehung-ri, Sangwon-kun; 4th Base, Kongpo-ri, Yonsan-kun; 5th Base, location unknown; 6th Base, Pangjong-ri, Yonsan-kun. At each base there are stationed ten companies, each of which is ninety-nine strong. Each company is divided into three platoons, each of thirty-three members, while each platoon has three squads.

124 Unit and Operations in South Korea

The first occasion on which 124 Unit launched what was intended to be a significant operation (and which, since it failed, revealed something of the nature and purposes of that formation) was an attempted raid on Chong Wa Dae Palace in Seoul, the residence of President Park. The intention was to assassinate Park on January 21, 1968.

In order to achieve this, a thirty-one-man team was thrown in that was composed of seven subgroups. The "Command," or leading subgroup, was in charge of Captain Kim Chong-ung, who had two orderlies (couriers) by him, while the 1st subgroup was headed by Lieut. Kim Chong-sik, with four subordinates. The 2nd subgroup was led by Lieut. Kim Sin-jo, who was, ultimately, the only survivor of the affair and who had been attached to it in a special capacity as a security officer. The 3rd, 4th, and 5th subgroups had five, five, and six members respectively, while the 6th consisted of three drivers.

As is so often the case with abortive irregular attacks, as this one proved to be, there had been a last-minute change of plans. But there is little doubt that if the original plan had gone through it would also have met with failure. Originally this task force was to have been part of an extremely ambitious plan, which was suddenly abandoned, whose characteristics were as follows:

An assault unit was to raid South Korea that would have had a strength of thirty-five men. It was to have been divided into five subgroups with objectives:

(1) The 1st subgroup (with fifteen members) was to raid Chong Wa Dae and murder President Park.
(2) The 2nd subgroup was to destroy the residence of the U.S.Ambassador and to murder him and his family.
(3) The 3rd subgroup (five men) had the task of demolishing Army H.Q. and murdering commanding generals.
(4) The 4th subgroup (five men) would blast open the front gate of Seoul Prison, free all prisoners, and then proceed to a special detention camp for North Korean agents at Sobin-go, southeast of Seoul, to rescue all agents.
(5) The 5th subgroup was arranged as a reinforcement and support unit in the actions described above.

However, this plan, which seems, on analysis, to be of a somewhat fanciful nature, was abandoned and a substitute plan introduced. It is anybody's guess whether the modified plan had any chance of success if it had been introduced originally and then consistently followed.

In the second plan a force of thirty-one men was divided into seven subgroups that were instructed to operate as follows:

(1) The 1st subgroup was to raid the second floor of Chong Wa Dae and murder the President.
(2) The 2nd subgroup was to occupy the first floor and kill all officials there.
(3) The 3rd subgroup was directed to attack the security office and murder all security officers there.
(4) The 4th subgroup had the task of entering the Secretary's office and killing all officials there.
(5) The guiding and command subgroup and the 5th subgroup were to assault security guards at the front gate, seize cars in Chong Wa Dae, and drive all members of the raid back to North Korea once the raid was over and the mission accomplished.
(6) All units or subgroups not assigned specific objectives were to remain in a support role and instructed to carry out diversionary or covering actions as necessary.

The timing for the above operation was to have been on a Sunday evening (January 21) at 8 P.M. and was scheduled to take about three

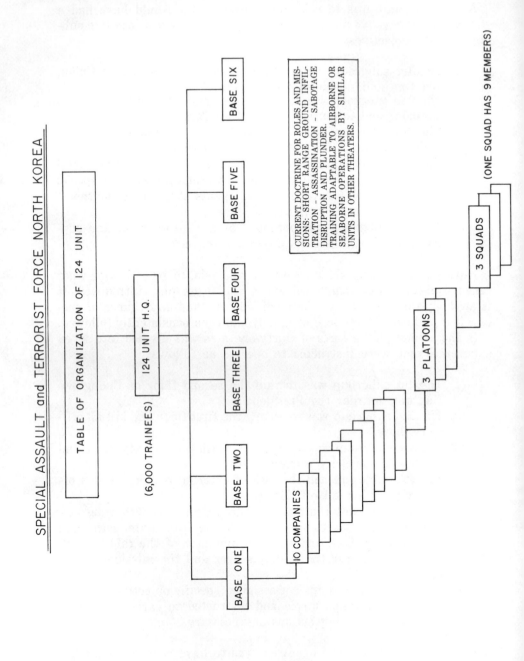

SPECIAL ASSAULT and TERRORIST FORCE NORTH KOREA

TABLE OF ORGANIZATION OF 124 UNIT

124 UNIT H.Q.

(6,000 TRAINEES)

BASE ONE

BASE TWO

BASE THREE

BASE FOUR

BASE FIVE

BASE SIX

10 COMPANIES

3 PLATOONS

3 SQUADS

(ONE SQUAD HAS 9 MEMBERS)

CURRENT DOCTRINE FOR ROLES AND MISSIONS: SHORT RANGE GROUND INFILTRATION - ASSASSINATION - SABOTAGE DISRUPTION AND PLUNDER. TRAINING ADAPTABLE TO AIRBORNE OR SEABORNE OPERATIONS BY SIMILAR UNITS IN OTHER THEATERS.

to four minutes, followed by rapid withdrawal across the Imjin the same night.

Each member of the force was equipped with a submachine gun, 300 rounds of ammunition, a Russian TT (Tula-Tokharets) pistol, an antitank grenade, eight hand grenades, and a knife.

The task of slipping through the DMZ and the approach to Seoul had taken longer than they anticipated on the night of the raid and they did not arrive at the Chahamun Pass near Seoul until 9:40 P.M. They were disguised as members of a South Korean intelligence agency.

While proceeding down the pass they were challenged by South Korean police who wanted to check their documents. The terrorists acted in a rather inept fashion by opening fire indiscriminately at the police and the public, throwing grenades into buses passing by and into nearby houses. Seven persons were killed immediately, including the chief of the police detachment at Chong-no police station and passengers on the buses. The R.O.K. troops responded promptly, after the infiltrators had scattered in all directions, by rounding up and killing twenty-nine of the thirty-one. One individual was posted as missing, while Lieut. Kim was captured.[30]

Another raid was mounted by 124 Unit some months later on Sunday morning, November 3, 1968, at 5:30 A.M. On that occasion a similar team arrived in the Ulchin and Samchok area. They selected as the objective for their attack Kosudong village. The intent was to terrorize the village into cooperating with them, and to recruit agents in the course of what they called a "small village revolution." As before, the operation ended in an orgy of indiscriminate slaughter of innocent and defenseless country people, including children and an old Buddhist nun. They did not last long and were all hunted down and killed in the course of a few days by R.O.K. antiguerrilla teams.

In some ways the procedure followed by the terrorists resembled the actions of the Viet Cong: infliction of terror in villages, attempts at recruiting members for "humanist" organizations such as "Women's Leagues, Youth Leagues for National Salvation, and Revolutionary Veterans Organizations," or the "Organization for Men of Culture" for intellectuals. From such bodies, the units recruit a network for intelligence operations. Selected members of the community were also to be kidnapped and taken to North Korea.

The tactical doctrine as it was formulated for assaulting army units was as follows:

124 Unit had designated as targets Infantry Battalion H.Q., Divisional H.Q., and Missile Bases. Special attention was to be paid to communications centers: attacks on switchboards, kidnapping of key post offi-

cers, and removal of documents relating to military operations or intelligence. Attacks on missile bases involve destruction of missiles, tractors, and launchers, and killing of key missile-men.

Such attacks are always to be preceded by careful reconnaissance covering exact location of any such units, storage points, key concentrations of manpower, etc. Teams are assembled in a form and in a strength appropriate to the task in hand, ranging from fifteen-man teams to units of company strength.

Timing, in order to achieve maximum surprise, is set for mealtimes, free time in the evenings, during weekends, or on public holidays. Attacks on special installations such as missile sites are mostly launched at night. Teams are usually composed of Command, Assault, and Covering subgroups. Operations are supposed to be completed in five to ten minutes, after which all personnel return to a rendezvous.

The investigations that have been made into 124 Unit, on the basis of its performance in 1968, have indicated that what at one time used to be espionage and stealthy infiltration has been turned into a particular form of guerrilla warfare waged by teams of selected specialized infantrymen who have been described as "murderous moving weapons." They are, in fact, a variant of the more traditional Korean "Ronin" of whom the Japanese used to be so conscious. From the moment of recruitment, they are imbued with the outlook of beings prepared to die in the cause of their mission "as sons of Kim Il-sung and his party," without betrayal. Recruits for 124 Unit are

(1) Strong young men in their twenties, thoroughly indoctrinated with the Communist ideology of North Korea.
(2) Sons and brothers of laborers and farmers devoted to the Peoples' Republic of North Korea.
(3) Individuals born in North Korea, with no relations in the South.
(4) Enlisted men of many years' service, with skill in driving vehicles or flying aircraft and in the operation of communications equipment.
(5) Infantrymen with sound experience in reconnaissance and intelligence work.

A rigid screening process takes place and those selected for training as guerrillas are introduced to the subject by orientation lectures compiled by Kim Il-sung himself on "Principles of Scouting." Armed espionage missions are euphemistically called "reconnaissance missions" and the agents themselves are called "scouts."

On April 6, 1968, Kim Il-sung drafted his ten-point doctrine to describe the basic qualifications for such agents operating on intelligence missions in South Korea:

(1) Scouts shall be trained in various conditions of weather and build up their bodies by rigorous training on steep mountains day and night.
(2) Scouts shall always be armed with the ideology of the Communist Party and be prepared to fulfill the mission even when threatened with death.
(3) For physical buildup, the scouts shall be adapted by all possible ways of physical training.
(4) Scouts shall be trained as able men to conduct military operations; that is, to fulfill all practical duties, to put up a fight in the rear of enemy territory.
(5) Scouts shall learn English, Japanese, and dialects and customs of all provinces.
(6) Scouts shall be trained in skills of destroying airports, atomic cannon, missiles, bridges, tunnels, and locomotives.
(7) Scouts shall be able to operate aircraft, locomotives, and all vehicles.
(8) Scouts shall always be able to operate boats in the sea and rivers as well as being able to swim.
(9) Scouts always study creative tactics in fulfillment of the missions, drawing on their combat experience.
(10) Scouts shall study political, economic, military, and geographic conditions in the South.

There is high topicality to the doctrines of terrorist groups. Special notice should be taken of the threat embodied in the current wave of Arab terrorism. The "Black September" movement recently employed a small group of Japanese assassins in a suicide role. There is obvious linkage between units such as belong to Black September and Far Eastern agents like the nefarious Japanese who indiscriminately killed twenty-seven civilians and wounded seventy-eight others at Israel's Lod Airport on May 30, 1972. Behind Black September, operating it, is a sinister organization called "Jihad al Rasd," or RASD for short ("Operation Network") that has a great interest in hashish, which together with oil helps to finance the movement. RASD runs narcotics into Europe to weaken its enemies in Western society and to enrich itself. It pushes a strong brand of hashish that has on its package labels a picture of an Arab guerrilla with an assault rifle at the ready. In action, many of its members are crazed with the same commodity or with other stimulants.

So far the special operations undertaken by this group, while spectacular and extremely provocative, are of the "one shot" variety and their principal characteristics have been speed and dash combined in ruthless and murderous intent rather than the direct attainment of major objectives. Yet the indirect results of their operations have been and can be quite portentous.

It is not well known that the secret army of "al-Fatah," the private army of the Husseini family, is strongly supported by the Chinese Reds. Such linkages stress the importance of making a detached examination of the Korean terrorists.

Both the Korean 124 Unit and the Arab terrorists owe much of their operational and tactical skill to Chinese instruction and strategic doctrine. The undercurrent of narcotics trading and usage runs not too far below the surface in both cases, while the Koreans are also prone to use certain stimulants while in action. However it should be noted that the current operations under review are really a type of "blitz" rather than the more orthodox Maoist conception of "protracted revolutionary warfare." This variation occurred after the "Six-Day" War, which started a wave of interest in "rapid warfare." Also, Lin Piao, whose star was in the ascendant at that time, was a specialist in the "short battle."

Since the Korean Peoples' Republic has very many guerrillas trained in the pattern of 124, although there are only about 3,000 on active service at one time, it is important that a rather serious view be taken of the formation. Especially so as, in the event of aggressive moves by North Korea, they have additional other units with somewhat similar training who could act in a supporting role in an attempt at a "pushover" in South Korea.

For example, there exists also the 283rd Unit that was established in March 1966. It was set up to train agents in five bases, through which some 2,000 agents have passed who have undergone tactical training similar to that of 124 Unit, although their role would probably be quite different. There are some 60 training sites near Pyongyang where squad-sized groups or individuals can be given weapons and tactical training. Altogether about 9,000 "Scouts" now exist in association with three group armies and there are also several score members of the Korean Residents Association in Japan, "Chocongryon," who are pro-Pyongyang.

After the failure of the attack on Chong Wa Dae, several other impending operations were called off. For instance, there was a plan to send another thirty-one-man team from 1st Base of the 124 Unit to Pusan to destroy police stations, the city hall, and the telephone offices.

Another project abandoned, after extensive espionage had been concluded, was a raid by a team 102-strong from 3rd Base of 124 Unit, with the object of attacking an army division at Taegu. This was to have left for the South in mid-January but was abandoned because of the initial failure.

Similarly two others were abandoned: an attack by a thirty-one-man team on the administration buildings at Samchok-up, Samchok-kun, and a mission by 200 guerrillas to launch a surprise attack on Kimpo Airport during the summer of 1968. In spite of these setbacks it is dangerous to underestimate the potential of this military trend, especially since in numerous instances they have caused Kim Il-sung to take personal command of the special units.

In view of the current attitudes of certain Arab guerrilla groups, we can expect further criminal attacks in Europe and in the Western Hemisphere. It is a sobering thought that courses of the kind about to be described have been given extensively in Africa, in Cuba, China, Korea, and elsewhere, perhaps even in Canada. And the United States is already heavily infiltrated by Chinese seamen and Cuban refugees, many of whom are involved in heroin trading by which they can both demoralize that target country and gain influence with its nationals. Paradoxically many of these Americans are members of "peace" movements, veterans of the Vietnam War, and other misled and disaffected citizens.

North Korean Training for Terrorists in a Guerrilla Warfare Role

In accordance with the Kim Il-sung doctrine outlined above, recruits for 124 Unit undergo a program of training in two stages that together fill 740 hours.

The object of the program is to produce guerrillas fully and rigorously trained as infantry scouts and as shock assault units in a combat role. These small units, which tend increasingly towards suicide missions, are taught how to infiltrate the South, to launch surprise attacks, and to carry out wholesale murder and destruction "without betrayal."

Some recruits undergo an exceptionally hard training schedule. It is designed to provide, in all, thirty-four weeks of training in the year, involving a total of 1,632 hours. Included are two army exercises, each one lasting one or two months.

During their basic-training course, the trainees learn as fundamental arts combat crossing of the DMZ, the deep infiltration approach, camping, shelter building, surprise attack, and preparation of protective cover to avoid discovery by pursuing forces. As a part of the general courses of study they are taught wireless communications, military engineering, marksmanship, geo-morphology (i.e., topography), counterintelligence, hygienics (including uses and properties of narcotics), "political science," "special training," and swimming. A part of the program is a scouting exercise carried out over a secret route. After this, all trainees are given tests concerned both with military knowledge and proficiency and political "understanding."

Military training of this kind is provided in a ratio of 10 percent lectures and instructional drills and 90 percent exercises. Field exercises are conducted at a specially constructed center where the trainees are taught how to surmount various obstacles and to move under fire. Eighty percent of the training is in night exercises. Equipped with knapsacks, weapons, compasses, maps, and shovels, the trainees are first shown how to cross the DMZ, and then training is conducted by company commanders for some 160 hours in the year.

"Scouts" are divided into three kinds of parties—"patrol," "nucleus," and "rear-guard." The patrol party finds obstacles to its infiltration (interference factors) and gets rid of them as instructed by liaison leaders. The nucleus party is the core of the team and is charged with the responsibility of commanding the team and of guarding the flanks while marching. The rear-guard group is charged with guard duty in the rear and with erasing traces that may show the march or transit of the guerrilla team.

They are instructed in obstacle clearance such as barbed-wire entanglements, fences, minor obstacles like marshes, MP checkpoints, enemy ambush-patrol-group dugouts, and early-warning systems with tripwires. (It may be noted here, perhaps, that inadequate attention has been paid to date by these adversaries to sophisticated sensory devices now being used for detection of infiltrating groups on defended frontiers.)

Despite the Korean Military Armistice Agreement, the Communists continually have been training such guerrilla and terrorist groups, intended for disruption and terror raids in the South, in violation of the terms. After the basic training in DMZ crossing is completed, the trainees attend drills on how to reach their target areas in a straight deep infiltration approach, i.e., how to get to their targets by means of short cuts when they have passed the DMZ. This topic is the subject of a major training course that is supposed to account for 40 percent of total training hours.

The advance to the target areas is conducted in the same formation in which the DMZ is crossed and takes place between sunset and sunrise. Trainees are supposed only to follow ridge lines on their march and are forbidden to use such normal routes as village pathways, valleys, roads, bridges, railroads, or tunnels. Their methods of infiltration are quite flexible, depending on geography and the situation in the area. They use a number of secret signals and such devices as changing the direction of footprints if this is required.

When they cross rivers, they come out at a landing point on the other side that is close to deep forest or near the conjunction of two mountains. When rivers are deep, they use flotation bags. Should they unexpectedly encounter checkpoints or sentries, they are supposed to continue marching but to be ready to fight. When challenged, advanced patrols simulate the identity of special units undergoing scouting training, a strategem aided by the fact that they wear R.O.K. uniforms.

If they are thought to be in danger of discovery, at a secret signal to be given by the leader they are to eliminate the obstacle either by action with knives or by shooting and then rapidly to move on. They are trained to approach guard posts at night without hesitation and to murder guards with knives or by shooting. Silencer-equipped weapons may be used. While camping, they site and construct dugouts at points that are optimal for defensive and offensive purposes, observation, and for access to drinking water and routes of advance or retreat.

They usually select ridges (higher than 30 metres) where there are many trees. They have a preference for yellow soil, and construct dugouts or foxholes where five team members may sleep together.

When they do not need to dig trenches or foxholes, they select furrows in fields; places where there are reeds, bushes, acacia trees; embankments near rivers; natural caves in the mountains; open spaces between large rocks; uninhabited small huts; shelters in the mountains only sometimes used by villagers; or graveyard sites. They are required to avoid places frequented by villagers; where people come to cut grass or pick mushrooms, where they cut firewood, or other frequented areas.

In case of an emergency when the majority of the team members are asleep, they are warned by the pull of a rope attached to them to wake and be ready for combat duty. If they are exposed to discovery by villagers, they are instructed to kill all of them and to bury their bodies, leaving no trace. They must be ready to move on if circumstances seem unfavorable. While stationed in their dugouts, the routine is to clean weapons, to review the achievements of the previous day, and to plan those of the forthcoming day.

They are supplied with food in a compact form, primarily rice. This they eat with water, cooking it in a covered pot, using chemical fuel. When they leave they take pains to restore the place to its original appearance. Guerrillas master these skills in eighty hours of training. Shelters that they build in target areas are of two kinds—main and reserve shelters. Main shelters are built at a considerable distance from the target, for use on long-term operational missions, preferably deep in mountain fastnesses. Conditions for the selection of sites are similar to those for normal dugouts. Reserve shelters are built at a distance several hundred yards from the main ones and are used when the latter are discovered by outside people.

Both shelters are of the same size and large enough to accommodate a force of platoon size. When in position in them, troops post so-called "bottom guards" who watch shelter entrances, "telescope guards" who watch the right and left flanks of shelters, and "roof guards" who watch for approaches from the rear. There is continual communication between these guards and the main body.

When the troops are out on an operational mission, two members are left behind to watch the shelter, and sometimes to cook. When doing this, if they need to conserve chemical fuel, they are taught to avoid any wood that will give off smoke.

A principal item in the training of terrorist guerrillas is the delivery of surprise attacks. The course is a hard one. Major targets may be police stations, communications facilities, railroad stations, food and ammunition storage areas or dumps, local administration offices, and military bases. They also aim at industrial facilities in order to sabotage the South Korean economy. Manpower for assaults on targets of this description may vary from three to nine. In the case of attacks on army units, guerrillas may be of platoon number for attacks on a company-sized military base. Equipped only with the necessary items for murder, destruction, plunder, and arson, the guerrilla team is divided into three squads: attack, support, and blockade.

As the attack squad is engaged in murder, plunder, destruction, or arson in its target area, the support squad provides protective cover for it near the target area. Members of the blockade squad conceal themselves near the main roads, trying to block the arrival on the scene of any enemy reinforcements and also to keep open the line of retreat for the attack and support squads upon the completion of their mission.

Under these arrangements, the blockade squad will make the first approach to the target area, where it buries mines at two places along the main supply roads. The attack begins at a preset time, sometimes by the firing of a single round as the signal. Attacks on railroad stations or junctions for food, fuel, or ammunition stores are usually carried out by squads. They are instructed to destroy railway points, station buildings, and locomotives and to murder railroad guards. They are to plunder food and ammunition loaded in freight cars, and to start fires using incendiary devices.

Attacks are supposed to be completed in five or six minutes and, on the signal for withdrawal being given, they are to converge on a designated nearby rendezvous, check their strength in order to assess their losses, and then retire rapidly to their shelters. After reorganization of the squads and packing of their kit, the guerrillas move some 40 km from their advanced-base camping site that same night.

If the surprise assault fails, they scatter in all directions and then concentrate again at their shelter, after which they move on to another place. Stragglers are supposed to go by themselves to a predesignated gathering point and to identify themselves and establish contact using a secret code. Training for such surprise assaults takes eighty hours. A similar period of eighty hours is also spent in ambush training aimed at the countering of action by pursuing enemy forces or the plundering of food or supplies from the enemy while in retreat.

It may be noted here that, from the first, Red Chinese guerrillas have been particularly adept at drawing pursuit after themselves, doing it deliberately in order to collect weapons and even recruits from their opponents.

The formation of ambush squads is dependent on the nature of the mission, the configuration of the terrain, the manpower available, and on enemy strength. An ambush squad is divided into three sections: the attack section (about 35 percent of available manpower), the plundering section, and a support section. The attack squad is responsible for the killing, while the support section provides protective cover for the other two formations and also helps to carry the booty.

Current practice calls for training a squad in tactics with which it can oppose a platoon and sometimes a company, while a platoon of guerrillas can be pitted against a company or even a battalion. When an ambush is in prospect the guerrillas usually reach their position before sunset and start digging their individual foxholes or hideouts. When the enemy target unit approaches they attack it on a given signal.

The first intent is to paralyze the enemy's ability to counterattack. Under optimum conditions, where, for example, they can be assisted by an effective and established intelligence network in the pinpointing of key command personnel who are singled out for elimination, this is their means of achieving paralysis. If the ambush is well placed and the enemy is in movement in marching order and taken by surprise, the chances of elimination of officers and key NCOs is very good.

However, even if operating without support from a well-disposed local population from which such intelligence would be forthcoming, a well-trained and observant ambush group, particularly if it can achieve full surprise and be aided by its own detached recon team, can produce a situation of complete shock and confusion that can last for at least several minutes. During this the guerrillas approach the enemy unit, destroy its vehicles and seize supplies. Usually, they attempt to take prisoners in order to gain intelligence of enemy formations. When they retreat rapidly from such an ambush they are trained to move at least 40 km during the day.

Large-Scale Field Exercises

After ambush training, the trainees will have completed 740 hours of basics and can be considered ready for tactical field exercises. The main object of these is to assess the combat capability of the troops in guerrilla warfare after their basic education, indoctrination, and training. Such capability is assessed at squad, platoon, and company level. Usually the exercises are conducted in cold weather to prepare the guerrillas for their missions in winter. It has been ascertained that the thirty-one-man team detailed for the attack on Chong Wa Dae and on President Park was forced to undertake a seventeen-day field exercise that started on December 12, 1967, and that went over the whole course of training twelve times.

It was conducted in six "kun," in the areas Kangdong-kun, Hoeching-kun, Sin pyung-kun, Suan-kun, Koksan-kun, and Yonsan-kun. The range involved shows the extremely wide area used for training troops by means of field exercises. Each exercise was divided into five steps:

(1) Training for infiltration and field camping. This lasted for three days and the guerrillas rehearsed crossing the DMZ and rapid straight infiltration to the objective area.
(2) Passing of checkpoints and foraging by seizing food. Two days.
(3) Digging of trenches, foxholes, shelters. Withdrawal after completion of mission. Two days.
(4) Ambush and plunder. This was an attack by a company-sized unit on a mining area.
(5) Return to base. Intended to demonstrate skills in returning to the North after a mission in the South.

Although the concepts underlying 124 Unit, its training, and various of its operations have been examined at some length, it must be recognized that this is only the briefest of accounts and that the details of training have been given in outline only. Enough has been said, however, to indicate the close resemblance between this force and similar organizations that have been projected elsewhere by the Chinese Communists, and with similar aims. The fact that there is now a discernible trend away from "protracted conflict" towards the "short battle" is not only significant but may prove portentous.

It has been shown by a number of researchers that the Chinese-operated guerrilla movements are often organized and financed by the proceeds of narcotics transactions, since they would otherwise prove much too expensive for their sponsors. What may be regarded as follow-up actions are often undertaken when clandestine smuggling operations have been under way for some time, conducted by intelligence networks that not only soften up the target population for the terrorist assault but provide the basic inputs to their strategic and tactical planning. At the worst, the preliminary intelligence operations produce a useful form of demoralization, and at best, the spread of influence by corruption at high levels on the other side and a degree of collaboration on the part of the target population.

Peking has, for several years, been on close terms in the Middle East with the Palestine Liberation Organization (PLO) which it has seen as a means of extending Red Chinese influence in a theater where Russian power has been advancing. It will be remembered that the PLO was created under the auspices of the late President Nasser at a conference held in Jerusalem during the period May 28–June 2, 1964. This was attended by about 400 Palestinian refugees from many countries.

A headquarters was set up in Cairo that assumed the status of a government in exile; its leading figure was treated by the Arabs as a head of state. Its first chairman was Ahmed Shukairy, who received a good many flattering attentions from Chou En-lai and Chen Yi. As a result, in March 1965 Shukairy led a six-man delegation of the PLO to Peking, where he conferred with Chang Hsi-jo, the chief of the Peoples' Foreign Relations Institute. He was promised material support, weapons, and training, and proceeded to open a liaison office for the PLO in Peking.

As a consequence of secret agreements that Shukairy and the Red Chinese leaders signed at that time and soon afterwards, several hundred Arab terrorists were sent immediately to the Chinese mainland to undergo courses in guerrilla warfare and terrorist tactics. It is understood that they had ideological instruction as well as military training. These trainees were regarded as cadres, or a leadership and elitist group, who would form a Red Chinese-oriented leadership category among the members of the rapidly growing Arab guerrilla movement.

This liaison was not a particularly new phenomenon; there had been constant contact in the past between Peking and the Arabs that had resulted in a rather solid Red Chinese contribution to the defeat of

France in Algeria. It may be noted that the Chinese Ambassador to the U.A.R. (now at the UN) attended a PLO meeting that was held in Gaza in May 1967.

Shukairy soon came to grief because of his own defects of character, failures in the '67 war and elsewhere, and also because of his close contacts with Peking at a period when the U.S.S.R. was in the ascendant in the Arab world. He was replaced by Yasir Arafat.

The Palestine guerrillas made an attempt to use Jordan as their main base because it was conveniently close to Iraq and Kuweit, both of which contributed to their support. But the guerrillas were badly mauled by King Hussein, who regarded them as a threat to his government and to traditional Arab values. After great reverses in Jordan they concentrated in Syria and Lebanon while retaining, of course, an important element in Egypt.

In order to underline the importance of these scattered terrorist movements in the Middle East and elsewhere and to clarify their special, but far from obvious, relevance to the international drug scene, it must be understood that the Chinese have always believed strongly in getting "barbarians to fight barbarians" and in military indirection. The Reds are, for example, extremely active now in Western Europe as well as the United States and do not seem to have forgotten the worldwide Lin Piao strategy (in spite of the demise of its author) of "the countryside against the cities." Terrorist movements, inspired by the "thought of Mao Tse-tung" and fueled by the Red Chinese drug traffic, are on the move and it is perhaps no coincidence that Munich, a newly developed storage-and-transit center of the international traffic, was also the scene of the Olympic Games terrorist operation.

At present the Arab organizations, of which there are many, are at a particularly critical stage in their history. They are in a mood of even-more-than-usual extreme desperation and are utterly frustrated by their many failures in their struggle against Israel and by what they consider to be treacherous opposition from many Arabs and some Arab states.

In particular, as Munich and the recent bombings in the Israeli Embassy in London have shown, they are turning their attention to other areas than the Middle East and now consider serious action against targets other than military. A new doctrine has appeared that may be called "diffused terrorism," which seems to extend as far as Ulster but which may soon cross the Atlantic, where, of course, much of the preparatory work has been done by others.

The best known of the Arab guerrilla movements has been al-Fatah, led by Yasir Arafat, which has the little-known, secret ally called Jihad al Rasd (RASD), also known as Operation Network. RASD has only been operating for three years and is now the largest and most advanced of all the Palestinian terrorist groups. It is, in fact, to RASD that the Black September group belongs and it was the latter that was behind the hijacking of the Sabena airliner on May 8, 1972; the despicable murder of Wasfi Tel, the Jordanian Prime Minister, in Cairo on November 28, 1971; and the sabotage of the oil refinery in Rotterdam on March 15, 1971. They are also supposed to have been behind the attempted murder of Zaid al Rifai, the Jordanian Ambassador in London, on December 15, 1971, and responsible for the attempted destruction of an El Al aircraft on August 16, 1972, and the destruction of part of an oil refinery in Trieste in the same month.

There is evidence to suggest that RASD, Black September, and PFLP (Popular Front for the Liberation of Palestine) all collaborated in organizing the massacre at Lod airport on May 30, 1972, that was perpetrated by Japanese gunmen. The same combination may also have been behind the Munich massacre of September 1972.

RASD itself dates back to 1962, not in its present form but in its origins, when its nucleus began as an intelligence organization principally intended to collect information and to screen recruits for al-Fatah. Its first members were trained by elements of the Egyptian Intelligence Service (EIS), which itself owed much of its own techniques and professional capabilities to a curious succession of SS and GRU mentors. Recent events connected with the departure of the "Soviet imperialists" from Egypt have indicated that the Egyptians proved themselves apt and well-qualified disciples.

On the whole, RASD has shown itself to be a rather successful business enterprise in the fields of kidnapping and paid assassination, as well as in dope-smuggling. Not only does it traffic in morphine and heroin of Lebanese and Albanian (i.e., Chinese) origin, but also in Lebanese hashish dispensed in half-pound packages gaily labeled with action pictures of Arab guerrillas with assault rifles (AK-47s) at the ready. RASD has accumulated a war chest of about $100 million that is reported to be deposited in Italy, West Germany, and Switzerland. Hassan es Sabah would certainly have approved of its mentality and methods.

This organization has recently been busy recruiting agents in Europe, many of whom are right-wing extremists: Germans affected by neo-Nazi points of view and Italians of the neo-Fascist persuasion. There now seems to be a large-scale International Terrorist Front in the making that paradoxically embodies both right- and left-wing elements. Within it, in spite of great differences in other areas, a curious working rapprochement seems to have developed even between feuding Soviet and Chinese exponents of "La Guerre Révolutionnaire."

The practical abolition of customs barriers and the commonality of labor forces in the Common Market in Europe are circumstances that seem, at present, to favor their operations.

In fact, it is said that RASD now has its "action cells" in several countries in Europe, where they have recruited local networks not identifiable as Arabs. Their main center is in Rome, where they are able to maintain contact with Arab diplomats at a "Diplomat's Club" that they own.

There are some 2,000 Arab terrorists in the Arkoub area in Lebanon that has recently (September 19, 1972) been under attack by the Israeli forces. Another 3,000 or so are concentrated near Mt. Hermon. In Syria there is the paramilitary "Saiqa" organization that has a strength of about 15-20,000 men. Actually, the more successful the Israelis prove to be in their counterguerrilla operations, the more likely will Arab long-range operations be and continue.

It is no accident that there has been a proliferation of guerrilla movements and activities by participants in the international traffic in the two great areas of origin and distribution of narcotics. And, so far, not nearly enough attention has been paid to two extremely dangerous and interrelated threats to the international order.

Southeast Asia has been a particularly fertile area for the spawning of guerrilla movements and in fact has been in recent years the proving ground in which the Maoist concept of "Protracted Peoples' War" has been submitted to its most searching test. If this doctrine of revolutionary warfare has been judged by the military analysts of the international Communist movement to have been the success and the panacea that its exponents claim it to be, we are likely to be plagued by a good deal more of it.

Violence—Ideological Aspect

The roots of the philosophy of revolutionary violence are extremely old but the modern phase can most realistically be traced back to the "Revolutionary Manifesto" by Nechaev, which can be said to have profoundly influenced the managers of the Bolshevik revolution in Russia and many of their successors today.

In 1967 international communism celebrated its 50th anniversary and in the November 1967 issue of *Political Affairs* it was stated that the Bolshevik Revolution brought about "a new and higher social order." In spite of this phraseology, it is well known and can be statistically documented that Bolshevism has brought about more bloodshed, terror, and human misery than any other political change in history. This is because at the root of the Communist movement lie hatred, force, violence, and terror as its professed means of gaining its objectives.

The most modern restatement of the philosophy has that which we must attribute to Mao when he said, "Power grows out of the barrel of a gun." The Chinese Reds are much more vociferous in their advocacy of this tenet than the Soviet ideologues, who in recent years have defined the boundary conditions encompassing the use of force somewhat differently. Indeed, their present views on the matter have led to considerable differences between the two largest "party states."

In the course of an address delivered by Karl Marx in 1872, known as the "Speech to the Hague Congress of the First International," he said, "Force must be the lever of our Revolution." Lenin always insisted that violence is an absolutely essential part of the Communist movement, declaring in his book *State and Revolution*, published in 1917, that "violent revolution lies at the root of the whole of Marx and Engels' teachings." Also, in *Selected Works*, Vol. II, p. 17, he said, "We have never rejected terror on principle nor can we do so. Terror is a form of military operation that may be usefully applied, or may even be essential in certain moments of the battle, under certain conditions." The point is, however, that terrorism is now advocated, not as one of the operations an army in the field must carry out in close connection with and in complete harmony with the whole system of fighting, but as an individual attack completely separated from any army whatsoever.

A typical example of the Leninist approach to terror was afforded by his "Note to Comrade Sklyanski" (August 1920). He ordered E. M. Sklyanski, then leading the Red Army, to assassinate large numbers of "kulaks," priests, and landlords, concealing, however, the actual nature of the operation and blaming it on a fictitious peasant force:

> Carry it out together with Dzerzinski [head of the Cheka]. Under the guise of "greens" [peasant guerrillas], we will later put the blame on them, we will advance 10-20 versts and summarily hang the kulaks, priests, and landlords. The premium 100,000 rubles for every one hanged.[31]

Khrushchev brought about a modification in the definitions regarding the use of violence. This may have been provoked, to an extent, by his need to expose the universal and indiscriminate use of violence and terror by his predecessor, Joseph Stalin. Nikita Khrushchev maintained that force and violence are essential to the process of establishing a Communist government only if the movement met with resistance. He asserted that if the opposition surrendered without resistance, violence would not be necessary. Before the Congress of the CPSU, he said in a speech:

> ...achieving this, the forces [of transition to socialism] need not be associated with civil war under all circumstances. Our enemies like to depict us Leninists as advocates of violence always and everywhere... There is no doubt that, in a number of capitalist countries, violent overthrow of the dictatorship of the bourgeoisie and the sharp aggravation of class struggle connected with this are inevitable. But the forms of social revolution vary and it is not true to say that we regard violence and civil war as the only way to remake society.
>
> Leninism teaches that the ruling classes do not surrender power voluntarily. However, the greater or lesser intensity which the struggle may assume, the use or non-use of violence in the transition to socialism depends on the resistance of the exploiters, or whether the exploiting class itself resorts to violence rather than the proletariat.[32]

There is also a reference to this kind of situation in the basic international Communist textbook *Fundamentals of Marxism-Leninism:*

> Thus a peaceful revolution has become feasible not because the ruling classes have somehow changed their nature and are now inclined to surrender their power voluntarily but because, in a number of countries, it is now possible to achieve such superiority... that realizing the hopelessness of resistance, the reactionary classes will have no alternative but to capitulate before the revolutionary people...[33]

Usually the CPSU holds to the opinion that the overthrow of the United States will require force. That viewpoint was given in *Political Affairs* as follows:

> U.S. imperialism will not collapse of its own weight. It will have to be overthrown...the forces for that task are maturing and growing.[34]

However, in view of the recent evidences of growing rapprochement between the higher echelons of U.S. government and the party chiefs of the countries implacably opposed to the U.S. and completely resolved on its downfall, the question may well be asked now whether the above assessment has been superseded by a more optimistic anticipation of a more peaceful takeover.

Nevertheless full-scale development continues of means for the exploitation of a revolutionary situation in the United States (and Canada). Among these can be seen the use of drugs, both as a tranquillizer or depressant that will weaken the will and the capability to resist and as a stimulant to reinforce the power of the guerrillas and terrorists. Also, it is clear that the enormous financial gains from the traffic here, as elsewhere, are channeled into the war chests of the forces of subversion, anarchy, and eventual coup d'état.

With the winding down of the war in Vietnam and the repatriation of large numbers of U.S. troops (many bringing with them acute heroin addiction), a considerable effort has been made by left-wing entertainers during the final phases of the withdrawal to instill feelings of defeatism and pacifism in the troops and to incite them against the "establishment." An example of this is the "Free the Army Show" that has been organized by Jane Fonda, Dick Gregory, and Dalton Trumbo.

Their attitudes, in particular those of Jane Fonda that have earned her the sobriquet of "Hanoi Hannah," do not need elaboration. The revolutionary potential in the armed services is being assiduously built up (greatly aided by the increasing indiscipline and racial conflict arising from drug abuse). A state of incipient armed struggle, with occasional lapses into serious terrorism, exists in the United States; a state that conceivably can be made to assume a much more dangerous form when the last of the GIs has returned and the demobilized residue returns to civilian life. There it brings with it combat experience and a sense of great frustration and dissatisfaction that will, in its turn, lead to vulnerability to the cleverly conceived propaganda of a number of subversive "veterans" organizations.

The armed struggle and disorder just mentioned can be said to have had their initial stages during the disturbances in the ghettos and the racial confrontations in 1967 and 1968. They had become more selective by the end of 1970. Besides the activities of the Black Panther Party, there have been manifestations such as those of the Venceremos Brigade—started by the SDS—that has been sending contingents of young "angries" to Cuba, ostensibly to level sugar cane but actually to undergo training in guerrilla tactics.

In the large-scale migrations to and from Cuba there have been literally thousands of disaffected young people involved, affiliated with such groups as the Weathermen; the Revolutionary Youth Movement II (RYM II—SDS); the Student Worker Alliance (SWA), an extreme Marxist faction of SDS; the CPUSA; the "Che Guevara-Patrice Lumumba Wing" of the CPUSA; the Trotskyite-Communist Socialist Workers Party (SWP); the Young Socialist Alliance (YSA), as well as others.

The amount of revolutionary training being carried out in Cuba is considerable; there are in the island some forty-three camps that have a total throughput of 10,000 activists a year. The basic course lasts about four months but there are longer courses for specialists. Students are taught to hate everything connected with the United States, and imbued with the nihilistic urge to destroy. They are incited to murder as many U.S. policemen as possible, thus bringing nearer the ultimate goal of total breakdown of the powers of law enforcement, powers already highly taxed by the mounting crime attendant on growing drug abuse and the simultaneous assault on the courts and prisons.

These training establishments are quite polyglot, with an extremely wide range of specializations. Basically, the subjects taught are Assault, Raids and Penetrations, Occupation of Premises or Military Works, Ambush, Street-fighting Tactics, Techniques of Strikes and Work Stoppages, Desertion, Diversionary Actions, Seizure of Equipment or Stores, Expropriation of Ammunition and Explosives, Liberation of Prisons, Execution, Kidnapping, Sabotage, Terrorism, Armed Propaganda, Hijacking, War of Nerves.

Among the instructors are Anton Skylarsky, a Russian and a specialist in demolition and explosives; and another Russian, "General" Enrico Lister (like Skylarsky, also an ex-member of the Red Army). Among the principal camps are the one at Pinar del Rio, also known as the 5th of May Camp; Tarara, 8 km east of Havana; La Gobernadora, 26 km west of Havana; and a fourth at Minas del Frio in Oriente Province.

There is, of course, worldwide liaison with other Communist training establishments and guerrilla and terrorist organizations. Hitherto, although the web of lawless violence has been operating worldwide, the U.S.S.R. and the Chinese Reds each has had its own version of a "partisan international," engaging in its own forms of competitive intrusion. Now a kind of synthesis is going on, with Arab guerrillas playing a somewhat unusual role by drawing sustenance from both large Communist powers, much as Hanoi has done. The recent disaster at the Olympic games in Munich has been a signal that the Palestinian guerrilla forces have extended the range of their operations and, blocked in the Middle East by Israeli competence and determination, are seeking new and more vulnerable objectives.

This trend is especially satisfactory to the Maoists, not only in China but in other countries, as it fits in well with their doctrine of worldwide struggle and the final reduction of the "cities" (Europe and America—possibly even Russia) by the "countryside" (the Third World and China). The Palestine Liberation groups have, so far, had Israel as their primary target, but their depredations against "imperialism, capitalism, and feudalism" have been rapidly growing in intensity on a broad front. Planning has been proceeding for some time and signs of their intentions have not been lacking to the discerning few.

Contacts that the Palestinians have had, as a result of their diaspora, have given them a revolutionary ideology that is not only irredentist but revolutionary, with a particular animosity towards large Western-owned oil companies and bourgeois Arab governments such as those of Jordan, Morocco, and Saudi Arabia. They have particular reason to detest that of Jordan since the well-merited punishment they sustained at the hands of King Hussein.

In 1969 there was a revolutionists' rally in Jordan, when a large number of subversive groups made visits to Palestinian guerrilla camps in that country. These groups were from European movements, including some from Great Britain. The primary deployment of the Arab groups has been in Jordan, Syria, and Lebanon, and in their camps there have been, from time to time, aspirants under training from the Black Panthers, the "Front de Libération de Québec," the West German Baader-Meinhoff Group, the Turkish "Peoples' Liberation Army," and others. There have been contacts and interchanges with the IRA "Provisionals," Kurdish groups, the Popular Front for the Liberation of Palestine (PFPL), the Eritrean Liberation Front, and the urban guerrillas of the U.S. Weathermen group.

Spain has been having unpleasant experiences of late caused by a Basque separatist and terrorist movement called "Euzkadi Ta Azkatasuna" (ETA), which it seems has had some dealings with the IRA. In April 1972 there were conferences between ETA and the PFPL. Furthermore, Richie Ryan, the spokesman of the Eire Fine Gael Party in Ireland, has said that he had reports that nine members of the PFPL visited Dublin in May to have discussions with an "illegal" organization. PFPL's wide-ranging contacts also extend to numbers of ultraleftist groups in Sweden, France, and West Germany, and also to the Red Army of Japan that provided the assassins for the massacre at Lod Airport. The manner in which that team made its way to Israel is of interest because it indicates how a bloody international "Murder Incorporated" is now operating. They traveled to their objective via Canada, Paris, Frankfurt, Rome, and Beirut.

Deeply involved in all this activity are the Trotskyists of the "Fourth International." With its headquarters in Brussels, this formidable and growing organization has other groups linked with it all over the world, principally in France, Great Britain, Eire, the United States, Canada, and Japan, as well as in Belgium. In Asia it has been strong in Ceylon and parts of India. It may have been behind some of the action in Bangla Desh.

Cuba, which has been for so long a primary base for subversive and terrorist operations, is now being reinforced by another base of operations, Marxist Chile. A new body with the innocuous name of the "Committee for International Affairs" has apparently been set up to coordinate the widespread operations of guerrilla groups in a number of Latin American countries: Argentina, Brazil, Bolivia, Ecuador, Peru, and Uruguay. There are persistent reports that Chile is becoming a major transit point for heroin and that its operations in this area are linked with the role of Paraguay as a new crossroads of delivery and transshipment. Quite recently an important operator belonging to the Union Corse, one M. Ricord, was held in custody in Paraguay, whence he has been extradited to face charges in the United States. While it seems very doubtful that this individual would have had much to do with activities such as those of the Tupamaros and others like them, he has evidently been dealing in a commodity that is linked with such actions.

Quite apart from the ostensible and visible effects of these activities, the factor that interests their leaders is the trauma and shock they can induce, eventual forms of social and economic paralysis leading to final revolutionary situations.

The Philippines

It has been pointed out earlier that the main target of subversion and Chinese Communist aggression in the Far East is Japan. However, the strategic planning of those who intend to detach that prosperous country from the sphere of influence of the United States calls for working hard, currently, to loosen the structure of the postwar defensive outworks established by the United States upon which the security of Japan depends. The more the credibility of the United States declines as a result of the Vietnam War, the inexplicable flirtation with Red China, and the Kremlin accords leading to the nuclear-arms-control treaties, the nearer comes Chinese domination of Japan.

The principal outworks in question are South Korea, Taiwan, Okinawa, and the Philippines. Already the situation in South Korea has deteriorated markedly since the United States served notice on Park's government that there is going to be a massive reduction in the U.S. presence in that country, and since Okinawa, of much significance to the defense of South Korea, has reverted to Japan. The Republic of China has been betrayed in the UN and now has very little reason to expect any support in the event of an attack by the Reds. In addition, there has been a major Communist political offensive taking place in the Philippines; the course of action being pursued there by the agents and networks of the Chinese Reds has persuaded some analysts that we are witnessing what may be a dress rehearsal for future aggressive moves against Japan.

On August 24, 1971, President Ferdinand Marcos of the Philippines said during a broadcast from Manila on a nationwide hookup:

> These subversive elements responsible for the recent wave of terrorist bombings are followers of Marx, Lenin and Mao and have the moral and material support of a foreign power and have infiltrated almost every level of Philippine society.

The organization responsible for the bombings to which President Marcos referred has been, in the main, the Maoist-controlled New Peoples Army (NPA), which has been especially active in Manila itself. It is the official view of the government community in Manila that this aggressiveness has been a bold response to the U.S. pullout in Vietnam and the wider implications of the "Nixon Doctrine," which is being interpreted in Asia as a sellout on an unprecedented scale. It has been remarked that the NPA, in its intensive recruiting campaign, has been concentrating on high school and university students. These, rather than workers or peasants, are the material from which they are obtaining their cadres.

There are, as usual, several different organizations, in accordance with the normal practice of creating confusion by multiplicity of groups. For example, there is the "Kabatsang Makabayan" or KM, a Maoist student organization that is, itself, responsible for coordinating a complex of components such as the Students Alliance for National Democracy (STAND) that was the spearhead of student activism in the recent demonstrations and riots. Also in the same complex are the "Samahang Demokratiko Ng Kabatan" (SDK) and the Movement for a Democratic Philippines (MDP).

In view of the current divergences between the Moscow- and the Peking-operated parties, it is important to note that most of the present day leaders are Maoist but that they were originally active in the Communist Party of the Philippines that is Moscow-controlled (now called the Traditional Party). Many of the newer recruits have been brought in from the Chinese population, which is officially admitted to be between 200,000 and 300,000 strong but which is actually about 800,000 strong.

Among them are many of the sons and daughters of wealthy Chinese merchants. Indeed, it has been noted that the polarization of the revolutionary movement in the Philippines into Maoist and "traditional" groups has been particularly evident in Manila.

Serious offensive and disruptive operations began in the Philippines in 1970, with students demonstrating in "shock masses" of 300-or-more at a time. In disturbances of this kind during the summer nine people were killed and some 200 injured. Molotov cocktails had been exploded in front of the U.S. Embassy in Manila in December 1969, announcing the beginning of the campaign.

Resulting investigations revealed that many of the demonstrators and activists were under the influence of drugs while confronting the civil power, having taken LSD, while others were under the influence of a stimulant called "Madrax." At the time there was also a truck-drivers' strike in progress, centered on the oil industry, that seemed, in its characteristics, like others that had been instigated in Montreal by the FLQ and, more recently, like still others in Puerto Rico directed against U.S.-owned industrial concerns on that island.

The Philippines Government was able to overrun a good many of the camps, tunnels, and hideouts constructed by the NPA. A good many documents were seized, together with a number of photographs of a KM leader, Arthur Garcia, under instruction in a Red Chinese training base for guerrillas. He was shown laying booby traps and constructing tunnels of the Chinese-guerrilla pattern, now much more familiar to the U.S. forces in Vietnam after the seizure of Viet Cong military works in Laos and Cambodia, as well as in South Vietnam.

Quite recently there has been a significant merger between survivors and second-generation members of the "Huk" (Hukbalahap) Movement and the new Maoists led by Jose Maria Sison (Amado Guerrero). This has resulted in the revival of the Communist Party of the Philippines that was dissolved after the defeat of the Huks by Magsaysay and his U.S. advisers. This new version of the CPP has become a contributor to a new clandestine military force called CPP/NPA. One of the important leaders of that body has been "Comrade Dante," a mysterious and charismatic figure held in high regard by the Maoist students whose real name is Bernardo Buscayno, a second-generation Huk.

The founder of KM, Jose Maria Sison, holds that it is essential for the fanatical activist students, a minority group, to integrate with the struggle of the masses and to merge with the workers and peasants. So far, the latter have been quite reluctant to join in any such combination. However, in view of the explosive situation in Manila and the Philippines generally, announced on September 23, 1972, when President Marcos introduced martial law, it seems probable that this merger, regarded as essential by Marxist planners before true revolutionary situations can be initiated, may now be in a more advanced status.

That President Marcos had been fully apprised of the situation for some time is shown by the statement he made on the nationwide radio-and-TV broadcast of August 24, 1971.

In view of these events and the more recent moves on the part of the Japanese Government to recognize Red China, thus throwing a militarily defenseless country (unless strongly supported by the United States) into the trap of Chinese subversion, the Philippine disorders may well be considered an exercise testing the actions that would be needed to take over Japan.

This may sound farfetched. It may prove impossible of achievement, but it is necessary to be aware of the almost incredible ambitions, aspirations, and designs of the Chinese Reds in spite of the smoke screens they are able to wrap around themselves. Also, it should be understood that left-wing organizations are far more deeply entrenched in Japanese society and potentially far more powerful than those in the Philippines, although the latter are now recognized as constituting a threat there to the survival of the state.

The Filipino revolutionaries have been trained in the Chinese training bases and those in North Korea that are directly concerned with longer-range plans directed against the survival of Japan. The United States laboriously and skillfully sponsored Japan over the years; now Japan's very existence as an independent nation is threatened, as is the pattern of U.S. security that emerged after the exertions and sacrifices of the U.S. armed forces in World War II. Nothing less is at stake. The probable course of events arising from the new trends that are in motion in the Far East could even involve major hostilities in that region.

Malaysia and Singapore

The governments of both these countries are highly aware of the international narcotics problem and intend to play their part responsibly as members of the international community. They have both inherited from the previous British colonial administration highly effective and well-trained police organizations experienced in resisting subversion and criminal activity of all kinds.

Principally the older Chinese indulge in opium smoking on an appreciable scale; very few of the younger generation of Chinese in either country seem to be showing any particular interest in the drug. Some of the Malays go in for bhang, another form of the hashish/marijuana/hemp fixation.

There is some morphine addiction, particularly in urban or industrial communities, and a small incidence of heroin addiction that does not, so far, seem to be on the increase. Well aware of the threat this has represented to young people and students elsewhere, the Singapore and Malaysian Governments are vigilant in their policies, directed towards protecting potential victims in these categories.

However, so far none of these measures have been able to check the establishment of trading organizations and the operations of smuggling rings that use these countries as transit areas, exploiting their situation. Penang, formerly a colony administered separately from the Malaysian establishment, has, traditionally, been a center of activity for Chinese secret societies and has also been of especial interest to opium traders.

Indonesia

In Indonesia the Chinese Communists have experienced what is probably their largest single political reverse in the gamut of their forward movement toward subversion in Southeast Asia. It would be interesting to know, in detail, what their internal comments on that affair have been.

The Chinese, in adopting the program that they installed, did so because the Soviet Union was quite active there and had made remarkable progress through arms dealing as they had been doing in Egypt. So the Chinese used an approach that was abnormal from their point of view. Instead of placing the main stress on "Peoples' War" and a liberation movement involving revolt against the established order, they adopted a Soviet-type strategy aimed at gaining control over President Sukarno. Their methods were as interesting as they were disreputable, although by no means unprecedented in history. Not only were they assiduous in pandering to the vices of the late Indonesian ruler, but made available all their traditional skill in the use of drugs most likely to be of service to Sukarno in the bedchamber, a procedure that, as it turned out, recoiled both on their political dupe and themselves.

Kang Sheng, who had much to do with this debacle and who attempted to retrieve the situation by seizing supreme power through elements of the services before the failing dictator became useless to their designs, had his fingers badly burned by the whole episode. It is as lurid a tale as any in the annals of subversive offensive operations; one day it may provide material for an unusual pornographic novel.

Chapter 6
References and Footnotes

1. For some aspects of French Army doctrine and attitudes towards irregular warfare and narcotics, see:
   (a) Paul Marie de la Gorce, *The French Army* (New York: Braziller, 1963); and
   (b) Alfred W. McCoy, *The Politics of Heroin in Southeast Asia* (New York: Harper & Row, 1972). This is interesting and informative but needs to be regarded with some circumspection, being wholly pejorative towards the U.S. and its allies and apparently unaware of Communist activity in the narcotics field.
2. Maj. Gen. Edward G. Lansdale, *In the Midst of Wars* (New York: Harper & Row, 1972), p. 112.
3. Report by Provost Marshal's Department, MACV, 1971.
4. *New York Times*, June 6, 1971.
5. *Ibid.*
6. *Ibid.*
7. *Ibid.*
8. *Ibid.*
9. *Washington Star*, January 5, 1972.
10. *Ibid.*
11. Senate Internal Security Subcommittee Hearings, August 14, 1972, p. 20.
12. *Ibid.*, pp. 21-23.
13. *Ibid.*, p. 23.
14. *Ibid.*, p. 27.
15. *Ibid.*, pp. 53 *et seq.*
16. Article in *Chi Yin Daily News*, Hong Kong, Dec. 17, 1952.
17. Article in *Kung Shang Jih Pao*, Hong Kong, Oct. 16, 1952.
18. Article in *Hsing Tao Pao*, Hong Kong, Sept. 20, 1952.
19. Percy Finch, *Shanghai and Beyond* (New York: Charles Scribner's Sons, 1953), p. 305.
20. *Ibid.*, p. 307.
21. See W. P. Morgan, *Triad Societies in Hong Kong* (Hong Kong: Government Press, 1960).

22. For addiction in Hong Kong, see Albert G. Hess, *Chasing the Dragon* (New York: The Free Press, 1965).
23. Richard Deverall, *Mao Tze-tung Stop This Dirty Opium Business* (Tokyo: Toyoh Printing and Bookbinding Co., 1954), p. 33.
24. *Ibid.*, p. 42.
25. *Ibid.*, p. 44.
26. Henry J. Anslinger, Memorandum to the UN, April 15, 1952.
27. Deverall, *op. cit.*, pp. 47-51.
28. Richard Deverall, Testimony presented to Senate Internal Security Subcommittee, May 13, 1955.
29. Donald B. Louria, *The Drug Scene* (New York: McGraw-Hill, 1968), Chapter 5, "Turning On in Stockholm."
30. 124 Unit information obtained privately.
31. Handwritten note, Trotsky Archives, Houghton Library, Cambridge, Mass.
32. Statement by Nikita Khrushchev, Proceedings of the 20th Congress CPSU, as reported in Keesing's Contemporary Archives, 1955-56 (Bristol, England), p. 17476.
33. *Fundamentals of Marxism-Leninism* (Moscow: Foreign Affairs Publishing House, 1970), p. 173.
34. *Political Affairs*, November 1969.

Impact of the Present Offensive on the U.S. Public After Decades of Preconditioning

The essential basis of Communist political warfare, including propaganda (or "agitprop" as they call it), rests upon their own research
and applications of their findings within the fields of psychoneurology
and behavioral science.

Edward Hunter, journalist, distinguished specialist in the field of
Communist political warfare, and editor of *Tactics*, in his book *Brainwashing in Red China* introduced the word "brainwashing" into the
English language for the first time. It is a literal translation of the
Chinese term "hsi-nao," meaning "wash-head." In his next book, *Brainwashing: From Pavlov to Powers*, Hunter has some particularly interesting observations to make about the consequences of the work of the
well-known Soviet physiologist Ivan Pavlov. He recounts that shortly
after the revolution in Russia, Lenin invited Pavlov to stay with him as a
guest at his house for three months.[1]

During that visit Lenin listened to Pavlov's views on the way he
hoped that his discoveries in the field of conditioned reflexes would
be remedial in their nature. Lenin had different views on their possibilities and asked his guest to write for him a special report on human
aspects of these discoveries. His guest complied and wrote a four-hun-

dred-page manuscript that has never been published and that has never left the Kremlin. On reading it, Lenin observed, "You have saved the Revolution."

To that point Lenin had been of the opinion that the changes in human nature made necessary by the ideological tenets of Bolshevism would not gain adequate acceptance for his purposes if individuals and groups were permitted freedom of choice. But Lenin saw in Pavlov's discoveries a means of enforcing ideological conformity and of creating "Soviet Man." In this regard Hunter mentions that the Chinese Reds have taken the whole matter even further than the Russians and that their application of mass conditioning of populations is more ambitious.

During his work Ivan Pavlov conducted many experiments on animals and on human beings, investigating conditioned reflexes with the object of inducing artificial neuroses. Writing in his book *Conditioned Reflexes*, he stated about such conditions (as induced in dogs) "this excitation could not be stopped in any way, whether by shouting, petting or striking the animal, which became absolutely *unrecognizable*."[2] "Now we produce the neurosis... during the experiment the dog was extremely excitable... [experiencing] chaotic condition of the nervous activity... the animal was *intolerant and uncontrollable*."[3] Again, "Its weakening results in an abnormal predominance of delay and other normal phenomena of which inhibition is a part, expressed also in the general behavior of the animal, struggling, impatience, unruliness and finally as pathological phenomena."[4]

Basically he employed three types of procedure to effect neuroses in animals, which he classified in three groups:

(1) An excitatory or sensitive group.
(2) An inhibitory group.
(3) A central group (of two types).

The procedures were

(a) Overstraining or overexciting the dogs of group (1), using strong stimuli.
(b) Overstraining dogs of group (2), using a very strong or sustained inhibition.
(c) The production of a clashing of the excitatory and inhibitory processes, producing neurosis.[5]

Pavlov defined the conditions for the transition into a morbid state as "quite definite. Two of these are well known. These are: very strong external stimuli and the collision of the excitatory and inhibitory process."[6]

Others of his statements on this question were

Experimental neuroses are usually permanent, affecting an animal for months and even years[7]

and also

In both cases the normal relation between excitation and inhibition has disappeared. We call this a nervous breakdown, and these destructions of equilibrium in the nervous system we consider as neuroses. They are real neuroses, one showing a predominance of excitation, the other of inhibition. It is a serious illness, continues months, and is one for which treatment is necessary.[8]

Ivan Petrovitch Pavlov was Director of the Physiological Laboratory at the Institute of Experimental Medicine and the Academy of Sciences, Leningrad; he was also Professor of Physiology at the Military Medical Laboratory, Leningrad, and a Member of the Academy of Sciences of the U.S.S.R. He has rightly been regarded as the initiator of an important new trend in the control of human behavior and the promotion of abnormal psychological states of mind for political purposes.

Another Soviet scientist who pursued Pavlov's methods, particularly as they could be applied to humans, was A. R. Luria, who worked with children as subjects in the period 1925–29. He was particularly interested in the effect of rhythmic sounds and sensory impressions and the hypnotic effects that could be induced. The findings of his experimental program were published. In his book Luria explains the effects of "nerve-jamming" in children and the artificial production of retardation.[9]

Luria, who was Professor of Psychology at the Academy of Communistic Education and a Research Associate of the State Institute of Experimental Psychology, Moscow, carried through a great many experiments to discover the nature of the stimuli needed to produce abnormal and neurotic behavior pertaining to what he termed the "affect" condition or state. About this he wrote as follows in a chapter called "The Investigation of Mass Affect":

The affect state causes a great disturbance in the associative processes which is only dispelled by a number of secondary processes; the associative process in the affective state is entirely another psychological structure than that which is seen in the association of ordinary subjects. In these cases, while for some reason

327

such a secondary elaboration of the associative process fails, it is plain why the subject should give a perverted series of the associative reactions entirely disorganised in character. We begin to see a chain of senseless extra-signalising responses: every accidental stimulus—the portfolio on the table, the eyeglasses of the experimenter, pictures drawn on the wall—all these begin to activate the subject, taking him away from the experiment and producing "accidental responses." We obtain an associative series ordinarily foreign to the cultivated adult and usually seen only in the earlier stage of development or in peculiar forms in definite neurotic states.[10]

Luria's method for producing mental retardation in children may be described as a process:

(1) Subjecting them to severe nervous tension.
(2) Creating artificial degrees of neurosis.

It was necessary to create artificially effects and models of experimental neuroses which made possible an analysis of the laws lying at the basis of *disintegration of behavior.*[11]

(3) Interfering with the normal maturing of the nervous system of the cortical (reasoning) section of the brain as against the subcortical (the impulsive uncontrolled section with animal instincts).
(4) Destruction of the normal inhibitory mechanism of the cerebral cortex.
(5) Hypnotic induction of sleep.

Another worker in a similar area of research was K. I. Platonov. He has always been regarded as one of the Soviet Union's leading authorities on hypnosis. Platonov worked in the Physiological Laboratory of the Ukrainian Psychological Institute (which was headed by M. Denisenko) and also in the Laboratory of Physiology of Higher Nervous Activity of the Department of Physiology of the Kharkov Pedigogical Institute (headed by Y. Katkov).

Many of his ideas can be found in his book called *The Word as a Psychological and Therapeutic Factor,* which begins with the following revealing statement:

Soviet psychotherapy has developed under conditions different from those in foreign countries and in prerevolutionary Russia. It is being built on the basis of dialectical materialism, a materialist teaching of the higher nervous activity, the unity of the mind and body and the determination of the consciousness by the conditions of life.[12]

The work of these three Soviet scientists produced a formidable corpus of knowledge on the art of producing a state of acute affect by means of certain prescribed forms of stimuli, and of destroying, sometimes finally, normal associative activity and throwing the subjects back into the most primitive psychological conditions.

There has been a good deal of adverse criticism in professional circles outside the Soviet Union of these and other similar highly dangerous and aggressive forms of tampering with the mind, with ultimate control and manipulation in view, to be accomplished either through visual symbols, rhythms, or various complementary sensory signals.

For example, a well-known neuropsychiatrist in Baltimore, Dr. Leon Freedom, is quoted by Hunter as saying that the Communists have originated nothing in brainwashing or in any other branch of psychiatry. "All they have done is to take what free science has developed and use it in a manner that would ordinarily be considered mad... there isn't anything original about what they are doing, only in the way they are doing it. Their single innovation has been to use what they copy in a diabolical order. Their object solely is to *make minds sick*, not healthy—to create frustration."[13]

Again Dr. Freedom is quoted, as saying, "The methods derived by the Free World to combat illness are used by the Communists to create it."[14] The word "menticide" has been aptly invoked to describe the process and is attributable to Dr. Joost A.M. Meerlos, a psychiatrist of Dutch origin. By it he means murder of the mind; it is described by Hunter: "...this atrocious quack science devised by the Reds to bring about the voluntary submission of people to an unthinking discipline and a robot-like involvement."[15] One of the most important agencies that has been employed has been sound—rhythmic and percussive.

The application of this "quack science" as a means of affecting and transforming human society through cultural and psychological demolition goes back a good many years. It stems from the foundation in Moscow of a body called the International Music Bureau, whose aims were revealed by the following statement published in *Soviet Music* in 1933:

We should not verge one single iota from a program of progressive class struggle. We can be successful in our efforts only if we know how to transplant our political slogans to the sphere of music.... We should prove that the only right road for artistic creations, which include also that of musicians, is the service to the objectives of proletarian revolution.[16]

One of the founders of that Music Bureau, Hanns Eisler, is quoted as saying, "Communist music becomes heavy artillery in the battle for communism."[17]

Some students of disruptive processes in society, particularly as these exist in the United States, have expressed the gravest concern about the influence of certain kinds of music on character and morality. The relationship has been recognized to some extent since the beginning of history, and the profoundest thinkers and philosophers, such as Aristotle and Confucius, understood it well.

One of the gifted and perceptive writers who have commented on this important matter in recent years has been David A. Noebel, who has much to say in his highly factual and illuminating work *Rhythm, Riots and Revolution.* In this book the Rev. Noebel carefully explores and fully documents evidence that there has been an extension of the techniques of inducing the conditioned reflex, menticide, and moral collapse, particularly in the young, by the mobilization of musical "art" forms.

Much of his argument is based on what is known of Soviet research in the field of applied psychology and on what is known about Communist participation in the organization of record companies. He contends that there has been a long-term plan in operation that goes back to the late 1940s and early '50s. The plan has intended to apply techniques of hypnosis and induce stress, disorientation, and hysteria in the young with an obsessive craving for "far out" forms of modern music. This amounts to a kind of addiction and causes a form of collective behavior that ends in depravity.

More recently, the same author has produced another shorter study on the same theme, called *The Beatles—A Study in Drugs, Sex and Revolution,* that underlines the conceptions explored in more detail in the first book and expands them to include a more specific approach to the whole question. It takes into account the type of "rock" music and its themes that the Beatles have done so much to popularize, and their influence on the sexual revolution and the drug subculture. In the second book Noebel writes

Music Professor Frank Garlock commented that "almost daily the newspapers report on neurotic behavior which has accompanied or followed a rock 'n' roll session." Social disrupters have used rock 'n' roll and its performers to promote revolution. "Rock 'n' roll," he says, "often acts as an accompaniment for teen-age wars, riots and sex orgies." Professor Garlock, in analyzing music in general and rock 'n' roll in particular, states that "the manner in which music affects the listener varies according to the proportion of tension and relaxation in the music. Good music has a balance of these two elements. The more exciting the piece of music, the more the elements of tension will be found in it, but no good music ever uses one to the exclusion of the other." He then states that it is difficult to put on paper the elements that make rock 'n' roll what it is, but in the following one may see some of the reasons for rock 'n' roll's results. Although he says that not everything in the rock 'n' roll column applies to all rock, everything in that column applies to the majority of it. And not unexpectedly all of the things listed in the rock 'n' roll column are for tension, none for relaxation. It is therefore "no wonder" he says, "that the kids scream, faint, gyrate and go into ecstatic convulsions."[18]

Aside from the deliberate attrition upon the individual nervous system and the enforcement (there is really no other word to describe it) of communal and bacchanalian attitudes, there is the perpetual stress on drug-taking that is repeated over and over again in their songs. Such drug-taking is deliberately harnessed to the interests of the promoters of revolution. There have been a good many groups active in this form of proselytizing, with one of the most active the Students for a Democratic Society (SDS). Noebel writes

> Even now the SDS is recruiting "freaks, bikers and greasers" who dig rock and smoke dope at the huge rock concerts being conducted throughout the nation. "Our political objective at a rock concert," says the SDS, "is to rap with as many people as possible and get out mass propaganda about the national action.... We have made a political presence at almost every large gathering of youth this summer, and many of the kids at our city-wide meetings have been people we met at these concerts. Many of the kids we have rapped with are coming along with us on our actions, and some have become full-blown organizers for the national action.[19]

Thus it is for the last ten years or so, during the Vietnam War be it noted, the youth of the nation have been subjected to a subtle yet powerful, most insidious form of progressive demoralization through lax sexual behavior, drugs, and revolutionary progaganda. It has been implanting in them an increasing alienation and a corresponding sense of loss of identity. To a great extent these come with the onset of the drug experience; they continue through vain attempts to rediscover identity by endless, fruitless, often fatal variants of the drug experience.

331

When all aspects of the propagandizing of marijuana and LSD are carefully reviewed, the conclusion is inescapable that these have been used deliberately as weapons of warfare by those whose interest it is to extinguish our form of society and the beliefs and values on which it is founded. Both these drugs and the attitudes that they bring, when regarded within the context of the "scene" and the malignant influences within it, are conditioning agents and precursors of heroin addiction; and heroin is the instrument leading to the coup de grâce.

During the Vietnam War, U.S. recruitment policies and the draft were highly derelict. Military forces, while they were supplied with the best and most modern *physical* armament the taxpayer could buy, were largely lacking the spiritual and *metaphysical* armament they greatly needed. They were exposed to enemy action of psycho-chemical warfare and interrelated propaganda, and were actually set up and preconditioned for the forms of attack that were delivered upon them with great skill.

During World War II, stringent precautions were taken because U.S. troops in the Pacific and Far Eastern theaters might become victims to drugs that were always known to be prevalent in areas where the Japanese forces operated. In this matter, most laudably, the U.S. forces and the State Department acted wisely and with foresight. They attempted to persuade their allies who had colonial possessions that they would probably reoccupy to consider precautions against the social evils that might come after the war, and to introduce appropriate legislation.

Despite that policy, it did not prevent the U.S. forces from coming under deliberate attack by their opponents in the Korean War, and this was made all too obvious by some of the reports issued by SCAP. In these circumstances and in view of the background and understanding of the subject that must have existed in the Pentagon, it is rather remarkable that the Chinese and their North Vietnamese allies could have inflicted the surprise that they did.

If any explanation is possible, it may be found in the enormously increased degree of civilian operational control over the armed forces—which has gone much too far, as the progress of a most unfortunate war has shown beyond dispute. Also, there is among strategic planners and military theorists in the United States, an unfortunate overstress upon physical aspects of waging war. This has almost eliminated from our armory other aspects that have always been recognized by the best military minds as being far more important.

In the course of official duties as an officer of Occupation Forces in West Germany, I often met with Russian officers acting in a similar capacity in their zone of occupation. During these encounters, in which

332

on occasion I was able to observe the Soviet phenomenon at closer quarters than usual, I noticed with considerable interest differences inherent in their system between the essential status of the armed forces and that occupied by other instrumentalities, such as special political departments and the propaganda services.

It was very clear that not only did the latter lead a life of privilege compared to the former, occupying a far higher position, but that this, to a large extent, arose from an attitude of conviction on the part of their sponsors in the Soviet Communist Party. The special services were, in fact, the decisive arm; they were much more likely to achieve the basic aims of communism than the armed forces, who were, of course, essential in a supporting role but not quite as important. It was obvious that the persons who were engaged in propaganda services or political warfare were carefully selected, highly trained, imaginative, and competent to a degree. At that time there still existed on the Western side certain counterparts to this sort of person, since we had been obliged to counter enemy propaganda and engage in some of our own, but there was a precipitous tendency to wind up all such forms of organization and discharge our specialists, a circumstance that boded ill for the years of conflict ahead.[20]

Very recently we have been reminded of this by the almost total collapse of the morale of the U.S. Army engaged in Vietnam. In part this is a tribute to the proficiency of the enemy's propaganda services; it also reflects the total inadequacy of our own, whether these be judged for maintenance of morale in our own forces or for attempts to attack that of the enemy. In this field, although well aware of methods and possibilities, we are not in the same league as our opponents. The situation has, of course, been seriously aggravated by the completely fallacious doctrine of "limited warfare" (i.e., "no-win" war) that was adopted and that has only reaped the consequences that were inevitable for it. It is quite easy to understand the frustrations and discontent of soldiers exposed to ordeals of this nature and it is indeed remarkable that the troops have performed as well as they have. But there are great perils yet implicit in the current situation.

During September 19 and 25, 1972, exceptionally important hearings were held before the Committee on Internal Security, U.S. House of Representatives, the topic being "Hearings Regarding H.R. 16742: Restraints on Travel to Hostile Areas." The hearings were called as a result of a high degree of dissatisfaction with the treasonable and seditious activities of Miss Jane Fonda during her visits to Hanoi. While there, she engaged, among other things, in a series of broadcasts that had been designed with the morale of members of the U.S. Armed Forces and, to a lesser extent, of the ARVN, in mind.

Miss Fonda's general political views were summarized by a statement she made in a speech delivered at Duke University, Durham,
N.C., on December 11, 1970:

> *I would think that if you understood what communism was, you
> would hope and pray on your knees that we would someday be
> Communist. I am a socialist, I think that we should strive toward
> a socialist society—all the way to communism.* [21]

Her attitude toward the Armed Services and the nature of the propaganda objectives for them for which she has been enlisted by the
enemy are further clarified by another statement. This she made at
the University of Texas on the "new breed" of soldiers. It was reported
in the *Dallas News* as follows:

> "No order is accepted unchallenged. No smart officer would send
> his men on a dangerous mission; ask them to cut their hair or
> beards or stop smoking pot because he would be shot." She further
> stated that "We've got to establish a socialistic economic structure
> that will limit private, profit-oriented businesses. Whether the
> transition is peaceful depends on the way our present governmen-
> tal leaders react. We must commit our lives to this transition." She
> added: "We should be very proud of our new breed of soldier. It's
> not organized but it's mutiny and they have every right." [22]

There is little point in repeating the monstrous fabrications and distortions for which she was responsible during the series of twelve
broadcasts she delivered in the period July 14–August 22, 1972. They
were so skillfully composed that they could only have been scripted
for her by the talented "agitprop" (now called "propagit") specialists
of COSVN* or of the Lao Dong.

However, it is profitable to take some account of the assessments
made of them by some of the psychological-warfare specialists on our
own side of the lines.

In his statement before the same hearings Edward Hunter carefully
defines the essential distinctions between overt or "white" propaganda;
"gray," or covert unattributable propaganda handed out to media or
to "opinion-makers" of one's own side ("backgrounders" are a good example of this technique); and "black" propaganda, the kind that is completely covert and injected into the enemy's information system.

With regard to the Fonda episode, Hunter says with great perception
that it represents an important innovation in the propaganda field. It

---

*A.U.S. acronym for Hanoi's general headquarters inside South Vietnam.

is of a somewhat unprecedented nature, to which no formal definition has yet been formally accorded, at least on our side. His complete grasp of the situation arises from his own important investigations into what he has called "privileged treason" in the United States, and in this instance he has the following to say:

> The enemy seeks to add credibility to his propaganda too, by putting an American citizen before the microphone, and by having him or her address the American troops. The purpose is the same as when everyday gossip from within one's own military camp is told by the enemy over his own radio. When a change of personnel or location can be told the troops before they have been even informed themselves the impact is even greater. When the American citizen, especially one with the glamour and the prestige value of a Jane Fonda, can travel back and forth between the United States and the enemy capital without interference or arrest by the American authorities, the effect is devastating.
>
> What comes from a source on one's own side commands attention, under any circumstances. When the enemy can obtain the assistance of a national of the country it is fighting to propagate its material in his or her own country, and also to broadcast it personally over the enemy's radio, going to its capital city to do so, it has achieved a form of war propaganda for which, as yet, there is no professional term—except, perhaps, the old-fashioned word, treason. Both the "white" and "black" propaganda forms are combined in it with great subtlety.
>
> The most appropriate term for this might be "enemy blue," a term that just now arises in my mind. A new label surely is needed, for what we have is an expanded kind of warfare with a new dimension added to it—the psychological—although it is yet to receive legislative or judicial recognition despite its obvious existence.[23]

Edward Hunter's analysis pursues, rigorously and with insight, the various features of the broadcasts such as identification, coordination, reinforcements and orchestration, professionalism, and reverse logic. Under the first of these items he points out that, in the circumstances described above:

> The mind of an American soldier in Vietnam is attacked this way from front and rear. The enemy is not only in front of him but behind him, in his homeland. At the same time those whom he is fighting are being portrayed to him as not really the enemy.
>
> If this weren't so, they obviously would be arrested wouldn't they? This is the confused picture that is being presented to the

335

typical soldier who is forced to do the fighting and dying. Such a moral dilemma can lead only to at least frustration. The ready outlet for frustration in Vietnam has been readily at hand and cheap—heroin, and he has heard how it is waiting for him back home in the U.S. too.[24]

There has been another opinion expressed about the impact of such propaganda, about the related drug phenomenon that lies at the root of most decay in military morale in that theatre, and about the growing understanding by the troops of the utterly self-defeating doctrine by which the war has been fought. It is a significant opinion from Brigadier S. L. A. Marshall, former Director of Orientation, U.S. Army. Among other things, in a letter addressed to Robert M. Hormer, Chief Investigator of the Committee on Internal Security, he stated

> I do know that we have an extremely sensitive situation in Indo-China, one probably without precedent in our history. On returning there in July 1970 to get a measure of troop morale and discipline the Chief of Staff, USA, felt so much alarm at what he found that on getting back to Washington he visited the President to warn him that "anything might happen. That would include large-scale mutiny. Where the balance is just that delicate, any act of aid and comfort to the enemy of the United States could become the fatal straw."[25]

The steady withdrawal of U.S. troops from Vietnam during the present administration has prevented anything of that nature from taking place, but it is obvious that there has been a considerable increase in forms of passive resistance to authority that would never have been tolerated under normal circumstances. Also there is the chilling prospect of large numbers of fully trained troops being discharged, many of whom have been thoroughly indoctrinated with propaganda designed to incite them against the established order.

Much is known about the existence of highly subversive and militant groups and of forms of racial bitterness that could take a particularly menacing turn. Given current levels of unemployment, and with the prospects of economic difficulties ahead arising both from causes that are easy to understand and from others that are almost inexplicable, an atmosphere of revolution is being engendered that may well result in violent nationwide explosion some day.

Considering this situation in conjunction with the opportunities being presented to potential interventionists in the Caribbean area, or even on the Canadian frontiers over which for the last few years some

25,000 illegal Chinese immigrants have been seeping, the prospect cannot be considered to be particularly good.

The attitude of Miss Fonda and the tenor of her statements was such that several commentators have expressed the view that they could be counterproductive, resulting in the service-hearer being turned off. In the course of a lengthy and penetrating "Theme Analysis of the Fonda Statements," addressed to Donald G. Sanders, Chief Counsel of the House Internal Security Subcommittee, Joseph E. Thach, a research analyst, referred to a presentation made in Hanoi by Miss Fonda on July 20, 1972, in which she gave an explanation of the 1954 Geneva Accords for Indo-China slanted in the Communist direction:

> If her text which was mainly the standard leftist "anti-Cold War" interpretation of U.S. involvement in Vietnam (complete with the old canard attributed to President Eisenhower on the popularity of Ho Chi Minh), failed to alienate American servicemen listeners, then her presentation certainly did. Based on my own background in psychological operations, it is quite possible we may have gained support among skeptical GIs. In fact, had Benedict Arnold listened to such an appeal during the American Revolution, we probably would have kept him in the fold.[26]

Edward Hunter, the distinguished editor of *Tactics*, spoke from the depth of his experience in psychological warfare. In the course of his careful examination of the Fonda case, submitted to the same subcommittee and called "Analysis of Jane Fonda Activities in North Vietnam," Hunter explored the basic propaganda doctrine as well as the technique and said

> Troops ordinarily discount anything known to come from the enemy's side. They know that the enemy has a harmful intent in telling it. The enemy knows this and so a number of devices are concocted to lend credibility to what emanates from its territory. When such material contains names and gossip, for instance from one's own regiment, it achieves the desired purpose, injuring morale. How did the enemy find out these details? Who is the traitor in their midst or, even more disturbing, at headquarters? Such questions are sure to arise in men's minds with a destructive impact on morale.[27]

It is not possible to give a complete or balanced account of the sources, operations, and aims of that most dangerous aspect of the international narcotics traffic, "the Red Chinese connection," without examining in more detail the assault on the U.S. Armed Forces. In its wider ramifications, this form of aggression is far more dangerous than the more obvious threat posed by enemy military action.

Although the impact of the enemy's drug-pushing on the forces is perhaps the most critical single factor in an all-out attempt to erode their morale and destroy their combat capability, it would not be nearly as effective as it is without a good many related operational methods that are being used with a disturbing degree of success.

In general, the principal means may be listed as follows:

(1) The narcotics weapon.

(2) Subversion by unsuitable entertainment.

(3) The promotion of racial conflict.

(4) Attacks on the military within Congress.

(5) Special forms of legal aid designed to incite and support the military in a "struggle" against the "establishment."

(6) Publications, i.e., propaganda—books, pamphlets, underground papers, etc.

(7) Infiltration and incitement, e.g., pitting draftees against "lifers." Building cells and "shadow" units and organizations.

(8) Communist-inspired "fronts"; special associations; groups or movements outside the armed services but designed to promote pacifism, dissaffection, "concern," or treason.

(9) Incitement to desert, and use of deserters.

(10) Special morale operations directed against relatives of POWs in North Vietnam. Mind-changing of POWs and public displays of disloyalty by POW and Peace Groups.

(11) Promotion of alienation of the general public from the armed forces; campaigns against recruitment. Portrayal of U.S. military policy as one of aggression. Constant harping on My Lai atrocities, bombing, etc.

(12) Campus warfare. Action against ROTC and military capabilities, research, special projects, etc., through peace groups and student activists and faculty activists of the professariat.

(13) Extension of (7) above into organization of "armies within the Army." Military training and experience exploited in order to make possible the building up of an effective revolutionary army.

Thus far, preliminary remarks have been made about military drug abuse in Vietnam, the theater in which the main attack on morale, discipline, and cohesiveness has been delivered. However, before enlarging on that subject, the point must be made that the problem is becoming one of worldwide significance, affecting U.S. servicemen in virtually all places of deployment. In particular, it has reached especially disturbing proportions in West Germany where an inactive garrison way-of-life presents a highly inviting target to those enemy interests out to disrupt and to produce breakdown in the Armed Forces.

A few typical incidents and situations will serve to illustrate the point. They are quoted from *Army in Anguish* by Haynes Johnson and George C. Wilson, both of the *Washington Post.* While the standpoint of that periodical on the war in Vietnam is well known and the tenor of this series of articles, which has been collected into a particularly depressing though informative book, does not diverge appreciably from that attitude, the information in it is both authoritative and irrefutable. Some of this, pertinent to the subject of psycho-chemical warfare and morale operations, is quoted below:

> Shortly before 4 P.M. on March 22nd three black soldiers entered room 312, building 7089, at the Army's Warner Barracks in Bamberg, Germany. At knifepoint they called out to four white GIs: "Give us your dope."
>
> As the intruders were leaving with no dope but with all the cash the soldiers had, $36, one of the bandits pressed his knife close to a victim and said: "You know the paper you signed? I think you're about three months behind on your insurance policy."
>
> The policy was an agreement to pay the gang leader $10 every payday to stay healthy—the old protection racket, right there in the Army barracks. The traditional refuge of the soldier when day is done is no longer safe.
>
> "Crimes of violence, such as robbery, are at an all-time high and climbing," said Maj. John T. Sherwood Jr., staff judge advocate at the Nuremberg Trial Center, which encompasses Bamberg. "I'd just hate to live in the barracks. The guy who just wants to be let alone isn't being left alone."
>
> A field officer who reads Army crime reports coming in from all over Germany said that much of the crime "is a matter of race—groups of blacks against whites."
>
> Such views were not universal among officers interviewed in Germany, with one black major who investigated the robbery-extortion ring in Bamberg stressing that it should not be considered typical of the type of crime being committed in the Army.
>
> However, the predominant viewpoint was that there are no longer safe firebreaks between black militancy, violence and drugs. They are all mixed together in an explosive combination. Idleness, broken-down vehicles, poor housing, German hostility, no sense of mission—all these facets of garrison life in Germany today seem to be aggravating the problem.
>
> Terror is such that one of the distinguishing features of the Bamberg robberies last March was that they were even reported at all. The bandits evidently felt that their knives would ensure silence,

because they hit two other rooms in the same barracks complex the next two nights. It was blacks robbing whites in those cases too.

"I gather this has been going on for a year," Sherwood said, "and no one has ever said anything to anyone. No one has ever turned it in."[28]

Although it can be said that GIs often enter the service with either an addiction or a predisposition towards drugs, it is important to realize that there is a very highly organized pushing of drugs not only in the immediate neighborhood of military units but also within them. Many soldiers turn to drugs because they are forced into it. For example:

The soldiers testify to something more than this physical neglect and disintegration.* They speak of a breakdown in spirits, in ethics and in discipline. One of the privates who talked about it is only 17. Thin, pale and frightened, he has been at Merrell less than a month. Already, he said, he has been beaten twice by fellow soldiers in senseless acts of violence.

"Sure I've got fear," he said as he stood in the darkened entry way of Merrell Barracks. "I'm afraid to walk around in here." Part of his fear stems from the organized drug traffic within his barracks.

"The first thing when a guy gets here, just arrived you know, the first thing is a pusher comes along and says he has some good stuff and wants you to use it. This happened to me on my second day here. They take you to their room, maybe to a certain spot where they've got their stuff, and they let you take a look at it.

"At first, you know, after they give you this inventory, they keep an eye on you for about a week—two weeks—three weeks. To make sure you're not either CID [Criminal Investigation Division] or an informer or something like that.

"Terror," the private explained, "is the pusher's weapon for achieving silence. They sent messages to one of my friends that 'if we find out you're CID we're going to do this or that.' Beat the——out of me. Make me feel like if I was an informer that I'd never be able to inform anybody of the stuff again."

After he refused the offer which he had never used before, and satisfied the pushers in his barracks that he was not an informer, the soldier said that they laced one of his regular cigarettes with hash without his knowing it.

"In your mind, it's almost a force the way they work," he says. "See, here in this building we've got juicers (who drink alcohol)

---

*Merrell Barracks is in an extremely dilapidated condition.

340

and heads (who take drugs). When I came in I was between them, a loner. I don't drink. See, alcohol I don't like.

"But I did smoke grass. So when they took me to that room and offered to share a bowl [of hashish, eight to ten times stronger than marijuana], I says, 'No thank you, I'm not familiar with what it does or doesn't do.' "

Now he admits he smokes hash regularly. He is a customer the pushers made for themselves right here in the Army barracks.

Drugs are a key factor in barracks crime, whether assaults or robberies. Few soldiers feel safe—either inside or outside their barracks.

Another soldier interviewed at Merrell picked up a bayonet from a desk in his room and said: "The only way I'd walk around here at night is if I'm carrying this with me."

He spoke of break-ins. "Do you see my door there? It's been jimmied, completely busted through two or three times. You see, sir, the Army doesn't pay very much and people get broke and they steal things to sell. You know for dope and stuff. And that's it right there."[29]

It has been estimated by official investigators who have been studying this unbelievable situation that 46 percent of all army personnel stationed in Europe have tried an illegal drug at least once; 16 percent are regularly using illegal drugs three times a week at least. Thirty percent of the latter category are on heroin or hashish. Also there is now beginning a considerable influx of opium.

The hashish comes from the Middle East and is described as "Turkish Green," "Afghanistan Black," or "Lebanon Red." In West Germany it costs $1.25 to $2.50 a gram but in the United States it could cost as much as $30 a gram. Many soldiers spend almost their entire paycheck on it. Heroin is only beginning now to become a problem in West Germany.

However, the position is different in Vietnam and also in the United States. It was observed during the heroin "blitz" in Vietnam that 10–15 percent of the GIs were on heroin; also it has been quite prevalent and easy to get at such U.S. centers as Fort Bragg and Fort Dix. But, be it noted, the price is far higher there and the imperatives to steal or commit other crimes correspondingly greater.

There are some particularly sinister undertones in all this. While, in the conditions that now obtain in the army, there has been a serious decline in the sense of national purpose and a growing, uncomfortable feeling of frustration and aimlessness, the same cannot be said about the mood of the underground forces being organized inside the Army. These are being readied to march to another drummer.

For example, the Black Panthers have their own shadowy contingent, no more obtrusive than several other special groups (some of which are white); they recognize one another by the usual method of signs, grips, and handshakes or other classical recognition signals. The Panthers do not openly profess communism but assert that they are for "revolutionary intercommunalism."

In an issue of *The Black Panther* an article appeared that discussed the "prospects for revolutionary intercommunal warfare" and stated that a necessary precondition for reaching this goal would be the defeat of "world enemy No. 1, the U.S." It draws comparisons with the Bolshevik conquest of Russia in 1917 and points out that one of the main reasons Tsarist Russia collapsed was "internal weakness of the armed forces which are supposed to protect the interest of the capitalist state."[30]

Another internal underground movement is a Communist-inspired and -led body known as Movement for a Democratic Military (MDM) that has been particularly active on the West Coast. The well-known defense correspondent of the North American Newspaper Alliance, Col. Robert Heinl, USMC (Ret.), who has made a close study of morale problems, writing in the Manchester, N. H. *Union Leader*, stated

> One militant West Coast group, Movement for a Democratic Military (MDM), has specialized in weapons theft from military bases in California. During 1970, large armory thefts were successfully perpetrated against Oakland Army Base, Fort Cronkhite and Fort Ord, and even the Marine Corps base at Camp Pendleton, where a team wearing Marine uniforms got away with nine M-16 rifles and a J-79 grenade launcher.[31]

MDM has aroused a good deal of approbation in Communist circles, and an article about its successes appeared in the Communist *Daily World* on January 15, 1972, that dealt with its activities at the Great Lakes Naval Training Center:

> The MDM staff members have ambitious goals for political education and mass organizing within the military.... Their program is based upon an analysis of imperialism and they have made a "deliberate effort to develop a revolutionary consciousness of working-class power."... MDM's influence is potentially enormous.... (It) has had a profound impact on Great Lakes since it was founded in June, 1970.[32]

Yet another highly subversive organization formed for the express purpose of destroying the U.S. Armed Forces from within and converting their trained manpower into a revolutionary arm is the American Servicemen's Union (ASU). Its national chairman, Andrew Stapp, attended a conference organized by the Black Panthers called the "Conference for a United Front Against Fascism." It was held in Oakland, July 18-20, 1969, and at it he said that the ASU was

> playing a leading role [in this fight against the U.S. military]... We have chapters...on 60 large military installations in the United States and 40 overseas.... Just as the Bolshevik Party organized through the Soviets in 1917... the American Servicemen's Union is organizing Soviets within the U.S. imperialist army.... And... right now the [ASU] is building an army within an army, a workers militia inside the U.S. Army, and along with the Panthers and others we are going to make that revolution.[33]

This menacing process is aided by a massive publishing program that provides a good many (well over 100) seditious publications that are made freely available on all military bases.

Quite apart from the questions that arise about the impact of the drug traffic on our society and on the armed forces, there is also the extremely important matter of the various attitudes taken towards the issue of Chinese complicity. This was discussed at some length, earlier, in Chapter 3. We have, on the one hand, a great deal of highly informative testimony given to the legislative branch of government by expert witnesses, the long record of criminal convictions obtained by the judicial branch, and much evidence implicating the Chinese Reds. Then, on the other hand, within the executive branch, particularly at the highest levels where foreign policy is determined, there is a totally different attitude.

For example, when he testified before a congressional committee in July 1971, Dr. Robert Baird, a specialist in drugs from a clinic in New York called The Haven, stated that the Chinese Communists were preparing to use drugs to demoralize the U.S. population, especially young people, for ideological purposes. He also said that we were being misled into believing that Turkey is the principal source of narcotics, and gave as his estimate that the Chinese Reds produce 55 to 65 percent of the world's hard drugs.

Furthermore, Rep. Seymour Halpern (R; N.Y.) reported to the House Foreign Affairs Committee that

> There is reason to believe that opium produced in Communist China, particularly in the Yunnan Province, does enter the Golden Triangle—Burma, Thailand, Laos—drugs conduit in Southeast Asia....

343

It has been difficult, because of China's great wall of isolation, to document the extent of her opium production in relation to her own consumption and to her medicinal requirements. Several experts have estimated, however, that the minimal medical needs for her huge population would require about 100 tons of opium production per year. It is known that the Peoples' Republic of China has the capacity for large cultivation, particularly in the Southern Provinces. There have been numerous rumors that a good portion of *China's vast crop* finds its way into illicit channels.[34]

Whenever U.S. Government spokesmen have been asked to comment on such rumors in recent years, and particularly during the administration that took office in 1968, they have rather pointedly denied any question of Chinese Communist complicity and have at the same time, as if by a sort of reflex, blamed Turkey.

As an example of this sort of procedure, on December 28, 1971, Dr. Nelson Gross, acting in his capacity as adviser to the Secretary of State and Coordinator for International Narcotics Matters, was asked during a press conference, "Do you have any evidence pro or con that any of the opium comes from China?" He replied

We have had no evidence that any opium is coming from China at all. In fact, we have even had reports that some has moved up from Burma across the border into China.* I might say here that the Chinese and our own government have had virtually an identity of interest and an identity of policy for a century. We have consistently been with the Chinese Government over the years in trying to eradicate not only production but obviously trafficking and use of opium and derivatives.[35]

The next question asked of Dr. Gross was, "How would you know if it were coming from China or not?" In reply he said

Well, our intelligence sources indicate that it is coming from those areas (indicating the "Golden Triangle" area on the map). There is more than enough supply in those areas to account for all of the material which comes either into Southeast Asia, into victim areas—South Vietnam or the United States. We have no reports—and we would tell from those who might be arrested as to where they were acquiring the material—we have no report of any coming from China.[36]

---

*Very likely it was moving in to be processed.

As a further example of this rather strange attitude on the part of the State Department, the following extract is quoted from a letter signed by the Chief of Public Enquiries Division. It was issued in reply to an inquiry on the facts about Red Chinese drug trading:

Over the last several years news stories have from time to time appeared purporting to give details of alleged dealings by Communist China in the international drug traffic. Some of these stories have achieved widespread credence and have been cited in support of their view that Peking is so implacable in its hostility to the United States as to rule out all possibility of an improvement in our relations.

The U.S. Government has been concerned by these stories and has made every effort to investigate their authenticity. These investigations have determined that there is no reliable evidence that the Communist Chinese have ever engaged in [sic] or sanctioned the illicit export of opium or its derivatives. Nor is there any evidence of that country exercising any control over or participating in the Southeast [Asian] opium trade. From our investigations, it appears that the drug traffic in Southeast Asia is carried on by individuals, some of them ethnically Chinese, who are inspired by motives of financial gain rather than political considerations.

The Peoples' Republic of China has no drug problem of its own. Chinese Communist authorities have for years strictly forbidden private production, consumption and distribution of opium and its derivatives. Stringent controls over opium poppy production and use were adopted at the 21st Session of the State Administrative Council of the Peoples' Republic of China on February 24, 1950. These were applied with great vigor in Han (ethnic Chinese) areas but, according to some reports, the use of opium in tribal areas where its use was already established continued to be permitted for several years afterward. After twenty years of rigorous effort to eliminate the last vestiges of narcotics addiction in that country, the Chinese Communist authorities authorize limited amounts of opium to be produced under strict government controls exclusively for medicinal purposes.

The date of this letter is October 1971, well before the Presidential visit. It is interesting that the word "illicit" in paragraph 2 seems to be correctly used because, of course, the Chinese program is fully legal in China and has the whole weight of the Government there behind it.

Somewhat earlier the Bureau of Narcotics and Dangerous Drugs (BNDD) had issued its Fact Sheet No. 2 called "Illegal Traffic in Narcotics and Dangerous Drugs," which contained the following:

There are two main currents of illicit traffic in opium and the opiates. One begins in the Middle East and ends in North America. The other pattern is from Southeast Asia directed to Hong Kong, Japan, China (Taiwan), and the West coast of America....in the Far East, opium is cultivated in vast quantities in the Yunnan Province of China and the Shan and Kachin States in Burma. Although much is consumed by opium smokers in the region, considerable amounts of the drug find their way to the United States.[37]

After some discussions that took place in Washington early in February 1972, during which the matter of Red Chinese involvement was discussed, an interesting memorandum made its appearance and was circulated among Members of Congress. It was unsigned, had no letterhead or indication of place of origin, was dated February 15, 1972, and was entitled "Alleged Involvement of the Peoples' Republic of China in Illicit Drug Traffic." It was couched in terms rather similar to the State Department letter quoted above, containing the words:

The Government of the Peoples' Republic of China has for years officially forbidden the private production [sic], consumption, and distribution of opium and its derivatives. There is no reliable evidence that the PRC has either engaged in [sic] or sanctioned the illicit export of opium or its derivatives to the Free World nor are there any indications of PRC control over the opium trade of Southeast Asia and adjacent markets.[38]

One of the Representatives to comment on this rather curious document was John Ashbrook (R; Ohio), who said that

The memo which was confirmed as a White House memo by my colleague was, interestingly enough, on plain white paper with no heading, no agency identification, no attribution—a real "backgrounder." It was real propaganda too.... The claim that the Chinese people are forbidden to produce opium for their own consumption is of course true... but the production of opium by the Red Chinese for illicit export is a long established policy which, of course, they deny.[39]

Mr. Ashbrook continued:

The memo does indicate that there is evidence that there has been "cross-border movement of opiates between China and Southeast Asia." This, of course, confirms to some extent the BNDD claims that illicit opium shipments have come from Yunnan Province. However, the White House memo puts the responsibility for

346

such shipments on individual Chinese efforts which, they infer, violate Red Chinese government regulations. Information shows... that such individual efforts would violate Government regulations only if such traffic were for domestic consumption in China, whereas illicit export is approved and encouraged by the Government of Red China.[40]

The "magic figure" of 80 percent Turkish heroin entering the United States is one that has been used by Ramsey Clark, ex-U.S. Attorney General, a recent visitor to Hanoi, and also by former Postmaster General Winton Blount. That they have helped to support this figure has had a marked effect on the Turkish and French Governments, particularly when Blount was adopting an especially hostile attitude towards France, urging economic sanctions.

In this connection Rep. Ashbrook is also quoted as having said

> When the President journeyed to Red China many of us who had observed the Red Chinese participation in the opium traffic hoped that at least Mr. Nixon would pressure the Red bandits to stop this illicit contribution to world misery.... It now appears that Mr. Nixon never even broached the subject... to Mao or Chou. Henry Kissinger vetoed bringing up the issue because it would have been too explosive at the initial meeting. The Communists won once more and American interests were subordinated.[41]

Commenting on the 80-percent figure, the Director of the Bureau of Narcotics and Dangerous Drugs, John E. Ingersoll, completely exploded the myth when he said

> That was the figure used by the old Bureau of Narcotics.... When I became Director of the new Bureau... I asked for data to support that precise figure and when it was not forthcoming I dropped the use of the 80 percent figure which has been used traditionally for some time. The best I can say now is that still the overwhelming majority comes from that source (Turkey) but whether it is 80 percent or whether it is 70 percent, I just cannot tell you.[42]

Dr. Gross' remarks, quoted shortly before, contain the phrase "identity of policy." The style and content of the State Department letter certainly appear to bear that out; so much so, in fact, that if the letterhead were changed it would not need much imagination to believe it had been drafted in the office of Chiao Kuan-hua, the Chinese Communist head of delegation at the UN. This would be a rather congenial form of exercise for that impressive personality since for some time

347

now he has been a member of the Department of Social Affairs and, concurrently, of the Ministry of Overseas Trade that is primarily responsible for "Special Products" (i.e., opium) trading abroad. What is more appropriate and, indeed, logical than that he should be posted at the earliest possible moment to a foreign assignment from which he can conduct further market research into the needs of his best customer.

It is a matter of some interest to be able to contrast the two rebuttals given above with statements issued by other agencies of the U.S. Government less concerned with public relations and more directly with professional aspects of the problem. For example, there is a statement submitted by the Bureau of Narcotics and Dangerous Drugs before the House Appropriations Subcommittee that was reviewing questions affecting the Department of State, the Departments of Justice and Commerce, and others. This outlined the overseas operations of BNDD, which are divided into three regions of operation:

> The third region is in Asia with a Regional Office in Bangkok and District offices in Seoul, Hong Kong and Singapore. The countries of Burma, Thailand, Laos and China (Yunnan Province) are sources of opium which moves to Bangkok, Macao and Hong Kong to be made into heroin which enters the West Coast of the United States.[43]

According to the syndicated columnist Paul Scott, the denials of Red Chinese complicity by the U.S. Government can be thus explained:

> Discussions of the heroin issue with the Chinese Communists also would contradict the official Nixon Administration position that "there is no hard traffic from the Asian mainland."[44]

This attitude, it seems, was adopted by the White House as part of the new Nixon policy towards Red China. According to Scott:

> Under this preconceived policy, government officials must not reveal any information of heroin traffic from China or the direct involvement of the Peking government.... Since the President's major foreign policy objective is to improve relations with Communist China, it is very doubtful that he will make any decision that might cause embarassment at this time.[45]

The immediately above all point inescapably to the conclusion that there is a moral issue of the greatest magnitude that confronts the nation. It is bad enough to have a declared enemy engaged in a silent, insidious assault, and undetected, but it is quite another thing to be faced with a situation in which one's own government, at the highest levels, not only refuses to admit such a possibility, but exculpates that enemy because, for reasons of power politics, it wishes to collaborate with that enemy. Previously, such situations could only arise after defeat and occupation. Now they produce similar results without the enemy having to fire a single shot or even to become directly and officially engaged.

Bilateral aspects apart, the situation is fraught with great dangers for the United States and for the Free World because the concept of the use of drugs as a weapon is not applied only in biological or psychochemical terms by our opponents within the Communist system. They have also evolved an extremely subtle political weapon capable of breaking up the target society and of destroying its alliances as well through techniques of deception and slander that lead to the alienation and fragmentation of coalitions or combinations of powers opposing themselves. There is a marked similarity, in some of the underlying theory of operations, with that used by the ancient, warlike, all-conquering state of Chin after which China has been named.

Although smaller than some of its adversaries, and even poorer than most of them, that tightly knit, highly disciplined belligerent power succeeded in destroying its enemies piecemeal. It understood the importance of disrupting opposing alliances, with great secrecy as to its intentions, and the importance of seizing the political and military initiative and retaining it. Chin ended up as the dominant power in China, leaving behind it a legacy of statecraft that is again becoming evident today.

Chapter 7
References and Footnotes

1. Edward Hunter, *Brainwashing in Red China* (New York: Vanguard Press, 1953) and *Brainwashing: From Pavlov to Powers* (Linden, N.J.: The Bookmailer, 1953).
2. Ivan P. Pavlov, *Conditioned Reflexes* (New York: Dover Publications, 1960), p. 398.
3. Ivan P. Pavlov, *Conditioned Reflexes and Psychology* (New York: International Publishers, 1963), p. 96.
4. Pavlov, *Conditioned Reflexes and Psychology*, p. 164.
5. Ivan P. Pavlov, *Lectures on Conditioned Reflexes* (New York: International Publishers, 1963), pp. 374, 375.
6. Pavlov, *Conditioned Reflexes and Psychology*, p. 52.
7. Pavlov, *Lectures on Conditioned Reflexes*, p. 375.
8. Pavlov, *Conditioned Reflexes*, p. 311.
   The statements and references from Pavlov may also be found quoted passim in David A. Noebel, *Rhythm, Riots and Revolution* (Tulsa, Okla.: Christian Crusade Publications, 1966).
9. A.R. Luria, *The Nature of Human Conflict—An Objective Study of Disorganisation and Control of Human Behaviour* (New York: Washington Square Press, 1967), Chapter 10, "The Development of the Reactive Processes."
10. *Ibid.*, p. 53.
11. *Ibid.*, p. xi.
12. K.I. Platonov, *The Word as a Psychological and Therapeutic Factor* (Moscow: Foreign Languages Publishing House, 1959), p. 1.
13. Hunter, *op. cit.*, p. 230.
14. *Ibid.*, p. 18.
15. *Ibid.*, p. 6.
16. Quoted in David A. Noebel, *Rhythm, Riots and Revolution* (Tulsa, Okla.: Christian Crusade Publications, 1966), p. 13.
17. *Ibid.*
18. David A. Noebel, *The Beatles—A Study in Drugs, Sex and Revolution* (Tulsa, Okla.: Christian Crusade Publications, 1969), 4th ed., 1970, p. 57. Quoted from *Voice*, XL, 6 (April 1967), p. 8.

19. *Ibid.*, p. 63. Quoted from *New Left Notes*, Aug. 29, 1969, p. 5.
20. In this connection, see Ian Greig, *The Assault on the West* (Richmond, Surrey, England: Foreign Affairs Publishing Co., 1968). This is an indispensable source on most aspects of Communist political warfare, based on unusually sound material.
21. Before the Committee on Internal Security, House of Representatives, September 19 and 25, 1972: Hearings Regarding H.R. 16742: "Restraints on Travel to Hostile Areas," p. 7680.
22. *Ibid.*, p. 7680.
23. *Ibid.*, p. 7582.
24. *Ibid.*, p. 7585.
25. *Ibid.*, p. 7602.
26. *Ibid.*, pp. 7675–76: "Theme Analysis of the Fonda Statements," by Joseph E. Thach.
27. *Ibid.*, p. 7582.
28. Haynes Johnson and George C. Wilson, *Army in Anguish (The Washington Post National Reports)* (New York: Pocket Books, 1972), Chapter 2, "GI Crime and Violence Overseas," pp. 31–32.
29. *Ibid.*, pp. 12–14.
30. *The Black Panther*, May 8, 1971. Quoted in "Intelligence Digest," Julian Williams, ed., *Christian Crusade Weekly*, Feb. 20, 1972.
31. Col. Robert Heinl, USMC (Ret.), article in Manchester, N.H., *Union Leader*, June 15, 1971.
32. Quoted in "Intelligence Digest," Julian Williams, ed., *Christian Crusade Weekly*, Feb. 20, 1972.
33. *Ibid.*
34. Quoted in Allan C. Brownfeld, *The Peking Connection: Communist China and the Narcotics Trade* (Washington, D.C.: The Committee for a Free China, 1972), p. 2.
35. *Ibid.*, pp. 10–11.
36. *Ibid.*, p. 11.
37. *Ibid.*, pp. 11–12.
38. *Ibid.*, p. 12.
39. *Ibid.*, pp. 12–13.
40. *Ibid.*, p. 13.
41. *Ibid.*, p. 24.
42. *Ibid.*, p. 14, Statement by the BNDD before the House Appropriations Subcommittee, June 2, 1971.
43. *Ibid.*, p. 11, BNDD statement.
44. *Ibid.*, p. 25.
45. *Ibid.*, p. 25.

The author acknowledges with thanks the services of Allan C. Brownfeld in gathering a most useful compendium of statements and quotations bearing on the traffic in narcotics, and especially on the manner in which it has become an "un-subject" insofar as Red Chinese participation is concerned.

8

Summary and Conclusion—Possible Courses of Action and of National and International Control

In spite of large-scale involvement by the Chinese Reds in the Vietnam War and in its subsidiary Laotian and Cambodian operations, the U.S. Government has consistently treated the Chinese Communists as non-belligerents and even as the de facto government of a country with which "improved relations" are desirable. This has been so much the case that the world was recently treated to the spectacle of a U.S. Commander in Chief paying social calls in Peking and wining and dining with professed enemies who have never let up for a moment in their abuse, either before or after the event. This of course took place while U.S. forces were engaged in combat with North Vietnam, which has been heavily backed at all times by the Chinese as well as the Russians, and where large numbers of Chinese antiaircraft gunners have been busily engaged in picking off U.S. planes.

The conduct of war under such strange circumstances can only continue if it embodies large elements not only of self-deception but of outright concealment from the electorate of a great many important issues. It is a matter of common knowledge, for example, that the USIA spent a good deal of time and public money on the production of a film about the savage Chinese aggression against Tibet. It included details about the flight of the Dalai Lama into India. This film has been suppressed at the direct instigation of Henry Kissinger, who clearly did not want his delicate negotiations with the Chinese to fail because of the inconvenient exposure of the appalling truth.

In the same way the well-known Chinese propensity to export narcotics has become an "un-subject." Just as it has been expedient to ignore direct and continuing Red Chinese involvement in the Indo-Chinese war and to conceal the results of U.S. research into the unprecedented genocide of a formerly free people in Tibet, so it has been thought inappropriate to support the allegations against the Chinese Reds in their role of global dealers in narcotics. Many of the denials and items of misinformation have already been examined.

However, all law-enforcement officers aware of the problem who have seen fit to express themselves publicly on it are unanimous in their view that drugs must be kept out of the trading and distribution channels that bring them to their victims. They have repeated over and over again that the evil must be checked at its source. So far the forms of action taken as a result of such statements have been directed only at known and "accepted" sources: Turkey (an ally of the United States) and France (another ally), both of whom have been highly cooperative in spite of slanderous aspects of the allegations leveled at them.

Similar allegations have continually been made against persons, and even governments, in other allied countries such as Laos, Cambodia, or Thailand. It should be noted here that the channels that dispense this information have always concentrated on countries, areas, or peoples under Western influence (with exceptions noted below) and have, for instance, ignored countries like Burma that, although plagued by Communist intrustions, are neutral. India, also "neutral," although less neutral than before since signing its pact with the Soviet Union, is also free from any attack, although it is an opium-growing country and one that exports opiates to the U.S.S.R. In order to qualify as an object of slander, a degree of commitment is necessary. Small wonder, therefore, that the CIA has come in for its share of abuse even when it has been engaged in attempts to suppress rather than foster the traffic (unfortunately with rather scant success so far).

It is almost amusing, if it were not so tragic, to note that now, in the opium "shell game" presently being played with undoubted skill by the public relations specialists of the international narcotics cartel, it suddenly becomes necessary to implant new myths in the public mind. It is no longer possible to sustain the old one—of the magic number of 80 percent of heroin deliveries to the United States being of Turkish origin—in view of the disappearance of the Turkish crop this year. New myths are now being invented and fostered by ingenious publicity. Now it is the Golden Triangle that is being invested with full accreditation as the primary source of heroin. Since there already has been a very considerable export from that area, which in fact made a sizable contribution to the above 80-percent figure, the shift of focus has not been very difficult. But the elevation of the minuscule and largely irrelevant town of Tachilek to world eminence as an opium metropolis shows an ingenuity and a touching estimate of the faith of the general public in the media by which it is kept up to date through the latest misinformation.

It is not only on opium couches that delusions arise caused by consumption of opium. Organs of public information are themselves addictive, and then able to convey the subtle opiates of deceit and false estimates of extremely dangerous situations, maintaining a constant parade of illusion. This serves to delude a highly gullible public whose powers of discernment and analysis are being progressively sapped. And whose leaders are also being affected by these means, as well as others much more selectively administered, that silence and immobilize them. Thus the weapons of psycho-chemical warfare move along their trajectories and their progress toward their chosen targets is made the surer.

What then needs to be done to rehabilitate our damaged polities, reeling from the blows of the narcotics offensive, assailed by soaring crime rates, racial cleavage in the nation, and approaching collapse of the judicial and penal systems? What can be done to preserve our youth from the mounting waves of degradation and death that threaten to overwhelm them and, indeed, before long, the very fabric of civilization itself—now on notice of survival and living on borrowed time?

It must, first be clearly recognized and stated in honest and unmistakable terms that there is in existence a politico-military operation of unprecedented dimensions within the field of psycho-chemical warfare. It has been shown in the course of this book that there are well-established historical precedents for the existence of operations of this kind on varying scales of magnitude. This one is undoubtedly the greatest so far achieved, and needs to be recognized as such. Next, the cowardly conspirators who have devised it must be unmasked and identified.

In the early days of British rule in India there was discovered a comparable cunningly hidden evil—the ancient cult of "Thuggee" that had claimed millions of lives over a period lasting many generations. Carried out in the name of the goddess Kali, or Durga, with its victims dedicated as human sacrifices, the movement strangely and rather inexplicably also had Muslim participants. All were consumed with a lust for blood as well as plunder. A growing situation of economic weakness and chaos, undoubtedly caused by the acts of the Thugs, led to further administrative breakdown of the Mogul Empire, although decay was already far advanced by the time the deadly traffic in terror was unmasked. Under the fear induced by the sinister marauders and assassins, whose trade was aided by its religious aspect, many native administrators in large tracts of central and upper India had lost control and were conniving with them.[1] India and its large vulnerable population had good reason to be thankful for the arrival of a new and determined power that demonstrated its clear intent to eradicate this monstrous threat to public order. From the operations of Major Sleeman in his remarkable campaigns, whole new concepts of police action emerged that took form, in India and elsewhere throughout territories under British jurisdiction, in the development of the Special Branch of the police and law-enforcement agencies. Its methods have been tried over and over again and have proved thoroughly worthwhile all over the world. The author has no hesitation in stating that withdrawal from the world stage of British Special Branch representatives has largely coincided with and has been partly responsible for an unprecedented growth in world lawlessness and terror. The agency that has allegedly been given a mandate to keep these forces in check, the UN, has so far been signally unsuccessful. It is, in some quarters, not unreasonably held suspect of having the desire to promote rather than to hinder such depredations.

Many very useful and potentially successful types of technical operations have already been proposed, but much more than technology is required. When the United States entered the world scene at the beginning of this century, it was imbued with the sense of high moral purpose with which the founding fathers were also equipped. It was the element of law enforcement and a definition of conditions of international law based on the highest moral standards that gave this country strength in that as well as in many other fields. Most regrettably, today that moral purpose has been largely abandoned and conditions of expediency rather than morality govern today's actions or the direction that those actions take. The situation will not improve unless a new crusade against drugs is launched that has as its base an outraged sense of justice and an absolute determination to apportion blame no matter where this needs to be done.

Such moral considerations apart, which are, of course, the most important, the practical resolution of the problem can be seen to be divisible into four clear fields of thought and action:

355

(a) Political
(b) Military
(c) Technical
(d) Social

Under (a), there exist already, as has been seen, a large number of international bodies and undertakings that, although excellent as far as they have been allowed to go, fall far short of the present requirement. They have suffered from being representational rather than operational bodies. For many years, beginning at the Shanghai Conference in 1909, the United States was unquestionably in the lead in the world crusade against drugs. The stature of the country was unassailable, held in the highest respect in the international community. This position was largely sustained until about 1962, when an entirely different attitude was noticeable that may well have coincided with the beginnings of the Indo-China war when the full apparatus of enemy propaganda and political warfare was brought to bear on America.

It is most regrettable, currently, that the former accuracy and assiduity in reporting the actual sources and nature of the drug traffic have become overlaid with inaccuracies and omissions. There can be little doubt, however, that if the original objectivity practiced by the United States in the world arena could be recovered, there would be an even stronger measure of support than already exists and the United States would regain an overwhelming lead in the matter. It is most essential that this situation be achieved and there are profound and, indeed, all-important ethical questions involved here that have a bearing on far wider issues even than the drug problem; and that is important enough.

In the military field, under (b), there is an opportunity for all the resources of military intelligence to be brought to bear on an unusual assignment that has not so far been properly targeted. Such instrumentalities can only function properly if correct and appropriate "requirements" are formulated and adequate "briefs" prepared that can set the machinery in motion and head it in the right direction. Indeed, nothing can be more dangerous or less rewarding than that such services and their considerable resources be headed, either inadvertently or by some fell intent, in the wrong direction. Any such tendencies must be detected and corrected; also the reasons for such errors need to be understood.

The resources that can be commanded by the military establishment, whether "in-house" or co-opted, are great indeed and can make most formidable contributions to the total suppression of the drug traffic, in conjunction with other partners, if suitably mobilized. There has been much talk lately in the United States about civil functions of the military and this is one of the most promising regions in which the military can serve the ultimate interests of the civil power, particularly in view of current estrangements from the public. Here is an opportunity to restore past harmonious relationships.

Discussion has been undertaken in this book of a capital question that all recognize to be of the most fateful consequence to the world community; it is closely connected with the survival and continuation of civilized values. So far it has not been viewed comprehensively in correct terms and, although much has been said and written, most of the dialogue has but led in the direction of half-measures and partial truths.

It is largely because the problem has been phrased for the most part in language that has embodied aspects of the sociological and medical. This is only natural in view of the grievous nature of the threat and it is only right that the first casualties have had "first aid" of this kind. Concurrently there has been considerable and most laudable activity at the law-enforcement and criminal-investigation levels. The problems to be resolved find themselves expressible in such terms but transcend them by several dimensions of magnitude. Unless they can clearly be perceived in politico-military terms—unless it can be seen that they embody elements of conscious intent and operational method and constitute a veiled form of aggression on the part of implacable and self-declared enemies of the public order in the United States and elsewhere—those who attempt to address themselves to the problem will fail. In spite of confident public statements to the contrary, which try to convey that imminent success is on the way, there will be massive failure and catastrophe.

Untold and unnecessary havoc has been caused by the U.S. Armed Forces in Vietnam, which have damaged friend and foe alike. This has come about because of unsound military doctrines that permitted the idea of indiscriminate fire in a friendly country infested with intruders and that set up "free fire zones." The first principle of war, and perhaps the most important of them all, the Principle of the Objective, has not only been forgotten but even officially interred by the "neo-strategists." In the circumstances it is not surprising that casualties arising from drug abuse have been regarded as "happenings" and the very concept of causality has been disregarded. Unless a very different, largely traditional, and highly selective form of approach is adopted, those who have made themselves responsible for the problem will continue to flounder. The casualties will mount. Two years ago the officially admitted figure for heroin addiction in the United States was "about 65,000." Now it is officially admitted by the White House Task Force to be 600,000. The author believes it is higher and has adopted a figure of 700,000 for some of his computations. But it must be remembered that this can be no static figure; it is, in fact, the index of a chain reaction. It is a factor in a strongly dynamic situation in which high concentration of addicts in one area can only spell rapid local increments in the stricken section of the population caught in the maelstrom of crime, degeneracy, and ultimate destruction dealt out by the swift current that bears them down. It is most alarming to consider that in New York City there are now 250,000 (some say twice as many) such addicts and that in Puerto Rico the incidence has been set at one in twenty-seven. These are regions of "critical mass" where the chain reaction will drive on to a situation of explosion. Who can forecast the range and consequences of apparently impending events of this kind?

For the last several years the United States has been engaged in a bitter, relentless, unrewarding struggle in Southeast Asia with the forces of communism that have been active in Vietnam, Laos, and Cambodia. The visible and most obvious opponent has been North Vietnam. For a long time there were considerable inhibitions, as there had been in Malaya when the British encountered and defeated a somewhat similar threat, against using the term "Communist," and a completely artificial term, "Viet Cong," was invented to meet the requirement.

Although North Vietnam is a small, industrially weak nation, it has been supported throughout by two large Communist powers and supplied to an ever-increasing extent with vast quantities of military equipment by the Soviet Union and China on a scale involving the expenditure of billions of dollars. The facts connected with this traffic have been well known to the U.S. military authorities and the intelligence agencies concerned, but it has never been fully accepted that this was the case in a manner that would lead to really effective countermeasures. Until recently, it has been a matter of usage that these have been largely "non-supplies" until they have actually found their way into the hands of the enemy and have been admitted to be pointed in our direction and seen to be firing. The enemy has had no such inhibitions and his penetration of our exposed and highly vulnerable home front has been conducted in depth with potentially devastating results not as yet fully apparent.

In this latter action, the delivery of drugs to the target population and the maintenance of an uninterrupted flow thereto have been vital factors. As related above, the aim has been to sap our will, weaken the national character, promote moral degeneration, cause an increase in the crime rate, subject the law enforcement and penal agencies of the country to an intolerable strain, and, above all, to corrupt and destroy our youth, turning them against their country. That this form of attrition has achieved striking success is witnessed by the mounting tides of racial tension and violence and the flight of large numbers of the younger generation abroad. In extreme cases they expire as hippies in the last stages of degradation somewhere on the Hashish Trail in Afghanistan or Nepal, spending their last resources on drugs that have been procured, more often than not, by the sale of their passports.[2]

In the ultimate, they are victims not only of the assault that our opponents have been mounting but of the refusal to identify the source of that assault by this country; victims of the half-truths that have been voiced about the nature of their predicament and the reasons for it. The same could be said about the fate of our armed forces in Vietnam, who have acquitted themselves honorably and well in spite of a few lapses and a devastating psychological-warfare assault that has attended their efforts. That assault has also been intended to isolate them from the body politic whose servants and defenders they have tried in most cases to be.

Until the real enemy is revealed, his policies and intentions recognized, and his basic doctrine and his strategy properly understood and analyzed, no amount of evasive rhetoric or self-deception and public deception can serve to restore the issue. For example, during the Vietnam War there has been large-scale and active participation on the part of the Chinese Reds.

For many years the Chinese Communists have been operating a large group of training establishments in Southwest China that have been indoctrinating and training North Vietnamese for the war; and they themselves have maintained there (i.e., in Vietnam) large military forces estimated by some to amount to some 74,000 men. The dispositions of these men include a command post, an entire infantry division, several antiaircraft divisions, an engineering division, railway regiments, and coastal-artillery regiments. Many of these troops have been actively engaged in defending the country against U.S. air attacks and have recently played a particularly important role after the North Vietnamese "spring offensive," when most of the North Vietnamese forces entered South Vietnam on their campaign of aggression designed to destroy the South Vietnamese Government and oust the United States from Southeast Asia. They have provided special technical services as a result of the U.S. mining of North Vietnamese ports, and vital cooperation in the field of logistics.

Quite apart from direct Chinese military involvement, there have been about 50,000 to 70,000 Red Chinese civilians: technicians, or special-service components who have had much to do with the operation of ordnance, of maintenance workshops, and with transport of supplies. The Chinese Reds have been able to maintain a flow of about 5,000 tons per day. In normal circumstances, this has been on the scale of 3,000 tons by rail and 2,000 tons by water.

These facts are given because, although well known and extremely hurtful to U.S. military interests in Vietnam, it has been politic, until very recently, to leave most of these arrangements "unnoticed" rather than to provoke the Chinese into intervention. Although a good amount of attention has been paid of late to fairly damaging interdiction missions, selection of targets and control of U.S. bombing at the highest levels has been designed to avoid inflicting damage on many obvious and worth-while military targets, including those mentioned above manned by the Chinese.

There is, indeed, a direct analogy that can be applied to analysis connected with narcotics trading. There is little doubt that to a large extent the Chinese Reds are able to hide from their own population the nature and existence of this traffic and have been engaged in the most able and effective measures of concealment. If we connive at this by assisting them in their task of falsifying the facts of history, we will be obliged to take the consequences—and the shape of those consequences is daily becoming more visible and menacing. There is little hope for nations that suicidally decline to avail themselves of their intelligence-gathering instrumentalities, to acquaint themselves with the facts, or that decline to take those findings into account when they are deemed inconvenient or politically uncomfortable.

In reference to the all-important intelligence aspects of the problem, in recent testimony submitted to the U.S. Senate, Maj. Gen. Lewis W. Walt, USMC (Ret.), has offered some extremely pertinent observations:

(1) Honest and conscientious men, looking at the same situation, come up with substantially different assessments.
(2) The classified files on any complex situation, therefore, will inevitably contain reports that differ significantly on details and even on fundamentals.
(3) Intelligence files will frequently also contain raw intelligence; that is, reports that come from a variety of sources which may or may not be true and which have to be substantiated before they can be considered to be hard intelligence.
(4) Those who have the responsibility of decision must weigh their intelligence files or their report files in aggregate, assiduously distinguishing between raw intelligence and hard intelligence.

(5) Reports that are six months to a year old must never by themselves be used as a guide to a current situation although their validity at the time may have been generally accepted. Situations can change radically in six months or even less.

(6) Reports, including task force reports, will vary enormously in quality. Some are outstanding; some are mediocre; some simply crumble before the test of time; some turn out to be odd mixtures of valid findings, and of findings that miss the mark completely. Each report and each section of each report, therefore requires careful evaluation.[3]

The above observations are of great value to anyone concerned with the task of assessing information and producing a carefully weighed situation report. It is most regrettable that they are not adhered to as fully as they might be. However, in the unraveling of a complex situation, wrapped in secrecy, such as the one with which we are contending, and where the promoters of the traffic in large measure have been improving the clandestinity of their operations, some vital and essential clues can be provided by historical research. This is particularly the case when our adversaries are pursuing long-range designs, even though the nature of the operation and the planning is different from most other commitments. For example—large-scale armament-development programs proceed according to well-defined phases of growth, and correct assessment of time scales, weapons characteristics, matters of doctrine, and impending threats of crisis must take into account a build-up of information collected over a considerable period of time. The process of collation in such circumstances is very different from that necessary under operational conditions where military dispositions may change or total shifts in policy may occur. Also, it may be noted that with the Chinese a decade is but an instant of time, and on their scale the U.S. intelligence services have been operating for about two and a half instants.

Mention has been made above of positive contributions that can be made by the military establishment here (and in other countries as well), and doubtless it will be found that collaborative research with a range of civilian bodies will be required.

Professionals in this area have been examining the possibilities of scientific aids to military intelligence or law enforcement, both at national and international levels. Taking their opinions into account, the technical approach to the problem could assume some or all of the following aspects:

(1) Worldwide location of opium crops (application of aerospace-surveillance techniques).

(2) Information on potential yields of opium crops.
(3) Determination of harvesting time and progress of harvesting; cropping cycles.
(4) Possible means of selective destruction of crops (herbicides or biological agents).
(5) Tracing action to detect and establish the pattern of distribution networks.
(6) Detection and sensing of concealed materials at points of transit or points of entry.
(7) Detection of clandestine laboratories. (Application of technical intelligence-tracer techniques in chemical supplies, monitoring of effluents, heliborne sensing methods, etc.)
(8) Rapid accumulation of inputs from widely distributed sources of acquisition and means of rapid data processing and retrieval. Computerized data-bank and worldwide intercommunications system.
(9) Identification of organizational and network sensitivities and vulnerabilities.
(10) Assessment of suppression and control measures or specification of devices or vehicles required to intensify, search, intercept, or capture—capabilities of law enforcement and preventive agencies.
(11) Formulation of doctrine and national and international training and development exercises.
(12) The organization, staffing, and equipping of an international "General Staff" able to employ adequate resources to conduct its task.

Crop Detection and Surveillance

Remote sensing and the use of optical or other similar devices using the electromagnetic spectrum have been in use for a good many years. Aerial photography, of course, has been used extensively as a tool in agricultural economic survey work and in resource investigations since the 1930s, but recent developments in the aerospace field have greatly increased the range of possibilities through such channels.

In particular, remote sensing from aircraft or from satellites is likely to prove of the highest importance in the location of opium fields although, of course as is well known, illicit cultivators have long been using a practice of mixed cropping and interspersal of poppies throughout more normal crops for purposes of concealment.

Tracers

Those faced with the responsibility of law enforcement would find their task greatly simplified if the source and the movement of the opiates and other narcotics products could be tagged through implantation of minute traces of substances detectable as a microconstituent by sensitive methods of chemical or physico-chemical analysis. For preference such substances should be introduced at the poppy field and followed during the process of delivery to world markets. Conceivably such substances could also be introduced within reagents or intermediates in general use in the refining industry. Here even null results could be made to have a certain significance. The application of this type of method would have relevance to (5), (6), and (7).

Sensors

Another technological approach to the resolution of the international drug problem is the possible use of refined sensors that can detect drugs at short distances. These would be used as well as the long-range type of sensor referred to above that is connected with aerial or satellite photography. Research of the kind now proceeding within the realms of industrial security and of environmental protection (i.e., air and water pollution) might be extended to include the development of devices to enable law enforcement officers to discover consignments of drugs hidden in suitcases, packages, letters, cars, aircraft, speedboats, or on the persons of smugglers. Such devices would need to embody features of selectivity, speed, and reliability, factors that often interfere with one another and that would need to be reconciled before effective designs could be established. There is much scope for investigation in this area.

Under the above procedures, reconnaissance aircraft and satellites have for some time now been equipped with elaborate multispectral survey devices. For example, those employed in ERTS, the Earth Resources Technology Satellite developed by NASA, will provide resolution of objects down to 300–400 feet. The smallest opium fields are somewhat smaller, being about a half-acre in size, say 150 x 150 feet. However the conditions under which opium is being grown in Thailand, Burma, and Laos, in areas under Communist control, are such that there is good possibility that photo-interpretation will reveal the presence of poppy fields. Large areas of North Vietnam are also known to be under cultivation and, under wartime conditions, there should be no particular difficulty in delimiting these areas. Experiments along these lines are beginning and there can be little doubt that their findings would be of the utmost value in throwing light on the situation in mainland China. An investigative program starting with Yunnan and Southwest China should be initiated on the utmost priority. The objectives of such a program would be to obtain data at first hand within the categories of (1), (2), and (3) above.

Selective Destruction of Crops

With regard to (4), a considerable amount of information already exists concerning defoliants and herbicides and biological agents such as molds or blights. Indeed, there are said to be highly selective agents specific to the poppy that could be used in the elimination of opium as a naturally occurring substance should international opinion ever progress to the point of demanding this. Although the Communist countries still depend on opiates for legitimate medical purposes more than do Western countries, there can be little doubt that opiates can be replaced by synthetics and that these would be far easier to control.

Laboratory Detection

While extremely difficult to detect by technical methods, small clandestine laboratories are, in fact, rather vulnerable to more classical police and security intelligence procedures. If pressure is maintained on them they are usually compelled to keep on the move, thus increasing their chances of being discovered. When the plants are larger and more of the established industrial type, intelligence or reconnaissance methods will become less tactical and more strategic in nature. Intensive research on personalities and on process details would be essential.

Most of the techniques connected with primary detection, as described above, could be classified as first-line devices or methods, as distinct from second-line ones, namely those that would be connected with the examination of samples of captured drugs in order to ascertain their characteristics or perhaps to exploit the tracer techniques previously mentioned. These would use such well-known methods as gas chromatography, mass spectroscopy, free-radical electron resonance, and other NMR (nuclear magnetic resonance) methods, as well as other sophisticated means of microanalysis. One in particular that has been suggested in connection with air-pollution problems, a multiple-reflection infrared spectroscope, appears to be a rather promising device.

Data Processing and Storage

The information provided by the first- and second-line installations would be used as inputs to the third-line system, which would be concerned both with storage and processing of information and with analysis. The information would be needed for network tracing and modeling to determine the features of each process of the traffic, logging the movement of opiates from the source to the consumer. In addition to the categories of information to be achieved under (1) to (12) above, this kind of operation, through well-established processes of data-bank design and economic analysis, could yield particularly useful deductions in connection with:

(a) Volume of traffic.
(b) Domestic storage and transit points and their disposition, capacity, stocks, etc.
(c) Economic and organizational analysis of the entire process and the assessment on a scientific basis of addiction rates vs. volume of deliveries.
(d) Formulation of the design premises for a concerted (i.e., national and international) and determined assault, based on proper evaluation of data for disruption of linkages or supply chains exposed to attack or countermeasures.
(e) Changes of policy or of routing, or of modes of deception, by expeditious processes rather than slow and laborious evaluation of field data.

Modern methods of communication, information theory, data processing, and computation provide an unprecedented opportunity for effective interchanges at an international level. If the large amounts of data involved were to be properly shared as well as stored; if information on production, distribution, and consumption of narcotics is to be quickly assessed, an international data-bank at the disposal of Interpol, International Narcotics Control Board, or any such interested or responsible agency already existing or to be created, would appear to be essential. However, systems of this kind need always to be regarded as high-powered and effective tools at the disposal of highly skilled professionals rather than a means of substituting for them or, indeed, of producing situations of overcentralization that would favor rather than check the traffic.

365

Operational Research and Analysis

The worldwide operations of the international drug traffic are comparable with other economic or military questions of a kind that have often been examined by well-known, proven methods of operations research and systems analysis. As we are aware, these can be exceptionally valuable means of resolving problems if they are tackled realistically; yet, on the other hand, they can deliver extraordinarily misleading results if the inputs, for one reason or another, are inappropriate. The security of the data-bank, its analytical processes, and the kind of management that would be associated with it would all be matters to be subjected to very serious scrutiny. The whole process would, for example, be quite vulnerable to subtle forms of deception unless properly protected.[4]

International Countermeasures

So far, the international countermeasures against the traffic have been the concern of two main bodies—the International Narcotics Control Board (INCB) and Interpol. The former is primarily concerned with the "regulation," as much as has so far proved possible, of the international traffic. It originally came into being as part of a world trend to which by far the most important contributor to date has been the United States. Its functions have been primarily directed toward implementation of the provisions of the Single Convention, which was first promulgated in 1961 but which became internationally effective on December 13, 1964.

In attempting to enforce the provisions of that Convention, which is particularly difficult because it has no enforcement powers, the INCB requests from both parties and non-parties to the Convention their estimates of all legitimate drug requirements; existing stocks; statistics of levels of production; figures of known or estimated consumption, licit and illicit; figures of addiction; particulars of quantities of seizure of illicit drugs.

The Convention, through its article 12(3), is empowered to fix estimates of the above figures if countries do not supply the data that they should, and also nominally has the power of imposing embargoes on imports and exports if any country is proved to have violated its provisions. The countries that are signatories to the Convention are supposed to issue licenses for all poppy cultivation and to be particularly scrupulous to issue export licenses only when exporters can produce import permits from the country of destination. There is a prohibition against transit of drugs through a third country unless it takes cognizance of proper documentation, i.e., the production of export licenses.

It must be understood, however, that the measures of enforcement and the powers of the Board are only nominal and that the Convention was really drawn up to monitor the production and distribution of legal opiates. From the first, the United States has quite rightly held that its provisions as directed towards the control of illicit drugs are totally inadequate.

The essence of the solution of the international problem is to change the substance and emphasis of the Convention. The powers of the INCB should be extended to give it the means of assessing the location of illegal production or diversion of drugs. It should be given the special case of Red China where the production of opium for export is legal but where its domestic consumption is not.

It is rather remarkable that the UN has proved extraordinarily slow in its approach towards any realistic attack on this grave international problem that many would consider to be well within its sphere of responsibility. It was only after a good deal of prodding by the United States that the UN eventually agreed to set up a "Special Fund for Drug Abuse Controls." While undoubtedly a move in the right direction, there has as yet been a most inadequate financial response. This is, perhaps, not unduly surprising because, so far, the objectives of the Fund have been somewhat unclear and certainly not directed towards the core of the main question—the task of finding the primary sources of opium and seeing that none of this deadly crop finds its way into the hands of the dealers and pushers. That applies whether it be in Turkey, Afghanistan, Iran, Burma, Laos, Thailand, North Vietnam, or Communist China. There is at least the interesting possibility that now that Red China is a member of the United Nations, as a newly arrived member of the international community it can be taxed publicly with its own responsibilities in this area.

Besides INCB there is another significant international body that has increasingly been drawn into matters connected with the traffic: namely the International Criminal Police Organization (Interpol). This interesting and potentially very important organization (in the field of narcotics) is located at St. Cloud, Paris, where it maintains a central headquarters and clearing house whose aim is to enable the police forces in all countries to coordinate their work in crime prevention and in law enforcement. It is not a very large body, having only about 100 full-time employees, only about a dozen of whom are fully engaged on narcotics problems.

One must realize that, although there is interest in the subject and quite often Interpol has rendered great assistance to individual governments that have been trying to suppress the traffic, it has been unable to contribute much on the policy plane. It has repeatedly urged that all governments should set up effective narcotics-control units of their own. When discussing this or any other related problems of crime or law enforcement, Interpol is always at pains to point out that national sovereignty must always be respected and that *cooperation* is the only possible basis for police efforts at an international level. The law-enforcement agency in each country must use its own resources and act in accordance with its own legislation.

In these circumstances, in the final analysis, Interpol feels that international cooperation in this as in all other fields can only be brought about by the *desire* of all concerned to cooperate. Unless this common desire can be obtained, the aims of international suppression campaigns cannot possibly be achieved whatever the methods used. Even when the consensus does exist, it will only be possible to obtain satisfactory results if the problems are systematized and effective common principles underlying international action can be formulated and accepted.

The General Secretariat of Interpol held a meeting in October 1970 that was devoted to problems of drugs, especially as these impinged on police training. Although the findings of that conference have not been made public, that Interpol has been giving the whole question extremely serious consideration is evidenced by the following, delivered at the Regional Conference on Drug Trafficking, Canberra, Australia, November 22–25, 1971, held at the instigation of the Australian Government:

Remarks by M.J. Nepote, Secretary General, Interpol:

Statement of Fundamental Principles

1st Principle: Coordination at National Level

Illicit drug traffic is carried on in complete secrecy, and is a "business" with numerous ramifications. Any isolated case of trafficking is in fact only one piece of a more complex puzzle.

This also applies to law enforcement in this field; it can only be of significance and value if all isolated measures and operations are linked and coordinated at a higher level.

At national level, it is essential that there should be one department—and one department only—to group together all in-

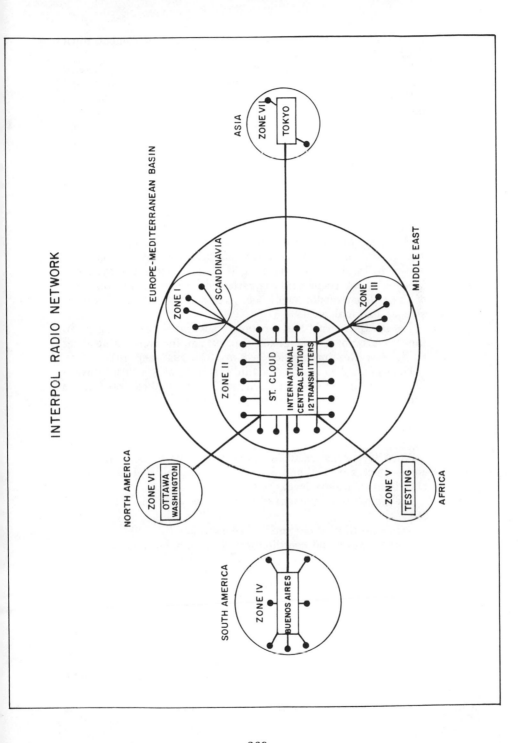

INTERPOL RADIO NETWORK

formation and data on operational measures to combat illicit drug traffic.

This department would then be in a position to keep lists of traffickers to build up an overall picture of their movements and activities, and to decide on general lines for the action to be taken.

If there is no such department, then either it must be set up, starting from scratch, or else the powers of an existing department must be extended. Whether or not this centralizing department is "operational" is another problem.

In the great majority of countries throughout the world, this task of centralization falls quite naturally to the national central police department responsible for law enforcement. In many countries, however, law enforcement with regard to illicit drug traffic falls within the jurisdiction of several different departments, sometimes coming under different administrations (such as the police or customs). In such circumstances the existence of a desire for cooperation is reflected by agreements that one of these departments should be invested with a kind of leadership at national level.

The ICPO-Interpol has constantly advocated the setting up in each country of a centralized department for combatting drug traffic (see Resolutions adopted in 1926, 1948 and 1957).*

The same policy is expressed in Article 11 of the 1936 Convention for the suppression of illicit traffic (national central offices) and in Article 25 of the 1961 Convention.

2nd Principle: Coordination at International Level

Since illicit drug traffic is by nature international, all the principles which are valid and desirable at national level are applicable at international level.

The logical consequences of coordination at international level are:

—rationalisation of channels of cooperation;

—centralisation and coordination of exchanges at international level.

(a) *Rationalisation of the channels of cooperation*

Despite their great importance, crimes of illicit drug traffic are, unfortunately, not the only ones requiring police cooperation. Crimes of murder, fraud, currency counterfeiting, theft and violence are also committed on an international scale. It is clearly impossible to set up separate cooperation machinery

---

*ICPO stands for International Chiefs of Police Organisations.

for each type of crime. This would be all the more illogical since in the majority of countries all these various types of crimes (including drugs offenses) are dealt with by the same general law enforcement departments (the central criminal police department). In addition international police cooperation has its own special requirements if it is to be effective (procedural rules, collective discipline, telecommunications, coded messages, etc.).

This naturally led the ICPO-Interpol to build up international police cooperation around one national agency in each country; in nearly all cases, the ICPO-Interpol National Central Bureaus.

Each Interpol National Central Bureau is a pivot of international police cooperation.

If the internal structures in any given country do not appear suited to such an arrangement, then—thanks to the desire for cooperation—ways will be found to adapt existing structures; the ICPO-Interpol will always encourage such efforts.

(b) *Centralisation and coordination of exchanges at international level*

At international level, overall coordination is effected by the ICPO-Interpol General Secretariat. Examination and filing of the information it receives enables it to carry out various tasks and studies connected with crime and criminals, which are of benefit to all member countries.

Since the movements of offenders do not correspond to any predetermined geographical criteria, it would be illogical and costly to envisage international cooperation on a regional basis, especially since the Interpol NCBs are entirely free to effect bilateral or multilateral liaisons according to the requirements of each individual case.

Finally, it should be emphasised that any international exchanges made through channels other than those described above are not centralised or coordinated; this is precisely what must be avoided.

3rd Principle: Rapidity of Exchanges

Nowadays, technical progress has reduced distances both for criminals and for law enforcement agencies.

With regard to the latter, it is still necessary for these agencies to acquire such technical equipment and furthermore to be willing to use it.

(a) *Equipment*

Firstly, of course, there are traditional methods of communication (telephone, telex). Over the years, however, the ICPO-Interpol has set up an independent instrument for international communications, the Interpol radio network (see separate memorandum). This enables us to make exchanges over the whole network and any country can be linked with any other country on the network.

There is no doubt that if—as has been suggested frequently—the NCBs of the Asian countries installed equipment to enable them to link up with the Tokyo Regional Station, then police cooperation throughout this part of the world would be greatly improved.

(b) *Its use*

Another condition must however be fulfilled if action is to be taken with the rapidity on which success depends: this concerns the human element, the use we make of the resources at our disposal.

For what is the use of linking two towns 5,000 kilometers apart, in the space of a few minutes, if the persons sending and receiving the messages are hampered by the maze of hierarchical structures, if the document is not used immediately, or if an excessive waste of time is caused by the forwarding of the document from one office to another in the next street?

Rapidity in handling cases is also proof of the desire for cooperation.

There are undoubtedly improvements to be made in this field and it is at national level—in accordance with the situation peculiar to each country—that measures can be taken (increased staff, departments operating a 24-hour service, simplification of hierarchical structures, etc.).

Contacts Through Interpol and "Direct" Contacts

On this particular point, there have been several errors of interpretation which have tended to create the belief that contact through Interpol machinery prevents or hinders direct contacts. This is a myth which should be swept away.

(a) *Border contacts*

This question was examined in the Report "The National Central Bureaus of the ICPO-Interpol: Policy," (page 13A) on relations between the police forces of different countries.

There may be *occasional* contacts and exchanges of information between local police forces, especially border forces on ac-

372

count of their opportunities or as a matter of tradition. The NCBs should always be kept informed; cooperation should be resumed through NCB channels as soon as possible.

It would be absurd to think that Interpol cooperation seeks to restrain or prohibit contacts between services on opposite sides of a common border. It is normal and, indeed, desirable that border services should exchange offenders operating in their common sector; we have only recommended that in serious cases, these contacts should be confirmed by messages and official exchange through Interpol channels so that the information is properly centralised at national and international level.

(b) *Meetings of investigators*

When dealing with certain complicated cases, it is highly desirable for an investigator in country A to visit country B (or even a third country C) and meet his colleagues there. He can then give them any information he could not let them have in writing and, if necessary, assist them unofficially in enquiries. Interpol cooperation is certainly not opposed to such meetings, indeed, one of its aims is to facilitate them. How? By giving advance notice of the officer's arrival and arranging that he is immediately directed to the appropriate department. Preparations of such missions abroad is one of the everyday tasks carried out by Interpol NCBs. Over the years many hundreds of these missions have been successfully arranged and if they are now less frequent, Interpol is in no way responsible.

In short, we would like to see efforts made along the following lines:

(1) In each country, the fight against illicit drug traffic should be centralised and coordinated by a specialized national service.

(2) In cases where this specialised service is not the one appointed as Interpol National Central Bureau, there should either be close and permanent contact between these two services, or the specialised department should be incorporated into the Interpol machinery.

(3) The Asian countries should join the Interpol radio network.

(4) The collective working methods and rapid information services of the Interpol General Secretariat should be respected.

(5) In international cases, efforts should be made to handle matters quickly at all levels.[5]

There are a number of difficulties with which Interpol must contend in its attempts to operate on an international plane. For example, member governments do not always provide it with enough information about domestic criminal cases, even when foreign nationals are being prosecuted. Also there is a tendency to withold information on smuggling and smugglers that would be of considerable international interest. In the narcotics field specifically, it is impeded in its efforts by

(1) Insufficient intercommunication between police units in member countries.
(2) Corrupt practices and bribery in some countries not only at the police level but also at very senior administrative and policy-making levels.
(3) Large tracts of territory in some countries in which the writ of the central government does not run and which may be under foreign control, as in Vietnam, Laos, Cambodia, and Burma.

Unquestionably, Interpol seems to provide a potential nucleus for greatly improved and more highly mechanized and sophisticated methods such as already have been described. However, the investment would need to be considerable and Interpol's budget at present is only some $1 million a year. In all possibility such enhancement of the capabilities of Interpol would throw the organization out of balance and perhaps make it less effective in other directions. Possibly the organization of a special department of Interpol and the foundation of what would amount to an international advisory agency of the RAND type, operated jointly by Interpol and INCB through a combined panel, would be of use but it would be necessary to draw careful distinctions between research and operations in such a case.

There are numerous other forms of action that also need to be taken to combat the drug traffic and the operations of the International Narcotics Cartel and the rings that act for it.

A good many countries are only partially aware of the nature of the problem; in many cases they even function as channels or conduits for the traffic. Where situations of this kind exist, it obviously is the duty of the United States or other responsible and right-thinking governments to furnish information as required and also to exert diplomatic pressure if necessary. This is the case with allied governments in Southeast Asia, where grave disabilities exist that have been allowed to develop to a dangerous level. Yet they could have been checked to a considerable extent if they had been foreseen and if the clear warnings about large-scale Red Chinese participation had been heeded.

Obviously, too, the UN should be stimulated to play a more active role in countering this traffic, just as it also must take account of the related question of terrorism. The level of financial support of the UN Special Fund should be raised; additionally, there are possibilities that the International Narcotics Control Board and the UN Commission on Narcotics Drugs could do much to study the social and agricultural implications of the suppression of opium crops, as well as providing inspectors for suspected areas.

Above all, the actual points of narcotics origin, including those in Red China, must be fearlessly exposed so that a massive delivery to the international traffic can be put under control and eliminated. Some excellent preliminary steps have been taken in Turkey and in France, countries that essentially are on the same "side" as the United States. Similar actions are in view in Southeast Asia, but in themselves all these measures will prove inadequate unless the newest member of the UN Security Council can be persuaded to abandon procedures that could only provoke the strongest reactions against it if the facts about it were known.

The maintenance of public order and the stability of the state is, in the first instance, the responsibility of the courts and the police power, which in periods of increasing disorder need to be fully supported by military action. All these safeguards have been threatened of late: the courts have been under attack, as have our penal institutions; the populace is constantly being incited against the police; great inroads have been made upon military morale, tending towards its destruction. In all these processes psycho-chemical warfare has been a primary arm. During the hearings on foreign relations of the U.S. Senate, held on July 1, 1971, from which some quotations have already been made, there was a particularly apposite statement made by Patrick V. Murphy, Police Commissioner of the City of New York, who said *inter alia:*

> What I do want to establish is that local police agencies cannot—
> I repeat cannot—effectively stem the flow of narcotics into our
> cities, much less into the veins of hundreds of thousands of young
> people. Only the national government can make truly effective
> strides toward breaking the chain of distribution that leads from
> the poppy fields of the Middle East and Indo-China into the bodies
> of wretched victims here in the United States. And until now noth-
> ing even remotely resembling effective action to realize this poten-
> tial has been taken by the Federal Government....
> Once opium poppies have been harvested abroad and placed into
> the hands of illegal trade, five or ten thousand miles from here,
> the battle is already lost and thousands of American addicts are
> already doomed to a life of continuing misery and often agonizing
> death.[6]

This scourge cannot be defeated and its promoters held responsible unless the whole nature of the monstrous traffic is truly understood to be an enemy action. The dual threat of psycho-chemical warfare and its related strategy of terror must be countered by strenuous and determined opposition in campaigns waged just as strongly as any in war. The will to victory must be revived, thus restoring to the United States and its allies an initiative vital to their survival. We have been on the defensive too long—we must now think and act offensively.

Chapter 8
References and Footnotes

1. For Thuggee, see: Maj. W.H. Sleeman, Commissioner for the Suppression of Thuggee, *Report on the Depredations of the Thug Gangs (of Upper and Central India)*, East India Company Document, Calcutta, 1840. W. H. Sleeman, *The Thugs or Phansigars of India* (Philadelphia, 1839). Louis B. Zoul, *Thugs and Communists* (Long Island City, N.Y.: Public Opinion, 1959).
2. See Suzanne Labin, *Hippies, Drugs and Promiscuity* (New Rochelle, N.Y.: Arlington House, 1972).
3. Hearings before the Senate Internal Security Subcommittee, August 14, 1972: "World Drug Traffic and Its Impact on U.S. Security," p. 5.
4. See Hearings before the Select Committee on Crime, U.S. House of Representatives, April 26-28, 1971: "Narcotics Research, Rehabilitation and Treatment," Part I.
5. Australian Government, Department of Customs and Excise, publication. Appendix D: "Report on the Regional Conference on Drug Trafficking," Canberra, November 22-25, 1971.
6. Hearings before the Committee on Foreign Relations, United States Senate, July 1, 1971: "International Traffic in Narcotics," p. 79.

Appendix I

National Government Mandate

These provisional regulations, drawn up by the Chinese National Government in the course of the Sino-Japanese conflict, indicate by their severity the importance attached by the authorities to the need for rigorously controlling the drug traffic and punishing offenders. They reflect the views of Chinese officials toward a major threat to national security.

Chungking
February 19, 1941

The Provisional Regulations on Penal Offenses Relating to Opium Suppression and the Provisional Regulations on Penal Offenses Relating to Suppression of Narcotics are hereby abolished.

The Provisional Regulations on Penal Offenses Relating to Suppression of Opium and Narcotics are hereby enacted and promulgated.

Provisional Regulations On Penal Offenses Relating To Suppression Of Opium And Narcotics

Article 1

The term "opium" used in the present Regulations refers to opium, poppy plants and poppy seeds. The term "narcotics" refers to morphine, cocaine, heroin and their derivatives including various kinds of colored narcotic pills.

Article 2

Persons cultivating poppies or manufacturing opium or narcotics shall be subject to the death penalty.

377

Article 3

Persons instigating mob resistance against the uprooting of poppy sprouts shall be dealt with as follows:
1. The ringleader or other persons directing the mob on the spot—the death penalty.
2. Rioters—imprisonment for a term of 7 or more years.
3. Those who demonstrate on the spot—imprisonment for a term of 3 to 7 years.

Article 4

Persons transporting or selling narcotics shall be subject to the death penalty; those possessing narcotics with the intention of selling same shall be given the death penalty or life imprisonment. Persons transporting or selling opium shall be given the death sentence or life imprisonment; those possessing opium with the intention of selling the same, imprisonment for a term of 10 or more years. Persons transporting or selling poppy seeds shall be sentenced to imprisonment for a term of 5 to 12 years; those possessing poppy seeds with the intention of selling the same, imprisonment for a term of 2 to 7 years. Persons exporting or importing poppy seeds to or from abroad shall be given the death penalty.

Article 5

Persons giving to others morphine injections or providing premises for others to smoke or to take narcotics for profit shall be given the death penalty; those providing premises for others to smoke opium shall be given the death penalty or life imprisonment.

Article 6

Persons taking morphine injections or smoking or using narcotics shall be given the death penalty.

Persons smoking opium shall be sentenced to imprisonment for a term of 1 to 5 years and may, in addition, be liable to a fine of not more than $1,000. Addicts may be sent to doctors for compulsory treatment, to be cured within a specified period; and those found to be addicted again after having been cured shall be given the death penalty or life imprisonment.

Article 7

Persons helping others to commit the offenses stipulated in Article

6 of the regulations shall be sentenced to imprisonment for a term of 1 to 7 years.

Article 8

Persons manufacturing, transporting, selling, or possessing with the intention of selling, paraphernalia exclusively used for morphine injection or taking of narcotics shall be sentenced to imprisonment for a term of 3 years or more and may, in addition be liable to a fine of not more than $3,000. Persons manufacturing, transporting, selling or possessing with the intention of selling paraphernalia exclusively used for opium smoking shall be sentenced to imprisonment for a term of not more than 5 years and may, in addition be liable to a fine of not more than $1,000.

Article 9

Persons possessing opium or narcotics without any evidence of committing other offenses shall be sentenced to imprisonment for a term of 1 to 5 years and may, in addition, be liable to a fine of not more than $1,000. Persons possessing paraphernalia exclusively used for opium smoking, smoking or taking of narcotics, or morphine in injection, without evidence of committing other offences shall be sentenced to imprisonment for a term of not more than 3 years or a fine of not more than $500.

Article 10

Persons placing the contraband in the possession of others or forging evidence with intent to bring false charges of violations of the present Regulations shall be subjected to the penalties provided for in the articles concerned. The same applies to persons acting as witnesses and examiners who make false statements or reports; but if the objective of their so doing is to the advantage of defendants, their penalties may be alleviated.

Persons committing the above two crimes who surrender themselves before judgments are established may have the penalties alleviated.

Article 11

Public functionaries, soldiers or police found violating Articles 3 to 5 shall be given the death penalty; those found violating paragraph 2 of Article 6 or Articles 7 to 10 shall be subjected to the maximum punishment specified therein.

379

Article 12

Public functionaries, soldiers or police found taking advantage of their official authority to force others to commit the offenses provided for in Article 2 shall be given the death penalty.

Article 13

Public functionaries, soldiers or police found affording protection to or demanding or receiving bribes from others thus permitting them to commit the offenses provided for in articles 2 to 8 of the present Regulations shall be given the death penalty.

The same penalties may also be applicable to public functionaries, soldiers or police found conniving in the freeing of offenders violating the present Regulations or pilfering, substituting or concealing the seized opium or narcotics.

Bribes involved in the commission of offenses stipulated in paragraph one of this Article shall be confiscated, the offender shall be required to pay the amount. If all or part of the bribes are not available at the time of confiscation the offender shall be required to pay the amount. If such payment cannot be made on account of financial difficulties properties shall be confiscated to cover it. When the value of properties is not sufficient to cover the amount so required, a sum necessary for the maintenance of their families shall be set aside.

Article 14

Persons committing the offenses referred to in article 2 of the present Regulations who disclose information regarding the origin of the poppy seeds or of the materials for narcotic preparation, thus leading to the discovery thereof may have their penalties alleviated. Persons committing the offenses referred to in Articles 4 to 7 of the present Regulations who disclose information regarding the origin of the opium or narcotics, thus enabling the discovery thereof, may have their penalties alleviated. Persons committing the offense referred to in paragraph 2 of Article 6 of the present Regulations who voluntarily have their addiction cured before their crime is discovered may have their penalties alleviated or exempted if such are confirmed by medical examination.

Article 15

Persons found guilty with criminal intent to violate Articles 2 to 5, 8, 12 and 13 of the present Regulations shall be punished.

Article 16

Poppy seeds, opium, narcotics and paraphernalia exclusively used for the manufacture or smoking of opium and narcotics involved in the commission of offenses stipulated in the present Regulations shall all be confiscated and destroyed by fire. The same provision shall apply to caffeine, milk sugar and quinine alkaloid and other substances which are identified with the exclusive use of manufacturing narcotics.

Article 17

Persons receiving imprisonment penalties for a term of 6 or more months, in accordance with Articles of the present Regulations shall be deprived of civil rights for a term of 1 to 10 years.

Article 18

Persons violating articles 2 to 5 of the present regulations may have their properties confiscated, in part or in whole. Such confiscation of property may be effected according to the provisions of the Law of Compulsory Enforcement.

Article 19

The death penalty may be effected by shooting.

Article 20

Offenses not stipulated in the present Regulations shall be governed by the provisions of other laws and ordinances.

Article 21

Opium, morphine, cocaine, heroin and their derivatives or preparations for medicinal and scientific use shall not be subjected to the present Regulations, but to the Regulations Governing Narcotic Drugs.

Article 22

Offenses coming within the present Regulations shall be tried by authorities invested with the right of military jurisdiction as designated by the Chairman of the Military Affairs Commission, or by various local governments deputized by the same authority.

The judgments rendered according to the provisions of the above paragraph shall not be enforced without the approval of the Chairman of the Military Affairs Commission.

Article 23

The period of enforcement of the present Regulations is fixed for three years.

Article 24

These Regulations shall become effective from the date of promulgation.

Appendix II

Ordinance Controlling Narcotics in China

These instructions on the control of narcotics, drafted by the Imperial Japanese Government, were promulgated several months after those issued by the Chinese National Government. It is clear that they were much more permissive insofar as drug traffic in the Chinese theatre was concerned.

(Promulgated in the KANPO or Official Gazette on August 13, 1941; translation made by the Okuyama Service, Tokyo, and checked against the original in Japanese. Minor changes were made as a result.)

We have sanctioned the *'Ordinance Controlling Narcotics in China'* and cause the same to be promulgated.

Imperial Sign Manual
Imperial Seal

August 12, 1941

Prime Minister,
Prince Fumimaro Konoye;
Minister for Foreign
Affairs,
Teijiro Toyoda

Ordinance Controlling Narcotics in China
(Imperial Ordinance No. 815)

Article 1

The control of narcotics and crude opium in China for Japanese subjects and Japanese corporations shall be governed by the stipulations of this Ordinance.

The kind of narcotics mentioned in the previous paragraph shall be determined by the Minister for Foreign Affairs.

Article 2

Narcotics and crude opium cannot be manufactured in China.
Poppies cannot be cultivated in China for the purpose of manufacturing crude opium.

Article 3

Narcotics and crude opium cannot be imported into China.

Article 4

Narcotics and crude opium cannot be exported from China.

Article 5

Narcotics cannot be transferred from the jurisdictional district of one consulate in China to the jurisdictional district of another consulate.

Article 6

Narcotics and crude opium which are in China cannot be assigned to others or obtained by transfer, nor can they be delivered or accepted.

Article 7

Those provisions of the preceding three articles which relate to narcotics shall not apply in cases where doctors, druggists or other persons who are designated by the Minister for Foreign Affairs, import, transfer, assign to others, obtain by transfer, deliver or accept narcotics in accordance with the stipulations made by the Minister for Foreign Affairs.

Article 8

Narcotics cannot be possessed in China for the purpose of selling except by druggists.
Crude opium cannot be possessed in China.

Article 9

Except in cases corresponding to any of the following numbers, narcotics cannot be administered to oneself or to other persons in China.
1. When a doctor administers them in his professional capacity.
2. When a patient or his nurse administers them according to the instructions of a doctor in his professional capacity.
3. In addition to the cases mentioned in the preceding two numbers, when a person designated by the Minister for Foreign Affairs administers them in accordance with the stipulations made by the Minister for Foreign Affairs.

Article 10

A doctor within the meaning of this Ordinance shall be a doctor, dentist or veterinary surgeon who is designated by the Minister for Foreign Affairs. A druggist within the meaning of this Ordinance shall be a person who is engaged in the business of manufacturing medicines or a person who is engaged in the sale of medicines and who is designated by the Minister for Foreign Affairs.

Article 11

A person who has acted in contravention of the provisions of articles 2-6, Article 8 or Article 9 shall be liable to penal servitude not exceeding one year or a fine not exceeding Yen 200.

An attempt to violate any of the offenses mentioned in the preceding paragraph shall also be punished.

Article 12

A person who has prepared a machine or raw materials in China for the purpose of manufacturing narcotics in China shall be liable to penal servitude not exceeding six months or to a fine not exceeding Yen 100.

Article 13.

In addition to the stipulations made in Article 2 to the preceding Article, other necessary matters concerning the control of narcotics shall be determined by the Minister for Foreign Affairs.

385

Supplementary Rule.

This Ordinance shall be enforced as from August 20, 1941.

Appendix III

Text of Statement
by Prime Minister Erim of Turkey

In recent years the abuse of narcotics in the world has assumed a very serious and dangerous condition. This situation has been described by the United Nations as almost an "explosion." Several times more production is made of narcotic drugs than is needed for legitimate and medical needs. For this reason, the lives of millions of persons who use narcotics end. In some countries, this deadly disaster is spreading rapidly, particularly among youth. It is noted that even 12-year old children are drawn to drugs. Countries which never used drugs ten years ago are now its victims. The tragedy has spread even as far as the African countries. Furthermore, addiction has begun to threaten all the members of the community. Youth, in particular must be protected from this addiction as a great duty for the sake of mankind.

We have seen what a great danger the world is facing. We touched on this in the government program which our Parliament passed: "And indicated that the problem of opium smuggling which has become a destructive tragedy for all young people in the world, will be seriously undertaken by the government, which believes before all else that this harms sentiments of humane consideration. Opium growers will be given support by showing them a better field for earning their living."

Indeed, Turkey has not remained a stranger to the development of the problem of narcotic drugs, to the international agreements made in this matter since the beginning of the 20th Century, and to the work of the United Nations. On the contrary, she has joined in the agreements and has taken decisions to end this disaster.

Turkey has participated in all the international agreements made on the subject of narcotics beginning with the Hague Agreement of 1912: those included agreements in 1925, 1931, 1936, 1946, 1948, 1953 and 1961.

An important provision of the 1961 Narcotics Single Convention, signed by 78 nations, is the article which binds the production of opium to the permission of the government.

Governments coming before us have fulfilled their commitments to international agreements and furnished all types of statistical information to the authorized organs of the UN. However, the needed law establishing a licensing system for planting in Turkey, which is a key point of this agreement, for some reason was not passed until this year. Our state was continually asked by internationally authorized organs to fulfil this commitment. This shortcoming was criticized in the parliaments of many countries and by their public opinion. The UN Secretary General, in the report he presented on this subject in 1970, based on these criticisms, said that an extensive amount of smuggling was being made from Turkey.

After this, matters took a rapid turn. In the Summer of last year the matter was first taken up at the UN Economic and Social Committee. The Committee on Narcotic Drugs was called to an extraordinary meeting. There, the critical situation in the world was taken up and it was decided to start a struggle by taking exceptional measures in three stages of the problem: production, supply and demand, and smuggling. It was stipulated that a fund was to be established to assure the financial means for these purposes. The subject was agreed upon at the General Council Meeting of the UN too.

In a law passed by the Turkish Grand National Assembly in 1966, Turkey ratified the international agreement signed in 1961. In this way, international commitments became a part of our national law. Accordingly, "in the event one of the parties fails to implement the provisions of the agreement and, through this, the object of the agreement is seriously harmed, the control body will ask that the situation be corrected and can go so far as to set up an embargo against this country."

Smuggling made from our country in recent years has become very distressing for us. Governments, which were unable to prevent smuggling, decreased the number of provinces where poppies were planted from 1960 on and gradually moved the planting of opium from regions close to the border to the center of Anatolia. Now planting has been reduced to four provinces. In this way it was hoped to prevent smuggling.

However, unfortunately, this system did not give results. During 1970 many things developed in favour of the smugglers. Although the soil-products office obtained 116 tons of opium from the poppies planted in 11 provinces in 1969, in 1970 the opium which reached the office from nine provinces was only 60 tons.

The whole world has been asking where the difference is going. The contraband opium seized by our security forces, which we learn about in radio and news reports, shows everyone the extent of the problem.

It is certain that a smugglers' gang, organized on an international scale, constitutes a political and economic problem for Turkey. They will not be permitted to play around with the prestige of our country any further.

This horrible network of smugglers fools our villagers either with the wish to make extra money or by force and it tries to use them for their own ends. Of the tremendous sums which revolve around these transactions, the poor, hard-working Turkish villager actually does not get much. The smugglers pay 400 to 500 liras for an illegal kilo of opium to the villagers whom they force to break the law. By the time this opium reaches Turkey's borders, the smugglers have made a profit many times multiplied. After it leaves our country and throughout its route, the value of the drug becomes augmented more and more; in the end, it reaches an unbelievable price. International smugglers are earning millions from the raw opium produced by the villagers, but the Turkish farmer gets only a paltry sum. In countries where health is endangered through this opium, because smuggling cannot be prevented in Turkey, anti-Turkish opinions are created.

The Turkish villager also naturally feels bitter against this problem created by the smugglers who make millions from the backs of our farmers. All Turkish citizens feel a moral pain that our country is being blamed for smuggling which is poisoning world youth.

The measures to be applied to control smuggling are extremely expensive. In general, poppies are planted in one corner of the field. For this reason, it is necessary to establish an organization which can control an area ten times that of a total poppy-farming area of 13 thousand donums which may actually be planted. Vehicles, gasoline, personnel and their salaries must not be forgotten. Smugglers, on the other hand, it must be remembered, will resort to any means. Until now foreign assistance was obtained for control purposes; even an airplane was obtained for our organization. But, unfortunately, the matter was impossible to control by these means, in spite of all the efforts which were made. Our nation, which is known for its honesty and integrity, is now under a grave accusation. The time when we must end the placing of blame for deaths in other countries on Turkey is long overdue.

We cannot allow Turkey's supreme interests and the prestige of our nation to be further shaken. Our government has decided to apply a clear and firm solution. It forbids completely the planting of poppies; they have already been reduced to four provinces. The agreement ratified in 1966 also stipulates this arrangement.

Poppies will not be planted in Turkey beginning next year. However, we have given careful consideration to the fact that the farmers have, until now, obtained a legitimate and additional source of income from the planting of poppies. For this reason, in order that the poppy-growers will not incur a loss in any way, the necessary formula has been developed. This formula is: in order to make up for the income farmers who are planting in provinces at present will lose, they will be given compensation beginning from the coming year. This compensation will work this way: the basis will be the value on the international market of the whole produce such as opium, seeds, stems, etc., that the planters will sell to the soil-products office this year.

Furthermore, in order to replace the income lost by farmers by other means and to provide them other means of earning a living, long-term investments will be made in the region. Until these investments bear fruit, villagers will continue to be given compensation. From among those who would normally plant this year, those who voluntarily give up planting in the coming Autumn will be given compensation on the same basis.

I am now addressing my villager citizens. In order that the plan may be successful and that it will be possible to establish real values for future-year compensations, and the criteria for investment, please turn over all your produce to the soil-products office. You will receive the necessary assistance in this respect. We have also raised our purchasing price. The larger the amount turned over to the office by all the poppy-producers, the larger the compensation they will receive in the coming years without planting. Besides, by selling all his produce to the TMO, the producer will prove he is not the tool of the smuggler, that the Turkish farmer at no time had the object of poisoning the whole world, nor that he encouraged that knowingly.

Dear Farmer Citizens, you will be the ones to save the prestige of our nation. The government will also, henceforth, give special importance to your problems. Our Government has taken precautions in order that in the end, not a single farmer family will bear a loss. Your income will be met without allowing any room for doubts; at the same time, it is planned to establish necessary installations to open new sources of income in the region. I ask you to carry out this plan and to sell all your opium products for this year to the Office at the high price established last month; thereby you will give this program a good start.

Turkish Opium Decree—June 30, 1971

On the basis of the letter of the Ministry of Agriculture dated 26/6/1971, Number 02-16/1-01/342: per law 3491 as amended by law 7368, Article 18; and per article 22 of Appendix Agreement dated 27/12/1966 to Law 812, the Council of Ministers has decided on June 30, 1971: definitely to forbid the planting and production of poppies within the borders of Turkey beginning from the Autumn of 1972. This will be done by specifying the provinces shown on the lists attached hereto.

1. To forbid poppy planting and opium producing in provinces where warning is given as of the Autumn of 1972: Afyon, Burdur, Isparta, Kutahya.

2. To forbid poppy planting and opium producing in the provinces where a warning has been given from the Autumn of 1971: Denizli, Konya, Usak.

3. To give a suitable compensation as proposed by the Ministry of Agriculture and by the decision of the Council of Ministers to the planters in these seven provinces where poppy planting and production has been forbidden. This will be on the basis of the opium they deliver this year to the Soil Products Office and on the basis of any other poppy by-products so that the farmers will not incur any loss of income.

4. To grant to the planters in the areas indicated in Paragraph 1, who voluntarily give up planting in the Autumn of 1971, the right to benefit from the compensation set forth in paragraph 3.

C. Sunay
President of the Republic

Appendix IV

Section A

Two Reports Submitted by the Honorable
Henry J. Anslinger,
U.S. Commissioner of Narcotics, to the
United Nations Commission on
Dangerous Drugs

Report No. I (April 19 to May 14, 1954)

Last year I told this Commission that the United States is a target of Communist China to be supplied with a flood of foreign-exchange-earning, health-and-morale-devastating heroin. For several years, I have presented documented facts which have established that narcotics trading from the Chinese mainland is an insidious, calculated scheme of the Chinese Communist regime to obtain operating funds and, at the same time, spread the debauchery of narcotic addiction among the free nations.

On April 5th of this year, in San Francisco, California, after several months of intensive undercover investigation, we made important inroads on this traffic when we arrested eight prominent Chinese and indicted Judah Isaac Ezra of Hong Kong who collaborated in supplying heroin from Communist China to addicts on our West Coast. Pure heroin seized in the raids or purchased as evidence amounted to six pounds.

Merchant seamen who frequented Ezra's establishment obtained heroin from Ezra and smuggled it into the United States for the illicit market. In most instances, the heroin was brought into the country concealed on the persons of seamen. Ornately carved camphor-wood chests with specially built compartments were also used for the smuggling operations.

One of the dealers arrested in San Francisco operated a florists shop and made his deliveries of heroin disguised as boxes of flowers. Other dealers made deliveries to undercover agents in the usual manner in such places as Chinese restaurants and meeting places for seamen. Arrangements for sales of heroin were often negotiated over elaborate Chinese dinners. Chinese social clubs were frequently the meeting places to arrange for the sale and delivery of the narcotics. One such social club is known to authorities as a gathering place for Communist Chinese and Chinese-alien smugglers.

The importance of this coup can be gauged by the fact that in the diluted form in which it reaches the addict through Thailand from mainland China, more opium moves to and around Chiengrai in northern Thailand than any other place in the world in illicit traffic. The opium reaches Bangkok by boat, truck, rail and plane and three to four tons can be delivered at any time to a point outside the harbor at Bangkok in the open sea. This opium is priced at U.S. $40,000 per ton and can be purchased in lots of 200 tons on a six-months basis.

Crude morphine is sold by traffickers in narcotics from mainland China at the rate of $475 per pound in Bangkok. This morphine has about the same appearance as a cheap cake of soap. There is usually a large "A" or "A1" on the surface of each cake as in the case of a large seizure in Japan in July 1954. Heroin from these traffickers sells for U.S. $2,000-$3,000 per pound in Japan and for U.S. $3,000-$5,000 in the United States. A group of these smugglers successfully smuggled twenty pounds of heroin to Japan at a profit of $30,000 after all expenses were paid.

In October 1953, an airline pilot in Bangkok was approached to make eight flights to Macao with opium from mainland China. At the end of 1953, a group of smugglers including an official of the Bank of Canton smuggled twenty-three pounds of heroin and morphine from Yunnan to Chiengrai to Bangkok and thence to another transshipment point. In July 1954, an airline hostess was arrested at a transshipment point with a two-pound package of morphine which she was transporting as a courier for aircraft-maintenance personnel, after information had been received that narcotics were reaching Tokyo, Japan, in this manner. In the early part of 1954, a Chinese courier arriving in Hong Kong by air was arrested with approximately seven pounds of pure heroin transshipped at Bangkok. Shortly thereafter, an American was arrested in Hong Kong with approximately forty pounds of opium and morphine which he was transporting as a courier for traffickers in narcotics from mainland China. The transshipment point was Bangkok.

Despite the efforts of the Burmese Government to control the illicit traffic in narcotics, hundreds of tons of cleaned and packaged opium in one-kilogram units are brought into Burma each year from Yunnan Province. Routes for the smuggling are through Myitkyina in the Kachin State and through Lashio on the old Burma Road in the Northern Shan States.

The hub of the traffic on the Yunnan side of the border is Tengyueh. Along the border are found trucks, military vehicles, carts, mules and pack trains used for transporting the opium.

About forty-three tons of opium are consumed annually in one small area along the Yunnan border, but the amount of opium in the traffic through Burma far surpasses the amount consumed within the country. Shareholders in illegally operated opium shops along the Yunnan border in Burma have been forced to forfeit their interests because caravans from Yunnan sell opium more cheaply than the opium shops.

Another route used by the traffickers in illicit narcotics from mainland China is through Kengtung and across Burma to river, road and rail connections below Mandalay. Much of the opium is brought down in river boats to Rangoon where it is transferred to coastal steamers for further transshipment at Penang and Singapore.

Large quantities of high-quality crude morphine are being manufactured under expert technical supervision in factories in Communist China. The morphine is processed according to pharmaceutical standards and methods under government supervision and not in clandestine laboratories. When the smugglers of this morphine near Rangoon, the contraband is transferred to fast launches to by-pass the city. The traffic is so well organized that the authorities state they would need a patrol plane to meet with any success in suppressing the traffic.

On August 4, 1953, a seizure of 16.8 kilograms of this high quality morphine was made about eighty miles south of Mandalay. On April 17, another seizure of 43.5 pounds was made about fifty miles from Rangoon. Authorities believe the morphine had been brought down the Burma Road through Lashio from Yunnan. Containers of the opium, which is readily converted into heroin, are stamped with the Elephant Brand and with the "1 A 27" mark.

Since the processing of opium is illegal in Burma, authorities attempted to dispose of approximately 44 tons of opium which had either been seized from the illicit traffic or purchased some years ago. They received an offer stating that the opium would be transferred to Macao where it would be manufactured into medicinal narcotics. Burmese authorities saw through this attempt to regain the opium for the international illicit traffic.

On December 18, 1953, excise officials in Mandalay, Burma, seized 140.8 kilograms of opium which was being transported in a Dodge jeep from Lashio on the Burma Road.

Traffic in heroin from the Communist Chinese regime of mainland China is increasing, according to enforcement authorities concerned with traffic through Canton, Macao, Bangkok and other ports. Within the past year other areas have assumed a place of equal importance, as Korea and Japan, where the heroin is furnished directly by Communist agents in the traffic.

Millions of dollars obtained through the sale of opium and other narcotics are used by the Communist regime in mainland China for political purposes and to finance agents who have been found actively engaged. An official of an airline in the Far East was found to be smuggling heroin and currency for the Chinese Communist regime. A trafficker in narcotics from mainland China attempted to arrange for an airlift of a ton of morphine to the United States. The pilot was offered an interest in an opium-processing plant if he would smuggle the morphine... Narcotic traffickers offered to charter a PBY in March 1954 to airlift ten tons of opium from an inaccessible river area to a worldwide narcotic smuggling group with headquarters in Macao. An effort was made by these traffickers to establish an airline to move opium held by the Communist regime of mainland China. Both opium and crude morphine were airlifted from otherwise inaccessible points under the control of the regime to transshipment points where the narcotics were loaded on surface craft.

During the year 1953, opium from Yunnan Province accounted for almost one hundred percent of the opium seized at some transshipment points. The Gulf of Martaban and the Gulf of Siam both were used to facilitate this traffic. Investigations of circumstances surrounding the larger seizures revealed that the opium was smuggled in ships operated by the traffickers in this opium who had headquarters and connections in many of the principal ports of the Far East. Opium trafficked through the transshipment points often sells at a rate of U.S. $400 per pound.

In Japan a member of the Communist Party revealed that her organization, with branches in all big hospitals in Tokyo, Yokohama, Nagoya, Kobe and Osaka operated as the Society for the Protection of Health and Peace with headquarters inside the Communist Party Headquarters in Tokyo. This trafficker stated that she and five other females of the group made expenses and tremendous profits for the Tokyo branch of this Communist organization through the sale of heroin.

At a meeting of this Communist organization a resolution was adopted that the organization would gain funds by selling narcotics to various hotels, cabarets, bars and other establishments patronized by American personnel in the Tokyo area. Large sales of heroin which were paid for by check to "Society Headquarters" were made to beer halls in Tachikawa and to agents in Fuchu City, which is located near Tokyo.

A Chinese, Po Kung Lung, directed the activities of the six females and provided the heroin, which was valued at $11 per gram and was sold to Koreans and Japanese for further distribution. One of these retailers of heroin was an executive member of a Tokyo District Group of the Communist Party and was engaged in the collection of Party funds.

The enforcement Division of the Narcotic Section in the Welfare Ministry of Japan reported that extensive surveillance of two Chinese in Tokyo resulted in their arrest and the seizure of 585 grams of 94.2 percent heroin and 275 grams of 92.4 percent heroin in March 1954. The seizure was made as one of the Chinese, Yang Jui An, was leaving the Kakyo Building in the heart of Tokyo. This building is a center for traffickers with Communist connections dealing in heroin and United States currency. Among these traffickers were Li Chin Sui and his group, who were arrested in Tokyo in July with thirty-three pounds of heroin and morphine. As early as 1951, enforcement agents had purchased U.S. $5,633 worth of heroin from traffickers operating from the Kakyo Building. The heroin was 85 percent pure and bore tags and seals of the "Red Lion Brand.".…

Ten seizures of heroin totaling fifty-eight grams were made January 14, 1954, at Iwakumi in Yamaguchi Prefecture in Japan. In connection with these seizures the Japanese authorities stated the majority of the prostitutes in and around the city of Iwakumi, which is located near the international airport, are addicted to narcotic drugs and stimulants and are spreading the habit of taking such drugs. A Chinese, Fang Jen Chun, living in Kobe had been supplying the heroin to retailers at Iwakumi.

Kyodo News Agency reported November 16, 1954, that in 1952 U.S. $70 million worth of narcotics were shipped out of Communist China.

Twenty-six percent of this amount was shipped to Japan and these funds constituted the chief source for financing secret Communist agents. At the same time Director Goichiro Fuji said the Communist regime sold $15.5 million worth of narcotics in Japan in 1952.

According to a Pyongyang radio broadcast of December 29, 1953, special factories are being built to extract morphine from opium in North Korea. On October 16, 1954, the South Korean authorities announced the arrest of a North Korean agent who stated that Communist China is furnishing technical specialists to North Korea to operate narcotic-manufacturing plants. It is through North Korea that tremendous quantities of heroin from Communist China have reached Korea and Japan since 1947. Recently, an American soldier stated that while stationed in Taegu, South Korea, he and at least thirty other persons were furnished with heroin of an almost pure quality without cost. Addiction was acquired, making hospitalization necessary upon return to the United States.

Heroin from Communist China has been seized on both coasts of the United States, as well as in the interior at St. Louis, Missouri. In connection with the seizure in St. Louis, the source trafficker in Japan stated he has been dealing with the Communist regime of mainland China for one and one-half years through the use of deck crews as couriers.

On February 2, 1954, in New York City, twenty ounces of heroin with the characteristic physical and chemical properties of heroin from Communist China laboratories were seized from a seaman as he attempted to smuggle the contraband ashore from the round-the-world steamship *President Arthur*. It was later learned the heroin had been obtained at one of the usual transshipment points for narcotics from the Communist Regime of mainland China....

For several years the attention of the free nations of the world has been focused on the position which the Communist regime of mainland China has assumed in carrying on a worldwide traffic in opium, morphine and heroin. Mere denials comprise no answer to the documentation of this traffic.

397

Section B

Report No. II (April 18 to May 13, 1955)

The Illicit Narcotics Traffic in the Far East

The Communist regime of mainland China, in a New China News Agency dispatch from Peking on July 2, 1954, again denied the documented charges made over the past several years by the United States Representative on the United Nations Commission on Narcotic Drugs and specifically denied the charge I made before this commission in May 1954 that the Communist regime of mainland China is distributing drugs abroad and ... selling heroin and opium in large quantities to the free countries of the world.

Actual conditions in Southeast Asian and other free countries refute this unsupported denial and clearly prove that the Communist regime of mainland China is pouring opium, morphine and heroin out through the Province of Yunnan to augment the already existing lines of traffic out of Tientsin, Tsingtao and Canton.

While varying amounts of narcotics reach the traffic from other sources in the Far East, mainland China is the uncontrolled reservoir supplying the worldwide illicit narcotics traffic.

Pharmaceutical plants have been established in Communist China to process opium into morphine and heroin and all these drugs, including raw opium, are used as bartering commodities. Traffickers operating in the free countries share the profit in the illicit traffic in narcotics with the Communist regime of mainland China. Officials of this regime are exacting a tremendous profit from the traffic over the prices paid opium growers according to the traffickers who obtain the narcotics for further sale. These traffickers use whole sections of crews of surface craft, such as the engine crew or the deck crew, to smuggle narcotics. Cooperation of air maintenance crews is considered essential when the smuggling is by air, although passenger couriers are often used when the way has been well prepared and the traffickers consider there is no danger of apprehension.

One of the principal targets of the traffic from mainland China is Thailand, where one hundred tons of opium are sold annually. Consumers of this opium pay the equivalent of U.S. $350,000 per ton for the contraband in the form of smoking opium. Opium is brought from

Yunnan Province to the border of Thailand by horse and mule train.

From 200 to 400 tons of raw opium are moved annually and this operation would have represented over a million addict doses of this deadliest of drugs. It offers additional proof that we are not here dealing with a petty adversary but with a formidable and far-reaching plot to gain foreign exchange and at the same time demoralize the people of the free world.

Spreading narcotic addiction and obtaining funds for political purposes through the sale of heroin and opium is not the policy of just one man in the Communist regime; it is the policy of the entire Communist regime in mainland China.

The now-well-known Communist Po I-po had become an important official among the Communists in China by 1938 and was one of the principle exponents of the sale and distribution of heroin for funds and for political purposes. At the time the distribution of heroin was carried on from an area controlled by the Communists in Shensi Province, at which place the sale of heroin was part of an agent's underground assignment. The agent received instruction in such activity along with other political propaganda. Po became Minister of Finance of the Communist regime in October 1949, in which position he was able to expand international narcotic traffic from Communist China to heretofore unimagined proportions. When he was relieved as Minister of Finance in 1953, Jung Tzu-ho became Minister of Finance.

After visiting Moscow for several months he returned to Peking to attend a meeting of the Central Committee of the Party. Before the meeting of this Committee, Jung had held a conference and perfected an improved plan for the export and sale of opium and heroin in conjunction with Yeh Li-chuang, Minister of Trade, and Fang Jung-ho, Chief of Special Trade. The latter term signifies narcotics. According to the report of Jung, during the year Communist China exported opium, morphine (large quantities of morphine base were shipped out because of the shortage of chemicals) and heroin with a value of U.S. $60 million, amounting to over 800 pounds. Jung stated that the shipments were 20 percent short of the goal.

The innovation in the present arrangements over the former operation of the Communist regime in narcotics traffic is that the Foreign Ministry has overall control over the whole program and directs the export and further distribution of the heroin and opium through the National Trading Company which has its headquarters in Peking.

At the time the Communist regime was promoting illicit narcotics traffic in the interior of China in the area controlled by the Communists in 1938, Chen Kwan-yuan, alias Chen Kun-yuen, alias Chen

San-yuan, was busily engaged in Tientsin smuggling narcotics off Taku Bar as circumstances permitted. He was still in Tientsin when the now-well-known "Lions Globe" brand of heroin began to reach Japan in large quantities. Since that time, he has become one of the most powerful representatives of the Communists in the narcotic traffic outside China and has built his fortune on narcotics through and under the cover of his far-flung Tin Shing Trading Company, moving heroin out of Communist China to all parts of the world in exchange for tires, rubber goods, trucks and other strategic material. He has all the brass and front of a gangster and relies principally on bribery and buying protective information to smooth the smuggling of some five to fifty pounds of heroin at one time. Crew members of various kinds of ships have been used for this operation in addition to individual Chinese couriers. One of these is a relative to Tze Oi-chan, alias Mrs. Wu, the international smuggler of narcotics who was arrested in 1953 and who, while awaiting trial, is now living in grand style through a portion of the profits of Chen Kwan-yuan who arranged for her movements from one country to another. The co-conspirator of Mrs. Wu, the infamous Li Sui-po, alias Lee Sau-fung, who was also arrested, was in the organization of Chen Kwan-yuan.

There are two principal groups exporting and distributing heroin and opium for the Communist regime in China, in addition to the group which deals almost exclusively in heroin and opium from Yunnan Province. All of these are under the direction of the National Trading Company. One of these exports directly from the North China ports of Tientsin (Taku) and Tsingtao and in this way avoids the jurisdiction and control of the more powerful group in South China. In this Northern group is Hsieh Chun-mu, who went to Peking in 1952 where he has become a powerful political agent continuing his narcotic trafficking through Communist representatives with whom he has been associated for many years.

The group in South China functions as the Trade Bureau of South China, a Department of the Communist regime in China. The Trade Bureau operates powerful trading companies as fronts and has the greatest concentration of stocks of heroin and opium in all of China stored at Canton, Chungsan and Shek-ki for export to affiliated trading companies and other enterprises, including banks, which these companies control.

Eighty percent of the heroin from Communist China flows from Canton to these trading companies. The South China Group and their affiliates control this flow of heroin by means of more trading companies and representatives in those free countries from which payment for the heroin is received. Some of these representatives have become rich and powerful and are able to negotiate directly with the Communist regime as well as with major distributors who control the traffic in other free countries. The close connection between these trading companies and the overall Communist control can best be illustrated by their method of either pooling or borrowing stocks of heroin from whichever company or representative is available in order to make delivery of large consignments. In this dirty business the dealers operate as legitimate enterprises in that each knows where additional stocks of heroin may be obtained as necessary.

The fanatical Communist narcotic traffickers have resorted to the extreme measure of cutting off the ears of those small-time traffickers who dared to reveal the identity of the supplying group. Another method has been to take them into a Communist organization, whereby they are sealed off and thereby silenced....

From the beginning the Communist purveyors of heroin have realized the dual purpose of its sale, since they have forbidden members of their own organization to use the drug. This was true in 1938 and it is true today. Communist traffickers in the drug on the wholesale level talk of the dual purpose of sale, and also of the fact that users lose their effectiveness. Like remarks are heard from coolies on the streets.

The close relationship between the heroin and the opium and political agents extends all the way to the top. In Chungjin, a city in the suburbs of Peking, a factory for the manufacture of heroin is located. Here, also, is the training center for Communist China's political agents. The same pattern involving Communist agents and the sale of heroin was followed in the cities of Rashin and Wonsan, North Korea.

One of the principal methods of distribution to the ultimate consumer continued to be through the use of brothels operated by Chinese Communists or supplied by Chinese Communists, who funneled the profits of the traffic to powerful traders and representatives in the organization in the principal cities. These traders and representatives were also aided by Chinese who ostensibly were traders, but who were actually operating on behalf of the Communist regime in China and could supply any amount of heroin. They negotiate directly with Communist bosses on the mainland for large supplies of opium. In the offices of these traders, which bear little resemblance to offices of legitimate commercial companies, the clerical force is composed of stooges and lookouts. One such company is the Aaron Trading Company which operates with a head office and a branch office, and which has a direct connection into Communist China for quantities of heroin and opium. This company, operated by two Chinese, endeavoured to establish connections directly into New York City, and proposed using letters of credit concealing final destination.

Li Chin-sui, who heads a Chinese export-import company, is one of the most active traffickers in the Far East, operating under the direction of the gigantic combine. Li Chin-sui, a Chinese, was forced out of Japan by investigating agents of the Enforcement Division of the Narcotics Section, Ministry of Welfare, after he had accumulated a fortune trafficking in Communist heroin in the Yokohama-Tokyo area. Li's company channels strategic material to Canton and takes charge of the movement of opium and heroin under the direction of the South China Trade Bureau, and representatives affiliated therewith.

Powerful Chinese closely associated both commercially and socially with top-notch Communist agents have accumulated fortunes of tremendous magnitude, even by Western standards, through feeding gold and strategic materials into Communist China in return for heroin and opium. The extent of this operation becomes clear when it is realized to be a cold fact that 200 tons of opium from Communist China are required annually to carry on the established business of these Chinese traffickers and their associates. Most of this opium is from Kwangtung, Kweichow, Szechuan and Kwangsi Provinces. In addition to this known quantity of 200 tons of opium, tremendous quantities of finished heroin with a high degree of purity. Heroin is later refined and channeled by these same traffickers to their Communist representatives in other countries. Large amounts are shipped on consignment and need not be paid for until they are d ributed to representatives through trading companies or couriers by the political activity committee members who collect the money or acquire strategic materials according to a pre-arranged plan.

The Communist regime has decided that the system of consignment will be eliminated as far as possible since some of the profits have been embezzled. A large portion of the profits will continue to be used as a special fund for various organizations under the control of the Communist bosses in the area where the heroin is sold, but there is a strict requirement that a set portion of the profits must be returned to the Finance Committee of the Communist regime in China. It has likewise been decided that the system of trade cooperatives and agents transporting and selling the heroin must be more efficient and close knit to avoid detection and to provide more funds for the organization. Special attention is being given to improving the technique of the Communist bosses in control of the smugglers who are to take more care in the use of bribes to permit the smooth flow of drugs. The same procedure applies to entry and exit papers to facilitate the movements of the operators. The equivalent of more than U.S. $1,000 is often used in such an operation.

Traffic in heroin and opium has been found to be so lucrative and otherwise effective by the Communist regime in China that they have taken great pains to improve the cultivation of the opium poppy. Not only does the opium come from beyond the Great Wall in the Provinces of Chahar, Jehol and Suiyuan but also from Tsinghai, Sinkiang, Shensi, Kansu, Ninghsia Provinces. Yunnan Province also produces immense quantities of opium under the direct control of the head of the secret police. In this area 500 tons of opium were shipped out in 1950 at the same time that 500 tons were being offered for sale in Canton. Opium caravans from Yunnan Province, numbering approximately 200 men, are moving at the rate of two or three a week. Recently morphine base has been moved out in large quantities by air, a continuation of the traffic over the past several years. A seizure of 418 pounds of opium from Yunnan was made from an air cargo in November 1953. Other seizures of Yunnanese opium were made in April, 1,700 pounds, and in June, 3,250 pounds.

Forty tons of Yunnanese opium were offered for sale through agents of the Communist regime in China in June 1953. It was stated that the morphine content would be 9 percent; that the opium would be packed in one-kilogram packages wrapped in cellophane: and that fifty pieces in a tin container would be boxed and covered with jute cloth stitched with string. This shipment was offered at U.S. $2 million.

In Szechuan Province the Governor controls the opium production and also operates a factory with a capacity of 150 kilograms. Heroin factories were established in Kwangsi Province and in Yunnan Province. In Kwangsi Province the opium poppy planting is about three times what it was in 1951. In Yunnan and Kweichow Provinces the Communist authorities have issued special instructions to increase the production of opium. Because the authorities have not shared the huge profits with the growers they have not obtained as much opium as was expected. The yield must be sold to the Communist cooperatives who with their agents openly sell the opium at prices ranging from U.S. $100 per pound in quantities of a few pounds. Heroin is from six to ten times this price. These prices are in line with quotations by the Bank of China offering opium at U.S. $72 per pound and heroin at U.S. $500 per pound.

Japan

Through international liaison, the Enforcement Division of the Narcotic Section, Ministry of Welfare, Japan, was able to effect the arrest of the notorious international narcotic smuggler from Shanghai, Li Sui-po, alias Lee Sau-fung, during the past year. Brilliant undercover work and surveillance preceded the arrest of this trafficker in possession of 500 grams of heroin. He is now on trial and is held on a Y10 million (U.S. $25,000) bond, the highest on record for narcotic traffickers in Japan. The authorities also have under arrest Li's co-conspirator Tze Oi Chan, alias Mrs. Wu, formerly of Shanghai.

Approximately 12 kilograms of heroin, 50 percent more than for any like period since the end of World War II, were seized from the unending flow of heroin to Japan from Communist China. In view of the state of enforcement in Japan, officials do not consider the seizure to be more than one percent of the total smuggled into Japan from Communist China. This means that a huge amount of Communist heroin is being sold in Japan in a twelve-month period. One member of the Communist organization stated that 120 pounds of heroin entered Japan in Niigata Province, arriving from Communist China through the North Korean port of Wonsan. The explanation of the manner of payment for such a quantity, about U.S. $300,000, was that no money or goods are paid until the heroin is distributed to the Communist bosses in the various cities. Strategic goods are preferred to money.

Chinese Communist bosses in control of the traffic, assuming the role of import-export merchants and businessmen, relied principally on their tremendous capital to facilitate the smuggling and distribution of heroin.

For the Communists, the traffic in heroin in Japan was highly profitable and successful but it was, at the same time, a grim, deadly serious project. It was here that traffickers who dared reveal the identity of the suppliers had their ears severed from their heads. This method proved effective in closing avenues of information concerning factories producing heroin, accurate estimates of areas devoted to poppy cultivation, and the extent of the activities of the opium buying and selling cooperatives in the interior of China. Even former employees dared not talk.

Heroin poured into the country through the ports of Yokohama, Kobe, Sasebo and smaller ports along the Japan Sea as well as through the airports. With this very real weapon, Chinese Communist collaborators, acting as representatives of the Communist regime in China, posed a threat to the health and safety of the nation. The Japanese press has begun to cry out against this dirty business of the Communist regime in China.

As late as February 1954 the Japanese authorities were seeking thirty kilograms of heroin and 3,000 revolvers reported to have been landed in Kyushu from Communist China during the first part of the month.

South Korea

South Korea is the target of tremendous quantities of heroin from North Korea. The trading companies in North Korea, as in China, controlled by the Communist regime insist that at least one-fourth of all goods leaving North Korea for South Korea must be either heroin or opium. The smugglers, usually agents operating both for information and monetary gain, have for the most part used the same route into South Korea since 1947. They obtain heroin in Kaesong and at small villages along the coast of North Korea, opposite Kanghwa Island, and enter South Korea at Inchon. Some have proceeded overland directly to Seoul and thence to Taegu and Pusan.

There is extensive cultivation of the opium poppy in the areas around Pyongyang in the West and Wonsan on the east coast. There is also considerable cultivation in the northeasternmost province of North Korea. Some of the opium is shipped to a factory in Communist China at Chungjin, near Peiping. But much of the opium is processed at a factory in Pyongyang. As much as five tons of heroin have been stored at this factory.

Heroin is purchased in North Korea from the Communist trading companies in exchange for commodities most needed by the Communist regime. One of these commodities is rubber shoes which, on one occasion were used in the amount of 3,000 pairs to obtain 2,000 grams of heroin and 1,500 grams of opium. The opium in this case came from Communist China. The heroin was of the coarse, granular, off-white type which has been sold into international traffic in North Korea since 1948. The heroin was originally in the familiar heavy tin cans with slip-over tops soldered and waxed to protect the contents. Communist trading stores in North Korea have trafficked in heroin in this kind of container since 1949 in wholesale quantities. The containers appear to have been hammered out of corrugated metal.

The 2,000 grams of heroin and the 1,500 grams of opium were seized early in January 1954. The heroin had been placed aboard a 23-ft. boat about an hour before departure from Heichampo, a small town with five or six docks capable of accomodating seventeen to eighteen small ships at one time, on the coast of North Korea between Kaesong and Kanghwa Island. The smuggler was so confident of the contraband and so accustomed to smuggling that he did not bother to examine the contents of the packages, which proved to be 85.2 percent heroin. The value of the rubber shoes traded for the opium and heroin was U.S. $1,200.

The smuggler stated that the Communist regime issues instructions to the trading companies in regard to the narcotics, which are the property of the government. Most of the smugglers average two trips monthly from North Korea to South Korea with narcotics. Young girls working as maids or prostitutes receive the narcotics on many occasions. At other times the narcotics are turned over to wholesale syndicates, some of which are made up of businessmen.

A police official in the National Police Headquarters, Republic of Korea, stated that from April 1, 1952, to March 31, 1953, 2,400 Communists from North Korea, most of them posing as refugees, were arrested in South Korea. These Communists had received six months training in Communist ideology, learning names of contacts, answers to police in case of arrest, etc., at a political-training school in northwest Korea.

Using the expression of this official, these Communist agents carried gold in one hand and heroin in the other. The gold was for traveling and living expenses; the heroin was for political activity, for "mental" purposes. Young girls from eighteen to twenty-three years of age had come down into South Korea from North Korea as Communist agents. Some of these became housemaids at appropriate homes of politicians, others became prostitutes, not in the true sense of the word for a living, but in order to accomplish their political purposes. When the Communist arrived with heroin they knew in advance where to deliver it.

On May 10, 1953, heroin of the same quality, texture and physical appearance, in the amount of 851 grams and in the same kind of containers mentioned above, was seized as it was being smuggled into South Korea. The detail of similarity in the containers extended even to the wax-paper sack fitted into a brown sack of a peculiar texture and fastened at the top with paper clips of an unusual variety.

On May 19, 1953, heroin in the amount of 22 grams was seized from a known Communist agent from North Korea.

Some of the narcotics sold by the Communist trading companies in North Korea is morphine base, which is usually delivered to guerillas in the mountains in southwest South Korea. On October 31, 1953, a crude clandestine plant utilized for processing this morphine into heroin at the rate of 250 grams daily was seized.

In September 1953, a seizure was made of 15.8 pounds of opium and 135 grams of 90-percent heroin which had been brought in from North Korea. The opium was in glass jars and was in the odd-shaped balls which are characteristic of opium grown and collected in North Korea.

The cultivators sell it in this form and it is usually cut through with a knife to prevent concealment of rocks for increased weight.

One distributor of heroin in wholesale lots in Seoul was a North Korean who spoke perfect Chinese and who operated a brothel over his flourishing trading store. The heroin was sold by the prostitutes on the premises, as well as directly by the operator of the business. It was established that this smuggler and wholesaler knew the heroin was manufactured in Pyongyang and was brought in through Kanghwa Island to Seoul, Taegu and Pusan. He had several customers on an every-other-day basis at the rate of U.S. $10 for one-half gram of heroin.

The heroin is sold at prices which the traffic will bear, which vary from U.S. $2.00 per 0.3 gram to about one-half that price when it is supplied to lepers, thieves, pickpockets and prostitutes in the "Ditch" at Pusan.

Hong Kong

While movements of heroin through Hong Kong, because of its geographical location, continue despite efforts of local police who acted vigorously, there has been a noticeable trend towards bypassing this area whenever possible with shipments to other free countries. Enforcement officials and the courts have taken a positive attitude to thwart the traffickers. On February 26, 1954, in the Victoria District Court, Judge J. Reynolds, in sentencing a defendant for possession and sale of twelve grams of heroin, said, "I regard this offense of possession and sale of narcotics as one of the most serious offenses to come before me, and you are sentenced to two years and six months on each charge."

Conclusion

The three-fold increase in some areas in the land devoted to the cultivation of the opium poppy in Communist China, the establishment of new heroin factories in Communist China, the continuation and expansion of a twenty-year plan to finance political activities and spread addiction among free peoples through the sale of heroin and opium by the Communist regime in China, and the extension of the same pattern of narcotic activity to areas coming under the jurisdiction of Communist China has mushroomed the narcotic menace from Communist China into a multi-headed dragon threatening to mutilate and destroy whole segments of population from whom the danger of addiction through ready availability of drugs had been removed by the uncompromising work of the narcotic-enforcement authorities in the free countries of the world.

Until this Communist traffic in narcotics is dried up, the agents of this menace, wherever found, must be apprehended and dealt with surely and severely as a means of bringing under control this unbridled monster.

(Subsequently quoted in *Congressional Record,*
August 4, 1971, pp. E 8892–E 8896.)

Section C

Rebuttals: Chinese and Russian Positions

After Henry J. Anslinger, U.S. Commissioner of Narcotics had submitted to the UN Commission on Narcotics Drugs, on May 5, 1952,[1] a meticulously compiled report charging the Chinese Reds with dumping opium, heroin, and morphine on the world market in order to earn foreign exchange to support their war industry, the Red Chinese replied saying that Mr. Anslinger

> "had the audacity to submit a fabricated report which slandered the Peoples' Republic of China..." They went on to charge that the entire report was "... a groundless fabrication." They then described the steps which they had taken to suppress the *domestic* traffic in and the consumption of opium. The Red Chinese Ministry of Foreign Affairs then maintained that the Anslinger report was nothing but "a categorical slander against New China."[2]

In substance the Chinese denial was correct, as far as it went, insofar as it denied that there was traffic in opium on the mainland, but at no point did it attempt to deny the charge that extensive export of drugs was taking place. Anslinger took advantage of this omission and in his own reply to the Chinese statement said that, although abusive, the Chinese Reds could not deny the irrefutable evidence given to the UN.

408

The Russians, who at that time were still on good terms with the Chinese Reds and were, in fact, beneficiaries of the Chinese narcotics trading, attempted to defend their ally and circulated a statement in which they said that the American report was "a baseless fabrication from start to finish"; "malicious slander"; "shameless dissemination of lying rumors," etc. Neither power attempted to answer the charges in specific terms nor tried to disprove them.

A year later the Russians returned again to the attack when the Soviet spokesman, Zonov, told the UN Commission on Narcotics Drugs that the "United States' representative's slanderous allegations about the Peoples' Republic of China were unworthy of any reply."[3]

It may be noted that, since the breach with China, the Russians have reversed their position and now make frequent and grave accusations about Chinese narcotics trading. The United States has also reversed its position and some spokesmen have gone so far as to deny that the Chinese Reds have ever been engaged in the traffic. The Chinese are said to be "austere" and uninterested in the use of drugs. However, almost anyone would be austere when the alternative is decapitation.

More recently, the Chinese Communists have shown considerable irritation because, on a number of occasions, Soviet commentators have adopted a particularly hostile attitude and charged their former allies with large-scale participation in the drug traffic.

For example, it was reported in *The New York Times* of January 14, 1973, that the Chinese delegation at the UN on January 13 had

> accused the Soviet press of trying to disrupt their growing friendships abroad by falsely charging that she is trafficking in illegal opium to obtain American dollars.
>
> Denying the Soviet press reports as lies and slander Peking quoted an American authority as saying that there was no evidence of any trafficking from China.

According to the *Times*, this rebuttal and attack on the Soviet press was made in a Hsinhua (Chinese Government Press Agency) statement that was circulated as a press release by the Chinese delegation.

> ...The Chinese dispatch said that the Soviet Union began spreading rumors last September first saying that China was "corrupting" the African people with opium and later that China was opening up an important new market for selling opium in Europe.
>
> What now merits attention, the Chinese dispatch declared, is that the Soviet press agency Tass on Dec. 27, spread a rumor that China had earned $12 billion to $15 billion a year by opium trade abroad.

Tass asserted that huge amounts of opium had been shipped to the United States through the ports of Hong Kong and Macao in return for concentrated uranium and equipment, the Chinese dispatch declared. It added:

"The wicked aim of Soviet revisionist social imperialism in these lowdown acts is very clear that it tries through such lies to impair China's international prestige and disrupt the daily growing friendship between the Chinese people and the people of various countries."

Declaring that "lies have short legs" the Chinese dispatch maintained that a strict Government policy of prohibition against narcotics trading had been in force since 1950. It also quoted Nelson G. Gross, the United States State Department's special coordinator, as saying that there was no evidence of any illicit trade from China into other areas.

However, in spite of these denials, and supporting statements from certain U.S. officials, the weight of evidence has been mounting, particularly since the arrival of the Red Chinese delegation at the UN, that numerous illegally entered Chinese have been particularly active in the import and distribution of drugs, particularly heroin.

This has been associated with an influx of about 4,000 to 5,000 Chinese seamen per year. They have been coming in from Canada or from U.S. ports principally on the West coast. According to a recent FBI report referred to in the *New York Daily News* of March 21, 1973, the Hong Kong Seamens' Union "is a front for Peking propaganda, subversion and clandestine intelligence operations"; furthermore, that "the HKSU has approved a policy of placing Communist seamen on Western ships for the purpose of sabotage or capture in the event of future hostilities."

> HKSU is a major distributor of Chi-Com (Chinese Communist) propaganda to union members, overseas Chinese and other sympathizers. HKSU has been able to penetrate many foreign shipping lines that recruit seamen in Hong Kong.

The *New York Daily News* article goes on to say that such men have been caught crossing the border in the Maine woods, at Niagara Falls, in the Detroit area, and near Blaine, Washington. Former members of the Red Guards are among the Hong Kong sailors who have appeared here. Trained in guerrilla warfare and terrorist tactics, these men have helped to organize the street gangs that have sprung up in Chinatown.

Some of these gangs are led by militant Maoists. Others consist of young thugs hired by the local "tongs," or business groups, as protection against the Maoists. Warfare between such gangs has resulted in the worst wave of Chinatown violence since the 1920s.

An example of the kind of events that are now in train is the case of Hung Moy, a wealthy businessman, who was stabbed to death in the Rickshaw Garage immediately opposite the Elizabeth Street police station in New York's Chinatown. Previously it had been observed that the victim of this murderous attack had been keeping company with several suspected drug dealers who had illegally entered the United States from China.

That a clear connection of this kind exists to individuals from China engaged in distributing drugs from the mainland was attested by Frank Rogers, the citywide prosecutor of narcotics cases, and by Frank Gold, Brooklyn District Attorney. The former stated positively, at a press conference in January 1973 referred to in a Faso and Meskil article in the *New York Daily News* of March 20, 1973, that a plastic bag marked "Peoples' Republic of China" had been seized that contained brown rock heroin; and that the evidence was conclusive for a "China Connection," based on tape recordings of phone conversations between dope-smugglers and dealers.

He said: "This is the first clear and substantive evidence that we have that Mainland China and Hong Kong (a British Colony) are being used as a means of getting heroin into the U.S." It was further stated that the "...boss of the smuggling ring... is an important Chinese national who makes frequent trips between the U.S., Canada and Peking where he confers with top government officials."

On March 22 the *Daily News* carried further information on the Kwa Lin case that was earlier described by Faso and Meskil in an article in *True* magazine (see p. 225). They state that in CIA custody Kwa Lin "had turned informer and provided the first major intelligence breakthrough concerning Peking's undercover operations in North America."

> "Interrogation of Kwa Lin has led to the arrests of at least 20 other members of his narcotics ring," a Federal source says. "All were ship-jumping seamen who were seized by U.S. agents who also seized forged documents, communist propaganda, narcotics and classified information..."

Faso and Meskil go on to say:

> The Nixon administration insists that Peking is not sending drugs or spies to the U.S. But agents of the FBI, CIA, Immigration and Naturalization Service, Bureau of Narcotics and Dangerous

Drugs, and other Federal agencies are still trying to find out what these ship-jumping seamen are up to.

The official Washington explanation for Chinese operations here is that the Hong Kong seamen caught selling heroin here and committing other crimes are professional criminals, not Peking agents. Yet, investigators have tailed several of these ship-jumping felons to secret meetings with members of China's United Nations Mission here and the Chinese Embassy in Ottawa. There is no official explanation for the conferences between Peking's diplomats and Hong Kong's extraordinary seamen.

So much for Red Chinese rebuttals. The picture becomes clearer, however, when the personnel and composition of the Red Chinese delegation to the UN is placed under close scrutiny. The proportion of trained and experienced intelligence operatives is a rather high one; there are even indications that the narcotics cartel itself is represented by persons who, in previous appointments, have been involved in "Overseas Trade" and in "Social Affairs."

1. See Henry J. Anslinger and William Tompkins, *The Traffic in Narcotics* (New York: Funk & Wagnalls, 1953), Chapter IV, pp. 69–76.
2. Chinese denial in Hsinhua daily news release, Peking, May 20, 1952.
3. United Nations Economic and Social Council, Commission on Narcotics Drugs; 8th Session, Summary Record of 212th Meeting, New York City, pp. 3–4.

APPENDIX V

Table I

Known Locations of Ordinary Opium Farms in Red China*

Location	Target No. **	District	Total Area (6.6 mou=1 acre)	Remarks
A. <u>Northeast</u>	F 1**	Yenchi		
	F 2	Fusung		
	F 3	Yian		
	F 4	Kuantien		
	F 5	Changpai	400,000 mou	
	F 6	Linkiang		
	F 7	Chingyu		
	F 8	Holung		
	F 9	Huichun		

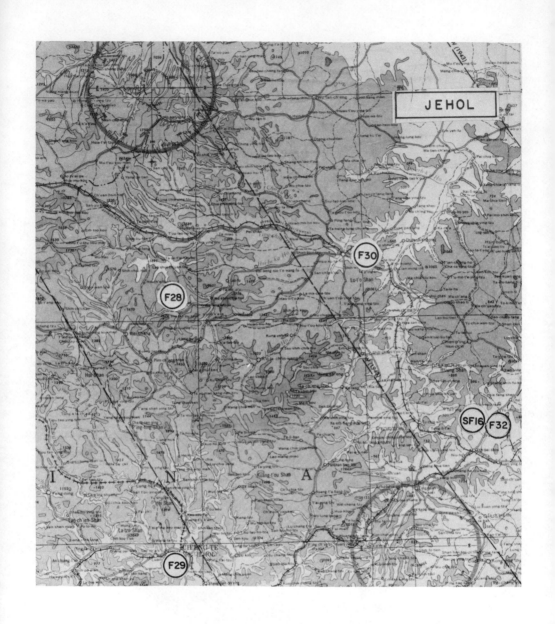

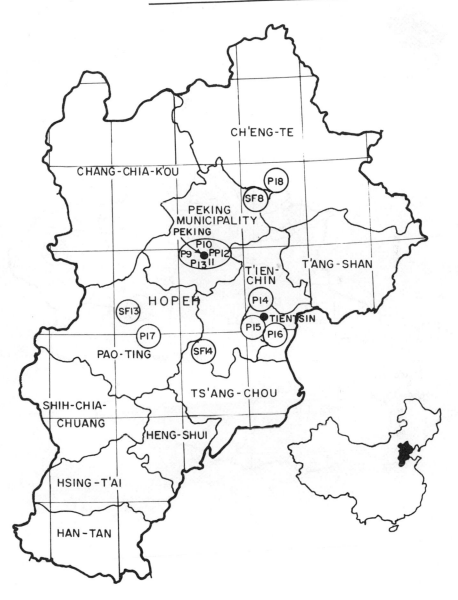

SINKIANG

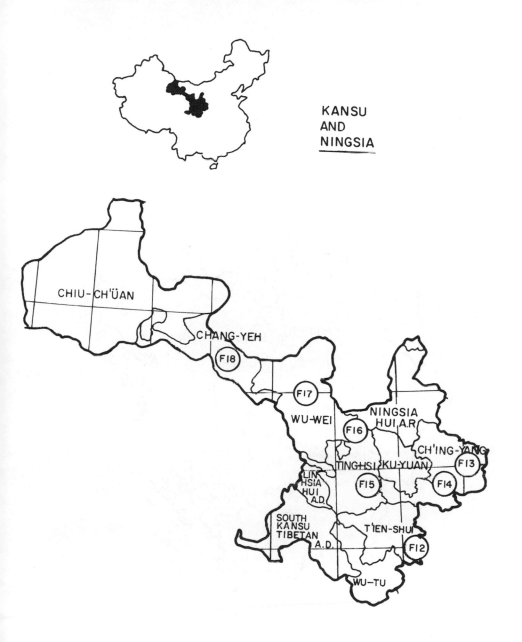

KANSU
AND
NINGSIA

CHEKIANG

F38
F37
F36
P24
P20
CHIA-HSING

HANG-CHOU SHIH
SHAO-HSING
NING-PO

CHIN-HUA
T'AI-CHOU

LI-SHUI
WEN-CHOU SHIH

WEN-CHOU

TSINGHAI

HAI-HSI MONGOL - TIBETAN - KAZAKH

HAI-PEI TIBETAN

HSI-NING SHIH

HAI-NAN TIBETAN

F25

HUANG-NAN TIBETAN

HO-NAN

HAI-HSIMONGOL TIBETAN- KAZAKH

YÜ-SHU TIBETAN

NGOLOG TIBE TIBETAN

F26

419

KWANGSI

SZECHWAN

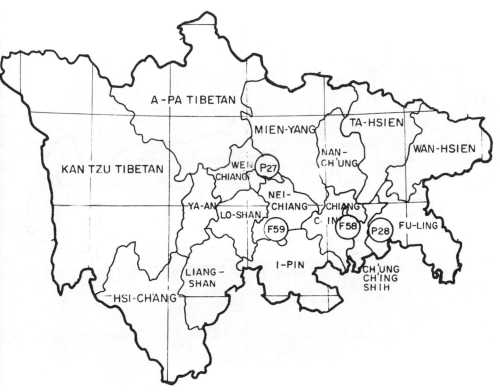

A-PA TIBETAN

MIEN-YANG

TA-HSIEN

KAN TZU TIBETAN

WAN-HSIEN

NAN-CH'UNG

WEN CHIANG

P27

YA-AN

NEI-CHIANG

CHIANG C IN

LO-SHAN

F59

F58

P28

FU-LING

I-PIN

LIANG-SHAN

CH'UNG CH'ING SHIH

HSI-CH'ANG

421

TIBET

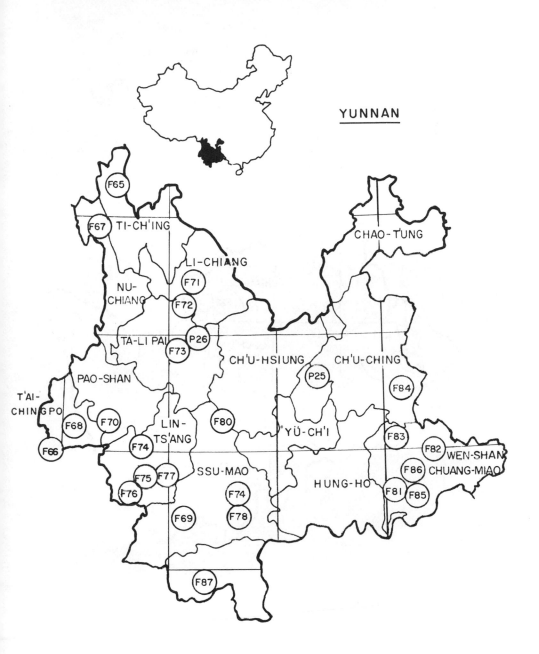

YUNNAN

HEILUNGKIANG

HEI-HO

CHIAMUSZU

SF22

NEN-CHIANG

I-CH'UN
SHIH

HO-CHIANG

SUI-HUA

SUNG-HUA-
CHIANG

MU-TAN-CHIANG

KWEICHOW

TSUN-I

T'UNG-JEN

F88

PI-CHIEH

SOUTHEAST
KWEICHOW
MIAO-T'UNG

AN-SHUN

SOUTH KWEICHOW
PUYI-MIAO

F89

HSING-I

F90

HONAN

AN-YANG

HSIN-HSIANG

K'AI-FENG

LO-YANG

SHANG-CH'IU

HSÜ-CH'ANG

CHOU-K'OU

F42

F40

F41

F39

NAN-YANG

CHU-MA-TIEN

HSIN-YANG

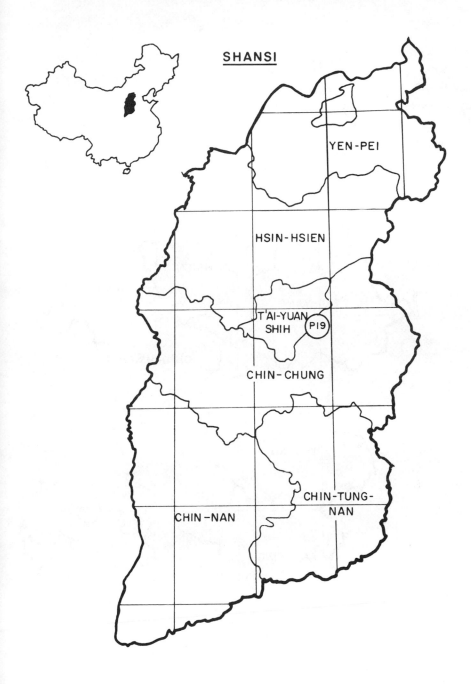

SHANSI

YEN-PEI

HSIN-HSIEN

T'AI-YUAN
SHIH   P19

CHIN-CHUNG

CHIN-TUNG-
NAN

CHIN-NAN

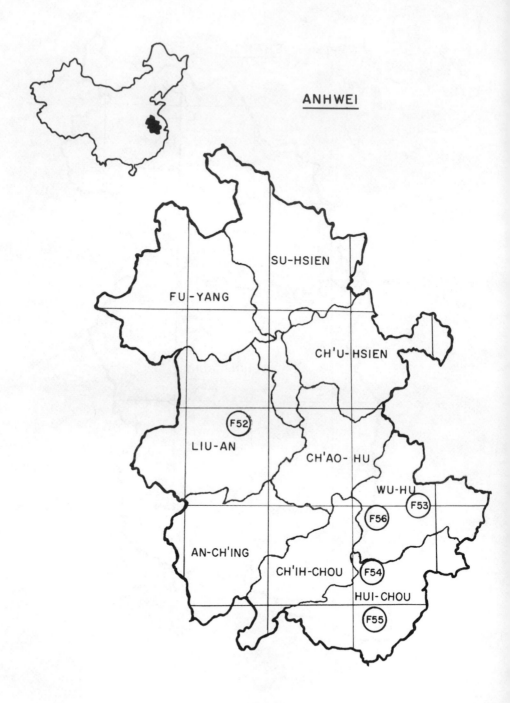

ANHWEI

SU-HSIEN

FU-YANG

CH'U-HSIEN

F52

LIU-AN

CH'AO-HU

WU-HU

F53

F56

AN-CH'ING

CH'IH-CHOU

F54

HUI-CHOU

F55

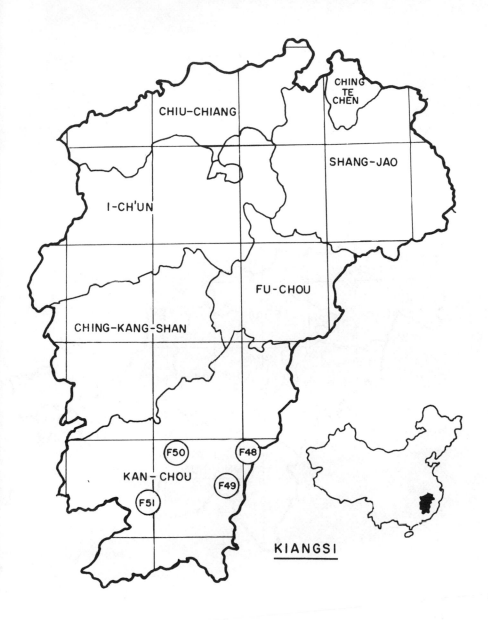

CHING TE CHEN

CHIU-CHIANG

SHANG-JAO

I-CH'UN

FU-CHOU

CHING-KANG-SHAN

F50

F48

KAN-CHOU

F49

F51

KIANGSI

KIRIN

PAI-CH'ENG

TE-HUI

SSU-PING

YUNG-CHI

P8

YEN-PIEN
KOREAN

F1

SF5

F9

F8

T'UNG-HUA

KIANGSU AND SHANGHAI

HSU-CHOU

F33 F34

SF25

F35

HUAI-YIN

YEN-CH'ENG

YANG-CHOU

LIU-HO

NAN-T'UNG

CHEN-CHIANG

SU-CHOU

SHANGHAI

P21

HUNAN

WEST HUNAN
T'UCHIA-MIAO
F97
F96
F98

CH'ANG-TE

F103

YÜEH-YANG

I-YANG

CH'ANG-SHA SHIH

CH'IEN-YANG

HSIANG-T'AN

CHU CHOU SHIH

F99

SHAO-YANG

HSIANG T'AN

F100

F101
F102

HENG-YANG

CH'EN-CHOU

LING-LING

HUPEH

KWANGTUNG

SHAO-KUAN

MEI-HSIEN

CHAO-CH'ING

HUI-YANG

SHAN-T'OU

FO'SHAN

HONG KONG

CHAN-CHIANG

MACAO

HAI-NAN

HAI-NAN LI-MIAO

434

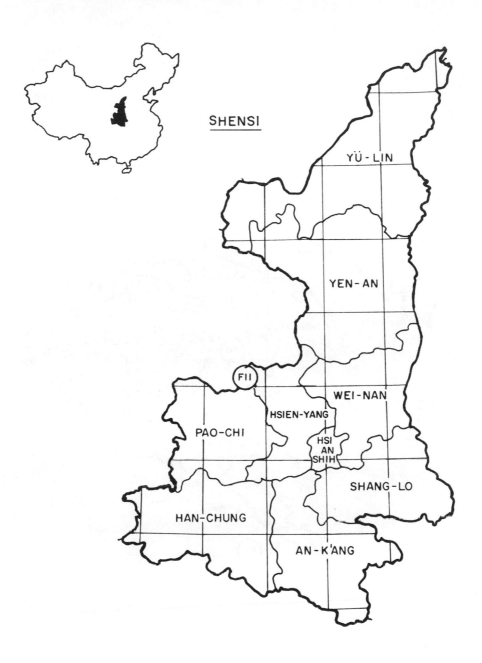

SHENSI

YÜ-LIN

YEN-AN

FII

WEI-NAN

HSIEN-YANG

PAO-CHI

HSI
AN
SHIH

SHANG-LO

HAN-CHUNG

AN-K'ANG

435

LIAONING

SHEN YANG

F2

FU-HSIN SHIH

SHEN-YANG SHIH

SF23

P3

FU-
SHUN
SHIH

F6

P4

F5

CH'AO-YANG

CHIN-CHOU

P5

P6

LIAO
YANG
SHIH

PEN-CH'I SHIH

CHIN
CHOU
SHIH

ANSHAN
SHIH

YING K'OU
SHIH

SF
1-2
3-4

TAN-TUNG SHIH

F3

F4

LIAO
NAN

P1

P2

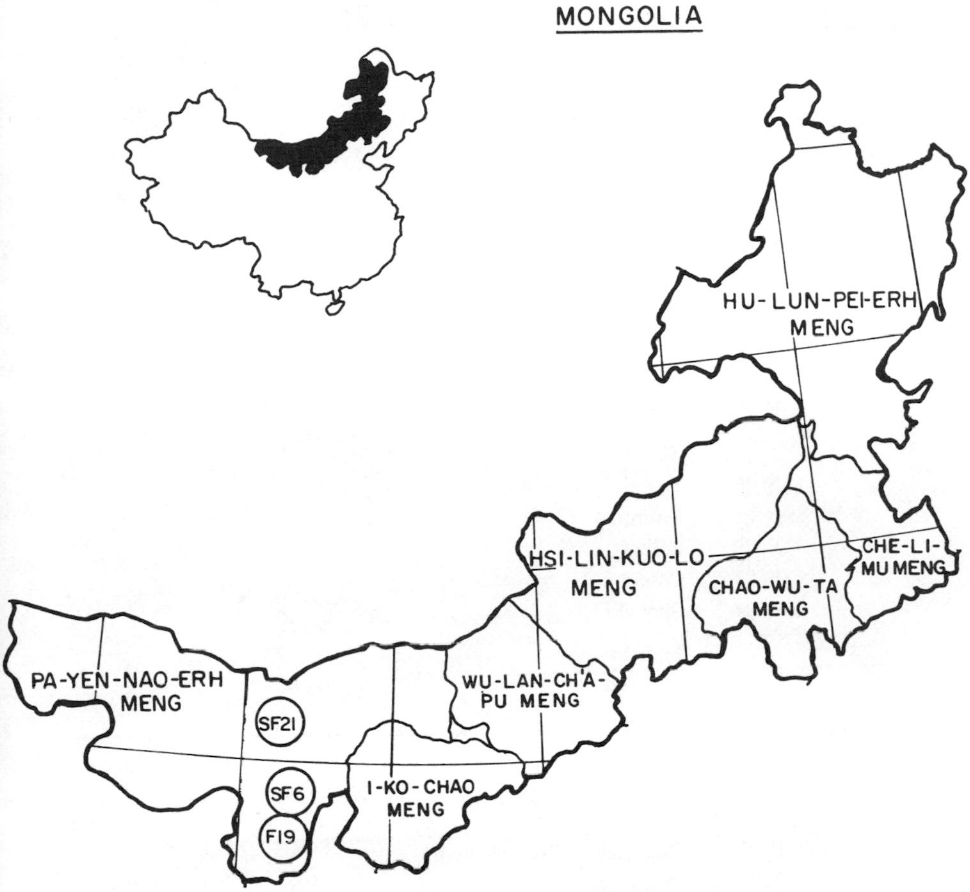

MONGOLIA

HU-LUN-PEI-ERH
MENG

HSI-LIN-KUO-LO
MENG

CHE-LI-
MU MENG

CHAO-WU-TA
MENG

PA-YEN-NAO-ERH
MENG

SF21

WU-LAN-CH'A-
PU MENG

SF6

I-KO-CHAO
MENG

F19

B. Northwest		Shensi	
	F 10	Lueyang	
	F 11	Changwu	
		Kansu	
	F 12	Liangkiang	250,000 mou
	F 13	Hoshui	
	F 14	Chingchuan	
	F 15	Huining	
	F 16	Chingyuan	
	F 17	Wuwei	
	F 18	Changyeh	
		Ninghsia	
	F 19	Chungwei	
		Sinkiang	
	F 20	Yuwei	
	F 21	Nanhu	
	F 22	Suikai	
	F 23	Chinghua	
	F 24	Chanchi	
		Tsinghai	
	F 25	Yungjen	
	F 26	Yushu	
C. North China		Jehol	
	F 28	Chaoyang	
	F 29	Chengteh	100,000 mou
	F 30	Chihfeng	
	F 31	Chinglung	
	F 32	Shanshu	
D. East China		Kiangsu	
	F 33	Tunghai	
	F 34	Kuanyun	
	F 35	Lienshui	100,000 mou
		Chekiang	
	F 36	Yuhang	
	F 37	Wukang	
	F 38	Anchi	
E. Central China		Honan	
	F 39	Nanyang	

F 40	Neihsiang		
F 41	Chech'uan		
F 42	Fangcheng		
	Hupeh	700,000 mou	
F 43	Anshih		
F 44	Laifeng		
F 45	Hofeng		
F 46	Tungshan		
F 47	Huangpeh		
	Kiangsi		
F 48	Juichin		
F 49	Juich'ang		
F 50	Yuntu		
F 51	Hsinfeng		
	Anwhei		
F 52	Liuho		
F 53	Hsuancheng		
F 54	Taiping		
F 55	Hsiuning		
F 56	Nanning		

F. Szechuan Basin		Szechuan		
	F 57	Lait'ung	30,000 mou	Formerly main center, now much reduced in importance as a producing area.
	F 58	Chiaching		
	F 59	Weiyuan		

G. Yunnan, Kwangsi, Kweichow		Kwangsi		
	F 60	Silin	2,000,000 mou	New main base, planned from point of view of accessibility of delivery routes into Southeast Asia, Macao, and Hong Kong.
	F 61	Silung		
	F 62	Tienpien		
	F 63	Paise		
	F 64	Huichi		
		Yunnan		
	F 65	Tehung		
	F 66	Juili		
	F 67	Kungshan		
	F 68	Lungchuan		
	F 69	Lantsang		
	F 70	Lungling		

439

	F 71	Lichiang	In mid-September 1970, Revolutionary Committee of Meng-Peng District, Mengla County, sent a production team of about 500 men to Sula village near the border area for reclamation and planting of opium poppies.
	F 72	Hotu	
	F 73	Tali	
	F 74	Chenkang	
	F 75	Kengma	
	F 76	Tsangyuan	
	F 77	Shuangchien	
	F 78	Szemao	
	F 79	Puerh	
	F 80	Chingtung	
	F 81	Wenshan	
	F 82	Kwangnan	
	F 83	Chiupei	
	F 84	Lopang	
	F 85	Makuan	
	F 86	Yenshan	
	F 87	Mengla	
		Kweichow	
	F 88	Pichieh	
	F 89	Chinglung	
	F 90	Hsingyi	
H. Tibet, Sikang		Sikang	
	F 91	Yaan	
	F 92	Sich'ang	
	F 93	Huili	50,000 mou
		Tibet	
	F 94	Langma	
	F 95	Tch'ing Tch'ing	
I. Western Hunan	F 96	Yungshun	
	F 97	Sangchih	
	F 98	Paoching	700,000 mou
	F 99	Chinyang	
	F 100	Huit'ung	
	F 101	Wukang	
	F 102	Hsinning	
	F 103	Ch'angteh	

J.	F 104	Tungwan	330,000 mou	Bhang is produced in India,
Kwangtung	F 105	Ch'ingyuan		Brazil, South Africa, and
Mountain	F 106	Yingteh		the U.S.S.R. In 1968 the
Area	F 107	Juyuan		Chinese Communists
	F 108	Yangshan		obtained seeds from India
	F 109	Lienshan		and Brazil and planted
	F 110	Lienhsien		them in Hainan. Production
	F 111	Kwangning		not yet known.
	F 112	Szehui		
	F 113	Yunfu		
	F 114	Yangkiang		
	F 115	Wuhua		
	F 116	Hsingning		
	F 117	Tzechin		
	F 118	Loch'ang		
	F 119	Yangchun		
	F 120	Fengchuan		
	F 121	Kaoyao		
	F 122	Loting		
	F 123	Lufeng		
	F 124	Huahsien		
		The mountain area between Canton and Whampoa, Hainan Is.		

Total Area of opium cultivation	5,830,000 mou (approximately 880,000 acres)

*Statements appear from time to time that Chinese narcotics trading and production are forms of private enterprise and are not conducted by the mainland regime. It cannot be emphasized too strongly that all production is either government-directed or -sponsored, as is distribution.

**Identification code:

F=Opium farm	P=Plant or Refinery	NK=Not Known
SF=Special farm	A, B, C=Grades of product	

(The identification numbers on this and succeeding tables are supplied by the author to correspond to markings on the provincial maps.)

Table II

Rural People's Communes Known to be Engaged in Opium Growing (as of Beginning of 1972)

Province	Hsien/City	Commune and/or Production Brigade
Kirin	Chi-an	Liang-shui-chuan Commune
		Lung-chao Commune
	Fu-sung	Tung-kang Commune
	Yen-chi	Yue-ching Commune, Shih-chien-ping Brigade
		Lao-tou-kou Commune
		Tung-sheng Commune
	Chang-pai	Lung-shui Commune, Hua-shu Brigade
		Shih-erh-tao-kou Commune
	Ho-lung	Lu-kuo Commune
	Hun-chun	Liang-shui Commune
Liaoning	Kuan-tien	Chang-tien Commune
		Tai-ping-hsiao Commune
	Pei-piao	Pa-chia-tzu Commune
Hopei	Ching-lung	Pan Cheng Commune
Shansi	Ho-chu	Liu-chia-ta Commune
		Tan-chai Commune
	Pao-teh	Tsao-hu Commune
	Hsing-hsien	Wa-tang Commune
		Lu-liang-kuang Vanguard Commune
	Wu-chai	Mi-feng Commune
		Sung-chia-kou Commune
		Wei-hsing Commune
Shensi	Tzu-chang	Hsi-kua-chieh Commune
	Ting-pien	Feng-chih-keng Commune
	Sui-teh	Kao-chien-tsun Commune
		San-chiao-ping Commune
	Mi-chih	Kao-miao-shan Commune
	Chang-wu	Hsiang-kung Commune, Hsiang-kung Brigade
		Yu-yuan Commune
	Chun-hua	Yu-yueh Commune, Ma-chia-po Brigade
		Jen-chen Commune, Kai-chu-ching Brigade
		Wu Chia Commune
		Hu-chia-pang Commune
	Lueh-yang	Kuan-yin-ssu Commune
		Ma-ti-wan Commune
		Shih-chia-yen Commune
Kansu	Ching-yang	Liang-feng Commune
		Tung-chih Commune
	Ning-hsian	Chiu-tou Commune
		Chiu-ling Commune
	Ching-yuan	San-ho Commune
		Tung-wan Commune

442

	Hui-ning	Chang-chuan Commune
		Ning-tu Commune
		Kan-kou Commune
		Chia-cheng Commune
		Tou-chai Commune
	Ching-chuan	San-shih-li-pu Commune
		Na-feng Commune
		Tu-tu Commune
		Shen-tzu Commune
	Wu-wei	Ching-yang Commune
		Yung-hsin Commune, Shih-pai Brigade
		Ta-liu Commune
		Fa-chan Commune, Lei-sheng Brigade
		Hsin-hua Commune, Chan-shen Brigade
		Po-shu Commune
		Wan-chun Commune
	Chang-yi	East Wind Commune, Great Leap Brigade
		Yao-wu Commune, Yao-wu Brigade
		Min-le Commune, Hua-yuan Brigade
		Kang-lung-ssu Commune
		Ta-man Commune
		Liang-chia-tun Commune
Ninghsia	Chung-wei	Hsi-yuan Commune
		Ching-chuang Commune
		Hsian-sheng Commune
		Teng-ta Commune
Sinkiang	Chang-chi	Hsin-hua Commune
		Yi-shui Commune
		Hu-hao Commune
		Tian-pa Commune, Kao-lai Brigade
		Wei-sheng Commune, Chang-lin Brigade
	Yi-wu	Wu-yi Commune
Ch'inghai	Tung-jen	Lien-sheng Commune
		Tung-feng Commune
	Yu-shu (Jyekundo)	Pa-tang Commune, La-sa-kan Brigade
		Chih-men-ta Commune
Kiangsu	Tung-hai	Ping-ming Commune, An-ying Brigade
		Pai-ta Commune, Pei-tou Brigade
		Shun-feng Commune, Tung-tai Brigade
		Wu-shan Commune, Kuan-miao Brigade
		Huang-chuan Commune, Chu-chiao Brigade
		Lin-chai Commune, Hsin-Hsing Brigade
	Kuan-yun	Lung-chu Commune, Lao-huo Brigade
		Pan-pu Commune, Tung-cheng Brigade
		Yun-tai Commune, Chu-kuang Brigade
		Sse-tui Commune, Chung-hsin Brigade
		Yi-shan Commune, Shan-tung Brigade
		Tung-hsing Commune, 5th Brigade

443

	Shu-yang	Ko-ping Commune, Tung-hsing Brigade
		Ching-yi-hu Commune
		Tai-ping Commune
		Sang-chu Commune
		Cha-hsia Commune, 3rd Brigade
	Lien-shui	Tung-feng Commune
		Nan-liu Commune
		Wu-kang Commune, Tsai-kung Brigade
Chekiang	Yu-hang	Kou-chuang Commune, Chung Hsin Brigade
		Liang-chung Commune, Tai-ping Brigade
		Wen-mei Commune, Lien-cheng Brigade
		Tung-shan Commune, Ying-chia-chung Brigade
	An-chi	Shuang-chien Commune, Suang-yi Brigade
		Kang-kou Commune, Wu-Ho Brigade
		Liang-chi Commune, Liang-cheng Brigade
		Ching-shan Commune, Wu-se Brigade
		Hsiao-tou Commune, Lung-chuan Brigade
	Chun-an	Wei-ping Commune
		Chin-feng Commune
Honan	Nan-yang	Liao-ho Commune
		Han-tung Commune, San-pa Brigade
		Wang-lin Commune, Fan-ying Brigade
	Fang-cheng	Ho-tsai Commune, Miao-tien-chuang Brigade
		Wan-hung Commune, Shang-lou Brigade
		Ho-feng Commune, Huang-yu Brigade
		Fang-chin-ku Commune
	Che-chuan	Chin-tien Commune
		Ma-tang Commune, Wang-yun Brigade
		Ma-shan Commune
		Nsia-kuan Commune
		Pei-tien-tzu Commune, Nan-chai Brigade
		Tung-kiang Commune, Tung-jung Brigade
		Wa-shu Commune, Li-chuang Brigade
	Hsi-shen	Mi-ping Commune
		Hsi-ping Commune
		Tsao-chang Commune
	Nan-tiao	Hsiao-tien Commune
Hupei	Huang-po	Mu-lan Commune
		Mu-li Commune, Ho-tien-fan Brigade
		Nieh-kou Commune, Hung-hsing Brigade
		Yuan-shou Commune, Lien-ho Brigade
		Shih-ho Commune, Hung-shou Brigade
		Tu-shan Commune
	Tung-shan	Hung-sheng Commune, Feng-kuang Brigade
		Hung-chi Commune
		Heng-shih Commune
	Lai-feng	Hsi-tun Commune, Tsung-ho Brigade
		Tou-ta Commune
		Tu-pao Commune
		Teng-tung Commune

444

	En-shih	Chang-ching Commune, Tsung-ho Brigade
		Hsin-tang Commune
		Lien-ho Commune, Ying-chun Brigade
		Wu-hsing Commune
		Hsin-chuan Commune
		Mao-shan Commune
	Li-chuan	Mou-tao Commune
	Ho-feng	Cha-yuan Commune, Cha-yuan Brigade
	Kan-feng	Chien-shan Commune
		Yang-ho Commune
Hunan	Hsi-ning	Shih-tien Commune
		Hui-lung-su Commune, Sheng-li Brigade
		San-tu Commune
	Wu-kang	Lung-kiang Commune
		Wu-tung Commune
		Kuo-jen Commune
		Hung-hsing Commune
		Hsin-teng Commune
		Shih-yang Commune
	Hui-tung	Hsiao-chia Commune, Heng-yen Brigade
		Hu-yung Commune, Ta-mu-tou Brigade
		Hu-wei Commune
		Kuang-ping Commune
	Chien-yang	Tai-ping Commune, Hsien-feng Brigade
		Hsia-chuang Commune, Chien-tien Brigade
		Chia-tung Commune, Tai-ho Brigade
		Hsin-ho Commune
		Wu-feng Commune
		Tuan-Chieh Commune
		Chi-nan Commune
	Chang-teh	Tung-feng Commune
		Hu-fu Commune
		Yung-feng Commune
		Chin-kang Commune
	Yung-shun	Shou-che Commune, Yu-li-ting Brigade
		Ta-wo Commune, Chang-lin Brigade
		Lien-tung Commune, Teh-shu Brigade
		Ai-chin Commune, Ai-chin Brigade
	Sang-chih	Chang-li Commune, Ti-tien Brigade
		Hsun-kuan Commune, Lung-tan Brigade
		Li-hsing Commune
		Chang-hsiu-tsai Commune
	Pao-ching	Hung-chi Commune, Fu-ye Brigade
		Ping-she Commune, Ko-le Brigade
		Mao-kung Commune, Mao-tu Brigade
		Lung-chi Commune, Tung-feng Brigade
		Chang-chin Commune, Wu-hsi-ho Brigade
		Ao-shang Commune, Yang-hai Brigade
		Mai-hua Commune, Li-fu Brigade

445

Kiangsi	Jui-chin	Sha-chou-pa Commune, Sha-chou-pa Brigade
		Chiu-pao Commune, Hsiao-po Brigade
		Lo-tang Commune, Hua-chia Brigade
		Kao-wei Commune, Kao-wei Brigade
		Yu-tung Commune, Tung-chi Brigade
		Hsieh-fang Commune, Huang-hsia Brigade
	Hsin-feng	Hsiao-ho Commune, Wu-hsing Brigade
		Tao-chiang Commune
		Cheng-feng Commune, Ao-shang Brigade
	Hui-chang	Lien-chih Commune, Ho-cheng Brigade
		Chung-chien Commune, Hsia-ying Brigade
		Ma-chuan Commune, Yi-pin Brigade
		Ma-chou Commune
	An-yuan	Lien-chiang Commune
	Yu-tu	Ma-an Commune
		Huang-lung Commune
Anhwei	Ho-fei	Ta-tu-shan Commune
	Huo-shan	Chu-ssu-yen Commune
		Fan-chung Commune
	Liu-an	Fan-tung-chiao Commune
	Feng-yang	Tai-yang-sheng Commune
		Hsien-feng Commune
	Ching-hsien	Yun-ling Commune
	Hsuan-cheng	Shuang-chiao Commune
	Hsiu-ning	Lung-tien Commune, Tao-lin Brigade
		Shuang-hu Commune
		Tan-chuan Commune
Szechuan	Chiang-chin	Liang-shan Commune
		Kao-chan Commune
	Tung-liang	Hsi-chuan Commune
	Hsi-shang	Hai-pin Commune
Kwangsi	Pai-se	Lung-tou Commune
		Ta-leng Commune, Pa-ping Brigade
		Pai-lan Commune, Hsin-hsin Brigade
		Ssu-tang Commune
	Ching-hsi	Hua-tung Commune
		Lung-pang Commune
		Jen-chuang Commune
		Ti-chuan Commune, Ho-kang Brigade
		Kuei-chou Commune, Chien-ling Brigade
		Ta-kang Commune
	Lung-lin	Hsin-ya Commune
Yunnan	Lo-ping	Chin-chi Commune
	Tsang-yuan	Ho-nan Commune
	Li-chiang	Lu-tien Commune
		Huang-shan Commune
		Yun-lung Commune
		Pai-hua Commune
	Ta-la	Tsang-shan Commune

	Ma-kuan	Hung-ho Commune
		Jen-ho Commune
		Tu-lung Commune
	Huang-nan	Chi-chieh Commune
	Wen-shan	Hung-chi Commune

Kweichow	Ching-lung	Lien-cheng Commune
		Wu-hsing Commune
	Hsing-yi	Chieh-shan Commune
		Ma-ling Commune
	Pi-chieh	Hsia-wu-tun Commune, Shuang-feng Brigade
		Yang-ching Commune, Shui-ching Brigade
		Sheng-li Commune, Sheng-li Brigade
		Tung-pu-ko Commune
		Lung-chang Commune
		Lin-kou Commune

Kwangtung	Chieh-hsi	Wu-ching-fu Commune
		Mien-hu Commune, Hsin-hu Brigade
	Chieh-yang	Chu-chi Commune, Chi-nan-shan Brigade
		Hsi-chang Commune
	Hua-hsien	Hua-tung Commune
		Chih-ni Commune, Hsi-chien Brigade
		Hua-shan Commune
	Tsung-hua	Chiang-pu Commune, Lien-hsing Brigade
		Liang-kou Commune
	Pan-yu	Ling-shan Commune
		Huang-feng Commune
	Shun-teh	Kuei-chou Commune
		Hsien-tung Commune
		Chang-chiao Commune
	Tung-wan	Ching-chi Commune
		Hou-chieh Commune
	Tzu-chin	Lan-tang Commune
	Le-chan	Chiu-feng Commune
		Yao-shan Commune
	Ching-yuan	Chin-tan Commune
		Yuan-tan Commune
	Ying-teh	Lin-li-tung Commune
		Wang-pu Commune
	Lien-hsien	Chi-po Commune
	Chao-yang	Hsia-shan Commune
		Hsi-lu Commune
		Lei-ling Commune
	Pu-ning	Nan-yang-shan Commune
		Li-hu Commune
		Yun-lo Commune
	Ling-feng	Ta-an Commune
	Wu-hua	Chi-ling Commune
		Ta-tien Commune
	Hsing-ning	Ta-ping Commune, Pai-yun Brigade
		Shui-ku Commune

447

Mei-hsien	Sung-kou Commune
	Pai-tu Commune, Feng-ling Brigade
	Chu-yang Commune, 1st Brigade
Ta-pu	Liu-huang Commune
	Hu-liao Commune, Lung-kang Brigade
	Kuang-fu Commune, Pa-li Brigade
Lo-ting	Su-lung Commune
Yung-fu	To-tung Commune
Feng-kai	Chang-kang Commune
Kuang-ning	Hou-chi Commune, Fen-yu Brigade
	Pin-keng Commune
Kao-yao	Pai-po Commune
	Tai-wan Commune, Kao-mao Brigade
Ssu-hui	Hsia-mao Commune, Yin-chai Brigade
	Chiang-ku Commune, Chu-chai Brigade
Yang-chiang	Ho-shan Commune
Yang-chun	Shih-wang Commune
Tun-chang	Wu-yuan Commune
	Huang-chen Commune
	Feng-yi Commune
Pao-ting	Hung-chi Commune, Shen-pao Brigade
	Tung-shen Commune, Fan-mao Brigade
	Nan-sheng Commune
Pai-sha	Chi-fang Commune
	Yuan-men Commune

Table III

Known Special Opium Farms

Organization in Charge	No.	Name of Farm	Area (in mou)	Remarks
Ministry of Agriculture		3rd Experimental Farm	20,000	
Water and Soil Conservancy Bureau		5th Experimental Farm	16,000	
Central Bureau of State Farms, Ministry of Agriculture	SF 1	Model Farm	12,000	
	SF 2	Chinchow Farm (Liaoning)	7,000	
	SF 3	Frog Pool Farm (Liaoning)	NK	

448

	SF 4	Hsungyu Farm (Liaoning)	NK
		Princess Ridge Farm (Kirin)	3,000
	SF 5	Chiuchan Farm (Kirin)	NK
	SF 6	Lingwu Farm (Ninghsia)	NK
	SF 7	Tarim Farm (Sinkiang)	NK
	SF 8	Kupeikou Farm (Hopei)	NK
	SF 9	Chihung Farm (Hopei)	NK
	SF 10	Huanghua Farm (Hopei)	NK
	SF 11	Yungnien Farm (Hopei)	NK
	SF 12	Kaoli Farm (Hopei)	NK
	SF 13	Paoting Farm (Hopei)	NK
	SF 14	Yellow River Valley Farm (Honan)	NK
	SF 14	Hulan Farm (Chekiang)	NK
	SF 15	Nanhsung Farms (Kwangtung; two farms in Sanshiang area, north of Nanhsung)	NK — These farms reported manned by political prisoners, April 1970.
Agricultural Products Bureau, Ministry of Agriculture		Special Farm under Central Authority	NK
	SF 16	Chaoyang Farm under Central Authority	NK
Northwest Agriculture and Forest Bureau, Ministry of Agriculture		2nd Farm	2,000
Academy of Sciences		Institute of Sciences Special Products Farm	800
		Botany Institute Experimental Farm for Narcotic Plants Seeds	NK

Sinkiang Military Region	SF 18	August First Farm	1,000
Tibet Military Region	SF 19	Chiangtze Farm	700
Inner Mongolia Military Region	SFi 20	Ko-erhsin Farm	1,500
		Taolin Farm	NK
Ninghsia	SF 21	Yinchuan Farm	500
Heilungkiang Peoples' Government	SF 22	Chiamuszu POW Farm	1,000
Liaoning Peoples' Government	SF 23	Peipiao Herb Farm	8,000
Hopei Peoples' Government	SF 24	Huachuan Water Conservancy Farm	NK
Kiangsu Peoples' Government	SF 25	Huapei Hsinjen Village Reclamation District	2,000

Table IV

Known Chinese Communist Narcotics Refineries

Area	No.	Name of Factory	Products
Northeast	P 1	Dairen Pharmaceutical Works	Opium, Morphine
	P 2	Dairen: Dashuang Pharmaceutical	Heroin
	P 3	Shenyang Pharmaceutical Works	Morphine
	P 4	Shenyang: China Company Nicotine Refinery	Nicotine
	P 5	Liaoning: Peipiao Pharmaceutical Works	Opium
	P 6	Liaoning: Chinchow Chemical and Pharmaceutical Works	Morphine, Opium
	P 7	Fusung, Kirin: Northeast Chemical and Pharmaceutical Works	Morphine, Ether
	P 8	Yenchi, Kirin: Special Product Refinery of Northeast Korean Nationality Autonomous District	Opium
North China	P 9	Peking: Narcotic Laboratory Affiliated with Medical Institute of Academy of Sciences (four branches)	Opium
	P 10	Peking: Narcotics Works under direct control of Pharmaceutical Bureau, Ministry of Health	Opium

	P 11	Peking: Raw Materials Works, Narcotics Control Bureau, Ministry of Health	Opium
	P 12	Peking: Narcotics Works of China Pharmaceutical Company (three branches)	Morphine, Opium
	P 13	Peking: Special Products Refinery	Opium, Heroin
	P 14	Tientsin: Special Products Manufactory	Heroin
	P 15	Chinese Products Export Co. Refinery, Ministry of Foreign Trade (five branches)	Opium
	P 16	Refinery under direct control of Monopoly Enterprises of Ministry of Commerce (nine branches)	Opium
	P 17	Chingwan, Hopei: Special Products Experimental Refinery	Opium
	P 18	Kupeikou, Hopei: Native Products Refinery	Opium, Morphine
	P 19	Taiyuan, Shansi: Shansi Chemical and Pharmaceutical Works	Morphine
East China	P 20	Hangchow: Chekiang Pharmaceutical Works	Opium, Morphine
	P 21	Shanghai Pharmaceutical Works	Opium, Morphine
South China	P 22	Poan, Kwangtung: Chemical and Pharmaceutical Works	Morphine, Heroin
	P 23	Canton: Kwangtung Chemical and Pharmaceutical Works	Morphine
Central China	P 24	Hankow: Special Products Purchase Bureau	Morphine
Southwest	P 25	Kunming: China Chemical Materials Company, Special Materials Refinery (four branches)	Morphine, Ether
	P 26	Tali: Yunnan Materials Company; China Pharmaceutical Company	Morphine, Ether
Northwest	P 27	Chengtu: Szechuan Pharmaceutical Works, Third Branch	Morphine
	P 28	Chungking: Opium Laboratory	Morphine
	P 29	Kangting, Sikang: Sikang Pharmaceutical Works	Opium
	P 30	Chiangtze, Tibet: Tibet Refinery, Second Branch	Opium

Table V

Known Brands of Narcotics Produced by the Chinese Communists

Product	Brand	Grade*
Opium	138	B
	139	A
	Ginseng	C
	South Pole	A
	Red Gold	B
	Gold Elephant	A
	Red Roc	B
	Silver Tripod	B
	Sun Feng	C
	Lao-Pei-ku	A
	Ta-chen	A
	Heng-tiao	C
	Camel	C
	Globe	C
	Greyhound	C
	Kang-fu	A
	Sung Pao	B
	Hung-hsing	A
	(Red Star)	
	Chin-feng	A
	(Gold Phoenix)	
	Fan Chuan	B
	(Sailboat)	
Morphine	Tsai-feng	B
	(Variegated Phoenix)	
	Yin-lung	B
	(Silver Dragon)	
	Chin-yin	B
	(Gold-Silver)	
	Lung-tze	A
	(Dragon Son)	
	Hei Chi	A
	(Black Chicken)	
	Lo-to	B
	(Camel)	
	Huang-shang-huang	C
	(King of Kings)	
	Hsung-chi	B
	(Cock)	
	Hung-shih	A
	(Red Lion)	
	999	A
	AAA	B
	OK	B

Heroin	Pei-chi	B
	(North Pole)	
	Hung Chin	A
	(Red Gold)	
	Yin-ting	A
	(Silver Tripod)	
	Shih Ch'iu	A
	(Lion Ball)	
	Hsiang-pin	A
	(Champion)	
	Chin-yü	B
	(Golden Fish)	
	Hsiang-nan	B

*Grade A represents the highest quality.

The above is not an exhaustive list; there are many others. Often the name and origin of a product is obscured by processes of repacking and redesignation. The Chinese Communists maintain plants abroad.

Most of the material and information in Appendix V is from a confidential memorandum, "Chinese Communist Production and Sale of Narcotics," by Peter Huang, specialist in Chinese Communist affairs. It is in part compiled from intelligence from the Chinese mainland, from Hong Kong and Macao, the Yunnan-Burma area, and other locations.

Appendix VI

Summary of the Chinese Communists'

20–Year Special Products Plan

Phase I: Development of the Base, 1950–56

  (a) Selection of poppies and standardization of practices. Planting of poppies on an increasing scale. Inauguration of new laboratories and opiates-processing plants in appropriate places. Reorganization and expansion of existing establishments. Training programs for operational personnel.

  (b) Exploratory actions in potential markets in
    i. The short range:
      Japan, South Korea, South Vietnam, Laos, Burma, Thailand, Philippines, Malaya, Singapore, etc.
    ii. The middle range:
      Middle East, Africa, Europe and Mediterranean Area, Soviet Union.
    iii. The long range:
      United States, Canada, Central and South America..

  (c) Policy-planning conference with "competitors."

Phase II: The Establishment of the Movement Pattern, 1956–63

The definition of the target areas, individuals, communities, and movements (contingent on findings of i, ii, and iii above). Setting up of correct organizational pattern to ensure deliveries to the above. Maintenance of flow. Control of the aims of flow.

Phase III: The Realization of the Objectives, 1963–70

Translation of the captured individuals and organizations into active or passive assets. Synchronization of action arising with psychological and ideological impulses; also with military action as required.

Notes:
During Phase I the aim will be to gain foreign exchange to service loans and to pay for purchases from the U.S.S.R. and from other foreign powers.

During Phase II the aim will be to lay the foundations of militant movements and fronts and to demoralize the enemy.

During Phase III the aim is active and revolutionary development and training for I(b)i. For example, action in the Philippines may be regarded as experimentation for the Japanese objective. The latter can serve as experience for U.S. and Canadian objectives.

Time scale on II and III subject to tactical adjustment and extension.

Final Planning Date: 1973.

Appendix VII

Extracts from Proceedings of Court-Martial of Major Delbert Fleener, April 1972

p.10.TC*: The general nature of the charges in this case is possession of opium on or about 24th February 1970; three specifications of introduction of opium into United States aircraft on or about the 21st, 22nd and 24th of February 1970; three specifications of introduction of opium into a military installation on or about the 21st, 22nd and 24th of February 1970; violation of MACV Directive 37-6, by possessing United States currency wrongfully on or about the 24th of February 1970; and an additional charge of violation of AFR 76-10 by transporting opium for personal financial gain on or about

---

*Identification code for initials used throughout this appendix:
TC=Trial Counsel
IDC=Individual Defense Counsel
MJ=Military Judge
WIT=Witness
OSI=Office of Special Investigations
MACV=Military Assistance Command, Vietnam
CAAG=A group or organization otherwise unidentified
BOQ=Bachelor Officers' Quarters
TDY=Temporary Duty

the 21st, 22nd and 23rd of February 1970. Charge I and Charge II were preferred by First Lieutenant Dennis L. Dufour; the additional charge and its specifications was preferred by Lieutenant Colonel Andrew C. Lynch. All of these charges were forwarded with recommendations as to disposition by Colonel Lynch; investigated by Major Charles E. Borie. The military judge will not be a witness for the prosecution.

p.17   Direct Examination

Questions by trial counsel:

Q. Would you state your name and grade?
A. My name is Roy P. Burnett, Major.

Q. Your organization?
A. My organization is Headquarters, Seventh Air Force, United States Air Force.

Q. Your station?
A. Tan Son Nhut Air Base, Republic of Vietnam.

Q. Do you know the accused in this case?
A. Yes, I do.

Q. If you see him in the courtroom would you point to him and call him by name?
A. Major Delbert W. Fleener. (The witness pointed to the accused.)

TC: The record should reflect that the witness did as requested.

Q. Major Burnett, when were you first stationed here at Tan Son Nhut?
A. I arrived at Tan Son Nhut 15 April '69, and have been here ever since.

Q. Was Major Fleener stationed there at that time?
A. Yes, he was.

Q. Are you assigned to the same organization as Major Fleener?
A. I was until the seventh of April of this year as a member

of the same organization, 6250th Support Squadron, Seatback Operations.

Q. You have known Major Fleener then since you were assigned?
A. I met Major Fleener shortly after I arrived at Tan Son Nhut,
shortly after 15th April '69.

Q. I would like to direct your attention to the twentieth of Febru-
ary 1970. Did you have occasion to fly with Major Fleener to
Bangkok?
A. Yes, sir, I did.

Q. When did you return from Bangkok?
A. I returned from Bangkok on the twenty-second of February.

Did Major Fleener come back with you?
A. No, sir, he did not.

Q. Was he still in Bangkok?
A. Yes, sir, he was.

Q. Did anything unusual occur in flight?
A. In flight back on the twenty-second? Yes, sir.

Q. Would you tell the court what that was?
A. Well four boxes had been placed on the aircraft, VC-54, serial
number 44-9149. They were placed on the crew bunk of the
aircraft. I recognized those four boxes as being the same four
boxes that had been in the room that Major Fleener and I
shared in the Chao Phaya Hotel on the day and the night
of 20 and 21 February. On that flight, the Aircraft Commander, Major Donald Cipra, and myself made the decision
to open one of them to see what was in it.

Q. How many boxes were there?
A. Four, total.

Q. And where were you when you first noticed those four boxes?
A. I was the crew navigator on that particular flight and the
boxes were about five feet behind the navigator's station in
the 54. They were sitting on the edge of the crew bunk.

Photographs of prepared opium seized in Vietnam. Chinese writing assures the buyer it is "Prepared under experienced guidance" and "We do not cheat young or old." Note: The Chinese "altar of heaven," which used to be ascended by the emperors, had three staircases of nine steps each — thus "999."

Q. Was the aircraft in flight en route from Bangkok to Tan Son Nhut?

A. Yes, sir, it was one and one-half hours after takeoff from Bangkok. That is when I first noticed the boxes.

Q. And who opened one of the boxes?

A. Who opened one of the boxes? I took the string from around the one box that was opened and removed the rope that was under the white cord.

Q. And what did you discover?

A. Several packages, small packages, approximately ten to fifteen in number, about the size of a household brick, wrapped in heavy paper, sealed at the seams with clear Scotch tape. They had an alphabetical number with a digit in the upper lefthand corner, and a number in the center written with a fine-line magic marker in red.

Q. Why did you and Major Cipra, in your opinion decide to open the boxes?

IDC: Wait just a minute. I object on the grounds that it is calling for a conclusion and no foundation has been laid.

TC: I will withdraw that question.

Q. What occurred then, next—when you discovered the contents of the box?

A. Well, we talked about the possible contents for a while and the result was that I instructed...

IDC: Just a minute. I object to any conversation on the grounds that it is hearsay.

MJ: Objection is overruled insofar as what he himself said. I believe he was about to state—you prefaced your remark by "you instructed?"

WIT: Yes.

IDC: Wouldn't that be hearsay as far as the accused is concerned?

MJ: No. I assume the witness is being called here regarding the motion on search and seizure. So I am going to permit the answer.

TC: Will you continue please with what you said?

A. I instructed Major Cipra to place the one small package that had been taken from the larger box and place it in my B-4 bag, the pocket of my B-4 bag which was laying on the same crew bunk with the four boxes. And he placed the one package in my B-4 bag.

Q. Did you remove any of the paper that you have described from around this object?

A. Yes, sir. The one small package that was removed from the larger box, the end was torn open where it was sealed at the seams with Scotch tape, and approximately twenty percent of the surface was exposed.

Q. Would you describe what you saw on the surface?

A. It was a hard substance, something of a plaster of Paris-type substance: irregular in color, brownish, somewhat like the panelling on the wall that you see in this room.

Q. What occurred then after Major Cipra placed the brick-like object in your B-4 bag? What occurred next?

A. Well, I examined the letter that was placed on the top of one box that was in an envelope that was folded in the middle and placed under the wrapping of one box. I attempted to read it without opening it, with a flashlight.

Q. Did you have anything to substantiate the ideas besides those two things.

A. No.

p. 27

Q. Really no. You got this brick, I understand and turned it over to the OSI?

A. Yes, sir.

Q. Why did you do that?

A. Why did I? Because I suspicioned that it was some sort of illegal material, some type of contraband.

461

Q. Now, when did you decide that?

A. Again, on the weight and the size, the numbering system that was contained on the outside of the package, the excessive weight, the excessive wrapping, the unmarked boxes except for the word "CAAG," written on the outside.

Q. As a matter of fact weren't those boxes—didn't you know they were going to Major Davis?

A. Yes, sir, Major Fleener had told me that Major Davis was going to take care of them.

Q. Have you ever seen anything like those bricks before?

A. No, sir. I have never seen a substance like this before.

IDC: I think that is all I have, but there is one other subject that I might go into by recalling him. If trial counsel has no objection I can take him over and put that on now.

MJ: I have no objection.

TC: Then I am going to object to improper cross-examination.

IDC: I didn't want an objection.

Major Burnett, when you came to the base, did you see the boxes after you got to the base? The four boxes?

A. Yes, sir.

Q. Where did you first see them?

A. I saw Major Davis place two of the four in the back of the pickup driven by Colonel Hamphill, who met the airplane.

Q. How about the other two? Did you see them unloaded?

A. No, I observed only two being unloaded before I departed the area momentarily.

Q. And did you go to the BOQ where they were taken from the truck?

A. Yes, sir.

Q. And how long have you known Major Davis?

A. I met Major Davis about the same time I met Major Fleener, shortly after 16 April '69.

Q. Major Davis was stationed here at Tan Son Nhut at that time?
A. Yes, sir.

Q. Do you know what his duties were at that time, or since?
A. Yes sir. He is a C-118 pilot, Aircraft Commander, Standardization Flight Examiner.

p. 30

Q. Assigned to the same organization as you are—you were as of the 20th through the 24th of February 1970?
A. Yes.

Q. Did you see who actually removed those four boxes that you referred to from the aircraft?
A. Two of the four boxes I observed Major Davis coming off the aircraft with them, one in each hand, and placing the same two boxes in the back end of Colonel Hamphill's pickup.

Q. This note that you referred to—or envelope, you called it— was it addressed to anyone?
A. It had Major Davis' name printed on the middle of it.

Q. Could you describe the envelope to any greater degree?

IDC: What would the best evidence be? Do you have the envelope?

TC: No, we do not.

WIT: The envelope was legal in size; it had a Chao Phaya Hotel return address in the upper lefthand corner. To the best I recall, it had airmail markings around the edges and it was addressed either with a pencil or a ballpoint pen to Major Davis. It did not have a complete address, including organization, mailroom number or box or APO.

Q. What part of the contents did you read?

463

A. Most likely it appeared...

Q. What words did you see?
A. I saw the word "A.H.Sing." That is "A" being a cap letter, "H" being a cap letter, "S" being a cap letter, S-i-n-g, the "ing" in small letters. It said "phone." I could not make out the numbers, but there were some numbers, and "in Kowloon."

Q. Where was the note located, again?
A. It was folded in the middle and placed under the rope and the white cord wrapping around one box.

Q. Would you describe the size of these boxes?
A. I would estimate the size, as best I recall, about twenty inches square and about sixteen to eighteen inches high. It would cover about four of those tiles. (Witness pointed to floor tiles in the courtroom.)

p. 33 The Article 39 (a) session recessed at 1602 hours, 20 April 1970.

TC: The Government calls Colonel Marek.

Colonel Frank R. Marek, Commander 377th Combat Support Group, Tan Son Nhut Air Base, Republic of Vietnam, a witness for the prosecution was sworn and testified as follows:

Direct Examination

Questions by the prosecution:

Q. Would you state your name and rank, please?
A. Frank E. Marek, Colonel, United States Air Force.

Q. Your organization, station and armed force?
A. Three seventy-seventh Combat Support Group, Tan Son Nhut Air Base, United States Air Force.

Q. Do you know the accused in this case?
A. No, sir.

Q. What are your duties here on Tan Son Nhut?
A. I am the United States Air Force Base Commander at Tan

Son Nhut Air Base and Commander of the 377th Combat Support Group.

Q. In that capacity, sir, and directing your attention to the 23rd of February 1970, were you approached by OSI agents?
A. Yes, sir.

(TC handed the reporter two documents which were marked as Appellate Exhibits 3 and 4.)

TC: I show to the defense what is marked as Appellate Exhibits 3 and 4.

(TC handed the documents to IDC for his examination.)

IDC: The defense has no objection to Exhibit 5. On Exhibit 5 we object on the grounds that it is irrelevant, immaterial and incompetent because the search was not of the possessions of the accused.

TC: Sir, these are marked Appellate Exhibits 3 and 4.

IDC: I will change it to: The defense has no objection to Appellate Exhibit 3, which is authority to search and seize in the case of Major Delbert W. Fleener. The defense objects to Appellate Exhibit 4 on the grounds that it is incompetent, immaterial and irrelevant to the issues of this case and concerns property not under the control of the accused.

MJ: Of course he hasn't identified them for my benefit. Colonel Edwards do you have any comments?

TC: Yes, sir. The Government intends to show that Colonel Marek authorized the search of Major Davis' room and similarly Major Fleener's; that this evidence is relevant because in Major Davis' room six boxes were found which were introduced into Tan Son Nhut Air Base by the accused, Major Fleener.

MJ: It is alleged, is that right?

TC: Yes, sir.

465

MJ: I will permit the trial counsel to continue subject to connecting it all up. You may proceed at this time.

TC: Colonel Marek, I show you Appellate Exhibit 3. Can you identify that document, sir?

(The witness examined Appellate Exhibit 3.)
WIT: Yes, sir.

Q. What is that?
A. This is a document that I signed authorizing OSI agents to search and seize any narcotics that may be in the possession of Major Fleener whether in person or in his quarters.

Q. How do you identify those two documents?
A. By my signature.

Q. When did you sign these documents, sir?
A. On the 23rd.

Q. Did you give them to anyone, or did you maintain possession of them?
A. May I have a repeat on that please?

Q. Did you give these documents to anyone after having signed them?
A. I gave them to the special Agents, Welch and Walsh.

Q. What information, if any, did Special Agents Welch and Walsh relay to you, or relate to you prior to your signing these two search warrants?
A. They came to me and informed me that they had received information from a navigator, Major Burnett. It appeared that Major Burnett extracted a brick from a package which in turn was turned over to the OSI. The OSI in turn took the brick to Long Binh for analysis. Based on the information they gave me, it was concluded that it was definitely opium.

TC: Prosection will call Pritchard.

Lt. Col. Robert P. Pritchard, OSI, District 50, Tan Son Nhut

Air Base, a witness for the prosecution, was sworn and testified, as follows:

Direct Examination

Questions by the prosecution:

Q. Colonel Pritchard, I direct your attention to the 23rd of February. Did a Major Burnett visit you on the morning of that day?
A. He did.

p. 56

Q. Would you tell me what occurred?
A. Major Burnett, about eight o'clock in the morning of the 23rd, came to my office and handed me a wrapped package which he told me he had obtained from an airplane and he suspected it to be some type of contraband. He wanted our office to determine what it was.

Q. Did you examine this package?
A. I opened the package. I observed the package and found out there was nothing inside it other than this brown crystalline-type substance. I took a sample off of the brick itself and released it to Major Bill Welch who transported it to the laboratory at Long Binh for analysis.

Q. Who is Major Welch?
A. Major Welch is my Chief of the Investigative Unit here at Tan Son Nhut.

Q. Where is Long Binh?
A. Long Binh is an Army camp about twenty miles away, which has a laboratory there.

Q. Did you obtain any results?
A. Yes, I made arrangements with Major Welch to have him phone me when the laboratory had made a field test. Approximately an hour to two hours later, Major Welch phoned and told me that the results were positive for an opiate or opium substance.

467

IDC: Will you strike that on the grounds that it is just hear-say—the last part about the Major and the composition was hearsay.

MJ: Overruled.

TC: Would you describe the appearance of this brick you were given by Major Burnett?

A. The brick was approximately six inches by two inches by four inches in size; weighed approximately a pound and a half; it had the raised numerals "999" on the surface of the brick; it was brownish in color and it had the appearance of plaster.

Q: Did the numerals "999" have any significance?

IDC: Just a minute. May I point out that the witness on this subject... May I talk to the witness on that subject? Colonel tell me your duties here on the post. Are you in any way a chemist?
WIT: No sir.

IDC: What are your specific duties?
WIT: I am the Deputy Commander of the OSI at Tan Son Nhut.

IDC: Now the question, I assume, is whether or not "999" has any significance? I would like to know what experience you have had in connection with the identification of those numerals?

p. 57

WIT: Approximately 1958 there was a case which the OSI ran on in Tokyo and Hong Kong involving an airman by the name of Wilmont. Wilmont was apprehended bringing bricks of "999" from Hong Kong into Japan. The bricks were seized by OSI up there and I was to later on see photographs of those bricks, and also when the case was adjudicated the bricks were passed around to the OSI districts in PACAF for examination.

Special Agent William C. Welch, Office of Special Investigations, District 50, Tan Son Nhut Air Base, Republic of Vietnam, a witness for the prosecution was sworn and testified as follows:

468

Direct Examination

Questions by the prosecution:

Q. State your name and occupation.
A. William C. Welch, Special Agent, Office of Special Investigations, District Office 50, Tan Son Nhut Air Base.

Q. You are employed by the United States Air Force?
A. Yes, sir.

Q. Do you have a rank?
A. Yes, sir, Major.

Q. How long have you been stationed here at Tan Son Nhut?
A. Approximately ten months.

Q. In February of 1970, were you performing your duties as an OSI agent.
A. Yes, sir.

Q. Now on the 23rd of February 1970, did you have occasion to go to Long Binh?
A. Yes, sir.

Q. Would you tell me what that occasion was?
A. Well, it was about ten o'clock in the morning of that date, Colonel Pritchard, who is our Deputy Commander, brought in a brick, small brick, to me and showed it to me as well as some others in the office; and this brick had the numerals "999" on the outside. It was partially opened and had a brown wrapping on the outside. He suspected that the brick might contain some sort of opium derivative. So Colonel Pritchard took a scraping off of this brick and it was placed in a small vial, with a decision to take it to Long Binh to the Army for examination in their laboratory. So I and Special Agent Billy Webber took the small bundle to Long Binh to the laboratory on that day, arriving there I suppose about twelve noon and gave it to the people at Long Binh. They examined it within five or ten minutes, using a reagent, they call it Mark E reagent. It involves placing a liquid over a certain part of the specimen being examined. The specimen

469

turned a deep purple colour, which the two examiners there told us...

p. 59

IDC: I object to the conversation up there on the grounds that it is incompetent, immaterial and irrelevant.

TC: I agree it's hearsay. The police and OSI must act upon hearsay, together with other statements made personally to them, but I think it pertinent for the court to know what this agent was informed by the laboratory because this forms the foundation of the entire knowledge known to the police at the time that they went to secure a search warrant.

MJ: Objection overruled.

WIT: The two gentlemen that made the test in front of us advised that the change in color indicated the presence of opium in the sample. They said they were not qualified from a testimonial standpoint as well as Camp Zama to come up with a thorough analysis and that this was only a field test. But that the change in color was such that it would be quite advisable to send the remaining portion of the sample to Camp Zama for further analysis.

Q. Was this done, to your knowledge?
A. Yes, sir.

Q. Did you then return to Tan Son Nhut?
A. Yes, I then returned to Tan Son Nhut.

Q. Did you have an occasion to go to Colonel Marek's office?
A. Yes, sir.

Q. Why was that?
A. The reason I went over to Colonel Marek's office specifically was to brief, not to brief but to introduce Special Agent Walsh to Colonel Marek, whom he had not met or had not seen for many years. On the tour he is still on he will see Colonel Marek on a daily basis and I thought that Major Walsh would be the likely one to brief Colonel Marek on the

470

case that was formulating at this time and it was quite likely that Major Walsh would be running the investigation. So my main purpose initially was simply to introduce him to Colonel Marek. Colonel Marek was of course briefed for the most part by Major Walsh.

Q. Would you tell me what Colonel Marek was informed, what he was advised?
A. He was advised essentially of two things, or three. One was the contents of the conversation that had taken place with Major Burnett earlier.

Q. Would you relate in detail what he was told?
A. He was told that as far as this conversation was concerned, that Major Burnett had come in initially and given Colonel Pritchard the brick of the "999" and later on came back earlier in the afternoon and related a story that, on the 20th of February he was a crew member on a plane that was going from Saigon to Bangkok. The plane was forced to remain, and the crew remained, for an engine change in Bangkok, so that three of the crew members stayed over in Bangkok until the 22nd of February. On the 21st of February, Major Burnett who was in the same room with Major Fleener, or one of the crew members, noticed him tying string about some packages. He asked what the packages were for and Major Fleener indicated that they were for the CAAGers. He noticed on the 22nd, early in the afternoon of the 22nd, the packages were no longer there. Major Burnett then was on his way out to the airport at Bangkok to go on as another
p. 60 crew member on the trip to Saigon. During the flight, Major Burnett had occasion to go back into the area where his B-4 bag was situated. In order to get back to the B-4 bag he had to move one of the packages that he had noticed in the room where he and Major Fleener had stayed, and he noticed the weight was exceptionally high in the packages. He talked to other crew members and it was decided to open up one of the packages and see what was inside. About fifteen or twenty bricks were noticed of this same size brick. One of the bricks was removed and the decision was made to seal the package up and take this one brick to the OSI the next day. Now the four packages were transported to Saigon, where Major Davis met the aircraft. The packages were loaded inside a carry-all van and the packages were trans-

471

ported to Major Fleener's quarters, his BOQ room. This was noticed by Major Burnett. As I mentioned, Major Burnett took the brick the next day down to the OSI. So this is essentially what was related to Colonel Marek. In addition, I pointed out what the results of the laboratory examination were at Long Binh. Also, we discussed the magnitude or possible magnitude of a case involving this much opium if it all was opium. And then Colonel Marek was given two sheets of paper to read over and sign if he decided to sign them. They were the authority for search and seizure regarding Major Davis' BOQ room and Major Fleener's BOQ room. I personally did not see what was recorded on these sheets of paper because these sheets had been made out during the period of time that I was in Long Binh. So I never saw what was on them. I assume what was on them was essentially what would be on any sheet of paper looking into an investigation of this nature with respect to authority for search and seizure.

TC: Don't tell us what you assumed. Tell us what you discussed.

A. Well, we discussed specifically what was to be looked into within the room, that is, any items or boxes containing narcotics, any documents, checks, shipping documents let us say, cancelled checks or anything that might pertain to money transactions. The search of the two individuals was required.

IDC: I move to strike that. To say the search of the individuals was required is irrelevant and immaterial.

MJ: I think you need a clarification. I will overrule it. You may finish the answer.

A. There was a discussion about the possibility of when having an individual who may be using narcotics, you may find narcotics in the room in such a state that the individual might use it, or the instruments of narcotics such as needles, that a search of the individual would be required, if for nothing else for your own safety.

p. 61

IDC: Would you strike that—the last part of the sentence—because it is incompetent and immaterial and calls for a conclusion of the witness. It is irrelevant.

472

TC: I certainly think it is relevant what this witness says that the Base Commander was informed on.

p. 62

Q. Was currency discussed?

IDC: That is a leading question. I object.

TC: I don't know how else to do it.

MJ: Continue.
TC: Was currency discussed?
A. As part of the instruments, this was also considered to be monetary and the possibility was suggested that money would be found. Yes.

IDC: I move to strike the last answer of the witness because it is incompetent, immaterial and irrelevant. It is speculative and imaginatory and does not state the contents of the conversation that would be important.

TC: I will concur and withdraw the question. Your witness.

Cross Examination

Questions by individual defense counsel:

Q. Will you clarify for us what the analysis showed this to be. Was it morphine or opium.
A. They weren't certain. All they could say was that it was an opium derivative. They suspected it was fairly pure opium.

Q. What did they tell you that it was? Did they make any mention of morphine?
A. No, sir, they didn't. They said, "It is opium, but we can't say what kind of opium. We would have to take it to Zama to find out specifically."

IDC: That is all.

p. 67

Special Agent Donald R. Walsh, Office of Special Investigations, District 50, Tan Son Nhut Air Base, Republic of Vietnam, a witness for the prosecution was sworn in and testified as follows:

Questions by the prosecution:

Q. Would you state your name and occupation?
A. Donald R. Walsh, Special Agent, District 50, Office of Special Investigation at Tan Son Nhut Air Base.

TC: Did you, Major Walsh, subsequently participate in the search of Major Fleener's person and room?
A. I did.

Q. When was this?
A. The search started at approximately 0115; between 0100 and 0130 hrs, 24th February.

Q. And where was this?
A. The search was conducted in room #1, BOQ #111, on Tan Son Nhut Air Base.

Q. At what time did you arrive.
A. It was approximately one o'clock.

Q. Was Major Fleener there?
A. No, sir, when I first arrived, he was not there.

Q. Did you ask for him?
A. Yes, sir. Inquiries were made in the BOQ as to his whereabouts.

Q. What action did you take then, if any?
A. I went from the BOQ up to the guard shack which is located to the left of the BOQ, and attempted to reach the Security Police desk sergeant to have a pickup order put on a white Toyota that Major Davis and Major Fleener were driving. However, prior to the desk sergeant responding to my request, I was called back to the BOQ by Mr. Casteluccio, indicating that Major Fleener had arrived at his quarters.

Q. Did you return to building #111?
A. I did, sir.

Q. Did you see Major Fleener?
A. I did, sir.

Q. Where was he at this time?
A. He was standing in the hallway in front of his room.

Q. Was there anyone else with him?
A. Yes, sir, Special Agents Casteluccio, Cundiff and Lieutenant Colonel Sills.

Q. What action did you take then, if any?
A. I identified myself as a Special Agent with the Office of Special Investigations. I asked Major Fleener to step in his room.

p. 70

Q. During this period did you watch Major Fleener and observe his movements?
A. Yes sir. He was standing directly in front of me.

Q. Did he attempt to remove anything from his pockets or make any motions toward you which endangered you?
A. No, sir, he did not.

Q. What did you remove from his person?
A. His billfold, two envelopes and other papers he had.

Q. Do you know what was in those envelopes?
A. Yes sir, United States green currency.

Q. What was in his billfold?
A. There was $539.00 in green currency and there were several cards and pieces of paper which had handwritten notes apparently made by Major Fleener.

Q. Did you seize any of this material?
A. Yes, sir, we did.

Q. The cards and the currency?
A. Yes, the cards and the currency were seized.

Q. Why did you take the cards?
A. Well, we thought that there was a good possibility that they might relate to the source of the opium.

Q. Did they contain any names or addresses or telephone numbers?

A. Yes they did. On one piece of paper was scribbled the name "Gutch" and "Hughes."

Q. Did there seem to be any financial computations on any of these documents?

A. Yes, sir, on that particular document there was an indication of so many boxes at such and such a price.

IDC: I'll object to that on the grounds that the document itself is the best evidence.

TC: Very well. I will withdraw the question.

Q. Did you seize any currency?

A. Yes, sir, we did.

Q. How much and what kind of currency?

A. Five hundred and thirty-nine dollars in American green currency was seized from his wallet. There were two envelopes; one had a "1M" on the outside of it and it contained $1000.00, the other envelope had "2M" on the front of it and it contained $2000.00. There was a total of $3,539.00 in American green currency seized from Major Fleener.

p. 127　　Charge I:　　Violation of the Uniform Code of Military Justice, Article 134

Specification 1: In that MAJOR DELBERT W. FLEENER, United States Air Force, 6250th Support Squadron, did at Tan Son Nhut, Republic of Vietnam, on or about 24th February, wrongfully have in his possession about 559 pounds, more or less, of a habit-forming drug, to wit: opium.

Specification 2: In that MAJOR DELBERT W. FLEENER, United States Air Force, 6250th Support Squadron, did, at Don Muang Airport, Thailand, on or about 21 February 1970, wrongfully introduce about 234 pounds, 7 ounces of a habit-forming narcotic drug, to wit: opium, into a military aircraft for the purpose of transport to Tan Son Nhut Airfield, Republic of Vietnam.

Specification 3: In that MAJOR DELBERT W. FLEENER, United States Air Force, 6250th Support Squadron, did, at Tan Son Nhut Airfield, Republic of Vietnam, on or about 21 February, 1970, wrongfully introduce about 234 pounds, 7 ounces of a habit-forming narcotic drug, to wit: opium, into a military installation, to wit: Tan Son Nhut Airfield, for the purpose of transfer.

Specification 4: In that MAJOR DELBERT W. FLEENER, United States Air Force, did at Don Muang Airport, Thailand, on or about 22 February 1970, wrongfully introduce about 141 pounds of a habit-forming narcotic drug, to wit: opium, into a United States Air Force aircraft for the purpose of transport to Tan Son Nhut Airfield, Republic of Vietnam.

Specification 5: In that MAJOR DELBERT W. FLEENER, United States Air Force, 6250th Support Squadron, did, at Tan Son Nhut Airfield, Republic of Vietnam, on or about February 22 1970, wrongfully introduce about 141 pounds of a habit-forming drug, to wit: opium, into a military installation, to wit: Tan Son Nhut Airfield, for the purpose of transfer.

Specification 6: In that MAJOR DELBERT W. FLEENER, United States Air Force, 6250th Support Squadron, did, at Don Muang Airport, Thailand, on or about 23 February 1970, wrongfully introduce about 491 pounds of a habit-forming narcotic drug, to wit: opium, into a United States Air Force aircraft for the purpose of transport to Tan Son Nhut Airfield, Republic of Vietnam.

Specification 7: In that MAJOR DELBERT W. FLEENER, United States Air Force, 6250th Support Squadron, did, at Tan Son Nhut Airfield, Republic of Vietnam, on or about 24 February 1970, wrongfully introduce about 491 pounds of a habit-forming narcotic drug, to wit: opium, into a military installation, to wit: Tan Son Nhut Airfield, for the purpose of transfer.

Charge II: Violation of the Uniform Code of Military Justice, Article 92

Specification: In that MAJOR DELBERT W. FLEENER, United States Air Force, 6250th Support Squadron, did, at Tan Son Nhut Airfield, Republic of Vietnam, on or about 24 February 1970, violate a lawful general regulation, to wit: Directive 37-6, dated 15 September 1969, paragraph 7A, Headquarters United States Military Assistance Command Vietnam, by wrongfully having in his possession $3,539.00 in United States currency.

Additional Charge: Violation of the Uniform Code of Military Justice, Article 92

Specification 1: In that MAJOR DELBERT W. FLEENER, United States Air Force, 6250th Support Squadron, did, on board C-123 aircraft #56-4375, on or about 21 February 1970, violate a lawful general regulation, to wit: Paragraph 1, Air Force Regulation 76-10, dated 25th April 1968, by causing 234 pounds, 7 ounces of opium to be transported by United States Air Force aircraft from Thailand to the Republic of Vietnam for the purpose of personal financial gain.

Specification 2: In that MAJOR DELBERT W. FLEENER, United States Air Force, 6250th Support Squadron, did on board VC-54 aircraft #44-9149, on or about 22 February 1970, violate a lawful general regulation, to wit: Paragraph 1, Air Force Regulation 76-10, dated 25th April 1968, by causing 1414 pounds of opium to be transported by United States Air Force aircraft from Thailand to the Republic of Vietnam for the purpose of personal financial gain.

Specification 3: In that MAJOR DELBERT W. FLEENER, United States Air Force, 6250th Air Support Squadron, did, on board VC-118 aircraft #51-3827, on or about 23 February 1970, violate a lawful general regulation, to wit: Air Force Regulation 76-10, dated 25th April 1968, by causing 491 pounds of opium to be transported by United States aircraft from Thailand to the republic of Vietnam for the purpose of personal financial gain.

p. 185
        TC: I will call Major Walsh.

        Special Agent Donald R. Walsh, Office of Special Investigation District 50, Tan Son Nhut Air Base, Republic of Vietnam, a witness for the prosecution, was sworn in and testified as follows:

Direct Examination

Questions by the prosecution:

        Q. State your name and grade, please.
        A. Donald R. Walsh, Major, United States Air Force.

        Q. You are assigned here at Tan Son Nhut?
        A. Yes, I am, sir.

        Q. What is your organization?
        A. District 50, Office of Special Investigations.

        Q. Do you know the accused in this case?
        A. Yes, sir, I do.

Q. If you see him in the courtroom would you point to him and call him by name?
A. Delbert Fleener. (The witness pointed to the accused.)

TC: The witness correctly identified the accused.

Q. What are your duties here at Tan Son Nhut, Major Walsh?
A. I am a Special Agent with the office of Special Investigations.

Q. How long have you been a Special Agent?
A. For approximately seven and one-half years.

Q. How long have you performed your duties here at Tan Son Nhut?
A. Since June 20th 1969.

Q. Now directing your attention to the 23rd of February 1970, did you have occasion to talk with a Major Burnett?
A. Yes, sir, I did.

Q. When and where was this?
A. At OSI District 50 office.

Q. At what time?
A. Approximately 1300 hours on the 23rd of February.

Q. Did Major Burnett furnish you with an oral and written statement?
A. Yes, sir, he did.

Q. Did he swear to the contents of the written statement?
A. He did, sir.

Q. Did you have occasion to visit the Base Commander?
A. I did, sir, the afternoon of 23 February 1970.

Q. At approximately what time?
A. 1500 hrs.

p. 186
Q. Was anyone with you?
A. Yes, sir, Major William C. Welch.

479

Q. Who is the Base Commander?
A. Colonel Frank E. Marek.

Q. He is the one you visited that day?
A. Yes, sir.

Q. Did you give him any briefing of any kind?
A. Yes, sir, I did.

Q. Without telling me what you said, did you relate to him what Major Burnett had told you?
A. I did, sir.

Q. Did you relate to him your understanding of the analysis at Long Binh?
A. I did, sir.

Q. Did you make any requests of the Base Commander?
A. Yes sir.

Q. What was that?
A. I requested authority to search and seize Major Fleener and Major Davis.

Q. Did you know where Major Fleener and Major Davis lived?
A. Yes, sir. BOQ #111, room #1 was Major Fleener's room and room #49 was Major Davis' room.

Q. Did you have occasion to search either one of those rooms?
A. I did, sir. I searched Major Fleener's room on the morning of 24 February 1970.

Q. At what time did you arrive at building #111?
A. At approximately 0100 hours.

Q. Did you see Major Fleener there?
A. No, sir, not at that time.

Q. Did you ask for him?
A. Yes, sir, I did.

Q. Did you subsequently see him?

A. Yes, sir, I did, at approximately one thirty—0130 hrs.

Q. On the morning of 24 February 1970?

p. 187

A. That is correct.

Q. Where was he when you first saw him?
A. He was standing in the hallway of BOQ #111, in front of the door to his room.

Q. What action did you take then, if any?
A. I identified myself as a Special Agent and asked him to step into his room. At that point I showed him the authority to search and seize which was signed by Colonel Marek. I asked him to read it. He acknowledged that he did. At that time I advised him of his rights under Article 31 UCMJ, and I asked him if he understood his rights. He stated he did. I asked him if he wanted a lawyer present. He stated he did not. I asked him if he was sure he understood his rights and he said "yes." I asked him again if he wanted a lawyer and he said "no." At that point I said to Major Fleener, "Would you please turn around and extend your hands spread-eagle on the wall locker" which was in the room. At that point I conducted a body search of Major Fleener.

Q. Who was present with you, if anyone?
A. Special Agent Jerome Casteluccio, Special Agent Ronald Cundiff, and Lieutentant Colonel Sills from Seventh Air Force.

Q. Why was he there?
A. He requested a disinterested officer to witness the search to assure that Major Fleener's rights were not violated.

Q. Were any of the three OSI Agents armed?
A. Yes, Special Agent Cundiff had a .38 caliber revolver on his hip.

Q. Did you remove anything from the person of Major Fleener?
A. Yes, sir, I did: his wallet and a couple of envelopes and other papers.

481

Q. I show you what has been marked as Prosecution Exhibits 2, 3, 4, 5 and 6 for identification, and ask you if you can identify these exhibits?

(TC handed Prosecution Exhibits 2 through 6 to the witness.)

A. Yes sir. These are papers which were taken from Major Fleener on the morning of the 24th.

Q. Where did they come from specifically?
A. I believe they came from his wallet or his pockets.

Q. Did you remove his wallet?
A. I did, sir.

Q. Did you remove the items from the wallet?
A. Either I or Mr. Casteluccio did.

Q. Is there anything else that you removed from the wallet?
A. Yes, sir, there were $539.00 in American green currency in the wallet which was removed.

Q. Did you remove anything else from his papers?
A. No, sir.

Q. You testified to one envelope—two envelopes—how many did you remove?
A. I believe there were two, sir.

p. 188

Q. Did you examine their contents?
A. Yes, sir.

Q. What did they contain?
A. One envelope contained $1000.00 in American green; the second one contained $2000.00 in American green. The denominations of the bills were $100s, $50s, $20s and $10s.

Q. Who did you give this money to, if anyone?
A. That money was counted by us and it was also counted by

482

Colonel Sills; an evidence tag was made out for the money by Mr. Casteluccio that morning.

Q. Who took possession of Prosecution Exhibits 2 through 6 for identification, if you know?
A. Mr. Casteluccio.

Q. What occurred next, then, Major Walsh, following the body search?
A. At that point, I picked up the two boxes which were located in front of his wall locker, placed them on his bunk, cut the bindings on the boxes. The boxes contained bricks identified with "999" on them.

Q. Describe these boxes as you first saw them there in the room.
A. There were two boxes. One was located on top of the other. They appeared to have Oriental writing on the boxes. The boxes were bound with brown twine and also a white twine—rope. They appeared to weigh about thirty pounds, maybe forty pounds.

Q. Would you look around the court room and see if you see those boxes?

(The witness left the stand and examined the exhibits in the court room.)

A. This is one of them.

(The witness lifted the exhibit and placed it beside the witness stand.)

A. This is the second one. These are the two boxes which I picked up from in front of the locker on the morning of the 24th.

Q. You have identified Prosecution Exhibits 16 and 15 for identification. How did you identify these?
A. My initials are on the flap, "DRW, 24 February 70."

Q. You are referring to the flap of the box?

A. Yes, sir, on the flap of the box.

p. 189

Q. At the time that you first saw these boxes, how were they wrapped?

A. They were wrapped with the brown twine and the white twine on the four sides.

Q. I show you some brown and white twine that is in Prosecution Exhibit 16. Does that appear to be the substance that was used?

A. Yes, sir, it does.

Q. Was there any tape sealing the top?

A. No, sir.

Q. Just the twine?

A. Yes, sir.

Q. Now, before you sit down, did you empty those boxes there in Major Fleener's room when you found them?

A. Yes, sir, I did. I initialled the brown wrapper on each brick. There were thirty-three bricks at that time; fifteen bricks in one box and eighteen in the second. I put my initials and "24 February 1970" on each wrapper.

Q. Can you tell me now which box contains fifteen bricks?

A. Yes, sir, it was this box. I made out an evidence tag for the bricks at the time that I went through the box.

Q. That is Prosecution Exhibit 16?

A. Yes, sir.

Q. And Prosecution Exhibit 15, do I understand that it contained eighteen bricks?

A. Yes, sir.

TC: You may resume your seat.

(The witness returned to the witness stand.)

Q. Have you had occasion recently to examine the contents of those boxes now?
A. I did, sir, last evening.

Q. Do they still contain fifteen and eighteen bricks?
A. No, sir. They contain fifteen and seventeen.

Q. Where is the missing brick?
A. One brick was turned over to the Bureau of Narcotics and Dangerous Drugs in Washington, D.C., and has not been returned as yet.

p. 190

TC: Now during the search, Major Walsh, did you ask Major Fleener any questions?
A. Yes, sir, I did.

Q. What questions did you ask?
A. I asked him if he had tied the boxes, if he had handled the contents. He replied no, he had not. I asked him if there were any shipping documents, envelopes, or other papers with the boxes that he was aware of, and he replied, "No." I asked him how he came into possession of the boxes. He related that a man in a Red Cross uniform between forty and forty-five years of age, weighing about one hundred and seventy pounds, asked him to deliver the boxes to Saigon from Bangkok. I asked him if he knew what the brick of "999" was, and he replied: "Opium, I guess, because that is what it said on the search warrant." He asked if he could see a brick and after I had peeled the wrapping from one brick I handed it to him and he looked at it.

Q. I show you what has been marked as Prosecution Exhibit 33 for identification. Can you identify that photograph?

(TC handed the witness Prosecution Exhibit 33 for identification.)

A. Yes, sir. This is a photograph that was taken on the morning of 24 February in Major Fleener's room; it is one of the two boxes we seized.

485

Q. Of the two you seized? Prosecution Exhibit 34 for identification?

(TC handed the witness Prosecution Exhibit 34 for identification.)

A. Yes, sir. This is also a photograph that was taken on the morning of 24 February in Major Fleener's room; it is one of the two boxes we seized.

Q. Upon completing the search of Major Fleener's room, you did what?
A. We transported the two boxes and their contents and Major Fleener to OSI District 50 office.

p. 192

Q. Did Major Fleener make any statements to you at that time?
A. Yes, sir, he did. He stated that he had flown to Bangkok on the 20th...

Q. Let me ask you this, Major Walsh, did he subsequently reduce what he said orally to a written statement?
A. Substantially, yes.

Q. Have you seen that written statement?
A. Yes, sir, I have.

Q. Are there any differences, substantial differences?
A. One difference that I did note after reading his statement and reviewing the notes which I took of the interview that morning, was a remark to the effect that Chou, an Oriental over in Bangkok, asked him to take the boxes from Bangkok to Saigon, and Major Fleener said he asked him what they were. And he said money and medicine. And Major Fleener asked him, "Is it dope?" and Chou replied, "No." This was one of the material omissions in the statement in comparison with the interview.

Q. When did this supposedly take place?
A. On 21 February in Bangkok.

486

Q. Is this what Major Fleener told you on the morning of the 24th in the OSI office?
A. That is correct.

Q. When did you review your notes and discover that difference?
A. About three days ago.

Q. During the interview with Major Fleener on that morning, did he direct your attention to any additional boxes?
A. Yes, sir. He volunteered that there were twelve additional boxes which he had brought in from Bangkok on the morning of the 23rd—the evening of the 23rd, and they were located in his wall locker at Seatback Operations.

Q. Now tell me again when this interview began, at what time?
A. I believe it was 0600 hrs, 24 February 70.

Q. When you first began to question him at OSI?
A. That is what I am talking about. That is correct. I would like to change that. It wasn't at 0600 hrs, it was closer to 0530.

Q. What questions did you initially ask Major Fleener after advising him of his rights?
A. I asked him to relate how he came into possession of the boxes which were seized from his room.

p. 193
Q. What did he say?
A. He related that he received these from a man with red hair dressed in a Red Cross uniform. He said that he received them from him in front of the Chao Phaya Hotel. He stated that he and the man had taken the four boxes up to his room for delivery to the CAAGers.

Q. Did he say when this was?
A. On the 21st. Later in the interview he stated that the story was a fabrication and that he actually did tie the bindings around the boxes in the Chao Phaya Hotel, and that he did send an envelope to Major Davis with the four boxes which were put on the aircraft on the 22nd February.

487

Q. At the beginning of the interview he again indicated what he had in the room, that is that he got the boxes from a Red Cross man?
A. Yes, that is what he said at the beginning of the interview.

Q. Did he again state that he had not wrapped the boxes?
A. When he was confronted with the fact that he had been seen tying twine around the boxes in the room by Major Burnett, when he was informed that there was an envelope attached under the bindings of one of the boxes, he changed his story and stated that he had been making up a story earlier and changed it.

Q. Now, when during the interview did he tell you about the boxes, the other boxes?
A. The twelve boxes? It was at the conclusion of the interview. He stated: "I have twelve more boxes down in my locker, and they are probably dope too." I asked him at that time if he would consent to a search of his locker and he said he would. He gave us written authorization to search his wall locker at Seatback. After he was again advised of his rights under article 31, after he was again asked if he would like a lawyer present, he signed the consent to search his wall locker at Seatback.

Q. At approximately what time of day was this?
A. Approximately six thirty in the morning.

Q. What action did you take then, if any?
A. He, Mr. Casteluccio, Special Agent, and myself drove down to his locker at Seatback. He went over to the locker, opened it and took one package from there and said: "Here it is." At that point, Major Fleener, Stevenson and I emptied the locker of the twelve boxes which were located therein.

Q. What building number is this locker located in, if you know?
A. Building #602 Tan Son Nhut Air Base.

Q. Do you know where Seatback Operations is?
A. Yes, sir, it is in the same building.

Q. Now where is this locker in relation to Seatback Operations?

A. It is in the rear of the building. It is enclosed within the building.

p. 194

Q. Is it a separate room, or a part of some other room?
A. It is a separate room.

Q. Would you look around the courtroom and tell me whether you see any boxes like the boxes you removed?
A. Yes, sir, they are located over there.
Q. Would you get up and look at them closely?

(The witness examined the exhibits he had indicated.)

Q. As you are examining those boxes, Major Walsh—after taking those boxes, did you open them and examine their contents?
A. Yes, sir, I did.

Q. Would you tell me then by referring to the prosecution exhibit numbers on them what you found them to contain?
A. Yes, sir, they all contained packages reflecting the trade mark "Lucky" brand.

Q. Would you demonstrate to the court one of those packages?

(The witness removed one of the packages and showed it to the court.)

Q. Now I notice that that package has been cut.
A. Yes, sir.

Q. Was it cut when you first saw it?
A. No, sir.

Q. Do you know who cut it?
A. No, sir, but it was subsequent to the time that I seized the package to determine if it did, in fact, contain tar.

Q. That block you removed from Prosecution Exhibit 17?
A. Yes, sir.

Q. When did you first open Prosecution Exhibit 17?

489

A. The morning of the 24th between seven thirty and nine.

Q. 0730 to 0900?
A. Yes, approximately that time.

p. 194

Q. Was this at the OSI office?
A. Yes, at the OSI office.

Q. What did you find Prosecution Exhibit 17 to contain? How many of these "Lucky" brands?
A. Twelve blocks.

Q. What are the numbers of the other boxes and what were their contents?
A. The contents of the other eleven boxes were also packages of "Lucky" brand.

Q. I understand, Prosecution Exhibit 19. How many "Lucky" brand tars did that contain?
A. Fifteen.

Q. Would you give me the contents of all the other boxes?
A. Prosecution Exhibit 18 contains 17 blocks; Prosecution Exhibit 20, 14; Prosecution Exhibit 22 contained 12 bricks; Prosecution Exhibit 21 contained 12 bricks; Prosecution Exhibit 24 contained 15 bricks; Prosecution Exhibit 23 contained 12 bricks; Prosecution Exhibit 27 contained 15 bricks; Prosecution Exhibit 25 contained 10 bricks; Prosecution Exhibit 26 contained 12; Prosecution Exhibit 28 contained 14 blocks.

p. 220

TC: I will call Specialist Kane.

Specialist 4 Michael Kane, 515 Military Police Detachment, United States Army, Japan, a witness for the prosecution, was sworn and testified as follows:

Questions by the prosecution:
Q. Would you state your name, rank and organization?

490

A. Specialist Michael Kane, Specialist Fourth Class, 515th Military Police Detachment, United States Army.

IDC: If it please the court, I am perfectly willing to make a stipulation as to what the chemical analysis of these bricks was shown to be by this witness if trial counsel wants to accept a stipulation.

TC: What is your stipulation, sir?

IDC: My stipulation is substantially this: That he examined a given number of bricks and his chemical analysis showed the presence of morphine, codeine, cryptopine, narceine, thebaine....

TC: I will try to limit it to a few questions.

IDC: All right.

TC: What are your duties, Specialist Kane?
A. I am a chemist, sir.

Q. How long have you been in the army?
A. Sixteen months, sir.

Q. Do you have any formal education?
A. Yes, sir.

Q. What is that?
A. I have a Bachelor of Science degree in Chemistry and six months of graduate school.

IDC: I am going to admit his qualifications.

TC: The government will stipulate then to his qualifications.

TC: Specialist Kane, did a Mr. Johns of the OSI here at Tan Son Nhut visit you?
A. Yes, sir.

491

Q. When was that?

A. On the 28th February and also on the 16th of April.

Q. Did he bring certain items for you?

A. Yes.

Q. Would you look in these boxes that are here in the courtroom and identify the items that he brought, if you can? Just lay each item on the top of the box. Go through each box and be sure that you can identify the item you examined.

(The witness examined the contents of the exhibits in the courtroom.)

p. 222

While he is doing that let's have a very brief recess.

(The court reconvened at 1512 hours, 23 April 1970.)

MJ: The court will come to order.

TC: Let the record reflect that all parties to the trial who were present when the court recessed are again present in court, and Specialist Kane is once again on the witness stand. You are reminded that you are still under oath.

WIT: Yes, sir.

TC: Now, Specialist Kane, you have removed a block of tar from each box here in the courtroom, "Lucky" brand tar, from each box that contains "Lucky" brand tar.

A. Yes, sir.

Q. Can you identify those?

A. Yes, sir.

Q. How do you identify them?

A. They have a laboratory case number marked on them, followed by a letter; my initials; the date, and also gross weight in grams.

Q. Now Prosecution Exhibits 13, 14, 15 and 16. Did you examine the contents of these boxes?

A. Yes, sir.

Q. Were they delivered to you also at Camp Zama by Mr. Johns?
A. Yes, sir.

Q. Did you perform a chemical analysis on each of these tars that you have identified and on all of that "999" in those four boxes?
A. Yes, sir.

Q. How many tests did you conduct?
A. On all the "999" blocks I conducted three tests. Excuse me, two tests. There was a spectroscopy and also an ultra-violet color test. These tests indicated that all blocks are identical and I further examined three of these blocks and on two of these I conducted what is known as thin-layer chromatography, separating various components having "999" and this indicated the presence of morphine and codeine. In an additional block I conducted an analysis to determine the percentage of morphine and the percentage of codeine.

Q. Now you are talking about the blocks which are contained in Prosecution Exhibit 16?

(TC showed the witness a brick from Prosecution Exhibit 16 for identification.)

p. 223

A. Yes, and I found the presence of morphine and codeine, and the percentage of morphine was 54 percent and the presence of codeine was 8 percent.

Q. Now what tests did you conduct of the "Lucky" brand tar?
A. On the "Lucky" brand tar, initially the thin layer chromatography separated the components; ultra-violet spectroscopy and the color test further identified these properties.

Q. Now there are sixteen of these tar bricks, I believe, are there not, that you analyzed?
A. Yes, sir.

Q. Did they all appear to be of similar composition?
A. Yes, sir.

Q. Now what was the result of your tests of the "999" and the "Lucky" brand tar?

A. I conclude that they are opium.

Q. Is there any doubt in your mind.
A. No, sir.

Q. Did you find any codeine or morphine in the "Lucky" brand tar?
A. Yes.

Q. What percentage?
A. I found approximately 20 percent morphine in one of the blocks of tar.

Q. Did you say how much codeine?
A. I did not conduct an analysis for codeine.

Q. What are the primary ingredients, say the two primary ingredients, of opium?
A. Morphine and codeine.

TC: That is all I have. Your witness.

IDC: I have no examination. I hope you make your Doctorate.

MJ: If there are no further questions, Specialist Kane, you may be excused. I don't anticipate either side will plan to recall you. Since you are on TDY, you may make the necessary arrangements to go back to Japan. You are excused.

(The witness, Specialist Fourth Class Michael Kane, withdrew from the courtroom.)

p. 242

(The court reconvened at 1013 hours, 24 April 1970).

MJ: The court will come to order.
TC: Let the record reflect that all members who were present when the court recessed yesterday are again present. The members of the court are again present. During the recess two out-of-court hearings were held.

MJ: Colonel Edwards, are you ready to proceed?

TC: Request permission to read to the court Appellate Exhibits 15, 16, 17 and 18.

IDC: Defense agrees.

MJ: Permission granted.

TC: "United States versus Major Delbert W. Fleener, Stipulation of Testimony: It is hereby stipulated by and between the prosecution and the defense, with the express consent of the accused, that if Mr. Jerry Brightwell were present in court he would testify under oath substantially as follows: I am Jerry L. Brightwell, a Special Agent of the OSI stationed at Tan Son Nhut Air Base. On 24 February, I weighed the contents of the following Prosecution Exhibits and received the following weights on the scale at the OSI office at Tan Son Nhut Air Base: Prosecution Exhibit 9, 55 pounds, 2 ounces; Prosecution Exhibit 10, 55 pounds, 3 ounces; Prosecution Exhibit 11, 74 pounds; Prosecution Exhibit 12, 55 pounds, 2 ounces; Prosecution Exhibit 13, 37 pounds, 12 ounces; Prosecution Exhibit 14, 35 pounds, 12 ounces; Prosecution Exhibit 15, 40 pounds, 15 ounces; Prosecution Exhibit 16, 27 pounds, 4 ounces: Exhibit 17, 37 pounds; Exhibit 18, 52 pounds, 5 ounces; 19, 45 pounds, 13 ounces; 20, 42 pounds, 14 ounces.

p. 244

TC: At this time, your honor, I request permission to read to the court Prosecution Exhibit 7 and Prosecution Exhibit 42.

MJ: If you desire to read it you may. It has been admitted into evidence and it can be furnished the court.

TC: To save time I thought I might read it so that all members will be aware of the contents at the same time. Prosecution Exhibit 7, gentlemen, is a Statement of Military Suspect. I will not read all of the printed matter. It purports to be a statement by the accused, Major Fleener. The body of the statement reads as follows: "Approximately five to six months ago"—and I note that the statement is signed 24 February 1970. "Approximately five to six months ago, I met a Thailand or Chinese man, Mr. Chou, in a poker game in Angeles City, Philippines. He asked a few questions such as what do I do. I told him I was a pilot and he asked where I was based and where I flew to. I told him I was based in Saigon and that I flew to Tokyo, Hong Kong and Bang-

495

kok and in Vietnam. He asked me when I was going to Hong
Kong and I told him approximately two to three weeks. He
gave me his 'phone number and asked me to call him in
p. 244 Hong Kong. Approximately three weeks later I was in Hong
Kong and called him. We again played poker. I lost
approximately four to five hundred dollars. He said he was
an importer and wanted to know when I was going to Bangkok. I told him I was going to Saigon and would probably
be in Bangkok within a week. He gave me a phone number
to call him in Bangkok. After making several trips to Bangkok, he called me at the Chao Phaya Hotel and told me he
was in the coffee shop. I met him and talked to him about
thirty minutes. He asked if there were a phone in Saigon
where he could call me. I gave him TSN number 2427. He
asked if I could carry some money and checks to Hong Kong
as Chinese and Thai people can only take out one thousand
dollars. He said he would pay me ten percent. I told him
I could not do it. After being in Saigon several days I received a note to call Saigon number 37263. The note was
to call Mr. Yao. I called him three or four days later and
he said that he had just come in from Bangkok and that
he was a friend of Mr. Chou's. He said that he wanted to
see me to give me a letter from Mr. Chou. I met him a few
days later at Caravelle Hotel lobby. The letter from Mr.
Chou said for me to call him next time in Bangkok as it
was important... A few weeks later I called Mr. Chou in
Bangkok and again he asked me to take a package to Hong
Kong for him. I asked him what was in the package and
he said checks and about four thousand dollars in Thai
money. I told him that I did not know when I would be
going to Hong Kong. Approximately three weeks later in
Saigon I received a note to call Mr. Yao at same number.
I did not call him. Several days later he called while I was
in the office and asked if he could see me as he wanted
to know how to contact some one on base about opening
up a gift shop. I told him to contact PX manager. Maybe
three or four weeks later Mr. Chou called me again at Chao
Phaya Hotel. Again he was in the lobby and asked if I
would take the same type package to Hong Kong. I asked
to see the package and was told he would show it to me
on my next Bangkok trip. My crew bus was waiting at Chao
Phaya and I told him I would see him next time. He asked
me to deliver a letter in Saigon to Mr. Yao. He gave me

a phone number and I called Mr. Yao in Saigon to give him letter. I met him in restaurant next to Continental Palace. He opened the letter that was written in Chinese or Japanese and said that Mr. Chou wanted him to explain to me about taking a box of cash and checks to Hong Kong, that he needed the money in Hong Kong. I told him that I wanted to see the box. He asked when I was going back to Bangkok and I told him within a week. I arrived in Bangkok and called a phone number that he gave me. He said he would meet me in lobby of Chao Phaya Hotel. He did within thirty or forty minutes. He said that he would show me the contents of the box. We went to Amarin Hotel and he showed me three boxes approximately the size of shoe boxes. One had checks and approximately five thousand dollars in Thai currency. The other two boxes were empty. I told him I was going back to Chao Phaya and do some shopping in PX. He asked if I would take the box to Hong Kong. I told him that I did not know exactly when I was going to Hong Kong but that I would be back in a few days and would phone him and let him know. I asked him how much ten percent would be. He told me approximately two to three hundred dollars. I returned to Saigon and then back to Bangkok and told him I would be going to Hong Kong within a few days. He asked if I could come over to pick up the package. I told him no, that he should bring it to Chao Phaya. He asked what time I would be leaving Chao Phaya Hotel to go to the airport. I told him 1430. He said he would meet me at 1400. He arrived approximately 1400 and gave me three boxes. He told me that Mr. Chou was

p. 245 in Hong Kong and gave me a number K650-434, and asked me to call or see Mr. Fong at the airport. If Mr. Fong did not meet the aircraft then I should call Mr. A. H. Sing at phone number K 650-434. When I arrived in Hong Kong I gave Mr. Fong three boxes. He asked which hotel I was staying and I told him Empress. He said Mr. Chou would call me. I got to Empress Hotel and Mr. Chou called and then came to my room. He gave me nine hundred dollars for carrying the three boxes. I returned to Saigon and received approximately four or five notes to call Mr. Yao. I disregarded the notes. Approximately two months later Mr. Chou and Mr. Yao met me in Chao Phaya Hotel lobby. They asked me to take more checks and money to Hong Kong and I said "No." Approximately 17 Feb. 1970, I received a phone call from Mr. Yao while I was in Seatback office. He asked if I could meet him in Saigon and take two letters to Bangkok and that Mr. Chou would pick them up at Chao Phaya. I met Mr. Yao in Saigon at restaurant near Continental Palace. He gave me two letters and asked me to call Mr. Chou when I got to Bangkok. I told him—he asked what day and time I would arrive in Bangkok, I told him approximately noon on the 20 Feb. When I arrived, I called Mr. Chou and told him I had the letters. He asked me to be on sidewalk in front of the Chao Phaya Hotel and that he would be there in a few minutes. I waited approximately five to ten minutes and a car drove up with Mr. Chou and Mr. Yao. He said that he had four more small packages in his car. I told him that I did not want to carry them. He offered me two thousand dollars to take them to Hong Kong. I asked him what was in the boxes. He said checks and some cash. I said I would do it. He then explained that he had four heavier boxes to go to Saigon and that the boxes contained film, dirty movies and literature, and some medicine. I agreed, and then he asked me if I could take approximately twelve to fifteen packages to Saigon and he would pay me three thousand five hundred dollars now and approximately two thousand dollars after I delivered four boxes of checks and money to Hong Kong and twelve to fifteen boxes in Saigon. I agreed. The next day, 21 Feb 1970, he brought eight boxes to the hotel and I put four of them in taxi cab and took to airport and put on aircraft number 13827. The other four I took to room in Chao Phaya and at approximately 1500 I gave to Major Sokol to take back on C-123. On 21 Feb. I gave my first four boxes to Major Sokol to take to Saigon on C-123. I put, parenthesis, 22 Feb. end of parenthesis four boxes to C-54 and asked Major Barzoloski to take them to Saigon for CAAG people. I then called Mr. Chou and told him that I would not be going to Hong Kong but I would ask Major Davis or Sergeant Taniguchi to give them to Mr. Fong at airport. I then called Major Davis and explained to him that I was sending some boxes to Saigon on C-54 and C-123 and asked him to meet the aircraft. I told him that there was some money involved and that I would share it with him. He said, quote, I will meet the aircraft and keep the boxes unquote. I told him I would explain it all to him when I arrived. I also sent him a note saying boxes marked CAAG should go to Hong

Kong. Next day, 23 Feb, Mr. Chou had fifteen boxes in his car. I put twelve boxes in taxi and told him I could not take other three. I put on aircraft number 13827, 23 Feb, while engine was being changed. Took off from Bangkok approximately 2140 L and landed TSN 0030. I drove Major Davis, Major Hagberg and Major Curtis to BOQ. I went back to aircraft and removed the twelve packages and put in my locker. I returned to BOQ and OSI agents asked to search my room. I consented. They opened the boxes. I was told that the boxes contained opium. I had no idea that the boxes contained dope or narcotics. I was under the impression that the boxes for Hong Kong contained checks and cash and the boxes for Saigon contained dirty movies and books and some medicine. On 23 Feb, approximately 1000 p. 246 to 1100 when I transferred twelve boxes from Mr. Chou's car he gave me thirty-five hundred U.S. dollars and said he would pay two thousand more in Saigon after all boxes were delivered. Chou Ph number Bangkok 57173 or 57371.

IDC: ... We will proceed by calling the accused, Major Fleener, first.

Major Delbert W. Fleener 6250th Support Squadron, United States Air Force, Tan Son Nhut Air Base, Republic of Vietnam, the accused in this case was sworn and took the witness stand and testified in his own behalf as follows:

TC: State your name and grade.

ACC: Delbert W. Fleener, Major, United States Air Force.

TC: Are you the accused in this case.

ACC: Yes, sir.

TC: Your witness.

p. 254

Q. Now, in flying between these cities, is there a custom with respect to flying cargo for other members of your squadron, or other members of the armed forces?
A. Well, expecially with trips to Hong Kong, we buy a lot of things for other people and you get phone calls in your hotel

from different people to carry things, and I am sure you could get almost every pilot to say that they have flown many boxes of unknown cargo and contents into this base and into many other bases. It is the same way from Tokyo into here and from Nepal into here.

Q. Now let's bring this down to the events which involve your presence here. Will you relate to the court the time and place where you first met any of these Oriental individuals who have been designated in the documents previously admitted in the court.

A. Yes sir. I was TDY over to Clark in the Philippines and I went to Angeles City one night. And in the back part of a bar there was a poker game with three or four American GIs and a couple of foreigners one of which introduced himself as Mr. Chou. I played poker with them for a couple of hours. When I quit playing I ended up with all Philippine pesos and I asked if they would change the money back into American money and nobody would. When I left the game I went inside the barroom part and I was in there all by myself maybe for ten or fifteen minutes. And this man Mr. Chou walked in there and sat down and talked to me for maybe thirty or forty minutes. I told him that I didn't like it because nobody would give me any American money and I was stuck with much pesos. So he gave me maybe forty or fifty dollars worth of American money. And he asked me a lot of questions. Was I based at Clark and I told him no. He asked where I was based, and I told him Saigon. He asked me what I was doing at Clark, I told him I was over there on TDY. He asked me what for and I told him the airplane was broken and needed some maintenance. He asked how often I got over to Clark and I told him not on a definite schedule, but if the airplane needed parts or to pick up a cargo we came in there. He asked me how often I got out of the country. I told him that I got out of the country quite a bit. He asked me where I flew to and I told him to Tokyo and to Taipei and to Hong Kong and a couple of times to Manila; to Kathmandu, Nepal; but mostly it was flying back and forth between Saigon and Bangkok.

Q. All right now, for the purpose of helping myself and the court, there are three or four Oriental names which appear in your exhibits: Now, Mr. Chou, tell us generally where did

500

you meet him or see him—in what cities?

A. I had seen him maybe two or three times in Hong Kong, but most of the times, six or eight times or maybe more, in Bangkok. I only saw him once in the Philippines.

Q. Now there is Mr. Sing. What would be the status of where he was meeting with you?

A. During the conversation I had with Mr. Chou at the Philippines, he asked me if I knew anybody to show me around in Hong Kong, or had I been sight-seeing. I told him no, I didn't know anybody and I usually did'nt have time to do p. 255 any sight-seeing. He asked me what I did with my time up there and I told him that I usually have one afternoon and one night and have to leave the next day. He asked me what I did and I said that I usually spend my time shopping. I have maybe six or eight shopping lists to buy things for people. He asked me what all I had to buy. I told him maybe as much as two dozen watches, cameras, hi-fi equipment. He asked me what store I go to, and I told him I normally go to the China Fleet Store. He asked me what I paid for these items that I picked up and I told him, a watch, for example, may be forty-five or fifty dollars. He told me that he was in the import and export business and he said he knew a lot of the shop owners up there and he could get me as much as two or maybe five dollars off on each item. He asked me if I was interested in him helping me and I said yes. And it was the same way with cameras and binoculars, things of this nature. He asked me—he said, "I've got to be going back up there. Why don't you give me a call?" I said. "O.K." He said he didn't know exactly where he would be living up there, or staying up there and gave me the number of A. H. Sing and his phone number. He said when you get there just call Mr. Sing and he will tell you where I can be located. He asked me exactly when I was going. I told him the schedule was uncertain, and that I never really knew more than one or two days in advance.

Q. And now did you only see Mr. Sing in Hong Kong?
A. Yes sir.

Q. Now let's find out about Mr. Yao. Y-o-u is that the way you pronounce it?
A. It is pronounced Yao, sir.

501

p. 255

A. After I met Mr. Chou in Hong Kong, I subsequently—the first time I met him he asked me would I be coming back to Hong Kong. I told him I didn't know exactly. He said "Where will you be going?" I said "Bangkok," and he told me he was also going to Bangkok. He asked me what hotel in Bangkok, and I said, "I don't stay overnight. It is usually a four or five-hour ground time and I go up to the Chao Phaya Hotel and maybe eat, and maybe get a haircut and shop at the PX and loaf around the swimming pool. He asked me when I was going back to Saigon and I told him that day. He asked me if I would deliver a letter back here to Saigon and he gave me the name and phone number of Mr. Yao. When I got back here I tried to call the phone number but it was a downtown Saigon number. I didn't dial it right. I couldn't get the phone to work; I don't know what it was. The next day I had to fly. I had also given Mr. Chou my phone number here on the base. The next couple of days I never called up the number he gave me in Saigon, but one of the despatchers up at the office gave me a note saying to call this man and it had a phone number on it which I have given to the OSI people. He asked me if I would meet him downtown and I did. I had to go down to the Embassy anyway with some passports and I met him. I believe it was in the lobby of the Caravelle Hotel. We walked around the street to a restaurant next door to the Continental Palace Hotel, and he read the letter I had brought to him. The second time that I had met Mr. Chou he kept complaining that he was only allowed to take $1,000 out of the country because that is all they are allowed and he had asked if I would take some money up to him. And I told him "No." He asked me— he said, "There is nothing illegal about that." I said mainly, "I cannot tell you. My schedule is too irregular. I can't tell you when I am going back to Hong Kong again." But anyway I delivered the letter to his friend Mr. Yao. Mr. Yao read the letter and said, "Mr. Chou wants me to explain to you that he can only take $1,000.00 out of Thailand and wants me to ask you if you would take some money back up to him." Again I told him I didn't know the schedule and I couldn't tell him. He gave me a letter to take back and he quickly jotted another letter, that I suppose was written in Thai or Chinese. I couldn't read it anyway. He put it in an enve-

lope and asked me if I would—he asked me when I was going
back to Bangkok and I told him within a couple of days. He
asked me if I would take these letters back and give to his
old friend Mr. Chou. By the time I got back over there and
called him and told him I had the letters for him, he said
I will be over there in thirty minutes to an hour—I forget
what it was. But he asked me to meet him out front. A car
came up that he described and Mr. Yao was in the car with
him. He had come to Bangkok between the couple of days
that had lapsed since he gave me the two letters. So that
is how I got acquainted with this Mr. Yao.

IDC: Well, now tell us about Mr. Fong.
A. He works for the Company at the Hong Kong Airport. When
you first arrive there and when you park your airplane, they
are the people who push the steps up to the airplane, they
are the people you deal with as far as buying gas and oil.
They are the people you have to pay your $2.00 for every
passenger you have on board. He asked me if I knew Mr.
Fong, and I told him "No." He described him to me and told
me where he worked, and I said, "Yes, I think I remember
him." Because I had been to Hong Kong many times.

p. 256

Q. Any contacts with him were limited entirely to the city of
Hong Kong?
A. Yes, sir.

Q. Now, in these preliminary dealings which you have had with
these men, was there anything about their conduct that
would have aroused your suspicion that maybe they were in
an illegitimate business?
A. No, sir. As a matter of fact Mr. Chou had done quite a few
favors for me is the reason I would trust him; time-consuming favors as far as taking you around to different jewelry
stores in Hong Kong, and camera stores. And if he didn't
think I was getting a good bargain, he would talk with the
man and tell him I had a list of twenty-five or thirty watches
to buy at once, and I would get them cheaper by two or three
dollars.

Q. Well, tell the court the first incident you had with these men
that involved the flying of any materials of any kind.

503

A. Well, sir I can't tell you the exact time, or even the month, but on one particular trip I went back to Bangkok and I can't say whether I called them or they called me, but they picked me up at the Chao Phaya Hotel and they took me over to the Amarin Hotel. Both of them stayed there maybe ten minutes then Mr. Chou had left. But they told me they had set up a temporary office in there and they had quite a few packages laying around. Some of them were open so that I could see that they had brochures of hi-fi equipment, and cameras, and I was sitting there looking at it. At this time they had asked me if I would take some—a box of money to Hong Kong, some checks and receipts and some office material—invoices and shipping documents—and I said I wanted to see. So they took me over there and I noticed three boxes, two of which were empty. One of them had some checks and receipts and shipping documents in it and some office paperwork and some brochures that I mentioned a while ago. And then there was a sack of—it looked like a money sack to me—I looked into the sack and there was a bunch of Hong Kong dollars in there. A sack maybe like this—six inches across. And there was, I figured, too there was a stack of bills there. I think he told me there was two or three thousand dollars. I forget the exact figures.

Q. Then what transpired?
A. He asked me if I would take it to Hong Kong for him, He said he would pay me ten percent. I said, "Well how much is that?" He said, "Maybe two or three hundred dollars." I said "O.K. I'll take it." So then I had to pick up some things at another store or I had to go back to the Chao Phaya to get a haircut, or the PX or something. He asked me what time I was leaving Bangkok and I told him the crew bus would pick me up at the Chao Phaya Hotel between 1400 and 1430, and he said "I will meet you over there at about 1430 and bring the box," and he did. But when he got there he had three boxes. Again he had given me the phone numbers and everything. My instructions were to give the three boxes to this guy Mr. Fong, at the airport and he would take care of the boxes. And I have to admit I agreed to do that and I agreed to take them there.

Appendix VIII

The International Police Radio Network in Asia

General Information

One of Interpol's most effective instruments is its international police radio network. It now comprises 35 stations and handles approximately 150,000 messages a year. Every NCB with a radio station is able to contact the other NCBs on the network quickly, easily, and quite cheaply. A short time after sending out a telegram a few lines long it can obtain the information requested by the NCBs contacted or have the latter carry out the action desired. Moreover, it receives all the general or zone broadcasts of interest to its region put out by the other NCBs or by the General Secretariat and is thus involved in the Organization's day-to-day activities. Experience has shown that an NCB can only be really efficient when it is linked to the network. The network uses the A1 system (Morse) only; this is the simplest, most reliable, and cheapest method, and the one best suited to our requirements.

The network is divided into regional networks that operate in coordination with the Central Station in Paris. Each regional network has a central regional station that acts as relay to all the national stations in its region and maintains contact with the rest of the network via the Central Station in Paris. This form of organization means that each NCB can keep the equipment of its station to a minimum—just enough to broadcast to the central region station. Only the central region station needs powerful equipment and sufficient staff to work with all the stations in the region and the Paris Central Station.

The regulations for operating on the network and the various procedures used by the Interpol stations are laid down by the International Police Radiocommunications Regulations adopted by the Interpol General Assembly in 1949. Heads of NCBs may obtain copies from the General Secretariat.

The Network in Asia

(a) Europe-Mediterranean network

Some stations—Beirut, Tehran, and Tel Aviv—are at present on the Europe-Mediterranean network because they are relatively near the Central Station.

(b) East Asia network

The Tokyo station is the central regional station for Southeast Asia; it has all the necessary technical staff and technical and operating equipment. Liaison with the Paris Central Station is excellent.

The Manila station (Philippines) and the Seoul station (Korea) are at present linked to the Tokyo station. A station in Saigon is currently carrying out tests and is expected to join the network in the near future.

Development of the Asian Network

It would be highly desirable if several Asian NCBs could open Interpol radio stations; this would greatly improve international police cooperation.

The Tokyo regional station is prepared to establish liaison with any stations wishing to do so.

Equipment needed to Open a Station

The minimum amount of equipment necessary for an international police radio station in liaison with Tokyo is as follows:

- 1 multifrequency transmitter of at least 1 kw. with relatively rapid frequency change (a few minutes).
- a narrow band-pass receiver.
- the corresponding aerials.
- a source of power.

It would be very useful to have an emergency transmitter and possibly an additional receiver.

Staff

Technicians are needed for the installation and—more important still—maintenance of equipment.

In addition, there must be at least two skilled operators.

Frequencies

Four to six frequencies are needed in order to establish liaison night and day all the year round. The choice of these frequencies is made in conjunction with the regional station, since regional frequencies must be different from those reserved for communications between networks.

It should be remembered that frequencies are never allocated to international organizations, but to individual governments. The national postal authorities of each country are usually responsible for notifying the International Frequency Registration Board (which is a part of ITU and has its Headquarters in Geneva) of the frequencies chosen for use by the various departments in that country.

Heads of NCBs may obtain additional information on the staff and equipment required from the Central Secretariat.

Appendix IX, A

Thai Legislation

The legal system in Thailand also gives the police ample authority to suppress narcotics trafficking and crossborder smuggling. The import of chemicals used in refining, such as acetic anhydride, is under import controls.

The 1970 UN Project Preparation Mission to Thailand in the Field of Narcotics Control estimated that Thailand has about 200,000 opium and heroin addicts. The government is attempting to control narcotics trafficking in the country to prevent the domestic problem from growing, as well as to help control the international traffic.

Thailand cooperates with international narcotics control programs. In August 1971 the Thai Foreign Ministry signed a statement with the U.S. Ambassador which publicly expressed concern over the growth of addiction and drug abuse. A US-Thai Memorandum of Understanding on International Narcotics Control was signed in Washington on 20th September 1971; a Drug Abuse Control Project Agreement was signed in Bangkok by the head of the Thai police and UN narcotics officials. Under the agreement the UN Fund for Drug Abuse Control will provide $2 million and Thailand will provide about $5 million— partly in kind—for drug control efforts during 1972-76.

World Opium Survey 1972.
Cabinet Committee on International Narcotics Control.
Washington, D.C.

Appendix IX, B

Thai Countermeasures

The presence of uncontrollable military forces in the Thai border regions [i.e., the CIF] and particularly their trafficking in opium has become an increasing source of embarrassment to the Royal Thai Government. As a result, Thai military authorities with jurisdiction over these regions began negotiations with two groups of Chinese Irregular Forces to obtain their permanent resettlement in Thailand and their integration into the mainstream of Thai culture and commerce.

These two groups, headed by self-appointed generals, consist of approximately 6,000 individuals, comprising men, women, and children. The effort to resettle them involves not only the allocation of land but also the development of new agricultural pursuits.

Late in December of 1971, negotiations reached the point where the Chinese generals agreed to the resettlement scheme and offered among other things to surrender 26 tons of harvested opium on hand from the most recent crop cultivation. The opium was to be exchanged for legal recognition, land, agricultural assistance, settlement of debts, and an immediate cash reserve for the housing and supplying the group during the initial resettlement period.

In view of American interests in suppressing the illicit opium traffic in Southeast Asia, our embassy was approached for assistance in facilitating this resettlement, and a tentative agreement was reached for providing the sum of $1 million.

From this point forward, it was determined that our bureau—the Bureau of Narcotics and Dangerous Drugs—should be the principal in arranging the transfer of funds and insuring the surrender of the 26 tons of opium. The necessary funds were transferred to our Bangkok office and Mr. William Wanzeck... entered into negotiations with General Kriangsak of the Royal Thai Army, who is responsible for the resettlement. This resulted in an agreement in early February whereby our officials would inspect the surrendered opium, witness its destruction, and receive evidence of the progress in resettling the two groups of Chinese Irregular Forces.

"World Drug Traffic and its Impact on U.S. Security."
Hearings before Senate Internal Security Subcommittee.
Aug. 14, 1972, p. 37.

Appendix IX, C

Thai Opium Burning

On March 6, Mr. Koles, accompanied by our regional Director, Mr. Wanzeck, visited the Chiang Mai artillery range where the sacks of opium were stored in a special area surrounded by barbed wire and armed troops.

Each burlap sack contained between 84 and 87 kilograms of opium in the form of 20 individually wrapped packages of opium. Mr. Koles and Mr. Wanzeck removed samples at random from each of the individual sacks which were 319 in number. The specimens were taken by first cutting into the bag with a knife and then withdrawing a small amount on a wooden applicator stick plunged at depth into the particular ball of opium which it happened to strike. All of these specimens were then placed into containers and secured for examination.

Subsequently, the samples were subjected to two different types of scientific tests in such a way as to ensure that all samples were tested at least once, and some of them twice. It was found that all of the samples were representative of unadulterated gum opium typical of the area. Our chemist was, therefore, able to conclude that the entire 26 tons of material in question was opium of a quality typical of Southeast Asia.

511

At this point I should explain that gum opium is a raw agricultural commodity which consists of a latex-type exudate from the opium poppy bulb and varies in morphine content from one geographic area to another. The most potent opium is produced in Turkey, having a morphine content sometimes in excess of 16 percent. Southeast Asia opium, although normally of lower quality, may have as high as 10 percent morphine content. The 26 tons of opium in question would, nevertheless, suffice for the manufacture of more than two tons of heroin.

Ten pyres were then constructed on the artillery range at Chiang Mai with stacks of logs approximately 12 feet in length. On top of these were placed the bags of opium which were then drenched with jet aviation fuel. On March 7 officers of our bureau together with Thai army officers and members of the Bangkok press corps stood witness as the mass was ignited for final destruction.

The decision to call in the Thai press had been made at the last moment and several bags were cut open for the benefit of a demonstration to them prior to the burning. The 26 tons burned for a total of 15 hours until, on the morning of the 8th, the modest residue was bulldozed into a pit and buried.

This ends the account of the largest single destruction of opium since Commissioner Lin touched off a war with Great Britain in the last century. More importantly, we hope that it is the beginning of the end of organized opium trafficking by irregular military forces operating in the Golden Triangle.

"World Drug Traffic and its Impact on U.S. Security," pp. 38–39.

Appendix IX, D

Laotian Actions

General WALT:

Looking at the situation which existed a year ago in Laos, no one could be blamed for deciding that the ingrained attitudes ran too deep to make any serious improvement possible. But then things began to happen.

The strength of the American reaction to the news of the heroin epidemic among our servicemen in Vietnam persuaded the Laotian leaders that they could no longer afford to remain indifferent or unmotivated if they wished to retain American support. And so, on Nov. 15, 1971, the Laotian Legislature took the revolutionary step of passing a law banning the production, sale, or use of opium. All of the Meo deputies, following the leadership of General Vang Pao, voted affirmatively on this measure.

Even before the law was passed, the Laotian Government had acted to curtail refinery operations, destroying two refineries and seizing large quantities of drugs in the process.

Alarmed by the evidence of mounting governmental pressure, several additional refineries closed down or moved their operations to Burma. Today, according to responsible officials who follow the situation in Laos on a day-to-day basis, there is no evidence to indicate that there is a single heroin lab currently active in the country of Laos.

While there are unquestionably some corrupt officials in the Laotian police force and the Laotian Armed Forces, everyone in the Embassy with whom I discussed the matter was completely convinced of the sincerity and motivation of Prime Minister Souvanna Phouma and General Vang Pao and of the key officials appointed to deal with the problem of opium suppression.

In Vientiane I was able to meet with a number of the Laotian officials now involved in their country's war against opium and the opium traffickers. Among them were His Royal Highness Tiao Mankhara Manivong, President of Narcotics Destruction; Mr. Chantaboun Luangraj, Director General of National Police and President of the Subcommission for Repression of the Narcotics Traffic; and Mr. Nith Sigharaj, President of the Interministerial Committee for Narcotics Control. I had a chat with each of these gentlemen and I may say that my conversations with them completely bore out what we had heard from Ambassador Godley and his staff, and that is, that the Laotian Government is now animated by a completely new spirit and that the officials assigned to deal with the problem have both a sophisticated understanding of it and the determination to really do something about it.

Despite the fact that they have had to build an anti-opium apparatus almost from scratch, and despite the demands of the war, the Laotian Government's operation has drawn blood since the first of the year in the form of repeated seizures of small and large quantities of opium.

"World Drug Traffic and its Impact on U.S. Security," pp. 22-23.

Appendix X

92D CONGRESS
1ST SESSION

H. R. 9588

IN THE HOUSE OF REPRESENTATIVES

JULY 1, 1971

Mr. STEELE (for himself, Mr. MURPHY of Illinois, and Mr. SARBANES) introduced the following bill; which was referred to the Committee on Armed Services

---

A BILL

To provide comprehensive treatment for servicemen and veterans who suffer from abuse of, or dependency on, narcotic drugs, and for other purposes.

1   *Be it enacted by the Senate and House of Represen-*
2   *tatives of the United States of America in Congress*
3   *assembled,* That (a) chapter 55 of title 10, United States
4   Code, is amended by adding at the end thereof the
5   following new section:

6   "**§ 1089. Care and treatment of narcotic drug depen-**
7   **dent members**

8   "(a) (1) The Secretary concerned, subject to the
9   overall direction and supervision of the Secretary of
10   Defense, shall take such action as may be necessary to
11   implement immediately comprehensive programs—

12   "(A) to detect narcotic drug abuse and drug de-
13   pendency among members on active duty by means
14   of periodic urinalysis of each member;

15   "(B) to provide acute care, detoxification, and
16   other appropriate treatment for members detected
17   to be suffering from drug abuse or drug dependency;

18   "(C) to provide basic rehabilitation services for
19   members provided treatment under clause (B) of
20   this subsection; and

21   "(D) to provide information with respect to the
22   dangers of drug abuse and drug dependency.

23   "(2) The comprehensive programs required to be
24   implemented under paragraph (1) of this subsection
25   shall be primarily administered by the Surgeon General
26   (or equivalent) of the armed force concerned.

1   "(b) (1) In the implementation of the compre-
2   hensive programs specified in subsection (a) of this sec-
3   tion, the Secretary concerned shall by regulation re-
4   quire that any member detected to be suffering from
5   drug abuse or drug dependency shall be immediately
6   placed under the jurisdiction of the Surgeon General (or
7   equivalent) for care and treatment. The Secretary shall
8   take any other action he deems appropriate to assure
9   strict compliance with this subsection, particularly at
10 the lower echelon levels within the armed force concerned.
11   "(2) The informational programs required under
12 subsection (a) (1) (D) of this section shall include—
13   "(A) the development, collection, and dis-
14   semination of appropriate materials (including but
15   not limited to films, pamphlets, posters, and radio
16   and television programs) on the dangers of drug
17   abuse, which materials shall be of general applica-
18   tion but, in cases where deemed necessary, may be
19   of special relevance to the drug control problems in-
20   digenous to any single military installation; and
21   "(B) the development and implementation of
22   regularly scheduled lecture and discussion group
23   programs (including group therapy sessions) to
24   deal with the individual's inclination to become,
25   and the reasons that he should resist becoming, in-
26   volved with narcotics. Such programs should be

1   directed toward the following four groups of
2   people:

3   "(i) the nonuser, who should be convinced
4   not to experiment with drugs;

5   "(ii) the experimenter or casual user, who
6   should be convinced not to continue his abuse;

7   "(iii) the addict, who should be convinced
8   to seek out professional assistance to help him
9   rid himself of his problem, and be informed of
10   the treatment and rehabilitative services
11   available to him; and

12   "(iv) the supplier, who should be convinced
13   to discontinue his involvement in drug
14   trafficking.
15 Such informational programs shall be under the super-
16 vision of appropriately trained personnel, including at
17 least one psychiatrist with experience in dealing with
18 users of narcotics, at least one enforcement officer, and
19 at least one person having experience in drug education.
20   "(c) At any time the capacity of the facilities of the
21 armed force concerned are not sufficient to carry out
22 the purposes of this section, the Secretary concerned,
23 after consultation with the Secretary of Defense, may
24 contract with any other Federal department or agency,
25 any State or political subdivision thereof, or any private
26 agency or institution for the provision of acute care,

1   detoxification, and rehabilitation services for members
2   entitled to care and treatment under this section.

3   "(d) In any case in which the Secretary concerned
4   determines that a member whose discharge or release
5   from active service is imminent (1) is likely to be a nar-
6   cotic addict within the meaning of section 301(a) of the
7   Narcotic Addict Rehabilitation Act of 1966, and (2)
8   would be best served by commitment for treatment un-
9   der title III of such Act, the Secretary concerned shall
10 be deemed to be a 'related individual' within the mean-
11 ing of section 301(i) of such Act for the purposes of filing
12 a petition on behalf of such member under section 302 of
13 such Act. If a hearing results from such petition and the
14 member is thereafter determined to be a narcotic addict
15 who is likely to be rehabilitated through treatment, the
16 United States district court concerned shall civilly com-
17 mit the member under title III of such Act to the
18 custody of the Administrator of Veterans' Affairs for
19 treatment (including posthospitalization treatment)
20 effective as of the date of his discharge or release from
21 active service. The Administrator shall exercise the
22 same functions and duties with respect to any person
23 committed to him for treatment pursuant to this sub-
24 section as would be exercised by the Secretary of
25 Health, Education, and Welfare with respect to such

1   person if such person were committed to the Secretary
2   for treatment pursuant to title III of such Act."

3   (b) The analysis of such chapter 55 is amended by
4   adding at the end thereof the following:

5   "1089. Care and treatment of narcotic dependent members."

6   (c) There are authorized to be appropriated, without
7   fiscal year limitation, such sums as may be necessary to
8   carry out the purposes of the amendment made by sub-
9   section (a) of this section.

10   (d) The Commandant of the Coast Guard shall im-
11 plement within the Coast Guard comprehensive
12 programs similar in effect to those required under sec-
13 tion 1089 of title 10, United States Code (as added by
14 subsection (a) of this section), except that any member
15 of the Coast Guard who needs acute care, detoxification,
16 or other appropriate treatment for drug abuse or drug
17 dependency shall be transferred to the Secretary of a
18 military department (subject to such arrangements as
19 may be mutually agreeable to the Commandant and the
20 Secretary) for such treatment.

21   SEC. 2. (a) (1) Chapter 47 (Uniform Code of Military
22 Justice) of title 10, United States Code, is amended by
23 adding immediately after section 933 (Article 133)
24 thereof the following:

25 "§ 933a. Art. 133a. Sale and possession for sale of
26   habit forming drugs and related materials

1   "Any person subject to this chapter who sells, or
2   possesses for sale, any habit-forming drug, any
3   materials or paraphernalia associated with the use of
4   any habit-forming drug, or any marijuana shall be
5   punished as a court-martial may direct, but may not be
6   sentenced to confinement at hard labor for more than 20
7   years in the case of an offense involving a habit-forming
8   drug or associated materials or paraphernalia, nor for
9   more than 5 years in the case of an offense involving
10 marijuana."
11   (2) The analysis of subchapter X of such chapter 47
12 is amended by inserting immediately before
13 "934. 134. General Article."
14 the following:
15 "933a. 133a. Sale and possession for sale of habit forming drugs."
16   (b) Notwithstanding any other provision of this
17 chapter, the personal use of a habit-forming drug
18 (including marijuana) by any person subject to chapter
19 47 of title 10, United States Code, or the possession of
20 any such drug by any such person for his personal use
21 shall not be deemed a punishable offense under the
22 Uniform Code of Military Justice.
23   (c) Notwithstanding any other provision of law,
24 neither (1) a condition of drug abuse or drug dependency
25 which is manifest with respect to any member of an
26 armed force while such member is on active duty, nor

1 (2) the personal use or possession for personal use of
2 any habit-forming drug (including marijuana) by any
3 member of any armed force on active duty, shall in
4 itself, be deemed to be reason or cause for a dis-
5 honorable, bad conduct, or undesirable discharge or
6 separation of such member from active duty. The
7 Secretary of Defense shall promulgate such regulations
8 as are necessary to cary out the provisions of this sub-
9 section, which regulations shall be of uniform applica-
10 tion throughout the Armed Forces.

11 SEC. 3. (a) Section 612 of title 38, United States
12 Code, is amended by inserting at the end thereof the
13 following new subsection:

14 "(i) Notwithstanding any other provision of this ti-
15 tle, the Administrator may provide medical services to
16 any eligible veteran who is dependent upon a narcotic
17 drug or has a drug abuse problem if such services are
18 applied for by the eligible veteran. Medical services
19 shall be provided to any eligible veteran under this sub-
20 section if his drug dependency or drug abuse problem
21 was discovered during the period of his active military,
22 naval, or air service or commenced at any time after his
23 discharge or separation from such service. An eligible
24 veteran shall be provided medical services under this
25 section for such period of time as the Administrator
26 deems necessary but the Administrator may terminate

1   any such services if an eligible veteran refuses to
2   cooperate with the conditions of the services prescribed
3   by the Administrator. As used in this subsection, the
4   term 'eligible veteran' means any person who served in
5   the active military, naval, or air service on or after
6   January 1, 1961, and who was discharged or released
7   therefrom and without regard to the nature of his dis-
8   charge or release, or to section 3103 of this title."

9   (b) There are authorized to be appropriated,
10 without fiscal year limitation, such sums as may be
11 necessary to carry out the purposes of the amendment
12 made by subsection (a) of this section.

Bibliography

Adrian, E.D., *The Physical Background of Perception.* London: Oxford University Press, 1947.

Amae, Hirayama, *History of Chinese Secret Societies (Chung Kuo pi-mi she-hui shih).* Mukden: South Manchurian Railway Research Department, 1925.

Anslinger, Henry J., *The Murderers.* New York: Farrar, Straus & Giroux, 1961.

———, *The Protectors.* New York: Farrar, Straus & Giroux, 1954.

——— and William Tompkins, *The Traffic in Narcotics.* New York: Funk & Wagnalls, 1953.

Asian Peoples' Anti-Communist League, *The Chinese Communist Plot to Drug the World.* Taipei: the League, 1972.

Ball, John C., C. D. Chambers and J. M. Ball, "The Association of Marihuana Smoking with Opiate Addiction in the United States," *Journal of Criminal Law, Criminology and Police Science,* LIX, June 1968, 172-182.

Barter, James T., G. L. Mizier and P. H. Werner, *Patterns of Drug Abuse Among College Students.* Washington: U.S. Department of Justice, Bureau of Narcotics and Dangerous Drugs, 1970.

Barth, Gunter, *Bitter Strength.* Cambridge, Mass.: Harvard University Press, 1964.

Bloomquist, E. R., *Marijuana.* Beverly Hills, Calif.: Glencoe Press, 1968.

Blum, Richard, and Associates, *Students and Drugs,* Vols. I & II. San Francisco: Jossey-Bass, 1964.

———, *Utopiates (The Use and Users of LSD-25).* New York: Atherton Press, 1964.

Blythe, Wilfred, *The Impact of Chinese Secret Societies in Malaya.* London: Oxford University Press, 1969.

Bogg, Richard, R. Smith and S. Russell, *Drugs and Michigan High School Students.* Lansing, Mich.: Michigan Legislature, Report of Study Conducted for Special Committee on Narcotics, 1968.

Brownfeld, Allan C., *The Peking Connection: Communist China and the Narcotics Trade.* Washington: The Committee for a Free China, 1972.

Bruce, Ronald, *The Pot Report.* New York: Universal Publishing & Distributing Corp. (Award Books), 1971.

Byass, Hugh, *Government by Assassination.* London: Allen & Unwin, 1943.

Canadian Government Commission of Enquiry, *The Non-Medical Use of Drugs* (Interim Report of the Commission). Harmondsworth, England: Penguin Books, 1971.

Candlin, A. H. Stanton, *Tibet at Bay*. New York: American-Asian Educational Exchange, 1971.

Chesneaux, J., *Les Sociètès secrètes en Chine*. Paris: Archives Juilliard, 1965.

Chu Lin, *Record of the Hung Family (Hung Men Chih)*. Shanghai: Chung Hua Book Co., 1947.

Clark, Ramsey, *Crime in America*. New York: Simon & Schuster, 1970.

Cocteau, J., *Opium*. New York: Grove Press, 1957.

Cohen Sidney, *The Drug Dilemma*. New York: McGraw Hill, 1969

Collis, M., *Foreign Mud* (An account of the opium imbroglio at Canton in the 1830s and the Anglo-Chinese War that followed). New York: Alfred Knopf, 1947.

Cooke, M. C., *The Seven Sisters of Sleep*. London: Blackwood, 1860.

Curtis, Wade, *Red Heroin*. New York: Berkley Publishing, 1969

Daraul, Arkon, *A History of Secret Societies*. New York: Pocket Books, 1969.

De la Gorce, Paul Marie, *The French Army*. New York: Braziller, 1963.

Demaris, Ovid, *Poso del Mundo (Inside the Mexican-American Border)*. New York: Pocket Books, 1970.

De Ropp, R. S., *Drugs and the Mind*. New York: Grove Press, 1960.

Deverall, Richard, *Mao Tze-tung Stop This Dirty Opium Business*. Tokyo: Toyoh Printing and Bookbinding Co., 1954.

De Vosjoli, P. L. Thyraud, *Lamia (The Story of KGB Infiltration Into SDECE)*. Boston: Little, Brown, 1970.

Dixon, S., and Otto Heilbrunn, *Communist Guerrilla Warfare*. London: Allen & Unwin, 1954.

Efron, D. H. (ed.), *Psychopharmacology: A Review of Progress, 1957-1967*. Washington: Government Printing Office, 1968.

Egyptian Government Central Narcotics Intelligence Bureau, *Annual Report for Year 1944*, Chapter VIII, "Hashish." Cairo: the Bureau, 1945.

Fehrenbach, T. R., *The Swiss Banks*. New York: McGraw Hill, 1966.

Finch, P., *Shanghai and Beyond*. New York: Scribner's, 1953.

Frankel, M., *Rights in Conflict* (The Walker Report). New York: Bantam, 1968.

Garit, J. P., *Opium*. New York: Brentano, 1927.

Goldstein, J., *The Social Psychology of Student Drug Use*. Pittsburgh: Carnegie Mellon University, Department of Psychology, 1970.

Green, T., *The World of Gold*. New York: Walker, 1968.

Greig, Ian, *The Assault on the West*. Richmond, Surrey, England: Foreign Affairs Publishing Co., 1968.

Heckethorne, C., *The Secret Societies of All Ages*, Vols. I & II. New Hyde Park, N.Y.: University Books, 1965.

Heilbrunn, O., *Warfare in the Enemy's Rear*. London: Allen & Unwin, 1965.

Hess, Albery G., *Chasing the Dragon*. New York: Free Press, 1965.

H.M.S.O. (British Government Official Publication), *Cannabis*. London: Wootton Committee, Report of the Advisory Committee on Drug Dependence, 1968.

Hong Kong Government, *The Problem of Narcotic Drugs in Hong Kong*. (a White Paper). Hong Kong: Legislative Council, 1959.

Hunter, E., *Attack By Mail*. Linden. N. J.: Bookmailer, 1966.

———, *The Black Book on Red China*. Linden, N. J.: Bookmailer, 1958.

———, *Brainwashing in Red China*. New York: Vanguard Press, 1953 (2d. ed.).

———, *Brainwashing: From Pavlov to Powers*. Linden, N. J.: Bookmailer, 1965.

Hutton, J. B., *The Subverters*. New Rochelle, N.Y.: Arlington House, 1971.

Indian Hemp Drugs Commission, *Marijuana Report of I.H.D.C. (1893-94)*. Baltimore: Waverly Press (reprint), 1969.

Jackson, J. H., *Selected Writings* (1932 ed.), Vol. 2, pp. 92-118, "Remarks on Evolution and Dissolution of the Nervous System." London: Hodder and Stoughton, 1887.

Johnson, H., and G. C. Wilson, *Army in Anguish (Washington Post* National Reports). New York: Pocket Books, 1972

Kalant, O. J., *The Amphetamines: Toxicity and Addiction.* Springfield, Ill.: Charles C. Thomas, 1966.

Kitson, F., *Low Intensity Operations.* London: Faber, 1971.

Kolb, L., and A. G. May, *The Prevalence and Trends of Drug Addiction in the United States and Factors Influencing It.* Washington: Government Printing Office, 1924.

Kornbluth, J., *Notes From the New Underground.* New York: Ace Books, 1968.

Labin, Suzanne, *Hippies, Drugs and Promiscuity.* New Rochelle, N.Y.: Arlington House, 1972.

Lansdale, E. G., *In the Midst of Wars.* New York: Harper & Row, 1972.

Lewin, L. *Phantastica: Narcotic and Stimulating Drugs.* New York: Dutton, 1931.

Liu, Leo Yueh-yun, *China as a Nuclear Power in World Politics.* London: Macmillan, 1972.

Liu Lien-k'o, *A History of Three Hundred Years Revolutionary Activities of the Secret Societies (Pang-hui san-pai-nien ke-ming-shih).* Macao: Liu Yuan Publishing Co., 1942.

Louria, D. B., *The Drug Scene.* New York: McGraw Hill, 1968.

Luria, A. R., *The Nature of Human Conflict.* New York: Washington Square Press, 1967.

Maas, P., *The Valachi Papers.* New York, Bantam Books, 1969.

McCoy, A. W., *The Politics of Heroin in Southeast Asia.* New York: Harper & Row, 1972.

Mechoulam, R., "Marijuana Chemistry," *Science,* 168:3936 (June 5, 1970), 1159-1166.

Merrill, Frederick T., *Japan and the Opium Menace.* New York: IPR/FPA, 1942.

Messick, Hank, *Lansky.* New York: Berkley Publishing, 1971.

Morgan, W. P., *Triad Societies in Hong Kong.* Hong Kong: Government Press, 1960.

Mullick, B. N., *The Chinese Betrayal.* Bombay and Calcutta: Allied Publishers, 1971.

Noebel, David A., *The Beatles: A Study in Drugs, Sex and Revolution.* Tulsa, Okla: Christian Crusade Publications, 1969 (4th ed. October 1970).

———, *Rhythm, Riots and Revolution.* Tulsa, Okla.: Christian Crusade Publications, 1966.

Nowlis, H., *Drugs on the College Campus.* New York: Doubleday (Anchor Books), 1969.

Oppenheimer, M., *The Urban Guerrilla.* Chicago: Quadrangle Books, 1969.

Pavlov, Ivan P., *Conditioned Reflexes.* New York: Dover Publications, 1960.

———, *Conditioned Reflexes and Psychology.* New York: International Publishers, 1963.

———, *Lectures on Conditioned Reflexes.* New York: International Publishers, 1963.

———, *Psychopathology and Psychiatry.* Moscow: Foreign Languages Publishing House, n.d.

Platonov, K. I., *The Word as a Psychological and Therapeutic Factor.* Moscow: Foreign Languages Publishing House, 1959. (A translation from the second Russian edition.)

Purcell, V., *The Chinese in Southeast Asia.* London: Oxford University Press, 1951.

Reid, E., *The Grim Reapers.* New York: Bantam, 1970.

———, *The Mistress of the Mafia.* New York: Bantam, 1971.

Rinkel, M., *Chemical Concepts and Psychosis.* New York: McDowell & Obolensky, 1952.

Rowan, R. W., *Terror in Our Time (The Secret Service of Surprise Attack).* New York: Longmans, Green, 1941.

Salerno, R. and J. Tompkins, *The Crime Confederation.* New York: Popular Library, 1969.

Sargant, W., *Battle For the Mind—A Physiology of Conversion and Brainwashing.* New York: Doubleday, 1957.

Schmitz, J. G., F. Thompson, and R. H. Zion, *The Vietnam War—Communist Subversion in the Peace Movement.* Congressional Record, April 21, 1971.

Sleeman, W. H., *Report on the Depredations of the Thug Gangs (of Upper and Central India).* East India Company Document, Calcutta, 1840.

Solomon, David, *L.S.D.—The Consciousness Expanding Drug.* New York: Berkley Publishing, 1966.

Taylor, Norman, *Narcotics—Nature's Dangerous Gifts.* New York: Dell, 1963.

Thi Yen-wei, *Chinese Gangs and Societies, Green, Red and Han Liu (Chung-kuo panghui Ch'ing, Hung Han Liu).* Shanghai: Shanghai Literature Co., 1948.

Turnbull, J. H., *Chinese Opium Narcotics (A Threat to the Survival of the West).* Richmond, Surrey, England: Foreign Affairs Publishing Co., 1972.

Vega, L. M., *Guerrillas in Latin America.* New York: Praeger, 1969.

Waley, A., *The Opium War Through Chinese Eyes.* London: Allen & Unwin, 1958.

Weston, P. B., *Narcotics U.S.A.* New York: Greenberg, 1952.

Weyl, N., *Traitors End.* New Rochelle, N.Y.: Arlington House, 1970.

Wolff, P.O., *Marijuana—Latin America and the Threat it Constitutes.* Washington: Linacre Press, 1949.

Zoul, Louis B., *Thugs and Communists.* Long Island City, N.Y.: Public Opinion, 1959.

INDEX

529

Ministry, 508; Free Thai Movement, 197, 199; government, 261, 509; Kriangsak, General, 510; Thai Liberation Movement, 244; U.S.-Thai Memorandum of Understanding, 508; Voice of Free Thailand, 259; "Voice of Thai Revolution," 259

Third World, 316

Tibet, 155, 352, 353; Tibetan Invasion, 190; Dalai Lama, 353; "17 Point Agreement," 155; Younghusband expedition, 33

Tracers and sensors, 363

Trucial Oman; Dubai, 283

Tsarist Russia, 342

Turkey, 14, 18, 113, 115, 129, 197, 213, 218, 240, 343, 344, 347, 353, 375; Anatolia, 388; "People's Liberation Army," 317

"United Front," 145, 184, 236; "United Front Against Fascism, Conference for a," 343

United Nations, 355, 367, 375; Chiao Kuan-hu 347; Commission on Narcotic Drugs, 69, 295, 375, 408, 409; Economic & Social Committee, 388; Huang Hua, 144; ILO, 272; Portugese Ambassador, 50; Secretary General, 388; Security Council, 375; Special Fund for Drug Abuse Controls, 367

United States, 19, 20, 36, 45, 51, 356-357, 358, 374; Abrams, General Creighton, 244; ACLU, 45; Adams, John Quincy, 31; AFL-CIO, 49; Ambrose, Customs Commissioner Myles J., 83; American Security Council, 110; American Servicemen's Union, 343; Anslinger, Hon. Henry J., 87-89. 90-95, 192, 205, 268, 289-290, 295, 408; armed forces, 357; Arnold, Benedict, 337; Ashbrook, Rep. John, 346, 347; Baird, Dr. Robert, 60, 343; Bananas, Joe, 167; Bartholomew, Frank H., 180; Bartimo, Frank A., 58; Bentley, Mrs. Helen, 246; "Bing Kong Tong," 85;

Black Panthers, 315, 317, 342, 343; Blount, Winston, 347; Boyle, John Hunter, 52; Brady, Phil, 242; Bunker, Ambassador Ellsworth, 60, 244; Bureau of Narcotics and Dangerous Drugs, 54, 84, 95, 106, 107, 182, 218, 222, 261, 345-346, 347, 348, 411, 485, 510;

Chief of Staff, 336; Chung Wing Fong, 85; Church, Senator Frank, 18; CIA, 220, 222-223, 229, 244, 245, 255, 353, 411; Civil Rights Law, 49; Clark, Ramsey, 347; Copley Newspapers, 110; Copp, De Witt, 109; CORE, 48; Cornell University, 208; Cosa Nostra, 168, 170, 171, 172, 173, 177; Courtney, Max, 172; Cramer, Rep. William C., 81; Crane, Rep. Philip R., 108; Democratic Military, Movement for a, 342; Deverall, Richard L.G., 90, 99, 104, 288, 290, 291; Dodd, Senator Thomas J., 59; Duke University, 334; Earth Resources Technology Satellite, 363; Eastland, Senator James, 90; Eisenhower, President Dwight D., 337; Emerson, Gloria, 57; Epstein, "Joe," 177; Faso, Frank, 225, 226, 411; FBI, 411; Federal Narcotic and Marijuana Law, 84; Federal Reserve Bank of New York, 284; Finch, Percy, 272, 273; Fleener, Major Delbert W., 243, 256-504; Fonda, Jane ("Hanoi Hannah"), 315, 333, 337; Foreign Assistance Act, 19; Fort Bragg, 341; Fort Dix, 341; "Free the Army Show," 315; Freedom, Dr. Leon, 329; Garlock, Professor Frank, 330; George Douglas Poole Case, 85; Gilbert, Rodney, 75, 76; Ginn, Jerry, 227; Godley, Ambassador, 514; Gold, Frank, 411; Great Lakes Naval Training Center, 342; Gregory, Dick, 315; Gross, Dr. Nelson, 344, 397, 410; Gurney, Senator, 263; "Hai Wai," 225; Hall, Rep. Durward G., 58; Halpern, Rep. Seymour, 55,

ILLUSTRATIONS

MAPS AND CHARTS

APPENDIXES